YBM 실전토익 LC1000 1

YBM
실전토익
LC 1000 1

발행인 이동현
발행처 YBM

문항 개발 Marilyn Hook, 백주선
편집 최정현
디자인 김혜경, 이현숙
마케팅 정연철, 박천산, 고영노, 박찬경, 김동진, 김윤하

개정판 초판 발행 2019년 10월 1일
개정판 4쇄 발행 2021년 5월 20일

신고일자 1964년 3월 28일
신고번호 제 300-1964-3호
주소 서울시 종로구 종로 104
전화 (02) 2000-0515 [구입문의] / (02) 2000-0563 [내용문의]
팩스 (02) 2285-1523
홈페이지 www.ybmbooks.com

ISBN 978-89-17-23212-7 978-89-17-95114-1 SET

토익 주관사가 제시하는 진짜 토익

YBM 실전토익 LC 1000 1을 발행하며

지난 30여 년간 우리나라에서 토익 시험을 주관하면서 토익 시장을 이끌고, 꾸준히 베스트셀러를 출간해 온 YBM에서 〈YBM 실전토익 LC 1000 1〉을 출간하게 되었습니다.

YBM 토익은 이렇게 다릅니다!

YBM의 명성에 자부심을 가지고 개발했습니다!

YBM은 지난 1982년부터 우리나라의 토익 시험을 주관해온 토익 주관사로서, 지난 30여 년간 400여 권의 토익 베스트셀러를 출판해왔습니다. 그 오랜 시간 토익 문제를 분석하고 교재를 출판하면서 쌓아온 전문성과 실력으로 이번에 〈YBM 실전토익 LC 1000 1〉을 선보이게 되었습니다.

토익 주관사로서의 사명감을 가지고 개발했습니다!

토익 주관사로서 사명감을 갖고 신토익 최신 경향을 철저히 분석하여 〈YBM 실전토익 LC 1000 1〉을 개발하였습니다. 실제 시험과 가장 유사한 문제 유형을 반영하였고, 핵심 출제 포인트를 해설집에 상세히 담았습니다.

ETS 교재를 출간한 노하우를 가지고 개발했습니다!

출제기관 ETS의 토익 교재를 독점 출간하는 YBM은 그동안 쌓아온 노하우를 바탕으로 〈YBM 실전토익 LC 1000 1〉을 개발하였습니다. 본 책에 실린 1000개의 문항은 출제자의 의도를 정확히 반영하였기 때문에 타사의 어떤 토익 교재와도 비교할 수 없는 퀄리티를 자랑합니다.

YBM의 모든 노하우가 집대성된 〈YBM 실전토익 LC 1000 1〉은 최단 시간에 최고의 점수를 수험자 여러분께 약속 드립니다.

YBM 토익연구소

토익의 구성과 수험 정보

TOEIC은 어떤 시험인가요?

Test of English for International Communication(국제적 의사소통을 위한 영어 시험)의 약자로서, 영어가 모국어가 아닌 사람들이 일상생활 또는 비즈니스 현장에서 꼭 필요한 실용적 영어 구사 능력을 갖추었는가를 평가하는 시험이다.

시험 구성

구성	Part	내용		문항수	시간	배점
듣기 (L/C)	1	사진 묘사		6	45분	495점
	2	질의 & 응답		25		
	3	짧은 대화		39		
	4	짧은 담화		30		
읽기 (R/C)	5	단문 빈칸 채우기(문법/어휘)		30	75분	495점
	6	장문 빈칸 채우기		16		
	7	독해	단일 지문	29		
			이중 지문	10		
			삼중 지문	15		
Total	**7 Parts**			**200문항**	**120분**	**990점**

TOEIC 접수는 어떻게 하나요?

TOEIC 접수는 한국 토익 위원회 사이트(www.toeic.co.kr)에서 온라인 상으로만 접수가 가능하다. 사이트에서 매월 자세한 접수 일정과 시험 일정 등의 구체적 정보 확인이 가능하니, 미리 일정을 확인하여 접수하도록 한다.

시험장에 반드시 가져가야 할 준비물은요?

신분증 규정 신분증만 가능
(주민등록증, 운전면허증, 기간 만료 전의 여권, 공무원증 등)

필기구 연필, 지우개 (볼펜이나 사인펜은 사용 금지)

시험은 어떻게 진행되나요?

09:20	입실 (09:50 이후는 입실 불가)
09:30 – 09:45	답안지 작성에 관한 오리엔테이션
09:45 – 09:50	휴식
09:50 – 10:05	신분증 확인
10:05 – 10:10	문제지 배부 및 파본 확인
10:10 – 10:55	듣기 평가 (Listening Test)
10:55 – 12:10	독해 평가 (Reading Test)

TOEIC 성적 확인은 어떻게 하죠?

시험일로부터 12일 후 인터넷과 ARS(060-800-0515)로 성적을 확인할 수 있다. TOEIC 성적표는 우편이나 온라인으로 발급 받을 수 있다(시험 접수시, 양자 택일). 우편으로 발급 받을 경우는 성적 발표 후 대략 일주일이 소요되며, 온라인 발급을 선택하면 유효기간 내에 홈페이지에서 본인이 직접 1회에 한해 무료 출력할 수 있다. TOEIC 성적은 시험일로부터 2년간 유효하다.

TOEIC은 몇 점 만점인가요?

TOEIC 점수는 듣기 영역(LC) 점수, 읽기 영역(RC) 점수, 그리고 이 두 영역을 합계한 전체 점수 세 부분으로 구성된다. 각 부분의 점수는 5점 단위이며, 5점에서 495점에 걸쳐 주어지고, 전체 점수는 10점에서 990점까지이며, 만점은 990점이다. TOEIC 성적은 각 문제 유형의 난이도에 따른 점수 환산표에 의해 결정된다.

신토익 경향 분석

PART1 사진 묘사 Photographs

총 6문제

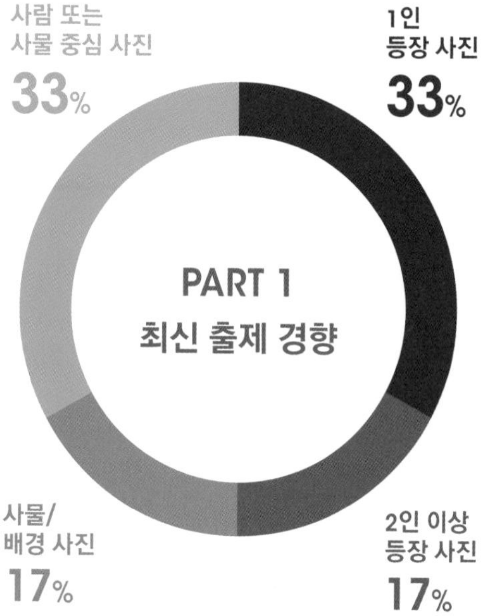

1인 등장 사진
주어는 He/She, A man/woman 등이며 주로 앞부분에 나온다.

2인 이상 등장 사진
주어는 They, Some men/women/people, One of the men/women 등이며 주로 중간 부분에 나온다.

사물/배경 사진
주어는 A car, some chairs 등이며 주로 뒷부분에 나온다.

사람 또는 사물 중심 사진
주어가 일부는 사람, 일부는 사물이며 주로 뒷부분에 나온다.

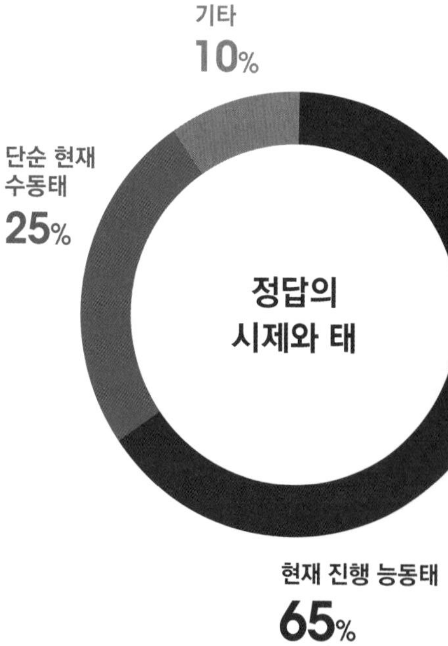

현재 진행 능동태
〈is/are + 현재분사〉 형태이며 주로 사람이 주어이다.

단순 현재 수동태
〈is/are + 과거분사〉 형태이며 주로 사물이 주어이다.

기타
〈is/are + being + 과거분사〉 형태의 현재 진행 수동태, 〈has/have + been + 과거 분사〉 형태의 현재 완료 수동태, '타동사 + 목적어' 형태의 단순 현재 능동태, There is/are와 같은 단순 현재도 나온다.

PART 2 질의 & 응답 Question-Response

총 25문제

평서문
질문이 아니라 객관적인 사실이나 화자의 의견 등을 나타내는 문장이다.

명령문
동사원형이나 Please 등으로 시작한다.

의문사 의문문
각 의문사마다 1~2개씩 나온다. 의문사가 단독으로 나오기도 하지만 What time ~?, How long ~?, Which room ~? 등에서처럼 다른 명사나 형용사와 같이 나오기도 한다.

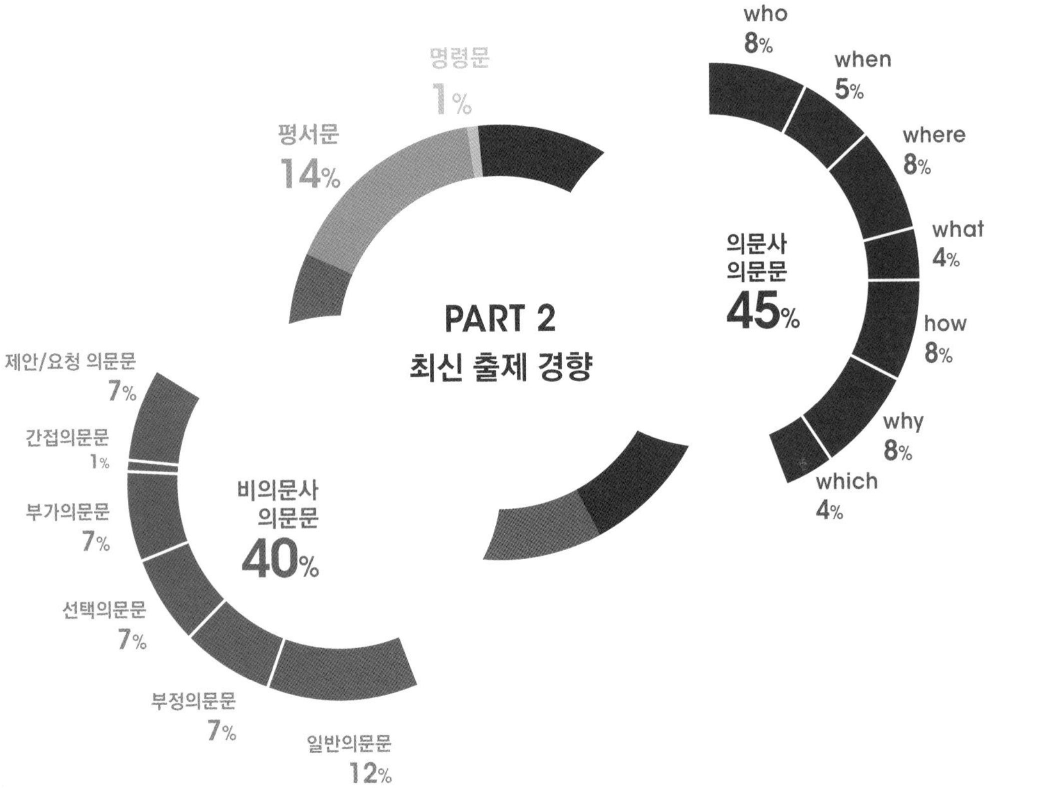

비의문사 의문문

일반(Yes/No) 의문문 적게 나올 때는 한두 개, 많이 나올 때는 서너 개씩 나오는 편이다.

부정의문문 Don't you ~?, Isn't he ~? 등으로 시작하는 문장이며 일반 긍정 의문문보다는 약간 더 적게 나온다.

선택의문문 A or B 형태로 나오며 A와 B의 형태가 단어, 구, 절일 수 있다. 구나 절일 경우 문장이 길어져서 어려워진다.

부가의문문 ~ don't you?, ~ isn't he? 등으로 끝나는 문장이며, 일반 부정 의문문과 비슷하다고 볼 수 있다.

간접의문문 의문사가 문장 처음 부분이 아니라 문장 중간에 들어 있다.

제안/요청 의문문 정보를 얻기보다는 상대방의 도움이나 동의 등을 얻기 위한 목적이 일반적이다.

PART 3 짧은 대화 Short Conversations

총 13대화문 39문제 (지문당 3문제)

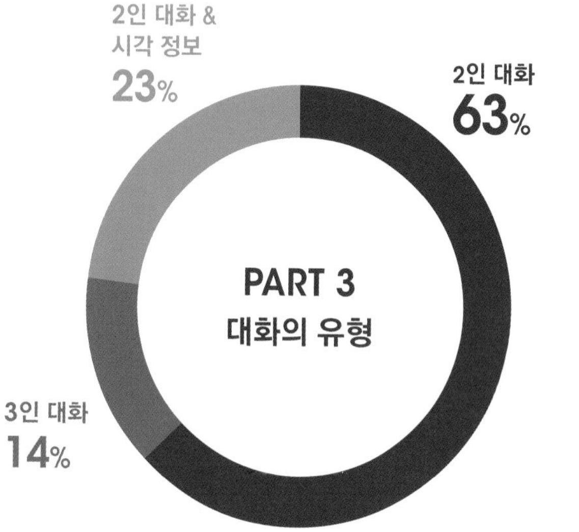

- 3인 대화의 경우 남자 화자 두 명과 여자 화자 한 명 또는 남자 화자 한 명과 여자 화자 두 명이 나온다. 따라서 문제에서는 2인 대화에서와 달리 the man이나 the woman이 아니라 the men이나 the women 또는 특정한 이름이 언급될 수 있다.
- 대화 & 시각 정보는 항상 파트의 뒷부분에 나온다.
- 시각 정보의 유형으로 chart, map, floor plan, schedule, table, weather forecast, directory, list, invoice, receipt, sign, packing slip 등 다양한 자료가 골고루 나온다.

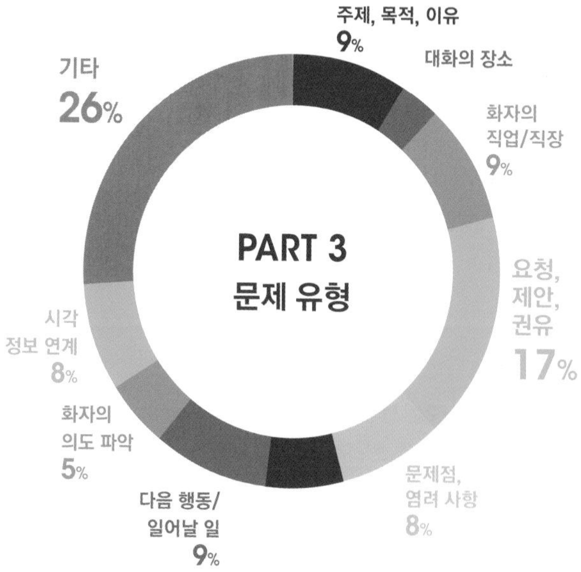

- 주제, 목적, 이유, 대화의 장소, 화자의 직업/직장 등과 관련된 문제는 주로 대화의 첫 번째 문제로 나오며 다음 행동/일어날 일 등과 관련된 문제는 주로 대화의 세 번째 문제로 나온다.
- 화자의 의도 파악 문제는 주로 2인 대화에 나오지만, 가끔 3인 대화에 나오기도 한다. 시각 정보 연계 대화에는 나오지 않고 있다.
- Part 3 안에서 화자의 의도 파악 문제는 2개 나오고 시각 정보 연계 문제는 3개 나온다.

PART 4 짧은 담화 Short Talks

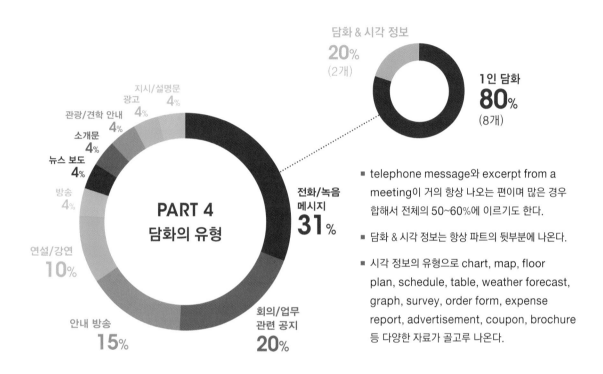

총 10지문 30문제 (지문당 3문제)

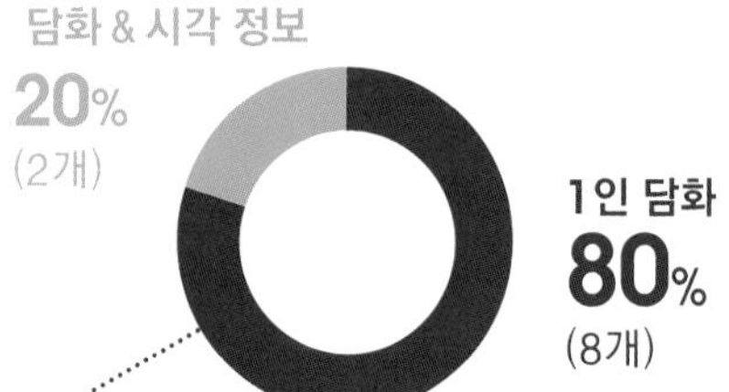

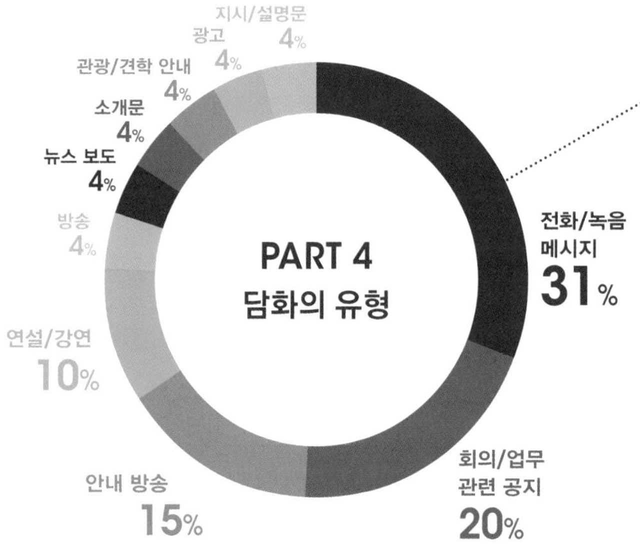

- telephone message와 excerpt from a meeting이 거의 항상 나오는 편이며 많은 경우 합해서 전체의 50~60%에 이르기도 한다.
- 담화 & 시각 정보는 항상 파트의 뒷부분에 나온다.
- 시각 정보의 유형으로 chart, map, floor plan, schedule, table, weather forecast, graph, survey, order form, expense report, advertisement, coupon, brochure 등 다양한 자료가 골고루 나온다.

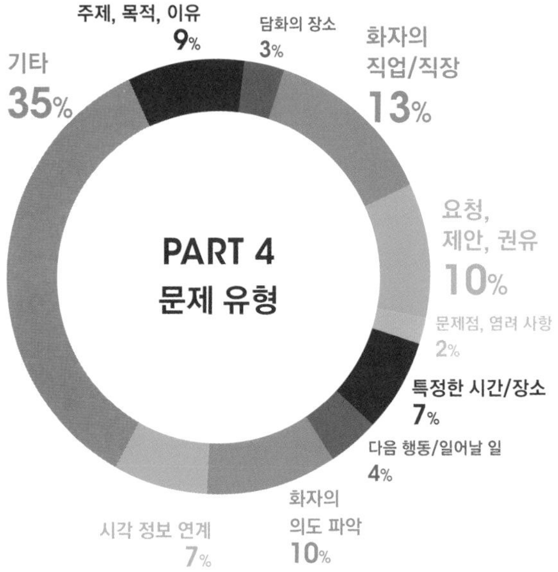

- 문제 유형은 기본적으로 Part 3과 거의 비슷하다.
- 주제, 목적, 이유, 담화의 장소, 화자의 직업/직장 등과 관련된 문제는 주로 담화의 첫 번째 문제로 나오며 다음 행동/일어날 일 등과 관련된 문제는 주로 담화의 세 번째 문제로 나온다.
- Part 4 안에서 화자의 의도 파악 문제는 3개 나오고 시각 정보 연계 문제는 2개 나온다.

PART 5 단문 빈칸 채우기 Incomplete Sentences

총 30문제

문법 문제

시제와 대명사와 관련된 문법 문제가 2개씩, 한정사와 분사와 관련된 문법 문제가 1개씩 나온다. 시제 문제의 경우 능동태/수동태나 수의 일치와 연계되기도 한다. 그 밖에 한정사, 능동태/수동태, 부정사, 동명사 등과 관련된 문법 문제가 나온다.

어휘 문제

동사, 명사, 형용사, 부사와 관련된 어휘 문제가 각각 2~3개씩 골고루 나온다. 전치사 어휘 문제는 3개씩 꾸준히 나오지만, 접속사나 어구와 관련된 어휘 문제는 나오지 않을 때도 있고 3개가 나올 때도 있다.

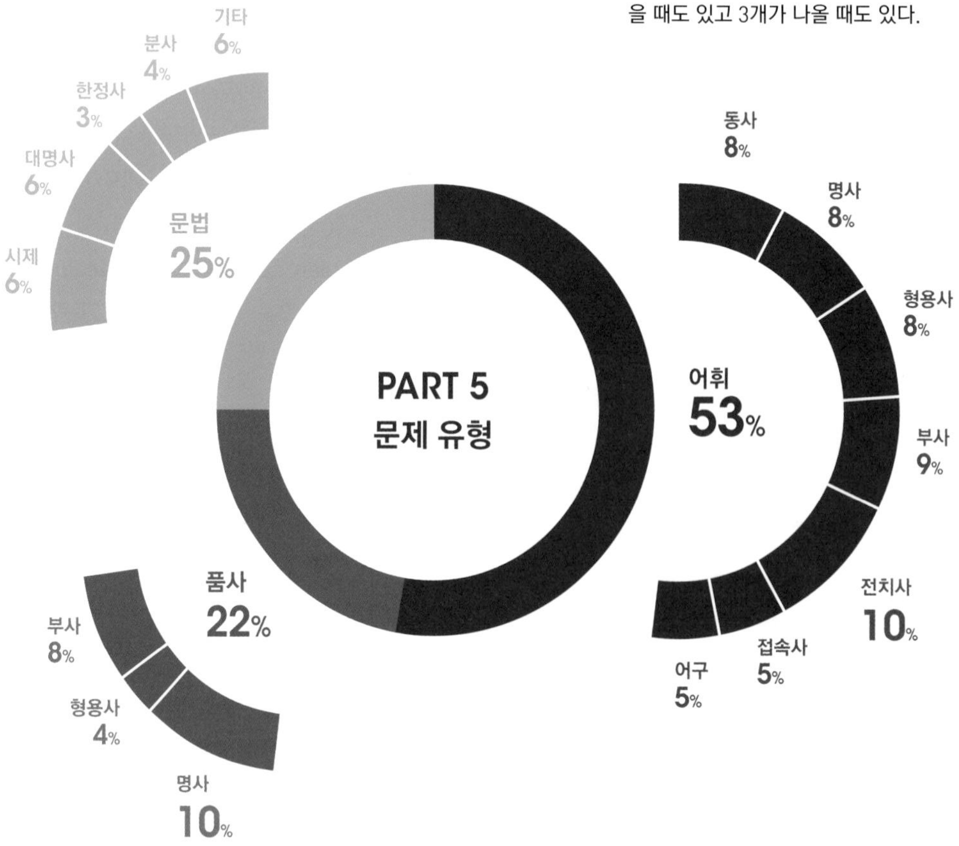

품사 문제

명사와 부사와 관련된 품사 문제가 2~3개씩 나오며, 형용사와 관련된 품사 문제가 상대적으로 적은 편이다.

PART 6 장문 빈칸 채우기 Text Completion

총 4지문 16문제 (지문당 4문제)

한 지문에 4문제가 나오며 평균적으로 어휘 문제가 2개, 품사나 문법 문제가 1개, 문맥에 맞는 문장 고르기 문제가 1개 들어간다. 문맥에 맞는 문장 고르기 문제를 제외하면 문제 유형은 기본적으로 파트 5와 거의 비슷하다.

어휘 문제

동사, 명사, 부사, 어구와 관련된 어휘 문제는 매번 1~2개씩 나온다. 부사 어휘 문제의 경우 therefore(그러므로)나 however(하지만)처럼 문맥의 흐름을 자연스럽게 연결해 주는 부사가 자주 나온다.

문맥에 맞는 문장 고르기

문맥에 맞는 문장 고르기 문제는 지문당 한 문제씩 나오는데, 나오는 위치의 확률은 4문제 중 두 번째 문제, 세 번째 문제, 네 번째 문제, 첫 번째 문제 순으로 높다.

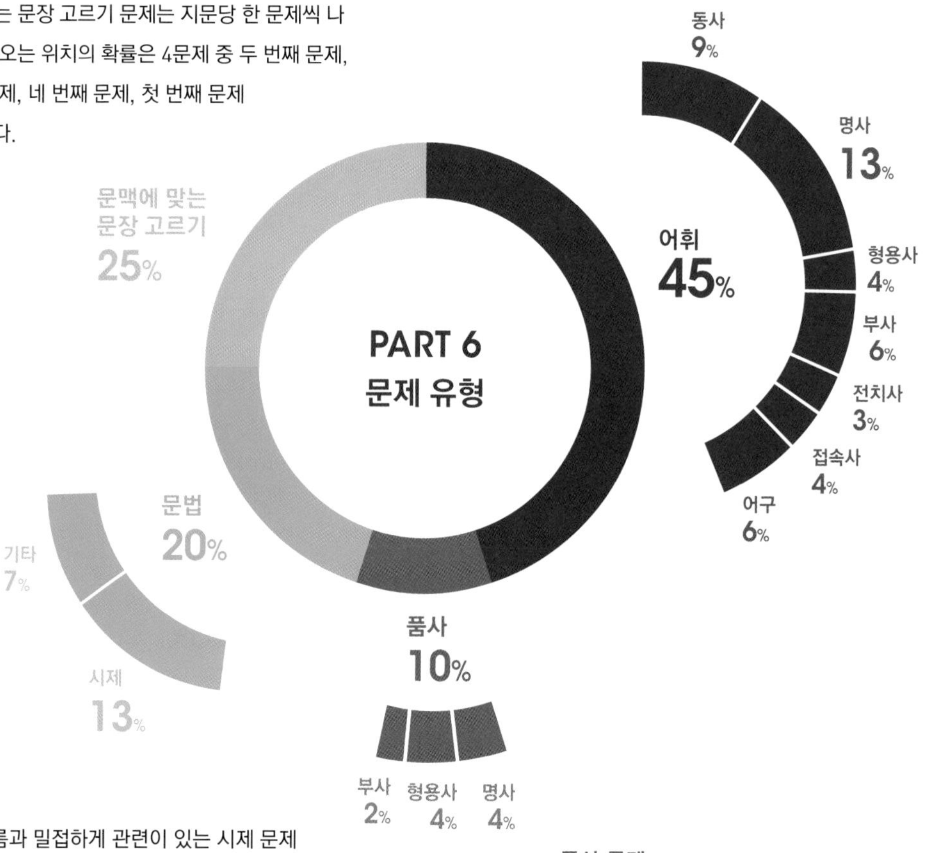

문법 문제

문맥의 흐름과 밀접하게 관련이 있는 시제 문제가 2개 정도 나오며, 능동태/수동태나 수의 일치와 연계되기도 한다. 그 밖에 대명사, 능동태/수동태, 부정사, 접속사/전치사 등과 관련된 문법 문제가 나온다.

품사 문제

명사나 형용사 문제가 부사 문제보다 좀 더 자주 나온다.

PART 7 독해 Reading Comprehension

총 15지문 54문제 (지문당 2~5문제)

지문 유형	지문당 문제 수	지문 개수	비중 %
단일 지문	2문항	4개	약 15%
	3문항	3개	약 16%
	4문항	3개	약 22%
이중 지문	5문항	2개	약 19%
삼중 지문	5문항	3개	약 28%

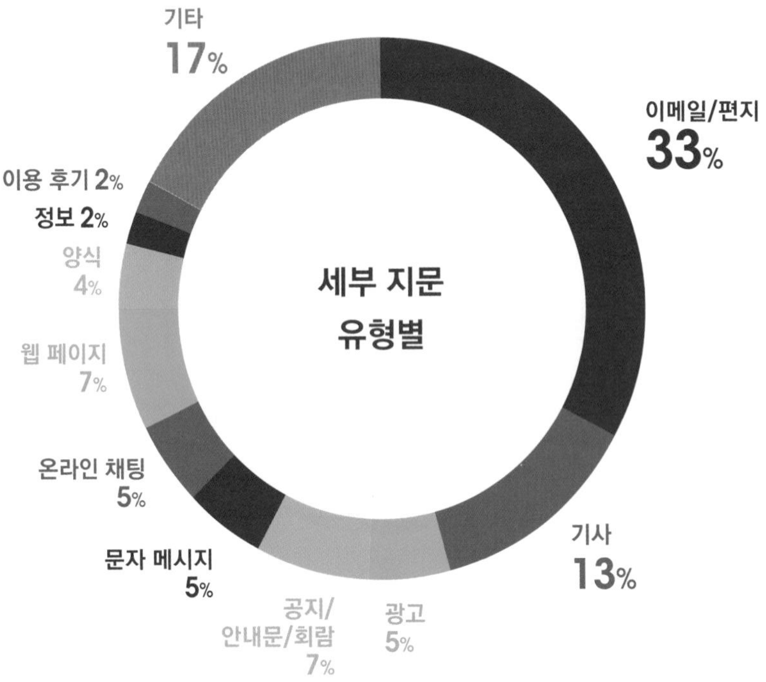

- 이메일/편지, 기사 유형 지문은 거의 항상 나오는 편이며 많은 경우 합해서 전체의 50~60%에 이르기도 한다.
- 기타 지문 유형으로 agenda, brochure, comment card, coupon, flyer, instructions, invitation, invoice, list, menu, page from a catalog, policy statement, report, schedule, survey, voucher 등 다양한 자료가 골고루 나온다.

(이중 지문과 삼중 지문 속의 지문들을 모두 낱개로 계산함 - 총 23지문)

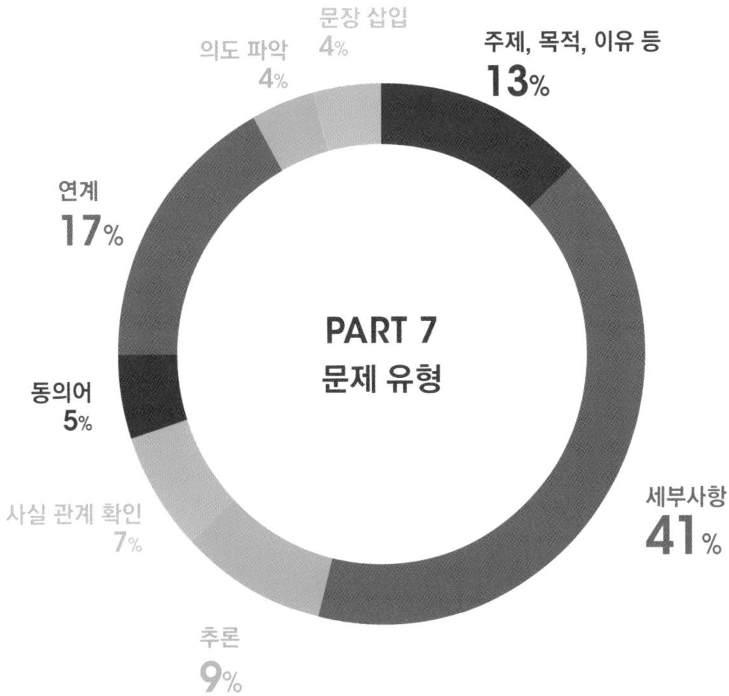

- 동의어 문제는 주로 이중 지문이나 삼중 지문에 나온다.
- 연계 문제는 일반적으로 이중 지문에서 한 문제, 삼중 지문에서 두 문제가 나온다.
- 의도 파악 문제는 문자 메시지(text-message chain)나 온라인 채팅(online chat discussion) 지문에서 출제되며 두 문제가 나온다.
- 문장 삽입 문제는 주로 기사, 이메일, 편지, 회람 지문에서 출제되며 두 문제가 나온다.

점수 환산표

LISTENING Raw Score (맞은 개수)	LISTENING Scaled Score (환산 점수)
96-100	480-495
91-95	435-490
86-90	395-450
81-85	355-415
76-80	325-375
71-75	295-340
66-70	265-315
61-65	240-285
56-60	215-260
51-55	190-235
46-50	160-210
41-45	135-180
36-40	110-155
31-35	85-130
26-30	70-105
21-25	50-90
16-20	35-70
11-15	20-55
6-10	15-40
1-5	5-20
0	5

READING Raw Score (맞은 개수)	READING Scaled Score (환산 점수)
96-100	460-495
91-95	410-475
86-90	380-430
81-85	355-400
76-80	325-375
71-75	295-345
66-70	265-315
61-65	235-285
56-60	205-255
51-55	175-225
46-50	150-195
41-45	120-170
36-40	100-140
31-35	75-120
26-30	55-100
21-25	40-80
16-20	30-65
11-15	20-50
6-10	15-35
1-5	5-20
0	5

* 이 환산표는 본 교재에 수록된 Test용으로 개발된 것이다. 이 표를 사용하여 자신의 실제 점수를 환산 점수로 전환하도록 한다. 즉, 예를 들어 Listening Test의 실제 정답 수가 61~65개이면 환산 점수는 240점에서 285점 사이가 된다. 여기서 실제 정답 수가 61개이면 환산 점수가 240점이고, 65개이면 환산 점수가 285점임을 의미하는 것은 아니다. 본 책의 Test를 위해 작성된 이 점수 환산표가 자신의 영어 실력이 어느 정도인지 대략적으로 파악하는 데 도움이 되긴 하지만, 이 표가 실제 TOEIC 성적 산출에 그대로 사용된 적은 없다는 사실을 밝혀 둔다.

CONTENTS

TEST 01 4

TEST 02 18

TEST 03 32

TEST 04 46

TEST 05 60

TEST 06 74

TEST 07 88

TEST 08 102

TEST 09 116

TEST 10 130

해설집

LC

TEST 1

LISTENING TEST

In the Listening test, you will be asked to demonstrate how well you understand spoken English. The entire Listening test will last approximately 45 minutes. There are four parts, and directions are given for each part. You must mark your answers on the separate answer sheet. Do not write your answers in your test book.

PART 1

Directions: For each question in this part, you will hear four statements about a picture in your test book. When you hear the statements, you must select the one statement that best describes what you see in the picture. Then find the number of the question on your answer sheet and mark your answer. The statements will not be printed in your test book and will be spoken only one time.

Statement (C), "They're sitting at a table," is the best description of the picture, so you should select answer (C) and mark it on your answer sheet.

Test 1

1.

2.

GO ON TO THE NEXT PAGE

3.

4.

5.

6.

GO ON TO THE NEXT PAGE

PART 2

Directions: You will hear a question or statement and three responses spoken in English. They will not be printed in your test book and will be spoken only one time. Select the best response to the question or statement and mark the letter (A), (B), or (C) on your answer sheet.

7. Mark your answer on your answer sheet.

8. Mark your answer on your answer sheet.

9. Mark your answer on your answer sheet.

10. Mark your answer on your answer sheet.

11. Mark your answer on your answer sheet.

12. Mark your answer on your answer sheet.

13. Mark your answer on your answer sheet.

14. Mark your answer on your answer sheet.

15. Mark your answer on your answer sheet.

16. Mark your answer on your answer sheet.

17. Mark your answer on your answer sheet.

18. Mark your answer on your answer sheet.

19. Mark your answer on your answer sheet.

20. Mark your answer on your answer sheet.

21. Mark your answer on your answer sheet.

22. Mark your answer on your answer sheet.

23. Mark your answer on your answer sheet.

24. Mark your answer on your answer sheet.

25. Mark your answer on your answer sheet.

26. Mark your answer on your answer sheet.

27. Mark your answer on your answer sheet.

28. Mark your answer on your answer sheet.

29. Mark your answer on your answer sheet.

30. Mark your answer on your answer sheet.

31. Mark your answer on your answer sheet.

PART 3

Directions: You will hear some conversations between two or more people. You will be asked to answer three questions about what the speakers say in each conversation. Select the best response to each question and mark the letter (A), (B), (C), or (D) on your answer sheet. The conversations will not be printed in your test book and will be spoken only one time.

32. Why is the woman calling?

(A) To place an order
(B) To check a delivery status
(C) To make an exchange
(D) To request a brochure

33. What does the man tell the woman about?

(A) A new service
(B) An additional fee
(C) A return policy
(D) A job opportunity

34. What does the man offer to do for the woman?

(A) Issue a receipt
(B) Recommend a product
(C) Write a message
(D) Search a storage room

---

35. What is the purpose of the woman's visit?

(A) To tour an office
(B) To interview for a position
(C) To give a demonstration
(D) To deliver a package

36. What does the man offer to do?

(A) Set up some equipment
(B) Reserve a conference room
(C) Help unload some items
(D) Look for his manager

37. What does the man tell the woman?

(A) A contract has already been drafted.
(B) A presentation's time slot was shortened.
(C) A meeting's location has changed.
(D) A group's size has increased.

---

38. What does the woman's company most likely manufacture?

(A) Hand tools
(B) Art supplies
(C) Office furniture
(D) Fashion accessories

39. Why was the woman disappointed with an advertising agency?

(A) It usually exceeded its budget.
(B) Its campaigns were not successful.
(C) It did not complete projects on time.
(D) Its ideas were not creative.

40. What will Todd most likely do next?

(A) Ask for more information
(B) Introduce an account team
(C) Suggest revisions to an agreement
(D) Present some market data

---

41. What does the man ask the woman to do?

(A) Review an invoice
(B) Schedule a delivery
(C) Sign a document
(D) Choose a payment option

42. What problem does the woman mention?

(A) An address is incorrect.
(B) Some goods are missing.
(C) A staff member is unavailable.
(D) Some boxes are very heavy.

43. What will the man do next?

(A) Start unpacking some containers
(B) Look in a vehicle for some items
(C) Contact his supervisor
(D) Print another shipping label

GO ON TO THE NEXT PAGE →

44. What is the purpose of the woman's call?

(A) To make a complaint
(B) To upgrade a service
(C) To inquire about rates
(D) To cancel a contract

45. What information does the man ask for?

(A) A total charge
(B) A street address
(C) An account number
(D) A transaction date

46. According to the man, how long will it take to make a change?

(A) Two days
(B) Five days
(C) One week
(D) Two weeks

---

47. Where most likely does the man work?

(A) At a construction business
(B) At an interior decorating firm
(C) At a real estate agency
(D) At a landscaping company

48. Why does the woman say, "He told me three days"?

(A) To show regret
(B) To clarify a schedule
(C) To answer a complaint
(D) To request a specific team

49. Why is the woman pleased?

(A) She is eligible for a discount on the work.
(B) She can join a customer loyalty program.
(C) The company will not charge a fee to make a change.
(D) The company returned her call quickly.

---

50. What is the woman unsure about?

(A) How to travel to the airport
(B) When a flight will depart
(C) Where a check-in counter is
(D) Which airline to fly with

51. What does the man offer to do?

(A) Share some news with a group of colleagues
(B) Reserve a type of transportation
(C) Consult an official Web site
(D) Create an electronic spreadsheet

52. What does the woman say she will do?

(A) Pack only one bag
(B) Prepare to leave soon
(C) Sit in a nearby waiting area
(D) Use an office messaging service

---

53. What are the women asked to do?

(A) Interview job candidates
(B) Design an advertisement
(C) Conduct a training session
(D) Prepare some work spaces

54. Why is the man concerned?

(A) The available time is limited.
(B) Some employees are absent today.
(C) The budget for an event is low.
(D) Some equipment is not working.

55. What will the women do to solve the problem?

(A) Send materials in advance
(B) Consult an expert
(C) Hire some temporary workers
(D) Adjust a printing schedule

---

56. Where most likely does the man work?

(A) At a carpet store
(B) At a car dealership
(C) At a clothing retailer
(D) At an appliance store

57. What is the woman worried about?

(A) Getting the wrong size
(B) Having to pay for repeated repairs
(C) Spending too much on energy
(D) Being confused by some instructions

58. According to the man, what special offer is available this week?

(A) A discounted price
(B) An extended warranty
(C) Complimentary installation
(D) Free samples

---

59. What project is the woman working on?

(A) Expanding a building
(B) Renovating a room
(C) Constructing a new house
(D) Decorating an office

60. What does the woman mean when she says, "It doesn't seem like much"?

(A) She is disappointed with the selection.
(B) She is unsure about the amount she needs.
(C) She thinks the prices are very affordable.
(D) She thought a process would take longer.

61. What does the man recommend doing?

(A) Browsing in a different section
(B) Taking advantage of a sale
(C) Visiting an online store
(D) Coming back another day

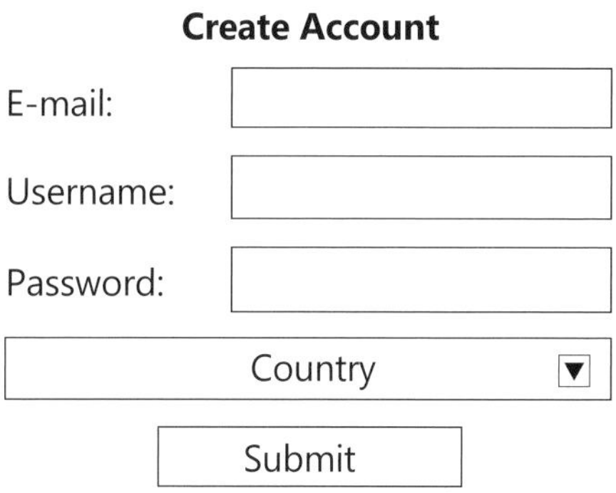

62. What was the woman doing earlier?

(A) Attending a client meeting
(B) Analyzing the results of a survey
(C) Watching a software demonstration
(D) Arranging a press conference

63. Look at the graphic. Which field will appear above "Submit" after the requested change?

(A) E-mail
(B) Username
(C) Password
(D) Country

64. What most likely is the purpose of the Web site being designed?

(A) To provide a place for discussion
(B) To give travel directions
(C) To sell a company's merchandise
(D) To allow users to search the Internet

GO ON TO THE NEXT PAGE →

Screen Replacement: Winona Phones	
Model	**Cost**
8R	$140
7R	$135
4L	$125
3L	$100

65. What will the woman do next week?

(A) Upgrade a phone plan
(B) Move to another city
(C) Start a new job
(D) Go on a business trip

66. Look at the graphic. Which phone model does the woman have?

(A) 8R
(B) 7R
(C) 4L
(D) 3L

67. What does the man ask the woman to do?

(A) Make a payment
(B) Provide a contact number
(C) Present a receipt
(D) Complete a form

Powell Theater Presents

the Meadow City Orchestra

Sunday, June 18 at 3:00 P.M.

Admit One: General Seating

68. What does the woman say about the tickets?

(A) She purchased some online.
(B) They will be sent by mail.
(C) They are sold out now.
(D) Their price was raised.

69. What does the man offer to do?

(A) Check a show's start time
(B) Call the woman when he arrives
(C) Buy some extra tickets
(D) Give the woman a ride

70. Look at the graphic. When does the man want to meet on Sunday?

(A) At 1:30 P.M.
(B) At 2:00 P.M.
(C) At 2:30 P.M.
(D) At 3:00 P.M.

PART 4

Directions: You will hear some talks given by a single speaker. You will be asked to answer three questions about what the speaker says in each talk. Select the best response to each question and mark the letter (A), (B), (C), or (D) on your answer sheet. The talks will not be printed in your test book and will be spoken only one time.

71. What has the speaker recently done?
(A) Evaluated staff members
(B) Run a marketing campaign
(C) Participated in a seminar
(D) Analyzed some figures

72. What does the speaker want to do?
(A) Launch a new product
(B) Monitor operating expenses
(C) Improve the magazine's layout
(D) Increase subscriptions

73. Why should the listeners e-mail the speaker?
(A) To share suggestions
(B) To get spending approval
(C) To confirm attendance
(D) To select a meeting time

---

74. What problem does the speaker mention?
(A) A shipment arrived late.
(B) Some items were the wrong model.
(C) A Web site is not working.
(D) Some merchandise was damaged.

75. What does the speaker want to do?
(A) Use a coupon
(B) Cancel an order
(C) Get a replacement
(D) Receive a refund

76. Why should the listener call the speaker back?
(A) To arrange a delivery
(B) To provide an estimate
(C) To explain a process
(D) To issue a code

77. According to the speaker, what will happen tomorrow?
(A) An inspection will take place.
(B) A branch will have a grand opening.
(C) The store will stay open late.
(D) A new product will be released.

78. Who most likely is Ms. Lansing?
(A) An inventor
(B) An assistant manager
(C) A journalist
(D) A business owner

79. What does the speaker say she will do?
(A) Provide some refreshments
(B) Confirm a work schedule
(C) Make copies of a manual
(D) Get feedback from customers

---

80. What is the broadcast mainly about?
(A) Shopping tips
(B) Party planning
(C) Home baking
(D) Cleaning techniques

81. According to the speaker, what will be posted on the Web site from next week?
(A) Previous broadcasts
(B) Discount offers
(C) Detailed instructions
(D) Photo collections

82. Why does the speaker say, "Be a part of it"?
(A) To encourage the listeners to give feedback
(B) To give a preview of the next show
(C) To promote a special event
(D) To urge the listeners to apply for a job opening

GO ON TO THE NEXT PAGE

83. What is the purpose of the event?

(A) To recognize an employee's achievement
(B) To celebrate a company anniversary
(C) To show appreciation for a retiring executive
(D) To publicize a business expansion

84. Who most likely is Mr. Kott?

(A) A lab employee
(B) A company president
(C) A salesperson
(D) A financial consultant

85. What does the speaker remind listeners to do?

(A) Indicate a meal preference
(B) Sign a greeting card
(C) Have their picture taken
(D) Review some information

---

86. What did the listener send the speaker?

(A) A questionnaire
(B) A magazine article
(C) A budget report
(D) An advertisement

87. What does the speaker imply when he says, "is this really it"?

(A) He thinks some information is missing.
(B) He is not pleased with a quality level.
(C) He cannot find the file he needs.
(D) He is surprised by a quick response.

88. What does the speaker ask the listener to do?

(A) Come to his desk
(B) Hire a professional
(C) E-mail some notes
(D) Work extra hours

---

89. What is the main topic of the broadcast?

(A) A mobile app
(B) Self-service machines
(C) A city regulation
(D) Bicycle lanes

90. According to Ms. Howell, why was a change made?

(A) To reduce some expenses
(B) To impress the organizers of an event
(C) To improve an area's air quality
(D) To shorten some wait times

91. How are some people responding to the change?

(A) They are buying more locally-made goods.
(B) They are asking others to sign an agreement.
(C) They have fulfilled some safety requirements.
(D) They plan to stop visiting a business.

---

92. What is the speaker calling about?

(A) A Web development project
(B) An upcoming trade show
(C) Office supplies spending
(D) Participation in a photo shoot

93. What does the speaker imply when she says, "a lot of them were left over afterwards"?

(A) The listener can obtain some equipment for free.
(B) She requires assistance with a task.
(C) A storage space is full.
(D) A proposal should be revised.

94. What does the speaker offer to send the listener?

(A) Some financial data
(B) A catalog
(C) An access code
(D) Some product accessories

Schedule	
8:00 A.M.	Session 1
9:00 A.M.	Session 2
10:00 A.M.	Session 3
11:00 A.M.	Session 4

95. Who most likely are the listeners?
(A) Conference presenters
(B) Lecture attendees
(C) Contest judges
(D) Workshop participants

96. What does the speaker say is especially important?
(A) Asking questions
(B) Following guidelines
(C) Using teamwork
(D) Taking notes

97. Look at the graphic. When will the listeners speak to Ms. Miller?
(A) At 8:00 A.M.
(B) At 9:00 A.M.
(C) At 10:00 A.M.
(D) At 11:00 A.M.

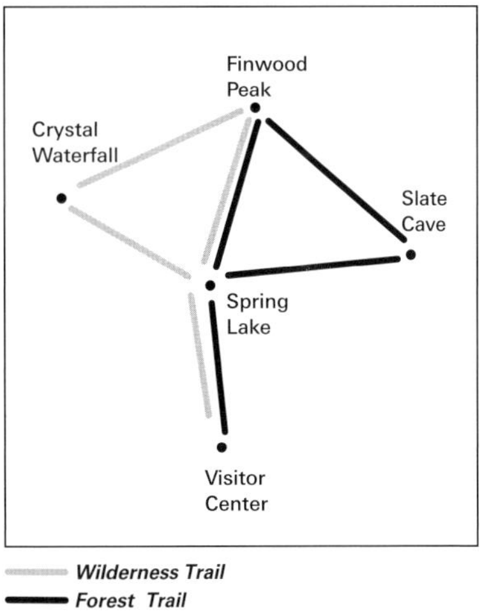

98. Why does the speaker apologize to the listeners?
(A) One of the hiking trails is closed.
(B) The group is larger than expected.
(C) Some reservations were lost.
(D) The tour is starting later than planned.

99. Look at the graphic. Which site is usually not included in the hike?
(A) Crystal Waterfall
(B) Finwood Peak
(C) Spring Lake
(D) Slate Cave

100. What does the speaker remind the listeners to do?
(A) Avoid touching plants
(B) Put on safety gear
(C) Bring along their cameras
(D) Stay on the trail

This is the end of the Listening test. Turn to Part 5 in your test book.

LC

TEST 2

LISTENING TEST

In the Listening test, you will be asked to demonstrate how well you understand spoken English. The entire Listening test will last approximately 45 minutes. There are four parts, and directions are given for each part. You must mark your answers on the separate answer sheet. Do not write your answers in your test book.

PART 1

Directions: For each question in this part, you will hear four statements about a picture in your test book. When you hear the statements, you must select the one statement that best describes what you see in the picture. Then find the number of the question on your answer sheet and mark your answer. The statements will not be printed in your test book and will be spoken only one time.

Statement (C), "They're sitting at a table," is the best description of the picture, so you should select answer (C) and mark it on your answer sheet.

1.

2.

GO ON TO THE NEXT PAGE

3.

4.

5.

6.

GO ON TO THE NEXT PAGE

PART 2

Directions: You will hear a question or statement and three responses spoken in English. They will not be printed in your test book and will be spoken only one time. Select the best response to the question or statement and mark the letter (A), (B), or (C) on your answer sheet.

7. Mark your answer on your answer sheet.

8. Mark your answer on your answer sheet.

9. Mark your answer on your answer sheet.

10. Mark your answer on your answer sheet.

11. Mark your answer on your answer sheet.

12. Mark your answer on your answer sheet.

13. Mark your answer on your answer sheet.

14. Mark your answer on your answer sheet.

15. Mark your answer on your answer sheet.

16. Mark your answer on your answer sheet.

17. Mark your answer on your answer sheet.

18. Mark your answer on your answer sheet.

19. Mark your answer on your answer sheet.

20. Mark your answer on your answer sheet.

21. Mark your answer on your answer sheet.

22. Mark your answer on your answer sheet.

23. Mark your answer on your answer sheet.

24. Mark your answer on your answer sheet.

25. Mark your answer on your answer sheet.

26. Mark your answer on your answer sheet.

27. Mark your answer on your answer sheet.

28. Mark your answer on your answer sheet.

29. Mark your answer on your answer sheet.

30. Mark your answer on your answer sheet.

31. Mark your answer on your answer sheet.

PART 3

Directions: You will hear some conversations between two or more people. You will be asked to answer three questions about what the speakers say in each conversation. Select the best response to each question and mark the letter (A), (B), (C), or (D) on your answer sheet. The conversations will not be printed in your test book and will be spoken only one time.

32. What has the man misplaced?

(A) A new smartphone
(B) A locker key
(C) A library card
(D) A borrowed book

33. What does the woman explain to the man?

(A) An advantage of a technology
(B) A reason for a refusal
(C) A cleaning routine
(D) A choice of options

34. What does the woman tell the man to do?

(A) Wait for several days
(B) Fill out some paperwork
(C) Search some study areas
(D) Post a notice on a bulletin board

---

35. Where does the man most likely work?

(A) At a bus station
(B) At a taxi service
(C) At a ferry terminal
(D) At an airport

36. Why is the woman calling?

(A) To inquire about a travel schedule
(B) To request a ticket exchange
(C) To report a billing problem
(D) To change a reservation

37. What does the man remind the woman to do?

(A) Wear waterproof clothing
(B) Arrive at the site early
(C) Bring some documents
(D) Check the weight of her luggage

---

38. Where is the conversation most likely taking place?

(A) At a history museum
(B) At an amusement park
(C) At a department store
(D) At a sports stadium

39. According to the man, what happened last year?

(A) Renovations were carried out.
(B) Operating hours were shortened.
(C) A celebrity filmed an advertisement.
(D) A lease was not renewed.

40. How will the man help the women?

(A) By giving them a brochure
(B) By guiding them to a location
(C) By issuing a public announcement
(D) By writing down some directions

---

41. What does the man's company specialize in?

(A) Property management
(B) Employee recruitment
(C) Financial consulting
(D) Medical research

42. What does the woman want to do on Thursday?

(A) Visit the man's office
(B) Update a database
(C) Start some training
(D) Conduct some interviews

43. What does the man offer to do?

(A) Waive a fee
(B) Check a calendar
(C) Send some résumés
(D) E-mail an invoice

GO ON TO THE NEXT PAGE

44. What problem does the man mention?
(A) A component is difficult to install.
(B) A product has been discontinued.
(C) A form was filled out incorrectly.
(D) A shipment has been delayed.

45. Why does the man recommend visiting a Web site?
(A) To place an order
(B) To read a policy
(C) To open an account
(D) To request a refund

46. What does the woman inquire about?
(A) A retail store
(B) A delivery period
(C) A warranty extension
(D) A price reduction

---

47. What is the main topic of the conversation?
(A) A safety procedure
(B) A business relocation
(C) A new vendor
(D) A loan agreement

48. What does the man mention about the speakers' company?
(A) Its workforce has grown.
(B) Its goods are popular.
(C) Its leadership has changed.
(D) Its building is modern.

49. What does the man suggest?
(A) Researching a competitor
(B) Walking around a site
(C) Drafting a memo
(D) Conducting a survey

---

50. Where most likely are the speakers?
(A) At a professional workshop
(B) At a board meeting
(C) At a job interview
(D) At a welcome reception

51. What achievement does the man describe?
(A) Improving employee productivity
(B) Increasing a company's sales
(C) Hiring a marketing specialist
(D) Reducing distribution costs

52. What does the man propose?
(A) Using newspapers to share coupons
(B) Targeting some current clients
(C) Holding a press conference
(D) Analyzing some financial data

---

53. Who most likely are the speakers?
(A) Moving consultants
(B) Real estate agents
(C) Interior designers
(D) Equipment suppliers

54. What does the woman mean when she says, "That'll make a big difference"?
(A) She wants additional workers to help.
(B) She hopes her recommendation is accepted.
(C) She is unsure about a final price.
(D) She needs to confirm some measurements.

55. What does the man say he will prepare?
(A) A cost estimate
(B) Some company brochures
(C) An updated contract
(D) Some product samples

---

56. What is the conversation mainly about?
(A) A colleague's promotion
(B) An investment bank
(C) An awards dinner
(D) A fund-raising campaign

57. What are the speakers having trouble doing?
(A) Arranging transportation
(B) Finding out some details
(C) Staying within a budget
(D) Making a decision

58. What does the woman suggest doing?
(A) Speaking with a supervisor
(B) Rescheduling a meeting
(C) Using a certain Web site
(D) Reviewing some records

59. What does the woman say about some sweaters?
(A) They are selling well.
(B) They are part of a window display.
(C) They are not yet available for purchase.
(D) They do not fit in a storage container.

60. What does the man mean when he says, "The changing rooms are always a mess"?
(A) More changing rooms are needed.
(B) He wants the woman to tidy up an area.
(C) The store is usually understaffed.
(D) He is disappointed with the customers.

61. What will the man probably do next?
(A) Take a short break
(B) Organize some clothing
(C) Unpack some boxes
(D) Call a coworker

Room	Guest Complaint
215	No hand soap
246	Sheets unchanged
320	Wet towels left on floor
334	Spots on dressing room mirror

62. What does the woman say about her department?
(A) Its workers need more training.
(B) It will be combined with another team.
(C) It does not have enough supplies.
(D) Its schedule must be revised.

63. Look at the graphic. In which room is Ms. Harper staying?
(A) Room 215
(B) Room 246
(C) Room 320
(D) Room 334

64. What does the man say he will do?
(A) Provide some free meals
(B) Clarify a hotel policy
(C) Give a discount on a room rate
(D) Collect additional feedback

GO ON TO THE NEXT PAGE

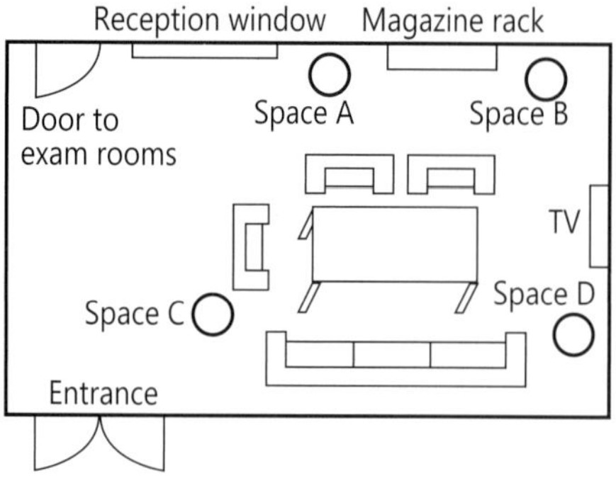

65. What kind of item are the speakers discussing?
(A) A potted plant
(B) A standing lamp
(C) A coat rack
(D) A small table

66. Look at the graphic. In which space will the woman put the item?
(A) Space A
(B) Space B
(C) Space C
(D) Space D

67. What does the woman say she will do in the afternoon?
(A) Sign for a delivery
(B) Make an announcement
(C) Set out some publications
(D) Read some instructions

Conifer Suites Building Directory	
1st Floor	Tukwila Enterprises
2nd Floor	Tech Limited
3rd Floor	Young & Associates
4th Floor	RTJ Insurance

68. What are the speakers doing?
(A) Repairing an appliance
(B) Cleaning some offices
(C) Inspecting the building
(D) Installing some equipment

69. Look at the graphic. According to the man, which company's office has a problem?
(A) Tukwila Enterprises
(B) Tech Limited
(C) Young & Associates
(D) RTJ Insurance

70. What does the woman suggest?
(A) Using some different materials
(B) Contacting a property owner
(C) Placing a supply request
(D) Finishing work for the day

PART 4

Directions: You will hear some talks given by a single speaker. You will be asked to answer three questions about what the speaker says in each talk. Select the best response to each question and mark the letter (A), (B), (C), or (D) on your answer sheet. The talks will not be printed in your test book and will be spoken only one time.

71. According to the speaker, what is the purpose of the event?
(A) To raise money
(B) To celebrate an achievement
(C) To vote on a plan
(D) To promote a competition

72. What has been posted around the hall?
(A) Estimated values
(B) A list of volunteers
(C) Photos of a neighborhood
(D) The results of a questionnaire

73. What does the speaker remind the listeners to do?
(A) Sit in assigned seats
(B) Register for a session
(C) Watch a short film
(D) Pick up a set of gifts

74. What is the talk mainly about?
(A) Tracking work hours electronically
(B) Participating in a conference call
(C) Creating videos of events
(D) Setting up an e-mail account

75. What does the speaker say about some technology?
(A) The listeners will try it out soon.
(B) It can only be used by an expert.
(C) He does not have access to it today.
(D) It will increase the company's efficiency.

76. What are the listeners asked to avoid doing?
(A) Running in the workplace
(B) Damaging a device
(C) Making unnecessary noise
(D) Losing a password

77. Why will the listener go to Mumbai?
(A) To attend a conference
(B) To inspect a factory
(C) To establish an office
(D) To sign a contract

78. According to the speaker, what should the listener do next week?
(A) Review an itinerary
(B) Visit a medical facility
(C) Book accommodations
(D) Renew a passport

79. What information does the speaker request?
(A) A seating preference
(B) An airline name
(C) A ticket number
(D) A hotel recommendation

80. What is the speaker giving an update on?
(A) Preparations for some promotional events
(B) Negotiations with a potential new hire
(C) The development of some consumer goods
(D) The attempted acquisition of a business

81. Why does the speaker say, "it isn't over yet"?
(A) To remind listeners of some unfinished tasks
(B) To express frustration with the speed of a process
(C) To give listeners hope of a positive end result
(D) To explain why she does not have some information

82. What does the speaker say about a government agency?
(A) It may fund a project.
(B) It oversees the healthcare industry.
(C) It is seeking a service provider.
(D) It may reject a proposal.

GO ON TO THE NEXT PAGE →

83. What is being announced?

(A) A start time has been postponed.
(B) A performance has been canceled.
(C) Some machinery is malfunctioning.
(D) Some merchandise is out of stock.

84. What are the listeners asked to do?

(A) Leave the area
(B) Show a form of identification
(C) Turn off their mobile phones
(D) Look at a display board

85. What will be given to the listeners?

(A) A refund of an entrance fee
(B) Directions to a convenience facility
(C) An express ticket to any other attraction
(D) A voucher for a souvenir shop

---

86. What is the speaker reporting on?

(A) A grand opening
(B) A product launch
(C) A restaurant's relocation
(D) A change in ownership

87. What does the speaker mean when she says, "They're going to be here for hours"?

(A) The business will remain open later than usual.
(B) There is enough time to take advantage of an offer.
(C) The business has a reputation for slow service.
(D) A lot of people are waiting to get into the business.

88. What is mentioned about the Chocolate Tower dessert?

(A) It has been discounted.
(B) It takes a long time to prepare.
(C) It uses foreign ingredients.
(D) It is already sold out.

---

89. What is the purpose of the call?

(A) To plan a celebration
(B) To show appreciation
(C) To extend an invitation
(D) To ask for some assistance

90. What does the speaker imply when he says, "I'd love to know where you got them printed"?

(A) He hopes printing costs are not over budget.
(B) He has to send a payment to a printer.
(C) He will need printing services in the future.
(D) He is having trouble selling a printing machine.

91. According to the speaker, what will happen next week?

(A) A new employee will begin work.
(B) The listener will give a talk at a meeting.
(C) Some office equipment will be replaced.
(D) The listener will have some time off.

---

92. What field does the Emerson Institute offer courses in?

(A) Software development
(B) Accounting practices
(C) Graphic design
(D) Creative writing

93. What is the Emerson Institute known for?

(A) Its opportunities for networking
(B) Its convenient class times
(C) Its wide selection of courses
(D) Its knowledgeable instructors

94. According to the advertisement, what will happen on February 6?

(A) An enrollment period will begin.
(B) An information session will be held.
(C) A course catalog will be published.
(D) A campus tour will be given.

Linens Request	
Item Type	**Quantity Needed**
Bar Towels	0
Kitchen Towels	0
Tablecloths	22
Napkins	0

Schedule of Departmental Talks	
9:00 A.M.	Sales
11:00 A.M.	R&D
12:30 P.M.	Lunch
1:30 P.M.	Marketing
3:30 P.M.	IT

95. Look at the graphic. Which branch made the request?

(A) Augusta
(B) Enfield
(C) Worthington
(D) Glendale

96. What is the speaker concerned about?

(A) Missing a deadline for an order
(B) Lacking the necessary storage space
(C) Paying high shipping charges
(D) Getting the wrong sizes

97. What is the listener asked to do?

(A) Report information to the managers
(B) Verify the contents of a package
(C) Choose a date for a gathering
(D) Monitor a branch's inventory

98. Who most likely are the listeners?

(A) Job candidates
(B) New employees
(C) Company executives
(D) Potential investors

99. Look at the graphic. When will Ms. Whitley give a talk?

(A) At 9:00 A.M.
(B) At 11:00 A.M.
(C) At 1:30 P.M.
(D) At 3:30 P.M.

100. According to the speaker, what will the listeners do at the end of the day?

(A) Go on a guided tour
(B) Receive some samples
(C) Take a written test
(D) Meet a business owner

This is the end of the Listening test. Turn to Part 5 in your test book.

LC

TEST 3

LISTENING TEST

In the Listening test, you will be asked to demonstrate how well you understand spoken English. The entire Listening test will last approximately 45 minutes. There are four parts, and directions are given for each part. You must mark your answers on the separate answer sheet. Do not write your answers in your test book.

PART 1

Directions: For each question in this part, you will hear four statements about a picture in your test book. When you hear the statements, you must select the one statement that best describes what you see in the picture. Then find the number of the question on your answer sheet and mark your answer. The statements will not be printed in your test book and will be spoken only one time.

Statement (C), "They're sitting at a table," is the best description of the picture, so you should select answer (C) and mark it on your answer sheet.

1.

2.

GO ON TO THE NEXT PAGE

3.

4.

5.

6.

GO ON TO THE NEXT PAGE

PART 2

Directions: You will hear a question or statement and three responses spoken in English. They will not be printed in your test book and will be spoken only one time. Select the best response to the question or statement and mark the letter (A), (B), or (C) on your answer sheet.

7. Mark your answer on your answer sheet.

8. Mark your answer on your answer sheet.

9. Mark your answer on your answer sheet.

10. Mark your answer on your answer sheet.

11. Mark your answer on your answer sheet.

12. Mark your answer on your answer sheet.

13. Mark your answer on your answer sheet.

14. Mark your answer on your answer sheet.

15. Mark your answer on your answer sheet.

16. Mark your answer on your answer sheet.

17. Mark your answer on your answer sheet.

18. Mark your answer on your answer sheet.

19. Mark your answer on your answer sheet.

20. Mark your answer on your answer sheet.

21. Mark your answer on your answer sheet.

22. Mark your answer on your answer sheet.

23. Mark your answer on your answer sheet.

24. Mark your answer on your answer sheet.

25. Mark your answer on your answer sheet.

26. Mark your answer on your answer sheet.

27. Mark your answer on your answer sheet.

28. Mark your answer on your answer sheet.

29. Mark your answer on your answer sheet.

30. Mark your answer on your answer sheet.

31. Mark your answer on your answer sheet.

PART 3

Directions: You will hear some conversations between two or more people. You will be asked to answer three questions about what the speakers say in each conversation. Select the best response to each question and mark the letter (A), (B), (C), or (D) on your answer sheet. The conversations will not be printed in your test book and will be spoken only one time.

32. Where most likely are the speakers?

(A) At a clothing store
(B) At a café
(C) At a dry cleaner's
(D) At a pharmacy

33. According to the woman, why is the man lucky?

(A) A business is open.
(B) A person is nearby.
(C) A sale is being held.
(D) A seat is empty.

34. What will the man most likely do next?

(A) Write down some instructions
(B) Choose between two items
(C) Consult a calendar
(D) Call a coworker

---

35. According to the woman, what has Haruto asked for?

(A) Information about profits
(B) Some customer profiles
(C) A travel itinerary
(D) A design proposal

36. What happened in May?

(A) Haruto was promoted.
(B) A merger took place.
(C) New merchandise was released.
(D) A financial period ended.

37. What does the man say he will do?

(A) Create a report
(B) Organize a meeting
(C) Contact Haruto
(D) Search for a form

---

38. What does the woman say she will do in New York City?

(A) Have a medical checkup
(B) Pick up a friend
(C) See tourist attractions
(D) Visit corporate headquarters

39. What does the man say the woman can do on Grand Street?

(A) Catch a taxi
(B) Rent a car
(C) Board a train
(D) Take a bus

40. Why does the woman ask about a train?

(A) She enjoys riding trains.
(B) She would prefer a shorter journey.
(C) She is concerned about prices.
(D) She has a lot of luggage.

---

41. What are the speakers preparing for?

(A) A regional contest
(B) Some market research
(C) Some training workshops
(D) A community service activity

42. Why has it been difficult to find participants?

(A) A low amount of compensation is being offered.
(B) Many people do not meet some requirements.
(C) Previous events did not go well.
(D) A location is far from a city.

43. What does the woman suggest doing?

(A) Providing a free shuttle bus ride
(B) Applying for a government grant
(C) Posting on a social networking service
(D) Hiring an advertising consultant

GO ON TO THE NEXT PAGE

44. What is the conversation mainly about?

(A) Receiving a discount
(B) Checking a credit card charge
(C) Exchanging a defective device
(D) Understanding a contract

45. What does the woman most likely give the man?

(A) A coupon
(B) A warranty
(C) A receipt
(D) A phone number

46. Why will the speakers speak to a manager?

(A) To process a complaint
(B) To inquire about some stock
(C) To confirm a store policy
(D) To obtain authorization

---

47. Where most likely do the speakers work?

(A) At a convention center
(B) At a shipping company
(C) At a journalism organization
(D) At a kitchen appliance manufacturer

48. What does the man say is a possible problem for an event?

(A) The budget
(B) The starting time
(C) The number of attendees
(D) The type of food to be served

49. What does Jen offer to do?

(A) Explain a Web site's features
(B) Design electronic invitations
(C) Carry some items to a nearby office
(D) Make some photocopies

---

50. What kind of products does the speakers' company make?

(A) Business stationery
(B) Travel bags
(C) Cosmetics
(D) Beverages

51. What does the woman imply when she says, "the plane leaves at five in the afternoon"?

(A) She thinks she will miss a flight.
(B) She intends to stay longer at an event.
(C) The speakers should try to take an earlier flight.
(D) The speakers do not have to worry about time.

52. What will the man probably do next?

(A) Stop by a print shop
(B) Order a meal for delivery
(C) Phone a taxi company
(D) Send some e-mails

---

53. Who most likely is the woman?

(A) A building owner
(B) A maintenance worker
(C) A safety inspector
(D) A real estate agent

54. What does the woman mention about some buildings?

(A) They are near transportation stops.
(B) They were recently renovated.
(C) They are well-known.
(D) They are tall.

55. What aspect of some spaces does the man ask about?

(A) Availability
(B) Cleanliness
(C) Security
(D) Size

---

56. What is the woman concerned about?
(A) Declining sales
(B) Computer problems
(C) Inventory shortages
(D) Customer complaints

57. Why does the man say, "what can I do"?
(A) To give advice
(B) To indicate regret
(C) To offer assistance
(D) To correct a misunderstanding

58. What does the woman say she will do in the afternoon?
(A) Rearrange some shelves
(B) Review a financial plan
(C) Distribute some flyers
(D) Meet with a local writer

---

59. What are the speakers discussing?
(A) Building a new parking area
(B) Changing a fee payment method
(C) Expanding employee benefits
(D) Establishing a business partnership

60. According to the woman, what is the advantage of accepting a proposal?
(A) A department would be able to save money.
(B) A manufacturing procedure would become more efficient.
(C) The company's public image would improve.
(D) Staff would be less inconvenienced.

61. What does the man want to know?
(A) When he has to make a decision
(B) What some competitors will do
(C) Whether other people agree with him
(D) Where some funding will come from

Directory	
Floor	**Category**
4	Magazines, Audiobooks
3	Nonfiction
2	Fiction, Special Collections
1	Children's Books

62. Look at the graphic. Which floor are the computers located on?
(A) 4
(B) 3
(C) 2
(D) 1

63. What problem does the man mention?
(A) He does not have a card.
(B) He did not return a book on time.
(C) He cannot find an audiobook.
(D) He could not reserve a study room.

64. What does the woman ask the man for?
(A) A log-in password
(B) The name of an author
(C) Personal identification
(D) A completed form

Test 3

GO ON TO THE NEXT PAGE

Orientation Agenda	
1. Welcome	Teri Duncan
2. Policies	Cindy Kim
3. Resources	Will Singleton
4. Systems	Ewa Kaminski

65. Why is the man speaking to the woman?
(A) To learn details about the orientation
(B) To receive an update on a project
(C) To request a special assignment
(D) To notify her of a revision to the agenda

66. Look at the graphic. Who will the man replace as a speaker?
(A) Teri Duncan
(B) Cindy Kim
(C) Will Singleton
(D) Ewa Kaminski

67. What does the man encourage the woman to do?
(A) Download some additional software
(B) Greet some new employees
(C) Negotiate a later deadline
(D) Concentrate on a development task

Juice	Price
Orange	$3.00
Mango	$3.50
Strawberry	$4.00
Grapefruit	$4.50

68. What problem are the speakers discussing?
(A) A product is not available.
(B) A shipment has been delayed.
(C) A machine is broken.
(D) A price has been miscalculated.

69. Look at the graphic. How much does a watermelon juice cost?
(A) $3.00
(B) $3.50
(C) $4.00
(D) $4.50

70. What does the man ask the woman to do tomorrow?
(A) Attach a notice to a menu
(B) Unpack some boxes
(C) Wash some fruit
(D) Ask a question

PART 4

Directions: You will hear some talks given by a single speaker. You will be asked to answer three questions about what the speaker says in each talk. Select the best response to each question and mark the letter (A), (B), (C), or (D) on your answer sheet. The talks will not be printed in your test book and will be spoken only one time.

71. What kind of business is the speaker calling?
(A) A magazine publisher
(B) A utility company
(C) A travel agency
(D) A bank

72. What does the speaker say he will do next week?
(A) Make a large purchase
(B) Go to another country
(C) Start a new job
(D) Renew a membership

73. What does the speaker want to change?
(A) A delivery method
(B) An account restriction
(C) Some reservation dates
(D) Part of an employment contract

---

74. What is the news report mainly about?
(A) An upcoming festival
(B) Some road maintenance
(C) A construction project
(D) Some weather conditions

75. What are some listeners advised to do?
(A) Take a different driving route
(B) Obtain a neighborhood map
(C) Bring some waterproof materials
(D) Contact a city government office

76. What will the listeners hear next?
(A) A song
(B) A traffic report
(C) An interview
(D) An advertisement

---

77. Where most likely is the announcement being given?
(A) At a music concert
(B) At a film screening
(C) At a cooking demonstration
(D) At a fashion show

78. Why does the speaker say, "it's a brand-new program"?
(A) To announce a schedule change
(B) To express excitement
(C) To encourage the listeners' participation
(D) To provide an excuse

79. According to the speaker, what will happen after an event?
(A) Registrations will be accepted.
(B) Refreshments will be served.
(C) Photographs will be taken.
(D) Prizes will be awarded.

---

80. Why is the company organizing a special meal?
(A) To congratulate a manager on his retirement
(B) To reward some excellent workers
(C) To welcome a new executive
(D) To celebrate its corporate anniversary

81. What does the speaker mention about the site of the meal?
(A) Booking it was difficult.
(B) Only invited guests will be allowed into it.
(C) It has audiovisual capabilities.
(D) It is spacious.

82. What does the speaker want the listeners to do after they arrive?
(A) Put up some decorations
(B) Sit with their department's employees
(C) Hand out party gifts
(D) Introduce themselves

GO ON TO THE NEXT PAGE →

83. What does the speaker's company most likely sell?

(A) Fitness clothing
(B) Sports nutrition products
(C) Home exercise equipment
(D) Stadium furnishings

84. What does the speaker mean when she says, "I think we can do a little better"?

(A) Her company's earnings are disappointing.
(B) Some preparations are progressing too slowly.
(C) She will inquire about other display options.
(D) She wants staff to attend skills workshops.

85. What does the speaker ask the listener to do?

(A) Proofread a press release
(B) Confirm a work schedule
(C) Clean a conference room
(D) Respond to a client's e-mail

---

86. What most likely is Mr. Branson's job?

(A) Web designer
(B) Hotel manager
(C) Architect
(D) Accountant

87. What does Mr. Branson intend to do next year?

(A) Teach a university course
(B) Remodel his office
(C) Relocate abroad
(D) Write a book

88. What will listeners most likely do next?

(A) Listen to a speech
(B) Enjoy a meal
(C) Watch a video
(D) Walk through a building

---

89. According to the speaker, what is new about Arbax Fitness Club?

(A) Its membership fees
(B) Its Web site
(C) Its floor plans
(D) Its range of classes

90. What are listeners encouraged to do?

(A) Arrange a consultation
(B) Sign a long-term agreement
(C) Take an online survey
(D) Download a voucher

91. What does the speaker imply when she says, "Don't let that stop you"?

(A) The club has long hours of operation.
(B) Club members can borrow workout clothes.
(C) There is a free trial period for new members.
(D) The club welcomes people of all fitness levels.

---

92. Who most likely are the listeners?

(A) Potential buyers
(B) Landscapers
(C) Journalists
(D) Paying tourists

93. What problem does the speaker mention?

(A) A garden is in poor condition.
(B) A set of stairs is steep.
(C) Many repairs are needed.
(D) There is no electricity.

94. What are the listeners encouraged to do?

(A) Point out damage to a property
(B) Take some promotional materials
(C) Turn off their mobile phones
(D) Get some directions

Best-selling Items in August	
Product	**Units Sold**
X190	620
Swiff B	455
Draco 1	390
BN237	110

95. Look at the graphic. What product is the speaker talking about?

(A) X190
(B) Swiff B
(C) Draco 1
(D) BN237

96. According to the speaker, what has influenced the sales of air conditioners?

(A) A discount
(B) The weather
(C) A marketing campaign
(D) The release of a new model

97. What does the speaker ask the listeners to do?

(A) Install some equipment
(B) Keep a handout
(C) Enter data into a computer
(D) Share some ideas

Meeting room B: Tuesday	
Time	**Event**
1:00 P.M.	Software Training
2:00 P.M.	Budget Discussion
3:00 P.M.	Focus Group Meeting
4:00 P.M.	Brainstorming Session

98. Where most likely does the speaker work?

(A) At a supermarket
(B) At an interior design firm
(C) At an advertising agency
(D) At a beverage company

99. Look at the graphic. What event did Jacob most likely reserve a room for?

(A) Software Training
(B) Budget Discussion
(C) Focus Group Meeting
(D) Brainstorming Session

100. What does the speaker offer to do?

(A) Edit a report
(B) Update a Web site
(C) Prepare a meeting space
(D) Submit an invoice

This is the end of the Listening test. Turn to Part 5 in your test book.

LC

TEST 4

LISTENING TEST

In the Listening test, you will be asked to demonstrate how well you understand spoken English. The entire Listening test will last approximately 45 minutes. There are four parts, and directions are given for each part. You must mark your answers on the separate answer sheet. Do not write your answers in your test book.

PART 1

Directions: For each question in this part, you will hear four statements about a picture in your test book. When you hear the statements, you must select the one statement that best describes what you see in the picture. Then find the number of the question on your answer sheet and mark your answer. The statements will not be printed in your test book and will be spoken only one time.

Statement (C), "They're sitting at a table," is the best description of the picture, so you should select answer (C) and mark it on your answer sheet.

1.

2.

GO ON TO THE NEXT PAGE

3.

booth
wireless
booth
wireless
ETC
ROGERS

4.

CHECK IN
DEPARTURES
1000
VICTORIA
SEAPLANE
TERMINAL
VICTORIA
VICTORIA
15
19

5.

6.

GO ON TO THE NEXT PAGE

PART 2

Directions: You will hear a question or statement and three responses spoken in English. They will not be printed in your test book and will be spoken only one time. Select the best response to the question or statement and mark the letter (A), (B), or (C) on your answer sheet.

7. Mark your answer on your answer sheet.

8. Mark your answer on your answer sheet.

9. Mark your answer on your answer sheet.

10. Mark your answer on your answer sheet.

11. Mark your answer on your answer sheet.

12. Mark your answer on your answer sheet.

13. Mark your answer on your answer sheet.

14. Mark your answer on your answer sheet.

15. Mark your answer on your answer sheet.

16. Mark your answer on your answer sheet.

17. Mark your answer on your answer sheet.

18. Mark your answer on your answer sheet.

19. Mark your answer on your answer sheet.

20. Mark your answer on your answer sheet.

21. Mark your answer on your answer sheet.

22. Mark your answer on your answer sheet.

23. Mark your answer on your answer sheet.

24. Mark your answer on your answer sheet.

25. Mark your answer on your answer sheet.

26. Mark your answer on your answer sheet.

27. Mark your answer on your answer sheet.

28. Mark your answer on your answer sheet.

29. Mark your answer on your answer sheet.

30. Mark your answer on your answer sheet.

31. Mark your answer on your answer sheet.

PART 3

Directions: You will hear some conversations between two or more people. You will be asked to answer three questions about what the speakers say in each conversation. Select the best response to each question and mark the letter (A), (B), (C), or (D) on your answer sheet. The conversations will not be printed in your test book and will be spoken only one time.

32. Where most likely do the speakers work?
(A) At a bookstore
(B) At a restaurant
(C) At a flower shop
(D) At a supermarket

33. According to the woman, what is the problem with the cash register?
(A) Some buttons are not working.
(B) Some money is missing.
(C) The screen has been broken.
(D) It does not open properly.

34. What will the man probably do next?
(A) Collect some receipts
(B) Call his manager
(C) Try to fix the cash register
(D) Give an explanation to customers

35. What is the man calling about?
(A) Buying a house
(B) Hiring new employees
(C) Remodeling an office
(D) Delaying a delivery

36. What does the woman say she has to do?
(A) Inspect some properties
(B) Order new products
(C) Meet with a consultant
(D) Review some written information

37. What does the woman say about the process?
(A) It takes longer than expected.
(B) It is expensive.
(C) It is rarely successful.
(D) It has recently changed.

38. Why does the man ask the woman for assistance?
(A) He missed a flight.
(B) His gate is far away.
(C) His bag was damaged.
(D) He misplaced his ticket.

39. What is the man's final destination?
(A) Toronto
(B) Moscow
(C) Frankfurt
(D) Warsaw

40. What does the woman suggest the man do?
(A) Use a mobile app
(B) Obtain reimbursement
(C) Take an airport shuttle
(D) Submit feedback

41. What is the conversation mainly about?
(A) A jobseeker's résumé
(B) A scientific report
(C) An employment contract
(D) A training manual

42. What is the problem with a document?
(A) It contains errors.
(B) It is not detailed enough.
(C) It has not been turned in yet.
(D) It is organized in a confusing way.

43. What does Odette explain to the man?
(A) She is unfamiliar with some processes.
(B) She is concerned about a budget.
(C) She has tested some software.
(D) She has adjusted an estimate.

GO ON TO THE NEXT PAGE

44. What kind of business is Bellardi's Best?

(A) An appliance retailer
(B) A furniture store
(C) A print shop
(D) A bakery

45. What does the woman mean when she says, "it's quite a large order"?

(A) Additional workers should be hired.
(B) There may not be enough materials.
(C) She would like further confirmation.
(D) The order qualifies for a bulk discount.

46. What will the woman probably do next?

(A) Mail a package
(B) Update a Web site
(C) Post a sign-up sheet
(D) Search for a client file

---

47. What does the woman ask about?

(A) A presentation topic
(B) The format of an agenda
(C) Some meeting invitations
(D) A venue reservation

48. What does the man ask permission to do?

(A) Download a document
(B) Delay a decision
(C) Notify other coworkers
(D) Return some equipment

49. Why was the woman unable to attend a previous meeting?

(A) She had to finish an assignment.
(B) She was on vacation.
(C) She was an intern.
(D) She did not know about it.

---

50. Where most likely is the conversation taking place?

(A) At a safety training facility
(B) At a sporting goods store
(C) At a building supply store
(D) At an event planning agency

51. What does the woman offer to do?

(A) Install a phone system
(B) Recruit an instructor
(C) Rent a larger space
(D) Redesign a display

52. What will the speakers probably do next?

(A) Set up some shelving
(B) Go to a checkout area
(C) Discuss some job candidates
(D) Attend a product demonstration

---

53. Why is the woman calling?

(A) To request a transportation service
(B) To change some travel dates
(C) To book accommodations
(D) To ask about meal options

54. What does the man suggest the woman do?

(A) Visit a Web site
(B) Postpone her arrival
(C) Join a waiting list
(D) Upgrade her reservation

55. What does the man offer to do?

(A) Waive a fee
(B) Expedite some paperwork
(C) Contact another branch
(D) Refund a deposit

---

56. What kind of company do the speakers most likely work for?

(A) A software developer
(B) A clothing maker
(C) A magazine publisher
(D) A photography studio

57. What did Marc-Dec Agency suggest the company do?

(A) Merge with another business
(B) Expand into overseas markets
(C) Advertise via social networking sites
(D) Discontinue several product lines

58. What does the man imply when he says, "we just renovated the lobby here"?

(A) He recommends publicizing an enhancement.
(B) He wants suggestions for future design projects.
(C) The company does not need to move its headquarters.
(D) The company's recent sales have been strong.

---

59. What does the woman say about a mobile app?

(A) A new version of it has been released.
(B) It won an industry competition.
(C) It can be downloaded for free.
(D) It conveniently stores business cards.

60. What problem does the man mention?

(A) A device has the wrong operating system.
(B) A screen layout cannot be customized.
(C) Some figures might not be accurate.
(D) Some customer reviews are negative.

61. What does the man say he is currently doing?

(A) Planning a team gathering
(B) Shopping for a new smartphone
(C) Reassigning some responsibilities
(D) Making some posts online

Locker Size	Price
Small	€4
Medium	€7
Large	€9
Extra Large	€12

62. What does the man recommend?

(A) Changing a departure time
(B) Visiting a tourist attraction
(C) Taking public transportation
(D) Purchasing items in the train station

63. Look at the graphic. Which size locker will the woman use?

(A) Small
(B) Medium
(C) Large
(D) Extra large

64. What does the woman need to do?

(A) Remember a code
(B) Fill out a form
(C) Exchange some money
(D) Get some directions

Test 4

GO ON TO THE NEXT PAGE

Title	Release Date
Amazing Arizona	April 3
Up Kinabalu	April 24
Cycling Spain	May 9
Tasmanian Lights	May 17

65. What did the man do yesterday?

(A) Read a manuscript
(B) Spoke to an author
(C) Returned from a trip
(D) Canceled a meeting

66. Look at the graphic. Which release date is no longer correct?

(A) April 3
(B) April 24
(C) May 9
(D) May 17

67. What does the woman ask the man to do?

(A) Upload an e-book to a Web page
(B) Study some consumer research
(C) Write a notification e-mail
(D) Place an advance order

Safety Rules

1. Wear appropriate eye protection.
2. Lift heavy loads safely.
3. Maintain the condition of your tools.
4. Keep your work space orderly.

68. What kind of device is the woman repairing?

(A) A hair dryer
(B) A coffee maker
(C) A digital camera
(D) A laptop computer

69. Look at the graphic. Which rule does the man refer to?

(A) Rule 1
(B) Rule 2
(C) Rule 3
(D) Rule 4

70. What does the woman say she will do next?

(A) Continue working on the device
(B) Check a cabinet for some safety gear
(C) Give a status report to a customer
(D) Remove some items from a table

PART 4

Directions: You will hear some talks given by a single speaker. You will be asked to answer three questions about what the speaker says in each talk. Select the best response to each question and mark the letter (A), (B), (C), or (D) on your answer sheet. The talks will not be printed in your test book and will be spoken only one time.

71. What is the speaker mostly talking about?
(A) A group presentation
(B) A staff directory
(C) A photo shoot
(D) A travel policy

72. What should the listeners do in the afternoon?
(A) Make a payment
(B) Consult a schedule
(C) Hold a practice session
(D) Send a text message

73. What does the speaker ask the listeners to pay special attention to?
(A) Their clothing
(B) A time limit
(C) A file size
(D) Their noise level

---

74. What service is being advertised?
(A) Interior decorating
(B) Landscaping
(C) Plumbing
(D) Cleaning

75. What is mentioned about the company?
(A) Its staff work part-time.
(B) It is located in a suburban area.
(C) It is owned by a local family.
(D) It has been in business for a long time.

76. According to the speaker, how can a listener receive a discount?
(A) By mentioning the advertisement
(B) By purchasing a package deal
(C) By referring a friend
(D) By paying with cash

---

77. What is being offered at a special discount?
(A) Printing services
(B) Stationery supplies
(C) Office furniture
(D) Product customization

78. Why does the speaker say, "we have a lot of shoppers here today"?
(A) To confirm the success of a sales event
(B) To apologize for long waiting lines
(C) To promote a store's new feature
(D) To warn about merchandise being out of stock

79. According to the speaker, what will the store do on Thursday?
(A) Extend its operating hours
(B) Move to another location
(C) Start a loyalty card program
(D) Provide home deliveries

---

80. What will be held on Friday?
(A) A film screening
(B) A concert
(C) An awards banquet
(D) A symposium

81. What is mentioned about the event?
(A) It will be recorded.
(B) It will be held outdoors.
(C) It will begin in the evening.
(D) It will have around 80 participants.

82. What is mentioned as one of Min-Joon's duties?
(A) Designing handouts
(B) Monitoring electronics
(C) Checking on refreshments
(D) Ushering audience members

GO ON TO THE NEXT PAGE

83. What kind of weather does the speaker forecast?

(A) Clear
(B) Rainy
(C) Snowy
(D) Windy

84. Why should listeners expect large crowds on Malton Beach?

(A) A sunset will be beautiful.
(B) A local celebrity will visit.
(C) There will be an athletic event.
(D) It is the last day of a festival.

85. What will listeners most likely hear next?

(A) A live music performance
(B) An update on traffic conditions
(C) A news report about sports
(D) A commercial for swimming gear

---

86. Why does the speaker apologize to the listener?

(A) He failed to notice an e-mail from her.
(B) He misplaced some papers.
(C) He misunderstood some guidelines.
(D) He did not send her a copy of the newsletter.

87. What does the speaker imply when he says, "I've only drafted a few articles so far"?

(A) It will be easy to make some revisions.
(B) Several potential topics have not been covered.
(C) An issue may be published late.
(D) He is not an experienced writer.

88. What does the speaker ask the listener to do?

(A) Write a short essay
(B) Grant a funding request
(C) Answer some questions
(D) Talk to an executive

---

89. Why should a listener contact the reception desk?

(A) To speak with Ms. Kennedy
(B) To hear a list of programs
(C) To set up a tour
(D) To obtain donation information

90. When does Ms. Kennedy say she is unavailable?

(A) On Monday mornings
(B) On Wednesday mornings
(C) On Friday afternoons
(D) On Saturday afternoons

91. What should a message for Ms. Kennedy include?

(A) The date and time
(B) The reason for contacting her
(C) A current course name
(D) A registration number

---

92. Who most likely is the speaker?

(A) An architect
(B) A travel agent
(C) A sales director
(D) A journalist

93. Why does the speaker say, "don't forget about Vancouver"?

(A) To suggest an addition to an article
(B) To remind listeners of a venue option
(C) To show concern about a person's workload
(D) To emphasize a person's accomplishments

94. What does the speaker say the business is known for?

(A) Its technological innovations
(B) Its promotional campaigns
(C) Its corporate culture
(D) Its growth rate

CORBIN ARENA

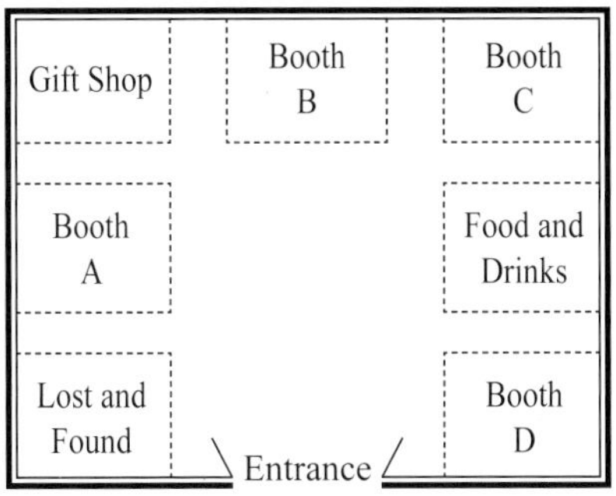

95. What event will take place at Corbin Arena on Saturday?

(A) A career fair
(B) A farmers market
(C) A hotel convention
(D) An art festival

96. What does the speaker ask the listener to do?

(A) Transport some goods
(B) Organize a storage room
(C) E-mail a work schedule
(D) Meet near an entrance

97. Look at the graphic. Which booth will the speaker occupy?

(A) Booth A
(B) Booth B
(C) Booth C
(D) Booth D

	Silver Membership	**Titanium Membership**	**Gold Membership**	**Platinum Membership**
Joining Fee	O	O	X	X
Membership Fee	$30	$45	$75	$100

98. Look at the graphic. Which membership level did the fitness center recently add?

(A) Silver
(B) Titanium
(C) Gold
(D) Platinum

99. What item will be given to new members?

(A) A T-shirt
(B) A bag
(C) A towel
(D) A water bottle

100. What will the speaker most likely do next?

(A) Distribute some documents
(B) Reveal a proposed logo
(C) Introduce a personal trainer
(D) Give an equipment demonstration

This is the end of the Listening test. Turn to Part 5 in your test book.

LC

TEST 5

LISTENING TEST

In the Listening test, you will be asked to demonstrate how well you understand spoken English. The entire Listening test will last approximately 45 minutes. There are four parts, and directions are given for each part. You must mark your answers on the separate answer sheet. Do not write your answers in your test book.

PART 1

Directions: For each question in this part, you will hear four statements about a picture in your test book. When you hear the statements, you must select the one statement that best describes what you see in the picture. Then find the number of the question on your answer sheet and mark your answer. The statements will not be printed in your test book and will be spoken only one time.

Statement (C), "They're sitting at a table," is the best description of the picture, so you should select answer (C) and mark it on your answer sheet.

1.

2.

GO ON TO THE NEXT PAGE

3.

4.

5.

6.

GO ON TO THE NEXT PAGE

PART 2

Directions: You will hear a question or statement and three responses spoken in English. They will not be printed in your test book and will be spoken only one time. Select the best response to the question or statement and mark the letter (A), (B), or (C) on your answer sheet.

7. Mark your answer on your answer sheet.
8. Mark your answer on your answer sheet.
9. Mark your answer on your answer sheet.
10. Mark your answer on your answer sheet.
11. Mark your answer on your answer sheet.
12. Mark your answer on your answer sheet.
13. Mark your answer on your answer sheet.
14. Mark your answer on your answer sheet.
15. Mark your answer on your answer sheet.
16. Mark your answer on your answer sheet.
17. Mark your answer on your answer sheet.
18. Mark your answer on your answer sheet.
19. Mark your answer on your answer sheet.
20. Mark your answer on your answer sheet.
21. Mark your answer on your answer sheet.
22. Mark your answer on your answer sheet.
23. Mark your answer on your answer sheet.
24. Mark your answer on your answer sheet.
25. Mark your answer on your answer sheet.
26. Mark your answer on your answer sheet.
27. Mark your answer on your answer sheet.
28. Mark your answer on your answer sheet.
29. Mark your answer on your answer sheet.
30. Mark your answer on your answer sheet.
31. Mark your answer on your answer sheet.

PART 3

Directions: You will hear some conversations between two or more people. You will be asked to answer three questions about what the speakers say in each conversation. Select the best response to each question and mark the letter (A), (B), (C), or (D) on your answer sheet. The conversations will not be printed in your test book and will be spoken only one time.

32. Where is the conversation taking place?
(A) At a car rental agency
(B) At a train terminal
(C) At a bus station
(D) At an airport

33. Why is the woman unable to use her credit card?
(A) It is not from a local bank.
(B) She has lost it.
(C) Its credit limit is too low.
(D) It has been damaged.

34. What will the woman probably do next?
(A) Exchange a ticket
(B) Locate a machine
(C) Buy a road map
(D) Make a phone call

---

35. Who most likely is the man?
(A) A production intern
(B) A human resources manager
(C) A business consultant
(D) A job applicant

36. What skill does the woman mention?
(A) Restoring antique art
(B) Supervising a team of people
(C) Analyzing survey results
(D) Recruiting staff from overseas

37. What does the man say about a job?
(A) It is well-paid.
(B) It is in a new department.
(C) It can be stressful.
(D) It may be done from home.

---

38. What is the woman unable to do?
(A) Turn on her laptop
(B) Find some files
(C) Upload some documents
(D) Log in to her account

39. What does the man say has caused the problem?
(A) An error made by staff
(B) A computer virus
(C) A power outage
(D) An increase in network users

40. What does the man suggest?
(A) Verifying the spelling of a name
(B) Contacting technical support
(C) Removing some software
(D) Updating a password

---

41. What are the speakers mainly discussing?
(A) A new executive
(B) A defective product
(C) An advertising campaign
(D) Some hiring policies

42. Why does the woman say a change is being made?
(A) An expert recommended it.
(B) Customers have asked for it.
(C) Technology has advanced.
(D) Extra funding is available.

43. According to the woman, what part of an agreement has not been decided?
(A) A start date
(B) A location
(C) A duration
(D) A fee

GO ON TO THE NEXT PAGE

44. What will Mallory most likely do this evening?

(A) Exercise
(B) Go shopping
(C) Work overtime
(D) Make vacation plans

45. Why does the man recommend asking Yoon-Hee for help?

(A) She has a lot of free time.
(B) She often visits a site.
(C) She owns a certain device.
(D) She has completed a course.

46. What does Mallory say she will do next?

(A) Photocopy some instructions
(B) Upgrade an operating system
(C) Send a group text message
(D) Conduct an Internet search

---

47. Where do the speakers most likely work?

(A) At a bookstore
(B) At a café
(C) At a hotel
(D) At a supermarket

48. What does the woman mean when she says, "the store next door is starting a big sale today"?

(A) She will not be able to fulfill a request.
(B) She is unhappy about some competition.
(C) She suggests visiting a neighboring business.
(D) She wants the man to do a task quickly.

49. What will the man most likely do next?

(A) Clear off a counter
(B) Assist a customer
(C) Put on a work uniform
(D) Set up a window display

---

50. Where most likely are the speakers?

(A) In an office
(B) In a house
(C) In a library
(D) In a museum

51. What do the speakers say about the new layout?

(A) It encourages collaboration.
(B) It provides greater privacy.
(C) It enhances security.
(D) It conserves energy.

52. According to the woman, what will happen next month?

(A) Another space will be rearranged.
(B) Some photographs will appear online.
(C) A commercial will be filmed.
(D) Some signs will be put up.

---

53. What problem does the woman mention?

(A) A loading area is disorganized.
(B) A shipment is missing.
(C) A door control is out of order.
(D) A delivery vehicle has been delayed.

54. What will the speakers most likely discuss at a meeting?

(A) Recruiting more part-time workers
(B) Starting a mentorship program
(C) Renting some industrial machinery
(D) Installing better lighting in a workplace

55. What does the woman say she will do tomorrow?

(A) Train a technician
(B) Give a facility tour
(C) Extend a meal break
(D) Create a slide show

---

56. According to the woman, what happened recently?

(A) A Web site was launched.
(B) A survey was administered.
(C) Renovations were completed.
(D) Contracts with suppliers were signed.

57. Why does the man say, "what brings them here"?

(A) He is excited.
(B) He is worried.
(C) He is frustrated.
(D) He is relieved.

58. What will the woman suggest at a meeting?

(A) Stocking more items in large sizes
(B) Selling more local produce
(C) Redesigning the store's logo
(D) Changing the store's hours

---

59. What is the conversation mainly about?

(A) A proposed law
(B) A company merger
(C) A trade show
(D) A current market trend

60. What does the woman advise the man to do?

(A) Avoid discussing an issue openly
(B) Decline an invitation politely
(C) Do further research
(D) Reply to an e-mail

61. What does the woman say about South Stark Industries?

(A) It has a long history.
(B) It sponsored an event.
(C) It recently expanded.
(D) It operates internationally.

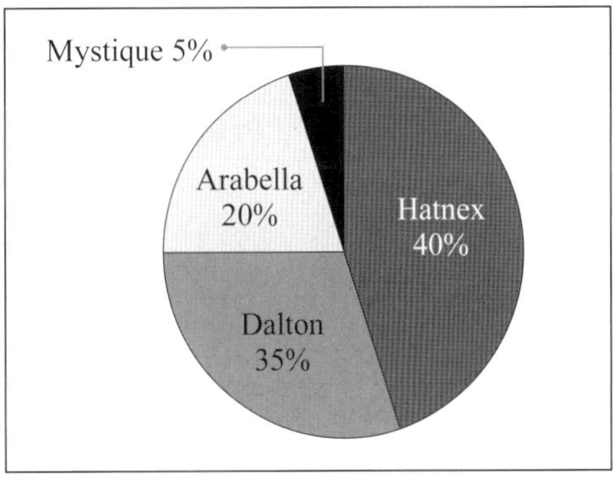

62. Look at the graphic. Which company do the speakers work for?

(A) Mystique
(B) Arabella
(C) Dalton
(D) Hatnex

63. What service does the woman want to start offering to customers?

(A) Styling consultations
(B) Expedited deliveries
(C) Clothing alterations
(D) Electronic catalogs

64. What does the man suggest the woman do on Monday?

(A) Temporarily suspend a project
(B) Introduce a topic during a meeting
(C) Hand out copies of a magazine article
(D) Look for unnecessary expenses in a budget

Test 5

GO ON TO THE NEXT PAGE

Ivory Office Max	
Item	**Price**
Clipboard	$9
Envelope	$13
Folder	$17
Printer paper	$48
Total:	$87

65. Why did the woman call the man?
(A) To check some inventory
(B) To revise an order
(C) To negotiate a price
(D) To ask about a misplaced item

66. What did the man do this morning?
(A) Repaired some equipment
(B) Made a cash deposit
(C) Hired a new employee
(D) Posted some sale signs

67. Look at the graphic. How much will the woman be refunded?
(A) $9
(B) $13
(C) $17
(D) $48

Room Assignments
Evening Group Classes

	6:00 – 7:20	7:30 – 8:50
Beginner	Classroom C	Classroom A
Intermediate 1	Classroom A	Classroom B
Intermediate 2	Classroom D	
Advanced	Classroom B	

68. Why has the woman arrived early at the language institute?
(A) She needs to take a level test.
(B) She has to purchase class materials.
(C) A trip took less time than expected.
(D) She misunderstood a schedule.

69. Look at the graphic. Which room is the woman's class most likely held in?
(A) Classroom A
(B) Classroom B
(C) Classroom C
(D) Classroom D

70. What does the man suggest that the woman do?
(A) Wait in the reception area
(B) Keep a registration receipt
(C) Sit in the front part of the classroom
(D) Leave a message for an instructor

PART 4

Directions: You will hear some talks given by a single speaker. You will be asked to answer three questions about what the speaker says in each talk. Select the best response to each question and mark the letter (A), (B), (C), or (D) on your answer sheet. The talks will not be printed in your test book and will be spoken only one time.

71. What is the reason for the announcement?
(A) A store is closing.
(B) There is a traffic problem.
(C) There is a special sale.
(D) A new service is available.

72. What does the speaker say a customer can do with a mobile app?
(A) Download a voucher
(B) Order some goods
(C) Compare some prices
(D) Access a floor plan

73. What can customers do to receive an additional discount?
(A) Use a self-checkout machine
(B) Supply their own bags
(C) Fill out a questionnaire
(D) Show a membership card

74. What is the message mainly about?
(A) A departmental restructuring
(B) A recent publication
(C) An office party
(D) A broken device

75. What does the speaker imply when she says, "it's a complicated process"?
(A) The listener will probably need help.
(B) The listener should provide some instructions.
(C) She should not be blamed for a mistake.
(D) She might miss a due date.

76. According to the speaker, what happened last week?
(A) The listener left for a business trip.
(B) The speaker's job transfer was announced.
(C) Changes to a financial plan were revealed.
(D) A company facility was sold.

77. What type of event will a law firm host?
(A) A lecture
(B) A fund-raiser
(C) A retirement banquet
(D) A job fair

78. Who most likely are the listeners?
(A) Tour organizers
(B) New lawyers
(C) Catering chefs
(D) Marketing employees

79. What difference from last year's project does the speaker mention?
(A) The client representative is new.
(B) The work will take longer.
(C) The payment is smaller.
(D) More paperwork will be required.

80. What did the listener order?
(A) Curtains
(B) Coffee
(C) Clothing
(D) Furniture

81. What has caused a delay?
(A) A payment was not received.
(B) A warehouse was damaged.
(C) A highway is undergoing roadwork.
(D) A material is out of stock.

82. What does the speaker give the listener?
(A) A partial refund
(B) An apology
(C) A phone number
(D) A choice of options

GO ON TO THE NEXT PAGE

83. Who is the talk intended for?
(A) Store clerks
(B) Cafeteria servers
(C) Movie theater staff
(D) Postal workers

84. Why does the speaker say, "Sometimes these sessions are over within five minutes"?
(A) To praise the listeners for their efficiency
(B) To reassure the listeners about an assignment
(C) To criticize the listeners for being careless
(D) To alert the listeners to a possible difficulty

85. What does the speaker instruct the listeners to do?
(A) Use a checklist
(B) Move some boxes
(C) Take some business cards
(D) Watch a video

---

86. What does the speaker say about the intended users of the product?
(A) They travel frequently.
(B) They manufacture computers.
(C) They exercise with headphones.
(D) They wear headphones for long periods.

87. According to the speaker, what is special about the product?
(A) It produces a loud sound.
(B) It does not break easily.
(C) It is very comfortable.
(D) It has a built-in microphone.

88. How can customers get a discount?
(A) By making a referral
(B) By buying many pairs of the product
(C) By using a coupon code
(D) By purchasing the product soon

---

89. What does the speaker say happened at his company recently?
(A) A product line was launched.
(B) A branch office was opened.
(C) A press conference was held.
(D) A sales trip was canceled.

90. What does the speaker imply when he says, "Seven thousand dollars is a lot of money"?
(A) He is disappointed with a negotiation's results.
(B) He understands other people's concerns.
(C) He will need to reduce operating costs.
(D) He is having doubts about a proposal.

91. What is scheduled for next Thursday?
(A) A factory inspection
(B) A training session
(C) A welcome reception
(D) A shareholders' meeting

---

92. Where most likely is the introduction taking place?
(A) In a restaurant
(B) In a park
(C) In an auditorium
(D) In a radio station

93. Why most likely is Mr. Woodruff being introduced?
(A) He recently returned from abroad.
(B) He has won an award.
(C) He is being promoted.
(D) He is retiring.

94. What does the speaker emphasize about Mr. Woodruff?
(A) His leadership
(B) His creativity
(C) His honesty
(D) His kindness

Tour Schedule	
Location	**Time**
Main House	10:45 A.M. – 11:45 A.M.
Roy Pavilion	11:45 A.M. – 12:00 P.M.
Mulberry Row	12:00 P.M. – 12:30 P.M.
Gertie Gardens	12:30 P.M. – 12:45 P.M.

95. Who was Ms. Mirasora?

(A) A painter
(B) A scientist
(C) A writer
(D) An architect

96. Look at the graphic. When will the listeners begin touring Stables Swimming Pool?

(A) At 10:45 A.M.
(B) At 11:45 A.M.
(C) At 12:00 P.M.
(D) At 12:30 P.M.

97. What does the speaker mention about Stables Swimming Pool?

(A) It is usually closed to the public.
(B) It has recently been renovated.
(C) It was expensive to build.
(D) It is cleaned twice a week.

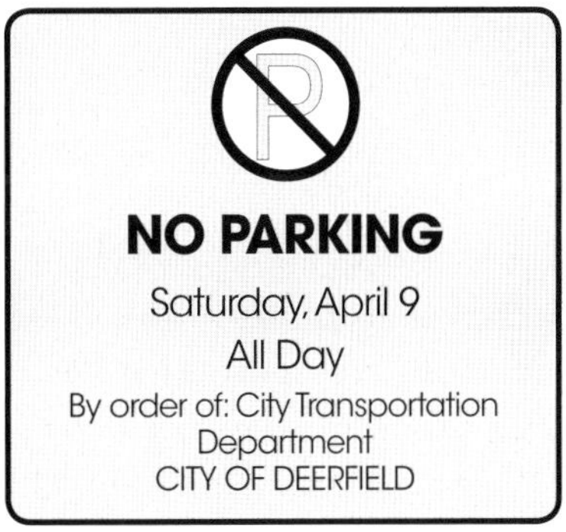

NO PARKING
Saturday, April 9
All Day
By order of: City Transportation Department
CITY OF DEERFIELD

98. What is happening in the city this Saturday?

(A) A holiday parade
(B) An automobile exposition
(C) An athletic event
(D) A music festival

99. Look at the graphic. On which street will the sign most likely be posted?

(A) Carson Avenue
(B) Maple Road
(C) Durden Lane
(D) Lyon Boulevard

100. What does the speaker encourage the listeners to do?

(A) Visit a Web site
(B) Call a city official
(C) Join an activity
(D) Use a residential road

This is the end of the Listening test. Turn to Part 5 in your test book.

LC

TEST 6

LISTENING TEST

In the Listening test, you will be asked to demonstrate how well you understand spoken English. The entire Listening test will last approximately 45 minutes. There are four parts, and directions are given for each part. You must mark your answers on the separate answer sheet. Do not write your answers in your test book.

PART 1

Directions: For each question in this part, you will hear four statements about a picture in your test book. When you hear the statements, you must select the one statement that best describes what you see in the picture. Then find the number of the question on your answer sheet and mark your answer. The statements will not be printed in your test book and will be spoken only one time.

Statement (C), "They're sitting at a table," is the best description of the picture, so you should select answer (C) and mark it on your answer sheet.

1.

2.

Test 6

GO ON TO THE NEXT PAGE

3.

4.

5.

6.

GO ON TO THE NEXT PAGE

PART 2

Directions: You will hear a question or statement and three responses spoken in English. They will not be printed in your test book and will be spoken only one time. Select the best response to the question or statement and mark the letter (A), (B), or (C) on your answer sheet.

7. Mark your answer on your answer sheet.

8. Mark your answer on your answer sheet.

9. Mark your answer on your answer sheet.

10. Mark your answer on your answer sheet.

11. Mark your answer on your answer sheet.

12. Mark your answer on your answer sheet.

13. Mark your answer on your answer sheet.

14. Mark your answer on your answer sheet.

15. Mark your answer on your answer sheet.

16. Mark your answer on your answer sheet.

17. Mark your answer on your answer sheet.

18. Mark your answer on your answer sheet.

19. Mark your answer on your answer sheet.

20. Mark your answer on your answer sheet.

21. Mark your answer on your answer sheet.

22. Mark your answer on your answer sheet.

23. Mark your answer on your answer sheet.

24. Mark your answer on your answer sheet.

25. Mark your answer on your answer sheet.

26. Mark your answer on your answer sheet.

27. Mark your answer on your answer sheet.

28. Mark your answer on your answer sheet.

29. Mark your answer on your answer sheet.

30. Mark your answer on your answer sheet.

31. Mark your answer on your answer sheet.

PART 3

Directions: You will hear some conversations between two or more people. You will be asked to answer three questions about what the speakers say in each conversation. Select the best response to each question and mark the letter (A), (B), (C), or (D) on your answer sheet. The conversations will not be printed in your test book and will be spoken only one time.

32. What does the woman want to do?

(A) Sell her personal vehicle
(B) Take driving lessons
(C) Arrange some repairs
(D) Return a rental vehicle

33. What does the man ask for?

(A) A payment
(B) Some identification
(C) Operating instructions
(D) A price quote

34. What does the man say he will do?

(A) Print a policy statement
(B) Bring out a supervisor
(C) Call a different branch
(D) Conduct an inspection

---

35. What does the man ask about?

(A) Upgrading a service package
(B) Suspending a membership
(C) Inviting guests to a club
(D) Beginning a trial period

36. What does the man imply when he says, "Here is the signed contract"?

(A) He thinks the woman is misinformed.
(B) He would like to join an organization.
(C) He cannot understand some rules.
(D) He has found a lost document.

37. What will the woman most likely do next?

(A) Shred some papers
(B) Take a photo
(C) Examine a credit card
(D) Issue a refund

---

38. What problem does the man describe?

(A) A medical professional is unavailable.
(B) A receptionist has made a mistake.
(C) A facility is temporarily unusable.
(D) A medication is out of stock.

39. Why does the woman need to see a doctor?

(A) An illness requires treatment.
(B) It is time for her regular checkup.
(C) She is about to start a new job.
(D) She has to travel overseas.

40. What does the man suggest doing?

(A) Resting at home
(B) Changing an appointment time
(C) Speaking to a doctor by phone
(D) Trying another clinic

---

41. Where most likely are the speakers?

(A) At a science museum
(B) At a hardware store
(C) At a photography studio
(D) At a research laboratory

42. What problem do the women have?

(A) They are not permitted to operate a machine.
(B) The cost of a service has increased.
(C) There is an error in a printed sign.
(D) An object's purpose is unclear.

43. What will Kyoko most likely do next?

(A) Read the results of a test
(B) Place an item back on a shelf
(C) Listen to an audio recording
(D) Go to the other side of the room

Test 6

GO ON TO THE NEXT PAGE

44. What does the man ask the woman about?
(A) Employee training
(B) A security procedure
(C) Product development
(D) An advertising campaign

45. What does the man suggest the woman's team do?
(A) Hire a special advisor
(B) Change a timeline
(C) Create some guidelines
(D) Limit access to some data

46. What does the woman say about the man's suggestion?
(A) There is not enough time for it.
(B) There is not enough money for it.
(C) She will mention it to her team.
(D) It would probably not be effective.

---

47. What does the man say can be found on a Web site?
(A) Customer reviews
(B) Product prices
(C) Branch locations
(D) Business hours

48. Why is the woman calling?
(A) To track a shipment
(B) To verify a discount
(C) To request an exchange
(D) To cancel an order

49. What does the woman say about herself?
(A) Her company needs some supplies.
(B) She lives outside the country.
(C) Her computer is malfunctioning.
(D) She has shopped at the store before.

---

50. What does the woman emphasize about a painting?
(A) Its texture
(B) Its colors
(C) Its subjects
(D) Its frame

51. What is mentioned about an art show?
(A) It will be publicized online.
(B) It will include a demonstration.
(C) It will take place outdoors.
(D) It will feature only one artist's work.

52. What will happen on July 1?
(A) The art show will end.
(B) A party will be held.
(C) Purchases will be delivered.
(D) A date will be announced.

---

53. Where is the conversation taking place?
(A) In a factory
(B) In a warehouse
(C) On a farm
(D) At a construction site

54. What does the woman ask the man about?
(A) His education
(B) His expected salary
(C) His work experience
(D) His career goals

55. What does the woman tell the man about a special position?
(A) It comes with a pay raise after six months.
(B) She is not certain that it is vacant.
(C) He is not yet eligible for it.
(D) It involves working at night.

---

56. Why is the man calling the woman?

(A) An order has been fulfilled.
(B) An event is about to begin.
(C) He wants some information.
(D) He received a text message from her.

57. What does the woman mean when she says, "I'm an hour away"?

(A) The man has misunderstood an itinerary.
(B) The man should handle a problem by himself.
(C) She cannot arrive before a store closes.
(D) She will have to communicate electronically.

58. What does the woman say is causing a delay?

(A) Heavy traffic
(B) Unreliable navigation
(C) Bad weather
(D) Car trouble

---

59. Who most likely is the woman?

(A) A house painter
(B) A landscaper
(C) A real estate agent
(D) An event planner

60. What does the woman ask about?

(A) The availability of parking
(B) The size of a structure
(C) The budget for a project
(D) The address of a property

61. Why will the job be difficult?

(A) Some materials are rare.
(B) Some surfaces are rough.
(C) A deadline cannot be changed.
(D) A location is inconvenient.

Thursday	Friday	Saturday	Sunday
25 °C	22 °C	18 °C	15 °C

62. What are the speakers planning to do together?

(A) Visit a market
(B) Take a walking tour
(C) Clean up an outdoor space
(D) Play a competitive sport

63. Look at the graphic. Which day do the speakers select?

(A) Thursday
(B) Friday
(C) Saturday
(D) Sunday

64. What does the man offer the woman?

(A) Transportation to a location
(B) Assistance with a work duty
(C) Some used equipment
(D) The key to a storage room

GO ON TO THE NEXT PAGE →

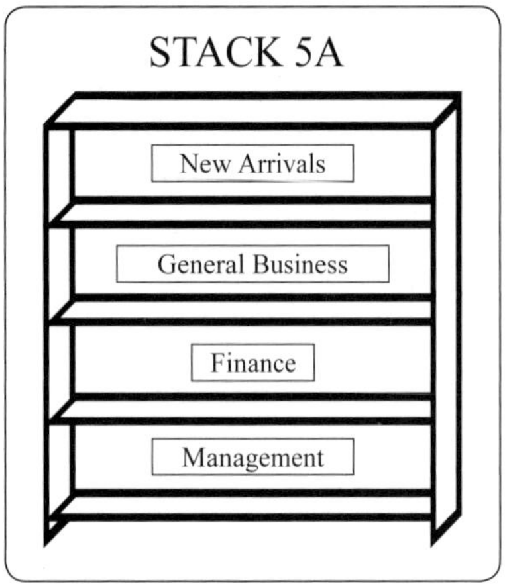

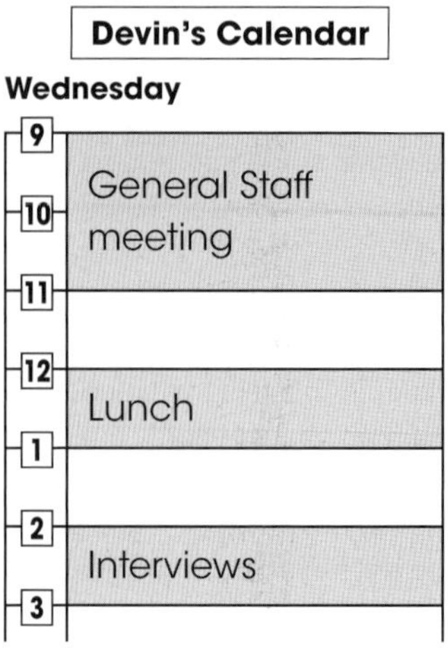

65. Look at the graphic. On which shelf does the man find the book?

(A) New Arrivals
(B) General Business
(C) Finance
(D) Management

66. What does the man say about the book?

(A) Its category was difficult to determine.
(B) It is popular with library patrons.
(C) It is unusually large.
(D) Its loan period cannot be extended.

67. Who most likely is Mr. Haskins?

(A) A writer of a book
(B) A librarian
(C) A newspaper reporter
(D) An organizer of a conference

68. What does the woman ask for help with?

(A) Preparing quarterly reports
(B) Scheduling a meeting
(C) Creating a presentation
(D) Reserving a venue

69. Look at the graphic. When will the speakers most likely meet?

(A) At 10:00 A.M.
(B) At 11:00 A.M.
(C) At 1:00 P.M.
(D) At 2:00 P.M.

70. What will the woman probably send the man?

(A) A press release
(B) A software update
(C) Some contact information
(D) Some visual materials

PART 4

Directions: You will hear some talks given by a single speaker. You will be asked to answer three questions about what the speaker says in each talk. Select the best response to each question and mark the letter (A), (B), (C), or (D) on your answer sheet. The talks will not be printed in your test book and will be spoken only one time.

71. Who most likely is the listener?

(A) A school administrator
(B) A bank supervisor
(C) A magazine editor
(D) A restaurant owner

72. What project is the speaker working on?

(A) Publishing an article
(B) Filling a job opening
(C) Conducting a survey
(D) Giving out an award

73. What does the speaker want to know about?

(A) An educational opportunity
(B) A marketing technique
(C) An organization's reputation
(D) A person's accomplishments

74. What is the speaker mainly discussing?

(A) Planning an orientation session
(B) Writing some employment advertisements
(C) Negotiating the terms of a contract
(D) Interviewing some candidates

75. Who most likely is Mr. Ramos?

(A) A client
(B) A job applicant
(C) An intern
(D) A department manager

76. What are the listeners asked to do?

(A) Volunteer for a task
(B) Shorten a list of names
(C) Review some feedback
(D) Prepare for a seminar

77. What is the speaker calling about?

(A) A laboratory policy
(B) A research experiment
(C) A piece of equipment
(D) A communication method

78. Why does the speaker say, "I'm usually good at that sort of thing"?

(A) To express surprise at a failure
(B) To show interest in a project
(C) To refuse an offer of help
(D) To provide a reason for a choice

79. Why does the speaker want to meet?

(A) To look for a missing item
(B) To make some plans
(C) To study a document
(D) To reorganize a room's layout

80. Where most likely is the announcement being made?

(A) At a fitness center
(B) At a television station
(C) At a sporting goods store
(D) At a stadium

81. What can listeners do today?

(A) Join a loyalty program
(B) Receive a consultation
(C) Use a promotional coupon
(D) Enter a trivia contest

82. What special offer is currently available?

(A) Free samples
(B) A customization service
(C) An online discount
(D) Ticket upgrades

GO ON TO THE NEXT PAGE

83. What is the main topic of this episode of the podcast?

(A) Luggage brands
(B) Travel photography
(C) A tourist destination
(D) A mobile app

84. What does the speaker imply when she says, "I'm looking at their plans right now"?

(A) An itinerary lists some exciting activities.
(B) A tourist has new goals for the future.
(C) A facility will make use of modern technology.
(D) A company's offerings are comprehensive.

85. What are listeners encouraged to do on the podcast's Web site?

(A) Follow a link
(B) Download a file
(C) Leave a comment
(D) Enter a code

---

86. What information does the speaker provide about the training sessions?

(A) How long they will last
(B) Where they will be held
(C) Who will lead them
(D) What participants should bring to them

87. Why should the listeners contact the speaker?

(A) To offer to assist with the upgrade
(B) To vote for one of three options
(C) To get a manual for the new system
(D) To schedule a separate training session

88. According to the speaker, what is better about the new system?

(A) It has more features.
(B) It is easier to use.
(C) It is less expensive.
(D) It requires less counter space.

---

89. How most likely did the speaker previously place an order?

(A) In person
(B) By phone
(C) Online
(D) By mail

90. What does the speaker imply when he says, "there's a race on Saturday"?

(A) He would like to invite the listener to an event.
(B) He is alerting the listener to a sponsorship opportunity.
(C) He needs some goods before the weekend.
(D) He would like to cancel an appointment.

91. What does the speaker request that Marcie do?

(A) Visit a Web site
(B) Confirm his new address
(C) Make a reservation
(D) Return his call

---

92. What field does Ms. Nomura most likely work in?

(A) Law
(B) Hospitality
(C) Technology
(D) Education

93. What will Ms. Nomura's lecture be about?

(A) Management techniques
(B) Customer satisfaction
(C) Workplace design
(D) Financial investing

94. What will Ms. Nomura do after her lecture?

(A) Attend a formal dinner
(B) Answer audience questions
(C) Lead some role-play exercises
(D) Read from her new book

Comparison of Company offerings

	Tasteen Snacks	Sandac Foods
Wholesale bulk ordering	✓	✓
Online shopping	✓	
Collectible gift boxes		✓
Seasonal promotions	✓	✓

95. According to the speaker, what did consumers like best about Healthy Crisps?

(A) Their taste
(B) Their packaging
(C) Their healthiness
(D) Their cost

96. Look at the graphic. Which area will the speaker discuss in the afternoon?

(A) Wholesale bulk ordering
(B) Online shopping
(C) Collectible gift boxes
(D) Seasonal promotions

97. What will the speaker probably do next?

(A) Take a lunch break
(B) Begin a videoconference
(C) Show a competitor's commercial
(D) Distribute some summaries

Area served	Bus color
A	Red
B	Yellow
C	Green
D	Blue

98. Where is the announcement taking place?

(A) In a subway station
(B) In an airport
(C) At a bus station
(D) On a train platform

99. Look at the graphic. What color is the bus that the affected passengers should take?

(A) Red
(B) Yellow
(C) Green
(D) Blue

100. According to the speaker, what should passengers show to a staff member?

(A) Meal receipts
(B) Completed forms
(C) Transportation passes
(D) Baggage claim tickets

This is the end of the Listening test. Turn to Part 5 in your test book.

LC

TEST 7

LISTENING TEST

In the Listening test, you will be asked to demonstrate how well you understand spoken English. The entire Listening test will last approximately 45 minutes. There are four parts, and directions are given for each part. You must mark your answers on the separate answer sheet. Do not write your answers in your test book.

PART 1

Directions: For each question in this part, you will hear four statements about a picture in your test book. When you hear the statements, you must select the one statement that best describes what you see in the picture. Then find the number of the question on your answer sheet and mark your answer. The statements will not be printed in your test book and will be spoken only one time.

Statement (C), "They're sitting at a table," is the best description of the picture, so you should select answer (C) and mark it on your answer sheet.

1.

2.

Test 7

GO ON TO THE NEXT PAGE

3.

4.

5.

6.

Test 7

GO ON TO THE NEXT PAGE

PART 2

Directions: You will hear a question or statement and three responses spoken in English. They will not be printed in your test book and will be spoken only one time. Select the best response to the question or statement and mark the letter (A), (B), or (C) on your answer sheet.

7. Mark your answer on your answer sheet.

8. Mark your answer on your answer sheet.

9. Mark your answer on your answer sheet.

10. Mark your answer on your answer sheet.

11. Mark your answer on your answer sheet.

12. Mark your answer on your answer sheet.

13. Mark your answer on your answer sheet.

14. Mark your answer on your answer sheet.

15. Mark your answer on your answer sheet.

16. Mark your answer on your answer sheet.

17. Mark your answer on your answer sheet.

18. Mark your answer on your answer sheet.

19. Mark your answer on your answer sheet.

20. Mark your answer on your answer sheet.

21. Mark your answer on your answer sheet.

22. Mark your answer on your answer sheet.

23. Mark your answer on your answer sheet.

24. Mark your answer on your answer sheet.

25. Mark your answer on your answer sheet.

26. Mark your answer on your answer sheet.

27. Mark your answer on your answer sheet.

28. Mark your answer on your answer sheet.

29. Mark your answer on your answer sheet.

30. Mark your answer on your answer sheet.

31. Mark your answer on your answer sheet.

PART 3

Directions: You will hear some conversations between two or more people. You will be asked to answer three questions about what the speakers say in each conversation. Select the best response to each question and mark the letter (A), (B), (C), or (D) on your answer sheet. The conversations will not be printed in your test book and will be spoken only one time.

32. Where does the man work?

(A) At a hotel
(B) At an airport
(C) At a hospital
(D) At a bookstore

33. Why most likely was a new policy introduced?

(A) To save money
(B) To satisfy a regulation
(C) To guarantee employees' safety
(D) To prevent customer complaints

34. What does the man offer to do?

(A) Call a service desk
(B) Supply reading materials
(C) Store the woman's belongings
(D) Cancel a reservation

---

35. What is the man concerned about?

(A) Keeping some costs low
(B) Keeping a workstation organized
(C) Keeping records of accomplishments
(D) Keeping track of appointments

36. According to the man, what is the problem with a notepad?

(A) It has been damaged.
(B) It is heavy to carry.
(C) It is easy to forget.
(D) It is almost full.

37. What does the woman tell the man to do?

(A) Visit her office
(B) Go to a Web site
(C) Post a reminder sign
(D) Change his daily schedule

---

38. What type of document has the woman created?

(A) A recommendation letter
(B) A training manual
(C) A press release
(D) A business document

39. Who is the man?

(A) A visiting researcher
(B) An outside vendor
(C) A prospective client
(D) A regional supervisor

40. What mistake did the woman make?

(A) She submitted a draft too early.
(B) She spelled a name incorrectly.
(C) She forgot to add her signature.
(D) She used the wrong date.

---

41. What did the man let the woman know by e-mail?

(A) He is unhappy with a fee increase.
(B) He plans to move away.
(C) He would like to carry out renovations.
(D) He discovered a problem with his apartment.

42. What does the woman want to do?

(A) Inspect a living space
(B) Notify a building's residents
(C) Check some paperwork
(D) Speak with a contractor

43. What will the man leave for the woman?

(A) Some keys
(B) A payment
(C) A container
(D) Some blueprints

GO ON TO THE NEXT PAGE

44. What did the woman recently do?

(A) She spoke at a conference.
(B) She designed a brochure.
(C) She reviewed survey results.
(D) She responded to e-mail inquiries.

45. Why does the man say, "I've been pretty busy with billing work"?

(A) To request extra help
(B) To provide an excuse
(C) To decline an invitation
(D) To correct an error

46. What will the woman suggest at a weekly meeting?

(A) Extending business hours
(B) Modifying a Web site
(C) Simplifying a hiring process
(D) Postponing an announcement

---

47. Who most likely is Mr. Aalders?

(A) A photographer
(B) A painter
(C) A fashion designer
(D) A sculptor

48. What does Elton mention about *Lilac*?

(A) It is very small in size.
(B) It is undergoing restoration.
(C) It is being shown at another institution.
(D) It is displayed in the main gallery.

49. What does Elton say he will do for the woman?

(A) Find some items
(B) Issue a refund
(C) Get an audio guide
(D) Explain an artistic technique

---

50. Who most likely are the speakers?

(A) Ushers
(B) Theater patrons
(C) Professional actors
(D) Backstage crew members

51. What does the woman mention about the play?

(A) It has been praised by critics.
(B) Its characters are interesting.
(C) Tickets for it have sold out.
(D) It has a positive theme.

52. What does the man want to see?

(A) Some sales figures
(B) A play program
(C) Some newspaper articles
(D) A copy of a script

---

53. What kind of business does the woman work for?

(A) A restaurant
(B) A food industry magazine
(C) A cooking school
(D) A kitchenware manufacturer

54. What does the woman highlight about the Multi-Pot?

(A) Its functions
(B) Its weight
(C) Its popularity
(D) Its available colors

55. What does the man ask the woman for?

(A) A promotional code
(B) A product sample
(C) A contact number
(D) A catalog

---

56. Where most likely are the speakers?

(A) At a medical clinic
(B) At a pharmacy
(C) At a fitness center
(D) At a health food store

57. Why does the man say, "I have been feeling tired lately"?

(A) To explain the reason for his visit
(B) To agree with the woman's analysis
(C) To apologize for a misunderstanding
(D) To indicate that an offer is attractive

58. What does the woman say she can do?

(A) Sign the man up for a class
(B) Give the man some free goods
(C) Demonstrate some exercises
(D) Search for a pamphlet

---

59. Why does the man ask Marissa for assistance?

(A) He is unable to operate a machine.
(B) He wants information about a product.
(C) He is confused about a policy.
(D) He does not know where a manager is.

60. What does Marissa mention about the Cleanster J9 ?

(A) It is being sold at a discount.
(B) It can be gift-wrapped at no additional cost.
(C) It is the store's best-selling vacuum.
(D) It is a relatively new model.

61. What will the man most likely do next?

(A) Help a customer carry a device
(B) Stock some shelves
(C) Guide a customer to another area
(D) Take some measurements

Your Order:

Item	Quantity	Total
Juice (large bottles)	25	$45
Pizza slice sampler	30	$80
Dessert package	50	$110
Sandwich platter	50	$135

62. What kind of event are the speakers planning?

(A) A store opening
(B) A music festival
(C) A staff picnic
(D) A charity fund-raiser

63. Why most likely does the man want to use Delmat Foods?

(A) They use high-quality ingredients.
(B) They offer reduced prices on large orders.
(C) They have a convenient parking facility.
(D) They provide a delivery service.

64. Look at the graphic. Which amount will be removed from the order?

(A) $45
(B) $80
(C) $110
(D) $135

Test 7

GO ON TO THE NEXT PAGE

☆ Ladden Supermarket ☆

Weeklong sale on select items!

- **5% off** .... flowers
- **10% off** .... cosmetics
- **15% off** .... baked goods
- **20% off** .... produce

65. What does the woman say will happen this weekend?

(A) Her friend will go out of town.
(B) Her hobby club will have a gathering.
(C) A movie will be broadcast on television.
(D) A housewarming party will take place.

66. Look at the graphic. Which price reduction will the woman try to receive?

(A) 5%
(B) 10%
(C) 15%
(D) 20%

67. What does the man offer to do for the woman?

(A) Write down a recipe
(B) Download a street map
(C) Lend her his loyalty card
(D) Assist with obtaining a coupon

FROM:	SUBJECT:
Mai Okazaki	Facility Tour Schedule
Sung-Chul Oh	ATTACHED: Sales Projections
Drew Langpro	Conference Planning Checklist
Hyun-Jin Seo	CANCELED: Computer Workshop

68. Why is the man unable to access an e-mail account?

(A) He does not have a valid password.
(B) His account's storage is full.
(C) He cannot get an Internet connection.
(D) He needs to install some new software.

69. Look at the graphic. Who sent the e-mail the speakers are discussing?

(A) Ms. Okazaki
(B) Mr. Oh
(C) Mr. Langpro
(D) Ms. Seo

70. What does the woman offer to do?

(A) Revise a document
(B) Print a data summary
(C) Arrange a team meeting
(D) Reply to a written request

PART 4

Directions: You will hear some talks given by a single speaker. You will be asked to answer three questions about what the speaker says in each talk. Select the best response to each question and mark the letter (A), (B), (C), or (D) on your answer sheet. The talks will not be printed in your test book and will be spoken only one time.

71. What does the speaker's business sell?
(A) Clothing
(B) Appliances
(C) Books
(D) Furniture

72. What is the problem?
(A) An address is incorrect.
(B) An item is unavailable.
(C) A price was misquoted.
(D) An invoice was not paid.

73. What does the speaker say the listener can see on her account page?
(A) Her balance of store credit
(B) Her contact preferences
(C) A set of instructions
(D) A shipping update

---

74. What department does the speaker most likely manage?
(A) Shipping and Receiving
(B) Maintenance
(C) Parking
(D) Security

75. What does the speaker imply when she says, "we need a new strategy"?
(A) A budget limit has been exceeded.
(B) A training program has received poor feedback.
(C) A recruiting attempt has not been successful.
(D) A technology is no longer free.

76. What will the listeners most likely do next?
(A) Greet a visitor
(B) Fill out a form
(C) Discuss a problem
(D) Conclude a meeting

---

77. What does the advertised program most likely teach?
(A) Graphic design
(B) Tax preparation
(C) Business management
(D) Computer engineering

78. What is mentioned about the program?
(A) It lasts more than one year.
(B) It offers some classes online.
(C) It includes career planning services.
(D) Its graduates receive a university degree.

79. What does the speaker say visitors to a Web site can do?
(A) Download an online course book
(B) Chat with academy staff
(C) Watch some videos
(D) Read course descriptions

---

80. What problem does the speaker describe?
(A) A presentation is not ready.
(B) A document is missing.
(C) A trip is delayed by weather.
(D) An itinerary contains an error.

81. What does the speaker ask the listener to do?
(A) Register for a conference
(B) Give a public talk
(C) Print out some graphs
(D) Modify a reservation

82. How can the listener get a file?
(A) By accessing it online
(B) By meeting the speaker
(C) By going to the post office
(D) By using a delivery service

GO ON TO THE NEXT PAGE

83. Who most likely is Mr. Stone?

(A) A financial advisor
(B) A legal expert
(C) A technical consultant
(D) A marketing specialist

84. Why does the speaker say Mr. Stone has been hired?

(A) To assist with a difficult decision
(B) To keep the company up-to-date
(C) To comply with environmental regulations
(D) To network with outside organizations

85. What are the listeners asked to do?

(A) Review some guidelines
(B) Gather again tomorrow
(C) Submit proposals for change
(D) Cooperate with Mr. Stone

---

86. What does the speaker ask the listeners to do?

(A) Arrange some boxes
(B) Collect some receipts
(C) Repair some equipment
(D) Check some inventories

87. What does the speaker mean when he says, "have you seen all the trucks"?

(A) He had to park his car far from a work site.
(B) He thinks that a work area is especially busy.
(C) He wants advice on purchasing new vehicles.
(D) He is concerned about some drivers' safety.

88. What will the speaker probably do next?

(A) Make a list
(B) Reschedule an appointment
(C) Clean a workstation
(D) Update a product description

---

89. What is the main topic of the broadcast?

(A) The advantages of public transportation
(B) The effects of personal electronics
(C) A new form of outdoor exercise
(D) Home improvement methods

90. According to the speaker, when should an activity be avoided?

(A) In the morning
(B) During lunch breaks
(C) In the afternoon
(D) At night

91. What will listeners probably hear next?

(A) An advertisement
(B) An interview
(C) A speech
(D) A song

---

92. What is the workshop mainly about?

(A) Environmental initiatives
(B) Business expansions
(C) Employee benefits
(D) Customer loyalty programs

93. What does the speaker imply when he says, "your customers will want to know about this kind of thing?"

(A) Some mistakes should be admitted.
(B) Some instructions should be clarified.
(C) Some achievements should be celebrated.
(D) Some positive efforts should be publicized.

94. What are the listeners asked to look at?

(A) A whiteboard
(B) A poster
(C) A handout
(D) A projector screen

Central Bus Terminal (departures)

Route	Destination	Departure time	Status
104	Trillburgh	1:55 P.M.	DEPARTED
312	Matford	2:10 P.M.	ON TIME
165	Dahlview	2:25 P.M.	ON TIME
981	Ledhurst	3:00 P.M.	DELAYED

95. Look at the graphic. Which bus route is the announcement for?

(A) 104
(B) 312
(C) 165
(D) 981

96. What are all travelers encouraged to do?

(A) Use vending machines
(B) Form lines in front of gates
(C) Buy tickets through a mobile app
(D) Complete a feedback survey

97. According to the speaker, what is temporarily available for free?

(A) Some refreshments
(B) Wireless Internet access
(C) Use of a storage locker
(D) Seating upgrades

Marv's Beach Gear Locations on Shunders Beach

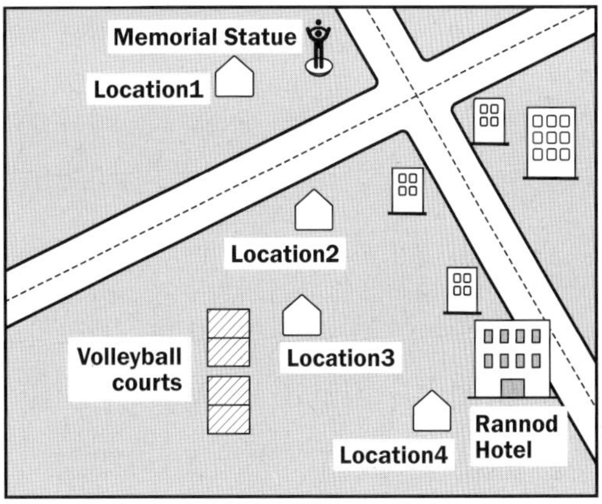

98. What does the speaker say about the upcoming event?

(A) This is the first year it has been held.
(B) It will be attended by a top city official.
(C) Marv's Beach Gear is supporting it financially.
(D) Some of Marv's Beach Gear's staff are participating in it.

99. Look at the graphic. Which location does the speaker believe will be the busiest?

(A) Location 1
(B) Location 2
(C) Location 3
(D) Location 4

100. According to the speaker, what will the listeners do before the event?

(A) Exchange shifts with each other
(B) Rehearse a performance
(C) Hang up some banners
(D) Move some stock

This is the end of the Listening test. Turn to Part 5 in your test book.

LC

TEST 8

LISTENING TEST

In the Listening test, you will be asked to demonstrate how well you understand spoken English. The entire Listening test will last approximately 45 minutes. There are four parts, and directions are given for each part. You must mark your answers on the separate answer sheet. Do not write your answers in your test book.

PART 1

Directions: For each question in this part, you will hear four statements about a picture in your test book. When you hear the statements, you must select the one statement that best describes what you see in the picture. Then find the number of the question on your answer sheet and mark your answer. The statements will not be printed in your test book and will be spoken only one time.

Statement (C), "They're sitting at a table," is the best description of the picture, so you should select answer (C) and mark it on your answer sheet.

1.

2.

Test 8

GO ON TO THE NEXT PAGE

3.

4.

5.

6.

Test 8

GO ON TO THE NEXT PAGE

PART 2

Directions: You will hear a question or statement and three responses spoken in English. They will not be printed in your test book and will be spoken only one time. Select the best response to the question or statement and mark the letter (A), (B), or (C) on your answer sheet.

7. Mark your answer on your answer sheet.

8. Mark your answer on your answer sheet.

9. Mark your answer on your answer sheet.

10. Mark your answer on your answer sheet.

11. Mark your answer on your answer sheet.

12. Mark your answer on your answer sheet.

13. Mark your answer on your answer sheet.

14. Mark your answer on your answer sheet.

15. Mark your answer on your answer sheet.

16. Mark your answer on your answer sheet.

17. Mark your answer on your answer sheet.

18. Mark your answer on your answer sheet.

19. Mark your answer on your answer sheet.

20. Mark your answer on your answer sheet.

21. Mark your answer on your answer sheet.

22. Mark your answer on your answer sheet.

23. Mark your answer on your answer sheet.

24. Mark your answer on your answer sheet.

25. Mark your answer on your answer sheet.

26. Mark your answer on your answer sheet.

27. Mark your answer on your answer sheet.

28. Mark your answer on your answer sheet.

29. Mark your answer on your answer sheet.

30. Mark your answer on your answer sheet.

31. Mark your answer on your answer sheet.

PART 3

Directions: You will hear some conversations between two or more people. You will be asked to answer three questions about what the speakers say in each conversation. Select the best response to each question and mark the letter (A), (B), (C), or (D) on your answer sheet. The conversations will not be printed in your test book and will be spoken only one time.

32. What did the speakers' company do last month?
(A) It redecorated its offices.
(B) It recruited new researchers.
(C) It merged some departments.
(D) It moved to a new location.

33. What information is incorrect on the man's business cards?
(A) A phone number
(B) An address
(C) A name
(D) A job title

34. What does the woman suggest the man do next?
(A) Read an instruction manual
(B) Write a note on a business card
(C) Log in to a computer system
(D) Call a technical support team

---

35. What did the man notice about the Maximus 94?
(A) A new version
(B) A recall announcement
(C) An additional color option
(D) A price decrease

36. What problem does the man have?
(A) He has misplaced a receipt.
(B) He forgot to bring a coupon.
(C) He cut a tag off a product.
(D) He does not have cash.

37. What does the woman say she will do next?
(A) Speak to a supervisor
(B) Exchange an item
(C) Check some inventory
(D) Give the man some paperwork

---

38. What does the woman say about a train?
(A) Its seats are uncomfortable.
(B) Its tickets are difficult to obtain.
(C) It does not serve a certain destination.
(D) It does not run frequently.

39. What does the woman want to avoid doing?
(A) Losing her luggage
(B) Using her time poorly
(C) Spending a lot of money
(D) Driving on narrow roads

40. Why does the man say, "the Grenzel compact car has a navigation system"?
(A) To suggest an alternative vehicle
(B) To explain a high rental fee
(C) To correct an inaccurate description
(D) To reassure the woman about a trip

---

41. Who most likely is the woman?
(A) A lawyer
(B) A reporter
(C) A scientist
(D) An architect

42. What does the man ask the woman to do?
(A) Consult with a manager
(B) Assist with a task
(C) Present some statistics
(D) Postpone a deadline

43. What will the woman most likely do next?
(A) Install a computer program
(B) Look through a database
(C) Send a package
(D) Take a break

GO ON TO THE NEXT PAGE →

44. Where does the conversation take place?

(A) At a bank
(B) At a real estate agency
(C) At a utility company
(D) At a newspaper office

45. What is the purpose of the man's visit?

(A) To propose a partnership
(B) To file a complaint
(C) To make an inquiry
(D) To open an account

46. What information does Ms. Jung ask the man for?

(A) A business's name
(B) A starting date
(C) An amount of money
(D) A property's location

---

47. What does the woman want to do in her restaurant?

(A) Increase convenience
(B) Reduce expenses
(C) Improve security
(D) Provide entertainment

48. What does the man mention about the G4 ?

(A) It is a wireless device.
(B) It has adjustable components.
(C) It is energy efficient.
(D) It comes in five colors.

49. What does the woman ask the man to do?

(A) Replace a machine part
(B) Give a demonstration
(C) Confirm a model number
(D) Arrange a shipment

---

50. Why did the woman visit Plath Corporation?

(A) To meet a former colleague
(B) To have an interview
(C) To deliver a package
(D) To speak with a client

51. What does the woman ask the man for?

(A) Some coins
(B) His signature
(C) Directions to a building
(D) Validation for parking

52. What problem does the man mention?

(A) A broken gate
(B) A slow machine
(C) A narrow exit path
(D) A road closure

---

53. What type of performance is the man interested in?

(A) Comedy
(B) Dance
(C) Acting
(D) Singing

54. Why does the man qualify for a discount?

(A) He is purchasing more than ten tickets.
(B) He has a membership card.
(C) He is attending a show in the daytime.
(D) He is buying tickets on the day of the performance.

55. What information does the woman ask the man for?

(A) A card number
(B) An e-mail address
(C) A pick-up time
(D) A seating preference

---

56. Who will visit the restaurant on Thursday?
(A) A food critic
(B) A photographer
(C) A television producer
(D) A politician

57. What concern does Miguel have about the signature dish?
(A) It must be prepared by the head chef.
(B) It takes too long to cook.
(C) It requires too many ingredients.
(D) It was already featured in a publication.

58. What will the men most likely do after the meeting?
(A) Inspect a kitchen
(B) Plan a business trip
(C) Review an advertisement
(D) Discuss a menu

---

59. What does the woman offer to do?
(A) Stock some shelves
(B) Clean a loading area
(C) Refill some cash registers
(D) Lead a store tour

60. What does the man say he did this morning?
(A) He assembled a display cabinet.
(B) He repaired some equipment.
(C) He placed a supply order.
(D) He visited a warehouse.

61. What does the woman imply when she says, "it's going to be a really big event"?
(A) The man will need several people to work in a booth.
(B) The man should make a reservation soon.
(C) She wants to help design an exhibit.
(D) She intends to request vacation time.

Table of Contents

1. E-mails and memos
2. Letters
3. Reports
4. Press releases

62. Look at the graphic. Which chapter will the woman most likely consult?
(A) Chapter 1
(B) Chapter 2
(C) Chapter 3
(D) Chapter 4

63. What does the man say is an advantage of *The Oliver Writing Handbook*?
(A) Its explanations are easy to understand.
(B) Its contents are approved by the company.
(C) It comes with membership in an online forum.
(D) It is available to employees for free.

64. What will the speakers' company do next month?
(A) Revise a personnel policy
(B) Negotiate a contract
(C) Launch a new product
(D) Stop offering a service

Test 8

GO ON TO THE NEXT PAGE

Training schedule for: *Mary Soto*	
Time	**Session title**
10:00 A.M.	Describing Products
1:00 P.M.	Taking Orders
2:00 P.M.	Handling Complaints
4:00 P.M.	Processing Refunds

65. What does the woman offer to do for the man?
    (A) Record a presentation
    (B) Prepare a work area
    (C) Photocopy a manual
    (D) Mail some invoices

66. Look at the graphic. Which session does the man plan to attend?
    (A) Describing Products
    (B) Taking Orders
    (C) Handling Complaints
    (D) Processing Refunds

67. What will the man probably do next?
    (A) Gather some training materials
    (B) Contact a sales representative
    (C) Proofread a report
    (D) Make some graphs

Notice—street closures

Street name	Reason for closing
Bay Avenue	Fallen tree
Tilden Drive	Parade
Dee Road	Construction
Nelson Way	Sign painting

68. Look at the graphic. Which street do the speakers most likely use to go to work?
    (A) Bay Avenue
    (B) Tilden Drive
    (C) Dee Road
    (D) Nelson Way

69. What does the woman say she will do this morning?
    (A) Deliver some packages
    (B) Host a videoconference
    (C) Interview job applicants
    (D) Purchase new furniture

70. Who most likely is Mr. Davidson?
    (A) A branch manager
    (B) A potential client
    (C) An incoming intern
    (D) A guest lecturer

PART 4

Directions: You will hear some talks given by a single speaker. You will be asked to answer three questions about what the speaker says in each talk. Select the best response to each question and mark the letter (A), (B), (C), or (D) on your answer sheet. The talks will not be printed in your test book and will be spoken only one time.

71. Where is the talk being given?

(A) In a store showroom
(B) On a factory floor
(C) At a museum
(D) In a recording studio

72. What will the speaker distribute to the listeners?

(A) Bags of snacks
(B) Audio devices
(C) Reusable passes
(D) Guide maps

73. According to the speaker, what will happen at two o'clock?

(A) A fund-raising auction
(B) An interactive performance
(C) A contest announcement
(D) A staff appreciation event

74. Where does the speaker work?

(A) At a public library
(B) At a community center
(C) At a nature reserve
(D) At a school

75. Why does the speaker say, "the registration period for new volunteers ended in June"?

(A) To express concern about a program
(B) To highlight a missed deadline
(C) To accept an invitation
(D) To justify a proposal

76. What does the speaker ask the listener to do?

(A) Take some photographs
(B) Revise a budget
(C) Come to her office
(D) Submit an online form

77. Who is the advertisement most likely intended for?

(A) Marketing specialists
(B) Property managers
(C) Store owners
(D) Jobseekers

78. What is the speaker mainly describing?

(A) A software program
(B) A series of workshops
(C) A security system
(D) A clothing line

79. What are listeners encouraged to do?

(A) Register for a trade show
(B) Make a phone call
(C) Visit a Web site
(D) Use a discount voucher

80. What does the speaker's store sell?

(A) Furniture
(B) Art supplies
(C) Hardware
(D) Plants

81. What does the speaker imply when he says, "our stock changes all the time"?

(A) He is proud of the staff's hard work.
(B) Some prices may not be marked accurately.
(C) Some of the store's aisles may be blocked.
(D) He wants to encourage repeat visits.

82. According to the speaker, what can customers obtain at the service desk?

(A) Sample goods
(B) Store coupons
(C) Order forms
(D) Job applications

GO ON TO THE NEXT PAGE

83. What most likely does the speaker work?

(A) At a convention center
(B) At a fitness club
(C) At a medical clinic
(D) At an interior design firm

84. What does the speaker say was upgraded?

(A) A parking area
(B) An audio system
(C) A floor surface
(D) A passenger elevator

85. What does the speaker encourage the listener to do?

(A) Complete a questionnaire
(B) Postpone an appointment
(C) Register for e-mail updates
(D) Go to an upcoming party

---

86. Where is the talk taking place?

(A) At a training seminar
(B) At a product demonstration
(C) At a focus group session
(D) At a board meeting

87. What problem does the speaker mention?

(A) Unnecessary information in some documents
(B) The large distance between two buildings in a complex
(C) The difficulty of maintaining healthy exercise habits
(D) A lack of communication between workers

88. What are the listeners asked to do?

(A) Take detailed notes
(B) Look at some charts
(C) Introduce themselves
(D) Volunteer for a committee

---

89. What is the broadcast mainly about?

(A) Upgrades to bicycle paths
(B) Tours of a neighborhood
(C) A business's reopening
(D) A sporting event

90. What does the speaker mean when he says, "Davis Gardens underwent extensive roadwork in May"?

(A) Some funds have already been spent.
(B) An improvement project is not unique.
(C) Some retailers were inconvenienced.
(D) A delay was unavoidable.

91. What will most likely happen next?

(A) Some songs will be played.
(B) Some advertisements will air.
(C) A telephone interview will begin.
(D) A traffic report will be given.

---

92. What will the listeners have the opportunity to do?

(A) Compete for an industry award
(B) Develop foreign language skills
(C) Influence hiring decisions
(D) Learn from senior employees

93. What does the speaker thank Francisco for?

(A) Making a suggestion
(B) Conducting some research
(C) Leading a special team
(D) Following some rules

94. What should interested listeners do?

(A) Submit an application
(B) Attend another meeting
(C) Talk to Francisco
(D) Read a memo

Coupon

Dardano's Inn

10% off banquet room rental

–For groups of 30⁺ guests
–Rent a private room for three hours!

Expires: July 1

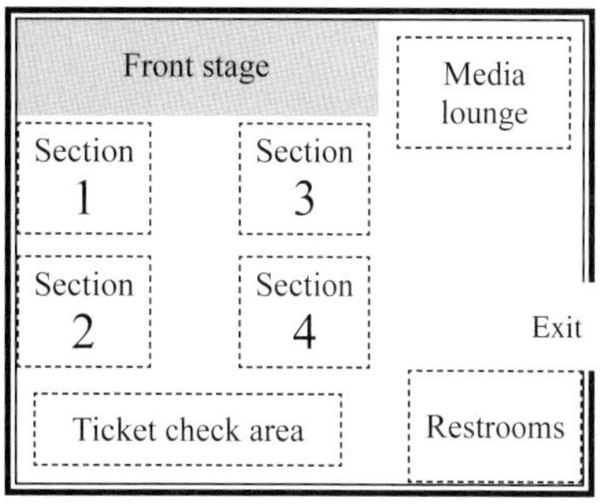

95. According to the speaker, why is the event being held?

(A) To recognize a staff member's retirement
(B) To celebrate a business anniversary
(C) To host some potential clients
(D) To promote new merchandise

96. Look at the graphic. Why will the speaker be unable to use the coupon?

(A) His group's size is too small.
(B) His group will require buffet service.
(C) The event is expected to last too long.
(D) The event will happen after an expiration date.

97. What does the speaker ask the listeners for?

(A) A cost estimate
(B) Some instructions
(C) A recommendation
(D) Some donations

98. Who most likely are the listeners?

(A) Lighting technicians
(B) Music journalists
(C) Performers
(D) Ushers

99. Look at the graphic. What section does the speaker tell the listeners to sit in?

(A) Section 1
(B) Section 2
(C) Section 3
(D) Section 4

100. What are the listeners asked to do after the show ends?

(A) Participate in a ceremony
(B) Share some feedback
(C) Return some equipment
(D) View an updated schedule

This is the end of the Listening test. Turn to Part 5 in your test book.

LC

TEST 9

LISTENING TEST

In the Listening test, you will be asked to demonstrate how well you understand spoken English. The entire Listening test will last approximately 45 minutes. There are four parts, and directions are given for each part. You must mark your answers on the separate answer sheet. Do not write your answers in your test book.

PART 1

Directions: For each question in this part, you will hear four statements about a picture in your test book. When you hear the statements, you must select the one statement that best describes what you see in the picture. Then find the number of the question on your answer sheet and mark your answer. The statements will not be printed in your test book and will be spoken only one time.

Statement (C), "They're sitting at a table," is the best description of the picture, so you should select answer (C) and mark it on your answer sheet.

1.

2.

Test 9

GO ON TO THE NEXT PAGE

3.

4.

5.

6.

Test 9

GO ON TO THE NEXT PAGE

PART 2

Directions: You will hear a question or statement and three responses spoken in English. They will not be printed in your test book and will be spoken only one time. Select the best response to the question or statement and mark the letter (A), (B), or (C) on your answer sheet.

7. Mark your answer on your answer sheet.

8. Mark your answer on your answer sheet.

9. Mark your answer on your answer sheet.

10. Mark your answer on your answer sheet.

11. Mark your answer on your answer sheet.

12. Mark your answer on your answer sheet.

13. Mark your answer on your answer sheet.

14. Mark your answer on your answer sheet.

15. Mark your answer on your answer sheet.

16. Mark your answer on your answer sheet.

17. Mark your answer on your answer sheet.

18. Mark your answer on your answer sheet.

19. Mark your answer on your answer sheet.

20. Mark your answer on your answer sheet.

21. Mark your answer on your answer sheet.

22. Mark your answer on your answer sheet.

23. Mark your answer on your answer sheet.

24. Mark your answer on your answer sheet.

25. Mark your answer on your answer sheet.

26. Mark your answer on your answer sheet.

27. Mark your answer on your answer sheet.

28. Mark your answer on your answer sheet.

29. Mark your answer on your answer sheet.

30. Mark your answer on your answer sheet.

31. Mark your answer on your answer sheet.

PART 3

Directions: You will hear some conversations between two or more people. You will be asked to answer three questions about what the speakers say in each conversation. Select the best response to each question and mark the letter (A), (B), (C), or (D) on your answer sheet. The conversations will not be printed in your test book and will be spoken only one time.

32. Who most likely is the man?
(A) A hotel clerk
(B) An airline employee
(C) A restaurant manager
(D) A rental car agent

33. Why is the woman calling?
(A) To cancel a reservation
(B) To complain about a policy
(C) To ask about a misplaced item
(D) To request a special meal

34. What does the man ask the woman to do?
(A) Provide a code
(B) Wait for a moment
(C) Send an e-mail
(D) Confirm an address

---

35. What does the man mention about the pens?
(A) They are too expensive.
(B) Their ink dries too slowly.
(C) Their design is unattractive.
(D) Using them is uncomfortable.

36. Why is the woman unable to return the pens?
(A) She cannot find a receipt.
(B) She lost one of them.
(C) The return period has ended.
(D) Their packaging has been opened.

37. What will the woman most likely do next?
(A) Rearrange a storage room
(B) Search for replacements
(C) Collect some boxes
(D) Write an online review

---

38. Where most likely does the man work?
(A) At a dry cleaner
(B) At a home appliance store
(C) At a fabric manufacturing company
(D) At a shoe shop

39. What is the purpose of the woman's call?
(A) To report a problem
(B) To inquire about the status of an order
(C) To verify some business hours
(D) To find out a price

40. What did the man do yesterday?
(A) Worked overtime
(B) Fixed a machine
(C) Called a customer
(D) Picked up some files

---

41. What does the woman say about the man's report?
(A) It covers one year of research.
(B) It includes some graphics.
(C) It will be released to the public.
(D) It was completed after a due date.

42. What does the woman most likely mean when she says, "most reports end with a list of recommendations"?
(A) She did not finish reading a report.
(B) She is suggesting a revision.
(C) She is confused by some results.
(D) She appreciates the man's creativity.

43. What will the woman most likely do on Friday?
(A) Proofread a document
(B) Host an event
(C) Move her office
(D) Issue some invoices

GO ON TO THE NEXT PAGE →

44. What did the man do in Madrid?

(A) He took a vacation.
(B) He met a client.
(C) He attended a workshop.
(D) He inspected a project site.

45. What happened at the office while the man was gone?

(A) A renovation project was started.
(B) A negotiation was rescheduled.
(C) A retirement was announced.
(D) Some supplies were damaged.

46. What will the man offer to Sarah?

(A) His assistance
(B) His congratulations
(C) Some instructions
(D) Some incentives

---

47. What are the speakers mainly discussing?

(A) Discontinuing facility tours
(B) Updating a software program
(C) Expanding a product line
(D) Holding a career fair

48. What does the woman ask Fred about?

(A) A potential venue
(B) A financial report
(C) A contract renewal
(D) An advertising approach

49. What will the speakers most likely do on Wednesday?

(A) Mail some documents
(B) Create a digital video
(C) Meet with a distributor
(D) Prepare a travel itinerary

---

50. Where did the man see a conference schedule?

(A) In a trade journal
(B) On a posted notice
(C) In an e-mail
(D) On a Web page

51. What does the man say about the conference center?

(A) It is nearby.
(B) It was built recently.
(C) It is owned by a city government.
(D) It has a good reputation.

52. What does the woman hope the conference includes?

(A) A networking opportunity
(B) A returning speaker
(C) A device demonstration
(D) A brainstorming session

---

53. What did Euphoria Factory do last month?

(A) It lowered its prices.
(B) It published a newsletter.
(C) It surveyed the public.
(D) It hired a new executive.

54. What were the women surprised by?

(A) A number of participants
(B) An increase in expenses
(C) The simplicity of a procedure
(D) The results of an analysis

55. According to the women, what will happen in February?

(A) Some consumers will win prizes.
(B) Some restaurants will open.
(C) A new item will become available.
(D) A retail store will have a sale.

---

56. What is the conversation mainly about?
(A) A business dinner
(B) Some sales data
(C) Some training sessions
(D) A reimbursement process

57. What does the man imply when he says, "I haven't done that, actually"?
(A) The woman has supplied helpful information.
(B) Another person deserves praise for a success.
(C) He was unable to meet a deadline.
(D) He is not qualified to give the woman advice.

58. What does the woman decide to do?
(A) Recalculate some estimates
(B) Approve some requests
(C) Upgrade a computer system
(D) Issue a written clarification

---

59. What are some customers having a difficult time doing?
(A) Finding some merchandise
(B) Understanding a policy
(C) Filling out some forms
(D) Identifying staff members

60. What will the woman most likely do tomorrow?
(A) Distribute a schedule
(B) Reserve a conference room
(C) Take a day off
(D) Set up some equipment

61. Where most likely do the speakers work?
(A) At an electronics store
(B) At a clothing retailer
(C) At a supermarket
(D) At a plant shop

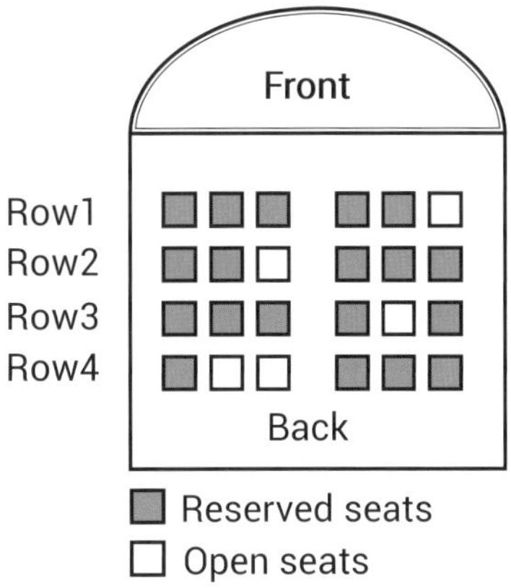

62. What does the woman inquire about?
(A) Using a dining service
(B) Bringing additional luggage
(C) Parking at the ferry terminal
(D) Accessing the Internet

63. What is the woman surprised to learn about the ferry?
(A) Its passengers must book a particular seat.
(B) There is a fee for using its electrical outlets.
(C) It departs at later times on weekends.
(D) It makes several stops along its route.

64. Look at the graphic. Which row will the woman sit in?
(A) Row 1
(B) Row 2
(C) Row 3
(D) Row 4

Test 9

GO ON TO THE NEXT PAGE

Building Directory	
Suite	**Company**
1	Garnet Associates
2	Osage Consulting
3	Madison Research
4	Spencer Solutions

65. What is the purpose of the man's visit?
(A) He is checking a security system.
(B) He is going to a job interview.
(C) He is making a delivery.
(D) He is repairing an elevator.

66. Look at the graphic. Which company will the man visit?
(A) Garnet Associates
(B) Osage Consulting
(C) Madison Research
(D) Spencer Solutions

67. What does the woman say about the parking areas?
(A) They are located behind the building.
(B) Some of them have a user fee.
(C) They are designated by color.
(D) They require printed permits.

Admission price per person	
University student	$5
Corporate sponsor	$8
Groups of 20 or more	$10
General admission	$15

68. What kind of event are the speakers discussing?
(A) A music concert
(B) A film festival
(C) A museum exhibit
(D) A theater performance

69. Look at the graphic. Which ticket price will the speakers most likely pay?
(A) $5
(B) $8
(C) $10
(D) $15

70. What will the woman probably do next?
(A) Rent a vehicle
(B) Print some paperwork
(C) Post a flyer on a wall
(D) Contact a coworker

PART 4

Directions: You will hear some talks given by a single speaker. You will be asked to answer three questions about what the speaker says in each talk. Select the best response to each question and mark the letter (A), (B), (C), or (D) on your answer sheet. The talks will not be printed in your test book and will be spoken only one time.

71. What will the listeners do soon?
(A) Travel abroad
(B) Reorganize a work space
(C) Answer inquiries from clients
(D) Vote on proposals

72. According to the speaker, what has changed about a process?
(A) The time frame
(B) The budget
(C) The supervising committee
(D) The method of communication

73. Why should the listeners speak to each other?
(A) To share their opinions
(B) To point out some mistakes
(C) To confirm some preparations
(D) To describe their roles

74. What kind of company does the speaker work for?
(A) A print shop
(B) A camera manufacturer
(C) A lighting equipment store
(D) A photography studio

75. What does the speaker say caused a problem?
(A) A broken piece of machinery
(B) A product redesign
(C) A delayed shipment
(D) A shortage of workers

76. What does the speaker offer the listener?
(A) A formal letter of apology
(B) An extended warranty
(C) Some discount rates
(D) Some free cleaning goods

77. Who most likely are the listeners?
(A) Graphic designers
(B) Freelance writers
(C) Career counselors
(D) Real estate developers

78. What is included with the seminar?
(A) Refreshments
(B) Transportation vouchers
(C) Online content
(D) In-person consulting

79. What does the speaker say she will distribute to the listeners?
(A) Promotional materials
(B) A list of topics
(C) A sign-up sheet
(D) Computer passwords

80. Where does the speaker most likely work?
(A) At a building cleaning service
(B) At a landscaping company
(C) At an automobile repair shop
(D) At a home improvement store

81. Why does the speaker urge the listener to visit a Web site?
(A) To obtain driving directions
(B) To watch an instructional video
(C) To complete a feedback survey
(D) To make an appointment

82. Why does the speaker say, "they're very popular with our customers"?
(A) To apologize for long waiting lines
(B) To encourage a quick purchase
(C) To suggest posting a user review
(D) To recommend a substitute item

GO ON TO THE NEXT PAGE →

83. What is the speaker trying to sell?

(A) Customized stationery
(B) Display furniture
(C) Packaging material
(D) Printing paper

84. According to the speaker, what is special about the product?

(A) It is imported.
(B) It is lightweight.
(C) It comes in many sizes.
(D) It is made from recycled goods.

85. How can listeners receive a discount?

(A) By placing a large order
(B) By using a special coupon
(C) By referring other customers
(D) By downloading a mobile app

---

86. What most likely is Ms. Tilden's area of expertise?

(A) Event coordination
(B) Data security
(C) Financial planning
(D) Fitness training

87. What does the speaker say will happen next month?

(A) A broadcast will have a guest host.
(B) A documentary will be released.
(C) A book will be published.
(D) A new class will be offered.

88. What are listeners encouraged to do?

(A) Donate to a charity organization
(B) Take a tour of a radio station
(C) Attend a regional conference
(D) Submit questions electronically

---

89. What department does the speaker most likely work in?

(A) Legal
(B) Purchasing
(C) Production
(D) Technical Support

90. What does the speaker imply when he says, "I've already completed your paperwork"?

(A) A problem has been resolved.
(B) A task was reassigned.
(C) A process is ahead of schedule.
(D) A change will be difficult to make.

91. What does the speaker instruct the listener to do?

(A) Send him another form
(B) Return his telephone call
(C) Cancel an upcoming trip
(D) Check his e-mail frequently

---

92. Who are the listeners?

(A) Truck drivers
(B) Computer technicians
(C) Customer service representatives
(D) Warehouse workers

93. What does the speaker imply when she says, "there's a big parade in the city"?

(A) A banner will be seen by many people.
(B) Some deliveries may take a long time.
(C) Some staff members may be absent.
(D) A neighborhood will be noisy.

94. What does the speaker ask the listeners to do?

(A) Put on a uniform
(B) Move some equipment
(C) Work with a partner
(D) Use a Web site

WEEKDAY SCHEDULE FOR FRANTINE STATION

Southbound Trains

Train	Departure Time
Train 315	5:00 A.M.
Train 383	5:18 A.M.
Train 324	5:30 A.M.
Train 379	5:45 A.M.

95. Look at the graphic. Which departure time does the announcement concern?

(A) 5:00 A.M.
(B) 5:18 A.M.
(C) 5:30 A.M.
(D) 5:45 A.M.

96. What is the speaker announcing?

(A) A permanent change to a route
(B) A delay caused by bad weather
(C) A plan for maintenance work
(D) A new feature available on a train

97. What does the speaker remind the listeners about?

(A) The locations of some timetables
(B) A way to give feedback
(C) The color of a special bus line
(D) Some rules for train passengers

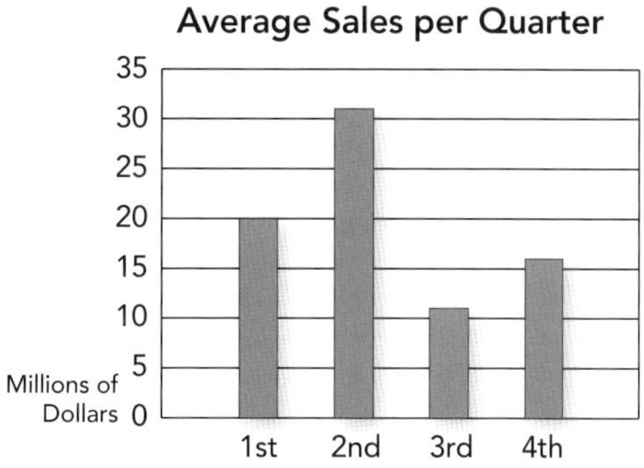

98. What type of products does the speaker's company most likely sell?

(A) Mobile phones
(B) Construction tools
(C) Inventory management software
(D) Casual footwear

99. Look at the graphic. When is the meeting taking place?

(A) In the first quarter
(B) In the second quarter
(C) In the third quarter
(D) In the fourth quarter

100. What does the speaker suggest?

(A) Offering additional price discounts
(B) Sponsoring a sporting event
(C) Participating in a trade show
(D) Advertising more on social media

Test 9

This is the end of the Listening test. Turn to Part 5 in your test book.

LC

TEST 10

LISTENING TEST

In the Listening test, you will be asked to demonstrate how well you understand spoken English. The entire Listening test will last approximately 45 minutes. There are four parts, and directions are given for each part. You must mark your answers on the separate answer sheet. Do not write your answers in your test book.

PART 1

Directions: For each question in this part, you will hear four statements about a picture in your test book. When you hear the statements, you must select the one statement that best describes what you see in the picture. Then find the number of the question on your answer sheet and mark your answer. The statements will not be printed in your test book and will be spoken only one time.

Statement (C), "They're sitting at a table," is the best description of the picture, so you should select answer (C) and mark it on your answer sheet.

1.

2.

Test 10

GO ON TO THE NEXT PAGE

3.

4.

5.

6.

Test 10

GO ON TO THE NEXT PAGE

PART 2

Directions: You will hear a question or statement and three responses spoken in English. They will not be printed in your test book and will be spoken only one time. Select the best response to the question or statement and mark the letter (A), (B), or (C) on your answer sheet.

7. Mark your answer on your answer sheet.
8. Mark your answer on your answer sheet.
9. Mark your answer on your answer sheet.
10. Mark your answer on your answer sheet.
11. Mark your answer on your answer sheet.
12. Mark your answer on your answer sheet.
13. Mark your answer on your answer sheet.
14. Mark your answer on your answer sheet.
15. Mark your answer on your answer sheet.
16. Mark your answer on your answer sheet.
17. Mark your answer on your answer sheet.
18. Mark your answer on your answer sheet.
19. Mark your answer on your answer sheet.
20. Mark your answer on your answer sheet.
21. Mark your answer on your answer sheet.
22. Mark your answer on your answer sheet.
23. Mark your answer on your answer sheet.
24. Mark your answer on your answer sheet.
25. Mark your answer on your answer sheet.
26. Mark your answer on your answer sheet.
27. Mark your answer on your answer sheet.
28. Mark your answer on your answer sheet.
29. Mark your answer on your answer sheet.
30. Mark your answer on your answer sheet.
31. Mark your answer on your answer sheet.

PART 3

Directions: You will hear some conversations between two or more people. You will be asked to answer three questions about what the speakers say in each conversation. Select the best response to each question and mark the letter (A), (B), (C), or (D) on your answer sheet. The conversations will not be printed in your test book and will be spoken only one time.

32. What does the man encourage the woman to do?

(A) Explore a new department
(B) Complete a customer survey
(C) Sample a product
(D) Join a rewards program

33. What problem does the woman have?

(A) She does not live nearby.
(B) She does not have much money.
(C) She is in a hurry.
(D) She has a health issue.

34. What does the man give to the woman?

(A) A free cosmetics item
(B) A sales receipt
(C) An application form
(D) A discount voucher

---

35. What does the woman say she likes about the café?

(A) The artwork on display
(B) The food
(C) The background music
(D) The furniture

36. Who is Ms. Martinez?

(A) A local performer
(B) A business owner
(C) A talent agent
(D) A café manager

37. What does the man say he will do for the woman?

(A) Bring her a menu
(B) Add her name to a list
(C) Clear her table
(D) Give her a schedule

---

38. What does the man want to know?

(A) Who will give a presentation
(B) When an event starts
(C) How to find some data
(D) Where a coworker is

39. What problem does the man mention?

(A) He is not feeling well.
(B) He is late for a meeting.
(C) He cannot set up some equipment.
(D) He has misplaced some files.

40. What does the woman say she will do?

(A) Review a slide show
(B) Prepare a conference room
(C) Send some contact information
(D) Confirm a number of attendees

---

41. What does the man mention about the exhibit?

(A) It will be closing for the day soon.
(B) Its ticket price has increased.
(C) Its venue has changed.
(D) It has sold out.

42. Why have the women come to Kemperling?

(A) To go to a conference
(B) To help with a festival
(C) To participate in a competition
(D) To spend time with friends

43. What does the man recommend?

(A) Walking through a garden
(B) Visiting a beach
(C) Attending a concert
(D) Opening a restaurant

GO ON TO THE NEXT PAGE

44. Why is the man calling the woman?

(A) To switch shifts with her
(B) To check a work schedule
(C) To request time off
(D) To inform her of a late arrival

45. According to the woman, why is the store busier than usual?

(A) A promotional sale has begun.
(B) Another employee is absent.
(C) New merchandise has been launched.
(D) A holiday is coming soon.

46. What does the man suggest?

(A) Hiring some temporary workers
(B) Assigning a task to a coworker
(C) Providing training to a colleague
(D) Asking another branch for assistance

---

47. What is the main topic of the conversation?

(A) A hotel policy
(B) An informational brochure
(C) A display stand
(D) A tour course

48. Why does the woman say, "most guests come in through the main entrance"?

(A) To emphasize the importance of cleaning an area often
(B) To recommend an angle for a photograph
(C) To express concern about an inconvenience
(D) To suggest a useful location for an item

49. What does the man say he will do?

(A) Move some decorations
(B) Try shopping online
(C) Make a price list
(D) Work overtime tonight

---

50. What is the conversation mainly about?

(A) A training session
(B) A contract renewal
(C) An interview process
(D) A software problem

51. What did the man do yesterday?

(A) He contacted a manufacturer.
(B) He summarized a manual.
(C) He issued a bill.
(D) He practiced a talk.

52. What does the woman mention about the business?

(A) Its workforce has recently expanded.
(B) It invests heavily in new technology.
(C) It will relocate to another city.
(D) It currently has several job openings.

---

53. What activity are the speakers discussing?

(A) Participating in a city event
(B) Registering for a government permit
(C) Revising some construction plans
(D) Reporting on a local news story

54. What information does Albert say he needs to verify?

(A) The budget for a project
(B) The next step of a procedure
(C) The start time of a meeting
(D) The name of an official

55. What will the woman most likely do next?

(A) Reschedule a dinner
(B) Drive to a building site
(C) Edit a draft of an article
(D) Look at some photographs

---

56. What has recently changed for the speakers?

(A) The length of their class sessions
(B) The skill level of their students
(C) The classrooms they teach in
(D) The textbooks they use

57. What is the man concerned about?

(A) Explaining a concept clearly
(B) Keeping listeners interested in a topic
(C) Finishing a certain number of lessons
(D) Impressing a supervisor

58. What does the woman imply when she says, "my class is about to start"?

(A) She cannot fulfill a request immediately.
(B) She needs to access some materials as soon as possible.
(C) The man is invited to observe her class.
(D) The man will have to leave the room.

---

59. Where most likely is the conversation taking place?

(A) At a bus stop
(B) At an industry event
(C) At the man's office
(D) At a personal celebration

60. What advantage of her new job is the woman especially pleased about?

(A) The short commute
(B) The flexible hours
(C) The high salary
(D) The friendly staff

61. What does the woman suggest?

(A) Having a meal together
(B) Collaborating on a proposal
(C) Sharing transportation
(D) Arranging a branch visit

Springer's Goods

Tents	10% off
Backpacks	20% off
Sleeping Bags	25% off
Flashlights	30% off

62. Why does the man thank the woman?

(A) She expedited an order for him.
(B) She checked a storage area for an item.
(C) She explained some product features.
(D) She gave him a coupon.

63. Look at the graphic. What is the man buying?

(A) A tent
(B) A backpack
(C) A sleeping bag
(D) A flashlight

64. What does the man ask about?

(A) An instruction manual
(B) A delivery option
(C) A return policy
(D) A closing time

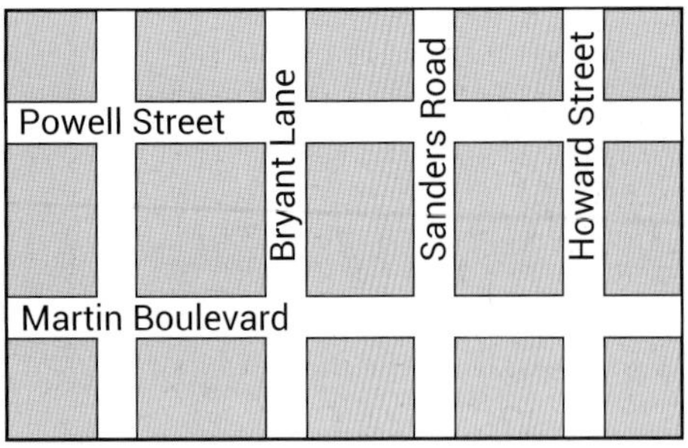

65. What will the speakers do at Mr. Wade's residence?
(A) Wash the windows
(B) Repair some plumbing
(C) Install an appliance
(D) Trim some trees

66. Look at the graphic. Which street is Mr. Wade's apartment on?
(A) Bryant Lane
(B) Sanders Road
(C) Howard Street
(D) Martin Boulevard

67. What does the man ask the woman to do when they arrive?
(A) Enter a building
(B) Unload some tools
(C) Wait in a vehicle
(D) Make a phone call

Department	Manager	Extension
Accounting	Angela Watkins	29
Human Resources	Jong-Kyu Kang	43
Marketing	Elias Cohen	18
Product Development	Prisha Acharya	37

68. What are the speakers mainly discussing?
(A) A company retreat
(B) Employee evaluations
(C) Design specifications
(D) A machine's performance

69. What problem does the woman mention?
(A) She is not authorized to give an approval.
(B) She does not have time to meet the man.
(C) She has not received the results of a test.
(D) She does not understand a document.

70. Look at the graphic. Who will the woman call?
(A) Ms. Watkins
(B) Mr. Kang
(C) Mr. Cohen
(D) Ms. Acharya

PART 4

Directions: You will hear some talks given by a single speaker. You will be asked to answer three questions about what the speaker says in each talk. Select the best response to each question and mark the letter (A), (B), (C), or (D) on your answer sheet. The talks will not be printed in your test book and will be spoken only one time.

71. Why most likely are the listeners visiting the park?

(A) To take a class
(B) To go on a hike
(C) To clean it up
(D) To conduct research

72. What has the speaker given to the listeners?

(A) A bag of supplies
(B) An admission ticket
(C) A map of a site
(D) An informational card

73. What does the speaker remind the listeners to do?

(A) Drink plenty of water
(B) Take regular breaks
(C) Stay in a group
(D) Wear sun protection

---

74. What type of event is taking place?

(A) A groundbreaking ceremony
(B) A shareholder meeting
(C) A product launch
(D) A guest lecture

75. What does the speaker say is included in a handout?

(A) A computerized image
(B) A detailed timeline
(C) A list of features
(D) A financial summary

76. What is Mr. Marsh famous for?

(A) Receiving an award
(B) Designing a building
(C) Managing a company
(D) Leading a media campaign

---

77. Who most likely are the listeners?

(A) Electronics technicians
(B) Corporate trainers
(C) Call center workers
(D) Retail salespeople

78. According to the speaker, what should the listeners focus on first?

(A) Promoting new merchandise
(B) Earning a customer's trust
(C) Identifying the problem
(D) Preparing a work space

79. What does the speaker plan to do next?

(A) Introduce a colleague
(B) Distribute handouts
(C) Assign groups
(D) Show a video

---

80. Who most likely is Mr. Finley?

(A) A city council member
(B) A journalist
(C) A professor
(D) A museum director

81. What does the speaker imply when she says, "It's five stories high"?

(A) A structure is easy to find.
(B) A building has a great view.
(C) Maintenance costs will be high.
(D) There is a lot of space to fill.

82. What are local residents asked to do?

(A) Donate everyday objects to a museum
(B) Share opinions about an exhibit
(C) Come to a fund-raising event
(D) Volunteer to work at an institution

GO ON TO THE NEXT PAGE →

83. According to the speaker, what will happen over the weekend?
(A) A construction project will begin.
(B) The business will move to another location.
(C) New office furniture will be delivered.
(D) Some rooms will be professionally painted.

84. Why does the speaker say, "there won't be much we can do"?
(A) To apologize for an error
(B) To give a warning
(C) To show disappointment
(D) To disagree with a suggestion

85. What does the speaker advise the listeners to do?
(A) Remove personal items from an office
(B) Report property damage to him
(C) Arrive early on Monday
(D) Indicate a brand preference

---

86. What kind of business is being advertised?
(A) A fitness facility
(B) An art school
(C) A hair salon
(D) A medical clinic

87. What does the speaker mention about the business?
(A) It has recently been renovated.
(B) Its hours of operation are convenient.
(C) Its practices are environmentally-friendly.
(D) It now offers a new service.

88. According to the speaker, what can Web site visitors do in April?
(A) See a floor plan
(B) Download an e-book
(C) Chat with a consultant
(D) Obtain a free pass

---

89. Why is the speaker calling?
(A) To notify the listener of a difficulty
(B) To inquire about a preference
(C) To invite the listener on a tour
(D) To confirm some flight details

90. What does the speaker say about the Ramsey Theater?
(A) It hosts live shows every evening.
(B) It is a popular destination for tourists.
(C) It offers discounts to its members.
(D) It is near the listener's accommodations.

91. What does the speaker say he will do?
(A) E-mail the listener
(B) Call the listener again
(C) Reserve some tickets
(D) Print a brochure

---

92. What is the broadcast mainly about?
(A) An economic development plan
(B) A business association
(C) A news provider
(D) A political contest

93. What does the speaker imply when she says, "Ms. Garza owns an expanding chain of laundry shops"?
(A) Ms. Garza is usually very busy.
(B) Ms. Garza could benefit from a proposal.
(C) Ms. Garza is a good candidate for a position.
(D) Ms. Garza does not require financial support.

94. According to the speaker, what did Ms. Garza say will happen soon?
(A) A new shop will open.
(B) An advertisement will be broadcast.
(C) A Web site will be launched.
(D) A public discussion will be held.

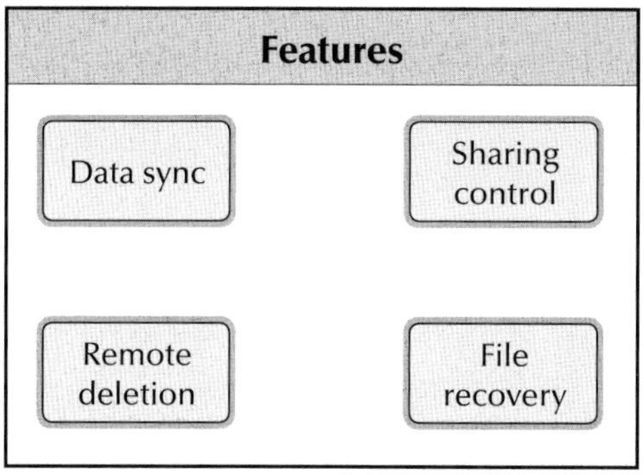

Jill's Flower Shop Order for Lynn International, March 2	
Item Description	**Quantity Requested**
Rose petals (pink, 20-ounce bag)	3
Entrance arch (white, 35 inches)	5
Summer Mix centerpiece	25
Individual rose (pink)	30

95. Where most likely does the speaker work?
(A) At a magazine publisher
(B) At a telecommunications firm
(C) At an architectural agency
(D) At a landscaping company

96. According to the speaker, what is the problem with some files?
(A) They cannot be located.
(B) They were deleted.
(C) They were released publicly.
(D) They are not being updated.

97. Look at the graphic. Which feature will the speaker talk about next?
(A) Data sync
(B) Sharing control
(C) Remote deletion
(D) File recovery

98. Why does the speaker want to change an order?
(A) She forgot to count one of the tables.
(B) A budget for supplies has been reduced.
(C) She has decided on a new theme for the party.
(D) More guests will attend than originally expected.

99. Look at the graphic. Which quantity does the speaker ask to change?
(A) 3
(B) 5
(C) 25
(D) 30

100. What does the speaker explain to the listener?
(A) What to bring for identification
(B) How to access a venue
(C) Where to mail an invoice
(D) When to make a delivery

This is the end of the Listening test. Turn to Part 5 in your test book.

ANSWER SHEET

YBM 실전토익 LC 1000

수험번호						

응시일자 : 20 년 월 일

성명	한 글	
	한 자	
	영 자	

Test 01 (Part 1~4)

1	ⓐ ⓑ ⓒ ⓓ	21	ⓐ ⓑ ⓒ	41	ⓐ ⓑ ⓒ ⓓ	61	ⓐ ⓑ ⓒ ⓓ	81	ⓐ ⓑ ⓒ ⓓ
2	ⓐ ⓑ ⓒ ⓓ	22	ⓐ ⓑ ⓒ	42	ⓐ ⓑ ⓒ ⓓ	62	ⓐ ⓑ ⓒ ⓓ	82	ⓐ ⓑ ⓒ ⓓ
3	ⓐ ⓑ ⓒ ⓓ	23	ⓐ ⓑ ⓒ	43	ⓐ ⓑ ⓒ ⓓ	63	ⓐ ⓑ ⓒ ⓓ	83	ⓐ ⓑ ⓒ ⓓ
4	ⓐ ⓑ ⓒ ⓓ	24	ⓐ ⓑ ⓒ	44	ⓐ ⓑ ⓒ ⓓ	64	ⓐ ⓑ ⓒ ⓓ	84	ⓐ ⓑ ⓒ ⓓ
5	ⓐ ⓑ ⓒ ⓓ	25	ⓐ ⓑ ⓒ	45	ⓐ ⓑ ⓒ ⓓ	65	ⓐ ⓑ ⓒ ⓓ	85	ⓐ ⓑ ⓒ ⓓ
6	ⓐ ⓑ ⓒ ⓓ	26	ⓐ ⓑ ⓒ	46	ⓐ ⓑ ⓒ ⓓ	66	ⓐ ⓑ ⓒ ⓓ	86	ⓐ ⓑ ⓒ ⓓ
7	ⓐ ⓑ ⓒ	27	ⓐ ⓑ ⓒ	47	ⓐ ⓑ ⓒ ⓓ	67	ⓐ ⓑ ⓒ ⓓ	87	ⓐ ⓑ ⓒ ⓓ
8	ⓐ ⓑ ⓒ	28	ⓐ ⓑ ⓒ	48	ⓐ ⓑ ⓒ ⓓ	68	ⓐ ⓑ ⓒ ⓓ	88	ⓐ ⓑ ⓒ ⓓ
9	ⓐ ⓑ ⓒ	29	ⓐ ⓑ ⓒ	49	ⓐ ⓑ ⓒ ⓓ	69	ⓐ ⓑ ⓒ ⓓ	89	ⓐ ⓑ ⓒ ⓓ
10	ⓐ ⓑ ⓒ	30	ⓐ ⓑ ⓒ	50	ⓐ ⓑ ⓒ ⓓ	70	ⓐ ⓑ ⓒ ⓓ	90	ⓐ ⓑ ⓒ ⓓ
11	ⓐ ⓑ ⓒ	31	ⓐ ⓑ ⓒ	51	ⓐ ⓑ ⓒ ⓓ	71	ⓐ ⓑ ⓒ ⓓ	91	ⓐ ⓑ ⓒ ⓓ
12	ⓐ ⓑ ⓒ	32	ⓐ ⓑ ⓒ ⓓ	52	ⓐ ⓑ ⓒ ⓓ	72	ⓐ ⓑ ⓒ ⓓ	92	ⓐ ⓑ ⓒ ⓓ
13	ⓐ ⓑ ⓒ	33	ⓐ ⓑ ⓒ ⓓ	53	ⓐ ⓑ ⓒ ⓓ	73	ⓐ ⓑ ⓒ ⓓ	93	ⓐ ⓑ ⓒ ⓓ
14	ⓐ ⓑ ⓒ	34	ⓐ ⓑ ⓒ ⓓ	54	ⓐ ⓑ ⓒ ⓓ	74	ⓐ ⓑ ⓒ ⓓ	94	ⓐ ⓑ ⓒ ⓓ
15	ⓐ ⓑ ⓒ	35	ⓐ ⓑ ⓒ ⓓ	55	ⓐ ⓑ ⓒ ⓓ	75	ⓐ ⓑ ⓒ ⓓ	95	ⓐ ⓑ ⓒ ⓓ
16	ⓐ ⓑ ⓒ	36	ⓐ ⓑ ⓒ ⓓ	56	ⓐ ⓑ ⓒ ⓓ	76	ⓐ ⓑ ⓒ ⓓ	96	ⓐ ⓑ ⓒ ⓓ
17	ⓐ ⓑ ⓒ	37	ⓐ ⓑ ⓒ ⓓ	57	ⓐ ⓑ ⓒ ⓓ	77	ⓐ ⓑ ⓒ ⓓ	97	ⓐ ⓑ ⓒ ⓓ
18	ⓐ ⓑ ⓒ	38	ⓐ ⓑ ⓒ ⓓ	58	ⓐ ⓑ ⓒ ⓓ	78	ⓐ ⓑ ⓒ ⓓ	98	ⓐ ⓑ ⓒ ⓓ
19	ⓐ ⓑ ⓒ	39	ⓐ ⓑ ⓒ ⓓ	59	ⓐ ⓑ ⓒ ⓓ	79	ⓐ ⓑ ⓒ ⓓ	99	ⓐ ⓑ ⓒ ⓓ
20	ⓐ ⓑ ⓒ	40	ⓐ ⓑ ⓒ ⓓ	60	ⓐ ⓑ ⓒ ⓓ	80	ⓐ ⓑ ⓒ ⓓ	100	ⓐ ⓑ ⓒ ⓓ

Test 02 (Part 1~4)

1	ⓐ ⓑ ⓒ ⓓ	21	ⓐ ⓑ ⓒ	41	ⓐ ⓑ ⓒ ⓓ	61	ⓐ ⓑ ⓒ ⓓ	81	ⓐ ⓑ ⓒ ⓓ
2	ⓐ ⓑ ⓒ ⓓ	22	ⓐ ⓑ ⓒ	42	ⓐ ⓑ ⓒ ⓓ	62	ⓐ ⓑ ⓒ ⓓ	82	ⓐ ⓑ ⓒ ⓓ
3	ⓐ ⓑ ⓒ ⓓ	23	ⓐ ⓑ ⓒ	43	ⓐ ⓑ ⓒ ⓓ	63	ⓐ ⓑ ⓒ ⓓ	83	ⓐ ⓑ ⓒ ⓓ
4	ⓐ ⓑ ⓒ ⓓ	24	ⓐ ⓑ ⓒ	44	ⓐ ⓑ ⓒ ⓓ	64	ⓐ ⓑ ⓒ ⓓ	84	ⓐ ⓑ ⓒ ⓓ
5	ⓐ ⓑ ⓒ ⓓ	25	ⓐ ⓑ ⓒ	45	ⓐ ⓑ ⓒ ⓓ	65	ⓐ ⓑ ⓒ ⓓ	85	ⓐ ⓑ ⓒ ⓓ
6	ⓐ ⓑ ⓒ ⓓ	26	ⓐ ⓑ ⓒ	46	ⓐ ⓑ ⓒ ⓓ	66	ⓐ ⓑ ⓒ ⓓ	86	ⓐ ⓑ ⓒ ⓓ
7	ⓐ ⓑ ⓒ	27	ⓐ ⓑ ⓒ	47	ⓐ ⓑ ⓒ ⓓ	67	ⓐ ⓑ ⓒ ⓓ	87	ⓐ ⓑ ⓒ ⓓ
8	ⓐ ⓑ ⓒ	28	ⓐ ⓑ ⓒ	48	ⓐ ⓑ ⓒ ⓓ	68	ⓐ ⓑ ⓒ ⓓ	88	ⓐ ⓑ ⓒ ⓓ
9	ⓐ ⓑ ⓒ	29	ⓐ ⓑ ⓒ	49	ⓐ ⓑ ⓒ ⓓ	69	ⓐ ⓑ ⓒ ⓓ	89	ⓐ ⓑ ⓒ ⓓ
10	ⓐ ⓑ ⓒ	30	ⓐ ⓑ ⓒ	50	ⓐ ⓑ ⓒ ⓓ	70	ⓐ ⓑ ⓒ ⓓ	90	ⓐ ⓑ ⓒ ⓓ
11	ⓐ ⓑ ⓒ	31	ⓐ ⓑ ⓒ	51	ⓐ ⓑ ⓒ ⓓ	71	ⓐ ⓑ ⓒ ⓓ	91	ⓐ ⓑ ⓒ ⓓ
12	ⓐ ⓑ ⓒ	32	ⓐ ⓑ ⓒ ⓓ	52	ⓐ ⓑ ⓒ ⓓ	72	ⓐ ⓑ ⓒ ⓓ	92	ⓐ ⓑ ⓒ ⓓ
13	ⓐ ⓑ ⓒ	33	ⓐ ⓑ ⓒ ⓓ	53	ⓐ ⓑ ⓒ ⓓ	73	ⓐ ⓑ ⓒ ⓓ	93	ⓐ ⓑ ⓒ ⓓ
14	ⓐ ⓑ ⓒ	34	ⓐ ⓑ ⓒ ⓓ	54	ⓐ ⓑ ⓒ ⓓ	74	ⓐ ⓑ ⓒ ⓓ	94	ⓐ ⓑ ⓒ ⓓ
15	ⓐ ⓑ ⓒ	35	ⓐ ⓑ ⓒ ⓓ	55	ⓐ ⓑ ⓒ ⓓ	75	ⓐ ⓑ ⓒ ⓓ	95	ⓐ ⓑ ⓒ ⓓ
16	ⓐ ⓑ ⓒ	36	ⓐ ⓑ ⓒ ⓓ	56	ⓐ ⓑ ⓒ ⓓ	76	ⓐ ⓑ ⓒ ⓓ	96	ⓐ ⓑ ⓒ ⓓ
17	ⓐ ⓑ ⓒ	37	ⓐ ⓑ ⓒ ⓓ	57	ⓐ ⓑ ⓒ ⓓ	77	ⓐ ⓑ ⓒ ⓓ	97	ⓐ ⓑ ⓒ ⓓ
18	ⓐ ⓑ ⓒ	38	ⓐ ⓑ ⓒ ⓓ	58	ⓐ ⓑ ⓒ ⓓ	78	ⓐ ⓑ ⓒ ⓓ	98	ⓐ ⓑ ⓒ ⓓ
19	ⓐ ⓑ ⓒ	39	ⓐ ⓑ ⓒ ⓓ	59	ⓐ ⓑ ⓒ ⓓ	79	ⓐ ⓑ ⓒ ⓓ	99	ⓐ ⓑ ⓒ ⓓ
20	ⓐ ⓑ ⓒ	40	ⓐ ⓑ ⓒ ⓓ	60	ⓐ ⓑ ⓒ ⓓ	80	ⓐ ⓑ ⓒ ⓓ	100	ⓐ ⓑ ⓒ ⓓ

ANSWER SHEET

YBM 실전토익 LC 1000

수험번호						

응시일자 : 20 년 월 일

성명	한 글	
	한 자	
	영 자	

Test 03 (Part 1~4)

1	ⓐ ⓑ ⓒ ⓓ	21	ⓐ ⓑ ⓒ	41	ⓐ ⓑ ⓒ ⓓ	61	ⓐ ⓑ ⓒ ⓓ	81	ⓐ ⓑ ⓒ ⓓ
2	ⓐ ⓑ ⓒ ⓓ	22	ⓐ ⓑ ⓒ	42	ⓐ ⓑ ⓒ ⓓ	62	ⓐ ⓑ ⓒ ⓓ	82	ⓐ ⓑ ⓒ ⓓ
3	ⓐ ⓑ ⓒ ⓓ	23	ⓐ ⓑ ⓒ	43	ⓐ ⓑ ⓒ ⓓ	63	ⓐ ⓑ ⓒ ⓓ	83	ⓐ ⓑ ⓒ ⓓ
4	ⓐ ⓑ ⓒ ⓓ	24	ⓐ ⓑ ⓒ	44	ⓐ ⓑ ⓒ ⓓ	64	ⓐ ⓑ ⓒ ⓓ	84	ⓐ ⓑ ⓒ ⓓ
5	ⓐ ⓑ ⓒ ⓓ	25	ⓐ ⓑ ⓒ	45	ⓐ ⓑ ⓒ ⓓ	65	ⓐ ⓑ ⓒ ⓓ	85	ⓐ ⓑ ⓒ ⓓ
6	ⓐ ⓑ ⓒ ⓓ	26	ⓐ ⓑ ⓒ	46	ⓐ ⓑ ⓒ ⓓ	66	ⓐ ⓑ ⓒ ⓓ	86	ⓐ ⓑ ⓒ ⓓ
7	ⓐ ⓑ ⓒ	27	ⓐ ⓑ ⓒ	47	ⓐ ⓑ ⓒ ⓓ	67	ⓐ ⓑ ⓒ ⓓ	87	ⓐ ⓑ ⓒ ⓓ
8	ⓐ ⓑ ⓒ	28	ⓐ ⓑ ⓒ	48	ⓐ ⓑ ⓒ ⓓ	68	ⓐ ⓑ ⓒ ⓓ	88	ⓐ ⓑ ⓒ ⓓ
9	ⓐ ⓑ ⓒ	29	ⓐ ⓑ ⓒ	49	ⓐ ⓑ ⓒ ⓓ	69	ⓐ ⓑ ⓒ ⓓ	89	ⓐ ⓑ ⓒ ⓓ
10	ⓐ ⓑ ⓒ	30	ⓐ ⓑ ⓒ	50	ⓐ ⓑ ⓒ ⓓ	70	ⓐ ⓑ ⓒ ⓓ	90	ⓐ ⓑ ⓒ ⓓ
11	ⓐ ⓑ ⓒ	31	ⓐ ⓑ ⓒ	51	ⓐ ⓑ ⓒ ⓓ	71	ⓐ ⓑ ⓒ ⓓ	91	ⓐ ⓑ ⓒ ⓓ
12	ⓐ ⓑ ⓒ	32	ⓐ ⓑ ⓒ ⓓ	52	ⓐ ⓑ ⓒ ⓓ	72	ⓐ ⓑ ⓒ ⓓ	92	ⓐ ⓑ ⓒ ⓓ
13	ⓐ ⓑ ⓒ	33	ⓐ ⓑ ⓒ ⓓ	53	ⓐ ⓑ ⓒ ⓓ	73	ⓐ ⓑ ⓒ ⓓ	93	ⓐ ⓑ ⓒ ⓓ
14	ⓐ ⓑ ⓒ	34	ⓐ ⓑ ⓒ ⓓ	54	ⓐ ⓑ ⓒ ⓓ	74	ⓐ ⓑ ⓒ ⓓ	94	ⓐ ⓑ ⓒ ⓓ
15	ⓐ ⓑ ⓒ	35	ⓐ ⓑ ⓒ ⓓ	55	ⓐ ⓑ ⓒ ⓓ	75	ⓐ ⓑ ⓒ ⓓ	95	ⓐ ⓑ ⓒ ⓓ
16	ⓐ ⓑ ⓒ	36	ⓐ ⓑ ⓒ ⓓ	56	ⓐ ⓑ ⓒ ⓓ	76	ⓐ ⓑ ⓒ ⓓ	96	ⓐ ⓑ ⓒ ⓓ
17	ⓐ ⓑ ⓒ	37	ⓐ ⓑ ⓒ ⓓ	57	ⓐ ⓑ ⓒ ⓓ	77	ⓐ ⓑ ⓒ ⓓ	97	ⓐ ⓑ ⓒ ⓓ
18	ⓐ ⓑ ⓒ	38	ⓐ ⓑ ⓒ ⓓ	58	ⓐ ⓑ ⓒ ⓓ	78	ⓐ ⓑ ⓒ ⓓ	98	ⓐ ⓑ ⓒ ⓓ
19	ⓐ ⓑ ⓒ	39	ⓐ ⓑ ⓒ ⓓ	59	ⓐ ⓑ ⓒ ⓓ	79	ⓐ ⓑ ⓒ ⓓ	99	ⓐ ⓑ ⓒ ⓓ
20	ⓐ ⓑ ⓒ	40	ⓐ ⓑ ⓒ ⓓ	60	ⓐ ⓑ ⓒ ⓓ	80	ⓐ ⓑ ⓒ ⓓ	100	ⓐ ⓑ ⓒ ⓓ

Test 04 (Part 1~4)

1	ⓐ ⓑ ⓒ ⓓ	21	ⓐ ⓑ ⓒ	41	ⓐ ⓑ ⓒ ⓓ	61	ⓐ ⓑ ⓒ ⓓ	81	ⓐ ⓑ ⓒ ⓓ
2	ⓐ ⓑ ⓒ ⓓ	22	ⓐ ⓑ ⓒ	42	ⓐ ⓑ ⓒ ⓓ	62	ⓐ ⓑ ⓒ ⓓ	82	ⓐ ⓑ ⓒ ⓓ
3	ⓐ ⓑ ⓒ ⓓ	23	ⓐ ⓑ ⓒ	43	ⓐ ⓑ ⓒ ⓓ	63	ⓐ ⓑ ⓒ ⓓ	83	ⓐ ⓑ ⓒ ⓓ
4	ⓐ ⓑ ⓒ ⓓ	24	ⓐ ⓑ ⓒ	44	ⓐ ⓑ ⓒ ⓓ	64	ⓐ ⓑ ⓒ ⓓ	84	ⓐ ⓑ ⓒ ⓓ
5	ⓐ ⓑ ⓒ ⓓ	25	ⓐ ⓑ ⓒ	45	ⓐ ⓑ ⓒ ⓓ	65	ⓐ ⓑ ⓒ ⓓ	85	ⓐ ⓑ ⓒ ⓓ
6	ⓐ ⓑ ⓒ ⓓ	26	ⓐ ⓑ ⓒ	46	ⓐ ⓑ ⓒ ⓓ	66	ⓐ ⓑ ⓒ ⓓ	86	ⓐ ⓑ ⓒ ⓓ
7	ⓐ ⓑ ⓒ	27	ⓐ ⓑ ⓒ	47	ⓐ ⓑ ⓒ ⓓ	67	ⓐ ⓑ ⓒ ⓓ	87	ⓐ ⓑ ⓒ ⓓ
8	ⓐ ⓑ ⓒ	28	ⓐ ⓑ ⓒ	48	ⓐ ⓑ ⓒ ⓓ	68	ⓐ ⓑ ⓒ ⓓ	88	ⓐ ⓑ ⓒ ⓓ
9	ⓐ ⓑ ⓒ	29	ⓐ ⓑ ⓒ	49	ⓐ ⓑ ⓒ ⓓ	69	ⓐ ⓑ ⓒ ⓓ	89	ⓐ ⓑ ⓒ ⓓ
10	ⓐ ⓑ ⓒ	30	ⓐ ⓑ ⓒ	50	ⓐ ⓑ ⓒ ⓓ	70	ⓐ ⓑ ⓒ ⓓ	90	ⓐ ⓑ ⓒ ⓓ
11	ⓐ ⓑ ⓒ	31	ⓐ ⓑ ⓒ	51	ⓐ ⓑ ⓒ ⓓ	71	ⓐ ⓑ ⓒ ⓓ	91	ⓐ ⓑ ⓒ ⓓ
12	ⓐ ⓑ ⓒ	32	ⓐ ⓑ ⓒ ⓓ	52	ⓐ ⓑ ⓒ ⓓ	72	ⓐ ⓑ ⓒ ⓓ	92	ⓐ ⓑ ⓒ ⓓ
13	ⓐ ⓑ ⓒ	33	ⓐ ⓑ ⓒ ⓓ	53	ⓐ ⓑ ⓒ ⓓ	73	ⓐ ⓑ ⓒ ⓓ	93	ⓐ ⓑ ⓒ ⓓ
14	ⓐ ⓑ ⓒ	34	ⓐ ⓑ ⓒ ⓓ	54	ⓐ ⓑ ⓒ ⓓ	74	ⓐ ⓑ ⓒ ⓓ	94	ⓐ ⓑ ⓒ ⓓ
15	ⓐ ⓑ ⓒ	35	ⓐ ⓑ ⓒ ⓓ	55	ⓐ ⓑ ⓒ ⓓ	75	ⓐ ⓑ ⓒ ⓓ	95	ⓐ ⓑ ⓒ ⓓ
16	ⓐ ⓑ ⓒ	36	ⓐ ⓑ ⓒ ⓓ	56	ⓐ ⓑ ⓒ ⓓ	76	ⓐ ⓑ ⓒ ⓓ	96	ⓐ ⓑ ⓒ ⓓ
17	ⓐ ⓑ ⓒ	37	ⓐ ⓑ ⓒ ⓓ	57	ⓐ ⓑ ⓒ ⓓ	77	ⓐ ⓑ ⓒ ⓓ	97	ⓐ ⓑ ⓒ ⓓ
18	ⓐ ⓑ ⓒ	38	ⓐ ⓑ ⓒ ⓓ	58	ⓐ ⓑ ⓒ ⓓ	78	ⓐ ⓑ ⓒ ⓓ	98	ⓐ ⓑ ⓒ ⓓ
19	ⓐ ⓑ ⓒ	39	ⓐ ⓑ ⓒ ⓓ	59	ⓐ ⓑ ⓒ ⓓ	79	ⓐ ⓑ ⓒ ⓓ	99	ⓐ ⓑ ⓒ ⓓ
20	ⓐ ⓑ ⓒ	40	ⓐ ⓑ ⓒ ⓓ	60	ⓐ ⓑ ⓒ ⓓ	80	ⓐ ⓑ ⓒ ⓓ	100	ⓐ ⓑ ⓒ ⓓ

ANSWER SHEET

YBM 실전토익 LC 1000

수험번호						

응시일자 : 20 년 월 일

성명	한 글	
	한 자	
	영 자	

Test 05 (Part 1~4)

1	ⓐ ⓑ ⓒ ⓓ	21	ⓐ ⓑ ⓒ	41	ⓐ ⓑ ⓒ ⓓ	61	ⓐ ⓑ ⓒ ⓓ	81	ⓐ ⓑ ⓒ ⓓ
2	ⓐ ⓑ ⓒ ⓓ	22	ⓐ ⓑ ⓒ	42	ⓐ ⓑ ⓒ ⓓ	62	ⓐ ⓑ ⓒ ⓓ	82	ⓐ ⓑ ⓒ ⓓ
3	ⓐ ⓑ ⓒ ⓓ	23	ⓐ ⓑ ⓒ	43	ⓐ ⓑ ⓒ ⓓ	63	ⓐ ⓑ ⓒ ⓓ	83	ⓐ ⓑ ⓒ ⓓ
4	ⓐ ⓑ ⓒ ⓓ	24	ⓐ ⓑ ⓒ	44	ⓐ ⓑ ⓒ ⓓ	64	ⓐ ⓑ ⓒ ⓓ	84	ⓐ ⓑ ⓒ ⓓ
5	ⓐ ⓑ ⓒ ⓓ	25	ⓐ ⓑ ⓒ	45	ⓐ ⓑ ⓒ ⓓ	65	ⓐ ⓑ ⓒ ⓓ	85	ⓐ ⓑ ⓒ ⓓ
6	ⓐ ⓑ ⓒ ⓓ	26	ⓐ ⓑ ⓒ	46	ⓐ ⓑ ⓒ ⓓ	66	ⓐ ⓑ ⓒ ⓓ	86	ⓐ ⓑ ⓒ ⓓ
7	ⓐ ⓑ ⓒ	27	ⓐ ⓑ ⓒ	47	ⓐ ⓑ ⓒ ⓓ	67	ⓐ ⓑ ⓒ ⓓ	87	ⓐ ⓑ ⓒ ⓓ
8	ⓐ ⓑ ⓒ	28	ⓐ ⓑ ⓒ	48	ⓐ ⓑ ⓒ ⓓ	68	ⓐ ⓑ ⓒ ⓓ	88	ⓐ ⓑ ⓒ ⓓ
9	ⓐ ⓑ ⓒ	29	ⓐ ⓑ ⓒ	49	ⓐ ⓑ ⓒ ⓓ	69	ⓐ ⓑ ⓒ ⓓ	89	ⓐ ⓑ ⓒ ⓓ
10	ⓐ ⓑ ⓒ	30	ⓐ ⓑ ⓒ	50	ⓐ ⓑ ⓒ ⓓ	70	ⓐ ⓑ ⓒ ⓓ	90	ⓐ ⓑ ⓒ ⓓ
11	ⓐ ⓑ ⓒ	31	ⓐ ⓑ ⓒ	51	ⓐ ⓑ ⓒ ⓓ	71	ⓐ ⓑ ⓒ ⓓ	91	ⓐ ⓑ ⓒ ⓓ
12	ⓐ ⓑ ⓒ	32	ⓐ ⓑ ⓒ ⓓ	52	ⓐ ⓑ ⓒ ⓓ	72	ⓐ ⓑ ⓒ ⓓ	92	ⓐ ⓑ ⓒ ⓓ
13	ⓐ ⓑ ⓒ	33	ⓐ ⓑ ⓒ ⓓ	53	ⓐ ⓑ ⓒ ⓓ	73	ⓐ ⓑ ⓒ ⓓ	93	ⓐ ⓑ ⓒ ⓓ
14	ⓐ ⓑ ⓒ	34	ⓐ ⓑ ⓒ ⓓ	54	ⓐ ⓑ ⓒ ⓓ	74	ⓐ ⓑ ⓒ ⓓ	94	ⓐ ⓑ ⓒ ⓓ
15	ⓐ ⓑ ⓒ	35	ⓐ ⓑ ⓒ ⓓ	55	ⓐ ⓑ ⓒ ⓓ	75	ⓐ ⓑ ⓒ ⓓ	95	ⓐ ⓑ ⓒ ⓓ
16	ⓐ ⓑ ⓒ	36	ⓐ ⓑ ⓒ ⓓ	56	ⓐ ⓑ ⓒ ⓓ	76	ⓐ ⓑ ⓒ ⓓ	96	ⓐ ⓑ ⓒ ⓓ
17	ⓐ ⓑ ⓒ	37	ⓐ ⓑ ⓒ ⓓ	57	ⓐ ⓑ ⓒ ⓓ	77	ⓐ ⓑ ⓒ ⓓ	97	ⓐ ⓑ ⓒ ⓓ
18	ⓐ ⓑ ⓒ	38	ⓐ ⓑ ⓒ ⓓ	58	ⓐ ⓑ ⓒ ⓓ	78	ⓐ ⓑ ⓒ ⓓ	98	ⓐ ⓑ ⓒ ⓓ
19	ⓐ ⓑ ⓒ	39	ⓐ ⓑ ⓒ ⓓ	59	ⓐ ⓑ ⓒ ⓓ	79	ⓐ ⓑ ⓒ ⓓ	99	ⓐ ⓑ ⓒ ⓓ
20	ⓐ ⓑ ⓒ	40	ⓐ ⓑ ⓒ ⓓ	60	ⓐ ⓑ ⓒ ⓓ	80	ⓐ ⓑ ⓒ ⓓ	100	ⓐ ⓑ ⓒ ⓓ

Test 06 (Part 1~4)

1	ⓐ ⓑ ⓒ ⓓ	21	ⓐ ⓑ ⓒ	41	ⓐ ⓑ ⓒ ⓓ	61	ⓐ ⓑ ⓒ ⓓ	81	ⓐ ⓑ ⓒ ⓓ
2	ⓐ ⓑ ⓒ ⓓ	22	ⓐ ⓑ ⓒ	42	ⓐ ⓑ ⓒ ⓓ	62	ⓐ ⓑ ⓒ ⓓ	82	ⓐ ⓑ ⓒ ⓓ
3	ⓐ ⓑ ⓒ ⓓ	23	ⓐ ⓑ ⓒ	43	ⓐ ⓑ ⓒ ⓓ	63	ⓐ ⓑ ⓒ ⓓ	83	ⓐ ⓑ ⓒ ⓓ
4	ⓐ ⓑ ⓒ ⓓ	24	ⓐ ⓑ ⓒ	44	ⓐ ⓑ ⓒ ⓓ	64	ⓐ ⓑ ⓒ ⓓ	84	ⓐ ⓑ ⓒ ⓓ
5	ⓐ ⓑ ⓒ ⓓ	25	ⓐ ⓑ ⓒ	45	ⓐ ⓑ ⓒ ⓓ	65	ⓐ ⓑ ⓒ ⓓ	85	ⓐ ⓑ ⓒ ⓓ
6	ⓐ ⓑ ⓒ ⓓ	26	ⓐ ⓑ ⓒ	46	ⓐ ⓑ ⓒ ⓓ	66	ⓐ ⓑ ⓒ ⓓ	86	ⓐ ⓑ ⓒ ⓓ
7	ⓐ ⓑ ⓒ	27	ⓐ ⓑ ⓒ	47	ⓐ ⓑ ⓒ ⓓ	67	ⓐ ⓑ ⓒ ⓓ	87	ⓐ ⓑ ⓒ ⓓ
8	ⓐ ⓑ ⓒ	28	ⓐ ⓑ ⓒ	48	ⓐ ⓑ ⓒ ⓓ	68	ⓐ ⓑ ⓒ ⓓ	88	ⓐ ⓑ ⓒ ⓓ
9	ⓐ ⓑ ⓒ	29	ⓐ ⓑ ⓒ	49	ⓐ ⓑ ⓒ ⓓ	69	ⓐ ⓑ ⓒ ⓓ	89	ⓐ ⓑ ⓒ ⓓ
10	ⓐ ⓑ ⓒ	30	ⓐ ⓑ ⓒ	50	ⓐ ⓑ ⓒ ⓓ	70	ⓐ ⓑ ⓒ ⓓ	90	ⓐ ⓑ ⓒ ⓓ
11	ⓐ ⓑ ⓒ	31	ⓐ ⓑ ⓒ	51	ⓐ ⓑ ⓒ ⓓ	71	ⓐ ⓑ ⓒ ⓓ	91	ⓐ ⓑ ⓒ ⓓ
12	ⓐ ⓑ ⓒ	32	ⓐ ⓑ ⓒ ⓓ	52	ⓐ ⓑ ⓒ ⓓ	72	ⓐ ⓑ ⓒ ⓓ	92	ⓐ ⓑ ⓒ ⓓ
13	ⓐ ⓑ ⓒ	33	ⓐ ⓑ ⓒ ⓓ	53	ⓐ ⓑ ⓒ ⓓ	73	ⓐ ⓑ ⓒ ⓓ	93	ⓐ ⓑ ⓒ ⓓ
14	ⓐ ⓑ ⓒ	34	ⓐ ⓑ ⓒ ⓓ	54	ⓐ ⓑ ⓒ ⓓ	74	ⓐ ⓑ ⓒ ⓓ	94	ⓐ ⓑ ⓒ ⓓ
15	ⓐ ⓑ ⓒ	35	ⓐ ⓑ ⓒ ⓓ	55	ⓐ ⓑ ⓒ ⓓ	75	ⓐ ⓑ ⓒ ⓓ	95	ⓐ ⓑ ⓒ ⓓ
16	ⓐ ⓑ ⓒ	36	ⓐ ⓑ ⓒ ⓓ	56	ⓐ ⓑ ⓒ ⓓ	76	ⓐ ⓑ ⓒ ⓓ	96	ⓐ ⓑ ⓒ ⓓ
17	ⓐ ⓑ ⓒ	37	ⓐ ⓑ ⓒ ⓓ	57	ⓐ ⓑ ⓒ ⓓ	77	ⓐ ⓑ ⓒ ⓓ	97	ⓐ ⓑ ⓒ ⓓ
18	ⓐ ⓑ ⓒ	38	ⓐ ⓑ ⓒ ⓓ	58	ⓐ ⓑ ⓒ ⓓ	78	ⓐ ⓑ ⓒ ⓓ	98	ⓐ ⓑ ⓒ ⓓ
19	ⓐ ⓑ ⓒ	39	ⓐ ⓑ ⓒ ⓓ	59	ⓐ ⓑ ⓒ ⓓ	79	ⓐ ⓑ ⓒ ⓓ	99	ⓐ ⓑ ⓒ ⓓ
20	ⓐ ⓑ ⓒ	40	ⓐ ⓑ ⓒ ⓓ	60	ⓐ ⓑ ⓒ ⓓ	80	ⓐ ⓑ ⓒ ⓓ	100	ⓐ ⓑ ⓒ ⓓ

ANSWER SHEET

YBM 실전토익 LC 1000

수험번호						

응시일자 : 20　　년　　월　　일

성명		
	한 글	
	한 자	
	영 자	

Test 07 (Part 1~4)

1	ⓐ ⓑ ⓒ ⓓ	21	ⓐ ⓑ ⓒ	41	ⓐ ⓑ ⓒ ⓓ	61	ⓐ ⓑ ⓒ ⓓ	81	ⓐ ⓑ ⓒ ⓓ
2	ⓐ ⓑ ⓒ ⓓ	22	ⓐ ⓑ ⓒ	42	ⓐ ⓑ ⓒ ⓓ	62	ⓐ ⓑ ⓒ ⓓ	82	ⓐ ⓑ ⓒ ⓓ
3	ⓐ ⓑ ⓒ ⓓ	23	ⓐ ⓑ ⓒ	43	ⓐ ⓑ ⓒ ⓓ	63	ⓐ ⓑ ⓒ ⓓ	83	ⓐ ⓑ ⓒ ⓓ
4	ⓐ ⓑ ⓒ ⓓ	24	ⓐ ⓑ ⓒ	44	ⓐ ⓑ ⓒ ⓓ	64	ⓐ ⓑ ⓒ ⓓ	84	ⓐ ⓑ ⓒ ⓓ
5	ⓐ ⓑ ⓒ ⓓ	25	ⓐ ⓑ ⓒ	45	ⓐ ⓑ ⓒ ⓓ	65	ⓐ ⓑ ⓒ ⓓ	85	ⓐ ⓑ ⓒ ⓓ
6	ⓐ ⓑ ⓒ ⓓ	26	ⓐ ⓑ ⓒ	46	ⓐ ⓑ ⓒ ⓓ	66	ⓐ ⓑ ⓒ ⓓ	86	ⓐ ⓑ ⓒ ⓓ
7	ⓐ ⓑ ⓒ	27	ⓐ ⓑ ⓒ	47	ⓐ ⓑ ⓒ ⓓ	67	ⓐ ⓑ ⓒ ⓓ	87	ⓐ ⓑ ⓒ ⓓ
8	ⓐ ⓑ ⓒ	28	ⓐ ⓑ ⓒ	48	ⓐ ⓑ ⓒ ⓓ	68	ⓐ ⓑ ⓒ ⓓ	88	ⓐ ⓑ ⓒ ⓓ
9	ⓐ ⓑ ⓒ	29	ⓐ ⓑ ⓒ	49	ⓐ ⓑ ⓒ ⓓ	69	ⓐ ⓑ ⓒ ⓓ	89	ⓐ ⓑ ⓒ ⓓ
10	ⓐ ⓑ ⓒ	30	ⓐ ⓑ ⓒ	50	ⓐ ⓑ ⓒ ⓓ	70	ⓐ ⓑ ⓒ ⓓ	90	ⓐ ⓑ ⓒ ⓓ
11	ⓐ ⓑ ⓒ	31	ⓐ ⓑ ⓒ	51	ⓐ ⓑ ⓒ ⓓ	71	ⓐ ⓑ ⓒ ⓓ	91	ⓐ ⓑ ⓒ ⓓ
12	ⓐ ⓑ ⓒ	32	ⓐ ⓑ ⓒ ⓓ	52	ⓐ ⓑ ⓒ ⓓ	72	ⓐ ⓑ ⓒ ⓓ	92	ⓐ ⓑ ⓒ ⓓ
13	ⓐ ⓑ ⓒ	33	ⓐ ⓑ ⓒ ⓓ	53	ⓐ ⓑ ⓒ ⓓ	73	ⓐ ⓑ ⓒ ⓓ	93	ⓐ ⓑ ⓒ ⓓ
14	ⓐ ⓑ ⓒ	34	ⓐ ⓑ ⓒ ⓓ	54	ⓐ ⓑ ⓒ ⓓ	74	ⓐ ⓑ ⓒ ⓓ	94	ⓐ ⓑ ⓒ ⓓ
15	ⓐ ⓑ ⓒ	35	ⓐ ⓑ ⓒ ⓓ	55	ⓐ ⓑ ⓒ ⓓ	75	ⓐ ⓑ ⓒ ⓓ	95	ⓐ ⓑ ⓒ ⓓ
16	ⓐ ⓑ ⓒ	36	ⓐ ⓑ ⓒ ⓓ	56	ⓐ ⓑ ⓒ ⓓ	76	ⓐ ⓑ ⓒ ⓓ	96	ⓐ ⓑ ⓒ ⓓ
17	ⓐ ⓑ ⓒ	37	ⓐ ⓑ ⓒ ⓓ	57	ⓐ ⓑ ⓒ ⓓ	77	ⓐ ⓑ ⓒ ⓓ	97	ⓐ ⓑ ⓒ ⓓ
18	ⓐ ⓑ ⓒ	38	ⓐ ⓑ ⓒ ⓓ	58	ⓐ ⓑ ⓒ ⓓ	78	ⓐ ⓑ ⓒ ⓓ	98	ⓐ ⓑ ⓒ ⓓ
19	ⓐ ⓑ ⓒ	39	ⓐ ⓑ ⓒ ⓓ	59	ⓐ ⓑ ⓒ ⓓ	79	ⓐ ⓑ ⓒ ⓓ	99	ⓐ ⓑ ⓒ ⓓ
20	ⓐ ⓑ ⓒ	40	ⓐ ⓑ ⓒ ⓓ	60	ⓐ ⓑ ⓒ ⓓ	80	ⓐ ⓑ ⓒ ⓓ	100	ⓐ ⓑ ⓒ ⓓ

Test 08 (Part 1~4)

1	ⓐ ⓑ ⓒ ⓓ	21	ⓐ ⓑ ⓒ	41	ⓐ ⓑ ⓒ ⓓ	61	ⓐ ⓑ ⓒ ⓓ	81	ⓐ ⓑ ⓒ ⓓ
2	ⓐ ⓑ ⓒ ⓓ	22	ⓐ ⓑ ⓒ	42	ⓐ ⓑ ⓒ ⓓ	62	ⓐ ⓑ ⓒ ⓓ	82	ⓐ ⓑ ⓒ ⓓ
3	ⓐ ⓑ ⓒ ⓓ	23	ⓐ ⓑ ⓒ	43	ⓐ ⓑ ⓒ ⓓ	63	ⓐ ⓑ ⓒ ⓓ	83	ⓐ ⓑ ⓒ ⓓ
4	ⓐ ⓑ ⓒ ⓓ	24	ⓐ ⓑ ⓒ	44	ⓐ ⓑ ⓒ ⓓ	64	ⓐ ⓑ ⓒ ⓓ	84	ⓐ ⓑ ⓒ ⓓ
5	ⓐ ⓑ ⓒ ⓓ	25	ⓐ ⓑ ⓒ	45	ⓐ ⓑ ⓒ ⓓ	65	ⓐ ⓑ ⓒ ⓓ	85	ⓐ ⓑ ⓒ ⓓ
6	ⓐ ⓑ ⓒ ⓓ	26	ⓐ ⓑ ⓒ	46	ⓐ ⓑ ⓒ ⓓ	66	ⓐ ⓑ ⓒ ⓓ	86	ⓐ ⓑ ⓒ ⓓ
7	ⓐ ⓑ ⓒ	27	ⓐ ⓑ ⓒ	47	ⓐ ⓑ ⓒ ⓓ	67	ⓐ ⓑ ⓒ ⓓ	87	ⓐ ⓑ ⓒ ⓓ
8	ⓐ ⓑ ⓒ	28	ⓐ ⓑ ⓒ	48	ⓐ ⓑ ⓒ ⓓ	68	ⓐ ⓑ ⓒ ⓓ	88	ⓐ ⓑ ⓒ ⓓ
9	ⓐ ⓑ ⓒ	29	ⓐ ⓑ ⓒ	49	ⓐ ⓑ ⓒ ⓓ	69	ⓐ ⓑ ⓒ ⓓ	89	ⓐ ⓑ ⓒ ⓓ
10	ⓐ ⓑ ⓒ	30	ⓐ ⓑ ⓒ	50	ⓐ ⓑ ⓒ ⓓ	70	ⓐ ⓑ ⓒ ⓓ	90	ⓐ ⓑ ⓒ ⓓ
11	ⓐ ⓑ ⓒ	31	ⓐ ⓑ ⓒ	51	ⓐ ⓑ ⓒ ⓓ	71	ⓐ ⓑ ⓒ ⓓ	91	ⓐ ⓑ ⓒ ⓓ
12	ⓐ ⓑ ⓒ	32	ⓐ ⓑ ⓒ ⓓ	52	ⓐ ⓑ ⓒ ⓓ	72	ⓐ ⓑ ⓒ ⓓ	92	ⓐ ⓑ ⓒ ⓓ
13	ⓐ ⓑ ⓒ	33	ⓐ ⓑ ⓒ ⓓ	53	ⓐ ⓑ ⓒ ⓓ	73	ⓐ ⓑ ⓒ ⓓ	93	ⓐ ⓑ ⓒ ⓓ
14	ⓐ ⓑ ⓒ	34	ⓐ ⓑ ⓒ ⓓ	54	ⓐ ⓑ ⓒ ⓓ	74	ⓐ ⓑ ⓒ ⓓ	94	ⓐ ⓑ ⓒ ⓓ
15	ⓐ ⓑ ⓒ	35	ⓐ ⓑ ⓒ ⓓ	55	ⓐ ⓑ ⓒ ⓓ	75	ⓐ ⓑ ⓒ ⓓ	95	ⓐ ⓑ ⓒ ⓓ
16	ⓐ ⓑ ⓒ	36	ⓐ ⓑ ⓒ ⓓ	56	ⓐ ⓑ ⓒ ⓓ	76	ⓐ ⓑ ⓒ ⓓ	96	ⓐ ⓑ ⓒ ⓓ
17	ⓐ ⓑ ⓒ	37	ⓐ ⓑ ⓒ ⓓ	57	ⓐ ⓑ ⓒ ⓓ	77	ⓐ ⓑ ⓒ ⓓ	97	ⓐ ⓑ ⓒ ⓓ
18	ⓐ ⓑ ⓒ	38	ⓐ ⓑ ⓒ ⓓ	58	ⓐ ⓑ ⓒ ⓓ	78	ⓐ ⓑ ⓒ ⓓ	98	ⓐ ⓑ ⓒ ⓓ
19	ⓐ ⓑ ⓒ	39	ⓐ ⓑ ⓒ ⓓ	59	ⓐ ⓑ ⓒ ⓓ	79	ⓐ ⓑ ⓒ ⓓ	99	ⓐ ⓑ ⓒ ⓓ
20	ⓐ ⓑ ⓒ	40	ⓐ ⓑ ⓒ ⓓ	60	ⓐ ⓑ ⓒ ⓓ	80	ⓐ ⓑ ⓒ ⓓ	100	ⓐ ⓑ ⓒ ⓓ

ANSWER SHEET

YBM 실전토익 LC 1000

수험번호						

응시일자 : 20 년 월 일

성명	한 글	
	한 자	
	영 자	

Test 09 (Part 1~4)

1	ⓐ ⓑ ⓒ ⓓ	21	ⓐ ⓑ ⓒ	41	ⓐ ⓑ ⓒ ⓓ	61	ⓐ ⓑ ⓒ ⓓ	81	ⓐ ⓑ ⓒ ⓓ
2	ⓐ ⓑ ⓒ ⓓ	22	ⓐ ⓑ ⓒ	42	ⓐ ⓑ ⓒ ⓓ	62	ⓐ ⓑ ⓒ ⓓ	82	ⓐ ⓑ ⓒ ⓓ
3	ⓐ ⓑ ⓒ ⓓ	23	ⓐ ⓑ ⓒ	43	ⓐ ⓑ ⓒ ⓓ	63	ⓐ ⓑ ⓒ ⓓ	83	ⓐ ⓑ ⓒ ⓓ
4	ⓐ ⓑ ⓒ ⓓ	24	ⓐ ⓑ ⓒ	44	ⓐ ⓑ ⓒ ⓓ	64	ⓐ ⓑ ⓒ ⓓ	84	ⓐ ⓑ ⓒ ⓓ
5	ⓐ ⓑ ⓒ ⓓ	25	ⓐ ⓑ ⓒ	45	ⓐ ⓑ ⓒ ⓓ	65	ⓐ ⓑ ⓒ ⓓ	85	ⓐ ⓑ ⓒ ⓓ
6	ⓐ ⓑ ⓒ ⓓ	26	ⓐ ⓑ ⓒ	46	ⓐ ⓑ ⓒ ⓓ	66	ⓐ ⓑ ⓒ ⓓ	86	ⓐ ⓑ ⓒ ⓓ
7	ⓐ ⓑ ⓒ	27	ⓐ ⓑ ⓒ	47	ⓐ ⓑ ⓒ ⓓ	67	ⓐ ⓑ ⓒ ⓓ	87	ⓐ ⓑ ⓒ ⓓ
8	ⓐ ⓑ ⓒ	28	ⓐ ⓑ ⓒ	48	ⓐ ⓑ ⓒ ⓓ	68	ⓐ ⓑ ⓒ ⓓ	88	ⓐ ⓑ ⓒ ⓓ
9	ⓐ ⓑ ⓒ	29	ⓐ ⓑ ⓒ	49	ⓐ ⓑ ⓒ ⓓ	69	ⓐ ⓑ ⓒ ⓓ	89	ⓐ ⓑ ⓒ ⓓ
10	ⓐ ⓑ ⓒ	30	ⓐ ⓑ ⓒ	50	ⓐ ⓑ ⓒ ⓓ	70	ⓐ ⓑ ⓒ ⓓ	90	ⓐ ⓑ ⓒ ⓓ
11	ⓐ ⓑ ⓒ	31	ⓐ ⓑ ⓒ	51	ⓐ ⓑ ⓒ ⓓ	71	ⓐ ⓑ ⓒ ⓓ	91	ⓐ ⓑ ⓒ ⓓ
12	ⓐ ⓑ ⓒ	32	ⓐ ⓑ ⓒ ⓓ	52	ⓐ ⓑ ⓒ ⓓ	72	ⓐ ⓑ ⓒ ⓓ	92	ⓐ ⓑ ⓒ ⓓ
13	ⓐ ⓑ ⓒ	33	ⓐ ⓑ ⓒ ⓓ	53	ⓐ ⓑ ⓒ ⓓ	73	ⓐ ⓑ ⓒ ⓓ	93	ⓐ ⓑ ⓒ ⓓ
14	ⓐ ⓑ ⓒ	34	ⓐ ⓑ ⓒ ⓓ	54	ⓐ ⓑ ⓒ ⓓ	74	ⓐ ⓑ ⓒ ⓓ	94	ⓐ ⓑ ⓒ ⓓ
15	ⓐ ⓑ ⓒ	35	ⓐ ⓑ ⓒ ⓓ	55	ⓐ ⓑ ⓒ ⓓ	75	ⓐ ⓑ ⓒ ⓓ	95	ⓐ ⓑ ⓒ ⓓ
16	ⓐ ⓑ ⓒ	36	ⓐ ⓑ ⓒ ⓓ	56	ⓐ ⓑ ⓒ ⓓ	76	ⓐ ⓑ ⓒ ⓓ	96	ⓐ ⓑ ⓒ ⓓ
17	ⓐ ⓑ ⓒ	37	ⓐ ⓑ ⓒ ⓓ	57	ⓐ ⓑ ⓒ ⓓ	77	ⓐ ⓑ ⓒ ⓓ	97	ⓐ ⓑ ⓒ ⓓ
18	ⓐ ⓑ ⓒ	38	ⓐ ⓑ ⓒ ⓓ	58	ⓐ ⓑ ⓒ ⓓ	78	ⓐ ⓑ ⓒ ⓓ	98	ⓐ ⓑ ⓒ ⓓ
19	ⓐ ⓑ ⓒ	39	ⓐ ⓑ ⓒ ⓓ	59	ⓐ ⓑ ⓒ ⓓ	79	ⓐ ⓑ ⓒ ⓓ	99	ⓐ ⓑ ⓒ ⓓ
20	ⓐ ⓑ ⓒ	40	ⓐ ⓑ ⓒ ⓓ	60	ⓐ ⓑ ⓒ ⓓ	80	ⓐ ⓑ ⓒ ⓓ	100	ⓐ ⓑ ⓒ ⓓ

Test 10 (Part 1~4)

1	ⓐ ⓑ ⓒ ⓓ	21	ⓐ ⓑ ⓒ	41	ⓐ ⓑ ⓒ ⓓ	61	ⓐ ⓑ ⓒ ⓓ	81	ⓐ ⓑ ⓒ ⓓ
2	ⓐ ⓑ ⓒ ⓓ	22	ⓐ ⓑ ⓒ	42	ⓐ ⓑ ⓒ ⓓ	62	ⓐ ⓑ ⓒ ⓓ	82	ⓐ ⓑ ⓒ ⓓ
3	ⓐ ⓑ ⓒ ⓓ	23	ⓐ ⓑ ⓒ	43	ⓐ ⓑ ⓒ ⓓ	63	ⓐ ⓑ ⓒ ⓓ	83	ⓐ ⓑ ⓒ ⓓ
4	ⓐ ⓑ ⓒ ⓓ	24	ⓐ ⓑ ⓒ	44	ⓐ ⓑ ⓒ ⓓ	64	ⓐ ⓑ ⓒ ⓓ	84	ⓐ ⓑ ⓒ ⓓ
5	ⓐ ⓑ ⓒ ⓓ	25	ⓐ ⓑ ⓒ	45	ⓐ ⓑ ⓒ ⓓ	65	ⓐ ⓑ ⓒ ⓓ	85	ⓐ ⓑ ⓒ ⓓ
6	ⓐ ⓑ ⓒ ⓓ	26	ⓐ ⓑ ⓒ	46	ⓐ ⓑ ⓒ ⓓ	66	ⓐ ⓑ ⓒ ⓓ	86	ⓐ ⓑ ⓒ ⓓ
7	ⓐ ⓑ ⓒ	27	ⓐ ⓑ ⓒ	47	ⓐ ⓑ ⓒ ⓓ	67	ⓐ ⓑ ⓒ ⓓ	87	ⓐ ⓑ ⓒ ⓓ
8	ⓐ ⓑ ⓒ	28	ⓐ ⓑ ⓒ	48	ⓐ ⓑ ⓒ ⓓ	68	ⓐ ⓑ ⓒ ⓓ	88	ⓐ ⓑ ⓒ ⓓ
9	ⓐ ⓑ ⓒ	29	ⓐ ⓑ ⓒ	49	ⓐ ⓑ ⓒ ⓓ	69	ⓐ ⓑ ⓒ ⓓ	89	ⓐ ⓑ ⓒ ⓓ
10	ⓐ ⓑ ⓒ	30	ⓐ ⓑ ⓒ	50	ⓐ ⓑ ⓒ ⓓ	70	ⓐ ⓑ ⓒ ⓓ	90	ⓐ ⓑ ⓒ ⓓ
11	ⓐ ⓑ ⓒ	31	ⓐ ⓑ ⓒ	51	ⓐ ⓑ ⓒ ⓓ	71	ⓐ ⓑ ⓒ ⓓ	91	ⓐ ⓑ ⓒ ⓓ
12	ⓐ ⓑ ⓒ	32	ⓐ ⓑ ⓒ ⓓ	52	ⓐ ⓑ ⓒ ⓓ	72	ⓐ ⓑ ⓒ ⓓ	92	ⓐ ⓑ ⓒ ⓓ
13	ⓐ ⓑ ⓒ	33	ⓐ ⓑ ⓒ ⓓ	53	ⓐ ⓑ ⓒ ⓓ	73	ⓐ ⓑ ⓒ ⓓ	93	ⓐ ⓑ ⓒ ⓓ
14	ⓐ ⓑ ⓒ	34	ⓐ ⓑ ⓒ ⓓ	54	ⓐ ⓑ ⓒ ⓓ	74	ⓐ ⓑ ⓒ ⓓ	94	ⓐ ⓑ ⓒ ⓓ
15	ⓐ ⓑ ⓒ	35	ⓐ ⓑ ⓒ ⓓ	55	ⓐ ⓑ ⓒ ⓓ	75	ⓐ ⓑ ⓒ ⓓ	95	ⓐ ⓑ ⓒ ⓓ
16	ⓐ ⓑ ⓒ	36	ⓐ ⓑ ⓒ ⓓ	56	ⓐ ⓑ ⓒ ⓓ	76	ⓐ ⓑ ⓒ ⓓ	96	ⓐ ⓑ ⓒ ⓓ
17	ⓐ ⓑ ⓒ	37	ⓐ ⓑ ⓒ ⓓ	57	ⓐ ⓑ ⓒ ⓓ	77	ⓐ ⓑ ⓒ ⓓ	97	ⓐ ⓑ ⓒ ⓓ
18	ⓐ ⓑ ⓒ	38	ⓐ ⓑ ⓒ ⓓ	58	ⓐ ⓑ ⓒ ⓓ	78	ⓐ ⓑ ⓒ ⓓ	98	ⓐ ⓑ ⓒ ⓓ
19	ⓐ ⓑ ⓒ	39	ⓐ ⓑ ⓒ ⓓ	59	ⓐ ⓑ ⓒ ⓓ	79	ⓐ ⓑ ⓒ ⓓ	99	ⓐ ⓑ ⓒ ⓓ
20	ⓐ ⓑ ⓒ	40	ⓐ ⓑ ⓒ ⓓ	60	ⓐ ⓑ ⓒ ⓓ	80	ⓐ ⓑ ⓒ ⓓ	100	ⓐ ⓑ ⓒ ⓓ

ANSWER SHEET

YBM 실전토익 LC 1000

수험번호						

응시일자 : 20 년 월 일

성명		
	한 글	
	한 자	
	영 자	

Part 1~4

1	ⓐ ⓑ ⓒ ⓓ	21	ⓐ ⓑ ⓒ	41	ⓐ ⓑ ⓒ ⓓ	61	ⓐ ⓑ ⓒ ⓓ	81	ⓐ ⓑ ⓒ ⓓ
2	ⓐ ⓑ ⓒ ⓓ	22	ⓐ ⓑ ⓒ	42	ⓐ ⓑ ⓒ ⓓ	62	ⓐ ⓑ ⓒ ⓓ	82	ⓐ ⓑ ⓒ ⓓ
3	ⓐ ⓑ ⓒ ⓓ	23	ⓐ ⓑ ⓒ	43	ⓐ ⓑ ⓒ ⓓ	63	ⓐ ⓑ ⓒ ⓓ	83	ⓐ ⓑ ⓒ ⓓ
4	ⓐ ⓑ ⓒ ⓓ	24	ⓐ ⓑ ⓒ	44	ⓐ ⓑ ⓒ ⓓ	64	ⓐ ⓑ ⓒ ⓓ	84	ⓐ ⓑ ⓒ ⓓ
5	ⓐ ⓑ ⓒ ⓓ	25	ⓐ ⓑ ⓒ	45	ⓐ ⓑ ⓒ ⓓ	65	ⓐ ⓑ ⓒ ⓓ	85	ⓐ ⓑ ⓒ ⓓ
6	ⓐ ⓑ ⓒ ⓓ	26	ⓐ ⓑ ⓒ	46	ⓐ ⓑ ⓒ ⓓ	66	ⓐ ⓑ ⓒ ⓓ	86	ⓐ ⓑ ⓒ ⓓ
7	ⓐ ⓑ ⓒ	27	ⓐ ⓑ ⓒ	47	ⓐ ⓑ ⓒ ⓓ	67	ⓐ ⓑ ⓒ ⓓ	87	ⓐ ⓑ ⓒ ⓓ
8	ⓐ ⓑ ⓒ	28	ⓐ ⓑ ⓒ	48	ⓐ ⓑ ⓒ ⓓ	68	ⓐ ⓑ ⓒ ⓓ	88	ⓐ ⓑ ⓒ ⓓ
9	ⓐ ⓑ ⓒ	29	ⓐ ⓑ ⓒ	49	ⓐ ⓑ ⓒ ⓓ	69	ⓐ ⓑ ⓒ ⓓ	89	ⓐ ⓑ ⓒ ⓓ
10	ⓐ ⓑ ⓒ	30	ⓐ ⓑ ⓒ	50	ⓐ ⓑ ⓒ ⓓ	70	ⓐ ⓑ ⓒ ⓓ	90	ⓐ ⓑ ⓒ ⓓ
11	ⓐ ⓑ ⓒ	31	ⓐ ⓑ ⓒ	51	ⓐ ⓑ ⓒ ⓓ	71	ⓐ ⓑ ⓒ ⓓ	91	ⓐ ⓑ ⓒ ⓓ
12	ⓐ ⓑ ⓒ	32	ⓐ ⓑ ⓒ ⓓ	52	ⓐ ⓑ ⓒ ⓓ	72	ⓐ ⓑ ⓒ ⓓ	92	ⓐ ⓑ ⓒ ⓓ
13	ⓐ ⓑ ⓒ	33	ⓐ ⓑ ⓒ ⓓ	53	ⓐ ⓑ ⓒ ⓓ	73	ⓐ ⓑ ⓒ ⓓ	93	ⓐ ⓑ ⓒ ⓓ
14	ⓐ ⓑ ⓒ	34	ⓐ ⓑ ⓒ ⓓ	54	ⓐ ⓑ ⓒ ⓓ	74	ⓐ ⓑ ⓒ ⓓ	94	ⓐ ⓑ ⓒ ⓓ
15	ⓐ ⓑ ⓒ	35	ⓐ ⓑ ⓒ ⓓ	55	ⓐ ⓑ ⓒ ⓓ	75	ⓐ ⓑ ⓒ ⓓ	95	ⓐ ⓑ ⓒ ⓓ
16	ⓐ ⓑ ⓒ	36	ⓐ ⓑ ⓒ ⓓ	56	ⓐ ⓑ ⓒ ⓓ	76	ⓐ ⓑ ⓒ ⓓ	96	ⓐ ⓑ ⓒ ⓓ
17	ⓐ ⓑ ⓒ	37	ⓐ ⓑ ⓒ ⓓ	57	ⓐ ⓑ ⓒ ⓓ	77	ⓐ ⓑ ⓒ ⓓ	97	ⓐ ⓑ ⓒ ⓓ
18	ⓐ ⓑ ⓒ	38	ⓐ ⓑ ⓒ ⓓ	58	ⓐ ⓑ ⓒ ⓓ	78	ⓐ ⓑ ⓒ ⓓ	98	ⓐ ⓑ ⓒ ⓓ
19	ⓐ ⓑ ⓒ	39	ⓐ ⓑ ⓒ ⓓ	59	ⓐ ⓑ ⓒ ⓓ	79	ⓐ ⓑ ⓒ ⓓ	99	ⓐ ⓑ ⓒ ⓓ
20	ⓐ ⓑ ⓒ	40	ⓐ ⓑ ⓒ ⓓ	60	ⓐ ⓑ ⓒ ⓓ	80	ⓐ ⓑ ⓒ ⓓ	100	ⓐ ⓑ ⓒ ⓓ

Part 1~4

1	ⓐ ⓑ ⓒ ⓓ	21	ⓐ ⓑ ⓒ	41	ⓐ ⓑ ⓒ ⓓ	61	ⓐ ⓑ ⓒ ⓓ	81	ⓐ ⓑ ⓒ ⓓ
2	ⓐ ⓑ ⓒ ⓓ	22	ⓐ ⓑ ⓒ	42	ⓐ ⓑ ⓒ ⓓ	62	ⓐ ⓑ ⓒ ⓓ	82	ⓐ ⓑ ⓒ ⓓ
3	ⓐ ⓑ ⓒ ⓓ	23	ⓐ ⓑ ⓒ	43	ⓐ ⓑ ⓒ ⓓ	63	ⓐ ⓑ ⓒ ⓓ	83	ⓐ ⓑ ⓒ ⓓ
4	ⓐ ⓑ ⓒ ⓓ	24	ⓐ ⓑ ⓒ	44	ⓐ ⓑ ⓒ ⓓ	64	ⓐ ⓑ ⓒ ⓓ	84	ⓐ ⓑ ⓒ ⓓ
5	ⓐ ⓑ ⓒ ⓓ	25	ⓐ ⓑ ⓒ	45	ⓐ ⓑ ⓒ ⓓ	65	ⓐ ⓑ ⓒ ⓓ	85	ⓐ ⓑ ⓒ ⓓ
6	ⓐ ⓑ ⓒ ⓓ	26	ⓐ ⓑ ⓒ	46	ⓐ ⓑ ⓒ ⓓ	66	ⓐ ⓑ ⓒ ⓓ	86	ⓐ ⓑ ⓒ ⓓ
7	ⓐ ⓑ ⓒ	27	ⓐ ⓑ ⓒ	47	ⓐ ⓑ ⓒ ⓓ	67	ⓐ ⓑ ⓒ ⓓ	87	ⓐ ⓑ ⓒ ⓓ
8	ⓐ ⓑ ⓒ	28	ⓐ ⓑ ⓒ	48	ⓐ ⓑ ⓒ ⓓ	68	ⓐ ⓑ ⓒ ⓓ	88	ⓐ ⓑ ⓒ ⓓ
9	ⓐ ⓑ ⓒ	29	ⓐ ⓑ ⓒ	49	ⓐ ⓑ ⓒ ⓓ	69	ⓐ ⓑ ⓒ ⓓ	89	ⓐ ⓑ ⓒ ⓓ
10	ⓐ ⓑ ⓒ	30	ⓐ ⓑ ⓒ	50	ⓐ ⓑ ⓒ ⓓ	70	ⓐ ⓑ ⓒ ⓓ	90	ⓐ ⓑ ⓒ ⓓ
11	ⓐ ⓑ ⓒ	31	ⓐ ⓑ ⓒ	51	ⓐ ⓑ ⓒ ⓓ	71	ⓐ ⓑ ⓒ ⓓ	91	ⓐ ⓑ ⓒ ⓓ
12	ⓐ ⓑ ⓒ	32	ⓐ ⓑ ⓒ ⓓ	52	ⓐ ⓑ ⓒ ⓓ	72	ⓐ ⓑ ⓒ ⓓ	92	ⓐ ⓑ ⓒ ⓓ
13	ⓐ ⓑ ⓒ	33	ⓐ ⓑ ⓒ ⓓ	53	ⓐ ⓑ ⓒ ⓓ	73	ⓐ ⓑ ⓒ ⓓ	93	ⓐ ⓑ ⓒ ⓓ
14	ⓐ ⓑ ⓒ	34	ⓐ ⓑ ⓒ ⓓ	54	ⓐ ⓑ ⓒ ⓓ	74	ⓐ ⓑ ⓒ ⓓ	94	ⓐ ⓑ ⓒ ⓓ
15	ⓐ ⓑ ⓒ	35	ⓐ ⓑ ⓒ ⓓ	55	ⓐ ⓑ ⓒ ⓓ	75	ⓐ ⓑ ⓒ ⓓ	95	ⓐ ⓑ ⓒ ⓓ
16	ⓐ ⓑ ⓒ	36	ⓐ ⓑ ⓒ ⓓ	56	ⓐ ⓑ ⓒ ⓓ	76	ⓐ ⓑ ⓒ ⓓ	96	ⓐ ⓑ ⓒ ⓓ
17	ⓐ ⓑ ⓒ	37	ⓐ ⓑ ⓒ ⓓ	57	ⓐ ⓑ ⓒ ⓓ	77	ⓐ ⓑ ⓒ ⓓ	97	ⓐ ⓑ ⓒ ⓓ
18	ⓐ ⓑ ⓒ	38	ⓐ ⓑ ⓒ ⓓ	58	ⓐ ⓑ ⓒ ⓓ	78	ⓐ ⓑ ⓒ ⓓ	98	ⓐ ⓑ ⓒ ⓓ
19	ⓐ ⓑ ⓒ	39	ⓐ ⓑ ⓒ ⓓ	59	ⓐ ⓑ ⓒ ⓓ	79	ⓐ ⓑ ⓒ ⓓ	99	ⓐ ⓑ ⓒ ⓓ
20	ⓐ ⓑ ⓒ	40	ⓐ ⓑ ⓒ ⓓ	60	ⓐ ⓑ ⓒ ⓓ	80	ⓐ ⓑ ⓒ ⓓ	100	ⓐ ⓑ ⓒ ⓓ

YBM
실전 토익
LC1000
1

TEST 1

1 (A)	**2** (B)	**3** (C)	**4** (B)	**5** (D)
6 (B)	**7** (A)	**8** (B)	**9** (A)	**10** (C)
11 (A)	**12** (B)	**13** (C)	**14** (A)	**15** (C)
16 (C)	**17** (C)	**18** (B)	**19** (A)	**20** (A)
21 (B)	**22** (C)	**23** (B)	**24** (A)	**25** (C)
26 (B)	**27** (C)	**28** (A)	**29** (C)	**30** (B)
31 (B)	**32** (A)	**33** (B)	**34** (C)	**35** (C)
36 (C)	**37** (D)	**38** (B)	**39** (C)	**40** (A)
41 (A)	**42** (B)	**43** (B)	**44** (B)	**45** (B)
46 (C)	**47** (D)	**48** (B)	**49** (A)	**50** (A)
51 (C)	**52** (B)	**53** (C)	**54** (A)	**55** (A)
56 (D)	**57** (C)	**58** (C)	**59** (B)	**60** (A)
61 (D)	**62** (A)	**63** (B)	**64** (A)	**65** (D)
66 (C)	**67** (A)	**68** (C)	**69** (D)	**70** (B)
71 (D)	**72** (D)	**73** (A)	**74** (D)	**75** (C)
76 (C)	**77** (D)	**78** (C)	**79** (A)	**80** (C)
81 (C)	**82** (A)	**83** (A)	**84** (A)	**85** (C)
86 (D)	**87** (B)	**88** (D)	**89** (B)	**90** (D)
91 (D)	**92** (B)	**93** (D)	**94** (B)	**95** (C)
96 (D)	**97** (D)	**98** (B)	**99** (A)	**100** (A)

PART 1

1 W-Br

(A) They're reviewing a document.
(B) They're moving some office furniture.
(C) They're writing on a whiteboard.
(D) They're facing the window.

(A) 사람들이 서류를 검토하고 있다.
(B) 사람들이 사무용 가구를 옮기고 있다.
(C) 사람들이 화이트보드에 글을 적고 있다.
(D) 사람들이 창문 쪽을 향하고 있다.

어휘 face ~ 쪽을 향하다, 마주 보다

해설 2인 이상 등장 사진 - 사람의 동작 묘사

(A) 두 사람이 책상에 앉아서 서류를 검토하고 있는(reviewing a document) 모습이므로 정답.

(B) 두 사람이 사무용 가구를 옮기고 있는(moving some office furniture) 모습은 아니므로 오답.

(C) 두 사람이 화이트보드에 글을 쓰고 있는(writing on a whiteboard) 모습이 아니므로 오답.

(D) 사진에 창문이 있지만 두 사람이 창문 쪽을 향하고 있는(facing the window) 모습이 아니므로 오답.

2 M-Au

(A) He's plugging in a laptop computer.
(B) He's sitting with his legs crossed.
(C) He's positioning his briefcase.
(D) He's arranging flowers in a vase.

(A) 남자가 노트북에 전원을 연결하고 있다.
(B) 남자가 다리를 꼬고 앉아 있다.
(C) 남자가 서류 가방을 자리에 두고 있다.
(D) 남자가 화병에 꽃을 꽂고 있다.

어휘 with one's legs crossed 다리를 꼬고 position ~을 적당한 장소에 놓다 briefcase 서류 가방 vase 화병

해설 1인 등장 사진 - 사람의 상태 묘사

(A) 남자가 노트북에 전원을 연결하고 있는(plugging in a laptop computer) 모습이 아니므로 오답.

(B) 남자가 다리를 꼬고(with his legs crossed) 앉아 있는 상태이므로 정답.

(C) 남자가 서류 가방을 특정 위치에 두고 있는(positioning his briefcase) 동작을 하고 있지 않으므로 오답.

(D) 남자가 화병에 꽃을 꽂고 있는(arranging flowers in a vase) 동작을 하고 있지 않으므로 오답.

3 M-Cn

(A) Some travelers are boarding a train.
(B) A man is carrying some luggage.
(C) Some people are using public transportation.
(D) A woman is placing her bag on a seat.

(A) 몇몇 여행객이 기차에 승차하고 있다.
(B) 남자가 짐을 나르고 있다.
(C) 몇 사람이 버스를 이용하고 있다.
(D) 여자가 자신의 가방을 좌석에 놓고 있다.

어휘 traveler 여행객 board (비행기, 기차, 배 등에) 타다 carry 들고 있다, 나르다, 운반하다 luggage 짐, 수하물 public transportation 대중교통 place 놓다, 두다

해설 2인 이상 등장 사진 - 사람의 동작 묘사

(A) 두 사람이 버스에 탑승한 상태이지 지금 기차에 승차하고 있는(are boarding a train) 모습이 아니므로 오답.

(B) 남자가 버스에 앉아 있는 상태이지 짐을 나르고 있는(is carrying some luggage) 모습이 아니므로 오답.

(C) 두 사람이 대중교통을 이용하고 있는(are using public transportation) 모습이므로 정답.

(D) 여자가 가방을 손에 들고 있는 상태이지 가방을 좌석에 놓고 있는(is placing her bag on a seat) 모습이 아니므로 오답.

4 W-Br

(A) The woman is cleaning a kitchen drawer.
(B) The man is repairing an appliance.
(C) The woman is putting a dish in an oven.
(D) The man is closing a tool box.

(A) 여자가 주방 서랍을 닦고 있다.
(B) 남자가 가전제품을 수리하고 있다.
(C) 여자가 오븐에 접시를 넣고 있다.
(D) 남자가 연장통을 닫고 있다.

어휘 drawer 서랍 repair 수리하다 appliance 가전제품 tool box 연장통

해설 2인 이상 등장 사진 – 사람의 동작 묘사

(A) 여자는 남자가 오븐을 수리하는 모습을 보고 있지 주방 서랍을 닦고 있는(is cleaning a kitchen drawer) 모습이 아니므로 오답.

(B) 두 사람 중 남자가 오븐을 수리하고 있는(is repairing an appliance) 모습이므로 정답.

(C) 사진에 오븐이 보이지만 여자가 접시를 넣고 있는(is putting a dish in an oven) 모습은 아니므로 오답.

(D) 남자 옆으로 연장통이 보이지만 남자가 연장통을 닫는(is closing a tool box) 모습이 아니므로 오답.

5 M-Cn

(A) A man is pushing a bench into a corner.
(B) Tourists are waiting in line to enter a gallery.
(C) Lights have been installed in a hallway.
(D) Some artwork has been hung on walls.

(A) 남자가 벤치를 구석으로 밀고 있다.
(B) 관광객들이 화랑에 입장하기 위해 줄을 서서 기다리고 있다.
(C) 복도에 조명이 설치됐다.
(D) 미술품 몇 개가 벽들에 걸려 있다.

어휘 corner 구석, 모서리 tourist 관광객 wait in line 줄을 서서 기다리다 gallery 화랑, 미술관 install 설치하다 hallway 복도 artwork 미술품

해설 2인 이상 등장 사진 – 사람 또는 사물 중심 묘사

(A) 남자가 벤치에 앉아 있지 벤치를 구석으로 밀고 있는(is pushing a bench into a corner) 모습이 아니므로 오답.

(B) 관광객들이 줄을 서서 기다리는(are waiting in line to enter a gallery) 모습이 아니므로 오답.

(C) 미술관에 조명이 설치가 되어 있지만 복도(have been installed in a hallway)가 아니라 천장에 설치되어 있으므로 오답.

(D) 사진 왼쪽과 뒤쪽 벽에 여러 개의 그림이 걸려 있는(has been hung on walls) 모습이므로 정답.

6 W-Am

(A) Some vehicles are being inspected.
(B) Some buildings are located near a construction site.
(C) Some trees are being planted in a garden.
(D) Some rocks have been loaded onto a truck.

(A) 차량 몇 대가 점검 받는 중이다.
(B) 몇몇 건물이 공사장 근처에 위치해 있다.
(C) 나무 몇 그루가 정원에 심어지고 있다.
(D) 바위 몇 개가 트럭에 실려 있다.

어휘 vehicle 차량 inspect 점검하다 construction site 공사장, 건설 현장 load (짐을) 싣다

해설 실외 사물/풍경 사진 – 다양한 사물의 상태 묘사

(A) 사진에 차량이 보이지만 현재 점검 받고 있는(are being inspected) 모습이 아니므로 오답.

(B) 몇몇 건물들이 공사장 근처에 있는(are located near a construction site) 모습이므로 정답.

(C) 나무를 심고 있는(are being planted) 모습이 아니므로 오답.

(D) 사진에 트럭(truck)이 보이지 않으므로 오답.

PART 2

7

W-Br What time is the next train to Liverpool?
M-Au (A) At six-thirty P.M.
(B) I've got a window seat.
(C) On the first platform.

리버풀 행 다음 열차가 몇 시에 있나요?
(A) 오후 6시 30분에요.
(B) 나는 창가쪽 자리예요.
(C) 첫 번째 승강장이에요.

어휘 platform 승강장, 플랫폼

해설 다음 기차 시간을 묻는 What time 의문문

(A) 정답. 리버풀 행 다음 열차(the next train)의 시간을 묻는 질문에 At six-thirty P.M.이라는 특정 시점을 언급하고 있으므로 정답.

(B) 연상 단어 오답. 질문의 the next train에서 연상 가능한 window seat를 이용한 오답.

(C) 연상 단어 오답. 질문의 the next train에서 연상 가능한 first platform을 이용한 오답.

8

M-Au Who approved the equipment purchase?

W-Am (A) Yes, two packaging machines.

(B) Probably Mr. Sullivan.

(C) In the main warehouse.

누가 장비 구입을 승인했나요?

(A) 네, 포장 기계 두 대예요.

(B) 아마 설리번 씨일 거예요.

(C) 가장 큰 창고에 있어요.

어휘 approve 승인하다 equipment purchase 장비 구입 packaging machine 포장 기계 probably 아마, 십중팔구 main 가장 큰 warehouse 창고

해설 승인자를 묻는 Who 의문문

(A) Yes/No 불가 오답. Who 의문문에 Yes/No 응답이 불가능하기 때문에 오답.

(B) 정답. 장비 구입(equipment purchase)의 승인자를 묻는 질문에 Mr. Sullivan이라는 특정 인물을 언급하고 있으므로 정답.

(C) 질문과 상관없는 오답. 장소를 묻는 Where 의문문에 어울리는 응답이므로 오답.

9

M-Cn Where did you get that desk calendar?

W-Br (A) A friend gave it to me.

(B) It's beautifully designed.

(C) It looks like everyone's free on Thursday.

그 탁상용 달력을 어디에서 구했나요?

(A) 친구가 줬어요.

(B) 디자인이 아름다워요.

(C) 목요일엔 모두가 시간이 되는 것 같군요.

어휘 look like ~처럼 보이다 free 다른 계획(약속)이 없는

해설 출처를 물어보는 Where 의문문

(A) 정답. 어디서 구했냐는 Where did you get 질문에 a friend가 주었다고 하였으므로 정답.

(B) 질문과 상관없는 오답. What do you think of ~?와 같은 의견을 묻는 질문에 적절한 응답이므로 오답.

(C) 연상 단어 오답. 질문의 calendar에서 연상 가능한 free on Thursday를 이용한 오답.

10

M-Cn Would you like a sample of our new ice cream flavor?

W-Am (A) I don't know him.

(B) That's a good example.

(C) I'll give it a try.

새로운 맛 아이스크림을 시식해 보시겠어요?

(A) 나는 그 남자를 몰라요.

(B) 그거 좋은 예로군요.

(C) 한번 먹어 볼게요.

어휘 sample 견본, 맛보기 flavor 맛, 풍미 give it a try 한번 해보다, 시도하다

해설 제안/권유의 의문문

(A) 질문과 상관없는 오답. him이 가리키는 대상이 질문에 없으므로 오답.

(B) 유사 발음 오답. 질문의 sample과 부분적으로 발음이 같은 example을 이용한 오답.

(C) 정답. 새로운 맛의 아이스크림(our new ice cream flavor)을 시식해 보라는 제안에 한번 먹어 보겠다(I'll give it a try.)는 긍정적인 응답을 하고 있으므로 정답.

11

M-Au Do you want a table outside or in the dining room?

W-Am (A) Inside is fine.

(B) A reservation for three.

(C) Sure, there's plenty.

바깥쪽과 식당 안쪽 중 어느 테이블을 원하세요?

(A) 실내가 좋아요.

(B) 3명 예약이요.

(C) 네, 많이 있어요.

어휘 dining room 식당 reservation 예약 plenty 다량, 풍부함

해설 구를 연결한 선택의문문

(A) 정답. 실외(outside)와 실내(in the dining room) 테이블 중 어떤 것을 원하는지에 대해 실내(Inside)를 선택한 것이므로 정답.

(B) 연상 단어 오답. 질문의 dining room에서 연상 가능한 reservation을 이용한 오답.

(C) Yes/No 불가 오답. 구를 연결한 선택의문문에는 Sure와 같은 긍정적 응답이 불가능하므로 오답.

12

W-Br When did you finish filming the promotional video?

M-Cn (A) A tour of company headquarters.

(B) We're not done yet, actually.

(C) It's for our Web site.

홍보 동영상 촬영은 언제 끝마쳤습니까?

(A) 본사 방문이에요.

(B) 사실은 아직 끝나지 않았어요.

(C) 웹 사이트용입니다.

어휘 finish 끝마치다 film 촬영하다 promotional 홍보의 headquarters 본사, 본부 yet 아직 actually 사실, 실제로

해설 시점을 물어보는 When 의문문

(A) 질문과 상관없는 오답. 시간을 묻는 질문에 tour라는 답변은 적절한 응답이 아니므로 오답.

(B) 정답. 언제 끝마쳤는지 시간을 물어보는 질문에, 아직 끝나지 않았다고 응답하고 있으므로 정답.

(C) 연상 단어 오답. 질문의 the promotional video에서 연상 가능한 Web site를 이용한 오답.

13

W-Am Which jackets are included in the sale?

M-Au (A) Until the end of the weekend.

(B) You'll be cold without it.

(C) The ones with price tags.

어떤 재킷들이 할인 판매하는 것들인가요?

(A) 주말이 끝날 때까지요.

(B) 그게 없으면 추울 거예요.

(C) 가격표가 붙은 것들이요.

어휘 be included 포함되다 price tag 가격표

해설 할인되는 재킷을 묻는 Which 의문문

(A) 연상 단어 오답. 질문의 sale에서 연상 가능한 the end of the weekend를 이용한 오답.

(B) 연상 단어 오답. 질문의 jackets에서 연상 가능한 cold without it을 이용한 오답.

(C) 정답. 어떤 재킷들이 할인되는지에 대해 가격표가 붙은 것(The ones with price tags)이라는 특정 상품을 지칭하고 있으므로 정답.

14

W-Am Who signed for the package when it arrived?

M-Cn (A) Someone at the front desk.

(B) Right after lunch.

(C) A box of supplies.

소포가 도착했을 때 누가 서명했나요?

(A) 안내 데스크에 있는 사람이 했어요.

(B) 점심 시간 직후에요.

(C) 물품 한 상자예요.

어휘 package 소포 front desk 안내 데스크 supplies 물품

해설 서명자를 묻는 Who 의문문

(A) 정답. 소포에 대한 서명자를 묻는 질문에 안내 데스크에 있는 사람(someone at the front desk)이라는 인물로 응답하고 있으므로 정답.

(B) 연상 단어 오답. 질문의 package와 arrived에서 연상 가능한 right after lunch를 이용한 오답.

(C) 연상 단어 오답. 질문의 package에서 연상 가능한 a box of supplies를 이용한 오답.

15

M-Cn Will you stay for all three days of the cosmetics fair?

W-Br (A) The entire sales team.

(B) Welcome back.

(C) I'm still thinking it over.

화장품 박람회 기간 사흘 동안 계속 머무실 건가요?

(A) 영업팀 전부 다요.

(B) 다시 오신 걸 환영합니다.

(C) 아직 생각 중이에요.

어휘 cosmetics fair 화장품 박람회 entire 전체의, 전부의 think over 잘[곰곰이] 생각하다

해설 체류 기간을 묻는 조동사(will) Yes/No 의문문

(A) 질문과 상관없는 오답. Who 의문문에 대한 응답이므로 오답.

(B) 질문과 상관없는 오답. 누군가 타지에서 돌아왔을 때 어울리는 응답이므로 오답.

(C) 정답. 사흘 동안 머무를 것인지에 대해 아직 생각 중(I'm still thinking it over.)이라는 불확실성 표현으로 응답하고 있으므로 정답.

16

W-Am Shouldn't we pick Ms. Jensen up at the airport?

M-Au (A) I'm a frequent flyer.

(B) Most of them do.

(C) She's renting a car there.

공항에서 젠슨 씨를 태워 와야 하지 않나요?

(A) 나는 항공사 상용 고객이에요.

(B) 그들 중 대부분이 그렇게 해요.

(C) 그녀가 그곳에서 차를 대여할 거예요.

어휘 pick up 태우러 가다, 마중하다 a frequent flyer 항공사 상용 고객 rent a car 차를 대여하다

해설 공항 픽업 여부를 묻는 부정의문문

(A) 연상 단어 오답. 질문의 airport에서 연상 가능한 frequent flyer를 이용한 오답.

(B) 질문과 상관없는 오답. them이 가리키는 대상이 질문에 없으므로 오답.

(C) 정답. 공항에서 젠슨 씨를 태워 와야 하는지에 대해 그녀가 차를 대여할 것(She's renting a car there.)이라는 말로 부정적 응답을 하고 있으므로 정답.

17

W-Br Why do I need a code to open this door?

M-Cn (A) Yes, for the next few days.

(B) Three or four times.

(C) I thought it was unlocked.

이 문을 여는 데 왜 암호가 필요하죠?

(A) 네, 앞으로 며칠 동안요.

(B) 서너 차례요.

(C) 나는 그게 열려 있는 줄 알았어요.

어휘 code 암호 be unlocked 열려 있다

해설 암호가 필요한 이유를 묻는 Why 의문문

(A) Yes/No 불가 오답. Why 의문문에 Yes/No 응답이 불가능하기 때문에 오답.

(B) 질문과 상관없는 오답. How often이나 How many times에 어울리는 응답이므로 오답.

(C) 정답. 문을 여는 데(open this door) 왜 암호(code)가 필요한지를 묻는 질문에 문이 열려 있는 줄 알았다(it was unlocked)는 말로 문이 잠겨 있던 것조차 몰랐다는 의미를 전달한 것이므로 정답.

18

M-Au Do you have replacement parts for laptops?

W-Am (A) No, I never learned how.

(B) It depends on the brand.

(C) I'll keep that in mind.

노트북 컴퓨터용 교체 부품이 있나요?

(A) 아뇨, 어떻게 하는지 배우지 못했어요.

(B) 브랜드에 따라 달라요.

(C) 명심할게요.

어휘 replacement part 교체 부품 laptop 노트북 컴퓨터 depend on ~에 달려 있다 keep in mind 명심하다

해설 부품 취급 여부를 묻는 조동사(do) Yes/No 의문문

(A) 연상 단어 오답. 질문의 replacement에서 연상 가능한 never learned how를 이용한 오답.

(B) 정답. 브랜드에 따라 달라서(depends on the brand) 교체 부품이 있을 수도, 없을 수도 있다는 뜻의 답변이므로 정답.

(C) 질문과 상관없는 오답. 상대방이 주의 사항이나 조언을 제공했을 때 어울리는 응답이므로 오답.

19

M-Cn Let's get front row seats for the rock concert.

W-Br (A) That'll be too expensive.

(B) One of my favorite singers.

(C) Did you have a good time?

앞줄에 있는 좌석을 구해서 그 록 콘서트를 봅시다.

(A) 그건 너무 비쌀 거예요.

(B) 내가 제일 좋아하는 가수들 중 한 명이에요.

(C) 좋은 시간 보내셨어요?

어휘 front row 앞줄 expensive 비싼 favorite 제일 좋아하는

해설 제안/권유의 평서문

(A) 정답. 앞줄 좌석을 구매하자는 제안에 그 자리는 너무 비쌀 것(too expensive)이라는 말로 부정적인 응답을 하고 있으므로 정답.

(B) 연상 단어 오답. 평서문의 rock concert에서 연상 가능한 my favorite singers를 이용한 오답.

(C) 연상 단어 오답. 평서문의 rock concert에서 연상 가능한 good time을 이용한 오답.

20

W-Br Haven't you seen the itinerary for the client visit?

M-Au (A) I know it includes a dinner.

(B) I explained our business operations.

(C) A two-week trip to Europe.

고객 방문 일정을 확인하지 않았나요?

(A) 저녁 식사가 포함되어 있다는 건 알아요.

(B) 저희 경영 활동에 대해 설명했습니다.

(C) 2주간의 유럽 여행이에요.

어휘 itinerary 여행 일정 business operation 경영 활동

해설 일정 확인을 묻는 조동사(have) 부정의문문

(A) 정답. 일정 확인에 관한 질문에 includes a dinner라는 세부 사항을 언급하였으므로 정답.

(B) 연상 단어 오답. 질문의 the client visit에서 연상 가능한 explained our business operations를 이용한 오답.

(C) 연상 단어 오답. 질문의 itinerary에서 연상 가능한 trip to Europe을 이용한 오답.

21

W-Am The sculpture exhibit will have its grand opening on Saturday.

M-Au (A) The one downtown.

(B) Will the artist attend it?

(C) Art class on weekends.

조각 전시회가 토요일에 개막할 거예요.

(A) 시내에 있는 거요.

(B) 그 작가도 참석하나요?

(C) 주말의 미술 수업이에요.

어휘 sculpture exhibit 조각 전시회 grand opening 개막, 개업 downtown 시내에, 시내의 attend 참석하다

해설 사실/정보 전달의 평서문

(A) 질문과 상관없는 오답. one이 가리킬 만한 대상이 평서문에 없으므로 오답.

(B) 정답. 조각 전시회(the sculpture exhibit)가 토요일에 개막할 것이라는 말에 그 작가(the artist)도 전시회에 참석하는지를 묻는 응답이므로 정답.

(C) 연상 단어 오답. 평서문의 sculpture에서 연상 가능한 art를 이용한 오답.

22

M-Cn Can you show me the shelf with Jim Arnold's new book?

W-Br (A) Sorry, he's busy right now.

(B) You have a point.

(C) It's already sold out.

짐 아놀드의 새 책이 있는 서가를 알려주시겠어요?
(A) 죄송해요, 그분은 지금 바쁘세요.
(B) 일리가 있군요.
(C) 이미 매진됐습니다.

어휘 shelf 서가, 책꽂이 have a point 일리가 있다 be sold out 다 팔리다, 매진되다

해설 부탁/요청의 의문문

(A) 질문과 상관없는 오답. 만날 수 있는지를 묻는 질문에 어울리는 답변이므로 오답.

(B) 질문과 상관없는 오답. 상대방이 중요 사항이나 핵심을 얘기했을 때 쓸 수 있는 표현이므로 오답.

(C) 정답. 특정 작가의 신간(Jim Arnold's new book)이 있는 곳을 알려달라고 했는데 그 책이 매진되었다(It's already sold out.)는 응답을 하고 있으므로 정답.

23

W-Am Why was there a work crew in the lobby this morning?

M-Au (A) In the area near the elevators.

(B) You should've gotten an e-mail about it.

(C) I wouldn't mind coming in early.

오늘 아침 로비에 작업반이 있던 이유가 뭐죠?
(A) 엘리베이터 근처 구역에서요.
(B) 그것에 관한 이메일을 받으셨어야 했는데요.
(C) 일찍 오는 것은 괜찮습니다.

어휘 work crew 작업반 mind 꺼리다

해설 작업반이 있던 이유를 묻는 Why 의문문

(A) 질문과 상관없는 오답. 이유에 대한 질문에 a work crew가 어디 있는지 장소에 관한 질문의 응답을 하고 있으므로 오답.

(B) 정답. 작업반이 있었던 이유를 묻는 질문에 이유가 기재된 이메일을 받았어야 했다면서 관련 이메일이 발송되었음을 알리고 있으므로 정답.

(C) 연상 단어 오답. 질문의 morning에서 연상 가능한 coming in early를 이용한 오답.

24

M-Cn Where did you put the final draft of the magazine cover?

W-Br (A) It's not due until tomorrow.

(B) He liked the photograph.

(C) I have a one-year subscription.

잡지 표지 최종 시안을 어디에 뒀지요?
(A) 내일까지 하면 돼요.
(B) 그가 사진을 마음에 들어 했어요.
(C) 나는 1년 정기구독을 하고 있어요.

어휘 final draft 최종 시안 not... until ~ 이후에야 비로소… due 마감 시한이 된 subscription 정기구독

해설 최종 시안이 있는 위치를 묻는 Where 의문문

(A) 정답. 잡지 표지(magazine cover)의 최종 시안이 어디에 있는지에 대한 질문에 마감 시한이 내일(not due until tomorrow)이라는 말로 아직 최종 시안이 나오지 않았다는 의미를 우회적으로 전달한 것이므로 정답.

(B) 질문과 상관없는 오답. He가 가리킬 만한 대상이 질문에 없으므로 오답.

(C) 연상 단어 오답. 질문의 magazine에서 연상 가능한 one-year subscription을 이용한 오답.

25

W-Br How will the ballroom be decorated for the annual banquet?

M-Au (A) Yes, to present staff awards.

(B) I appreciate your help.

(C) Jenny could tell you that.

연례 연회 때 무도회장을 어떻게 장식할 건가요?
(A) 네, 직원들에게 포상을 하려고요.
(B) 도와 주셔서 감사합니다.
(C) 제니가 말해줄 수 있을 거예요.

어휘 ballroom 무도회장 be decorated 장식되다 annual banquet 연례 연회 present 주다, 수여하다 staff awards 직원 포상 appreciate 감사하게 여기다

해설 무도회장 장식 방법을 묻는 How 의문문

(A) Yes/No 불가 오답. How 의문문은 Yes/No 응답이 불가능하므로 오답.

(B) 질문과 상관없는 오답. 무도회장(ballroom)의 장식 방법을 묻는 How 의문문에 감사하다(appreciate)는 응답을 할 수 없으므로 오답.

(C) 정답. 직접적인 응답 대신 제 3자인 Jenny가 장식 방법을 말해줄 수 있을 것(could tell you that)이라는 우회적 답변을 한 것이므로 정답.

26

M-Cn This software lets you record voice memos, doesn't it?

W-Am (A) You should save it regularly.

(B) No, it's the old version.

(C) The paper copies of those records.

이 소프트웨어로 음성 메모 녹음할 수 있는 거 맞죠?
(A) 규칙적으로 저장해야 해요.
(B) 아뇨, 옛날 버전이에요.
(C) 그 기록들의 종이 사본요.

어휘 record 녹음하다, 기록하다; 기록 save 저장하다 regularly 규칙적으로, 꼬박꼬박

해설 음성 메모 녹음 가능 여부를 확인하는 부가의문문

(A) 질문과 상관없는 오답. 소프트웨어에 음성 메모(voice memo) 녹음 기능이 있는지를 묻는 질문에 규칙적으로 저장해야 한다(save it regularly)는 답변은 질문의 맥락에서 벗어난 것이므로 오답.

(B) 정답. 음성 메모 녹음 기능이 있는지에 대한 질문에 먼저 No라는 부정적인 응답을 한 후, 소프트웨어가 구 버전(old version)이라서 녹음을 할 수 없다는 부연 설명을 하고 있으므로 정답.

(C) 단어 반복 오답. 질문에 쓰인 record의 다른 의미를 이용한 오답.

27

M-Au Could I leave my bicycle in the hallway?

M-Cn (A) He rides to and from work.

(B) The last apartment.

(C) Yes, but not overnight.

복도에다 자전거를 둬도 될까요?
(A) 그가 출퇴근용으로 타고 다녀요.
(B) 맨 마지막 아파트요.
(C) 네, 하지만 밤새도록 두면 안 돼요.

어휘 hallway 복도 ride to and from work 출퇴근용으로 타다 overnight 밤새도록

해설 부탁/요청의 의문문

(A) 연상 단어 오답. 질문의 bicycle에서 연상 가능한 rides를 이용한 오답.

(B) 질문과 상관없는 오답. 장소를 묻는 Where 의문문에 어울리는 응답이므로 오답.

(C) 정답. 자전거를 복도(hallway)에 둘 수 있는지에 대한 질문에 먼저 Yes로 긍정적인 응답을 한 후, 밤새도록(overnight) 둘 수는 없다는 조건을 제시한 응답이므로 정답.

28

W-Br How long is the drive to Grand Rapids Resort?

M-Au (A) Haven't you been there before?

(B) No, there isn't much traffic.

(C) Anytime after four o'clock.

그랜드 래피즈 리조트까지 차로 얼마나 걸리나요?
(A) 전에 그곳에 가본 적 있지 않나요?
(B) 아니요, 교통 체증이 심하지 않아요.
(C) 4시 이후에는 언제라도 괜찮아요.

어휘 resort 리조트, 유원지 anytime 언제든지, 언제라도

해설 운전 시간을 묻는 How long 의문문

(A) 정답. 목적지인 그랜드 래피즈 리조트(Grand Rapids Resort)까지의 운전 시간을 묻는 질문에 전에 그곳에 가본 적 있지 않냐며 질문자에게 역질문을 하고 있으므로 정답.

(B) 연상 단어 오답. 질문의 drive에서 연상 가능한 traffic을 언급한 오답.

(C) 질문과 상관없는 오답. 시점을 묻는 When 의문문에 대한 응답이므로 오답.

29

W-Am Would Soon-Hee prefer the necklace or the earrings for her birthday?

W-Br (A) At a popular jewelry store.

(B) Thanks for inviting me.

(C) A bracelet would be better.

순희가 생일선물로 목걸이와 귀걸이 중 어느 것을 더 좋아할까요?
(A) 인기 있는 보석상에서요.
(B) 초대해 주셔서 감사해요.
(C) 팔찌가 더 나을 것 같아요.

어휘 prefer 더 좋아하다, 선호하다 necklace 목걸이 earrings 귀걸이 bracelet 팔찌

해설 단어를 연결한 선택 의문문

(A) 연상 단어 오답. 질문의 necklace와 earrings에서 연상 가능한 jewelry를 이용한 오답.

(B) 연상 단어 오답. 질문의 birthday를 듣고 생일파티 초대로 잘못 이해했을 때 연상 가능한 답변이므로 오답.

(C) 정답. 질문에서 선택 사항으로 언급된 목걸이(necklace)나 귀걸이(earrings) 대신 팔찌(bracelet)라는 제 3의 선택 사항을 제시한 것이므로 정답.

30

M-Cn I'm thinking of moving to a smaller apartment to save some money.

W-Am (A) A local moving service.

(B) I had the same idea.

(C) Yes, opening a savings account.

더 작은 아파트로 이사해서 돈을 좀 아껴볼까 생각 중이에요.
(A) 지역 이사 서비스요.
(B) 나도 같은 생각을 했어요.
(C) 네, 예금 계좌 개설이요.

어휘 move to ~로 이사하다 save 저축하다, 아끼다 savings account 예금 계좌

해설 의견 제시의 평서문

(A) 단어 반복 오답. 질문에 나온 moving을 반복 이용한 오답.

(B) 정답. 돈을 절약하기 위해(save the money) 더 작은 아파트로 이사할까 생각 중(thinking of moving)이라는 말에 응답자도 같은 생각(the same idea)을 했었다는 동감을 나타낸 것이므로 정답.

(C) 유사 발음 오답. 질문의 save와 부분적으로 발음이 동일한 savings를 이용한 오답.

31

M-Au Ms. Clarence has reviewed my budget proposal, hasn't she?

W-Am (A) How much did it cost?

(B) I'll remind her to do it.

(C) Yes, the view is wonderful.

클래런스 씨가 내 예산안을 검토했겠죠?
(A) 얼마가 들었어요?
(B) 잊지 말고 검토하라고 할게요.
(C) 네, 경치가 멋져요.

어휘 review 검토하다 budget proposal 예산안 remind 상기시키다 view 경치, 전망

해설 제안서 검토 여부를 확인하는 부가의문문

(A) 연상 단어 오답. budget이 나오는 질문에 cost에 대해 언급하고 있는 오답.

(B) 정답. 클래런스 씨가 예산안(budget proposal)을 검토했는지를 묻는 질문에 그녀에게 그 일에 관해 다시 말해 주겠다(remind her)고 응답한 것이므로 정답.

(C) 유사 발음 오답. 질문의 reviewed와 부분적으로 발음이 동일한 view를 이용한 오답.

Part 3

32-34

W-Br Good morning. [32]**I'd like to send a dozen pink roses to a friend of mine.** Do you deliver to Berkshire?

M-Au Yes, we do, but [33]**there's an extra charge of fifteen pounds because it's outside our normal delivery zone.**

W-Br That's fine. I'd like them delivered on Friday morning to her office. I want to include a personal message on the card, but I'd rather not come into your shop in person.

M-Au That's not an issue. [34]**If you tell me what you want, I can write it for you.** Go ahead when you're ready.

여: 안녕하세요. **친구에게 분홍색 장미 12송이를 보내고 싶은데요.** 버크셔까지 배달해 주시나요?

남: 네, 하지만 **기본 배달구역 밖이라서 15파운드 추가 요금이 있습니다.**

여: 좋아요. 금요일 아침에 친구의 사무실로 배달해 주세요. 개인적인 메시지를 담은 카드도 포함시키고 싶은데, 가게에 직접 가고 싶지는 않군요.

남: 문제 될 것 없습니다. **원하시는 내용을 말씀하시면 제가 대신 적어드릴 수 있어요.** 준비되시면 말씀하세요.

어휘 dozen 12개 deliver 배달하다 extra charge 추가 요금 normal delivery zone 기본 배달구역 include 포함하다 I'd rather not 차라리 ~하지 않겠다 in person 몸소, 직접 issue 문젯거리

32

Why is the woman calling?

(A) To place an order
(B) To check a delivery status
(C) To make an exchange
(D) To request a brochure

여자가 전화한 이유는 무엇인가?

(A) 주문을 하려고
(B) 배송 상황을 확인하려고
(C) 교환하려고
(D) 안내 책자를 요청하려고

어휘 status 상태 exchange 교환

해설 전체내용 관련 – 전화 통화의 이유

여자의 첫 번째 대사에서 친구에게 분홍색 장미 12송이를 보내고 싶다(I'd like to send a dozen pink roses to a friend of mine.)고 했는데 이를 통해 여자가 꽃 주문을 목적으로 전화를 한 것임을 알 수 있으므로 정답은 (A)이다.

33

What does the man tell the woman about?

(A) A new service
(B) An additional fee
(C) A return policy
(D) A job opportunity

남자는 여자에게 무엇에 관해 말하는가?

(A) 새로운 서비스
(B) 추가 비용
(C) 반품 정책
(D) 일자리

해설 세부 사항 관련 – 남자가 여자에게 하는 말

남자의 첫 번째 대사에서 기본 배달구역 밖이라서 15파운드 추가 요금이 있다(there's an extra charge of fifteen pounds because it's outside our normal delivery zone.)고 했으므로 정답은 (B)이다.

▸▸ **Paraphrasing** 대화의 an extra charge
→ 정답의 an additional fee

34

What does the man offer to do for the woman?

(A) Issue a receipt
(B) Recommend a product
(C) Write a message
(D) Search a storage room

남자는 여자를 위해 무엇을 하겠다고 말하는가?

(A) 영수증 발급하기
(B) 제품 추천하기
(C) 메시지 적기
(D) 창고 찾아보기

해설 세부 사항 관련 – 남자가 여자를 위해 할 일

대화 마지막에 남자가 여자에게 원하는 내용을 말하면 대신 적어주겠다(If you tell me what you want, I can write it for you.)고 했으므로 정답은 (C)이다.

35-37

W-Am Good morning. I'm Seiko Nimiya from Delaney Tech. [35]**I'm scheduled to demonstrate how to use our new video projection system to your sales team at 10 A.M.**

M-Cn Yes, Ms. Nimiya. We're ready for you in conference room 3. [36]**Do you need any assistance in unloading the equipment?**

W-Am Thanks, but I'm fine. It's quite compact, so this cart is all I need.

M-Cn All right. And you should know that [37]**in addition to our sales team, a few other managers have decided to sit in on your presentation.**

W-Am Great. The more people to see it, the better.

여: 안녕하세요. 델라니 테크의 세이코 니미야입니다. **제가 오전 10시에 귀사의 영업팀을 상대로 저희의 새로운 비디오 영사 시스템의 사용법을 보여드릴 예정입니다.**

남: 네, 니미야 씨. 3번 회의실에서 당신을 맞을 준비를 해 놓았습니다. **장비를 내리는 데 도움이 필요하신가요?**

여: 감사합니다만 괜찮습니다. 장비가 소형이라 이 카트만 있으면 됩니다.

남: 좋습니다. 그리고 **우리 영업팀 외에 다른 매니저 몇 명이 당신의 발표를 참관하기로 결정했으니** 알아 두십시오.
여: 잘됐군요. 보는 사람이 많으면 많을수록 더 좋으니까요.

어휘 be scheduled to + 동사원형 ~할 예정이다, ~하기로 되어 있다 demonstrate 시범을 보이다, 실연하다 video projection system 비디오 영사 시스템 be ready for ~준비가 되어 있다 conference room 회의실 assistance 도움 unload 짐을 내리다 compact 소형의 in addition to ~에 더해, ~외에 sit in on ~을 참관하다

35

What is the purpose of the woman's visit?

(A) To tour an office
(B) To interview for a position
(C) To give a demonstration
(D) To deliver a package

여자의 방문 목적은 무엇인가?
(A) 사무실을 둘러보려고
(B) 구직 면접을 보려고
(C) 시범을 보이려고
(D) 소포를 배달하려고

해설 세부 사항 관련 - 여자의 방문 목적
여자의 첫 번째 대사에서 오전 10시에 영업팀을 상대로 새로운 비디오 영사 시스템의 사용법을 보여드릴 예정(I'm scheduled to demonstrate how to use our new video projection system to your sales team at 10 A.M.)이라고 했으므로 정답은 (C)이다.

36

What does the man offer to do?

(A) Set up some equipment
(B) Reserve a conference room
(C) Help unload some items
(D) Look for his manager

남자는 무엇을 해 주겠다고 제안하는가?
(A) 장비 설치
(B) 회의실 예약
(C) 물품 하역 돕기
(D) 매니저 찾기

해설 세부 사항 관련 - 남자의 제안 사항
남자의 첫 번째 대사에서 장비를 내리는 데 도움이 필요한지(Do you need any assistance in unloading the equipment?) 물어봤으므로 정답은 (C)이다.

▸▸ **Paraphrasing** 대화의 **the equipment** → 정답의 **some items**

37

What does the man tell the woman?

(A) A contract has already been drafted.
(B) A presentation's time slot was shortened.
(C) A meeting's location has changed.
(D) A group's size has increased.

남자는 여자에게 무슨 말을 하는가?
(A) 계약서의 초안이 이미 준비되어 있다.
(B) 발표 시간이 단축되었다.
(C) 회의 장소가 바뀌었다.
(D) 집단의 인원수가 늘었다.

어휘 draft 초안을 작성하다 slot 시간(대), 자리, 틈 location 장소

해설 세부 사항 관련 - 남자가 여자에게 하는 말
남자의 두 번째 대사에서 영업팀 외에 다른 매니저 몇 명이 발표를 참관하기로 결정했다(in addition to our sales team, a few other managers have decided to sit in on your presentation.)고 했다. 이를 통해 단체의 규모가 더 커졌다는 것을 알 수 있으므로 정답은 (D)이다.

38-40 3인 대화

M-Cn Ms. Gilligan, thank you for this opportunity. [38]**You know, our creative department loves your products—especially your colored pencils and sketchbooks.**

W-Br I'm glad to hear that. We enjoy your advertising campaigns.

M-Cn Thank you. Now, I'll be overseeing your account, but it will mainly be handled by Todd here. Todd, why don't you get the meeting started?

M-Au Sure, Alejandro. Ms. Gilligan, why did you decide to find a new advertising agency?

W-Br I was disappointed by our previous agency's performance. [39]**They had good ideas, but their campaigns were never ready on schedule.**

M-Au I see. We'll take that into account. Now, if you don't mind, [40]**I have some questions about your target market.**

남1: 길리건 씨, 기회를 주셔서 감사합니다. **아시겠지만 저희 광고부서는 귀사의 제품, 특히 색연필과 스케치북이 매우 마음에 듭니다.**
여: 그렇게 말씀해 주시니 기쁩니다. 귀사의 광고 캠페인 잘 봤습니다.
남1: 감사합니다. 이제 제가 귀사를 관리할 텐데요, 여기 계신 토드가 주로 맡아 주실 겁니다. 토드, 회의를 시작하는 게 어떨까요?
남2: 네, 알레한드로. 길리건 씨, 새로운 광고대행사를 찾기로 결심하신 이유가 무엇입니까?
여: 예전 대행사의 업무 수행이 실망스러웠습니다. **아이디어는 좋았지만 캠페인이 예정대로 준비된 적이 없어요.**
남2: 알겠습니다. 그 점을 참고하겠습니다. 괜찮으시다면 **이제 귀사의 표적 시장에 관한 질문을 드리겠습니다.**

어휘 opportunity 기회 creative 창의적인 department 부서 especially 특히 oversee 감독하다, 관리하다 account 고객, 이용 계정 mainly 주로 handle 다루다, 취급하다 be disappointed 실망하다 previous 이전의 performance (과제 등의) 수행, 실행 be ready 준비가 되다 on schedule 예정대로 take ~ into account ~을 고려하다, 참작하다 target market 표적 시장

38

What does the woman's company most likely manufacture?

(A) Hand tools
(B) Art supplies
(C) Office furniture
(D) Fashion accessories

여자의 회사는 무엇을 제조하겠는가?

(A) 수공구
(B) 미술용품
(C) 사무용 가구
(D) 패션 액세서리

어휘 manufacture 제조하다 hand tool 수공구 art supplies 미술용품

해설 전체 내용 관련 – 여자의 직업

대화 처음 남자의 말에서 상대방 여자의 회사 제품에 대한 언급을 하고 있으며(You know, our creative department loves your products) 이어서 여자 회사의 제품에 대한 구체적인 내용(especially your colored pencils and sketchbooks.)을 말하고 있어 여자의 회사는 미술용품을 제조한다는 사실을 알 수 있으므로 정답은 (B)이다.

39

Why was the woman disappointed with an advertising agency?

(A) It usually exceeded its budget.
(B) Its campaigns were not successful.
(C) It did not complete projects on time.
(D) Its ideas were not creative.

여자가 광고대행사에 실망한 이유는?

(A) 통상적으로 예산을 초과했다.
(B) 캠페인이 성공을 거두지 못했다.
(C) 프로젝트를 제때 완료하지 못했다.
(D) 아이디어가 창의적이지 않았다.

어휘 exceed 초과하다 budget 예산 successful 성공적인, 성공을 거둔 complete 완료하다 on time 시간을 어기지 않고

해설 세부 사항 관련 – 여자가 실망한 이유

여자의 두 번째 말에서 예전 대행사는 아이디어는 좋았지만 캠페인이 예정대로 준비된 적이 없다(They had good ideas, but their campaigns were never ready on schedule)고 하며 시간을 지키지 않은 것에 대해 이야기를 하였으므로 정답은 (C)이다.

40

What will Todd most likely do next?

(A) Ask for more information
(B) Introduce an account team
(C) Suggest revisions to an agreement
(D) Present some market data

토드는 다음으로 무엇을 하겠는가?

(A) 더 자세한 정보 요청하기
(B) 계정팀 소개하기
(C) 계약서 수정 사항 제안하기
(D) 시장 데이터 제시하기

어휘 suggest 제안하다 revision 수정, 변경 present 보여주다, 제시하다

해설 세부 사항 관련 – 남자가 할 일

대화 마지막에 토드가 이제 귀사의 표적 시장에 관한 질문을 드리겠다(I have some questions about your target market)고 하였으므로 정답은 (A)이다.

Test 1

41-43

M-Au All right. I've got your delivery unloaded. Here's the invoice. [41] **Please look it over and make sure everything is correct.**

W-Am Let's see. Um... [42] **it looks like there's supposed to be two more boxes of the seedless grapes.**

M-Au Oh, you're right. Sorry about that. [43] **Maybe I left them in the back of my truck. Let me check that.** I'll be back in a moment.

W-Am All right. I'll wait here, and I won't unpack anything until it's all here.

남: 됐습니다. 배달 물품을 내려놨어요. 여기 송장이 있습니다. **살펴보시고 모든 게 정확한지 확인해 주세요.**
여: 어디 보자. 음… **씨 없는 포도가 두 상자 더 있어야 하는 것 같은데요.**
남: 오, 당신 말이 맞아요. 미안합니다. **아마 제가 트럭 뒤쪽에 남겨둔 모양입니다. 확인해 보겠습니다.** 잠시 후에 돌아오죠.
여: 좋아요. 여기서 기다릴게요. 물건이 전부 여기에 올 때까지 풀어보지 않을래요.

어휘 delivery 배달 물품 unload 내리다, 하역하다 invoice 송장, 청구서 look over 자세히 살피다 make sure 확실히 하다 be supposed to + 동사원형 ~하기로 되어 있다 seedless grape 씨 없는 포도 unpack 포장을 풀다

41

What does the man ask the woman to do?

(A) Review an invoice
(B) Schedule a delivery
(C) Sign a document
(D) Choose a payment option

남자는 여자에게 무엇을 하라고 요청하는가?

(A) 송장 검토하기
(B) 배달 일정 잡기
(C) 문서에 서명하기
(D) 대금 지불 방법 선택하기

해설 세부 사항 관련 – 남자의 요청 사항

남자의 첫 대사에서 여자에게 송장을 살펴보고 모든 게 정확한지 확인해 달라(Please look it over and make sure everything is correct.)고 했다. 이 문장에서 it은 앞 문장의 the invoice(송장)를 가리키는 것이므로 정답은 (A)이다.

▸▸ **Paraphrasing** 대화의 **look over** → 정답의 **review**

42

What problem does the woman mention?

(A) An address is incorrect.
(B) Some goods are missing.
(C) A staff member is unavailable.
(D) Some boxes are very heavy.

여자는 어떤 문제를 언급하는가?

(A) 주소가 부정확하다.
(B) 일부 물품이 없다.
(C) 스텝 한 명이 부재중이다.
(D) 상자 몇 개가 아주 무겁다.

해설 세부 사항 관련 – 여자가 언급하는 문제점

여자의 첫 번째 대사에서 씨 없는 포도가 두 상자 더 있어야 할 것 같다(it looks like there's supposed to be two more boxes of the seedless grapes.)고 했다. 이를 통해 일부 물품이 빠진 것을 알 수 있으므로 정답은 (B)이다.

▸▸ Paraphrasing 대화의 **two more boxes of the seedless grapes** → 정답의 **Some goods**

43

What will the man do next?

(A) Start unpacking some containers
(B) Look in a vehicle for some items
(C) Contact his supervisor
(D) Print another shipping label

남자는 다음에 무엇을 하겠는가?

(A) 컨테이너 몇 개를 풀기 시작한다.
(B) 물품을 찾기 위해 차 안을 살핀다.
(C) 관리자에게 연락한다.
(D) 운송 라벨을 하나 더 출력한다.

어휘 supervisor 관리자, 감독관

해설 세부 사항 관련 – 남자의 다음 행동

남자의 두 번째 대사에서 아마 트럭 뒤쪽에 남겨둔 것 같으니 확인해 보겠다(Maybe I left them in the back of my truck. Let me check that.)고 했으므로 정답은 (B)이다.

▸▸ Paraphrasing 대화의 **check** → 정답의 **Look in**

44-46

W-Br Hi. My name is Teresa Hahm. I've been a Redhawk Communications customer for about six months, and [44]**I'm interested in upgrading to your high-speed Internet package.**

M-Cn All right, Ms. Hahm. Let me just look you up in the system. [45]**Where is the service being used?**

W-Br [45]**At 386 Hillcrest Drive.** That's here in San Diego. How long does it take to be switched over?

M-Cn The crew is about two days behind schedule at the moment, so [46]**it'll take about seven days before you can use the new service.** But you'll still be able to access the Internet in the meantime. Also, there's no installation fee, but of course your monthly rates will go up.

여: 안녕하세요. 제 이름은 테레사 함입니다. 약 6개월 동안 레드호크 통신을 이용하고 있는데, **귀사의 고속 인터넷 상품으로 업그레이드를 해볼까 하고요.**

남: 좋습니다, 고객님. 시스템에서 성함을 좀 찾아보겠습니다. **서비스를 이용하시는 곳이 어디인가요?**

여: **힐크레스트 드라이브 386번지예요.** 여기 샌디에이고에 있어요. 바꾸는 데 얼마나 걸리나요?

남: 기사들이 현재 이틀 정도 일이 밀려 있어서 **대략 7일은 지나야 새로운 서비스를 이용하실 수 있을 겁니다.** 하지만 그동안에도 여전히 인터넷은 사용하실 수 있습니다. 또 설치비는 무료지만, 당연히 월 사용료가 올라갑니다.

어휘 customer 고객 look up (컴퓨터에서) ~를 찾아보다 switch over 바꾸다, 전환하다 crew 작업반 behind schedule 일정에 뒤처진, 일정이 늦은 in the meantime 그동안에, 그 사이에 installation fee 설치비 access 이용하다, 접근하다 monthly rates 한 달 요금, 월 사용료

44

What is the purpose of the woman's call?

(A) To make a complaint
(B) To upgrade a service
(C) To inquire about rates
(D) To cancel a contract

여자가 전화한 목적은 무엇인가?

(A) 불만을 제기하려고
(B) 서비스를 업그레이드하려고
(C) 요금에 관해 문의하려고
(D) 계약을 취소하려고

어휘 complaint 불평 inquire 묻다 rate 요금

해설 전체 내용 관련 – 전화 통화의 목적

여자의 첫 번째 대사에서 고속 인터넷 상품으로 업그레이드를 하고 싶다(I'm interested in upgrading to your high-speed Internet package.)고 했으므로 정답은 (B)이다.

45

What information does the man ask for?

(A) A total charge
(B) A street address
(C) An account number
(D) A transaction date

남자는 어떤 정보를 요구하는가?
(A) 전체 비용
(B) 거리 주소
(C) 계좌번호
(D) 거래 일자

어휘 transaction 거래

해설 세부 사항 관련 - 남자가 요청하는 정보

남자의 첫 번째 대사에서 여자에게 서비스를 이용하는 곳이 어디인지(Where is the service being used?) 물어봤다. 이에 대해 여자가 힐크레스트 드라이브 386번지(At 386 Hillcrest Drive.)라고 대답했으므로 정답은 (B)이다.

46

According to the man, how long will it take to make a change?

(A) Two days
(B) Five days
(C) One week
(D) Two weeks

남자에 따르면, 교체 작업이 얼마나 걸릴 것인가?
(A) 2일
(B) 5일
(C) 1주일
(D) 2주일

해설 세부 사항 관련 - 변경 작업 소요 시간

남자의 마지막 대사에서 대략 7일은 지나야 새로운 서비스를 이용하실 수 있을 것(it'll take about seven days before you can use the new service.)이라고 했으므로 정답은 (C)이다.

▸▸ **Paraphrasing** 대화의 **seven days** → 정답의 **one week**

47-49

M-Cn Hi, Ms. Ashford. This is Richard from Peterson Company. I got your message saying that [47]**you needed a work crew to mow your yard and trim some bushes at your property.** [48]**We can send a team there sometime next week.**

W-Am Actually, I already got a call earlier from someone at your company, Robert. He told me three days.

M-Cn Let me check our system. Oh, you're right. He's got you listed for Friday at 9 A.M. And you should know that [49]**since you're a new customer, you will get ten percent off the fee.**

W-Am [49]**I really appreciate that.**

남: 안녕하세요, 애시포드 씨. 피터슨 컴퍼니의 리처드입니다. **귀댁의 마당 잔디를 깎고 관목을 손질할 작업반이 필요하시다는** 메시지를 받았는데요. **저희가 다음 주쯤 한 팀을 보낼 수 있습니다.**

여: 실은, 로버트라는 귀사의 어떤 분한테서 진작에 전화를 받았어요. 그분은 제게 사흘 뒤라고 하던데요.

남: 저희 시스템을 확인해 보겠습니다. 아, 맞아요. 그가 손님을 금요일 오전 9시 명단에 올려 놨군요. 그리고 **손님은 신규 고객이시라 비용에서 10%를 할인해 드릴 테니** 그렇게 알고 계세요.

여: **그래 주신다니 정말 고마워요.**

어휘 mow 잔디를 깎다 yard 마당 trim 손질하다, 다듬다 bush 관목, 덤불 property 부동산 get someone listed ~를 명단에 올리다 fee 요금

47

Where most likely does the man work?

(A) At a construction business
(B) At an interior decorating firm
(C) At a real estate agency
(D) At a landscaping company

남자가 일하는 곳은 어디겠는가?
(A) 건설 회사
(B) 인테리어 회사
(C) 부동산 중개업소
(D) 조경 회사

어휘 firm 회사 real estate 부동산

해설 전체 내용 관련 - 남자의 근무지

대화 첫 부분에서 남자가 여자에게 마당의 잔디를 깎고 관목을 손질할 작업반이 필요하다(you needed a work crew to mow your yard and trim some bushes at your property.)는 여자의 메시지를 받았다고 했다. 이 문장에서 mow와 trim이라는 단어를 통해 남자가 조경 회사(landscaping company)에 근무한다는 것을 알 수 있으므로 정답은 (D)이다.

48

Why does the woman say, "He told me three days"?

(A) To show regret
(B) To clarify a schedule
(C) To answer a complaint
(D) To request a specific team

여자는 왜 "그분은 제게 사흘 뒤라고 하던데요"라고 말하는가?
(A) 유감을 표하려고
(B) 일정을 분명히 하려고
(C) 불만에 답하려고
(D) 특정한 팀을 요청하려고

어휘 clarify 분명히 하다 specific 특정한

해설 화자의 의도 파악 - 사흘 뒤라는 말의 의미

남자의 첫 번째 대사에서 다음 주쯤 한 팀을 보낼 수 있다(We can send a team there sometime next week.)고 했다. 이에 대해 여자는 로버트라는 직원은 자신에게 사흘 뒤(He told me three days.)라고 말했다 했다. 즉, 여자는 조경 작업이 다음 주인지 아니면 사흘 뒤인지 정확히 알고 싶어서 인용문을 말한 것이므로 정답은 (B)이다.

49

Why is the woman pleased?

(A) She is eligible for a discount on the work.
(B) She can join a customer loyalty program.
(C) The company will not charge a fee to make a change.
(D) The company returned her call quickly.

여자가 기뻐하는 이유는?

(A) 작업 비용을 할인 받을 자격이 있어서
(B) 회원 우대 프로그램에 가입할 수 있어서
(C) 회사가 변경 사항에 따른 비용을 청구하지 않을 거라서
(D) 회사가 신속하게 응답 전화를 해 줘서

어휘 be eligible for ~에 자격이 있다

해설 세부 사항 관련 - 여자가 기뻐하는 이유

남자의 두 번째 대사에서 여자가 신규 고객이기 때문에 비용에서 10% 할인을 받게 된다(since you're a new customer, you will get ten percent off the fee)고 하자 이에 대해 여자가 고맙다(I really appreciate that.)고 했다. 즉, 여자는 할인 받을 수 있는 것에 대해 기뻐하는 것이므로 정답은 (A)이다.

▸▸ **Paraphrasing** 대화의 **ten percent off the fee**
→ 정답의 **a discount on the work**

50-52

W-Br Alex, have you seen the news? [50]**There's a problem with the metro's airport line. I'm not sure we'll be able to take it to catch our flight.** I mean, we have to check in by four P.M.

M-Au Hmm... OK, [51]**why don't I check the metro's "Notices" Web page?** It should have the most up-to-date information. Then we can decide whether we should take a bus or a taxi instead.

W-Br That's a good idea. Either way, [52]**we should head out sooner than we planned. I'm going to go get my suitcase and close up my office.** I'll be back in five minutes.

여: 알렉스, 뉴스 보셨나요? **지하철 공항 노선에 문제가 생겼어요. 지하철을 타면 비행기에 탑승할 수 있을지 잘 모르겠어요.** 오후 4시까지는 탑승 수속을 해야 하거든요.

남: **음… 제가 지하철 웹 페이지의 공지 사항을 확인해 볼까요?** 최신 정보가 있을 거예요. 그러면 버스를 탈지, 대신 택시를 탈지 결정할 수 있죠.

여: 좋은 생각이네요. **어떤 쪽이든 계획했던 것보다 일찍 출발해야 해요. 저는 가서 여행 가방을 가져오고 사무실 문을 닫을게요.** 5분 후 돌아오겠습니다.

어휘 metro 지하철 airport 공항 catch a flight 비행기에 탑승하다 notice 공지, 알림 up-to-date 최신의 instead 대신 either (둘 중) 어느 하나의 head out 출발하다 close up 문을 닫다

50

What is the woman unsure about?

(A) How to travel to the airport
(B) When a flight will depart
(C) Where a check-in counter is
(D) Which airline to fly with

여자는 무엇에 대해 확신하지 못하는가?

(A) 공항까지 갈 방법
(B) 비행기 출발 시간
(C) 체크인 카운터 위치
(D) 이용할 항공사

어휘 unsure 확신하지 못하는 flight 항공편 depart 출발하다 airline 항공사

해설 세부 사항 관련 - 여자가 언급하는 문제

여자의 첫 번째 대사에서 지하철의 공항 노선에 문제가 생겨 지하철을 타면 비행기에 탑승할 수 있을지 잘 모르겠다(There's a problem with the metro's airport line. I'm not sure we'll be able to take it to catch our flight.)고 하였다. 이로써 여자는 지하철을 이용하는 것에 확신이 없음을 나타내고 있으므로 정답은 (A)이다.

51

What does the man offer to do?

(A) Share some news with a group of colleagues
(B) Reserve a type of transportation
(C) Consult an official Web site
(D) Create an electronic spreadsheet

남자는 무엇을 하겠다고 제안하는가?

(A) 동료들에게 뉴스 공유하기
(B) 교통편 예약하기
(C) 공식 웹 사이트 확인하기
(D) 전자 스프레드시트 만들기

어휘 share 공유하다 colleague 동료 reserve 예약하다 transportation 교통 consult 찾아보다

해설 세부 사항 관련 - 남자가 제안하는 일

첫 번째 여자의 대사에서 지하철 공항 노선에 문제가 생겼다고 하자 이에 대해 남자가 지하철 웹 페이지의 공지 사항을 확인해 보겠다(why don't I check the metro's "Notices" Web page?)고 했으므로 정답은 (C)이다.

52

What does the woman say she will do?

(A) Pack only one bag
(B) Prepare to leave soon
(C) Sit in a nearby waiting area
(D) Use an office messaging service

여자는 무엇을 하겠다고 말하는가?

(A) 가방 하나만 꾸리기
(B) 곧 떠날 준비하기
(C) 인근 대기구역에 앉아 있기
(D) 오피스 메시지 서비스 이용하기

어휘 pack 싸다, 꾸리다 prepare 준비하다 nearby 인근의

해설 세부 사항 관련 – 여자가 할 일

대화 마지막에 여자가 계획했던 것보다 일찍 출발해야 한다(we should head out sooner than we planned)고 하면서 자신은 가서 여행 가방을 가져오고 사무실 문을 닫겠다(I'm going to go get my suitcase and close up my office)고 하였으므로 (B)가 정답이다.

53-55 3인 대화

M-Cn Hi, Gwen. Hi, Verna. As you know, we're in the process of hiring eight new people for the advertising team. [53]**I'd like you two to train the new staff members.**

W-Br Sure. When will they be starting work here?

M-Cn October ninth. But Mr. Sardana wants everything done in just two days. [54]**I'm worried that it's not enough time to cover all the necessary topics.** What do you think?

W-Am Yeah, that would really be a tight schedule, but it's not impossible. [55]**We could e-mail the new employees all of the necessary handouts ahead of time.** Then they could review them at home before their first day.

M-Cn Good idea. I think that's our best option.

남: 안녕하세요, 그웬. 안녕하세요, 버나. 알다시피 우리는 광고 팀에 8명을 새로 채용하는 과정에 있어요. **두 사람이 새로운 직원들을 교육시켜 주면 좋겠어요.**

여1: 물론이죠. 그들이 언제부터 이곳에서 일을 시작하나요?

남: 10월 9일부터요. 하지만 사르다나 씨가 이틀 만에 모든 걸 끝내 놓길 원하세요. **필요한 주제를 모두 다루기에는 시간이 넉넉하지 않아서 걱정이에요.** 당신 생각은 어떤가요?

여2: 네, 일정이 정말 빠듯하겠네요. 하지만 불가능한 일은 아니에요. **새로 채용된 사람들에게 필요한 자료를 사전에 모두 이메일로 보낼 수 있을 거예요.** 그러면 그들이 첫 출근일 전에 집에서 그 자료들을 살펴볼 수 있잖아요.

남: 좋은 생각이에요. 내 생각에도 그게 가장 좋은 선택인 것 같아요.

어휘 as you know 알다시피 be in the process of ~하는 과정에 있다 hire 채용하다 be worried 걱정하다, 우려하다 cover 다루다, 망라하다, 포함하다 tight schedule 빠듯한[빡빡한] 일정 ahead of time 미리, 사전에 option 선택

53

What are the women asked to do?

(A) Interview job candidates
(B) Design an advertisement
(C) Conduct a training session
(D) Prepare some work spaces

여자들은 무엇을 하라는 요청을 받았는가?

(A) 구직자 면접
(B) 광고 디자인
(C) 교육 과정 진행
(D) 작업 공간 마련

해설 세부 사항 관련 – 여자들이 받은 요청 사항

대화 첫 부분에서 남자가 여자들에게 새로운 직원들을 교육시켜 주면 좋겠다(I'd like you two to train the new staff members.)고 했으므로 정답은 (C)이다.

▸▸ Paraphrasing 대화의 train the new staff members → 정답의 conduct a training session

54

Why is the man concerned?

(A) The available time is limited.
(B) Some employees are absent today.
(C) The budget for an event is low.
(D) Some equipment is not working.

남자가 우려하는 이유는?

(A) 쓸 수 있는 시간이 제한되어 있다.
(B) 일부 직원들이 오늘 결근했다.
(C) 행사 예산이 작다.
(D) 장비가 작동하지 않는다.

어휘 concern 걱정시키다, 관련시키다 absent 결근한, 결석한 budget 예산

해설 세부 사항 관련 – 남자가 우려하는 이유

남자의 두 번째 대사에서 필요한 주제를 모두 다루기에는 시간이 넉넉하지 않아서 걱정된다(I'm worried that it's not enough time to cover all the necessary topics.)고 했으므로 정답은 (A)이다.

▸▸ Paraphrasing 대화의 not enough time → 정답의 The available time is limited.

55

What will the women do to solve the problem?

(A) Send materials in advance
(B) Consult an expert
(C) Hire some temporary workers
(D) Adjust a printing schedule

여자들은 문제를 해결하기 위해 무엇을 할 것인가?

(A) 자료 미리 보내기
(B) 전문가와 상의하기
(C) 임시직 몇 명 고용하기
(D) 인쇄 일정 조정하기

어휘 solve 해결하다 in advance 사전에, 미리 consult 상담하다 expert 전문가 temporary 임시의 adjust 조정하다

해설 세부 사항 관련 – 문제 해결을 위한 제안 사항

두 번째 여자의 대사에서 새로 채용된 사람들에게 필요한 자료를 사전에 모두 이메일로 보낼 수도 있다(We could e-mail the new employees all of the necessary handouts ahead of time.)고 했으므로 정답은 (A)이다.

▸▸ Paraphrasing 대화의 ahead of time → 정답의 in advance

56-58

W-Am Hello. [56]**My washing machine broke down, and I need to buy a new one.** Could you help me with that?

M-Au Sure. [56]**Did you have a particular brand in mind?**

W-Am Not really. But [57]**I need one that's efficient. I don't want to have high electricity bills.**

M-Au I completely understand. This one here has one of the best ratings in the industry. And it can handle a lot of different clothing types.

W-Am That looks good to me. And the price is reasonable. Do you deliver?

M-Au Of course. And you came at the right time. [58]**This week only, we're offering free installation on orders over two hundred dollars.**

여: 안녕하세요. **세탁기가 고장 나서 새것을 사야 하는데요.** 좀 도와주시겠어요?
남: 물론이죠. **특별히 생각하고 계시는 브랜드가 있나요?**
여: 아뇨. 하지만 **효율적인 제품이 필요해요. 전기료가 많이 나오는 건 원치 않거든요.**
남: 십분 이해합니다. 여기 있는 이 제품이 업계에서 가장 평가가 좋은 제품들 중 하나입니다. 매우 다양한 종류의 옷들을 세탁할 수 있죠.
여: 좋아 보이네요. 가격도 합리적이고요. 배달해 주시나요?
남: 물론이죠. 마침 제때에 오셨네요. **이번 주만 200달러가 넘는 제품을 주문하시면 설치비가 무료거든요.**

어휘 washing machine 세탁기 break down 고장 나다 have ~ in mind ~을 마음에 두다 efficient 효율적인 electricity bills 전기요금 청구서 rating 평가, 순위, 등급 handle 처리하다, 다루다 reasonable 합리적인 at the right time 제때에 offer free installation 무료로 설치해 주다 order 주문(품)

56

Where most likely does the man work?

(A) At a carpet store
(B) At a car dealership
(C) At a clothing retailer
(D) At an appliance store

남자가 일하는 곳은 어디겠는가?

(A) 카페트 가게
(B) 자동차 대리점
(C) 옷 소매점
(D) 가전제품 가게

해설 **전체 내용 관련 - 남자의 근무지**

여자의 첫 번째 대사에서 세탁기가 고장 나서 새 것을 사야 한다(My washing machine broke down, and I need to buy a new one.)고 했다. 이에 대해 남자가 여자에게 특별히 생각하는 브랜드가 있는지(Did you have a particular brand in mind?) 물어봤다. 이를 통해 남자가 가전제품 판매점에서 근무한다는 것을 알 수 있으므로 정답은 (D)이다.

57

What is the woman worried about?

(A) Getting the wrong size
(B) Having to pay for repeated repairs
(C) Spending too much on energy
(D) Being confused by some instructions

여자는 무엇을 염려하는가?

(A) 잘못된 용량의 제품을 구입하는 것
(B) 수리비를 재차 내야 하는 것
(C) 에너지를 너무 많이 쓰는 것
(D) 설명서로 인해 헷갈리는 것

어휘 instructions 설명, 지침

해설 **세부 사항 관련 - 여자의 염려 사항**

여자의 두 번째 대사에서 효율적인 제품이 필요하며 전기료가 많이 나오는 건 원치 않는다(I need one that's efficient. I don't want to have high electricity bills.)고 했다. 즉, 여자는 에너지를 너무 많이 사용하여 비용이 많이 드는 것에 대해 염려하는 것이므로 정답은 (C)이다.

58

According to the man, what special offer is available this week?

(A) A discounted price
(B) An extended warranty
(C) Complimentary installation
(D) Free samples

남자에 따르면, 이번 주에 특별히 제공되는 것은 무엇인가?

(A) 할인가
(B) 보증 기간 연장
(C) 무료 설치
(D) 무료 견본품들

어휘 extended 연장된 complimentary 무료의

해설 **세부 사항 관련 - 특별 제공 사항**

대화 마지막에 남자가 이번 주만 200달러가 넘는 제품을 주문하면 설치비가 무료(This week only, we're offering free installation on orders over two hundred dollars.)라고 했으므로 정답은 (C)이다.

▸▸ **Paraphrasing** 대화의 **free installation**
→ 정답의 **complimentary installation**

59-61

W-Br Excuse me. [59]**I'm doing a pantry renovation in my home,** and I have a question about your inventory.

M-Cn Certainly, ma'am. How can I help you?

W-Br Well, [60]**I was looking at the ceramic tile you offer, over on the shelves in the corner.** It doesn't seem like much. [60]**Do you really have just a few patterns to choose from?**

M-Cn We just had our big annual sale, so we are out of stock on a lot of goods at the moment. [61]**We'll be getting more in next week, so it would be better to stop by again then.** I'm sure you'd be able to find something that suits your needs.

여: 실례합니다. **제가 집에서 식료품 저장실을 개조하고 있는데,** 재고 문의 좀 하려고요.

남: 물론입니다, 부인. 어떻게 도와드릴까요?

여: 음, **제가 구석의 선반들 위쪽에 있는 세라믹 타일을 보고 있는데요.** 많지 않은 것 같네요. **고를 수 있는 문양이 정말 몇 가지밖에 없는 건가요?**

남: 대규모 연례 할인행사가 막 끝나서 현재 많은 물품이 재고가 없습니다. **다음 주에는 더 들어올 테니 그때 다시 들르시는 게 나을 겁니다.** 분명히 필요에 맞는 물건을 찾으실 수 있을 거예요.

어휘 pantry 식료품 저장실 renovation 개조, 보수 shelf 선반 seem like much 많아 보이다 pattern 문양, 무늬 choose from ~에서 고르다[택하다] annual sale 연례 할인행사 out of stock 재고가 없는 goods 물품, 제품 stop by 들르다, 방문하다 suit one's needs ~의 필요에 맞다

59

What project is the woman working on?

(A) Expanding a building
(B) Renovating a room
(C) Constructing a new house
(D) Decorating an office

여자는 어떤 작업을 하고 있는가?

(A) 건물 확장
(B) 공간 개조
(C) 새 집 건축
(D) 사무실 장식

해설 세부 사항 관련 - 작업의 종류

대화 첫 부분에서 여자가 집에서 식료품 저장실을 개조하고 있다(I'm doing a pantry renovation in my home)고 했으므로 정답은 (B)이다.

▸▸ **Paraphrasing** 대화의 a pantry renovation
→ 정답의 Renovating a room

60

What does the woman mean when she says, "It doesn't seem like much"?

(A) She is disappointed with the selection.
(B) She is unsure about the amount she needs.
(C) She thinks the prices are very affordable.
(D) She thought a process would take longer.

여자가 "많지 않은 것 같네요" 라고 말한 의도는 무엇인가?

(A) 상품 구색에 실망했다.
(B) 필요한 양이 확실하지 않다.
(C) 가격이 아주 적당하다고 생각한다.
(D) 공정이 더 오래 걸릴 것으로 생각했다.

어휘 disappointed 실망한

해설 화자의 의도 파악 - 많지 않은 것 같다는 말의 의미

인용문 앞 문장에서 여자가 구석의 선반들 위쪽에 있는 세라믹 타일을 보고 있다(I was looking at the ceramic tile you offer, over on the shelves in the corner.)고 했다. 그리고 인용문 뒤 문장에서 여자가 남자에게 고를 수 있는 타일 문양이 정말 몇 가지밖에 없는지(Do you really have just a few patterns to choose from?) 물어봤다. 이 두 문장을 통해 '많지 않은 것 같다(It doesn't seem like much.)'는 말의 의도는 타일에 대한 선택사항이 많지 않아 실망스럽다는 의미를 나타낸 것이므로 정답은 (A)이다.

61

What does the man recommend doing?

(A) Browsing in a different section
(B) Taking advantage of a sale
(C) Visiting an online store
(D) Coming back another day

남자는 무엇을 하라고 권하는가?

(A) 다른 섹션 살펴보기
(B) 할인 판매 활용하기
(C) 온라인 매장 방문하기
(D) 다른 날 다시 오기

해설 세부 사항 관련 - 남자의 권고 사항

대화 마지막에 남자가 여자에게 다음 주에는 물건이 더 들어올 테니 그때 다시 오는 게 낫다(We'll be getting more in next week, so it would be better to stop by again then.)고 했으므로 정답은 (D)이다.

▸▸ **Paraphrasing** 대화의 stop by again
→ 정답의 Coming back another day

62-64 대화 + 웹 페이지

M-Au Alicia, [62]**I saw you sitting down with Ms. Buchanan in the conference room just now.** How did it go?

W-Br It went very well. [62]**She likes how the Web site is looking so far and said she's glad she hired us to build it.**

M-Au Great! Did she request any changes?

W-Br A few. [63]**For example, on the "Create Account" page, she wants us to remove the "Country" menu entirely, and switch the positions of the "Username" and "Password" fields.**

M-Au Sure, that's easy.

W-Br Well, [64]**tomorrow we also need to make some tricky changes to the forum pages so that it's easier for users to respond to each other's posts and comments.** I'll e-mail you the details.

남: 앨리샤, **회의실에 뷰캐넌 씨와 함께 있는 걸 방금 봤는데요.** 어떻게 됐나요?

여: 아주 잘됐어요. **지금까지의 웹 사이트 모양새에 만족하고 있고요. 웹 사이트 구축하는 데 저희를 고용해서 기쁘다고 말씀하셨어요.**

남: 잘됐네요! 요구하신 변경사항이 있나요?

여: 조금요. **예를 들어 "계정 생성" 페이지에서 "국가" 메뉴를 완전히 삭제하고 "사용자명"과 "패스워드" 필드 위치를 바꿨으면 하십니다.**

남: 알겠습니다. 간단한 작업이네요.

여: 저, **내일은 사용자들이 서로의 게시물과 댓글에 응답하기 쉽도록 포럼 페이지를 수정하는 좀 어려운 작업도 해야 해요.** 자세한 내용은 이메일로 보내겠습니다.

어휘 conference room 회의실 so far 지금까지 hire 고용하다 build 구축하다 request 요청하다, 요구하다 for example 예를 들어 remove 삭제하다 entirely 완전히 switch 바꾸다 tricky 다루기 힘든, 교묘한 respond to ~에 응답하다 post 게시물 comment 댓글 detail 세부 사항

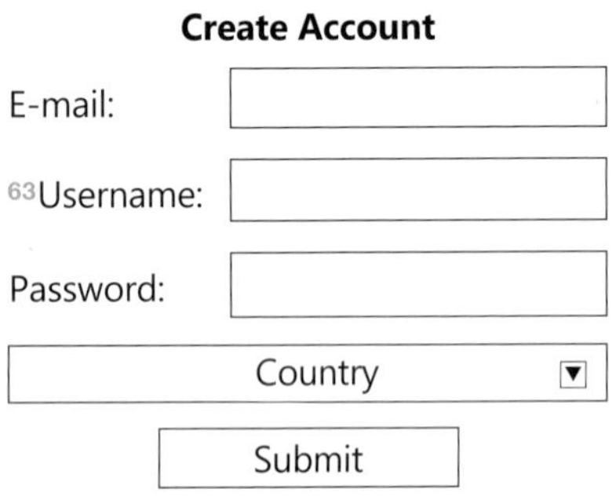

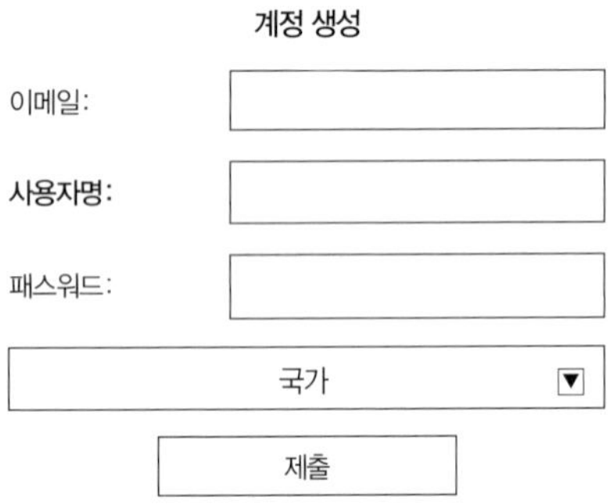

62

What was the woman doing earlier?

(A) Attending a client meeting
(B) Analyzing the results of a survey
(C) Watching a software demonstration
(D) Arranging a press conference

여자는 앞서 무엇을 하고 있었는가?

(A) 고객 회의 참석하기
(B) 설문조사 결과 분석하기
(C) 소프트웨어 시연 관람하기
(D) 기자회견 주선하기

어휘 attend 참석하다 client 고객 analyze 분석하다 survey 설문조사 demonstration 시연 arrange 마련하다, 주선하다 press conference 기자회견

해설 세부 사항 관련 – 여자가 하고 있던 일

남자의 첫 번째 대사에서 회의실에 뷰캐넌 씨와 함께 있는 걸 방금 봤다(I saw you sitting down with Ms. Buchanan in the conference room just now.)고 하였고 이에 대해 여자는 뷰캐넌 씨가 지금까지의 웹 사이트 모양새에 만족하고 있고 웹 사이트 구축하는 데 우리를 고용해서 기쁘다고 말씀하셨다(She likes how the Web site is looking so far and said she's glad she hired us to build it.)고 했다. 이로써 여자는 고객과 회의에 참석했다는 것을 알 수 있으므로 정답은 (A)이다.

63

Look at the graphic. Which field will appear above "Submit" after the requested change?

(A) E-mail
(B) Username
(C) Password
(D) Country

시각 정보에 의하면, 요청에 따른 변경 후 "제출" 위에 어떤 필드가 나타나겠는가?

(A) 이메일
(B) 사용자명
(C) 패스워드
(D) 국가

어휘 appear 나타나다

해설 시각 정보 연계 – 필드 위치 변경

여자의 두 번째 대사에서 "국가" 메뉴를 삭제하고 "사용자명"과 "패스워드"의 필드 위치를 바꿨으면 한다(For example, ~ she wants us to remove the "Country" menu entirely, and switch the positions of the "Username" and "Password" fields.)고 했다. 그러므로 표를 보면 "제출" 위에는 "사용자명"이 오게 되므로 정답은 (B)이다.

64

What most likely is the purpose of the Web site being designed?

(A) To provide a place for discussion
(B) To give travel directions
(C) To sell a company's merchandise
(D) To allow users to search the Internet

웹 사이트 디자인의 목적으로 가장 알맞은 것은?

(A) 토론의 장을 제공하기 위해
(B) 이동 방향을 알려 주기 위해
(C) 회사 상품을 판매하기 위해
(D) 사용자들이 인터넷 검색을 할 수 있도록 하기 위해

어휘 purpose 의도 discussion 토론 direction 방향 merchandise 상품 allow 허락하다 search 검색하다

해설 세부 사항 관련 – 웹 사이트 디자인

여자의 마지막 대사에서 내일은 웹 사이트 사용자들이 서로의 게시물과 댓글에 응답하기 쉽도록 포럼 페이지를 수정하는 좀 어려운 작업도 해야 한다(tomorrow we also need to make ~ each other's posts and comments.)고 하였으므로 정답은 (A)이다.

65-67 대화 + 가격표

W-Am Hello. I cracked my phone's screen, and [65]**since I'm going out of town on business next week**, I need to get it fixed quickly.

M-Au All right. I'll have to look at the phone to see if we have the right part for it in stock.

W-Am Here you are. The brand is Winona.

M-Au This is a very popular model, so we do have screens in stock. [66]**It'll be one hundred twenty-five dollars.**

W-Am OK. Do I just give you my home phone number so you can call me when it's ready?

M-Au Actually, we're not busy now, so you could just stop back in about an hour. But [67]**you'll have to pay for the work up front.**

여: 안녕하세요. 제 휴대폰 액정이 깨졌는데 **다음 주에 타지로 출장을 갈 예정이라** 빨리 수리를 맡겨야 해요.

남: 알겠습니다. 저희에게 알맞은 부품이 있는지 보려면 휴대폰을 살펴봐야 합니다.

여: 여기 있어요. 위노나 제품이에요.

남: 이건 아주 인기 있는 모델이라 저희에게 액정 재고가 있습니다. **가격은 125달러입니다.**

여: 좋아요. 휴대폰이 준비되면 제게 전화하실 수 있게 집 전화번호를 알려드리기만 하면 될까요?

남: 실은, 지금 저희가 바쁘지 않으니 1시간 정도 후에 다시 오시면 됩니다. 하지만 **작업에 대한 비용은 선불입니다.**

어휘 crack 금이 가(게 하)다, 깨(지)다 go out of town 타지로 나가다 on business 업무차 in stock 재고가 있는 up front 선불로

Screen Replacement:
Winona Phones

Model	Cost
8R	$140
7R	$135
[66]4L	$125
3L	$100

액정 교체:
위노나 휴대폰

모델	가격
8R	140달러
7R	135달러
4L	**125달러**
3L	100달러

65

What will the woman do next week?

(A) Upgrade a phone plan
(B) Move to another city
(C) Start a new job
(D) Go on a business trip

여자는 다음 주에 무엇을 할 것인가?

(A) 휴대폰 요금제 업그레이드
(B) 다른 도시로 이사하기
(C) 새로운 일 시작하기
(D) 출장 가기

해설 세부 사항 관련 – 여자의 다음 주 계획

대화 첫 부분에서 여자가 다음 주에 출장을 갈 예정(since I'm going out of town on business next week)이라고 했으므로 정답은 (D)이다.

▸▸ **Paraphrasing** 대화의 going out of town on business
→ 정답의 Go on a business trip

66

Look at the graphic. Which phone model does the woman have?

(A) 8R
(B) 7R
(C) 4L
(D) 3L

시각 정보에 따르면, 여자는 어떤 휴대폰 모델을 가지고 있는가?

(A) 8R
(B) 7R
(C) 4L
(D) 3L

해설 시각 정보 연계 – 휴대폰 모델

남자의 두 번째 대사에서 액정 가격이 125달러(It'll be one hundred twenty-five dollars.)라고 했다. 가격표를 보면 125달러에 해당하는 모델이 4L이므로 정답은 (C)이다.

67

What does the man ask the woman to do?

(A) Make a payment
(B) Provide a contact number
(C) Present a receipt
(D) Complete a form

남자는 여자에게 무엇을 하라고 요청하는가?

(A) 비용 지불하기
(B) 연락할 번호 제공하기
(C) 영수증 제시하기
(D) 양식 완성하기

어휘 present 제시하다 receipt 영수증 complete 완료하다

해설 세부 사항 관련 – 남자의 요청 사항

대화 맨 마지막에 남자가 여자에게 작업에 대한 비용을 선불로 지불해야 한다(you'll have to pay for the work up front.)고 했으므로 정답은 (A)이다.

▸▸ **Paraphrasing** 대화의 pay for the work
→ 정답의 Make a payment

68-70 대화 + 티켓

M-Cn I'm really looking forward to the Meadow City Orchestra concert this weekend. The online reviews have been fantastic.

W-Am Yeah, it'll be great. And it seems like we were lucky to get tickets. [68]**Some of the salespeople on the fourth floor tried to buy them yesterday, but there were none left.**

M-Cn That's too bad. I guess a lot of people are interested in the concert. [69]**Do you need me to pick you up on Sunday? I'll be driving.**

W-Am No, thanks. I'll just take the bus. But what time do you want to meet? Will two-thirty be too late?

M-Cn [70]**How about an hour before the show starts?** Then we can be sure to get good seats. I'll wait for you at the main entrance.

남: 이번 주말에 있을 메도우 시티 오케스트라의 연주회를 정말 고대하고 있어요. 인터넷에 올라온 감상평들이 아주 훌륭하거든요.

여: 네, 굉장한 연주회가 될 거예요. 입장권을 구하다니 우리가 운이 좋았던 것 같아요. **4층에 있는 영업부 직원 몇 명이 어제 표를 구하려고 했지만 남은 표가 없었대요.**

남: 안됐군요. 이 연주회에 많은 사람이 관심을 보이나 봐요. **일요일에 내가 데리러 갈까요? 차를 가지고 갈 거예요.**

여: 아뇨, 고맙지만 괜찮아요. 그냥 버스를 탈래요. 그런데 몇 시에 만날까요? 2시 30분은 너무 늦을까요?

남: **연주회가 시작되기 1시간 전쯤은 어때요?** 그러면 분명히 좋은 좌석을 차지할 수 있을 거예요. 정문에서 기다릴게요.

어휘 look forward to + (동)명사 ~을 고대하다 it seems like ~인 것 같다 be interested in ~에 관심이 있다 be sure to + 동사원형 확실히 ~하다 main entrance 정문

Powell Theater Presents

the Meadow City Orchestra

Sunday, June 18 at [70]3:00 P.M.

Admit One: General Seating

파월 극장 공연 안내

메도우 시티 오케스트라

6월 18일 일요일 오후 3시

1인 입장권: 일반 좌석

68

What does the woman say about the tickets?

(A) She purchased some online.
(B) They will be sent by mail.
(C) They are sold out now.
(D) Their price was raised.

여자는 입장권에 관해 뭐라고 말하는가?

(A) 그녀는 몇 장을 온라인으로 구입했다.
(B) 우편으로 발송될 것이다.
(C) 이제 매진되었다.
(D) 가격이 올랐다.

해설 세부 사항 관련 - 입장권에 대한 언급

여자의 첫 번째 대사에서 4층에 있는 영업부 직원 몇 명이 어제 표를 구하려고 했지만 남은 표가 없었다(Some of the salespeople on the fourth floor ~ there were none left.)고 했으므로 정답은 (C)이다.

▸▸ **Paraphrasing** 대화의 none left → 정답의 sold out

69

What does the man offer to do?

(A) Check a show's start time
(B) Call the woman when he arrives
(C) Buy some extra tickets
(D) Give the woman a ride

남자는 무엇을 하겠다고 제안하는가?

(A) 공연 시작 시간 확인하기
(B) 도착해서 여자에게 전화하기
(C) 추가로 입장권을 몇 장 더 사기
(D) 여자를 차에 태워 주기

해설 세부 사항 관련 - 남자의 제안 사항

남자의 두 번째 대사에서 남자가 여자에게 일요일에 차로 데리러 갈지(Do you need me to pick you up on Sunday? I'll be driving.) 제안을 했으므로 정답은 (D)이다.

▸▸ **Paraphrasing** 대화의 pick you up
→ 정답의 Give the woman a ride

70

Look at the graphic. When does the man want to meet on Sunday?

(A) At 1:30 P.M. (B) At 2:00 P.M.
(C) At 2:30 P.M. (D) At 3:00 P.M.

시각 정보에 따르면, 일요일에 남자가 만나기 원하는 때는 언제인가?

(A) 오후 1시 30분 **(B) 오후 2시**
(C) 오후 2시 30분 (D) 오후 3시

해설 시각 정보 연계 - 남자가 원하는 약속 시간

대화 맨 마지막에 남자가 여자에게 공연 시작 1시간 전쯤에 만나는 게 어떨지(How about an hour before the show starts?) 물어봤다. 그리고 입장권을 보면 공연 시작 시간이 오후 3시(3:00 P.M.)로 나와 있다. 따라서 남자는 2시에 만나고 싶어 하는 것이므로 정답은 (B)이다.

PART 4

71-73 회의 발췌

W-Am I'd like to wrap up this meeting with a comment about the status of our magazine. [71]**I've just finished an analysis of our circulation numbers**, and... um... there's definitely room for improvement. Over the next few months, [72]**my goal is to add at least ten percent more people to our subscription list**. One way to do this is by offering special discounts to the friends and family members of people who already read our magazine. [73]**I'm open to hearing your ideas about this as well,** so please e-mail them to me this week. Then [73]**we can discuss them at the next meeting**, which is scheduled for September eighth.

우리 잡지의 현황을 말씀드리며 이 회의를 마치려고 합니다. **제가 판매 부수에 관한 분석을 막 끝냈는데**… 음… 확실히 개선의 여지가 있습니다. 앞으로 몇 개월 동안 **저의 목표는 우리 구독자 명단의 인원수를 적어도 10퍼센트 늘리는 것입니다.** 이렇게 하는 한 가지 방법은 이미 우리 잡지를 읽고 있는 사람들의 친구와 가족들을 상대로 특별 할인을 제공하는 겁니다. **이에 관해 기꺼이 여러분의 생각도 들을 테니** 이번 주에 제게 이메일로 알려주시기 바랍니다. 그러면 9월 8일로 잡혀 있는 **다음 회의 때 우리가 논의할 수 있을 겁니다.**

어휘 wrap up 마무리하다, 매듭짓다 comment 언급, 논평 status 상황 analysis 분석 circulation number 판매부수 definitely 분명히, 확실히 there's room for ~할 여지가 있다 subscription list 구독자 명단 as well 역시, 또한 be scheduled for ~로 일정이 잡혀 있다

71

What has the speaker recently done?

(A) Evaluated staff members
(B) Run a marketing campaign
(C) Participated in a seminar
(D) Analyzed some figures

화자가 최근에 한 일은 무엇인가?

(A) 직원 평가
(B) 마케팅 캠페인 진행
(C) 세미나 참석
(D) 수치 분석

어휘 evaluate 평가하다 participate 참가하다 analyze분석하다

해설 세부 사항 관련 - 화자가 최근에 한 일

지문 초반부에 화자가 판매부수에 관한 분석을 막 끝냈다(I've just finished an analysis of our circulation numbers)고 했으므로 정답은 (D)이다.

▸▸ **Paraphrasing** 지문의 **circulation numbers**
→ 정답의 **some figures**

72

What does the speaker want to do?

(A) Launch a new product
(B) Monitor operating expenses
(C) Improve the magazine's layout
(D) Increase subscriptions

화자가 하고 싶어 하는 일은 무엇인가?

(A) 신제품 출시
(B) 운영비 모니터링
(C) 잡지 레이아웃 개선
(D) 구독자 늘리기

어휘 launch 출시하다, 시작하다 operating expenses 운영비

해설 세부 사항 관련 - 화자가 원하는 것

지문 중반부에 화자가 자신의 목표는 구독자 명단의 인원 수를 적어도 10% 늘리는 것(my goal is to add at least ten percent more people to our subscription list.)이라고 했으므로 정답은 (D)이다.

▸▸ **Paraphrasing** 지문의 **add** → 정답의 **Increase**

73

Why should the listeners e-mail the speaker?

(A) To share suggestions
(B) To get spending approval
(C) To confirm attendance
(D) To select a meeting time

청자들이 왜 화자에게 이메일을 보내야 하는가?

(A) 제안 사항을 공유하려고
(B) 지출 승인을 받으려고
(C) 출석을 확인하려고
(D) 회의 시간을 택하려고

해설 세부 사항 관련 - 청자들이 이메일을 보내야 하는 이유

지문 후반부에 화자가 청자들의 의견도 기꺼이 들을 것(I'm open to hearing your ideas about this as well)이라고 했다. 그리고 청자들의 아이디어들을 다음 회의 때 논의할 수 있다(we can discuss them at the next meeting)고 했다. 즉, 청자들의 제안 사항을 공유하려는 목적으로 이메일을 보내라고 한 것이므로 정답은 (A)이다.

▸▸ **Paraphrasing** 지문의 **ideas** → 정답의 **suggestions**

74-76 전화 메시지

M-Cn Hi, my name is Theo Schultz. I put in an order on your Web site a few days ago for a twenty-seven-inch computer monitor from Olaxi Company. The delivery arrived this morning as scheduled. But when I opened the package, [74]**I saw that there was a crack in the base.** I still really want this model, so [75]**I'd like to return this one and get a new one.** [76]**I'm not sure what I need to do to process an exchange, so could**

someone please call me back to tell me about it? My number is 555-0170. Thanks.

안녕하세요. 제 이름은 시오 셜츠입니다. 며칠 전 귀사의 웹 사이트에서 올랙시 컴퍼니의 27인치짜리 컴퓨터 모니터를 주문했습니다. 배송품은 예정대로 오늘 아침에 도착했고요. 하시만 포장을 열어보니 **밑부분에 금이 간 게 보였습니다.** 그래도 정말 이 모델을 갖고 싶어서 **이것을 반품하고 새것을 받고 싶습니다. 교환 절차를 밟기 위해 무엇을 해야 하는지 잘 모르니 제게 전화해서 알려 주시겠습니까?** 제 번호는 555-0170입니다. 감사합니다.

어휘 put in an order for ~을 주문하다 as scheduled 예정대로, 일정대로 open a package 포장을 열어보다 crack 금 process an exchange 교환 절차를 진행하다

74

What problem does the speaker mention?

(A) A shipment arrived late.
(B) Some items were the wrong model.
(C) A Web site is not working.
(D) Some merchandise was damaged.

화자는 무슨 문제를 언급하는가?

(A) 배송품이 늦게 도착했다.
(B) 일부 물품들의 모델이 잘못되었다.
(C) 웹 사이트가 작동하지 않는다.
(D) 어떤 상품이 손상되었다.

해설 세부 사항 관련 - 화자가 언급하는 문제점

지문 중반부에서 화자가 밑부분에 금이 간 게 보였다(I saw that there was a crack in the base.)고 했으므로 정답은 (D)이다.

▸▸ Paraphrasing 지문의 **there was a crack**
→ 정답의 **Some merchandise was damaged.**

75

What does the speaker want to do?

(A) Use a coupon
(B) Cancel an order
(C) Get a replacement
(D) Receive a refund

화자가 하고 싶어 하는 일은 무엇인가?

(A) 쿠폰 사용
(B) 주문 취소
(C) 물품 교환
(D) 환불 받기

해설 세부 사항 관련 - 화자의 희망 사항

지문 중반부에서 화자가 물건을 반품하고 새것을 받고 싶다(I'd like to return this one and get a new one.)고 했으므로 정답은 (C)이다.

▸▸ Paraphrasing 지문의 **get a new one**
→ 정답의 **Get a replacement**

76

Why should the listener call the speaker back?

(A) To arrange a delivery
(B) To provide an estimate
(C) To explain a process
(D) To issue a code

청자가 화자에게 다시 전화해야 하는 이유는?

(A) 배송 주선
(B) 견적 제공
(C) 절차 설명
(D) 암호 발행

해설 세부 사항 관련 - 청자가 전화해야 하는 이유

지문 후반부에 화자가 청자에게 반납 절차에 대해 잘 모르니 전화해서 알려 달라(I'm not sure ~ call me back to tell me about it?)고 했으므로 정답은 (C)이다.

▸▸ Paraphrasing 지문의 **tell me about it**
→ 정답의 **explain a process**

77-79 공지

W-Br I have a brief announcement, everyone. [77]**The K-88 smartphone from Keyata Tech hits the market tomorrow. We are one of just three stores in the country that will be carrying it,** so it's a big deal for us. The assistant manager and I are expecting a lot of customers throughout the day. [78]**I've spoken with Debra Lansing from the *Waynesville Times*, and she'll be here to cover the event.** She may even wish to interview some of you. Please double-check the schedule —as we're opening an hour early, your shift may be different from usual. And to show my appreciation for all of your hard work, [79]**I'll be bringing in coffee and doughnuts tomorrow.**

간단히 공지하겠습니다, 여러분. **케야타 테크에서 나온 K-88 스마트폰이 내일 시장에 출시됩니다. 우리는 그것을 취급하게 될 전국에 3개밖에 없는 매장 중 하나이며,** 따라서 우리에게는 아주 중요한 일입니다. 부점장과 나는 하루 종일 많은 고객들이 찾을 것으로 예상하고 있습니다. 내가 **〈웨인스빌 타임스〉 지의 데브라 랜싱 기자에게 이야기했으니 그녀가 행사를 취재하러 이곳에 올 겁니다.** 그녀는 여러분 중 몇 명과 인터뷰를 하고 싶어 할지도 모릅니다. 우리가 1시간 일찍 문을 열고 근무조가 평소와 다를 수 있으니 시간표를 재차 확인해 주세요. 그리고 여러분 모두의 노고에 감사를 표하기 위해 **내일 내가 커피와 도넛을 가져오겠습니다.**

어휘 have a brief announcement 간단히 공지하다 hit the market 출시되다 carry 취급하다 assistant manager 부점장, 대리 throughout the day 하루 종일 cover 취재하다 double-check 재차 확인하다 shift 교대 근무조 show one's appreciation 감사를 표하다

77
According to the speaker, what will happen tomorrow?
(A) An inspection will take place.
(B) A branch will have a grand opening.
(C) The store will stay open late.
(D) A new product will be released.

화자에 따르면, 내일 어떤 일이 있을 예정인가?
(A) 점검이 이루어진다.
(B) 지점이 개장한다.
(C) 가게를 늦게까지 연다.
(D) 신제품이 출시된다.

어휘 inspection 점검 take place 일어나다, 발생하다 branch 지점 release 출시하다

해설 세부 사항 관련 – 내일 발생할 일
지문 초반부에서 화자가 케야타 테크에서 나온 K-88 스마트폰이 내일 시장에 출시되는데 화자의 매장이 그것을 취급하게 될 전국 3개 매장 중 하나(The K-88 smartphone from Keyata Tech ~ that will be carrying it)라고 했다. 즉, 내일 신제품이 출시될 예정이므로 정답은 (D)이다.

78
Who most likely is Ms. Lansing?
(A) An inventor
(B) An assistant manager
(C) A journalist
(D) A business owner

랜싱 씨는 누구이겠는가?
(A) 발명가
(B) 부점장
(C) 기자
(D) 업주

해설 전체 내용 관련 – 데브라 랜싱의 신분
지문 중반부에서 화자가 〈웨인스빌 타임스〉 지의 데브라 랜싱 기자에게 이야기했으니 그녀가 행사를 취재하러 이곳에 올 것(I've spoken with Debra Lansing ~ here to cover the event.)이라고 했다. 이를 통해 데브라 랜싱이 기자라는 것을 알 수 있으므로 정답은 (C)이다.

79
What does the speaker say she will do?
(A) Provide some refreshments
(B) Confirm a work schedule
(C) Make copies of a manual
(D) Get feedback from customers

화자는 무엇을 할 것이라고 말하는가?
(A) 다과 제공
(B) 작업 일정 확인
(C) 사용설명서 복사
(D) 고객 의견 수렴

해설 세부 사항 관련 – 화자가 앞으로 할 일
지문 마지막에서 화자가 내일 커피와 도넛을 가져오겠다(I'll be bringing in coffee and doughnuts tomorrow.)고 했으므로 정답은 (A)이다.

▸▸ **Paraphrasing** 지문의 **coffee and doughnuts**
→ 정답의 **some refreshments**

80-82 방송

W-Br Welcome back to *Magic Moments*. I'm your host, Connie Gibson. [80]**Today on the show, I'm teaching you how to bake a delicious cake right in your own kitchen.** It's perfect for special occasions or just as a tasty dessert to surprise your family. And all of the ingredients are easy to find. I'm also pleased to announce that next week we'll be adding a new section to our Web site. [81]**There you will find step-by-step recipes for everything we talk about on the show.** And don't forget that [82]**our listeners can share their opinions and ideas on our "Listeners' Voices" page.** Be a part of it. There's no better way to let us know what you think.

〈매직 모먼츠〉를 다시 찾아 주신 여러분 환영합니다. 저는 진행을 맡은 코니 깁슨입니다. **오늘 쇼에서는 바로 여러분의 부엌에서 맛있는 케이크를 굽는 법을 알려드리겠습니다.** 특별한 경우를 위해서나 단순히 가족에게 놀라움을 선사할 맛있는 디저트로 딱 좋습니다. 게다가 재료가 모두 찾기 쉬운 것들입니다. 저는 또한 다음 주에 저희 웹 사이트에 새로운 섹션이 추가될 예정이라는 것을 알려드리게 되어 기쁩니다. **저희가 쇼에서 말씀드리는 모든 음식의 단계별 조리법들을 그곳에서 찾아보실 수 있습니다.** 그리고 **청취자 분들은 저희 "청취자의 목소리" 페이지에서 의견과 아이디어를 나눌 수 있다**는 사실을 잊지 마세요. **동참해 주시기 바랍니다.** 저희에게 여러분의 생각을 알릴 수 있는 가장 좋은 방법입니다.

어휘 welcome back to ~에 다시 온 걸 환영하다 bake 굽다 delicious 맛있는(= tasty) special occasion 특별한 경우[때] ingredient 재료, 성분 announce 발표하다, 공표하다 add A to B B에 A를 더하다 step-by-step 단계별 recipe 조리법 Be a part of it. 동참[참여]해 주세요. There's no better way to + 동사원형 ~하는 가장 좋은 방법이다

80
What is the broadcast mainly about?
(A) Shopping tips
(B) Party planning
(C) Home baking
(D) Cleaning techniques

방송은 주로 무엇에 관한 내용인가?
(A) 쇼핑 정보
(B) 파티 기획
(C) 가정식 제빵
(D) 청소 기술

해설 전체 내용 관련 - 방송 내용

지문 초반부에 화자가 오늘 쇼에서는 바로 청취자들의 부엌에서 맛있는 케이크를 굽는 방법을 알려주겠다(Today on the show, I'm teaching you how to bake a delicious cake right in your own kitchen.)고 했으므로 정답은 (C)이다.

81

According to the speaker, what will be posted on the Web site from next week?

(A) Previous broadcasts
(B) Discount offers
(C) Detailed instructions
(D) Photo collections

화자에 따르면, 다음 주부터 웹 사이트에 올라갈 내용은 무엇인가?

(A) 예전 방송분
(B) 할인 제안
(C) 자세한 설명
(D) 사진 모음

어휘 previous 이전의 broadcast 방송; 방송하다

해설 세부 사항 관련 - 웹 사이트 게시 사항

지문 중반부에서 화자가 웹 사이트에 새로운 섹션이 추가될 것이라고 했다. 그리고 그 섹션에서 쇼에서 다루는 모든 음식의 단계별 조리법들을 찾아볼 수 있다(There you will find step-by-step recipes for everything we talk about on the show.)고 했으므로 정답은 (C)이다.

▸▸ Paraphrasing 지문의 step-by-step recipes
→ 정답의 Detailed instructions

82

Why does the speaker say, "Be a part of it"?

(A) To encourage the listeners to give feedback
(B) To give a preview of the next show
(C) To promote a special event
(D) To urge the listeners to apply for a job opening

화자가 "동참해 주시기 바랍니다"라고 말한 이유는 무엇인가?

(A) 청취자들의 의견 개진을 장려하려고
(B) 다음 쇼의 내용을 예고하려고
(C) 특별 행사를 홍보하려고
(D) 청취자들이 일자리에 지원하도록 권고하려고

어휘 encourage 장려하다 preview 예고, 미리 보기 promote 홍보하다 urge 촉구하다 apply for ~에 지원하다

해설 화자의 의도 파악 - 동참해 달라고 말한 이유

인용문 바로 앞 문장에서 청취자들이 "청취자의 목소리" 페이지에서 서로 의견과 아이디어를 나눈다(our listeners can share their opinions and ideas on our "Listeners' Voices" page)라고 했다. 그런 다음 동참해 달라(Be a part of it.)고 했는데 문맥상 청취자들의 의견 개진을 권장하기 위한 것이므로 정답은 (A)이다.

83-85 연설

M-Au Good evening, ladies and gentlemen, and thank you for being here. [83]**We decided to hold this banquet to highlight the fine work of one of our employees, Stanley Kott.** [84]**Mr. Kott has been working in our laboratory for the past five years**, and he has recently been nominated for the prestigious Bozeman Science Award. This is quite an honor, and we're very proud of him. I'll invite Mr. Kott to say a few words in a moment. And don't forget that [85]**we'll be taking a group photo after the meal. Please stick around so you can be in that.**

안녕하십니까, 신사 숙녀 여러분. 이 자리에 와 주셔서 감사합니다. **우리는 우리 직원 중 한 명인 스탠리 콧의 훌륭한 성과를 집중 조명하기 위해 이 연회를 베풀기로 했습니다. 콧 씨는 지난 5년 동안 우리 연구실에 근무하고 있으며,** 최근에 권위 있는 보즈먼 과학상의 후보에 올랐습니다. 이는 커다란 영광이며 우리는 그가 매우 자랑스럽습니다. 콧 씨를 모셔서 잠시 몇 말씀 듣도록 하겠습니다. 그리고 **식사 후에 단체사진을 찍을 예정이니** 잊지 마시기 바랍니다. **가지 마시고 촬영에 함께해 주시기를 부탁드립니다.**

어휘 hold a banquet 연회를 베풀다 highlight 집중 조명하다, 강조하다 laboratory 연구실 recently 최근에 be nominated for ~의 후보가 되다 prestigious 권위 있는, 명망 있는 honor 영광 be proud of ~을 자랑스러워하다 take a group photo 단체사진을 찍다 stick around 가지 않고 머물다

83

What is the purpose of the event?

(A) To recognize an employee's achievement
(B) To celebrate a company anniversary
(C) To show appreciation for a retiring executive
(D) To publicize a business expansion

행사의 목적은 무엇인가?

(A) 한 직원의 성취를 표창하려고
(B) 회사 창립 기념일을 축하하려고
(C) 은퇴하는 임원에게 감사를 표하려고
(D) 사업 확장을 알리려고

어휘 recognize 표창하다, 인정하다 achievement 성취 appreciation 감사 executive 임원 publicize 공표하다

해설 전체 내용 관련 - 행사의 목적

지문 초반부에 화자가 직원 중 한 명인 스탠리 콧의 훌륭한 성과를 집중 조명하기 위해 이 연회를 베풀기로 했다(We decided to hold this banquet to highlight the fine work of one of our employees, Stanley Kott.)고 했으므로 정답은 (A)이다.

▸▸ Paraphrasing 지문의 fine work → 정답의 achievement

84
Who most likely is Mr. Kott?
(A) A lab employee
(B) A company president
(C) A salesperson
(D) A financial consultant

콧 씨는 누구이겠는가?
(A) 실험실 직원
(B) 회사 사장
(C) 영업 사원
(D) 금융 컨설턴트

해설 전체 내용 관련 - 콧 씨의 신분
지문 초반부에 콧 씨는 지난 5년 동안 연구실에서 근무했다(Mr. Kott has been working in our laboratory for the past five years)고 했으므로 정답은 (A)이다.

85
What does the speaker remind listeners to do?
(A) Indicate a meal preference
(B) Sign a greeting card
(C) Have their picture taken
(D) Review some information

화자는 청자들에게 무엇을 하라고 상기시키는가?
(A) 선호 식단 명시
(B) 인사장에 인사말 쓰기
(C) 사진 촬영
(D) 정보 검토

어휘 indicate 나타내다 preference 선호(도)

해설 세부 사항 관련 - 화자가 상기시키는 내용
지문 마지막에서 화자가 청자들에게 식사 후에 단체사진을 찍을 예정이니 가지 말고 함께 촬영해 주길 바란다(we'll be taking a group photo after the meal. So please stick around so you can be in that.)고 했으므로 정답은 (C)이다.

▸▸ Paraphrasing 지문의 photo → 정답의 picture

86-88 전화 메세지

M-Cn Hi, Sandy. It's Donald. 86**I just opened the attachment on the e-mail you sent, the one with our ad that's scheduled to appear in *Home Space Magazine*.** I'm looking at the file now, but... um... is this really it? 87**It seems that some of the images are not the right size, and the color needs to be adjusted as well.** It just doesn't look professional in its current state. So, 88**I'm afraid I'm going to need you to work overtime this evening to fix these problems.** I'll e-mail you some detailed notes.

안녕하세요, 샌디. 도널드입니다. **당신이 보낸 이메일에 첨부된 파일, 그러니까 〈홈 스페이스 매거진〉에 실릴 예정인 광고가 들어 있는 파일을 방금 열어 봤어요.** 지금 그 파일을 살펴보고 있는데… 음…. **이게 정말 그건가요? 사진 중 몇 장이 정확한 크기가 아니고 색상도 조정할 필요가 있어 보이는데요. 현재 상태로는 전문가의 솜씨로 보이지가 않아요.** 그래서 말인데, **오늘 저녁에 당신이 시간 외 근무를 해서라도 이 문제를 해결해야 할 것 같아요.** 내가 자세한 내용을 이메일로 보낼게요.

어휘 attachment 첨부 파일 be scheduled to + 동사원형 ~할 예정이다 adjust 조정하다 as well ~도, ~역시 professional 전문가의 솜씨로 보이는 current state 현재 상태 work overtime 시간 외 근무를 하다 fix 해결하다, 고치다 detailed 자세한, 상세한

86
What did the listener send the speaker?
(A) A questionnaire
(B) A magazine article
(C) A budget report
(D) An advertisement

청자가 화자에게 보낸 것은 무엇인가?
(A) 설문지
(B) 잡지 기사
(C) 예산 보고서
(D) 광고

해설 세부 사항 관련 - 청자가 보낸 자료
지문 초반부에 화자가 청자가 보낸 이메일에 첨부된 파일, 즉 〈홈 스페이스 매거진〉에 실릴 광고를 방금 열어 봤다(I just opened the attachment ~ in Home Space Magazine.)고 했으므로 정답은 (D)이다.

87
What does the speaker imply when he says, "is this really it"?
(A) He thinks some information is missing.
(B) He is not pleased with a quality level.
(C) He cannot find the file he needs.
(D) He is surprised by a quick response.

화자가 "이게 정말 그건가요?"라고 말한 의도는 무엇인가?
(A) 그가 볼 때 일부 정보가 빠졌다.
(B) 품질 수준이 만족스럽지 않다.
(C) 필요한 파일을 찾을 수 없다.
(D) 답장이 빨리 와서 놀랍다.

해설 화자의 의도 파악 - 맞는 파일인지를 물어본 이유
인용문 바로 뒤 문장에서 화자는 사진 몇 장이 정확한 크기가 아니고 색상도 조정할 필요가 있어 보인다(It seems that some of the images ~ needs to be adjusted as well.)고 했다. 즉, '이게 정말 그건가요?'라는 인용문은 청자가 보낸 파일에 대한 불만을 나타낸 것이므로 정답은 (B)이다.

88

What does the speaker ask the listener to do?

(A) Come to his desk
(B) Hire a professional
(C) E-mail some notes
(D) Work extra hours

화자는 청자에게 무엇을 하라고 요청하는가?

(A) 그의 책상으로 올 것
(B) 전문가를 고용할 것
(C) 내용을 이메일로 보낼 것
(D) 연장 근무를 할 것

해설 세부 사항 관련 - 청자에게 요청하는 것

지문 마지막에 화자가 청자에게 오늘 저녁에 시간 외 근무를 해서라도 문제를 해결해야 할 것 같다(I'm afraid I'm going to need you to work overtime this evening to fix these problems.)고 했으므로 정답은 (D)이다.

▸▸ **Paraphrasing** 지문의 **work overtime**
→ 정답의 **work extra hours**

89-91 뉴스 보도

M-Au In local news, a new service at Bartner Grocery Store is unpopular with some Polkes Lake residents. [89]**The store replaced two of its checkout lanes with four self-checkout kiosks.** Customers who use the kiosks scan their own purchases and handle payment themselves. [90]**Robin Howell, Bartner's vice president of marketing, wrote in a press release that the machines will allow customers to spend less time in checkout lines.** However, some customers who have used them say they actually slow down the checkout process. [91]**In their online group opposing the change, these customers say they intend to buy their groceries at other stores unless the kiosks are removed.** Bartner did not grant our request for comment.

바트너 식료품점의 새 서비스가 폴크스 레이크 일부 주민들에게 호응을 얻지 못하고 있다는 지역 소식입니다. **바트너 식료품점은 계산대 줄 두 곳을 네 대의 셀프 계산 단말기로 교체했습니다.** 셀프 계산 단말기를 이용하는 고객은 자신이 구입한 제품을 스캔하고 지불도 직접 합니다. **바트너 식료품점의 마케팅 부사장인 로빈 하월 씨는 보도 자료를 통해 셀프 계산 단말기는 소비자들이 계산 줄에서 기다리는 시간을 줄여 줄 것이라고 밝혔습니다.** 그러나 이를 이용한 일부 고객은 사실상 계산 절차가 더 느리다고 말합니다. **변경사항에 반대하는 온라인 모임에서 이 소비자들은 셀프 계산 단말기를 없애지 않으면 다른 매장에서 식료품을 구매하겠다고 말합니다.** 바트너는 입장을 표명하라는 요청을 수락하지 않았습니다.

어휘 local 지역의 grocery 식료품 unpopular 인기가 없는 resident 거주자, 주민 replace 교체하다 kiosk (무인 거래가 가능한) 단말기 purchase 구입한 것, 구입 handle 처리하다, 다루다 vice president 부사장 press release 보도 자료 process 과정, 절차 oppose 반대하다 intend to + 동사원형 ~할 작정이다 remove 제거하다 grant 승인하다, 허락하다

89

What is the main topic of the broadcast?

(A) A mobile app
(B) Self-service machines
(C) A city regulation
(D) Bicycle lanes

방송의 주제는 무엇인가?

(A) 모바일 앱
(B) 셀프 서비스 기계
(C) 시의 규제
(D) 자전거 전용도로

어휘 regulation 규정, 규제 lane 길, 도로

해설 전체 내용 관련 - 방송의 주제를 묻는 질문

지문의 두 번째 문장에서 바트너 식료품점이 계산대 줄 두 곳을 네 대의 셀프 계산 단말기로 교체했다(The store replaced two of its checkout lanes with four self-checkout kiosks)고 하면서 이와 관련된 내용이 있으므로 정답은 (B)이다.

90

According to Ms. Howell, why was a change made?

(A) To reduce some expenses
(B) To impress the organizers of an event
(C) To improve an area's air quality
(D) To shorten some wait times

하월 씨에 따르면, 변화를 꾀한 이유는?

(A) 비용을 절감하기 위해
(B) 행사 주최 측에게 감동을 주기 위해
(C) 지역 내 공기 질을 향상시키기 위해
(D) 대기 시간을 줄이기 위해

어휘 reduce 감소시키다, 줄이다 expense 비용 impress 감동을 주다 organizer 주최자 improve 향상시키다 shorten 짧게 하다

해설 세부 사항 관련 - 변화를 준 이유

지문 중반부에서 바트너 식료품점의 마케팅 부사장인 로빈 하월 씨가 보도 자료를 통해 셀프 계산 단말기는 소비자들이 계산대 줄에서 기다리는 시간을 줄여 줄 것이라고 밝혔다(Robin Howell, Bartner's vice president ~ to spend less time in checkout lines.)고 했으므로 정답은 (D)이다.

91

How are some people responding to the change?

(A) They are buying more locally-made goods.
(B) They are asking others to sign an agreement.
(C) They have fulfilled some safety requirements.
(D) They plan to stop visiting a business.

일부 사람들은 변화에 대해 어떤 반응을 보이는가?

(A) 지역 생산품을 더 많이 사고 있다.
(B) 다른 사람들에게 합의서 체결을 요청하고 있다.
(C) 안전 요건을 충족했다.
(D) 매장을 앞으로 방문하지 않을 계획이다.

어휘 locally-made goods 지역 생산품 sign an agreement 합의서를 체결하다 fulfill 충족하다 safety requirement 안전 요건

해설 세부 사항 관련 – 변화에 대한 일부 사람들의 반응

후반부에서 계산대 변경사항에 반대하는 온라인 단체의 소비자들이 셀프 계산 단말기를 없애지 않으면 다른 매장에서 식료품을 구매하겠다(In their online group opposing the change, ~ unless the kiosks are removed.)고 했으므로 정답은 (D)이다.

▸▸ **Paraphrasing** 지문의 **intend to buy their groceries at other stores**
→ 정답의 **plan to stop visiting a business**

92-94 전화 메시지

W-Am Hi, Hyun-Soo. [92]**I'm looking over the proposal you made for our participation in the Boston Web Design Expo.** For the most part, it's great. I like your idea of displaying two similar photographs of our office in the exhibition booth and giving prizes to visitors who find the differences between them. [93]**But about the plan to use company logo T-shirts as prizes... When we tried giving them away last year,** a lot of them were left over afterwards. So I was thinking... [94]**I have a booklet from Johnston Promotional Supplies that has some really interesting products. Would you like me to put it in your inbox?**

안녕하세요, 현수 씨. **보스턴 웹 디자인 엑스포 참가를 위해 작성하신 제안서를 살펴보고 있는데요. 대부분 훌륭합니다.** 전시 부스에 비슷한 사무실 사진 두 장을 게시하고 차이점을 찾아내는 방문객에게 경품을 주자는 아이디어가 좋습니다. **하지만 회사 로고 티셔츠를 경품으로 사용하자는 계획 말인데요. 작년에 선물로 나눠주려고 했는데** 나중에 수량이 많이 남았어요. 그래서 제 생각엔… **저에게 존스턴 홍보용품 책자가 있는데 정말 재미있는 제품들이 있더라고요. 제가 우편함에 넣어드릴까요?**

어휘 look over 살펴보다 proposal 제안서, 제안 participation 참가 similar 비슷한 exhibition 전시 difference 차이점 give away 선물로 주다 be left over 남다 afterwards 나중에 booklet 소책자 promotional supplies 홍보용품 inbox 우편 수신함, 받은 편지함

92

What is the speaker calling about?

(A) A Web development project
(B) An upcoming trade show
(C) Office supplies spending
(D) Participation in a photo shoot

화자는 무엇에 관해 전화를 걸고 있는가?

(A) 웹 개발 프로젝트
(B) 다가오는 무역 박람회
(C) 사무용품 지출
(D) 사진 촬영 참여

어휘 development 개발 upcoming 다가오는 trade show 무역박람회 office supplies 사무용품

해설 세부 사항 관련 – 전화 메시지의 내용

지문 초반부에서 화자는 보스턴 웹 디자인 엑스포 참가를 위해 청자가 작성한 제안서를 살펴보고 있다(I'm looking over the proposal you made for our participation in the Boston Web Design Expo.)고 했으므로 정답은 (B)이다.

93

What does the speaker imply when she says, "a lot of them were left over afterwards"?

(A) The listener can obtain some equipment for free.
(B) She requires assistance with a task.
(C) A storage space is full.
(D) A proposal should be revised.

화자가 "나중에 수량이 많이 남았어요"라고 말한 의도는 무엇인가?

(A) 청자는 장비를 무료로 얻을 수 있다.
(B) 업무에 관해 도움이 필요하다.
(C) 보관 장소가 꽉 찼다.
(D) 제안서를 수정해야 한다.

어휘 obtain 얻다 assistance 도움 storage 보관 revise 수정하다, 개정하다

해설 화자의 의도 파악 – 수량이 아직 남았다고 말한 의도

지문 중반부에서 화자는 회사 로고 티셔츠를 경품으로 사용하자는 계획에 대해 작년에 선물로 나눠줬는데 나중에 수량이 많이 남았다(But about the plan ~ a lot of them were left over afterwards.)고 했다. 인용문은 화자가 제안서를 수정해야 한다는 의도를 드러낸 것이므로 정답은 (D)이다.

94

What does the speaker offer to send the listener?

(A) Some financial data
(B) A catalog
(C) An access code
(D) Some product accessories

화자는 청자에게 무엇을 보내겠다고 말하는가?

(A) 재무 자료
(B) 카탈로그
(C) 접속 코드
(D) 제품 액세서리

어휘 financial 금융의, 재무의 access 접속

해설 세부 사항 관련 - 화자가 청자에게 보낼 것

지문 후반부에서 화자가 존스턴 홍보용품 책자가 있는데 정말 재미있는 제품들이 있으므로 이것을 우편함에 넣어드리겠다(I have a booklet from Johnston Promotional Supplies ~ in your inbox?)고 제안하였으므로 정답은 (B)이다.

▸▸ **Paraphrasing** 지문의 **booklet** → 정답의 **catalog**

95-97 회의 발췌 + 일정표

W-Am Good morning, and thank you all for agreeing to take part in our community center's writing competition. [95]**We need experts like you to identify the best entries and decide who should be the winner.** In session 1, you'll review the entries individually. There are a lot of submissions to cover, so [96]**it's important to take detailed notes so you'll be able to refer to them later.** In session 2, there will be a discussion to narrow down the entries. Then you'll review them again in session 3. The final decision will be made in session 4. [97]**The director of the community center, Joan Miller, will join you for the fourth session to hear your opinions.** Let's get started.

안녕하십니까. 저희 주민 센터의 글짓기 경연대회에 참석하기로 해 주셔서 감사합니다. **저희는 가장 뛰어난 참가작들을 가려내고 누가 우승자가 되어야 할지 결정하기 위해 여러분 같은 전문가들이 필요합니다.** 1부에서는 참가작들을 개별적으로 검토하시게 됩니다. 다뤄야 할 출품작이 많으므로 **나중에 참조하실 수 있도록 자세히 기록해 두시는 것이 중요합니다.** 2부에서는 참가작들의 범위를 좁히기 위해 토론을 벌일 예정입니다. 그런 다음 3부에서 참가작들을 다시 검토하게 됩니다. 최종 결정은 4부에서 내려질 것입니다. **4부에서는 조운 밀러 주민 센터장이 여러분의 의견을 듣기 위해 함께하실 겁니다.** 시작하시죠.

어휘 take part in ~에 참석[참가]하다 community center 주민 센터 writing competition 글짓기 경연대회 expert 전문가 identify 식별하다, 확인하다 entry 참가작, 참가자 session (특정 활동을 위한) 시간 submission 출품작 take detailed notes 자세히 기록하다 refer to ~을 참조하다 narrow down 범위를 좁히다 join 합류하다 get started 시작하다

Schedule	
8:00 A.M.	Session 1
9:00 A.M.	Session 2
10:00 A.M.	Session 3
[97]11:00 A.M.	Session 4

일정	
오전 8시	1부
오전 9시	2부
오전 10시	3부
오전 11시	4부

95

Who most likely are the listeners?

(A) Conference presenters
(B) Lecture attendees
(C) Contest judges
(D) Workshop participants

청자들은 누구일 것 같은가?

(A) 회의 발표자들
(B) 강의 참석자들
(C) 대회 심사위원들
(D) 워크숍 참가자들

어휘 lecture 강의 judge 심사위원 participant 참가자

해설 전체 내용 관련 - 청자의 신분

지문 초반부에 화자가 청자들에게 가장 뛰어난 참가작들을 가려내고 누가 우승자가 되어야 할지 결정하기 위해 여러분과 같은 전문가들이 필요하다(We need experts like you ~ who should be the winner.)고 했다. 이를 통해 청자들이 대회 심사위원임을 알 수 있으므로 정답은 (C)이다.

96

What does the speaker say is especially important?

(A) Asking questions
(B) Following guidelines
(C) Using teamwork
(D) Taking notes

화자는 무엇이 특히 중요하다고 말하는가?
(A) 질문하기
(B) 지침에 따르기
(C) 팀워크 활용
(D) 기록하기

해설 세부 사항 관련 - 화자가 언급한 중요 사항
지문 중반부에 화자가 청자들에게 나중에 참조할 수 있도록 자세히 기록해 두는 것이 중요하다(it's important to take detailed notes so you'll be able to refer to them later.)고 했으므로 정답은 (D)이다.

97

Look at the graphic. When will the listeners speak to Ms. Miller?
(A) At 8:00 A.M.
(B) At 9:00 A.M.
(C) At 10:00 A.M.
(D) At 11:00 A.M.

시각 정보에 따르면, 청자들이 언제 밀러 씨에게 말하게 되는가?
(A) 오전 8시
(B) 오전 9시
(C) 오전 10시
(D) 오전 11시

해설 시각 정보 연계 - 청자들이 말하는 시간
지문 후반부에 화자가 4부에서는 조운 밀러 주민 센터장이 청자들의 의견을 듣기 위해 함께할 것(The director of the community center, Joan Miller, will join you for the fourth session to hear your opinions.)이라고 했다. 그리고 일정표를 보면 4부는 11시에 시작되므로 정답은 (D)이다.

98-100 담화 + 지도

M-Cn Good morning, everyone, and welcome to Rinaldi National Park. I'm Thomas, your guide. [98]**I know you were supposed to be organized as two private hikes, but I'm afraid we had to combine you because one of our guides is sick.** I'm very sorry about this, but I do have some good news. To show our appreciation for your understanding, we're going to visit an extra site. [99]**Usually this hike only covers Forest Trail, but we'll be taking the Wilderness Trail today as well.** Now, you'll see a lot of beautiful plants throughout the hike, but [100]**you shouldn't touch them. Some of them are harmful to people.** This rule is for your safety.

안녕하세요, 여러분. 리날디 국립공원에 오신 것을 환영합니다. 저는 여러분을 안내할 토머스입니다. **여러분이 두 개의 개별 등산팀으로 꾸려져야 한다는 것을 알고 있지만, 안내원 중 한 명이 몸이 아파서 유감이지만 여러분을 한 데 합쳐야만 했습니다.** 이 점이 매우 유감스럽지만 제게 좋은 소식이 있습니다. 여러분이 양해해 주신 데 감사하기 위해 추가로 한 곳을 더 방문할 예정입니다. **평소 이 등산 여행에는 포레스트 트레일만 포함되지만, 오늘은 윌더니스 트레일로도 가게 될 겁니다.** 자, 이제 여러분은 등산을 하는 동안 아름다운 식물들을 많이 보시게 될 건데 **만지시면 안 됩니다. 그 중 몇몇 식물들은 사람에게 해롭습니다.** 이 규칙은 여러분의 안전을 위한 것입니다.

어휘 guide 안내원 be supposed to + 동사원형 ~하기로 되어 있다, ~해야 한다 organize 조직하다, 구성하다 private 개인의, 개별적인 hike 등산, 도보 여행 combine 합치다 appreciation 감사 extra 추가의 cover 포함하다, 망라하다 harmful 해로운 safety 안전

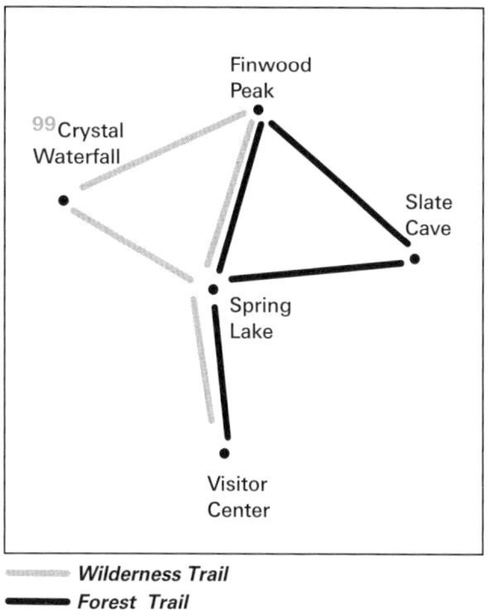

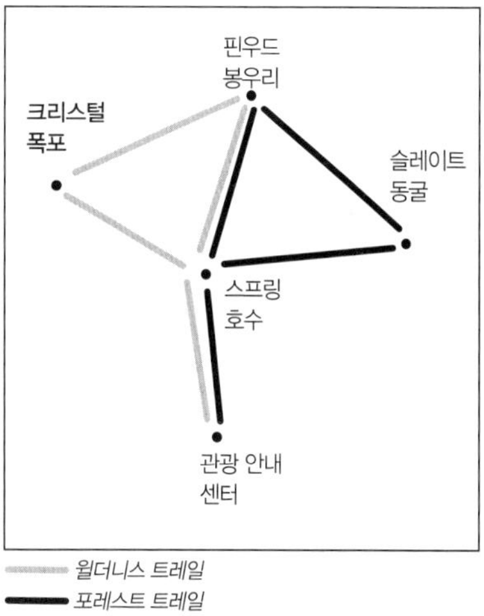

98

Why does the speaker apologize to the listeners?
(A) One of the hiking trails is closed.
(B) The group is larger than expected.
(C) Some reservations were lost.
(D) The tour is starting later than planned.

화자가 청자들에게 사과하는 이유는?

(A) 등산로 중 하나가 폐쇄되었기 때문에
(B) 집단 규모가 예상보다 크기 때문에
(C) 일부 예약이 누락되었기 때문에
(D) 여행이 계획보다 늦게 시작되기 때문에

해설 세부 사항 관련 – 화자의 사과 이유

지문 초반부에 화자가 청자들에게 원래 두 개의 등산팀이 꾸려져야 하지만 안내원 중 한 명이 몸이 아파서 유감이지만 하나로 합쳐야만 했다(I know you were ~ because one of our guides is sick.)고 했다. 즉, 화자가 청자들에게 예상보다 집단의 규모가 커진 것에 대해 사과하는 것이므로 정답은 (B)이다.

99

Look at the graphic. Which site is usually not included in the hike?

(A) Crystal Waterfall
(B) Finwood Peak
(C) Spring Lake
(D) Slate Cave

시각 정보에 따르면, 평소 등산에 포함되지 않는 장소는 어디인가?

(A) 크리스탈 폭포
(B) 핀우드 봉우리
(C) 스프링 호수
(D) 슬레이트 동굴

해설 세부 사항 관련 – 평소 등산에 포함되지 않는 장소

지문 중반부에 화자가 평소 등산 여행에는 포레스트 트레일만 포함되지만, 오늘은 윌더니스 트레일로도 가게 될 것(Usually this hike only covers Forest Trail, but we'll be taking the Wilderness Trail today as well.)이라고 했다. 그리고 지도를 보면 윌더니스 트레일로 가게 되면 크리스탈 폭포가 있으므로 정답은 (A)이다.

100

What does the speaker remind the listeners to do?

(A) Avoid touching plants
(B) Put on safety gear
(C) Bring along their cameras
(D) Stay on the trail

화자는 청자들에게 무엇을 하라고 상기시키는가?

(A) 식물 건드리지 않기
(B) 안전 장비 착용하기
(C) 카메라 가져오기
(D) 등산로에서 벗어나지 않기

해설 시각 정보 연계 – 청자들에게 상기시키는 것

지문 후반부에 화자가 청자들에게 그 중 몇몇 식물들은 사람에게 해로우니 만지면 안 된다(you shouldn't touch them. Some of them are harmful to people.)고 했으므로 정답은 (A)이다.

▸▸ **Paraphrasing** 지문의 **shouldn't touch them**
→ 정답의 **Avoid touching plants**

TEST 2

1 (B)	2 (C)	3 (D)	4 (C)	5 (A)
6 (B)	7 (B)	8 (B)	9 (C)	10 (A)
11 (B)	12 (A)	13 (C)	14 (C)	15 (B)
16 (A)	17 (B)	18 (A)	19 (C)	20 (B)
21 (C)	22 (A)	23 (A)	24 (B)	25 (B)
26 (C)	27 (A)	28 (C)	29 (C)	30 (A)
31 (B)	32 (D)	33 (D)	34 (B)	35 (C)
36 (A)	37 (C)	38 (D)	39 (A)	40 (B)
41 (B)	42 (D)	43 (C)	44 (B)	45 (A)
46 (B)	47 (B)	48 (A)	49 (D)	50 (C)
51 (B)	52 (B)	53 (C)	54 (C)	55 (D)
56 (C)	57 (D)	58 (A)	59 (C)	60 (B)
61 (D)	62 (A)	63 (B)	64 (A)	65 (A)
66 (B)	67 (D)	68 (D)	69 (C)	70 (B)
71 (A)	72 (A)	73 (D)	74 (B)	75 (A)
76 (C)	77 (B)	78 (B)	79 (A)	80 (D)
81 (C)	82 (D)	83 (C)	84 (A)	85 (C)
86 (A)	87 (D)	88 (C)	89 (B)	90 (C)
91 (A)	92 (C)	93 (D)	94 (A)	95 (D)
96 (B)	97 (A)	98 (D)	99 (C)	100 (A)

PART 1

1 M-Au

(A) He's drinking some coffee.
(B) He's preparing a beverage.
(C) He's putting on an apron.
(D) He's wiping off the counter.

(A) 남자가 커피를 마시고 있다.
(B) 남자가 음료수를 준비하고 있다.
(C) 남자가 앞치마를 두르고 있다.
(D) 남자가 조리대를 닦고 있다.

어휘 prepare (요리 등을) 준비하다 beverage 음료수 put on 착용하다, 입다 apron 앞치마 wipe off 닦다, 훔치다

해설 1인 등장 사진 – 사람의 동작 묘사

(A) 남자가 커피를 내리고 있지, 마시고 있는(is drinking some coffee) 모습은 아니므로 오답.

(B) 남자가 주전자로 물을 따르며 음료수를 준비하고 있는(is preparing a beverage) 모습이므로 정답.

(C) 남자가 앞치마를 두르는(is putting on an apron) 모습이 아니라 이미 착용한 상태(is wearing an apron)이므로 오답.

(D) 남자가 조리대를 닦고 있는(is wiping off the counter) 모습이 아니므로 오답.

2 W-Br

(A) A woman is leaving a meeting.
(B) A man is cleaning his glasses.
(C) A woman is holding a pen.
(D) A man is adjusting a clipboard.

(A) 여자가 회의 장소를 떠나고 있다.
(B) 남자가 안경을 닦고 있다.
(C) 여자가 펜을 쥐고 있다.
(D) 남자가 클립보드를 조정하고 있다.

어휘 adjust 조정하다 clipboard 클립보드(위에 집게가 달려 있어서 종이를 끼울 수 있는 판)

해설 2인 이상 등장 사진 – 사람의 동작 묘사

(A) 여자가 회의 장소에서 나가고 있는(is leaving a meeting) 모습이 아니므로 오답.

(B) 남자가 안경을 닦고 있는(is cleaning his glasses) 모습이 아니므로 오답.

(C) 여자가 오른손에 펜을 쥐고 있는(is holding a pen) 모습이므로 정답.

(D) 사진에 클립보드가 보이지만 남자가 클립보드를 조정하고 있는(is adjusting a clipboard) 모습은 아니므로 오답.

3 W-Am

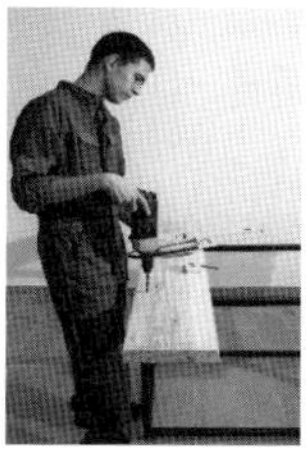

(A) A hole is being made in a wall.
(B) A wooden board is being polished.
(C) A worker is measuring a metal rack.
(D) A man is using an electric tool.

(A) 벽에 구멍이 뚫리고 있다.
(B) 나무판자가 매끄럽게 다듬어지고 있다.
(C) 작업자가 금속 걸이대의 길이를 재고 있다.
(D) 남자가 전동 공구를 사용하고 있다.

어휘 wooden board 나무판자 polish 윤을 내다, 매끄럽게 다듬다 measure (치수를) 재다 metal rack 금속 걸이대 electric tool 전동 공구

해설 1인 등장 사진 – 사람 또는 사물 중심 묘사
(A) 남자가 벽(in a wall)이 아닌 나무판자에 구멍을 뚫고 있는 모습이므로 오답.
(B) 남자가 나무판자를 매끄럽게 다듬고 있지(is being polished) 않으므로 오답.
(C) 남자가 금속 걸이대의 길이를 재고 있지(is measuring a metal rack) 않으므로 오답.
(D) 남자가 전동 공구를 사용하고 있는(is using an electric tool) 모습이므로 정답.

4 M-Au

(A) Some people are exiting an airplane.
(B) A woman is tying a scarf.
(C) A suitcase is being put in a storage area.
(D) All of the overhead compartments are closed.

(A) 몇 사람이 비행기에서 내리고 있다.
(B) 여자가 스카프를 매고 있다.
(C) 여행 가방이 보관 장소 안에 넣어지고 있다.
(D) 머리 위 짐칸들이 모두 닫혀 있다.

어휘 exit 나가다 tie 매다, 묶다 suitcase 여행 가방 storage area 보관 장소 overhead compartment 머리 위 짐칸

해설 2인 이상 등장 사진 – 사람 또는 사물 중심 묘사
(A) 사람들이 비행기에서 내리고 있는(are exiting an airplane) 모습이 아니므로 오답.
(B) 승무원이 이미 스카프를 착용한 상태이지 현재 스카프를 매고 있는(is tying a scarf) 모습은 아니므로 오답.
(C) 승객과 승무원이 함께 여행 가방을 보관 장소 안에 넣고 있는(is being put in a storage area) 모습이므로 정답.
(D) 머리 위 짐칸들이 모두 닫혀 있는(are closed) 상태가 아니라 하나는 열려 있으므로 오답.

5 W-Am

(A) Trees are lined up along a walkway.
(B) Some people are swimming in the water.
(C) Some boats are docked at a pier.
(D) A waterway is being constructed.

(A) 나무들이 보행로를 따라 늘어서 있다.
(B) 사람 몇 명이 물에서 수영을 하고 있다.
(C) 배 몇 대가 부두에 대져 있다.
(D) 수로가 건설되고 있다.

어휘 be lined up 줄지어 있다, 늘어서 있다 along ~을 따라서 walkway 보행로, 보도 dock (배를) 부두에 대다 pier 부두 waterway 수로 construct 건설하다

해설 사물/배경 사진 – 사람 또는 사물 중심 묘사
(A) 사진 왼쪽에 보이는 보행로(walkway)를 따라 나무들이 늘어서 있는(are lined up) 모습이므로 정답.
(B) 사진에는 물에서 수영하고 있는(swimming in the water) 사람들이 보이지 않으므로 오답.
(C) 사진에 부두(a pier)가 없으므로 오답
(D) 수로(waterway)가 현재 건설되고 있는(is being constructed) 모습이 아니므로 오답.

6 M-Cn

(A) There is a paint can sitting on the ground.
(B) Work gloves have been placed on a boot.
(C) Some potted plants are being watered.
(D) Gardening items have been left by a shed.

(A) 바닥에 페인트 통이 하나 있다.
(B) 작업용 장갑이 부츠 위에 놓여 있다.
(C) 화분에 심은 식물들에 물이 주어지고 있다.
(D) 원예용 도구들이 헛간 옆에 놓여 있다.

어휘 potted plant 화분에 심은 식물 water 물을 주다 gardening 원예, 정원 가꾸기 leave 두다, 두고 가다 shed 헛간

해설 사물/배경 사진 – 사물의 위치 묘사
(A) 바닥에 페인트 통(a paint can)은 보이지 않으므로 오답.
(B) 작업용 장갑이 부츠 위에 놓여 있는(have been placed on a boot) 모습이므로 정답.
(C) 화분이 바닥에 있지만 물이 주어지고 있는(are being watered) 모습이 아니므로 오답.
(D) 원예용 도구들이 바닥에 꽂혀 있는 상태이지 헛간 옆(by a shed)에 놓여 있는 상태는 아니므로 오답.

PART 2

7

M-Au Where is the best place to park near the stadium?
W-Br (A) Usually on weekdays.
(B) On Sixteenth Avenue.
(C) A big soccer game.

경기장 근처 어디에 주차하는 것이 가장 좋을까요?
(A) 대개 주중에요.
(B) 16번가에요.
(C) 큰 축구 경기요.

어휘 park 주차하다 on weekdays 주중에 avenue 거리, -가

해설 주차 장소를 묻는 Where 의문문

(A) 질문과 상관없는 오답. When 의문문에 대한 응답이므로 오답.

(B) 정답. 주차 장소를 묻는 질문에 On Sixteenth Avenue라는 구체적인 장소로 응답하고 있으므로 정답.

(C) 연상 단어 오답. 질문의 stadium에서 연상 가능한 soccer game을 이용한 오답.

8

W-Br Could you help me set up my online account?

M-Cn (A) Your user name and password.

(B) I'd be happy to.

(C) Yes, she's an accountant.

저의 온라인 계정 생성을 도와 주실 수 있으세요?

(A) 당신의 사용자명과 패스워드요.

(B) 그럴게요.

(C) 네, 그녀는 회계사입니다.

어휘 set up an online account 온라인 계정을 생성하다 user name 사용자명 accountant 회계사

해설 부탁/요청의 의문문

(A) 연상 단어 오답. 온라인 계정 생성(set up my online account)에서 연상 가능한 user name and password를 이용한 오답.

(B) 정답. 온라인 계정 생성(set up my online account)을 도와달라는 요청에 대해 수락의 의미로 I'd be happy to라고 응답하고 있으므로 정답.

(C) 유사 발음 오답. 질문의 account와 부분적으로 발음이 동일한 accountant를 이용한 오답.

9

M-Au You watched Brian's news report, didn't you?

W-Am (A) He's a reporter.

(B) I'll wash them now.

(C) Unfortunately, I missed it.

브라이언의 뉴스 보도를 보셨죠, 그렇지 않나요?

(A) 그는 기자입니다.

(B) 제가 그것들을 지금 씻을게요.

(C) 안타깝게도 못 봤네요.

어휘 news report 뉴스 보도 reporter 기자 unfortunately 안타깝게도 miss (기회를) 놓치다

해설 뉴스 시청 여부를 확인하는 부가의문문

(A) 파생어 오답. 질문의 report와 파생어 관계인 reporter를 이용한 오답.

(B) 유사 발음 오답. 질문의 watched와 부분적으로 발음이 유사한 wash를 이용한 오답.

(C) 정답. 뉴스 보도(news report)를 봤는지에 대해 그것을 놓쳤다(I missed it)면서 부정적 응답을 하고 있으므로 정답.

10

W-Am When does the offer expire?

M-Cn (A) It's printed on the coupon.

(B) Not as far as I know.

(C) A discount on office furniture.

할인 기간이 언제 끝나나요?

(A) 쿠폰에 인쇄돼 있어요.

(B) 내가 아는 한 아니에요.

(C) 사무용 가구에 대한 할인입니다.

어휘 offer (일정 기간의) 할인 expire (기한이) 만료되다 office furniture 사무용 가구

해설 끝나는 시점을 묻는 When 의문문

(A) 정답. 할인 기간이 끝나는 시점에 대한 질문에 쿠폰에 인쇄돼 있다(on the coupon)는 우회적 표현으로 응답하고 있으므로 정답.

(B) 질문과 상관없는 오답. 쿠폰의 할인 기간이 만료되었냐는 질문에 어울리는 응답이므로 오답.

(C) 연상 단어 오답. 질문의 the offer에서 연상 가능한 discount를 이용한 오답.

11

M-Cn Why did you leave your briefcase on the table?

W-Br (A) I wish I could.

(B) Because I'm coming right back.

(C) Mostly business contracts.

왜 서류 가방을 테이블에 두고 가셨나요?

(A) 저도 그럴 수 있으면 좋겠네요.

(B) 금방 다시 돌아올 거라서요.

(C) 대부분 사업 계약서입니다.

어휘 briefcase 서류 가방 mostly 주로, 대개 business contract 사업 계약(서)

해설 가방을 놓고 간 이유를 묻는 Why 의문문

(A) 질문과 상관없는 오답. 어떤 일을 희망하지만 실제로 할 수는 없을 때 쓰는 표현이므로 오답.

(B) 정답. 서류가방(briefcase)을 놓고 간 이유에 대해 금방 다시 돌아올 것이기 때문(Because I'm coming right back.)이라는 구체적인 이유를 제시하고 있으므로 정답.

(C) 연상 단어 오답. 질문의 briefcase에서 연상 가능한 business contracts를 이용한 오답이다.

12

M-Au Has the construction firm applied for the building permit?

W-Br (A) No, but they'll do it today.

(B) I work in another building.

(C) The renovations look fantastic.

그 건설회사는 건축 허가를 신청했나요?

(A) 아니요, 오늘 할 겁니다.

(B) 저는 다른 건물에서 일합니다.

(C) 개조한 모습이 멋지군요.

어휘 construction firm 건설회사 apply for 신청하다 building permit 건축 허가 renovation 개조, 보수

해설 건축 허가 신청 여부를 묻는 조동사(have) Yes/No 의문문

(A) 정답. 건설회사(construction firm)가 건축 허가(building permit)를 신청했는지에 대해 먼저 No로 부정적인 응답을 한 후, 그 회사가 오늘 할 것(they'll do it today)이라는 부연 설명을 하고 있으므로 정답.

(B) 단어 반복 오답. 질문의 building을 반복 이용한 오답.

(C) 연상 단어 오답. 질문의 construction에서 연상 가능한 renovations를 이용한 오답.

13

M-Cn I have to pay the enrollment fee in advance, don't I?

W-Am (A) In the student handbook.

(B) Delivery is free.

(C) That's correct.

입회비는 미리 내야 하죠, 그렇지 않나요?

(A) 학생 편람에요.

(B) 배달은 무료예요.

(C) 맞아요.

어휘 enrollment fee 입회비, 등록비 student handbook 학생 편람 delivery 배달

해설 입회비 선납 여부를 묻는 부가의문문

(A) 연상 단어 오답. enrollment fee에서 연상 가능한 student handbook을 이용한 오답.

(B) 유사 발음 오답. 질문의 fee와 발음이 유사한 free를 이용한 오답.

(C) 정답. 입회비(enrollment fee)를 미리(in advance) 납부해야 하는지에 대해 맞다(That's correct.)는 긍정적 응답을 하고 있으므로 정답.

14

M-Au When does the next issue of the magazine come out?

W-Br (A) A variety of articles.

(B) We're completely sold out.

(C) Not until next week.

그 잡지의 다음 호는 언제 나오나요?

(A) 다양한 기사요.

(B) 완판되었습니다.

(C) 다음 주에나 나와요.

어휘 issue 호 a variety of 다양한 article 기사 completely 완전히 not until ~가 되어서야 (비로소)

해설 잡지 출간 시점을 묻는 When 의문문

(A) 연상 단어 오답. 질문의 magazine에서 연상 가능한 a variety of articles를 이용한 오답.

(B) 연상 단어 오답. 질문의 magazine에서 연상 가능한 sold out를 이용한 오답.

(C) 정답. 발행 시점을 묻는 질문에 다음 주에나 나온다(Not until next week.)는 구체적인 시점을 언급하고 있으므로 정답.

15

W-Am Which drawer holds employee records?

M-Au (A) Yes, and schedules too.

(B) The top one.

(C) I'll hold it for you.

어느 서랍에 직원 기록이 들어 있나요?

(A) 네, 일정표들도요.

(B) 맨 위 서랍이요.

(C) 제가 당신을 위해 갖고 있을게요.

어휘 drawer 서랍 hold ~을 담다, 잡다 employee record 직원 기록

해설 서류가 담긴 서랍이 어느 것인지 묻는 Which 의문문

(A) Yes/No 불가 오답. Which 의문문에 Yes/No 응답이 불가능하기 때문에 오답.

(B) 정답. 직원 기록(employee records)이 어느 서랍에 들어 있는지에 대한 질문에 맨 위 서랍(The top one.)이라고 구체적으로 응답하므로 정답.

(C) 단어 반복 오답. 질문의 동사 hold를 반복 이용한 오답.

16

M-Cn You cannot enter this area of the factory.

W-Am (A) Sorry, I didn't know.

(B) Assembly line workers.

(C) Near the entrance.

공장 이쪽 구역에는 들어오실 수 없습니다.

(A) 죄송해요, 몰랐어요.

(B) 조립 라인 작업자들요.

(C) 입구 근처에요.

어휘 enter ~에 들어가다 assembly line 조립 라인 entrance 입구

해설 사실/정보 전달의 평서문

(A) 정답. 공장 이쪽 구역(this area of the factory)에 들어올 수 없다는 말에 죄송하다고, 몰랐다(Sorry, I didn't know.)고 사과하고 있으므로 정답.

(B) 연상 단어 오답. 공장(factory)에서 연상 가능한 조립 라인(assembly line)을 이용한 오답.

(C) 파생어 오답. 평서문의 enter와 파생어 관계에 있는 entrance를 이용한 오답.

17

M-Au How can I find the fastest route to the museum?

W-Br (A) That seems reasonable.

(B) Try searching for a map on the Internet.

(C) We're going to an art exhibition.

박물관으로 가는 가장 빠른 길은 어떻게 찾나요?

(A) 타당한 것 같군요.

(B) 인터넷으로 지도를 찾아보세요.

(C) 저희는 미술 전시회에 갑니다.

어휘 the fastest route to ~로 가는 최단 경로 reasonable 타당한 search for ~를 찾다 art exhibition 미술 전시회

해설 길 찾는 방법을 묻는 How 의문문

(A) 질문과 상관없는 오답. 상대방이 이치에 맞는 의견이나 적당한 가격을 제시했을 때 어울리는 응답이므로 오답.

(B) 정답. 박물관으로 가는 가장 빠른 길(the fastest route)을 어떻게 찾는지 묻는 질문에 인터넷으로 지도를 찾아보라(Try searching for a map on the Internet.)고 응답하고 있으므로 정답.

(C) 연상 단어 오답. 질문의 museum에서 연상 가능한 art exhibition을 이용한 오답.

18

M-Cn Where can I buy stationery like this?

W-Am (A) It was specially made.

(B) I appreciate that.

(C) No, I don't have time.

이런 문구류는 어디에서 살 수 있죠?

(A) 그건 특별 제작된 거예요.

(B) 감사합니다.

(C) 아니요, 저는 시간이 없어요.

어휘 stationery 문구류 specially made 특별 제작된 appreciate 감사하다

해설 문구류 구매 장소를 묻는 Where 의문문

(A) 정답. 특정 문구류(stationery)의 구매 장소를 묻는 질문에 일반적인 상품이 아니라 특별 제작된(specially made) 것이라며 매장에서 구입할 수 있는 제품이 아님을 알려주고 있으므로 정답.

(B) 질문과 상관없는 오답. 상대방이 도움을 주거나 호의를 베풀었을 때 어울리는 응답이므로 오답.

(C) Yes/No 불가 오답. Where 의문문에 Yes/No 응답이 불가능하기 때문에 오답.

19

W-Am Could we add labels to the sections of the storage room?

M-Au (A) Where are the paper clips?

(B) Yes, my favorite store.

(C) I don't see why not.

창고 구획에 라벨을 붙여도 될까요?

(A) 종이 클립들이 어디 있어요?

(B) 네, 제가 제일 좋아하는 가게예요.

(C) 안될 이유가 없죠.

어휘 label 라벨, 표 section 구역, 구획 storage room 창고

해설 제안/권유의 의문문

(A) 연상 단어 오답. label에서 연상 가능한 paper clips를 이용한 오답.

(B) 유사 발음 오답. 질문의 storage와 부분적으로 발음이 동일한 store를 이용한 오답.

(C) 정답. 라벨(labels)를 붙여도 되는지에 대해 '안될 이유가 없죠(I don't see why not.)'라는 긍정적 응답을 하고 있으므로 정답.

20

W-Br Would you inform the front desk staff of the change?

M-Cn (A) A copy of this form.

(B) Can Paul handle that?

(C) We're changing our checkout policy.

안내 데스크 직원에게 변동 사항을 알려 주시겠어요?

(A) 이 양식 한 장이요.

(B) 폴이 그 일을 처리해도 될까요?

(C) 저희는 체크아웃 규정을 바꾸는 중이에요.

어휘 inform A of B A에게 B를 알리다 copy (동일한 것의) 한 부 form 양식 handle 처리하다 policy 정책, 규정

해설 부탁/요청의 의문문

(A) 유사 발음 오답. 질문의 inform과 부분적으로 발음이 동일한 form를 이용한 오답.

(B) 정답. 안내 데스크 직원(front desk staff)에게 변동 사항(change)을 알려 주라는 요청에 대해, 부정적 응답 대신 폴(Paul)이 그 일을 처리해도 되는지 상대방에게 되묻고 있으므로 정답.

(C) 연상 단어 오답. front desk에서 연상 가능한 checkout을 이용한 오답.

21

W-Am Are the vegetables in the refrigerator still fresh?

W-Br (A) On the counter.

(B) The weekly farmer's market.

(C) Ask the head chef.

냉장고 안의 야채들은 아직 신선한가요?

(A) 조리대 위에요.

(B) 주 1회 하는 농산물 직판장요.

(C) 주방장에게 물어보세요.

어휘 vegetable 야채 counter 조리대, 계산대 farmer's market 농산물 직판장

해설 신선도를 묻는 be동사 Yes/No 의문문

(A) 질문과 상관없는 오답. vegetables의 위치를 묻는 질문에 어울리는 응답이므로 오답.

(B) 연상 단어 오답. 질문의 vegetables에서 연상 가능한 farmer's market을 이용한 오답.

(C) 정답. 야채가 신선한지를 묻는 질문에 직접적인 답변 대신 주방장에게 물어보라(Ask the head chef.)는 우회적 응답을 하고 있으므로 정답.

22

W-Am Was it your idea to give out T-shirts at the event?

M-Cn (A) I wasn't on the planning committee.

(B) No, thanks—we got ours earlier.

(C) Place two teachers in each classroom.

행사에서 티셔츠를 나눠주자는 건 당신 제안이었어요?

(A) 저는 기획 위원회에 있지 않았어요.

(B) 됐습니다. 우리 건 일찍 받았어요.

(C) 각 학급에 두 명의 교사를 배치하세요.

어휘 give out 나눠주다 planning committee 기획 위원회 place 배치하다

해설 상대방의 제안인지를 묻는 be동사 Yes/No 의문문

(A) 정답. 직접적인 답변 대신 자신은 기획 위원회에 있지 않았다며 우회적으로 부정의 응답을 하고 있으므로 정답.

(B) 연상 단어 오답. 질문의 give out T-shirts에서 연상 가능한 we got ours earlier를 이용한 오답.

(C) 질문과 상관없는 오답. 방법을 묻는 How 의문문에 대한 응답이므로 오답.

23

W-Br Aren't you coming with me to meet the real estate agent?

M-Au (A) I thought you canceled the appointment.

(B) It's included in the rental price.

(C) The woman in the blue suit.

저랑 같이 부동산 중개인 만나러 가는 거 아닌가요?

(A) 난 당신이 약속을 취소한 줄 알았는데요.

(B) 임대료에 포함되어 있어요.

(C) 파란색 정장을 입은 여자요.

어휘 real estate agent 부동산 중개인 rental price 임대료 suit 정장

해설 동행 여부에 대한 부정의문문

(A) 정답. 부동산 중개인을 만나러 같이 가는 거 아니냐는 질문에 대해 약속을 취소한 줄 알았다고 응답을 하고 있으므로 정답.

(B) 연상 단어 오답. 질문의 real estate agent에서 연상 가능한 rental price를 이용한 오답.

(C) 연상 단어 오답. 질문의 real estate agent에서 연상 가능한 woman in a blue suit를 이용한 오답.

24

W-Br Did Ms. Holbert accept any of our suggestions?

M-Cn (A) Yes, I agree.

(B) She's still considering them.

(C) I suggested getting new computers.

홀버트 씨가 저희 제안 중 수락한 것이 있었나요?

(A) 네, 동의합니다.

(B) 그녀는 아직 고려 중입니다.

(C) 저는 새 컴퓨터를 구입할 것을 제안했습니다.

어휘 accept 수락하다 suggestion 제안 consider 고려하다

해설 제안 수락 여부를 묻는 조동사(Do) Yes/No 의문문

(A) 질문과 상관없는 오답. 상대방의 의견이나 제안에 대해 긍정적 반응을 할 때 어울리는 응답이므로 오답.

(B) 정답. 홀버트 씨가 우리 제안(our suggestions)을 수락했는지에 대해 그녀가 여전히 고려 중(She's still considering them.)이라는 불확실성 표현으로 응답하고 있으므로 정답.

(C) 파생어 오답. 질문의 suggestions와 파생어 관계인 suggested를 이용한 오답.

25

M-Au Who's making the speech before the employee awards?

W-Am (A) The sales manager's office is over here.

(B) It's the founder of the company.

(C) That's great—you deserve it!

직원상 시상 전에 누가 연설을 하나요?

(A) 영업 매니저의 사무실은 이쪽에 있어요.

(B) 회사 창립자분이요.

(C) 잘됐군요! 당신은 그걸 받을 만하죠.

어휘 make a speech 연설하다 award 상 founder 창립자 deserve ~을 받을 만하다

해설 연설자를 묻는 Who 의문문

(A) 질문과 상관없는 오답. 연설자가 누구인지를 묻는 질문에 근무 장소로 대답할 수 없으므로 오답.

(B) 정답. 연설자를 묻는 질문에 회사 창립자(the founder of the company)라는 구체적인 인물로 응답하고 있으므로 정답.

(C) 연상 단어 오답. 질문의 employee awards에서 연상 가능한 답변을 이용한 오답.

26

W-Br The budget presentation hasn't started yet, has it?

M-Au (A) The graphics are hard to understand.

(B) The spending estimates for next year.

(C) We're waiting for the director to arrive.

예산안 발표 아직 시작 안 한 거죠, 그렇죠?

(A) 그래픽이 이해하기 어려워요.

(B) 내년 지출 추정치요.

(C) 저희는 이사님이 도착하기를 기다리고 있어요.

어휘 budget 예산, 예산안 spending 지출 estimate 추정(치) director 이사, 감독자

해설 예산안 발표 시작에 대해 묻는 부가의문문

(A) 연상 단어 오답. 질문의 presentation에서 연상 가능한 graphics를 이용한 오답.

(B) 연상 단어 오답. 질문의 budget에서 연상 가능한 spending estimates를 이용한 오답.

(C) 정답. 발표를 아직 시작하지 않았냐는 질문에 이사님의 도착을 기다리고 있다는 우회적인 답변을 하고 있으므로 정답.

27

W-Br Should I send the invoice by mail or by e-mail?

M-Cn (A) What's the client's preference?

(B) The total is two hundred euros.

(C) That's more than enough.

청구서는 우편으로 보낼까요, 아니면 이메일로 보낼까요?
(A) 고객이 무엇을 선호하나요?
(B) 합계는 200유로예요.
(C) 충분하고도 남아요.

어휘 invoice 청구서 client 고객 preference 선호, 희망하는 것 more than enough 너무 많은

해설 구를 연결한 선택의문문

(A) 정답. 청구서(invoice)를 우편과 이메일 중 어떤 방식으로 발송할지를 묻는 질문에 고객이 선호하는 방법(the client's preference)이 무엇인지 되물으며 고객이 원하는 대로 하자는 우회적 응답을 하고 있으므로 정답.

(B) 연상 단어 오답. 질문의 invoice에서 연상 가능한 two hundred euros를 이용한 오답.

(C) 질문과 상관없는 오답. 상대방이 먼저 특정 수량을 제시했을 때 어울리는 응답이므로 오답.

28

W-Am Are you going to Sunday's orchestra concert?

M-Au (A) She plays the violin.
(B) How was it?
(C) Only if I can get a ticket.

일요일 오케스트라 공연에 갈 거예요?
(A) 그녀는 바이올린을 연주해요.
(B) 그건 어땠어요?
(C) 표를 구할 수만 있다면요.

어휘 only if ~할 경우에 한해

해설 공연을 볼 것인지를 묻는 be동사 Yes/No 의문문

(A) 연상 단어 오답. 질문의 orchestra concert에서 연상 가능한 violin을 이용한 오답.

(B) 질문과 상관없는 오답. 상대방이 공연을 봤다고 했을 때 되물어볼 만한 질문이므로 오답.

(C) 정답. 공연을 보러 갈 것인지를 묻는 질문에 표를 구할 수만 있다면(Only if I can get a ticket.) 가겠다는 응답을 하고 있으므로 정답.

29

M-Au We need a professional to make these repairs.

M-Cn (A) There are a few pairs on this shelf.
(B) The leaking water pipes.
(C) That might be rather expensive.

우리는 이것들을 수리할 전문가가 필요해요.
(A) 이 선반에 몇 쌍 있어요.
(B) 새는 수도관들이요.
(C) 꽤 비쌀 텐데요.

어휘 professional 전문가 make a repair 수리하다 pair 쌍, 짝 leak 새다 rather 얼마간, 다소, 꽤, 상당히

해설 의견 제시의 평서문

(A) 유사 발음 오답. 평서문의 repairs와 부분적으로 발음이 동일한 pairs를 이용한 오답.

(B) 연상 단어 오답. 평서문의 repairs에서 연상 가능한 'leaking water pipes'를 이용한 오답.

(C) 정답. 수리를 할 전문가(professional)가 필요하다는 의견에 대해 전문가를 고용하면 꽤 비쌀 것(rather expensive)이라는 우려를 나타내고 있으므로 정답.

30

M-Cn How many security cameras will I need to install?

W-Am (A) It depends on the size of your property.
(B) Oh, this software updates automatically.
(C) Up to five days of filming.

보안 카메라를 몇 개 설치해야 할까요?
(A) 소유하시는 건물 크기에 따라 다릅니다.
(B) 아, 이 소프트웨어는 자동으로 업데이트가 돼요.
(C) 최대 5일간의 촬영이요.

어휘 security 보안, 경비 install 설치하다 depend on ~에 달려 있다 property 부동산, 건물 automatically 자동적으로 up to 최대 ~까지 film 촬영하다

해설 설치해야 할 보안 카메라의 수를 묻는 How many 의문문

(A) 보안 카메라를 몇 개 설치해야 할지를 묻는 질문에 건물 크기에 달려 있다는 우회적인 의미의 답변을 하고 있으므로 정답.

(B) 연상 단어 오답. 질문의 install에서 연상 가능한 software updates를 이용한 오답.

(C) 연상 단어 오답. 질문의 cameras에서 연상 가능한 filming을 이용한 오답.

31

W-Am I'm not sure if this layout looks good for the cover.

M-Au (A) Actually, Kiyoshi covered for her.
(B) Why don't you try something else?
(C) Because it will attract readers' interest.

표지에 이 배치가 괜찮은지 모르겠어요.
(A) 사실 키요시가 그녀를 대신했어요.
(B) 다른 걸 시도해 보면 어떨까요?
(C) 그게 독자들의 관심을 끌 거니까요.

어휘 layout 레이아웃, 배치 cover for ~를 대신하다 attract 마음을 끌다 interest 관심

해설 의견 제시의 평서문

(A) 파생어 오답. 평서문의 cover와 파생어 관계인 covered를 이용한 오답.

(B) 정답. 레이아웃(layout)이 표지에 어울리는지에 대해 다른 걸 시도해 보면 어떻겠느냐(Why don't you try something else?)고 우회적으로 부정의 응답을 하고 있으므로 정답.

(C) 연상 단어 오답. 평서문의 layout looks good에서 연상 가능한 attract readers' interest를 이용한 오답.

PART 3

32-34

M-Cn Hi. I'm here to report that [32]**I've lost a paperback that I checked out of your library two weeks ago.** I think I left it on an airplane, so I doubt that it will show up.

W-Am OK. [33]**You can either pay a flat fee of fifty dollars so that we can buy a replacement copy, or you can buy a new copy yourself.**

M-Cn Hmm... I'll buy a new copy.

W-Am Great. [34]**Please complete this form to give us official notice that the item has been lost.** Then you'll have thirty days to find a replacement copy.

남: 안녕하세요. **2주 전에 이 도서관에서 대출한 페이퍼백 책을 분실했다는** 걸 말씀드리려고 왔습니다. 비행기에 놓고 내린 거 같아서 책이 나타날 거 같지는 않네요.

여: 네. **저희가 대체 도서를 구입할 수 있게 균일 수수료 50달러를 내시든지, 아니면 새 책을 직접 구입해주셔도 됩니다.**

남: 음… 새 책을 구입할게요.

여: 좋습니다. **물품이 분실됐음을 알리는 공식적인 고지로 이 양식을 작성해 주세요.** 그러고 나서 대체 도서를 30일 안에 구하시면 됩니다.

어휘 report 알리다 paperback 페이퍼백(종이 한 장으로 표지가 되어 있는 책) check out (책을) 대출하다 show up 나타나다 flat fee 균일 요금[수수료] replacement 대체(물), 교체(물) complete (양식을) 작성하다

32

What has the man misplaced?

(A) A new smartphone

(B) A locker key

(C) A library card

(D) A borrowed book

남자는 무엇을 잃어버렸는가?

(A) 새 스마트폰 (B) 사물함 열쇠

(C) 도서관 카드 (D) 대출한 책

어휘 misplace (잘못 두어) 잃어버리다 borrowed 빌린

해설 세부 사항 관련 – 남자가 잃어버린 물건

남자의 첫 번째 대사에서 이 도서관에서 대출한 페이퍼백 책을 분실했다(I've lost a paperback that I checked out of your library two weeks ago.)고 했으므로 정답은 (D)이다.

33

What does the woman explain to the man?

(A) An advantage of a technology

(B) A reason for a refusal

(C) A cleaning routine

(D) A choice of options

여자는 남자에게 무엇을 설명하는가?

(A) 기술의 이점

(B) 거절 사유

(C) 청소 관례

(D) 선택 사항들

어휘 advantage 이점 refusal 거절 routine 관례, 판에 박힌 일 option 선택 사항, 옵션

해설 세부 사항 관련 – 여자가 설명하는 내용

여자의 첫 번째 대사에서 대체 도서를 구입할 수 있게 균일 수수료 50달러를 내든지 아니면 직접 구입해도 된다(You can either pay a flat fee ~ buy a new copy yourself.)고 하였으므로 정답은 (D)이다.

34

What does the woman tell the man to do?

(A) Wait for several days

(B) Fill out some paperwork

(C) Search some study areas

(D) Post a notice on a bulletin board

여자는 남자에게 무엇을 하라고 말하는가?

(A) 며칠간 기다리기

(B) 서류 작성하기

(C) 자습 구역 찾아보기

(D) 게시판에 공지 올리기

어휘 fill out 작성하다 paperwork 서류, 서류 작업 post a notice 공지를 올리다 bulletin board 게시판

해설 세부 사항 관련 – 여자가 요청하는 내용

대화 마지막에 여자가 물품이 분실됐다는 공식 고지로 이 양식을 작성해 달라(Please complete this form ~ the item has been lost.)고 했으므로 정답은 (B)이다.

▸▸ Paraphrasing 대화의 complete this form
→ 정답의 Fill out some paperwork

35-37

W-Br Hello. [35]**I'm interested in taking the ferry from Barth to Zingst.** [36]**I'd like to know what route times are available for this Thursday.**

M-Au Let's see... On weekdays, we have departures to Zingst at eight A.M., three P.M., and seven P.M., and a one-way trip costs fourteen euros. Will you be traveling alone?

W-Br Actually, I'll be bringing my dog with me in a carrier.

M-Au All right. In that case, [37]**be sure to bring the health records from your veterinarian to prove that the animal has had all of the necessary medical treatments.** Otherwise, it will not be allowed on board.

여: 안녕하세요. **저는 바르트에서 징스트로 가는 여객선을 타고 싶은데요. 이번 목요일에 어떤 시간대가 이용 가능한지 알고 싶어요.**
남: 어디 한번 보죠. 주중에는 오전 8시, 오후 3시, 오후 7시에 징스트로 출발합니다. 편도에 14 유로입니다. 혼자 가실 건가요?
여: 사실 캐리어에 개를 넣어 갈 예정이에요.
남: 알겠습니다. 그럼 **개가 필수적인 치료를 전부 받았다는 것을 증명하는 건강기록지를 수의사로부터 꼭 받아오세요.** 그렇지 않으면 배에 태울 수 없을 겁니다.

어휘 ferry 여객선 available 이용 가능한 on weekdays 주중에는 departure 출발 one-way trip 편도여행 health record 건강기록 veterinarian 수의사 prove 증명하다 necessary 필요한, 필수의 medical treatment 치료, 진료 otherwise 그렇지 않으면 allow 허가[허용]하다 on board 승선한

35

Where does the man most likely work?

(A) At a bus station
(B) At a taxi service
(C) At a ferry terminal
(D) At an airport

남자는 어디서 일하겠는가?

(A) 버스 정류장
(B) 택시 회사
(C) 여객선 터미널
(D) 공항

해설 전체 내용 관련 - 남자가 일하는 장소

여자의 첫 번째 대사에서 바르트에서 징스트로 가는 여객선을 타고 싶다(I'm interested in taking the ferry from Barth to Zingst.)고 했는데 이를 통해 남자가 여객선 터미널에서 근무함을 알 수 있으므로 정답은 (C)이다.

36

Why is the woman calling?

(A) To inquire about a travel schedule
(B) To request a ticket exchange
(C) To report a billing problem
(D) To change a reservation

여자는 왜 전화를 걸고 있는가?

(A) 여행 스케줄에 대해 문의하기 위해
(B) 표 교환을 요청하기 위해
(C) 청구서 문제를 알리기 위해
(D) 예약을 변경하기 위해

해설 전체 내용 관련 - 통화의 목적

여자의 첫 번째 대사에서 이번 주 목요일에 어떤 시간대가 이용 가능한지 알고 싶다(I'd like to know what route times are available for this Thursday.)고 했으므로 정답은 (A)이다.

37

What does the man remind the woman to do?

(A) Wear waterproof clothing
(B) Arrive at the site early
(C) Bring some documents
(D) Check the weight of her luggage

남자는 여자에게 무엇을 하라고 상기시키는가?

(A) 방수 의류 착용
(B) 현장에 일찍 도착
(C) 문서 지참
(D) 수하물 무게 확인

해설 세부 사항 관련 - 남자가 여자에게 상기시키는 것

대화 마지막에 남자가 여자에게 개가 필수적인 치료를 전부 받았다는 것을 증명하는 건강기록지를 수의사로부터 꼭 받아오라(be sure to bring the health records ~ the necessary medical treatments.)고 했으므로 정답은 (C)이다.

▸▸ **Paraphrasing** 대화의 **the health records**
→ 정답의 **some documents**

38-40 3인 대화

W-Am Excuse me—do you work here?
M-Cn Yes, I do. Can I help you ladies with something?
W-Am Yes, thank you. [38]**We're hoping to visit the team gift shop before the game starts, but we can't find it.** Isn't it near this entrance?
M-Cn It used to be, [39]**but the complex was remodeled last year.** A lot of facilities were moved around.
W-Br Ah, that explains why everything looks so different. We thought it was just because we hadn't been to a game in a while.
W-Am So, where's the gift shop now?
M-Cn It's over on the west side. [40]**I'm actually heading in that direction—would you like me to walk you over there?**
W-Br That would be great.

여1: 실례합니다. 여기서 일하시나요?
남: 네, 그런데요. 뭘 도와드릴까요?
여1: 네, 고맙습니다. **경기 시작하기 전에 팀 기념품점을 방문하고 싶은데, 찾을 수가 없네요.** 이 출입구 가까이 있지 않나요?
남: 그랬었는데, **이 단지가 작년에 리모델링 됐어요.** 여러 편의시설이 자리를 옮겼습니다.
여2: 아, 그래서 모든 게 그렇게 달라 보였네요. 우리가 한동안 경기를 보러 오지 않아서 그런가 했어요.
여1: 그러면, 기념품점은 지금 어디에 있죠?
남: 저기 서쪽 편에 있습니다. **사실은 저도 그 방향으로 가는 길인데, 그쪽까지 같이 걸어가드릴까요?**
여2: 그거 좋겠는데요.

어휘 entrance 출입구 used to + 동사원형 (예전에) ~이었다 complex 복합 건물, 단지 remodel 개조하다 facilities (편의)시설 in a while 한동안 head 향하다

38

Where is the conversation most likely taking place?

(A) At a history museum
(B) At an amusement park
(C) At a department store
(D) At a sports stadium

대화는 어디에서 일어나겠는가?

(A) 역사 박물관
(B) 놀이 공원
(C) 백화점
(D) 경기장

어휘 amusement park 놀이 공원 sports stadium 경기장

해설 전체 내용 관련 - 대화 장소

첫 번째 여자의 두 번째 대사에서 경기 시작하기 전에 팀 기념품점을 방문하고 싶은데, 찾을 수가 없다(We're hoping to visit the team gift shop ~ we can't find it.)고 했다. 이로써 대화가 경기장에서 이루어지고 있음을 알 수 있으므로 정답은 (D)이다.

39

According to the man, what happened last year?

(A) Renovations were carried out.
(B) Operating hours were shortened.
(C) A celebrity filmed an advertisement.
(D) A lease was not renewed.

남자에 의하면, 작년에 무슨 일이 있었는가?

(A) 보수 공사가 이루어졌다.
(B) 운영 시간이 단축되었다.
(C) 한 유명 인사가 광고를 촬영했다.
(D) 임대차 계약이 갱신되지 않았다.

어휘 renovation 수리, 보수 carry out 수행하다 operating hours 운영 시간 celebrity 유명 인사 lease 임대차 계약 renew 갱신하다

해설 세부 사항 관련 - 작년에 일어난 일

남자의 두 번째 대사에서 이 단지가 작년에 리모델링 됐다(the complex was remodeled last year.)고 했으므로 정답은 (A)이다.

▸▸ **Paraphrasing** 대화의 **remodeled** → 정답의 **Renovations**

40

How will the man help the women?

(A) By giving them a brochure
(B) By guiding them to a location
(C) By issuing a public announcement
(D) By writing down some directions

남자는 여자들을 어떻게 도와줄 것인가?

(A) 안내 자료를 줘서
(B) 장소로 안내해서
(C) 안내 방송을 해서
(D) 찾아가는 방법을 적어서

어휘 brochure (안내용) 작은 책자 issue 발표하다 public announcement 안내 방송 directions 길 안내, 가는 길

해설 세부 사항 관련 - 남자가 도와줄 방법

대화 마지막에 남자가 사실은 자신도 그 방향으로 가는 길인데, 그쪽까지 같이 걸어가자(I'm actually heading in that direction—would you like me to walk you over there?)고 했으므로 정답은 (B)이다.

41-43

W-Am Good morning. I'm Niyati Pandit, the owner of Lux Finance. I'm looking for a temporary worker to cover for an employee who's on extended medical leave. [41]**Your Web site said that you can fill openings fast.**

M-Cn That's right, Ms. Pandit. We have an extensive database of potential applicants. I'm sure we can find the right person for you.

W-Am Great! I need the person to start next Monday with some brief training, so [42]**I'd like to interview potential workers by phone on Thursday.**

M-Cn All right. After you send me the job description, I'll check our database for the best résumés. [43]**How about I send you the top five by the end of the day?**

여: 안녕하세요, 저는 럭스 파이낸스의 소유주인 니야티 판디트입니다. 장기 병가 중인 직원을 대신할 임시직 근로자를 찾고 있는데요. **귀사의 웹 사이트에 공석을 빨리 채울 수 있다고 되어 있어서요.**

남: 맞습니다, 판디트 씨. 저희는 폭넓은 잠재 지원자 데이터베이스를 확보하고 있습니다. 귀사에 적합한 사람을 찾을 수 있으리라 확신합니다.

여: 좋습니다. 다음 주 월요일 간단한 교육을 받고 일을 시작할 사람이 필요해요. 그래서 **목요일에 가능성 있는 근로자들을 전화로 면접 보고 싶습니다.**

남: 알겠습니다. 직무 기술서를 보내 주신 후에 저희 데이터베이스에서 최적의 이력서들을 찾아보겠습니다. **제가 오늘까지 상위 다섯 명의 이력서를 보내드리면 어떨까요?**

어휘 temporary worker 임시직 근로자, 비정규직 근로자 cover for ~를 대신하다 extended 장기의 medical leave 병가 opening 공석 extensive 광범위한, 폭넓은 potential 잠재적인 applicant 지원자 job description 직무 기술서 résumé 이력서

41

What does the man's company specialize in?

(A) Property management
(B) Employee recruitment
(C) Financial consulting
(D) Medical research

남자의 회사는 무엇을 전문으로 하는가?

(A) 부동산 관리
(B) 직원 채용
(C) 금융 컨설팅
(D) 의료 연구

해설 전체 내용 관련 – 남자 회사의 전문 분야

여자의 첫 번째 대사에서 남자 회사의 웹 사이트에 공석을 빨리 채울 수 있다고 되어 있다(Your Web site said that you can fill openings fast.)고 했으므로 정답은 (B)이다.

42

What does the woman want to do on Thursday?

(A) Visit the man's office
(B) Update a database
(C) Start some training
(D) Conduct some interviews

여자는 목요일에 무엇을 하고 싶어 하는가?

(A) 남자의 사무실 방문
(B) 데이터베이스 업데이트
(C) 교육 시작
(D) 면접 실시

해설 세부 사항 관련 – 여자가 목요일에 원하는 일

여자의 두 번째 대사에서 목요일에 가능성 있는 근로자들을 전화로 면접 보고 싶다(I'd like to interview potential workers by phone on Thursday.)고 했으므로 정답은 (D)이다.

▸▸ **Paraphrasing** 대화의 **interview** → 정답의 **conduct some interviews**

43

What does the man offer to do?

(A) Waive a fee
(B) Check a calendar
(C) Send some résumés
(D) E-mail an invoice

남자는 무엇을 해주겠다고 하는가?

(A) 요금 면제해주기
(B) 달력 확인하기
(C) 몇 개의 이력서 보내기
(D) 청구서를 이메일로 보내기

어휘 waive 면제하다, (권리 등을) 포기하다

해설 세부 사항 관련 – 남자의 제안

대화 마지막에 남자가 오늘까지 상위 다섯 명의 이력서를 보내주겠다(How about I send you the top five by the end of the day?)는 제안을 하고 있으므로 정답은 (C)이다.

44-46

M-Au Thank you for calling the Hayden Electronics helpline. How may I be of assistance?

W-Br I'm wondering where I can get spare parts for my e-reader. It's the T-70 model.

M-Au I'm sorry, but [44]**we don't manufacture that model anymore,** so we don't sell replacements parts either. What is the problem with the device?

W-Br It's actually just the charger that needs to be replaced. I lost it while I was on vacation.

M-Au Oh, that won't be a problem at all. [45]**The new models use the same charger. So, you can just order one from our Web site.**

W-Br All right, great! [46]**About how long would it take to get to me?**

M-Au Usually around three business days.

남: 헤이든 전자 상담센터에 전화 주셔서 감사합니다. 무엇을 도와드릴까요?

여: 제 전자책 단말기의 부품을 어디서 구할 수 있는지 궁금해서요. T-70 모델이에요.

남: 죄송하지만 **그 모델은 더 이상 생산하지 않아요.** 그래서 교체 부품도 판매하지 않습니다. 기기에 어떤 문제가 있나요?

여: 사실 교체할 것은 충전기뿐이에요. 휴가 중에 잃어버렸거든요.

남: 아, 그렇다면 전혀 문제 될 것이 없습니다. **신형 모델에도 동일한 충전기가 사용되니까요. 저희 웹 사이트에서 주문하실 수 있습니다.**

여: 좋아요, 잘됐네요! **저한테 도착하기까지 대략 얼마나 걸릴까요?**

남: 영업일 기준으로 보통 3일 정도 걸립니다.

어휘 be of assistance 도움이 되다 spare part (여분의) 부품 e-reader 전자책 단말기 manufacture 제조하다, 생산하다 replacement 교체 device 기기 charger 충전기 replace 교체하다 business day 영업일

44

What problem does the man mention?

(A) A component is difficult to install.
(B) A product has been discontinued.
(C) A form was filled out incorrectly.
(D) A shipment has been delayed.

남자는 어떤 문제를 언급하는가?

(A) 부품이 설치하기 어렵다.
(B) 제품이 단종되었다.
(C) 양식이 잘못 작성되었다.
(D) 배송이 지연되었다.

어휘 component 부품, 요소 discontinue 중단하다 incorrectly 부정확하게 shipment 배송 delay 미루다

해설 세부 사항 관련 – 남자가 언급하는 문제점

남자의 두 번째 대사에서 여자가 언급한 모델을 더 이상 제조하지 않는다(we don't manufacture that model anymore)고 했으므로 정답은 (B)이다.

▸▸ **Paraphrasing** 대화의 **don't manufacture**
→ 정답의 **discontinued**

45

Why does the man recommend visiting a Web site?

(A) To place an order
(B) To read a policy
(C) To open an account
(D) To request a refund

남자가 웹 사이트 방문을 권한 이유는?
(A) 주문을 하기 위해
(B) 정책을 읽어보기 위해
(C) 계정을 개설하기 위해
(D) 환불을 요청하기 위해

해설 **세부 사항 관련 – 남자가 웹 사이트 방문을 권하는 이유**
남자의 세 번째 대사에서 여자에게 신형 모델에도 동일한 충전기가 사용되므로 웹 사이트에서 주문할 수 있다(The new models use the same charger. So, you can just order one from our Web site.)고 했으므로 정답은 (A)이다.

▸▸ **Paraphrasing** 대화의 **order** → 정답의 **place an order**

46

What does the woman inquire about?

(A) A retail store
(B) A delivery period
(C) A warranty extension
(D) A price reduction

여자는 무엇에 대해 문의하는가?
(A) 소매점
(B) 배송 기간
(C) 품질보증 연장
(D) 가격 인하

어휘 retail 소매 extension 연장 reduction 감소

해설 **세부 사항 관련 – 여자의 문의**
여자의 세 번째 대사에서 남자에게 상품이 도착하는 데 대략 얼마나 걸리는지(About how long would it take to get to me?) 물어보고 있으므로 정답은 (B)이다.

47-49

W-Am Kevin, [47]**I really appreciate your help with finding a new site for our office.**
M-Cn It's my pleasure.
W-Am Now, you should know that the lease on our current building is up in just three months.
M-Cn That's not a lot of time, but [47, 48]**it'll be nice to have a large space since we've nearly doubled our staff size.**
W-Am Right. There are a few neighborhoods to consider, but... um... I'm not sure which one would be best.
M-Cn [49]**How about making a questionnaire for employees so they can give their opinions?**
W-Am Great idea!

여: 케빈, **사무실 새 부지를 찾는 데 도움을 주셔서 정말 고마워요.**
남: 도움이 돼서 기쁘네요.
여: 현 건물의 임대차 계약이 3개월만 있으면 끝난다는 걸 아실 거예요.
남: 시간이 많진 않군요. 하지만 **직원 규모가 거의 두 배로 늘어났으니 공간이 넓은 곳으로 가면 좋겠네요.**
여: 맞아요. 인근에 고려할 곳이 몇 군데 있는데… 음… 어디가 가장 좋을지 잘 모르겠어요.
남: **직원들도 의견을 낼 수 있도록 설문지를 만들면 어떨까요?**
여: 좋은 생각이네요!

어휘 site 장소, 부지 lease 임대차 계약 current 현재의 up (기간이) 다 된 nearly 거의 double 두 배로 만들다 neighborhood 인근 questionnaire 설문지 opinion 의견

47

What is the main topic of the conversation?

(A) A safety procedure
(B) A business relocation
(C) A new vendor
(D) A loan agreement

대화의 주제는 무엇인가?
(A) 안전 수칙
(B) 회사 이전
(C) 신규 공급업체
(D) 대출 계약

어휘 relocation 재배치, 이전, 전근 vendor 공급업체 loan 대출 agreement 계약(서), 동의

해설 **전체 내용 관련 – 대화의 주제**
여자의 첫 번째 대사에서 남자에게 사무실 새 부지를 찾는 데 도움을 줘서 고맙다(I really appreciate your help with finding a new site for our office.)고 했다. 그리고 남자의 두 번째 대사에 직원이 거의 두 배로 늘었기 때문에 넓은 공간이 좋을 것(it'll be nice to have a large space since we've nearly doubled our staff size.)이라고 했다. 화자들이 회사 이전에 대해 대화하고 있음을 알 수 있으므로 정답은 (B)이다.

48

What does the man mention about the speakers' company?

(A) Its workforce has grown.
(B) Its goods are popular.
(C) Its leadership has changed.
(D) Its building is modern.

남자가 화자들의 회사에 대해 언급한 것은 무엇인가?
(A) 직원이 증가했다.
(B) 상품의 인기가 좋다.
(C) 지도부가 바뀌었다.
(D) 건물이 현대적이다.

해설 세부 사항 관련 - 회사에 대한 남자의 언급
남자의 두 번째 대사에서 직원이 거의 두 배로 늘었기 때문에 넓은 곳으로 가면 좋겠다(it'll be nice to have a large space since we've nearly doubled our staff size.)고 했으므로 정답은 (A)이다.

▸▸ Paraphrasing 대화의 doubled our staff size
→ 정답의 workforce has grown

49
What does the man suggest?
(A) Researching a competitor
(B) Walking around a site
(C) Drafting a memo
(D) Conducting a survey

남자는 무엇을 제안하는가?
(A) 경쟁사 조사
(B) 현장 답사
(C) 메모 초안 작성
(D) 설문조사 실시

어휘 competitor 경쟁자 draft 초안을 작성하다

해설 세부 사항 관련 - 남자의 제안
남자의 세 번째 대사에서 직원들도 의견을 제시할 수 있도록 설문지를 만들자(How about making a questionnaire for employees so they can give their opinions?)는 제안을 하고 있으므로 정답은 (D)이다.

▸▸ Paraphrasing 대화의 making a questionnaire
→ 정답의 Conducting a survey

50-52

W-Br Mr. Anderson, [50]**please tell me more about how you've used social media in past jobs.**

M-Au In my last position, I used our accounts to improve engagement with customers and spread awareness of our specials. [51]**Our sales went up eight percent, with most of it connected to the coupon codes we shared only through social media.**

W-Br That's a major accomplishment. [50]**If you are hired, how do you think you could apply that approach to our company?**

M-Au First, [52]**I would work with your marketing specialist to come up with a similar strategy to build a better relationship with the clients you already have.** Then, I would consider ways to reach new customers.

여: 앤더슨 씨, **전 직장들에서 소셜 미디어를 어떻게 활용했는지 좀 더 자세히 얘기해 주세요.**

남: 직전 직장에서 저는 고객들과의 관계를 향상시키고 특별 상품들에 대한 인지도를 높이기 위해 회사의 계정들을 활용했습니다. **매출이 8퍼센트 상승했는데, 대부분 저희가 소셜 미디어만을 통해 공유한 쿠폰 코드와 연결된 것이었습니다.**

여: 중대한 성과를 거뒀군요. **귀하가 채용된다면 그 접근법을 우리 회사에서 어떻게 적용할 수 있겠습니까?**

남: 첫째로 **귀사의 마케팅 전문가와 협력해 유사한 전략을 마련하여 기존 고객들과 더 나은 관계를 구축하도록 할 것입니다.** 그러고 나서 신규 고객을 확보할 방법들을 모색해 내겠습니다.

어휘 position 직책 account 계정 improve 향상시키다 engagement 관여, 참여 spread 확산시키다 awareness 인지도 connected to ~와 연결된 accomplishment 업적, 성취 apply A to B A를 B에 적용하다 approach 접근법 specialist 전문가 come up with 마련하다, 제안하다 strategy 전략 build a better relationship with ~와 더 나은 관계를 구축하다

50
Where most likely are the speakers?
(A) At a professional workshop
(B) At a board meeting
(C) At a job interview
(D) At a welcome reception

화자들은 어디에 있겠는가?
(A) 전문인력 워크숍
(B) 이사회 회의
(C) 채용 면접
(D) 환영회

해설 전체 내용 관련 - 대화의 장소
여자의 첫 번째 대사에서 남자에게 전 직장에서 소셜 미디어를 어떻게 활용했는지 좀 더 자세히 얘기해 달라(please tell me more about how you've used social media in past jobs)고 했다. 그리고 여자의 두 번째 대사에서 만약 채용된다면 남자의 접근법을 어떻게 여자의 회사에 적용할 수 있을지(If you are hired, how do you think you could apply that approach to our company?) 물어봤다. 이를 통해 화자들이 채용 면접 중임을 알 수 있으므로 정답은 (C)이다.

51
What achievement does the man describe?
(A) Improving employee productivity
(B) Increasing a company's sales
(C) Hiring a marketing specialist
(D) Reducing distribution costs

남자는 어떤 성과를 설명하는가?
(A) 직원 생산성 향상
(B) 회사의 매출 증대
(C) 마케팅 전문가 고용
(D) 유통비 절감

어휘 achievement 성과, 업적 productivity 생산성 distribution 유통, 배급

Test 2

해설 세부 사항 관련 - 남자가 설명하는 성과

남자의 첫 번째 대사에서 매출이 8퍼센트 상승했는데, 대부분 소셜 미디어만을 통해 공유한 쿠폰 코드와 연결된 것(Our sales went up eight percent ~ only through social media.)이라고 했으므로 정답은 (B)이다.

▶▶ **Paraphrasing** 대화의 **went up** → 정답의 **Increasing**

52

What does the man propose?

(A) Using newspapers to share coupons
(B) Targeting some current clients
(C) Holding a press conference
(D) Analyzing some financial data

남자는 무엇을 제안하는가?

(A) 신문을 활용해 쿠폰 나누어 주기
(B) 기존 고객 일부를 겨냥하기
(C) 기자 회견 열기
(D) 금융 정보 분석하기

해설 세부 사항 관련 - 남자의 제안

남자의 두 번째 대사에서 마케팅 전문가와 협력해 유사한 전략을 마련하여 기존 고객들과 더 나은 관계를 구축하도록 하겠다(I would work with your marketing specialist ~ with the clients you already have.)는 제안을 하고 있으므로 정답은 (B)이다.

▶▶ **Paraphrasing** 대화의 **the clients you already have**
→ 정답의 **some current clients**

53-55

M-Cn Katie, Ms. Spencer called this morning. [53]**She loved our ideas for redecorating her living room, and she wanted to get a final quote for the work.**

W-Am I'm still waiting to find out if we can get the cherry wood flooring we want from the supplier. [54]**If he has it, the price will be quite reasonable, but otherwise we'll have to import it.** That'll make a big difference.

M-Cn I understand. Well, since Ms. Spencer's budget isn't very flexible, [55]**I'll prepare some alternative wood samples for her to choose from,** just in case we can't use her first choice.

남: 케이티, 스펜서 씨가 오늘 아침 전화했어요. **그녀는 거실 새 단장에 대한 우리의 아이디어가 마음에 들어서 작업에 대한 최종 견적을 받고 싶어 했어요.**

여: 공급업자로부터 우리가 원하는 체리목 바닥재를 받을 수 있을지 여부를 아직 기다리고 있어요. **그가 바닥재를 갖고 있다면 가격이 꽤 저렴해지겠지만 만약 없다면 바닥재를 수입해야 해요.** 거기서 큰 차이가 날 거예요.

남: 알겠어요. 음, 스펜서 씨의 예산이 크게 변하지 않을 테니 **그녀가 선택할 수 있는 대체 목재 샘플들을 준비할게요.** 그녀가 처음 고른 것을 사용 못 할 경우에 대비해서요.

어휘 redecorate 실내장식을 바꾸다 quote 견적(액) flooring 바닥재 supplier 공급업자 reasonable 적정한 otherwise 그렇지 않으면 import 수입하다 make a big difference 큰 차이를 내다 budget 예산 flexible 유연한 alternative 대안이 되는

53

Who most likely are the speakers?

(A) Moving consultants
(B) Real estate agents
(C) Interior designers
(D) Equipment suppliers

화자들은 누구겠는가?

(A) 이사 관련 컨설턴트
(B) 부동산 중개인
(C) 인테리어 디자이너
(D) 장비 공급업자

해설 전체 내용 관련 - 화자들의 직업

남자의 첫 번째 대사에서 스펜서 씨가 거실 새 단장에 대한 아이디어가 마음에 들어서 작업에 대한 최종 견적을 받고 싶어 했다(She loved our ideas for redecorating her living room, and she wanted to get a final quote for the work.)고 했으므로 정답은 (C)이다.

54

What does the woman mean when she says, "That'll make a big difference"?

(A) She wants additional workers to help.
(B) She hopes her recommendation is accepted.
(C) She is unsure about a final price.
(D) She needs to confirm some measurements.

여자가 "거기서 큰 차이가 날 거예요"라고 말한 의도는 무엇인가?

(A) 추가 인부들이 도와 주기를 바란다.
(B) 자신이 추천한 것이 받아들여지기를 바란다.
(C) 최종 가격에 대해 확신이 없다.
(D) 몇몇 치수를 확인해야 한다.

해설 화자의 의도 파악 - 거기서 큰 차이가 날 것이라는 말의 의미

여자의 대사에서 공급업자가 바닥재를 갖고 있다면 가격이 꽤 저렴하겠지만 만약 없다면 바닥재를 수입해야 한다(If he has it, the price will be quite reasonable, but otherwise we'll have to import it.)고 했다. 즉, 큰 차이가 날 것이라는 말은 아직 최종 가격을 확신할 수 없다는 의미이므로 정답은 (C)이다.

55

What does the man say he will prepare?

(A) A cost estimate
(B) Some company brochures
(C) An updated contract
(D) Some product samples

남자는 무엇을 준비하겠다고 말하는가?
(A) 비용 견적
(B) 회사의 안내 책자 몇 부
(C) 갱신된 계약서
(D) 몇 개의 제품 샘플

해설 세부 사항 관련 – 남자가 준비할 것
대화 마지막에 남자가 스펜서 씨가 선택할 수 있는 대체 목재 샘플들을 준비하겠다(I'll prepare some alternative wood samples for her to choose from)고 했으므로 정답은 (D)이다.

▸▸ **Paraphrasing** 대화의 some alternative wood samples
→ 정답의 some product samples

56-58 3인 대화

M-Au [56]**I'm really looking forward to the banquet next week.**

M-Cn Me, too. [56]**It'll be nice to be able to recognize the employees who have contributed to the company's success this year.**

W-Br Yeah, but we still haven't completed the list of award recipients, have we?

M-Au Not yet. Most of the categories had a clear winner, but [57]**for Employee of the Year, I really don't know what we should do.**

M-Cn [57]**It was hard enough narrowing it down to Mr. Davis and Ms. Reid.** They both deserve it. How can we choose just one?

W-Br We've got to find a way. [58]**How about meeting with Anthony Lindale, the manager of their department?** His perspective should be valuable.

남1: **다음 주에 있을 만찬이 정말 기대돼요.**
남2: 저도요. **올해 회사의 성과에 기여한 직원들을 표창할 수 있어 좋을 거예요.**
여: 네, 하지만 수상자 명단을 아직 완료하지 못했죠, 그렇죠?
남1: 아직이요. 거의 모든 부문에 확실한 수상자가 있지만 **'올해의 직원상'은 어떻게 해야 할지 정말 모르겠어요.**
남2: **데이비스 씨와 리드 씨로 좁히는 것만으로도 충분히 힘들었어요.** 둘 다 자격이 충분해요. 어떻게 한 명을 선택할 수 있을까요?
여: 방법을 찾아야죠. **그들의 부서장인 앤서니 린데일을 만나보는 건 어떨까요?** 그의 의견은 소중한 정보가 될 거예요.

어휘 look forward to ~를 고대하다 banquet 연회, 만찬 recognize 공로를 인정하다, 표창하다 contribute to ~에 기여하다 complete 완료하다 award recipient 수상자 narrow down 좁히다 deserve 자격이 있다 have got to + 동사원형 ~해야 하다 perspective 관점, 시각 valuable 소중한

56

What is the conversation mainly about?
(A) A colleague's promotion
(B) An investment bank
(C) An awards dinner
(D) A fund-raising campaign

대화는 주로 무엇에 관한 내용인가?
(A) 동료의 승진
(B) 투자은행
(C) 시상식 저녁 만찬
(D) 모금 운동

어휘 colleague 동료 promotion 승진 investment 투자 fund-raising 모금(의)

해설 전체 내용 관련 – 대화의 주제
대화 맨 처음에 남자가 다음 주에 있을 만찬이 정말 기대된다(I'm really looking forward to the banquet next week.)고 했고, 두 번째 남자 또한 올해 회사의 성과에 기여한 직원들을 표창할 수 있어 좋을 것(It'll be nice to be able ~ to the company's success this year.)이라고 했다. 이를 통해 화자들이 시상식 만찬에 대해 얘기하고 있음을 알 수 있으므로 정답은 (C)이다.

57

What are the speakers having trouble doing?
(A) Arranging transportation
(B) Finding out some details
(C) Staying within a budget
(D) Making a decision

화자들이 곤란을 겪는 문제는 무엇인가?
(A) 교통편 마련
(B) 세부 사항 확인
(C) 예산 범위를 벗어나지 않기
(D) 의사 결정

해설 세부 사항 관련 – 화자들이 겪는 어려움
첫 번째 남자가 두 번째 대사에서 올해의 직원상은 어떻게 해야 할지 정말 모르겠다(for Employee of the Year ~ we should do.)고 하자 두 번째 남자가 두 명으로 좁히는 것만으로도 충분히 힘들었다(It was hard ~ Ms. Reid.)고 했으므로 정답은 (D)이다.

58

What does the woman suggest doing?
(A) Speaking with a supervisor
(B) Rescheduling a meeting
(C) Using a certain Web site
(D) Reviewing some records

여자는 무엇을 제안하는가?
(A) 관리자와 얘기하기
(B) 회의 일정 변경하기
(C) 특정 웹 사이트 이용하기
(D) 기록 검토하기

어휘 supervisor 관리자, 상사

해설 세부 사항 관련 - 여자의 제안

대화 마지막에 여자가 부서장인 앤서니 린데일을 만나 의견을 들어보는 게 어떻겠냐(How about meeting with Anthony Lindale, the manager of their department?)는 제안을 하고 있으므로 정답은 (A)이다.

▸▸ **Paraphrasing** 대화의 **the manager** → 정답의 **a supervisor**

59-61

W-Am Mr. Aimes, I've finished unpacking all of the new sweaters in the storeroom. [59]**I heard that they don't need to go on display until the sale starts on Saturday.** So, [60]**is there anything else you need me to do?** My shift doesn't end until four o'clock.

M-Au Let's see. The changing rooms are always a mess.

W-Am OK. I'll work on that until the end of my shift. I just need to fold the clothes or put them back on hangers and then return them to their correct displays, right?

M-Au Yes, that's right. Why don't you start in the women's department first? [61]**I'll call the manager there to let her know that you're heading over.**

여: 에임즈 씨, 창고에 있는 모든 신상 스웨터의 포장을 풀었습니다. **토요일 판매 시작 때까지 진열할 필요가 없다고 들었어요.** 그럼, **제가 해야 할 다른 일이 있나요?** 제 근무 시간은 4시가 되어야 끝납니다.

남: 어디 봅시다. 탈의실들이 항상 엉망이더군요.

여: 알겠습니다. 제 근무 시간이 끝날 때까지 정리할게요. 옷을 개거나 옷걸이에 다시 걸어두고 제자리에 다시 진열해 두면 되는 거죠?

남: 네, 맞아요. 여성복 쪽부터 시작하는 게 어때요? **그쪽 매니저에게 전화해서 당신이 지금 간다고 알릴게요.**

어휘 unpack 꺼내다, 풀다 storeroom 창고 display 진열 changing room 탈의실 mess 엉망인 상태 shift 교대 근무 시간 fold 접어 개다 hanger 옷걸이 head 향하다

59

What does the woman say about some sweaters?

(A) They are selling well.
(B) They are part of a window display.
(C) They are not yet available for purchase.
(D) They do not fit in a storage container.

여자는 스웨터에 대해 무엇이라고 말하는가?

(A) 잘 팔리고 있다.
(B) 진열창 안의 물품 중 일부이다.
(C) 아직 구매할 수 없다.
(D) 사이즈상 보관함 안에 넣을 수 없다.

해설 세부 사항 관련 - 여자가 한 말

여자의 첫 번째 대사에서 남자에게 토요일 판매 시작 때까지 새 스웨터를 진열할 필요가 없다고 들었다(I heard that they don't need to go on display until the sale starts on Saturday.)고 했다. 즉, 스웨터를 아직 구매할 수 없으므로 정답은 (C)이다.

60

What does the man mean when he says, "The changing rooms are always a mess"?

(A) More changing rooms are needed.
(B) He wants the woman to tidy up an area.
(C) The store is usually understaffed.
(D) He is disappointed with the customers.

남자가 "탈의실들이 항상 엉망이더군요"라고 말한 의미는 무엇인가?

(A) 탈의실이 더 많이 필요하다.
(B) 남자는 여자가 어떤 구역을 정리했으면 한다.
(C) 매장은 평상시에 스텝이 부족하다.
(D) 남자는 손님들에게 실망했다.

어휘 tidy up ~을 말끔히 정돈하다 understaffed 인력이 부족한

해설 화자의 의도 파악 - 남자의 탈의실 언급 의도

여자의 첫 번째 대사에서 남자에게 해야 할 다른 일이 있는지(is there anything else you need me to do?) 물어보자 남자가 탈의실들이 항상 엉망(The changing rooms are always a mess.)이라고 대답했다. 즉, 남자는 여자가 탈의실을 정리해 주길 원하는 것이므로 정답은 (B)이다.

61

What will the man probably do next?

(A) Take a short break
(B) Organize some clothing
(C) Unpack some boxes
(D) Call a coworker

남자는 다음에 무엇을 하겠는가?

(A) 짧은 휴식 취하기
(B) 옷 정리
(C) 상자들 풀기
(D) 동료에게 전화하기

해설 세부 사항 관련 - 남자의 다음 행동

대화 마지막에 남자가 여성복 매니저에게 전화해서 여자가 지금 그곳으로 간다고 얘기하겠다(I'll call the manager there to let her know that you're heading over.)고 했으므로 정답은 (D)이다.

▸▸ **Paraphrasing** 대화의 **the manager** → 정답의 **a coworker**

62-64 대화 + 목록

M-Cn Ms. McCarty, I'm afraid your department, housekeeping, is still having a lot of problems. What can we do about that?

W-Am [62]**I guess I need to hold a workshop so the new staff members can review the cleaning procedures.** Is there anything in particular I should focus on?

M-Cn Well, just now I had a call from Ms. Harper. [63]**She said that the housekeeping staff didn't put clean sheets on her bed.** And that's just one example on this list of complaints.

W-Am All right. I'll organize something for this week.

M-Cn In the meantime, [64]**I'm going to give a voucher for a free breakfast to each of the guests who had a problem.** I hope that'll satisfy them.

남: 맥카티 씨, 당신이 맡고 있는 객실 관리부에 아직도 문제가 많은 것 같습니다. 어떻게 하면 좋을까요?
여: **워크숍을 열어서 새로운 직원들이 청소 절차를 재확인하도록 해야 할 것 같습니다.** 제가 특별히 중점을 둬야 할 사항이 있나요?
남: 음, 방금 하퍼 씨로부터 전화를 받았어요. **객실 관리 직원이 자기 침대에 깨끗한 시트를 깔지 않았다고 하더군요.** 그리고 그건 이 고객 불만 사항 목록에 나온 하나의 사례에 불과합니다.
여: 알겠습니다. 이번 주에 뭔가 마련할게요.
남: 그러는 동안 **저는 문제가 있었던 고객 각각에게 무료 아침식사 쿠폰을 제공하겠습니다.** 그들이 만족했으면 좋겠네요.

어휘 housekeeping 객실 청소·관리(부) hold a workshop 워크숍을 열다 procedure 절차 in particular 특별히 complaint 불만 organize 준비하다, 정리하다 in the meantime 그동안에 voucher 상품권, 쿠폰 satisfy 만족시키다 spot 얼룩 dressing room 탈의실

Room	Guest Complaint
215	No hand soap
[63]246	Sheets unchanged
320	Wet towels left on floor
334	Spots on dressing room mirror

객실	고객 불만 사항
215	손 비누가 없음
246	시트를 갈지 않음
320	바닥에 젖은 수건이 떨어져 있음
334	탈의실 거울에 얼룩이 있음

62

What does the woman say about her department?

(A) Its workers need more training.
(B) It will be combined with another team.
(C) It does not have enough supplies.
(D) Its schedule must be revised.

여자는 자신의 부서에 대해 무엇이라고 말하는가?

(A) 직원들이 교육을 더 받아야 한다.
(B) 다른 팀과 합쳐질 것이다.
(C) 물품이 충분치 않다.
(D) 스케줄이 수정되어야 한다.

어휘 be combined with ~와 합쳐지다

해설 세부 사항 관련 – 여자가 하는 말

여자의 첫 번째 대사에서 워크숍을 열어서 새로운 직원들이 청소 절차를 재확인할 수 있도록 해야겠다(I guess I need to hold a workshop so the new staff members can review the cleaning procedures.)고 했으므로 정답은 (A)이다.

▸▸ Paraphrasing 대화의 new staff members
→ 정답의 workers

63

Look at the graphic. In which room is Ms. Harper staying?

(A) Room 215
(B) Room 246
(C) Room 320
(D) Room 334

시각 정보에 의하면, 하퍼 씨는 어느 방에 투숙 중인가?

(A) 215호
(B) 246호
(C) 320호
(D) 334호

해설 시각 정보 연계 – 하퍼 씨가 묵고 있는 방

남자의 두 번째 대사에서 하퍼 씨에 따르면 객실 관리 직원이 자기 침대에 깨끗한 시트를 깔지 않았다(She said that the housekeeping staff didn't put clean sheets on her bed.)고 했다. 그리고 고객 불만 사항 목록을 보면 246호실의 불만 사항이 시트를 갈지 않은(Sheets unchanged) 것으로 나와 있으므로 정답은 (B)이다.

64

What does the man say he will do?

(A) Provide some free meals
(B) Clarify a hotel policy
(C) Give a discount on a room rate
(D) Collect additional feedback

남자는 무엇을 할 것이라고 말하는가?

(A) 무료 식사 제공
(B) 호텔 정책 명확히 설명하기
(C) 객실 요금 할인
(D) 추가 피드백 수집

해설 세부 사항 관련 – 남자가 하겠다는 일

대화 마지막에 남자가 문제가 있었던 고객 모두에게 무료 아침식사 쿠폰을 제공하겠다(I'm going to give a voucher for a free breakfast to each of the guests who had a problem.)고 했으므로 정답은 (A)이다.

▸▸ **Paraphrasing** 대화의 **a free breakfast**
→ 정답의 **some free meals**

65-67 대화 + 배치도

W-Br Dr. Choi, [65]**the bamboo palm we ordered for the waiting room just arrived. It's already in the pot,** so we just need to decide where to put it.

M-Au Let's see... How about that corner between the sofa and the TV?

W-Br That's an awfully small space. [66]**What would you think about the corner next to the magazine rack?** That way the leaves will have more room to breathe.

M-Au [66]**Sure, that's a good idea.** And you're going to be taking care of it, right?

W-Br Yes, that's right. [67]**The nursery included a little booklet of care instructions with the delivery. I'll look over it this afternoon.**

M-Au Thanks, Patty. I appreciate it.

여: 최 선생님, **대기실용으로 주문한 대나무 야자가 방금 도착했어요. 이미 화분 안에 심어져 있어서** 어디에 놓을지만 결정하면 됩니다.
남: 봅시다… 소파와 TV 사이 모퉁이가 어떨까요?
여: 거긴 굉장히 좁은 공간이네요. **잡지꽂이 옆 모퉁이는 어떻게 생각하세요?** 그렇게 하면 나뭇잎들이 숨 쉴 공간이 좀 더 생길 거 같네요.
남: **네, 좋은 생각입니다.** 그리고 당신이 나무 돌보기로 한 거 맞죠?
여: 네, 맞습니다. **묘목장에서 작은 관리 지침 책자를 나무 배달할 때 함께 보냈어요. 오늘 오후에 훑어봐야겠어요.**
남: 고마워요, 패티. 감사합니다.

어휘 bamboo palm 대나무 야자 awfully 대단히 rack 받침대, 선반 breathe 숨을 쉬다 nursery 묘목장 booklet 소책자 instructions 지시, 지침 look over 훑어보다

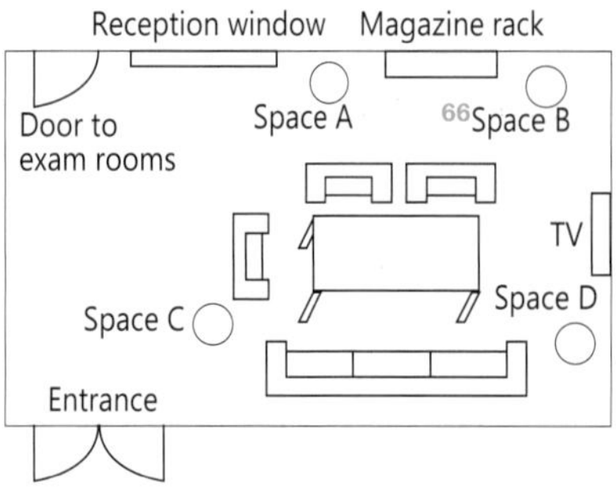

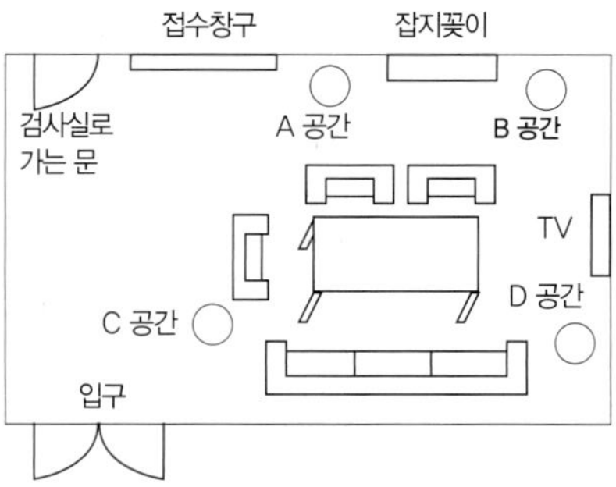

65

What kind of item are the speakers discussing?

(A) A potted plant
(B) A standing lamp
(C) A coat rack
(D) A small table

화자들은 어떤 물건에 대해 얘기하고 있는가?

(A) 화분에 심은 식물
(B) 스탠딩 램프
(C) 코트 걸이
(D) 작은 테이블

어휘 standing lamp (사람 키 높이의) 램프

해설 전체 내용 관련 – 배송된 물건의 종류

여자의 첫 번째 대사에서 대기실용으로 주문한 대나무 야자가 방금 도착했는데 이미 화분 안에 심어져 있다(the bamboo palm we ordered for the waiting room ~ in the pot)고 했으므로 정답은 (A)이다.

66

Look at the graphic. In which space will the woman put the item?

(A) Space A
(B) Space B
(C) Space C
(D) Space D

시각 정보에 의하면, 여자는 어느 공간에 물건을 놓을 것인가?

(A) A 공간
(B) B 공간
(C) C 공간
(D) D 공간

해설 시각 정보 문제 – 위치

여자가 두 번째 대사에서 잡지꽂이 옆 모퉁이에 두는 게 어떻겠냐(What would you think about the corner next to the magazine rack?)고 물었는데 남자가 좋다(Sure, that's a good idea.)고 했으므로 정답은 (B)이다.

67

What does the woman say she will do in the afternoon?

(A) Sign for a delivery
(B) Make an announcement
(C) Set out some publications
(D) Read some instructions

여자는 오후에 무엇을 하겠다고 말하는가?
(A) 배달물 받고 서명하기
(B) 발표하기
(C) 출판물 진열하기
(D) 지침서 읽기

어휘 set out 정돈하다, 진열하다 publication 출판물

해설 세부 사항 관련 – 여자가 할 일
여자의 마지막 대사에서 묘목장에서 작은 관리 지침 책자를 나무 배달할 때 함께 보냈고 오늘 오후에 훑어보겠다(The nursery included a little booklet ~ look over it this afternoon.)고 했으므로 정답은 (D)이다.

68-70 대화 + 안내판

M-Au Hey, Jane. [68]**Are you almost done with the security camera installation on the fourth floor?**

W-Br [68]**Yeah, I just have a few things to finish up.** Why? Do you need some help with yours? I can give you a hand in a minute.

M-Au Well, [69]**I'm here on the third floor, and I've run into a major issue.** I was about to connect the camera to the building's power source, but this wiring looks out of date. I don't think it's up to code.

W-Br In that case, [70]**we'd better call Ms. Fletcher. As the owner of this building, she'll have to hire someone to fix that.** Do you have her number?

남: 제인, **4층에 보안카메라 설치하는 일 거의 다 됐어요?**
여: **네, 마무리할 일만 몇 가지 있어요.** 왜요? 당신 일에 도움이 필요한가요? 곧 도와드릴 수 있어요.
남: 음, **제가 여기 3층에 있는데 중대한 문제에 부딪혔어요.** 카메라를 건물의 전원에 막 연결하려던 참이었는데 이 배선이 오래된 것 같아요. 규정에 맞지 않는 것 같은데요.
여: 그럼 **플레처 씨에게 전화하는 편이 좋겠어요. 그녀가 이 건물 소유주니까 수리할 사람을 고용해야 할 거예요.** 그분의 전화 번호 혹시 아세요?

어휘 be done with ~를 끝마치다 security camera 보안카메라 installation 설치 give A(사람) a hand A를 돕다[거들어주다] in a minute 곧 run into 만나다, 직면하다 power source 전력원 wiring 배선 out of date 낡은, 오래된 up to code 규정에 맞는

Conifer Suites Building Directory

1st Floor	Tukwila Enterprises
2nd Floor	Tech Limited
[69]3rd Floor	Young & Associates
4th Floor	RTJ Insurance

코니퍼 스위트 건물 안내판

1층	투퀼라 엔터프라이지즈
2층	테크 리미티드
3층	영 앤 어소시에이츠
4층	RTJ 보험

68

What are the speakers doing?
(A) Repairing an appliance
(B) Cleaning some offices
(C) Inspecting the building
(D) Installing some equipment

화자들은 무엇을 하고 있는가?
(A) 기기 수리
(B) 사무실 청소
(C) 건물 점검
(D) 장비 설치

해설 전체 내용 관련 – 화자들이 하고 있는 일
남자의 첫 번째 대사에서 여자에게 4층에 보안카메라 설치를 거의 다 끝냈는지(Are you almost done with the security camera installation on the fourth floor?) 물었고 여자는 마무리할 일만 몇 가지 남았다(Yeah, I just have a few things to finish up.)고 대답했다. 이를 통해 화자들이 장비를 설치하고 있음을 알 수 있으므로 정답은 (D)이다.

▸▸ **Paraphrasing** 대화의 the security camera
→ 정답의 some equipment

69

Look at the graphic. According to the man, which company's office has a problem?
(A) Tukwila Enterprises
(B) Tech Limited
(C) Young & Associates
(D) RTJ Insurance

시각 정보를 보라. 남자에 따르면, 어느 회사의 사무실에 문제가 있는가?
(A) 투퀼라 엔터프라이지즈
(B) 테크 리미티드
(C) 영 앤 어소시에이츠
(D) RTJ 보험

해설 시각 정보 연계 – 문제가 있는 사무실
남자의 두 번째 대사에서 자신이 3층에 있는데 중대한 문제에 부딪혔다(I'm here on the third floor, and I've run into a major issue.)고 했다. 건물 안내판을 보면 3층에 영 앤 어소시에이츠(3rd Floor - Young & Associates)가 있으므로 정답은 (C)이다.

Test 2

70

What does the woman suggest?

(A) Using some different materials
(B) Contacting a property owner
(C) Placing a supply request
(D) Finishing work for the day

여자는 무엇을 제안하는가?

(A) 다른 재료 사용하기
(B) 건물주에게 연락하기
(C) 물품 요청하기
(D) 금일 근무 종료하기

해설 세부 사항 관련 - 여자의 제안

대화 마지막에 여자가 플레처 씨에게 전화하는 편이 좋겠다고 하면서 그녀가 건물 소유주니까 수리할 사람을 고용해야 할 것(we'd better call Ms. Fletcher. As the owner of this building, she'll have to hire someone to fix that.)이라고 했으므로 정답은 (B)이다.

▸▸ **Paraphrasing** 대화의 **call** → 정답의 **contact**

PART 4

71-73 안내

W-Br Welcome, everyone, to the Lawrence Community Center's annual event. [71]**With the funds we collect tonight, we'll be able to make essential repairs to our building.** We have a lot of beautiful artwork to auction off this evening. [72]**We've put up posters around the hall listing the approximate value of each piece.** Of course, that's just the starting point. We hope you'll be even more generous with your bids. [73]**Don't forget, we've prepared a gift bag for each ticket holder, so be sure to grab yours on the way out.** All right, enjoy your evening.

여러분, 로렌스 지역 주민회관 연례 행사에 오신 것을 환영합니다. **오늘 밤 조성되는 기금으로 건물에 꼭 필요한 수리를 할 수 있을 것입니다.** 오늘 저녁 경매에 부칠 아름다운 미술품이 많이 있습니다. **홀 곳곳에 각 작품의 개산 가격을 적은 포스터들을 붙여 두었습니다.** 물론 이것은 시작 가격일 뿐입니다. 이보다 훨씬 더 후하게 입찰하시길 바랍니다. **모든 티켓 소지자들을 위해 선물 꾸러미를 하나씩 준비했으니 잊지 마시고 나가시는 길에 여러분의 선물을 꼭 챙겨가십시오.** 그럼, 즐거운 시간 보내시기 바랍니다.

어휘 annual 연례의 fund 기금 essential 필수적인 artwork 미술품 auction off 경매로 팔다 approximate value 개산 가격, 근사치 generous 후한 bid 입찰, 가격 제시 be sure to + 동사원형 꼭 ~하다 grab 잡다 on the way out 나가는 길에

71

According to the speaker, what is the purpose of the event?

(A) To raise money
(B) To celebrate an achievement
(C) To vote on a plan
(D) To promote a competition

화자에 따르면, 행사의 목적은 무엇인가?

(A) 모금을 하기 위해
(B) 성과를 축하하기 위해
(C) 계획을 표결에 부치기 위해
(D) 경연 대회를 홍보하기 위해

해설 세부 사항 관련 - 행사 개최 목적

지문 초반부에 오늘 밤 조성되는 기금으로 건물에 꼭 필요한 수리를 할 수 있을 것(With the funds we collect tonight, we'll be able to make essential repairs to our building.)이라고 했으므로 정답은 (A)이다.

▸▸ **Paraphrasing** 지문의 **the funds we collect**
→ 정답의 **raise money**

72

What has been posted around the hall?

(A) Estimated values
(B) A list of volunteers
(C) Photos of a neighborhood
(D) The results of a questionnaire

홀 주변에는 무엇이 게시되어 있는가?

(A) 예상 가격
(B) 자원봉사자 명단
(C) 동네 사진들
(D) 설문지 결과

어휘 estimated 예상의, 어림의

해설 세부 사항 관련 - 홀 곳곳에 게시된 것

지문 중반부에 홀 곳곳에 각 작품의 대략적인 가격을 적어 놓은 포스터들을 붙여 두었다(We've put up posters around the hall listing the approximate value of each piece.)고 했으므로 정답은 (A)이다.

▸▸ **Paraphrasing** 지문의 **the approximate value**
→ 정답의 **Estimated values**

73

What does the speaker remind the listeners to do?

(A) Sit in assigned seats
(B) Register for a session
(C) Watch a short film
(D) Pick up a set of gifts

화자는 청자들에게 무엇을 하라고 상기시키는가?

(A) 지정석 착석
(B) 세션에 등록하기
(C) 단편 영화 관람
(D) 선물 세트 가져가기

어휘 assigned 할당된 register for ~에 등록하다

해설 세부 사항 관련 – 청자들에게 상기시키는 사항

지문 마지막에 화자가 티켓 소지자들을 위해 선물 꾸러미를 준비했으니 나가는 길에 잊지 말고 꼭 가져가라(Don't forget, we've prepared a gift bag ~ on the way out.)고 했으므로 정답은 (D)이다.

▸▸ **Paraphrasing** 지문의 **grab yours**
→ 정답의 **Pick up a set of gifts**

74-76 담화

M-Cn OK, everyone. As you know, [74]**we've been asked to start teleconferencing regularly with other branches, so today I'm going to discuss how to do that.** The technological side is pretty simple—you just call the dial-in number and then provide the access code. [75]**You're going to practice that with our IT specialist here in a few minutes, when she gets the equipment set up.** Until then, let's talk about what else you can do to make the calls run smoothly. For example, [76]**you should stay quiet unless you need to speak.** Otherwise, you'll make it hard for everyone to hear the other participants.

자, 여러분, 아시다시피, **우리는 다른 지사들과 정기적인 원격 회의를 시작해 달라는 요청을 받았습니다. 그래서 오늘은 어떻게 하는지 얘기하려고 하는데요.** 기술적인 측면은 아주 간단합니다. 여러분이 직통 전화번호로 전화해서 접속 번호만 제공하면 됩니다. **여러분은 잠시 후에 우리 IT 전문가가 장비를 설치하는 대로 함께 이 자리에서 실행을 해 볼 거예요.** 그때까지, 통화를 순조롭게 하기 위해 그 밖에 뭘 할 수 있는지 얘기해 보겠습니다. 이를테면, **자신이 말해야 할 때가 아니면 조용히 해 주셔야 합니다.** 그렇지 않으면, 여러분 때문에 모든 사람이 다른 참여자들의 말을 듣는 게 어려워질 겁니다.

어휘 teleconferencing 원격 (화상) 회의 branch 지사 dial-in number 직통 전화번호 access code 접속 번호 stay quiet 조용히 하다 participant 참가자

74

What is the talk mainly about?

(A) Tracking work hours electronically
(B) Participating in a conference call
(C) Creating videos of events
(D) Setting up an e-mail account

담화의 주된 내용은 무엇인가?

(A) 컴퓨터로 근무 시간 추적하기
(B) 전화 회의 참석하기
(C) 행사 비디오 제작하기
(D) 이메일 계정 개설하기

어휘 track 추적하다 electronically 전자적으로, 컴퓨터로 conference call 전화 회의

해설 전체 내용 관련 – 담화의 주제

지문 초반부에 화자는 다른 지사들과 정기적인 원격 회의를 시작해 달라는 요청을 받았고 그래서 오늘은 어떻게 하는지 얘기하려고 한다(we've been asked to start teleconferencing ~ discuss how to do that.)고 했으므로 정답은 (B)이다.

75

What does the speaker say about some technology?

(A) The listeners will try it out soon.
(B) It can only be used by an expert.
(C) He does not have access to it today.
(D) It will increase the company's efficiency.

화자는 장비에 대해 무엇을 말하는가?

(A) 청자들이 곧 사용해 볼 것이다.
(B) 전문가만 사용할 수 있다.
(C) 오늘은 사용할 수 없다.
(D) 회사의 효율성을 높여줄 것이다.

어휘 technology 기술, 장비 try out 시험적으로 사용해 보다 expert 전문가 have access to ~을 사용할 수 있다 efficiency 효율성

해설 세부 사항 관련 – 장비에 대해 언급된 사항

지문 중반부에서 화자가 잠시 후에 IT 전문가가 장비를 설치하는 대로 함께 그 자리에서 실행을 해 볼 것(You're going to practice that with our IT specialist ~ the equipment set up.)이라고 했으므로 정답은 (A)이다.

▸▸ **Paraphrasing** 지문의 **practice** → 정답의 **try it out**

76

What are the listeners asked to avoid doing?

(A) Running in the workplace
(B) Damaging a device
(C) Making unnecessary noise
(D) Losing a password

청자들은 무엇을 지양하라고 요청받았는가?

(A) 사내에서 뛰는 것
(B) 장치를 손상시키는 것
(C) 불필요한 소음을 내는 것
(D) 비밀번호를 분실하는 것

어휘 workplace 직장 damage 손상시키다 device 장치

해설 세부 사항 관련 – 청자들이 지양해야 할 것

지문의 마지막 부분에서 화자가 자신이 말해야 할 때가 아니면 조용히 해 주셔야 한다(you should stay quiet unless you need to speak.)고 했으므로 정답은 (C)이다.

77-79 전화 메시지

M-Au Hi, Ms. Najera. This is Ron from the administration office. [77]**I'm making the arrangements for your upcoming trip for the assembly plant inspection in Mumbai.** There are some vaccinations you'll need to get before your trip, so [78]**I've booked you an appointment next week with Dr. Herbert at the Central Clinic.** That's for two P.M. on Tuesday. Also, I want to purchase your airline tickets as soon as possible. [79]**Would you like to sit by the window or by the aisle?** Please call me back to let me know. I'm at extension 22. Thanks.

안녕하세요, 나제라 씨. 총무부의 론입니다. **저는 곧 있을 귀하의 뭄바이 조립 공장 시찰 출장을 준비해 드리고 있습니다.** 여행하시기 전 맞으셔야 할 백신이 몇 가지 있어서 **다음 주 센트럴 클리닉의 허버트 박사께 예약을 해 두었습니다.** 화요일 오후 2시입니다. 아울러 가능한 한 빨리 항공권을 구입하고자 합니다. **창가 쪽 좌석이 좋으십니까, 아니면 통로 쪽 좌석이 좋으십니까?** 전화로 알려주시기 바랍니다. 제 내선번호는 22번입니다. 감사합니다.

어휘 administration office 총무부, 행정실 make the arrangements for ~를 준비하다 upcoming 다가오는 assembly plant 조립 공장 inspection 시찰 vaccination 백신 (예방) 접종 book 예약하다 appointment 약속 aisle 통로, 복도 extension 내선, 구내전화

77

Why will the listener go to Mumbai?

(A) To attend a conference
(B) To inspect a factory
(C) To establish an office
(D) To sign a contract

청자는 왜 뭄바이에 갈 것인가?

(A) 컨퍼런스에 참석하기 위해
(B) 공장을 시찰하기 위해
(C) 사무소를 설립하기 위해
(D) 계약을 체결하기 위해

해설 세부 사항 관련 - 청자가 뭄바이에 가는 이유

지문 초반부에 화자가 청자에게 곧 있을 뭄바이 조립 공장 시찰에 대한 출장 준비를 하고 있다(I'm making the arrangements for your upcoming trip ~ in Mumbai.)고 했으므로 정답은 (B)이다.

▸▸ **Paraphrasing** 지문의 **the assembly plant**
→ 정답의 **a factory**

78

According to the speaker, what should the listener do next week?

(A) Review an itinerary
(B) Visit a medical facility
(C) Book accommodations
(D) Renew a passport

화자에 따르면, 청자는 다음 주에 무엇을 해야 하는가?

(A) 여행 일정 검토
(B) 의료 시설 방문
(C) 숙소 예약
(D) 여권 갱신

어휘 itinerary 여행 일정(표) accommodations 숙박 시설 renew 갱신하다

해설 세부 사항 관련 - 청자가 다음 주에 해야 할 일

지문 중반에 화자가 청자를 위해 다음 주 센트럴 클리닉의 허버트 박사에게 진료 예약을 해 두었다(I've booked you an appointment next week with Dr. Herbert at the Central Clinic.)고 했으므로 정답은 (B)이다.

▸▸ **Paraphrasing** 지문의 **the Central Clinic**
→ 정답의 **a medical facility**

79

What information does the speaker request?

(A) A seating preference
(B) An airline name
(C) A ticket number
(D) A hotel recommendation

화자는 어떤 정보를 요청하는가?

(A) 선호하는 좌석
(B) 항공사명
(C) 티켓 번호
(D) 호텔 추천

해설 세부 사항 관련 - 화자가 요청한 정보

지문 후반부에 화자가 청자에게 창가 쪽과 통로 쪽 좌석 중 어떤 것을 선호하는지(Would you like to sit by the window or by the aisle?) 물어봤으므로 정답은 (A)이다.

80-82 회의 발췌

W-Am Good morning, everyone. [80]**I've called this meeting in response to the bad news regarding our bid to acquire Erlon Digital Advertising.** As I'm sure you've all heard, [80]**Erlon has entered into serious negotiations with Chelps Online instead.** [81]**Obviously, this is disappointing. Still,** it isn't over yet. [81]**The two companies may not manage to come to an agreement.** And even if they do, [82]**the government agency that oversees mergers and acquisitions might not approve of the plan.** So I think we shouldn't give up on Erlon at this point. What are your thoughts?

안녕하세요, 여러분. **얼론 디지털 애드버타이징 인수를 위한 경쟁 입찰과 관련해 좋지 않은 소식이 있어서 회의를 소집했습니다.** 여러분 모두 들었으리라 생각합니다만, **얼론은 대신 첼프스 온라인과 진지한 협상에 들어갔습니다. 이건 당연히 실망스럽죠. 하지만 아직 끝난 건 아닙니다. 그 두 회사가 합의를 이뤄내지 못할 수도 있습니다.** 그리고 합의를 한다 **해도 기업 인수 합병을 감독하는 정부 기관이 이 안을 승인하지 않을 수도 있고요.** 그러니까 우리는 현 시점에서 얼론을 포기해서는 안 된다고 생각합니다. 여러분 생각은 어떤가요?

어휘 in response to ~에 대응해 bid 경쟁 입찰 acquire 획득[취득]하다 enter into ~을 시작하다 negotiation 협상 instead 대신에 obviously 명백하게 disappointing 실망스러운 still 그런데도 manage to + 동사원형 간신히 ~해내다 come to an agreement 합의에 이르다 agency 기관 oversee 감독하다 mergers and acquisitions 기업 인수 합병(M&A) approve of 찬성하다, 승인하다

80

What is the speaker giving an update on?

(A) Preparations for some promotional events
(B) Negotiations with a potential new hire
(C) The development of some consumer goods
(D) The attempted acquisition of a business

화자는 무엇에 관해 최신 정보를 알려 주는가?

(A) 홍보 행사 준비
(B) 잠재 신입사원과의 협상
(C) 소비재 상품 개발
(D) 미수로 그친 업체 인수

어휘 potential 잠재적인 hire 신입사원 consumer goods 소비재 attempted 미수의, 시도된

해설 세부 사항 관련 – 화자가 알려주는 정보

지문 초반부에서 화자가 얼론 디지털 애드버타이징 인수를 위한 경쟁 입찰과 관련해 좋지 않은 소식이 있어서 회의를 소집했다(I've called this meeting ~ to acquire Erlon Digital Advertising.)면서 얼론은 대신 첼프스 온라인과 진지한 협상에 들어갔다(Erlon has entered into serious negotiations with Chelps Online instead.)고 했으므로 정답은 (D)이다.

81

Why does the speaker say, "it isn't over yet"?

(A) To remind listeners of some unfinished tasks
(B) To express frustration with the speed of a process
(C) To give listeners hope of a positive end result
(D) To explain why she does not have some information

화자가 "아직 끝난 건 아닙니다"라고 말한 이유는 무엇인가?

(A) 청자들에게 마무리되지 않은 과제를 상기시키려고
(B) 처리 속도에 대한 불만을 표시하려고
(C) 청자들에게 긍정적인 최종 결과에 대한 희망을 주려고
(D) 자신이 정보를 갖고 있는 않은 이유를 설명하려고

어휘 remind A of B A에게 B를 상기시키다 frustration 불만, 좌절 process 절차 positive 긍정적인

해설 화자의 의도 파악 – 아직 끝난 것이 아니라고 말한 이유

화자는 인용문 바로 앞 문장에서 현황이 당연히 실망스럽다(Obviously, this is disappointing.)고 했다. 그리고 인용문 뒤 문장에서는 그 두 회사가 합의를 이뤄내지 못할 수도 있다(The two companies may not manage to come to an agreement.)고 했다. 따라서 최종 결과에 대한 희망을 주려는 의미임을 알 수 있으므로 정답은 (C)이다.

82

What does the speaker say about a government agency?

(A) It may fund a project.
(B) It oversees the healthcare industry.
(C) It is seeking a service provider.
(D) It may reject a proposal.

화자는 정부 기관에 대해 무엇을 말하는가?

(A) 프로젝트 자금을 댈 수도 있다.
(B) 의료업계를 감독한다.
(C) 서비스 제공 업체를 찾고 있다.
(D) 제안을 거절할 수도 있다.

어휘 fund 자금을 대다 healthcare industry 의료업계

해설 세부 사항 관련 – 정부 기관에 관한 내용

지문 후반부에서 화자가 기업 인수 합병을 감독하는 정부 기관이 이 안을 승인하지 않을 수도 있다(the government agency that oversees mergers and acquisitions might not approve of the plan.)고 했으므로 정답은 (D)이다.

▸▸ **Paraphrasing** 지문의 **not approve of the plan**
→ 정답의 **reject a proposal**

83-85 안내 방송

M-Cn [83]**Attention, guests waiting in line to ride the Silver Eagle Roller Coaster. Unfortunately, this attraction has broken down.** Our technicians are attempting to repair it, but they do not expect it to reopen before the park closes today. [84]**Please exit the waiting area by turning around and following the same route through which you entered.** We are very sorry for the inconvenience. [85]**As a token of apology, each of you will be issued a single-use Speedy Pass. This will allow you to enter any other ride in the park without waiting in line.** Thank you, and we hope you enjoy the rest of your day at Reinholt Amusement Park.

실버 이글 롤러코스터를 타려고 줄 서서 기다리시는 방문자 여러분. 유감스럽게도 이 인기 놀이 기구가 고장이 났습니다. 저희 기술자들이 수리하려고 노력 중이지만, 오늘 공원 문을 닫기 전에 재가동이 될 거라고 생각되지는 않습니다. **뒤로 돌아서 여러분이 들어왔던 그 길을 따라 대기 구역에서 나가주시기 바랍니다.** 불편함을 드려 대단히 죄송합니다. **사과의 표시로 한 분 한 분께 1회 사용 스피디 패스를 지급해 드리겠습니다. 이를 제시하시면 줄 서서 기다리지 않고 공원 안에 있는 다른 어떤 놀이기구든 타실 수 있습니다.** 감사합니다. 라인홀트 놀이 공원에서 오늘 하루 남은 시간 즐겁게 보내시기 바랍니다.

어휘 ride 타다; 놀이기구 attraction 명소, 명물 break down 고장 나다 reopen 재개하다 exit 나가다 turn around 돌아서다 inconvenience 불편함 as a token of ~의 표시로 issue 발급하다, 지급하다

83

What is being announced?

(A) A start time has been postponed.
(B) A performance has been canceled.
(C) Some machinery is malfunctioning.
(D) Some merchandise is out of stock.

무슨 내용이 방송되고 있는가?
(A) 시작 시간이 연기되었다.
(B) 공연이 취소되었다.
(C) 기계가 제대로 작동하지 않는다.
(D) 상품의 재고가 없다.

어휘 malfunction (기계가) 제대로 작동하지 않다 merchandise 상품 out of stock 재고가 없는

해설 전체 내용 관련 – 방송 공지의 내용
지문 초반부에서 화자는 실버 이글 롤러코스터를 타려고 줄 서서 기다리시는 방문자께 유감스럽게도 그 인기 기구가 고장이 났다는 내용을 알린다(Attention, guests waiting in line ~ this attraction has broken down.)고 했으므로 정답은 (C)이다.

▸▸ Paraphrasing 지문의 attraction has broken down
→ 정답의 machinery is malfunctioning

84

What are the listeners asked to do?

(A) Leave the area
(B) Show a form of identification
(C) Turn off their mobile phones
(D) Look at a display board

청자들은 무엇을 하라고 요청받는가?
(A) 구역 떠나기
(B) 신분증 제시
(C) 휴대전화 끄기
(D) 게시판 보기

어휘 identification 신분 증명 display board (전광) 게시판

해설 세부 사항 관련 – 청자들이 요청받은 사항
지문 중반부에서 화자가 청자들에게 뒤로 돌아서 들어왔던 그 길을 따라 대기 구역에서 나가주길 바란다(Please exit the waiting area ~ through which you entered.)고 했으므로 정답은 (A)이다.

85

What will be given to the listeners?

(A) A refund of an entrance fee
(B) Directions to a convenience facility
(C) An express ticket to any other attraction
(D) A voucher for a souvenir shop

청자들에게 무엇이 제공될 것인가?
(A) 입장료 환불
(B) 편의 시설까지 가는 길 안내
(C) 다른 인기 놀이기구 급행 이용권
(D) 기념품 가게 상품권

어휘 convenience 편의 express ticket 급행권 souvenir shop 기념품 가게

해설 세부 사항 관련 – 청자들에게 제공되는 것
지문 후반부에서 화자가 사과의 표시로 1회 사용 스피디 패스를 지급할 것이고, 이를 제시하면 줄 서서 기다리지 않고 공원 안에 있는 어떤 놀이기구든 탈 수 있다(As a token of apology, each of you ~ in the park without waiting in line.)고 했으므로 정답은 (C)이다.

86-88 뉴스 보도

W-Am Good evening. This is Kaitlyn Brown from Prime Radio. [86]**I'm here with a live report from Pisani Bistro for its highly anticipated opening day.** The restaurant is owned by world-renowned chef Isabella Pisani, and food critics and diners alike are excited to taste the mouthwatering dishes she has created. [87]**Diners without reservations are lined up out the door.** They're going to be here for hours, but everyone I've spoken to says it'll be well worth it. [88]**Many of them are looking forward to trying Ms. Pisani's signature Chocolate Tower dessert, which features imported chocolate mixed with the perfect balance of exotic spices.** From Pisani Bistro, this has been Kaitlyn Brown reporting.

안녕하세요. 프라임 라디오의 케이틀린 브라운입니다. **저는 지금 큰 기대를 모으는 개점일 상황을 생중계하기 위해 피사니 비스트로에 나와 있습니다.** 이 식당은 세계적으로 유명한 요리사 이사벨라 피사니 씨가 소유하고 있는데요. 음식 비평가들과 손님들 모두 그녀가 새롭게 만든 군침 도는 요리를 맛보게 돼서 흥분해 있습니다. **예약하지 않은 손님들이 입구 밖에 줄을 서 있는데요.** 여기서 몇 시간 동안 기다려야 할 겁니다. 하지만 제가 얘기 나눠 본 사람들은 모두 충분히 그럴 만한 가치가 있을 거라고 입을 모읍니다. **이들 중 많은 수가 피사니 씨의 가장 유명한 초콜릿 타워 디저트를 고대하고 있습니다. 여기에는 완벽하게 조화를 이룬 이국적 향신료들과 어우러진 수입 초콜릿이 들어갑니다.** 피사니 비스트로에서, 케이틀린 브라운이었습니다.

어휘 live report 생중계 highly anticipated 매우 기대되는 world-renowned 세계적으로 유명한 food critic 음식 비평가 diner 식사하는 사람, 음식점 손님 A and B alike A도 B도 mouthwatering 군침을 돌게 하는 well worth it 그만한 가치가 충분하다 signature dish 요리사의 가장 유명한 요리 feature 특별히 포함하다 imported 수입된 exotic 이국적인 spice 향신료

86

What is the speaker reporting on?

(A) A grand opening
(B) A product launch
(C) A restaurant's relocation
(D) A change in ownership

화자는 무엇에 대해 보도하고 있는가?
(A) 매장 개점
(B) 제품 출시
(C) 식당 이전
(D) 소유주 변경

해설 전체 내용 관련 - 보도 내용
지문 초반부에 화자가 큰 기대를 모으는 개점일 상황을 생중계하기 위해 피사니 비스트로에 나와 있다(I'm here with a live report from Pisani Bistro for its highly anticipated opening day.)고 했으므로 정답은 (A)이다.

▸▸ Paraphrasing 지문의 opening day → 정답의 grand opening

87

What does the speaker mean when she says, "They're going to be here for hours"?
(A) The business will remain open later than usual.
(B) There is enough time to take advantage of an offer.
(C) The business has a reputation for slow service.
(D) A lot of people are waiting to get into the business.

화자가 "여기서 몇 시간 동안 기다려야 할 겁니다"라고 말한 의미는 무엇인가?
(A) 매장이 평소보다 늦게까지 열려 있을 것이다.
(B) 할인을 이용할 시간이 충분하다.
(C) 매장은 서비스가 느리다는 평을 듣는다.
(D) 많은 사람들이 매장에 들어가기 위해 기다리고 있다.

어휘 remain ~인 채로 남아있다 take advantage of ~을 이용하다 reputation 평판

해설 화자의 의도 파악 – 몇 시간 동안 기다려야 할 거라는 말
지문 중반부에 예약하지 않은 손님들은 입구 밖에 줄을 서 있다(Diners without reservations are lined up out the door.)고 했다. 그러므로 그들이 몇 시간 동안 기다려야 할 것이라는 인용문은 많은 손님들이 식당에 들어가기 위해 대기하고 있다는 의미이므로 정답은 (D)이다.

88

What is mentioned about the Chocolate Tower dessert?
(A) It has been discounted.
(B) It takes a long time to prepare.
(C) It uses foreign ingredients.
(D) It is already sold out.

초콜릿 타워 디저트에 대해 언급된 것은 무엇인가?
(A) 가격이 할인되었다.
(B) 준비하는 데 오래 걸린다.
(C) 외국산 재료를 사용한다.
(D) 이미 매진되었다.

해설 세부 사항 관련 - 디저트에 대해 언급된 내용
지문 마지막에 초콜릿 타워 디저트에는 완벽하게 조화를 이룬 이국적 향신료와 어우러진 수입 초콜릿이 들어간다(Chocolate Tower dessert, which features imported chocolate mixed with the perfect balance of exotic spices.)고 했으므로 정답은 (C)이다.

▸▸ Paraphrasing 지문의 exotic spices
→ 정답의 foreign ingredients

89-91 전화 메세지

M-Au Hi, Anika. [89]**I just wanted to thank you again for all the help you gave me with Ms. Stanton's retirement banquet.** Everyone was commenting on how beautiful the invitations were. I'd love to know where you got them printed! [90]**I have more events coming up, and it's always important to make a good impression.** Anyway, enjoy the rest of the weekend, and I'll see you at work. [91]**I'm looking forward to meeting Ms. Stanton's replacement, who starts next week.**

안녕하세요, 아니카. **스탠튼 씨의 은퇴 기념 연회를 위해 제게 주신 모든 도움에 대해 다시 한번 감사드립니다.** 모두들 초대장이 정말 멋지다고 이야기했어요. 어디서 인쇄하셨는지 무척 알고 싶습니다. **앞으로 행사가 더 있을 예정이고, 좋은 인상을 남기는 일은 항상 중요하거든요.** 아무튼 남은 주말 잘 보내시고 회사에서 뵐게요. **다음 주에 출근할 스탠튼 씨의 후임을 빨리 만나보고 싶네요.**

어휘 retirement 은퇴 comment on ~에 대해 언급하다 come up (행사 등이) 다가오다 make a good impression 좋은 인상을 주다 rest 나머지 at work 일터에서 replacement 후임자

89

What is the purpose of the call?
(A) To plan a celebration
(B) To show appreciation
(C) To extend an invitation
(D) To ask for some assistance

전화를 건 목적은 무엇인가?
(A) 축하 행사를 계획하기 위해
(B) 감사를 표하기 위해
(C) 초대를 하기 위해
(D) 도움을 청하기 위해

어휘 celebration 축하 assistance 도움

해설 전체 내용 관련 - 전화를 건 목적
지문 초반부에 화자가 청자에게 스탠튼 씨의 은퇴 기념 연회에 대해 도움을 줘서 다시 한번 감사드린다(I just wanted to thank you again for all the help you gave me with Ms. Stanton's retirement banquet.)고 했으므로 정답은 (B)이다.

90

What does the speaker imply when he says, "I'd love to know where you got them printed"?
(A) He hopes printing costs are not over budget.
(B) He has to send a payment to a printer.
(C) He will need printing services in the future.
(D) He is having trouble selling a printing machine.

화자가 "어디서 인쇄하셨는지 무척 알고 싶습니다"라고 말한 의도는 무엇인가?

(A) 인쇄비가 예산을 초과하지 않기를 바란다.
(B) 인쇄소에 대금을 지불해야 한다.
(C) 향후 인쇄 서비스가 필요할 것이다.
(D) 인쇄기를 판매하는 데 어려움이 있다.

해설 화자의 의도 파악 - 어디서 인쇄했는지 알고 싶다는 말의 의미

지문 중반부에서 앞으로 행사가 더 있을 예정이고, 좋은 인상을 남기는 일은 항상 중요하다(I have more events coming up, and it's always important to make a good impression.)고 했다. 즉, 어디서 초대장을 인쇄했는지 알고 싶다는 말은 화자가 앞으로 있을 행사를 위해 인쇄 서비스가 필요하다는 의미를 담고 있는 것이므로 정답은 (C)이다.

91

According to the speaker, what will happen next week?

(A) A new employee will begin work.
(B) The listener will give a talk at a meeting.
(C) Some office equipment will be replaced.
(D) The listener will have some time off.

화자에 따르면, 다음 주에 무슨 일이 있을 것인가?

(A) 새로운 직원이 업무를 시작할 것이다.
(B) 청자는 회의에서 연설을 할 것이다.
(C) 사무용 기기가 교체될 것이다.
(D) 청자는 얼마간의 휴식을 가질 것이다.

해설 세부 사항 관련 - 다음 주에 발생할 일

지문 마지막에 화자가 다음 주에 출근할 스탠튼 씨의 후임자를 빨리 만나보고 싶다(I'm looking forward to meeting Ms. Stanton's replacement, who starts next week.)고 했으므로 정답은 (A)이다.

▸▸ **Paraphrasing** 지문의 **Ms. Stanton's replacement**
→ 정답의 **a new employee**

92-94 광고

W-Br Take control of your future by developing career-enhancing skills at [92]**the Emerson Institute, the region's leading provider of classes on graphic design.** Whether you plan to work as a freelancer or join a company, you can be confident that the Emerson Institute will help you create the foundation you need for success. [93]**We're famous for our teachers, who are experts in their field, with more experience than those of any of our competitors.** They'll share their expertise and insights with you. Find out more at our January twenty-eighth informational meeting on campus, where you can get your questions answered. Then [94]**you can make an informed decision just in time for the February sixth to seventeenth registration.**

이 지역에서 그래픽 디자인 강좌를 제공하는 선도적인 에머슨 인스티튜트에서 커리어를 넓혀줄 기술을 개발하여 여러분의 미래를 지배하십시오. 여러분이 프리랜서로 일하려고 하든, 회사에 입사하고자 하든, 에머슨 인스티튜트가 여러분께서 성공에 필요한 기반을 닦는 데 도움이 될 것이라고 확신하셔도 좋습니다. **저희는 각 분야의 전문가들로서 어떤 경쟁업체보다 경험이 풍부한 강사들로 유명합니다.** 여러분은 강사들을 통해 전문 지식을 쌓고 통찰력을 기르게 될 것입니다. 1월 28일 캠퍼스에서 있을 설명회에 오셔서 더 자세한 내용을 알아보세요. 여러분의 궁금증에 대하여 답을 들을 수 있습니다. 그러면 **2월 6일~17일 등록 기간에 맞춰 현명한 결정을 내릴 수 있을 것입니다.**

어휘 take control of ~를 지배하다 career-enhancing 커리어를 넓혀 주는 leading 선도하는 confident 자신 있는 foundation 기초, 토대 competitor 경쟁 회사 expertise 전문 지식 insight 통찰력 informational meeting (정보) 설명회 informed decision (정보에 입각한) 현명한 결정 just in time for ~에 맞춰, 늦지 않게

92

What field does the Emerson Institute offer courses in?

(A) Software development
(B) Accounting practices
(C) Graphic design
(D) Creative writing

에머슨 인스티튜트는 어떤 분야의 강좌를 제공하는가?

(A) 소프트웨어 개발
(B) 회계 실무
(C) 그래픽 디자인
(D) 문예 창작

해설 세부 사항 관련 - 제공되는 강좌의 분야

지문 초반부에 에머슨 인스티튜트가 지역에서 그래픽 디자인 강좌를 제공하는 선도 기관(the Emerson Institute, the region's leading provider of classes on graphic design.)이라고 소개했으므로 정답은 (C)이다.

93

What is the Emerson Institute known for?

(A) Its opportunities for networking
(B) Its convenient class times
(C) Its wide selection of courses
(D) Its knowledgeable instructors

에머슨 인스티튜트는 무엇으로 유명한가?

(A) 인적 네트워크 형성 기회
(B) 편리한 강좌 시간
(C) 다양한 강좌
(D) 정통한 강사진

어휘 networking (정보나 조언을 얻기 위한) 인적 정보망의 형성 knowledgeable 정통한, 박식한

해설 세부 사항 관련 - 에머슨 인스티튜트가 유명한 이유

지문 중반부에 에머슨 인스티튜트는 각 분야의 전문가들로서 어떤 경쟁업체보다 경험이 풍부한 강사들로 유명하다(We're famous for our teachers ~ any of our competitors.)고 했으므로 정답은 (D)이다.

▸▸ **Paraphrasing** 지문의 **teachers** → 정답의 **instructors**

94

According to the advertisement, what will happen on February 6?

(A) An enrollment period will begin.
(B) An information session will be held.
(C) A course catalog will be published.
(D) A campus tour will be given.

광고에 따르면, 2월 6일에 무슨 일이 있을 것인가?

(A) 등록 기간이 시작될 것이다.
(B) 설명회가 개최될 것이다.
(C) 수강 카탈로그가 발행될 것이다.
(D) 캠퍼스 견학이 있을 것이다.

해설 세부 사항 관련 - 2월 6일에 있을 일

지문 마지막에 2월 6일에서 17일까지의 등록 기간에 맞춰 현명한 결정을 내릴 수 있다(you can make an informed decision ~ sixth to seventeenth registration.)고 했다. 2월 6일에 등록이 시작됨을 알 수 있으므로 정답은 (A)이다.

▸▸ **Paraphrasing** 지문의 **registration** → 정답의 **enrollment**

95-97 전화 메시지 + 주문서

W-Am Hi, Sean. It's Hisako. I've forwarded you the requests from the managers of each of our restaurant branches so you can place the linen order. [95]**Augusta and Enfield need more of everything, Worthington only needs bar towels, and Glendale only needs tablecloths.** Usually we send everything to our office to verify the contents, but the order's a lot bigger this time. [96]**I'm worried that we won't have enough space for everything.** So, please have the items delivered to the individual branches instead. Also, the managers want to know when the items will arrive. So, [97]**please call them as soon as you find out the delivery date.** Thanks!

안녕하세요, 션. 히사코입니다. 저희 식당의 각 지점 매니저들로부터 요청 사항을 받아 보내드렸으니 리넨 제품을 주문하시면 됩니다. **어거스타와 엔필드 지점은 모든 물품이 더 필요하다고 하고, 워딩턴 지점은 바 수건만, 글렌데일 지점은 테이블보만 필요합니다.** 보통은 내용물 확인을 위해 저희 사무실로 모든 물품을 보냅니다만, 이번에는 주문량이 훨씬 많아 **물품 일체를 둘 공간이 충분치 않을 것 같아 염려됩니다.** 그러니 물품이 사무실 대신 각 지점으로 배송되도록 해 주십시오. 아울러 매니저들은 물품이 언제 도착할지 알고 싶어합니다. 그러니 **배송 일자가 나오는 대로 매니저들에게 전화해 주십시오.** 감사합니다.

어휘 forward 전달하다 verify 확인하다 content 내용물 individual 각각의 quantity 수량

Linens Request

Item Type	Quantity Needed
Bar Towels	0
Kitchen Towels	0
[95]Tablecloths	22
Napkins	0

리넨 요청 사항

품목	필요 수량
바 수건	0
키친 타월	0
테이블보	22
냅킨	0

95

Look at the graphic. Which branch made the request?

(A) Augusta
(B) Enfield
(C) Worthington
(D) Glendale

시각 정보에 의하면, 어느 지점의 요청 사항인가?

(A) 어거스타
(B) 엔필드
(C) 워딩턴
(D) 글렌데일

해설 시각 정보 연계 - 요청을 한 지점

지문 초반부에 어거스타와 엔필드 지점은 모든 물품이 더 필요하고, 워딩턴 지점은 바 수건만, 글렌데일 지점은 테이블보만 필요하다(Augusta and Enfield need ~ Glendale only needs tablecloths.)고 했는데, 주문 양식을 보면 다른 물품에 대한 주문은 없고 테이블보만 22장 주문한 것으로 되어 있으므로 정답은 (D)이다.

96

What is the speaker concerned about?

(A) Missing a deadline for an order
(B) Lacking the necessary storage space
(C) Paying high shipping charges
(D) Getting the wrong sizes

화자는 무엇에 대해 염려하는가?

(A) 주문 기한을 넘기는 것
(B) 필요한 보관 공간이 부족한 것
(C) 비싼 배송료를 지불하는 것
(D) 틀린 사이즈의 물품들을 받는 것

해설 세부 사항 관련 - 화자의 염려

지문 중반부에 물품 일체를 둘 공간이 충분치 않을 것 같아 염려된다(I'm worried that we won't have enough space for everything.)고 했으므로 정답은 (B)이다.

97

What is the listener asked to do?

(A) Report information to the managers
(B) Verify the contents of a package
(C) Choose a date for a gathering
(D) Monitor a branch's inventory

청자는 무엇을 하라고 요청받았는가?

(A) 매니저들에게 정보 제공
(B) 소포 안의 내용물 확인
(C) 모임 날짜 선택
(D) 지점의 물품 목록 모니터링

해설 세부 사항 관련 - 청자에 대한 요청
지문 마지막에 화자가 청자에게 배송일자가 나오는 대로 매니저들에게 전화해 달라(please call them as soon as you find out the delivery date.)고 했으므로 정답은 (A)이다.

▸▸ **Paraphrasing** 지문의 the delivery date
→ 정답의 information

98-100 회의 발췌 + 일정표

M-Au Good morning, everyone, and welcome. Thank you for being here today. My name is Jared Brannon, and I'm the head of the sales team here at Mallory Industries. [98]**We're pleased that you are considering investing in our business.** Throughout the day, you'll be learning more about our operations, and we encourage you to ask questions at any time. I've passed out a schedule of the talks from directors of various departments. [99]**I'm sure you'll be particularly interested to hear from Rachel Whitley, our head of marketing.** [100]**After all the talks are over, I'll show you around the building so you can get a taste of what goes on behind the scenes.** If everyone's ready, let's get started.

안녕하세요, 여러분, 환영합니다. 오늘 와 주셔서 감사합니다. 제 이름은 재러드 브래넌이고, 이곳 말로리 인더스트리즈에서 영업팀장을 맡고 있습니다. **여러분께서 저희 회사에 투자를 고려하고 계셔서 기쁩니다.** 오늘 하루 동안 여러분은 저희 회사의 운영에 대해 더욱 많이 알게 되실 것이며 언제든지 질문을 해 주시기 바랍니다. 여러 부서장들의 발표 일정을 나눠 드렸습니다. **분명 저희 마케팅 부서장인 레이첼 위틀리의 발표에 특히 관심이 많으실 텐데요. 모든 발표가 끝나면 건물을 구경시켜 드려 이면에서 어떤 일들이 일어나고 있는지 엿볼 수 있도록 할 예정입니다.** 모두 준비되셨으면 시작하겠습니다.

어휘 invest 투자하다 operation 운영 encourage A to + 동사원형 A가 ~하도록 권장하다 at any time 언제라도 pass out 나눠 주다 particularly 특별히 show around ~을 구경시켜 주다 get a taste of ~을 엿보다 behind the scenes 이면에서

Schedule of Departmental Talks

9:00 A.M.	Sales
11:00 A.M.	R&D
12:30 P.M.	Lunch
[99]1:30 P.M.	Marketing
3:30 P.M.	IT

부서 발표 일정

오전 9시	영업부
오전 11시	연구개발부
오후 12시 30분	점심시간
오후 1시 30분	**마케팅부**
오후 3시 30분	IT부

98

Who most likely are the listeners?

(A) Job candidates
(B) New employees
(C) Company executives
(D) Potential investors

청자들은 누구겠는가?

(A) 입사 지원자들
(B) 신규 직원들
(C) 회사의 임원들
(D) 잠재적 투자자들

해설 전체 내용 관련 - 청자들의 정체
지문 초반부에 화자의 회사에 투자를 고려해 줘서 기쁘다(We're pleased that you are considering investing in our business.)고 했다. 청자들이 잠재 투자자임을 알 수 있으므로 정답은 (D)이다.

99

Look at the graphic. When will Ms. Whitley give a talk?

(A) At 9:00 A.M.
(B) At 11:00 A.M.
(C) At 1:30 P.M.
(D) At 3:30 P.M.

시각 정보에 의하면, 위틀리 씨는 언제 발표할 것인가?

(A) 오전 9시
(B) 오전 11시
(C) 오후 1시 30분
(D) 오후 3시 30분

해설 시각 정보 연계 - 위틀리 씨의 발표 시간
지문 후반부에서 화자가 청자들에게 마케팅 부서장인 레이첼 위틀리의 강연에 특히 관심이 많을 것(I'm sure you'll be particularly interested to hear from Rachel Whitley, our head of marketing.)이라고 했는데 일정표를 보면 마케팅부의 발표 시간이 오후 1시 30분으로 되어 있으므로 정답은 (C)이다.

100

According to the speaker, what will the listeners do at the end of the day?

(A) Go on a guided tour
(B) Receive some samples
(C) Take a written test
(D) Meet a business owner

화자에 따르면, 청자들은 일과 마지막에 무엇을 할 것인가?

(A) 안내원이 딸린 견학
(B) 샘플 받기
(C) 필기시험 치르기
(D) 기업주 만나기

해설 세부 사항 관련 – 청자들의 마지막 일과

지문 후반부에서 모든 발표가 끝나면 이면에서 어떤 일들이 일어나고 있는지 엿볼 수 있도록 건물을 구경시켜 주겠다(After all the talks are over ~ of what goes on behind the scenes.)고 했으므로 정답은 (A)이다.

Test 2

TEST 3

1 (D)	2 (C)	3 (A)	4 (B)	5 (D)
6 (B)	7 (A)	8 (B)	9 (C)	10 (C)
11 (A)	12 (C)	13 (B)	14 (A)	15 (C)
16 (C)	17 (A)	18 (A)	19 (C)	20 (A)
21 (B)	22 (B)	23 (A)	24 (B)	25 (C)
26 (A)	27 (B)	28 (B)	29 (C)	30 (C)
31 (B)	32 (A)	33 (C)	34 (B)	35 (A)
36 (C)	37 (A)	38 (D)	39 (D)	40 (B)
41 (B)	42 (B)	43 (C)	44 (A)	45 (C)
46 (D)	47 (D)	48 (C)	49 (A)	50 (C)
51 (D)	52 (D)	53 (D)	54 (A)	55 (A)
56 (A)	57 (C)	58 (B)	59 (B)	60 (D)
61 (C)	62 (B)	63 (A)	64 (C)	65 (B)
66 (D)	67 (D)	68 (A)	69 (C)	70 (D)
71 (D)	72 (B)	73 (B)	74 (C)	75 (A)
76 (D)	77 (A)	78 (D)	79 (B)	80 (C)
81 (B)	82 (D)	83 (B)	84 (C)	85 (B)
86 (C)	87 (C)	88 (C)	89 (C)	90 (A)
91 (A)	92 (A)	93 (D)	94 (B)	95 (A)
96 (B)	97 (D)	98 (D)	99 (B)	100 (C)

PART 1

1 W-Br

(A) She's eating some baked goods.
(B) She's cleaning the glass.
(C) She's pointing at a cupboard.
(D) She's looking at a display.

(A) 여자가 제과류를 먹고 있다.
(B) 여자가 유리를 닦고 있다.
(C) 여자가 찬장을 가리키고 있다.
(D) 여자가 진열품을 보고 있다.

어휘 baked goods 제과류 point 가리키다 cupboard 찬장 display 진열, 전시

해설 1인 등장 사진 – 사람의 동작 묘사

(A) 여자가 제과류를 먹고 있는(is eating some baked goods) 모습이 아니므로 오답.

(B) 여자가 유리를 닦고 있는(is cleaning the glass) 모습이 아니므로 오답.

(C) 사진에 찬장(cupboard)이 보이지 않으므로 오답.

(D) 여자가 진열된 제품을 보고 있는(is looking at a display) 모습이므로 정답.

2 W-Am

(A) A speaker is standing behind a podium.
(B) A meeting room is being set up.
(C) People are seated on both sides of a table.
(D) A man is passing out some documents.

(A) 화자가 연단 뒤에 서 있다.
(B) 회의실이 준비되고 있다.
(C) 사람들이 테이블 양편에 앉아 있다.
(D) 남자가 서류를 나눠주고 있다.

어휘 podium 연단 set up 준비하다 both sides of ~의 양쪽에 pass out 나눠주다

해설 2인 이상 등장 사진 – 사람의 상태 묘사

(A) 사진에 연단(podium)이 보이지 않으므로 오답.

(B) 회의실이 지금 준비되고 있는(is being set up) 상황이 아니므로 오답.

(C) 사람들이 테이블 양쪽에(on both sides of a table) 앉아 있는(are seated) 상태이므로 정답.

(D) 남자가 서류를 나눠주고 있는(is passing out some documents) 모습이 아니므로 오답.

3 M-Cn

(A) Some curtains have been pulled open.
(B) The floor is completely covered with carpeting.
(C) A lamp has been placed on a desk.
(D) Four chairs are stacked in a corner.

(A) 커튼이 열려 있다.
(B) 바닥이 카펫으로 완전히 덮여 있다.
(C) 램프가 책상 위에 놓여 있다.
(D) 구석에 네 개의 의자가 쌓여 있다.

어휘 pull open 당겨서 열다 floor 바닥 carpeting 카펫류 place 놓다, 두다 stack 쌓다

해설 실내 사물 사진 – 다양한 사물의 상태 묘사

(A) 커튼이 열려 있는(have been pulled open) 상태이므로 정답.

(B) 사진에 카펫류(carpeting)가 보이지만 완전히 덮고(is completely covered) 상태가 아니므로 오답.

(C) 사진 왼쪽에 램프(lamp)가 보이지만 책상 위에(on a desk) 놓여 있는 상태가 아니므로 오답.

(D) 네 개의 의자가 구석에 쌓여 있는(are stacked in a corner) 상태가 아니므로 오답.

4 M-Au

(A) Some boxes are being labeled.
(B) Items are being loaded into a truck.
(C) A man is repairing some equipment.
(D) A warehouse worker is relaxing on a platform.

(A) 상자 몇 개에 라벨이 붙여지고 있다.
(B) 물건들이 트럭에 실리고 있다.
(C) 남자가 장비를 수리하고 있다.
(D) 창고 근무자가 플랫폼 위에서 쉬고 있다.

어휘 label 라벨을 붙이다 load 싣다 repair 수리하다 equipment 장비 warehouse 창고

해설 1인 등장 사진 – 사람의 동작 묘사
(A) 사진에 상자들이 보이지만 지금 라벨이 붙여지고 있는(are being labeled) 모습이 아니므로 오답.
(B) 물건들이 트럭에 실리고 있는(are being loaded into a truck) 모습이므로 정답.
(C) 남자가 장비를 수리하고 있는(is repairing some equipment) 모습이 아니므로 오답.
(D) 창고 근무자가 일을 하고 있는 중이지 쉬고 있는(is relaxing) 모습이 아니므로 오답.

5 W-Br

(A) A man is bending over to pick up a bottle.
(B) A woman is writing on a piece of paper.
(C) Lab coats have been hung on a coat rack.
(D) Some people are organizing items on shelves.

(A) 남자가 병을 집으려고 몸을 굽히고 있다.
(B) 여자가 종이에 글씨를 쓰고 있다.
(C) 실험실 가운들이 옷걸이에 걸려 있다.
(D) 사람들이 선반에 물건을 정리하고 있다.

어휘 bend over 허리를 구부리다 lab coat 실험실 가운 hang 걸다, 걸리다 organize 정리하다 item 물건 shelf 선반

해설 2인 이상 등장 사진 – 사람의 동작 묘사
(A) 남자가 몸을 굽히는(is bending over) 모습이 아니므로 오답.
(B) 사진에 종이가 보이지만 여자가 글씨를 쓰는(is writing) 모습이 아니므로 오답.
(C) 두 사람이 실험실 가운을 입고 있지, 가운이 걸려 있는(have been hung) 모습이 아니므로 오답.
(D) 두 사람이 팔을 뻗어 선반에 물건을 정리하는(are organizing items) 모습이므로 정답.

6 M-Cn

(A) Lines have been painted on a road.
(B) A train is stopped at a station.
(C) Passengers are getting on a bus.
(D) A man is walking toward a ticket office.

(A) 도로 위에 선들이 그려져 있다.
(B) 기차가 역에 멈춰 있다.
(C) 승객들이 버스에 타고 있다.
(D) 남자가 매표소를 향해 걷고 있다.

어휘 passenger 승객 get on ~에 타다 toward ~를 향해 ticket office 매표소

해설 1인 등장 사진 – 사람의 동작 묘사
(A) 도로 위(on a road)에 그려진 선들이 보이지 않으므로 오답.
(B) 기차가 역에 멈춰 있는(is stopped at a station) 모습이므로 정답.
(C) 승객이 기차 앞에 있는 모습이지 승객들이 버스(on a bus)에 타고 있는 모습이 아니므로 오답.
(D) 남자가 매표소를 향해(toward a ticket office) 걷고 있는 모습이 아니므로 오답.

PART 2

7

M-Au When are you coming in to the office tomorrow?

W-Am (A) Not until nine-fifteen.

(B) To organize my files.

(C) The marketing department.

내일 몇 시에 출근할 건가요?

(A) 9시 15분은 되어야 할 거예요.

(B) 제 서류들을 정리하려고요.

(C) 마케팅 부서요.

어휘 not until ~이 되어서야 비로소, ~ 이후에

해설 출근 시간을 묻는 When 의문문

(A) 정답. 내일 출근 시간을 묻는 질문에 nine-fifteen이라는 구체적인 시점으로 응답하고 있으므로 정답.

(B) 질문과 상관없는 오답. 이유를 묻는 Why 의문문에 대한 응답이므로 오답.

(C) 연상 단어 오답. 질문의 office에서 연상 가능한 marketing department를 이용한 오답.

8

W-Br Did you get my e-mail about the conference?

M-Cn (A) The post office was closed.

(B) No, I've been away.

(C) All of the presenters.

회의에 관한 제 이메일 받았나요?

(A) 우체국이 문을 닫았어요.

(B) 아뇨, 제가 자리에 없었어요.

(C) 발표자 전부요.

어휘 conference 회의 post office 우체국 be away 부재중이다, 출타중이다 presenter 발표자

해설 이메일 수신 여부에 대한 조동사(do) Yes/No 의문문

(A) 연상 단어 오답. 질문의 e-mail을 mail로 잘못 들었을 경우 연상 가능한 post office를 이용한 오답.

(B) 정답. 회의에 관한 이메일(e-mail about the conference)을 받았는지에 대해 먼저 No로 부정적 응답을 한 후, 자리에 없었다(I've been away.)라는 구체적인 이유를 제시했으므로 정답.

(C) 질문과 상관없는 오답. Who 의문문에 대한 응답이므로 오답.

9

M-Au Where should we send the car to pick up the clients?

W-Am (A) By express mail.

(B) I'll pick it up this morning.

(C) To the Greel Plaza Hotel.

고객들을 마중 나갈 차를 어디로 보내야 하나요?

(A) 속달 우편으로요.

(B) 아침에 내가 가지러 갈게요.

(C) 그릴 플라자 호텔로요.

어휘 pick up 마중 나가다, 가지러 가다 client 고객 express mail 속달 우편

해설 차를 보낼 장소를 묻는 Where 의문문

(A) 연상 단어 오답. 질문의 send에서 연상 가능한 express mail을 이용한 오답.

(B) 단어 반복 오답. 질문의 pick up을 반복 이용한 오답.

(C) 정답. 고객을 픽업하기 위해(to pick up the clients) 차를 어디로 보내야 할지를 묻는 질문에 Greel Plaza Hotel라는 구체적인 장소로 응답하고 있으므로 정답.

10

M-Au Can't you take an earlier train on Friday afternoon?

W-Br (A) Because it's scheduled for Friday.

(B) All staff have attended the training.

(C) I'll need to check when I can leave work.

금요일 오후에 열차를 더 일찍 탈 수 있지 않나요?

(A) 금요일로 예정되어 있어서요.

(B) 모든 직원이 교육에 참석했어요.

(C) 내가 언제 퇴근할 수 있는지 확인해 봐야 해요.

어휘 take a train 기차를 타다 be scheduled for ~로 예정되어 있다 attend 참석하다 leave work 퇴근하다

해설 좀 더 이른 기차를 탈 수 있는지를 묻는 부정의문문

(A) 단어 반복 오답. 질문의 Friday를 반복 이용한 오답.

(B) 유사 발음 오답. 질문의 train과 부분적으로 발음이 동일한 training을 이용한 오답.

(C) 정답. 좀 더 이른 기차(an earlier train)를 탈 수 있는지에 대해 직접적인 답변을 피한 채 퇴근 시점을 확인해 봐야 한다(I'll need to check)는 불확실성 표현으로 응답하고 있으므로 정답.

11

W-Br Will Ms. Dillinger give us more details about the company trip soon?

M-Cn (A) Well, it's still six months away.

(B) Try your confirmation code.

(C) It was quite nice of her.

딜린저 씨가 곧 회사 여행에 관해 더 자세히 알려줄까요?

(A) 음, 아직 6개월이나 남았잖아요.

(B) 확인 코드를 쳐 보세요.

(C) 그분께서 잘해 주셨어요.

어휘 give more details about ~에 관해 더 자세히 알려주다 confirmation code 확인 코드

해설 정보 제공 여부를 묻는 조동사(will) Yes/No 의문문

(A) 정답. 회사 여행에 관해 곧 세부 내용을 알려 줄지(give us more details)에 대해 여행이 6개월이나 남았다(it's still six months away)는 말로 우회적인 부정적 응답을 하고 있으므로 정답.

(B) 질문과 상관없는 오답. 방법을 묻는 How 의문문에 대한 응답이므로 오답.

(C) 연상 단어 오답. 질문의 give에서 연상 가능한 nice를 이용한 오답.

12

M-Cn Do you think you can repair the copy machine, or will we need to buy a new one?

M-Au (A) About an hour.

(B) Yes, it was very affordable.

(C) I'm certain it can be fixed.

복사기를 수리할 수 있을 것 같은가요, 아니면 새 걸로 사야 할까요?

(A) 한 시간쯤이요.

(B) 네, 아주 저렴했어요.

(C) 확실히 고칠 수 있어요.

어휘 copy machine 복사기 affordable 저렴한 be certain 확신하다

해설 문장을 연결한 선택의문문

(A) 질문과 상관없는 오답. How long will it take to ~ ? 의문문에 어울리는 응답이므로 오답.

(B) 연상 단어 오답. 질문의 buy에서 연상 가능한 affordable을 이용한 오답.

(C) 정답. 복사기를 수리할지, 아니면 새 것을 구입해야 할지를 묻는 질문에 고칠 수 있다(it can be fixed)는 말로 복사기 수리를 선택한 응답이므로 정답.

13

M-Au Who posted the notice in the break room?

W-Br (A) Sure, go ahead and take a break.

(B) Someone from Personnel.

(C) Above the water cooler.

누가 휴게실에 공지문을 붙였나요?

(A) 물론이죠, 어서 쉬세요.

(B) 인사과 사람이요.

(C) 정수기 위에요.

어휘 post a notice 공지를 올리다[붙이다] take a break 잠시 쉬다 Personnel 인사부 water cooler 정수기

해설 공지문의 게시자를 묻는 Who 의문문

(A) 단어 반복 오답. 질문의 break를 반복 이용한 오답.

(B) 정답. 공지문의 게시자가 누군지를 묻는 질문에 인사과의 누군가(someone from Personnel)가 붙였다고 응답하고 있으므로 정답.

(C) 질문과 상관없는 오답. 장소를 묻는 Where 의문문에 어울리는 응답이므로 오답.

14

W-Am How do you report a problem with this software?

M-Cn (A) What kind of problem are you having?

(B) Since the last update.

(C) She's a newspaper reporter.

이 소프트웨어의 문제점은 어떻게 신고합니까?

(A) 어떤 종류의 문제가 있나요?

(B) 지난번 업데이트 이후로요.

(C) 그녀는 신문 기자입니다.

어휘 report 보고하다, 신고하다 what kind of 어떤 종류의 ~ since ~이래로 reporter 기자

해설 문제점을 신고하는 방법을 묻는 How 의문문

(A) 정답. 어떻게 신고하는지 묻는 질문에 어떤 종류의 문제가 있는지를 되묻는 응답이므로 정답.

(B) 연상 단어 오답. 질문의 software에서 연상 가능한 update를 이용한 오답.

(C) 파생어 오답. 질문의 report와 파생어 관계인 reporter를 이용한 오답.

15

W-Br Where will this year's summer charity concert be held?

W-Am (A) Usually in the middle of July.

(B) We plan to offer free music classes.

(C) I heard it'll be in Baxter Park.

올 여름 자선 음악회는 어디에서 열릴 예정인가요?

(A) 대개 7월 중순에요.

(B) 무료 음악 강좌를 제공할 계획이에요.

(C) 백스터 공원에서 열린다고 들었어요.

어휘 charity 자선 be held (행사가) 열리다 usually 대체로, 대개 in the middle of ~ 중순에, ~ 한가운데에

해설 음악회 장소를 묻는 Where 의문문

(A) 질문과 상관없는 오답. 시점을 묻는 When 의문문에 어울리는 응답이므로 오답.

(B) 연상 단어 오답. 질문의 charity concert에서 연상 가능한 music을 이용한 오답.

(C) 정답. 올 여름 자선 음악회(this year's summer charity concert)의 개최 장소를 묻는 질문에 Baxter Park라는 구체적인 장소로 응답하고 있으므로 정답.

16

W-Br Which airline did you use when you flew to the Bahamas?

M-Cn (A) I always stay on the beach.

(B) Just one large suitcase.

(C) It was SlimJet Air.

바하마 군도에 갈 때 어떤 항공사를 이용하셨어요?

(A) 저는 항상 해변에 머물러요.

(B) 큰 여행 가방 하나만요.

(C) 슬림젯 항공이었어요.

어휘 airline 항공사 fly to ~까지 비행기를 타고 가다 suitcase 여행 가방

해설 항공사를 묻는 Which 의문문

(A) 연상 단어 오답. 질문의 the Bahamas에서 연상 가능한 beach를 이용한 오답.

(B) 질문과 상관없는 오답. 여행에 가져간 물품을 묻는 의문문에 어울리는 응답이므로 오답.

(C) 정답. 어떤 항공사를 이용했는지에 대해 SlimJet Air라는 구체적인 항공사 이름으로 응답하고 있으므로 정답.

17

W-Am It's not supposed to rain this evening, is it?

M-Cn (A) I haven't checked the forecast.

(B) They're running late.

(C) Oh, was I supposed to?

저녁에 비가 오지 않겠죠, 그렇죠?

(A) 일기예보를 확인해 보지 못했네요.

(B) 그들은 늦을 거예요.

(C) 아, 제가 하는 거였어요?

어휘 be supposed to+동사원형 ~할 것으로 예상되다, ~하기로 되어 있다 forecast 일기예보 run late 늦다

해설 비가 올지를 묻는 부가의문문

(A) 정답. 저녁에 비가 올지(rain this evening)에 대해 일기예보를 확인해 보지 않았다(I haven't checked the forecast.)는 불확실성 표현으로 응답하고 있으므로 정답.

(B) 유사 발음 오답. 질문의 rain과 부분적으로 발음이 비슷한 late를 이용한 오답.

(C) 단어 반복 오답. 질문의 supposed to를 반복 이용한 오답.

18

M-Au Who's going to enter these expenses into the database?

W-Am (A) None of us has access to it.

(B) Wow, that is expensive.

(C) Through the building's side entrance.

이 경비 지출 건은 누가 데이터베이스에 입력할 예정입니까?

(A) 저희 중 누구도 데이터베이스 접근 권한이 없어요.

(B) 와! 비싸긴 하네요.

(C) 건물 옆쪽 출입구를 통해서요.

어휘 enter 입력하다 expense 비용, 경비 have access to ~에 접근할 수 있다 expensive 비싼 entrance 입구

해설 지출 건을 입력할 사람을 묻는 Who 의문문

(A) 정답. 누가 입력할지를 묻는 질문에 아무도 접근 권한이 없다는 우회적인 답변을 하고 있으므로 정답.

(B) 파생어 오답. 질문의 expenses와 파생어 관계인 expensive를 이용한 오답.

(C) 파생어 오답. 질문의 enter와 파생어 관계인 entrance를 이용한 오답.

19

W-Br Why was our plant in Taiwan closed down?

M-Au (A) No, I don't think so.

(B) The one near the harbor.

(C) It didn't pass an important inspection.

대만 공장이 왜 문을 닫았죠?

(A) 아뇨, 난 그렇게 생각하지 않아요.

(B) 항구 근처에 있는 것이요.

(C) 중요한 감사를 통과하지 못했어요.

어휘 plant 공장 be closed down 문을 닫다, 폐쇄되다 harbor 항구 inspection 감사, 검열

해설 공장 폐쇄 이유를 묻는 Why 의문문

(A) Yes/No 불가 오답. 이유를 묻는 Why 의문문에는 Yes/No 응답이 불가능하기 때문에 오답.

(B) 질문과 상관없는 오답. Which 또는 Where 의문문에 어울리는 응답이므로 오답.

(C) 정답. 공장의 폐쇄 이유를 묻는 질문에 중요한 감사를 통과하지 못했다(It didn't pass an important inspection.)는 구체적인 이유로 응답하고 있으므로 정답.

20

M-Cn How often should we clean out the staff refrigerator?

W-Am (A) At least once a month.

(B) The chicken sandwich is mine.

(C) Cleaning supplies are in the storage closet.

직원용 냉장고 안을 얼마나 자주 청소해야 하나요?

(A) 적어도 한 달에 한 번요.

(B) 치킨 샌드위치는 제 겁니다.

(C) 청소용품들은 벽장 안에 있어요.

어휘 refrigerator 냉장고 at least 적어도 cleaning supplies 청소용품들 storage closet 벽장

해설 청소 빈도를 묻는 How often 의문문

(A) 정답. 직원 냉장고(staff refrigerator) 안을 얼마나 자주 청소해야 하는지에 대해 적어도 한 달에 한 번(At least once a month.)이라는 구체적인 빈도로 응답하고 있으므로 정답.

(B) 연상 단어 오답. 질문의 refrigerator에서 연상 가능한 sandwich를 이용한 오답.

(C) 파생어 오답. 질문의 clean과 파생어 관계인 cleaning을 이용한 오답.

21

M-Au Has all of the ink for the printer been used up already?

W-Br (A) It hasn't been decided yet.

(B) Yes, but we've ordered more.

(C) Handouts for the seminar.

프린터용 잉크를 벌써 다 사용했나요?

(A) 아직 결정되지 않았어요.

(B) 네, 하지만 더 주문했어요.

(C) 세미나를 위한 인쇄물요.

어휘 use up 다 쓰다 handout 인쇄물

해설 잉크 소모 여부를 묻는 조동사(have) Yes/No 의문문

(A) 연상 단어 오답. 질문의 already에서 연상 가능한 yet을 이용한 오답.

(B) 정답. 잉크가 떨어졌는지(used up)에 대해 먼저 Yes로 긍정적 답변을 한 후, 하지만 더 주문해 놓았다는 부연 설명을 하고 있으므로 정답.

(C) 질문과 상관없는 오답. 잉크를 다 썼는지 묻는 질문에 세미나를 위한 인쇄물이라는 말은 맥락에서 벗어난 응답이므로 오답.

22

W-Am Ms. Shin has been transferred to the Berlin branch, hasn't she?

M-Au (A) The responsibilities of her new position.
(B) She started working there yesterday.
(C) How much did she send?

신 씨가 베를린 지사로 전근되었지요, 그렇지 않나요?
(A) 그분이 새 직책에서 맡은 일들요.
(B) 그분은 어제부터 거기에서 근무하기 시작했어요.
(C) 그분은 얼마를 보냈나요?

어휘 transfer 전근시키다 branch 지사 responsibilities 맡은 일들 position 직책

해설 전근 여부를 묻는 부가의문문

(A) 연상 단어 오답. 질문의 transferred에서 연상 가능한 new position을 이용한 오답.

(B) 정답. 신 씨가 베를린 지사로 전근을 갔는지에 대해 Yes를 생략한 채 그녀가 어제부터 그곳에서 근무를 시작했다(She started working there yesterday.)는 우회적 응답을 하고 있으므로 정답.

(C) 연상 단어 오답. 질문의 transferred를 송금이라고 잘못 이해했을 경우 연상 가능한 send를 이용한 오답.

23

M-Cn I'll let you know when your table is ready.

W-Br (A) Thanks—we'll wait here.
(B) I've been to that restaurant before.
(C) A darker brown wood.

테이블이 준비되면 알려드리겠습니다.
(A) 고마워요. 여기서 기다릴게요.
(B) 저는 그 식당에 가본 적이 있어요.
(C) 더 짙은 갈색의 목재요.

어휘 be ready 준비되다, 마련되다 darker brown 더 짙은 갈색

해설 계획/약속의 평서문

(A) 정답. 테이블이 준비되면(when your table is ready) 알려 주겠다는 말에 Thanks로 고마움을 나타낸 후, 여기서 기다리겠다(we'll wait here)는 문맥상 적절한 응답을 하고 있으므로 정답.

(B) 질문과 상관없는 오답. 테이블이 준비되면 알려 주겠다는 말에 그 식당에 가본 적이 있다는 말은 맥락에서 벗어난 응답이므로 오답.

(C) 연상 단어 오답. 평서문의 table에서 연상 가능한 wood를 이용한 오답.

24

W-Am Why don't you give this assignment to our intern?

M-Au (A) I'll put up a few more signs.
(B) He already has enough to do.
(C) Researching our competitors.

우리 인턴에게 이 임무를 맡기는 게 어때요?
(A) 표지판을 몇 개 더 세울 거예요.
(B) 그는 이미 할 일이 많은 걸요.
(C) 우리의 경쟁사들에 대해 조사하는 것이요.

어휘 Why don't you+동사원형? ~하는 게 어때요? assignment 임무 put up a sign 표지판[팻말]을 세우다 research 조사하다 competitor 경쟁 상대

해설 제안/권유 의문문

(A) 유사 발음 오답. 질문의 assignment와 부분적으로 발음이 동일한 signs를 이용한 오답.

(B) 정답. 인턴에게 this assignment(이 임무)를 맡기자는 제안에 대해 No를 생략한 채 그는 이미 할 일이 많다(He already has enough to do.)며 우회적인 부정적 응답을 하고 있으므로 정답.

(C) 질문과 상관없는 오답. 인턴에게 이 임무를 맡기자는 제안에 우리의 경쟁사들에 대해 조사하는 것이라는 말은 맥락에서 벗어난 응답이므로 오답.

25

M-Cn Do you want to buy my tickets for the film premiere this weekend?

W-Br (A) It's the best film I've seen in a while.
(B) The "Tickets" page of the Web site.
(C) I'm not sure I'll be able to go.

이번 주말에 개봉하는 영화의 관람권이 내게 있는데 사시겠어요?
(A) 한동안 내가 본 영화 중 가장 훌륭한 영화예요.
(B) 웹 사이트의 "표" 페이지요.
(C) 나는 갈 수 있을지 모르겠어요.

어휘 film premiere 영화 개봉 in a while 한동안 be able to+동사원형 ~할 수 있다

해설 티켓 구입 의사를 묻는 조동사(do) Yes/No 의문문

(A) 단어 반복 오답. 질문의 film을 반복 이용한 오답.

(B) 질문과 상관없는 오답. 장소를 묻는 where 의문문에 어울리는 응답이므로 오답.

(C) 정답. 영화 티켓 구입 의사가 있는지에 대한 질문에 No를 생략한 채 갈 수 있을지 모르겠다(I'm not sure I'll be able to go.)며 우회적인 부정적 응답을 하고 있으므로 정답.

26

W-Am This uniform design is the most popular with employees.

M-Au (A) Let's hope customers like it, too.
(B) Which brand does she design for?
(C) The red shirt and black pants.

이 유니폼 디자인이 직원들에게 가장 인기가 많아요.
(A) 손님들도 그 디자인을 좋아하기를 바랍시다.
(B) 그녀는 어느 회사를 위해 디자인 일을 하나요?
(C) 빨간 셔츠와 검은 바지요.

어휘 popular 인기가 많은 employee 직원 customer 손님, 고객

해설 사실/정보 전달의 평서문

(A) 정답. 이 유니폼 디자인이 직원들에게 가장 인기가 많다는 말에 손님들도 그 디자인을 좋아하길 바란다는 말은 적절한 응답이므로 정답.

(B) 단어 반복 오답. 질문에 나온 design을 반복한 오답.

(C) 연상 단어 오답. 질문의 uniform design에서 연상 가능한 red shirt and black pants를 이용한 오답.

27

M-Au Should I begin the workshop by introducing myself or the agenda?

W-Am (A) OK—my name's Camille and I'm an engineer.

(B) A quick game might relax the participants.

(C) The session on leadership begins at three P.M.

제 소개를 하며 워크숍을 시작할까요, 아니면 안건을 말씀드리며 시작할까요?

(A) 좋아요. 제 이름은 카밀이고요, 엔지니어입니다.

(B) 간단한 게임을 하면 참가자들의 긴장이 풀릴 거예요.

(C) 리더십 모임은 오후 3시에 시작합니다.

어휘 introduce 소개하다 agenda 회의 안건 participant 참가자

해설 단어를 연결한 선택의문문

(A) 연상 단어 오답. 질문의 introducing에서 연상 가능한 my name's Camille과 I'm an engineer를 이용한 오답.

(B) 정답. 질문에 선택 사항으로 언급된 introducing myself나 the agenda 대신 제3의 선택 사항을 제시한 것이므로 정답.

(C) 단어 반복 오답. 질문에 나온 begin을 반복한 begins를 이용한 오답.

28

M-Cn This set of keys belongs to you, doesn't it?

W-Br (A) No, not that long.

(B) Yes, where did you find them?

(C) There's a spare set at the reception desk.

이 열쇠 꾸러미가 당신 것 맞죠, 아닌가요?

(A) 아뇨, 그렇게 길지 않아요.

(B) 네, 어디에서 발견했나요?

(C) 접수대에 여분의 꾸러미가 있어요.

어휘 a set of keys 열쇠 꾸러미 belong to ~의 소유이다 spare 여벌의, 남는 reception desk 접수처

해설 열쇠 주인을 확인하는 부가의문문

(A) 유사 발음 오답. 질문의 belongs와 부분적으로 발음이 동일한 long을 이용한 오답.

(B) 정답. 열쇠 꾸러미(set of keys)의 주인을 확인하는 질문에 먼저 Yes로 긍정적 응답을 한 후, 열쇠를 어디에서 찾았는지(where did you find them?) 되묻고 있으므로 정답.

(C) 단어 반복 오답. 질문의 set를 반복 이용한 오답.

29

W-Am Why did the delivery person come up the stairs?

M-Cn (A) He'll arrive just before lunch.

(B) Please move them somewhere else.

(C) The elevator must be out of order.

배달원이 왜 계단으로 올라왔을까요?

(A) 그는 점심 먹기 직전에 도착할 거예요.

(B) 그것들을 다른 곳으로 옮겨 주세요.

(C) 승강기가 고장 난 게 틀림없어요.

어휘 come up the stairs 계단으로 올라오다 somewhere else 다른 곳으로[에서] must be ~인 게 틀림없다 out of order 고장 난

해설 계단을 이용한 이유를 묻는 Why 의문문

(A) 질문과 상관없는 오답. 시점을 묻는 when 의문문에 대한 응답이므로 오답.

(B) 연상 단어 오답. 질문의 delivery에서 연상 가능한 move를 이용한 오답.

(C) 정답. 배달원(delivery person)이 왜 계단을 이용했는지에 대해 승강기가 고장 났을(out of order) 것이라는 이유를 제시하고 있으므로 정답.

30

M-Au How about meeting at the coffee shop to discuss the project?

W-Am (A) She said we've sold ten cups so far.

(B) We talked about several topics.

(C) I'd rather use the meeting room.

커피숍에서 만나서 그 프로젝트를 논의하는 건 어떨까요?

(A) 그녀 말로는 지금까지 열 잔을 팔았다고 하는군요.

(B) 우리는 몇 가지 주제에 관해 이야기를 나눴어요.

(C) 저는 그냥 회의실에서 논의하고 싶어요.

어휘 discuss 논의[상의]하다 so far 현재까지 would rather+동사원형 차라리 ~하겠다

해설 커피숍에서 만나자는 제안 의문문

(A) 연상 단어 오답. 질문의 coffee shop에서 연상 가능한 커피 판매 개수를 이용한 오답.

(B) 질문과 상관없는 오답. 커피숍에서 만나서 그 프로젝트를 논의하자는 제안에 우리는 몇 가지 주제에 관해 이야기를 나눴다는 말은 맥락에서 벗어난 응답이므로 오답.

(C) 정답. 커피숍에서 만나자는 제안에 대해 부정어 No를 생략한 채 차라리 회의실(meeting room)에서 논의하고 싶다고 했으므로 정답.

31

W-Br Have we found enough volunteers for the focus group?

M-Cn (A) They'll test our newest products.

(B) I believe Chris is still searching.

(C) That should be plenty of space.

포커스 그룹에 들어갈 자원자들을 충분히 찾았나요?

(A) 그들은 우리의 최신 제품들을 시험할 거예요.

(B) 크리스가 아직 찾고 있을 거예요.

(C) 그 정도면 공간이 넉넉할 거예요.

어휘 volunteer 자원자 focus group 포커스 그룹(시장[여론] 조사를 위해 각 계층을 대표하도록 뽑은 소수의 사람들로 구성된 집단)

해설 자원자 확보 여부를 묻는 조동사(have) Yes/No 의문문

(A) 질문과 상관없는 오답. 포커스 그룹에 들어갈 자원자들을 충분히 찾았냐는 질문에 대해 그들은 우리의 최신 제품들을 시험할 거라는 말은 맥락에서 벗어난 응답이므로 오답.

(B) 정답. 포커스 그룹(focus group)에 들어갈 자원자를 충분히 확보했는지에 대해 No를 생략한 채 크리스가 여전히 찾고 있다(Chris is still searching)며 우회적으로 응답을 하고 있으므로 정답.

(C) 연상 단어 오답. 질문의 enough에서 연상 가능한 plenty를 이용한 오답.

PART 3

32-34

M-Cn [32]**Excuse me, could you help me find the dress shirts?** I need something appropriate to wear under a suit for a dinner tonight. The shirt I was planning to wear got stained.

W-Br Of course, they're right over here. [33]**You're in luck because we're currently having a buy-one-get-one-free promotion.** What color are you looking for?

M-Cn Hmm, I'm not sure whether blue or white would look better. [34]**Could you get me one of each to try on? That would help me decide.** I'm a size medium.

남: **실례합니다만 와이셔츠 찾는 걸 도와주시겠어요?** 오늘 밤 만찬에서 입을 정장에 어울리는 게 필요합니다. 입고 가려던 셔츠에 얼룩이 졌거든요.

여: 물론이죠. 바로 이쪽에 있습니다. **저희가 현재 '원 플러스 원' 행사를 진행하고 있는데 운이 좋으시네요.** 어떤 색상을 찾고 계신가요?

남: 음, 파란색이 나을지 흰색이 나을지 잘 모르겠군요. **한번 입어 보게 하나씩 갖다 주시겠어요? 그러면 결정하는 데 도움이 되겠네요.** 저는 미디움 사이즈예요.

어휘 dress shirt 정장용 셔츠, 와이셔츠 appropriate 적절한, 적합한 suit 정장 get stained 얼룩이 지다 be in luck 운이 좋다 a buy-one-get-one-free promotion 원 플러스 원 행사 whether A or B A일지 B일지 try on 입어 보다

32

Where most likely are the speakers?

(A) At a clothing store
(B) At a café
(C) At a dry cleaner's
(D) At a pharmacy

화자들이 어디에 있겠는가?

(A) 옷가게
(B) 카페
(C) 세탁소
(D) 약국

해설 전체 내용 관련 – 화자들의 대화 장소

남자의 첫 대사에서 여자에게 와이셔츠 찾는 걸 도와달라(Excuse me, could you help me find the dress shirts?)는 부탁을 했으므로 정답은 (A)이다.

33

According to the woman, why is the man lucky?

(A) A business is open.
(B) A person is nearby.
(C) A sale is being held.
(D) A seat is empty.

여자에 따르면 남자는 왜 운이 좋은가?

(A) 가게가 열려 있다.
(B) 사람이 근처에 있다.
(C) 할인 행사를 하고 있다.
(D) 빈 자리가 있다.

해설 세부 사항 관련 – 남자가 운이 좋은 이유

여자의 대사에서 현재 '원 플러스 원' 행사를 진행하고 있어서 남자가 운이 좋다(You're in luck because we're currently having a buy-one-get-one-free promotion.)고 했으므로 정답은 (C)이다.

▸▸ **Paraphrasing** 대화의 **a buy-one-get-one-free promotion** → 정답의 **a sale**

34

What will the man most likely do next?

(A) Write down some instructions
(B) Choose between two items
(C) Consult a calendar
(D) Call a coworker

남자가 다음에 무엇을 하겠는가?

(A) 지시사항 적기
(B) 두 가지 품목 중에서 선택하기
(C) 달력 보기
(D) 동료에게 전화하기

해설 세부 사항 관련 – 남자의 다음 행동

대화 마지막에 남자가 한번 입어 보게 하나씩 갖다 주면 결정하는 데 도움이 될 것(Could you get me one of each to try on? That would help me decide.)이라고 했다. 즉, 남자는 두 가지 색의 와이셔츠를 입어 보고 결정하겠다는 것이므로 정답은 (B)이다.

▸▸ **Paraphrasing** 대화의 **decide** → 정답의 **choose**

35-37

W-Am Tim, [35]**Haruto upstairs needs to know what percentage of our earnings are coming from the new line of women's watches.**

M-Cn That's no problem. I have a spreadsheet cataloguing that. Here it is. What time period does he want to see data from?

W-Am [36]**He'd like to see it from May, when the line launched, up through this month.**

M-Cn OK, [37]**I'll organize this into a report** so that he can see the percentage for each month as well as overall. That way he can see how the sales have trended.

여: 팀, **위층에 있는 하루토가 우리 수익 중 몇 퍼센트가 새로운 여성 시계 라인에서 나오는지 알고 싶어 해요.**

Test 3

남: 걱정 마세요. 그걸 정리한 스프레드시트가 제게 있으니까요. 여기요. 그가 어느 기간의 자료를 보고 싶어 하는 건가요?

여: **제품이 출시된 5월부터 이번 달까지의 자료를 보고 싶어 해요.**

남: 좋아요. **이걸 보고서로 정리해서** 그가 전체는 물론이고 월별 백분율까지 살펴볼 수 있도록 할게요. 그러면 판매 동향이 어떤지 알 수 있을 테니까요.

어휘 upstairs 위층에 있는 percentage 퍼센트, 백분율 earnings 수익 line (상품의) 종류 spreadsheet 스프레드시트(엑셀 표) catalogue 목록으로 정리하다, 분류하다 launch (제품을) 출시하다 organize ~ into a report ~을 보고서로 정리하다 A as well as B B뿐만 아니라 A도 overall 전체, 전부 that way 그렇게 하면, 그런 식으로 trend 동향을 나타내다, 추세를 따르다

35

According to the woman, what has Haruto asked for?

(A) Information about profits
(B) Some customer profiles
(C) A travel itinerary
(D) A design proposal

여자에 따르면, 하루토가 무엇을 요청했는가?

(A) 수익 정보
(B) 고객 정보
(C) 여행 일정
(D) 디자인 제안서

해설 세부 사항 관련 - 하루토가 요청한 것

여자의 첫 번째 대사에서 위층에 있는 하루토가 수익 중 몇 퍼센트가 새로운 여성 시계 라인에서 나오는지 알고 싶어 한다(Haruto upstairs needs ~ from the new line of women's watches.)고 했으므로 정답은 (A)이다.

▸▸ Paraphrasing 대화의 earnings → 정답의 profits

36

What happened in May?

(A) Haruto was promoted.
(B) A merger took place.
(C) New merchandise was released.
(D) A financial period ended.

5월에 무슨 일이 일어났는가?

(A) 하루토가 승진했다.
(B) 합병이 일어났다.
(C) 신상품들이 출시됐다.
(D) 회계 기간이 끝났다.

해설 세부 사항 관련 - 5월에 발생한 일

여자의 두 번째 대사에서 하루토가 제품이 출시된 5월부터 이번 달까지의 자료를 보고 싶어 한다(He'd like to see it from May, when the line launched, up through this month.)고 했다. 이를 통해 5월에 신상품들이 출시되었음을 알 수 있으므로 정답은 (C)이다.

▸▸ Paraphrasing 대화의 launch → 정답의 release

37

What does the man say he will do?

(A) Create a report
(B) Organize a meeting
(C) Contact Haruto
(D) Search for a form

남자는 무엇을 할 것이라고 말하는가?

(A) 보고서 작성
(B) 회의 주선
(C) 하루토에게 연락하기
(D) 문서 찾기

해설 세부 사항 관련 - 남자가 할 일

대화 마지막에 남자가 자료를 정리해 보고서로 만들겠다(I'll organize this into a report)고 했으므로 정답은 (A)이다.

38-40

W-Am [38]**I have to go to our head office in New York City for a meeting,** but I'm not sure the best way to get there.

M-Au By bus. [39]**You can take one from the terminal over on Grand Street straight to Penn Station,** where you can catch the subway. It takes about two and a half hours.

W-Am Hmm, [40]**my meeting is at 9:30 A.M. and I don't want to leave that early. Is there a train I can take instead?**

M-Au There is a train, but you have to drive over to Rosedale to catch it. It doesn't save much time, all things considered.

여: **회의 때문에 뉴욕 시에 있는 본사에 가야 하는데,** 어떤 방법으로 가는 게 가장 좋을지 모르겠어요.

남: 버스로 가세요. **저쪽 그랜드 가에 있는 터미널에서 버스를 타고 펜 역까지 곧장 가면** 거기에서 지하철을 탈 수 있어요. 두 시간 반 정도 걸릴 거예요.

여: **음, 회의가 오전 9시 30분이라 그렇게 일찍 출발하고 싶지는 않아요. 그 대신에 탈 만한 기차가 있나요?**

남: 기차도 있지만, 그걸 타려면 로즈데일까지 차로 가야 해요. 모든 걸 고려할 때 시간도 많이 절약되지는 않아요.

어휘 head office 본사 straight 곧장 catch the subway 지하철을 타다 take a train 기차를 타다 instead 대신에 drive over to ~ 차를 몰고 ~까지 가다 all things considered 모든 걸 고려할 때

38

What does the woman say she will do in New York City?

(A) Have a medical checkup
(B) Pick up a friend
(C) See tourist attractions
(D) Visit corporate headquarters

여자는 뉴욕 시에서 무엇을 할 것이라고 말하는가?
(A) 건강 검진 받기
(B) 친구 마중 나가기
(C) 관광 명소들 구경하기
(D) 회사 본사 방문하기

해설 세부 사항 관련 - 여자가 뉴욕 시에서 할 일
대화 맨 처음에 여자가 회의 때문에 뉴욕 시에 있는 본사에 가야 한다(I have to go to our head office in New York City for a meeting)고 했으므로 정답은 (D)이다.

▸▸ **Paraphrasing** 대화의 **go to our head office**
→ 정답의 **Visit corporate headquarters**

39
What does the man say the woman can do on Grand Street?
(A) Catch a taxi
(B) Rent a car
(C) Board a train
(D) Take a bus

남자는 여자가 그랜드 가에서 무엇을 할 수 있다고 하는가?
(A) 택시 승차
(B) 자동차 임대
(C) 기차 탑승
(D) 버스 승차

해설 세부 사항 관련 - 여자가 그랜드 가에서 할 수 있는 것
남자의 첫 번째 대사에서 여자에게 그랜드 가에 있는 터미널에서 버스를 타고 펜 역까지 곧장 갈 수 있다(You can take one from the terminal over on Grand Street straight to Penn Station)고 했으므로 정답은 (D)이다.

40
Why does the woman ask about a train?
(A) She enjoys riding trains.
(B) She would prefer a shorter journey.
(C) She is concerned about prices.
(D) She has a lot of luggage.

여자가 기차에 관해 물어본 이유는?
(A) 기차 타는 것을 즐긴다.
(B) 보다 짧은 이동 방법을 선호한다.
(C) 요금이 염려된다.
(D) 짐이 많다.

해설 세부 사항 관련 - 여자가 기차에 관해 물어본 이유
여자의 두 번째 대사에서 남자에게 자신의 회의가 오전 9시 30분이라 그렇게 일찍 출발하고 싶지는 않다(my meeting is at 9:30 A.M. and I don't want to leave that early.)며 기차는 있는지(Is there a train I can take instead?)에 대해 물어봤다. 즉, 더 짧은 이동 방법을 알고 싶어 기차에 대해 물어본 것이므로 정답은 (B)이다.

41-43 3인 대화

W-Br Alvin, [41]**Mario and I are almost finished planning the activities for our consumer focus groups.** How is participant recruitment going?

M-Au Not well. [42]**There just aren't a lot of people who fit the age and career profile we're looking for.** We're still about fifteen participants short.

M-Cn Hmm, what could we do to reach the type of person we need?

M-Au We'll have to find a better place to advertise.

W-Br Oh, [43]**how about uploading the ad to our Crowdmoon page? The platform's users could share the post with their connections who match the profile.**

M-Cn It's like they'd be helping with our search. That's a good idea. Let's give it a try.

여: 앨빈, **마리오와 저는 소비자 포커스 그룹의 활동 계획을 거의 끝마쳤어요.** 참가자 신규 모집은 어떻게 되어 가고 있나요?
남1: 잘 안 되고 있어요. **우리가 찾는 연령과 직업에 들어맞는 사람이 많지 않네요.** 아직도 참가자가 15명 정도 모자랍니다.
남2: 음… 우리가 필요로 하는 유형의 사람에게 알리려면 뭘 해야 할까요?
남1: 광고 장소로 보다 나은 곳을 찾아야 할 겁니다.
여: 아, **크라우드문 페이지에 광고를 올리는 건 어때요? 플랫폼 사용자들이 아는 인맥 중 프로필이 맞는 사람과 게시물을 공유할 수 있으니까요.**
남2: 그들이 우리의 검색 작업을 도와주는 셈이군요. 좋은 생각입니다. 한번 해봅시다.

어휘 activity 활동 consumer 소비자 focus group 포커스 그룹 (시장 조사나 여론 조사를 위해 각 계층을 대표하도록 뽑은 소수의 사람들로 이뤄진 그룹) participant 참가자 recruitment 채용, 신규 모집 fit 꼭 맞다 look for ~을 찾다 short 부족한 reach (어떤 사람의 관심권 내에) 들어가다 post 게시물 connection 연이 닿는 사람 search 검색 give it a try 한번 해보다

41
What are the speakers preparing for?
(A) A regional contest
(B) Some market research
(C) Some training workshops
(D) A community service activity

화자들은 무엇을 준비하고 있는가?
(A) 지역 대회
(B) 시장 조사
(C) 교육 워크숍
(D) 지역 사회 봉사 활동

Test 3

어휘 prepare for ~를 준비하다 regional 지역의 market research 시장 조사 community service 지역 사회 봉사

해설 전체 내용 관련 – 준비 사항

여자의 첫 번째 대사에서 마리오랑 여자가 소비자 포커스 그룹의 활동 계획을 거의 끝마쳤다(Mario and I are almost finished planning the activities for our consumer focus groups.)고 했다. 이로써 대화가 시장 조사를 위함임을 알 수 있으므로 정답은 (B)이다.

42

Why has it been difficult to find participants?

(A) A low amount of compensation is being offered.
(B) Many people do not meet some requirements.
(C) Previous events did not go well.
(D) A location is far from a city.

참가자를 찾기가 어려웠던 이유는 무엇인가?

(A) 지급되는 보상금이 적다.
(B) 요건을 충족하는 사람이 많지 않다.
(C) 이전 행사가 순조롭게 진행되지 않았다.
(D) 장소가 도심과 멀리 떨어져 있다.

어휘 a low amount of ~ 적은 액수의 compensation 보상 requirement 요구 사항, 요건 previous 이전의 be far from ~에서 멀리 떨어져 있다

해설 세부 사항 관련 – 참가자를 찾기 어려웠던 이유

첫 번째 남자가 찾는 연령과 직업에 들어맞는 사람이 많지 않다(There just aren't a lot of people who fit the age and career profile we're looking for.)고 했으므로 정답은 (B)이다.

43

What does the woman suggest doing?

(A) Providing a free shuttle bus ride
(B) Applying for a government grant
(C) Posting on a social networking service
(D) Hiring an advertising consultant

여자는 무엇을 하자고 제안하는가?

(A) 무료 셔틀버스 서비스 제공하기
(B) 정부 보조금 신청하기
(C) SNS에 글 올리기
(D) 광고 컨설턴트 고용하기

어휘 provide 제공하다 apply for ~에 지원하다, ~를 신청하다 government grant 정부 보조금 hire 채용하다, 고용하다

해설 세부 사항 관련 – 여자가 제안하는 일

여자의 마지막 대사에서 크라우드문 페이지에 광고를 올리는 건 어떠냐며 플랫폼 사용자들이 아는 인맥 중 프로필이 맞는 사람과 게시물을 공유할 수 있다(how about uploading the ad ~ with their connections who match the profile.)고 했으므로 정답은 (C)이다.

44-46

W-Am [44]**I just bought a new television from your store on Wednesday and then I saw in your Sunday ad that the same television is now on sale. Is there anything you can do for me?**

M-Cn Yes. [44]**It's within a week of the item going on sale, so I'm allowed to give you the reduced price.** [45]**Do you have the receipt from the purchase?**

W-Am [45]**Yes, here it is.** Can you return the difference to my credit card?

M-Cn Yeah, we can definitely do that. [46]**Let's take this to the manager, since she's the one who can approve your refund.** Follow me.

여: **수요일에 이 점포에서 텔레비전을 새로 산 다음 보니까 일요일 광고에 똑같은 텔레비전을 할인하고 있더군요. 제게 뭐 해 주실 수 있나요?**

남: 네. **해당 상품을 할인 판매한 지 일주일 내이기 때문에 손님께 할인가를 적용해 드릴 수 있습니다. 구매 영수증을 갖고 계신가요?**

여: **네, 여기 있어요.** 차액을 제 신용카드로 환불해 주실 수 있나요?

남: 네, 물론이죠. **이것을 관리자에게 가져가죠. 그녀가 환불을 승인할 수 있는 사람이거든요.** 이쪽으로 오세요.

어휘 ad 광고(= advertisement) be allowed to + 동사원형 ~하도록 허락 받다 reduced price 할인가 receipt 영수증 purchase 구매, 구입 return the difference 차액을 되돌려주다 approve 승인하다

44

What is the conversation mainly about?

(A) Receiving a discount
(B) Checking a credit card charge
(C) Exchanging a defective device
(D) Understanding a contract

대화의 주된 내용은 무엇인가?

(A) 할인 받는 것
(B) 신용카드 요금 확인
(C) 불량품 교환
(D) 계약서 이해하기

어휘 charge 요금 exchange 교환하다 defective 결함 있는 device 장치

해설 전체 내용 관련 – 대화의 주 내용

여자의 첫 번째 대사에서 수요일에 텔레비전을 샀는데 일요일 광고에서 똑같은 텔레비전을 할인하고 있는 걸 봤다면서 매장에서 여자에게 해줄 수 있는 게 있는지(I just bought a new television ~ anything you can do for me?) 물어봤다. 이에 대해 남자의 첫 번째 대사에서 해당 상품을 할인 판매한 지 일 주일 이내이기 때문에 여자에게 할인가를 적용해 드릴 수 있다(It's within a week ~ the reduced price.)고 했으므로 정답은 (A)이다.

▸▸ **Paraphrasing** 대화의 **the reduced price**
→ 정답의 **a discount**

45

What does the woman most likely give the man?

(A) A coupon
(B) A warranty
(C) A receipt
(D) A phone number

여자는 남자에게 무엇을 주겠는가?

(A) 쿠폰
(B) 보증서
(C) 영수증
(D) 전화번호

해설 세부 사항 관련 – 여자가 남자에게 줄 것
남자의 첫 번째 대사에서 여자에게 구매 영수증을 갖고 있는지(Do you have the receipt from the purchase?) 물어보니 여자가 갖고 있다(Yes, here it is.)고 대답했으므로 정답은 (C)이다.

46

Why will the speakers speak to a manager?

(A) To process a complaint
(B) To inquire about some stock
(C) To confirm a store policy
(D) To obtain authorization

화자들은 왜 관리자와 이야기할 것인가?

(A) 불만을 처리하려고
(B) 재고품에 대해 문의하려고
(C) 점포의 방침을 확인하려고
(D) 승인을 받으려고

어휘 complaint 불평, 불만 inquire 문의하다 stock 재고품 obtain 얻다 authorization 승인

해설 세부 사항 관련 – 관리자와 이야기하는 이유
대화 마지막에 남자가 여자에게 영수증을 관리자에게 가져가자고 하며 그녀가 환불을 승인할 수 있는 사람(Let's take this to the manager, since she's the one who can approve your refund.)이라고 했으므로 정답은 (D)이다.

47-49 3인 대화

M-Au [47]**For our product launch, I got a demonstration model of the new toaster oven. I'll focus on how it complements our current lines of juice makers and microwaves.**

W-Am That's terrific, Dean. And how are the rest of the event preparations going?

M-Au [48]**We're inviting key editors of trade publications, so our audience size keeps growing. There could be a problem with seating.**

W-Am Oh, Jen can help. She showed me a useful Web site, Seating-Smart.com. It helps plan seating layouts. Right, Jen?

W-Br Right. Dean, [49]**I'll walk you through all the site's features.** Let me open it on my laptop.

남: **제품 출시 행사를 위해 새로운 오븐 토스터의 전시용 모델을 받았어요. 저는 그것이 현재 우리 회사의 주스 메이커와 전자레인지들을 어떻게 보완하는지에 초점을 맞출 거예요.**
여1: 훌륭해요, 딘. 나머지 행사 준비는 어떻게 돼 가고 있나요?
남: **업계 출판물들의 핵심 편집자들을 초대할 거라서 청중의 규모가 계속 늘고 있어요. 좌석 배치에 문제가 생길 수도 있어요.**
여1: 아, 젠이 도와줄 수 있어요. 젠이 제게 Seating-Smart.com이라는 유용한 웹 사이트를 보여줬어요. 그게 좌석 배치도를 짜는 데 도움이 돼요. 그렇죠, 젠?
여2: 네, 딘, **제가 그 사이트의 기능들을 하나하나 설명해드릴게요.** 제 노트북 컴퓨터에서 해당 사이트를 열어보죠.

어휘 product launch 제품 출시 demonstration model 전시용 모델 toaster oven 오븐 토스터 focus on ~에 초점을 맞추다 complement 보완하다 current 현재의 microwave 전자레인지 terrific 멋진 trade 업계 publication 출판물 audience 청중 walk A through B A에게 B를 자세히 설명해주다 feature 기능, 특징

47

Where most likely do the speakers work?

(A) At a convention center
(B) At a shipping company
(C) At a journalism organization
(D) At a kitchen appliance manufacturer

화자들은 어디에서 근무하겠는가?

(A) 컨벤션 센터
(B) 운송 회사
(C) 언론 단체
(D) 주방용 가전기기 제조업체

해설 전체 내용 관련 – 화자들의 근무지
대화 맨 처음에 남자가 새로운 오븐 토스터의 전시용 모델을 받았고 그것이 현재 회사의 주스 메이커와 전자레인지들을 어떻게 보완하는지에 초점을 맞출 것(For our product launch ~ juice makers and microwaves.)이라고 했다. 이를 통해 화자들이 주방용 가전기기 제조업체에서 근무한다는 것을 알 수 있으므로 정답은 (D)이다.

▸▸ Paraphrasing 대화의 **toaster oven, juice makers and microwaves** → 정답의 **kitchen appliance**

48

What does the man say is a possible problem for an event?

(A) The budget
(B) The starting time
(C) The number of attendees
(D) The type of food to be served

남자는 행사를 진행함에 있어 무엇이 문제가 될 수 있다고 말하는가?

(A) 예산
(B) 시작 시간
(C) 참석 인원 수
(D) 제공되는 음식 종류

해설 세부 사항 관련 - 남자가 말하는 문제점

남자의 두 번째 대사에서 업계 출판물들의 핵심 편집자들을 초대할 거라서 청중의 규모가 계속 늘고 있고 좌석 배치에 문제가 생길 수도 있다(We're inviting key editors ~ a problem with seating.)고 했으므로 정답은 (C)이다.

▸▸ Paraphrasing 대화의 our audience size
→ 정답의 the number of attendees

49

What does Jen offer to do?

(A) Explain a Web site's features
(B) Design electronic invitations
(C) Carry some items to a nearby office
(D) Make some photocopies

젠은 무엇을 해 주겠다고 제안하는가?

(A) 웹 사이트의 특징 설명하기
(B) 전자 초대장 디자인하기
(C) 인근 사무실에 물품 들고 가기
(D) 복사하기

해설 세부 사항 관련 - 젠의 제안사항

대화 맨 마지막에 젠이 해당 사이트의 기능들을 하나하나 설명해주겠다(I'll walk you through all the site's features.)고 했으므로 정답은 (A)이다.

▸▸ Paraphrasing 대화의 walk through → 정답의 explain

50-52

M-Au OK. I just packed the extra luggage for the trade show. [50]**It has the deluxe samples of all our company's makeup and skin care products.**

W-Am Good. And the print shop will deliver our final batch of brochures by 10 A.M. sharp.

M-Au Oh. We should pack those before heading to the airport. But [51]**will we have time for that?**

W-Am Well... the plane leaves at five in the afternoon.

M-Au Ah! [51]**We're all right then.**

W-Am Yeah, the airport taxi arrives here at two, so we can even have a sit-down lunch.

M-Au Great. For now, [52]**I'll e-mail some last-minute invitations to potential attendees.**

남: 됐어요. 제가 방금 무역박람회에 가져갈 짐을 추가로 챙겼어요. **우리 회사의 전체 색조 화장품과 기초 화장품의 고급 샘플들이 들어 있어요.**
여: 좋아요. 그리고 인쇄소에서 우리의 최종 안내 책자 묶음을 오전 10시 정각에 배달해 줄 거예요.
남: 아, 공항에 가기 전에 그것도 챙겨야 해요. 하지만 **그럴 시간이 있을까요?**
여: 음… 비행기는 오후 5시에 출발하잖아요.
남: 아! **그럼 괜찮겠네요.**
여: 네, 공항 택시가 2시에 여기 도착하니까 편히 앉아서 점심식사도 할 수 있어요.
남: 잘 됐네요. 그럼 이제 **참석할 만한 사람들에게 이메일로 마지막 초대장을 몇 장 보낼게요.**

어휘 pack 짐을 싸다 luggage 짐, 수화물 trade show 무역박람회 deluxe sample 고급 샘플 makeup 색조 화장 skin care 기초 화장 print shop 인쇄소 batch 묶음 brochure 안내 책자, 브로셔 sharp 정각에 head to ~로 가다 have a sit-down lunch 편히 앉아서 점심식사를 하다 last-minute invitation 막판에 보내는 초대장 potential attendee 참석할 가능성이 있는 사람

50

What kind of products does the speakers' company make?

(A) Business stationery
(B) Travel bags
(C) Cosmetics
(D) Beverages

화자들이 다니는 회사는 어떤 종류의 제품을 만드는가?

(A) 사무용 문구
(B) 여행용 가방
(C) 화장품
(D) 음료수

해설 세부 사항 관련 - 회사가 제조하는 상품의 종류

남자의 첫 번째 대사에서 짐 안에 회사의 색조 화장품과 기초 화장품의 고급 샘플들이 들어 있다(It has the deluxe samples of all our company's makeup and skin care products.)고 했으므로 정답은 (C)이다.

▸▸ Paraphrasing 대화의 makeup and skin care products
→ 정답의 cosmetics

51

What does the woman imply when she says, "the plane leaves at five in the afternoon"?

(A) She thinks she will miss a flight.
(B) She intends to stay longer at an event.
(C) The speakers should try to take an earlier flight.
(D) The speakers do not have to worry about time.

여자가 "비행기는 오후 5시에 출발하잖아요"라고 말한 의도는 무엇인가?

(A) 자신이 비행기를 놓칠 거라고 생각한다.
(B) 행사장에 더 오래 머물려고 한다.
(C) 화자들이 더 이른 항공편을 잡으려고 해야 한다.
(D) 화자들이 시간에 대해 걱정하지 않아도 된다.

해설 화자의 의도 파악 - 비행기가 오후 5시에 출발한다는 말의 의미

남자의 두 번째 대사에서 공항에 가기 전에 안내 책자를 챙길 시간이 있을지(will we have time for that?) 물어봤다. 이에 대해 여자가 비행기가 오후 5시에 출발한다(the plane leaves at five in the afternoon.)고 하니 남자가 그럼 괜찮겠다(We're all right then.)고 했다. 즉, 비행기가 5시에 출발한다는 여자의 인용문은 시간적 부담을 가질 필요가 없다는 의도를 전달한 것이므로 정답은 (D)이다.

52

What will the man probably do next?

(A) Stop by a print shop
(B) Order a meal for delivery
(C) Phone a taxi company
(D) Send some e-mails

남자가 다음에 무엇을 하겠는가?

(A) 인쇄소에 들르기
(B) 식사 배달 주문하기
(C) 택시 회사에 전화하기
(D) 이메일 몇 통 보내기

해설 세부 사항 관련 – 남자의 다음 행동

대화 마지막에 남자가 참석할 만한 사람들에게 이메일로 최종 초대장을 보내겠다(I'll e-mail some last-minute invitations to potential attendees.)고 했으므로 정답은 (D)이다.

▸▸ **Paraphrasing** 대화의 **email some last-minute invitations**
→ 정답의 **send some e-mails**

53-55

M-Cn [53]**I'm interested in renting a new office space.** We need about three thousand square feet, and we'd like to be downtown with easy access to public transportation.

W-Br [53]**I know of spaces in two office buildings that might suit your needs.** [54]**One is two blocks from a stop on the underground train. The other isn't near the train but three bus lines run past it.**

M-Cn Both of those sites sound like good possibilities. [55]**Are the spaces in them currently vacant?**

W-Br Yes, they are. When would you be free to look at them? We can get you a discount if you're ready to move in within one month.

남: **새로운 사무 공간을 빌리는 데 관심이 있는데요.** 면적이 대략 3,000평방 피트에, 대중 교통을 쉽게 이용할 수 있는 시내에 위치했으면 합니다.

여: **손님의 필요에 맞을 만한 사무용 건물 두 곳에 있는 공간을 알고 있습니다. 하나는 지하철 정거장에서 두 구역 떨어져 있고요. 다른 하나는 지하철 근처는 아니지만 그곳을 지나는 버스 노선이 세 개 있습니다.**

남: 두 곳 다 괜찮은 것 같군요. **둘 다 현재 비어 있습니까?**

여: 네, 비어 있어요. 언제쯤 시간을 내서 살펴보실 수 있나요? 한 달 내로 입주하시면 할인해 드릴 수 있습니다.

어휘 rent (집, 토지 등)을 임차하다, 빌리다 square feet 평방 피트 downtown 시내에 with easy access to ~을 쉽게 이용할 수 있는 public transportation 대중교통 suit one's needs ~의 필요에 맞다 underground train 지하철 site 장소, 현장 vacant 비어 있는 move in 입주하다, 이사를 들어오다

53

Who most likely is the woman?

(A) A building owner
(B) A maintenance worker
(C) A safety inspector
(D) A real estate agent

여자는 누구겠는가?

(A) 건물 주인
(B) 관리 직원
(C) 안전 조사관
(D) 부동산 중개업자

해설 전체 내용 관련 – 화자의 신분

남자의 첫 번째 대사에서 새로운 사무실을 빌리고 싶다(I'm interested in renting a new office space.)고 했고 여자가 남자의 필요성에 맞을 만한 사무용 건물 두 곳에 있는 공간을 알고 있다(I know of spaces in two office buildings that might suit your needs.)고 했다. 이를 통해 여자가 부동산 중개인임을 알 수 있으므로 정답은 (D)이다.

54

What does the woman mention about some buildings?

(A) They are near transportation stops.
(B) They were recently renovated.
(C) They are well-known.
(D) They are tall.

여자는 건물들에 관해 무슨 말을 하는가?

(A) 정류장들 근처에 있다.
(B) 최근에 보수되었다.
(C) 유명하다.
(D) 고층이다.

해설 세부 사항 관련 – 건물에 대한 여자의 언급

여자의 첫 번째 대사에서 한 건물은 지하철 정거장에서 두 구역 떨어져 있고 다른 하나는 지하철 근처는 아니지만 그곳을 지나는 버스 노선이 세 개 있다(One is two blocks ~ three bus lines run past it.)고 했다. 즉, 두 건물이 모두 정류장들 근처에 있다는 말이므로 정답은 (A)이다.

▸▸ **Paraphrasing** 대화의 **underground train, bus**
→ 정답의 **transportation**

55

What aspect of some spaces does the man ask about?

(A) Availability
(B) Cleanliness
(C) Security
(D) Size

남자는 공간들의 어떤 점에 관해 물어보는가?

(A) 입주 가능성
(B) 청결함
(C) 보안
(D) 규모

해설 세부 사항 관련 – 공간에 대한 남자의 질문

남자의 두 번째 대사에서 여자에게 현재 빈 공간이 있는지(Are the spaces in them currently vacant?)를 물어봤으므로 정답은 (A)이다.

56-58

W-Br Frank, I'm concerned. [56]**Our bookstore's sales have dropped three months in a row.** To improve them and help sell this piled-up inventory, we need to hold an in-store special event. [57]**It could include author readings and prize contests...**

M-Au Oh, good idea. Uh... what can I do?

W-Br Let's see. I can create the promotional flyers. You're good at photography. How about taking pictures at the event?

M-Au Sure. We should consider having live music, too.

W-Br Yes, perhaps a local folk band. [58]**This afternoon, when it's not busy, I'll look over our store budget and see what we can afford.**

여: 프랭크, 걱정이네요. **우리 서점의 매출이 세 달 연속으로 줄었어요.** 매출을 올리고 이렇게 잔뜩 쌓인 재고를 판매하는 데 도움이 되도록 매장 내 특별 행사를 해야겠어요. **저자의 책 낭독과 경품 추첨 행사를 포함할 수도 있고요…**

남: 아, 좋은 생각이에요. 음… 저는 무엇을 할까요?

여: 어디 봅시다. 제가 홍보 전단지를 만들 수 있어요. 당신은 사진을 잘 찍잖아요. 행사 때 사진을 찍는 건 어떨까요?

남: 좋아요. 생음악을 연주하는 것도 고려해 봐요.

여: 네, 아마 이 지역 민속음악 밴드가 괜찮겠죠. **오늘 오후에 바쁘지 않을 때 우리 서점 예산을 살펴보고 우리 형편으로 무엇을 할 수 있는지 볼게요.**

어휘 be concerned 걱정하다, 우려하다 drop 떨어지다 in a row 연속으로 piled-up inventory 잔뜩 쌓인 재고 author 저자 prize contest 경품 추첨 행사 promotional flyer 홍보 전단지 folk 민속음악 budget 예산 afford ~할 형편이 되다

56

What is the woman concerned about?

(A) Declining sales
(B) Computer problems
(C) Inventory shortages
(D) Customer complaints

여자는 무엇을 염려하는가?

(A) 매출 감소
(B) 컴퓨터 문제
(C) 재고 부족
(D) 고객 불만

해설 세부 사항 관련 – 여자의 걱정거리

여자의 첫 번째 대사에서 서점 매출이 세 달 연속으로 줄었다(Our bookstore's sales have dropped three months in a row.)며 걱정하고 있으므로 정답은 (A)이다.

▸▸ **Paraphrasing** 대화의 **dropped** → 정답의 **Declining**

57

Why does the man say, "what can I do"?

(A) To give advice
(B) To indicate regret
(C) To offer assistance
(D) To correct a misunderstanding

남자가 "저는 무엇을 할까요?"라고 말한 의도는 무엇인가?

(A) 조언을 하려고
(B) 유감을 표명하려고
(C) 도와주려고
(D) 오해를 바로잡으려고

해설 화자의 의도 파악 – 무엇을 해야 할지를 물은 이유

여자의 첫 번째 대사에서 매장 내 특별 행사로 저자의 책 낭독과 경품 추첨 행사를 포함할 수도 있다(It could include author readings and prize contests)고 했다. 이 말을 듣고 남자가 자신은 무엇을 할 수 있을지(what can I do)를 물어본 이유는 여자에게 도움을 주기 위한 것이므로 정답은 (C)이다.

58

What does the woman say she will do in the afternoon?

(A) Rearrange some shelves
(B) Review a financial plan
(C) Distribute some flyers
(D) Meet with a local writer

여자는 오후에 무엇을 할 것이라고 말하는가?

(A) 서가 재배치
(B) 재무 계획서 검토
(C) 전단지 배포
(D) 지역 작가와의 만남

해설 세부 사항 관련 – 여자가 오후에 할 일

대화 맨 마지막에 여자가 오늘 오후에 바쁘지 않을 때 서점 예산을 살펴보고 서점 형편에 맞게 무엇을 할 수 있는지 알아보겠다(This afternoon, when it's not busy, I'll look over our store budget and see what we can afford.)고 했으므로 정답은 (B)이다.

▸▸ **Paraphrasing** 대화의 **look over** → 정답의 **review**

59-61

M-Cn Hi, Tonya. Have a seat. So, your e-mail said that you have a proposal for improving the company parking permit system.

W-Am That's right. [59]**I'd like to suggest that we take the fee for permits directly out of**

employees' paychecks, instead of asking them to pay it separately.

M-Cn That's an interesting idea. Tell me more.

W-Am [60]**Well, currently, staff have to remember to go to the Building and Grounds Department every six months to pay for their permits. My proposal would save them that time and energy.**

M-Cn It sounds good to me, but [61]**I'd like to know what everyone else thinks before making a decision.** I'll have managers discuss it with their teams.

남: 안녕하세요, 토냐. 앉으세요. 회사 주차 허가증 시스템을 개선하기 위한 제안 사항이 있다고 이메일을 보내셨죠.

여: 맞습니다. **직원들에게 허가증 비용을 따로 내라고 요청하는 대신 급여에서 직접 공제할 것을 제안합니다.**

남: 흥미로운 의견이네요. 좀 더 자세히 말씀해 주세요.

여: **음, 현재 직원들은 기억했다가 6개월마다 건물 관리 부서로 가서 주차 허가증 비용을 납부해야 합니다. 제 제안을 통해 직원들이 시간과 에너지를 아낄 수 있을 겁니다.**

남: 저는 괜찮은 생각 같은데, **결정을 내리기 전에 다른 사람들은 어떻게 생각하는지 알고 싶네요.** 관리자들이 팀원들과 의논할 수 있도록 하겠습니다.

어휘 have a seat 자리에 앉다 proposal 제안 improve 개선하다 parking permit 주차 허가증 fee 수수료, 요금 take A out of B B에서 A를 공제하다 directly 직접 paycheck 급여 separately 별도로, 따로 currently 현재 grounds (큰 건물의) 구내 make a decision 결정을 내리다, 결심하다

59

What are the speakers discussing?

(A) Building a new parking area
(B) Changing a fee payment method
(C) Expanding employee benefits
(D) Establishing a business partnership

화자들은 무엇에 관해 이야기하는가?

(A) 새로운 주차구역 만들기
(B) 요금 납부 방법 변경하기
(C) 직원 혜택 늘리기
(D) 사업상의 협력관계 구축하기

어휘 payment method 납부 방법 expand 확장시키다 benefit 혜택, 특전 establish 구축하다

해설 전체 내용 관련 – 논의하고 있는 문제

여자의 첫 번째 대사에서 직원들에게 허가증 비용을 따로 내라고 요청하는 대신 급여에서 직접 공제할 것을 제안한다(I'd like to suggest that we take the fee ~ asking them to pay it separately.)고 했고 이와 관련된 내용이 이어지고 있으므로 정답은 (B)이다.

60

According to the woman, what is the advantage of accepting a proposal?

(A) A department would be able to save money.
(B) A manufacturing procedure would become more efficient.
(C) The company's public image would improve.
(D) Staff would be less inconvenienced.

여자에 따르면, 제안을 수락했을 때 어떤 이점이 있는가?

(A) 부서가 비용을 아낄 수 있다.
(B) 제조 공정의 효율성이 높아질 것이다.
(C) 회사의 대외적인 이미지가 개선될 것이다.
(D) 직원들의 불편이 줄어들 것이다.

어휘 advantage 이점 manufacturing 제조 procedure 절차 efficient 효율적인 be inconvenienced 불편을 느끼다

해설 세부 사항 관련 – 제안 수락의 이점

여자의 두 번째 대사에서 직원들은 기억했다가 6개월마다 건물 관리 부서로 가서 주차 허가증 비용을 납부해야 하는데 자신의 제안을 통해 직원들이 시간과 에너지를 아낄 수 있다(staff have to remember to go to ~ for their permits. My proposal would save them that time and energy.)고 했으므로 정답은 (D)이다.

▸▸ **Paraphrasing** 대화의 **save them that time and energy**
→ 정답의 **less inconvenienced**

61

What does the man want to know?

(A) When he has to make a decision
(B) What some competitors will do
(C) Whether other people agree with him
(D) Where some funding will come from

남자는 무엇을 알고 싶어하는가?

(A) 의사 결정을 내려야 하는 시기
(B) 경쟁업체들의 향후 동향
(C) 다른 사람들의 동의 여부
(D) 앞으로 들어와야 할 자금의 출처

어휘 competitor 경쟁자 agree 동의하다 funding 자금

해설 세부 사항 관련 – 남자가 알고 싶어 하는 사항

남자의 마지막 대사에서 결정을 내리기 전에 다른 사람들은 어떻게 생각하는지 알고 싶다(but I'd like to know what everyone else thinks before making a decision.)고 하였으므로 정답은 (C)이다.

62-64 대화+층별 안내판

W-Br Welcome to Gould Library. How can I help you today?

M-Au Hello, I'd like to use one of the computers here to access the Internet.

Test 3

W-Br Sure. [62]**Our computers are located upstairs next to our nonfiction books.**

M-Au Great. Is there a limit on how long I can use the computers?

W-Br Yes—it's one hour. When you log in with your library card number, the computer will automatically calculate the time for you.

M-Au Oh, [63]**I don't have a library card.** Do I need one?

W-Br Unfortunately, you can't use our computers without one. But I can help you make one right now. [64]**I just need proof of your identity.** Do you have a driver's license?

여: 굴드 도서관에 오신 것을 환영합니다. 무엇을 도와드릴까요?
남: 안녕하세요. 여기 있는 컴퓨터 중 한 대로 인터넷에 접속하고 싶은데요.
여: 그러세요. **컴퓨터들은 위층 논픽션 섹션 옆에 있습니다.**
남: 잘됐네요. 컴퓨터를 사용하는 데 시간 제한이 있나요?
여: 네, 한 시간이요. 도서관 카드 번호로 로그인하실 때 컴퓨터가 자동으로 시간을 계산할 겁니다.
남: 어, **저는 도서관 카드가 없는데요.** 있어야 하나요?
여: 안타깝지만 카드가 없으면 컴퓨터를 사용하실 수 없습니다. 하지만 지금 당장 만들게 도와드릴 수 있습니다. **신분증만 있으면 됩니다.** 운전면허증 있으세요?

어휘 access 접속, 접근; 접근하다, 접속하다 upstairs 위층에 next to ~옆에 nonfiction 논픽션, 비소설 limit 제한 library card 도서관 출입증 automatically 자동으로 calculate 계산하다 unfortunately 안타깝게도, 유감스럽게도 proof of identity 신분증

Directory	
Floor	**Category**
4	Magazines, Audiobooks
[62]3	Nonfiction
2	Fiction, Special Collections
1	Children's Books

층별 안내판	
층	분야
4	잡지, 오디오북
3	**논픽션**
2	소설책, 특별 컬렉션
1	어린이 책

62

Look at the graphic. Which floor are the computers located on?

(A) 4
(B) 3
(C) 2
(D) 1

시각 정보에 따르면, 컴퓨터는 몇 층에 있는가?
(A) 4층
(B) 3층
(C) 2층
(D) 1층

해설 시각 정보 연계 – 컴퓨터가 있는 층
여자의 두 번째 대사에서 도서관 컴퓨터들은 위층 논픽션 섹션 옆에 있다(Our computers are located upstairs next to our nonfiction books.)고 했다. 그리고 층별 안내판을 보면 3층에 Nonfiction이 있으므로 정답은 (B)이다.

63

What problem does the man mention?

(A) He does not have a card.
(B) He did not return a book on time.
(C) He cannot find an audiobook.
(D) He could not reserve a study room.

남자는 어떤 문제를 언급하는가?
(A) 카드를 가지고 있지 않다.
(B) 책을 제때 반납하지 않았다.
(C) 오디오북을 찾을 수 없다.
(D) 열람실을 예약하지 못했다.

해설 세부 사항 관련 – 남자가 언급하는 문제점
남자의 세 번째 대사에서 도서관 카드를 갖고 있지 않다(I don't have a library card.)고 했으므로 정답은 (A)이다.

64

What does the woman ask the man for?

(A) A log-in password
(B) The name of an author
(C) Personal identification
(D) A completed form

여자는 남자에게 무엇을 요구하는가?
(A) 접속 비밀번호
(B) 작가의 이름
(C) 개인 신분증
(D) 작성된 양식

해설 세부 사항 관련 – 여자의 요구사항
대화 맨 마지막에 여자가 남자에게 신분증만 있으면 된다(I just need proof of your identity.)고 했으므로 정답은 (C)이다.

▸▸ **Paraphrasing** 대화의 **proof of your identity**
→ 정답의 **Personal identification**

65-67 대화 + 회의 안건

M-Cn So, 65**how is the development of the internal software platform coming along? Will it be ready for launch on schedule?**

W-Am Actually, we're a little behind. My team ran into some problems setting up the recording storage feature.

M-Cn That platform is our department's number-one priority. Is there anything I can do to help you get back on track?

W-Am Umm... oh, yes. 66**I'm supposed to give a talk on our systems at the new employee orientation tomorrow.** Could you find someone to take over for me?

M-Cn Sure. 66**In fact, I'll do it myself.** Don't give it another thought. 67**You just focus on getting the software ready on time.**

W-Am Thanks, Hugh. I will.

남: 자, **내부 소프트웨어 플랫폼 개발은 어떻게 되어 가고 있습니까? 예정대로 출시 준비가 되겠습니까?**

여: 사실 좀 늦어지고 있습니다. 저희 팀이 기록 저장 기능을 구축하는 데 몇 가지 문제가 생겼어요.

남: 해당 플랫폼은 우리 부서에서 최우선 사항입니다. 정상화를 위해 제가 도울 일이 있나요?

여: 음… 네. **제가 내일 신입사원 오리엔테이션에서 저희 시스템에 관한 강연을 하기로 되어 있는데요.** 저 대신 맡을 분을 구해주실 수 있나요?

남: 물론이죠. **제가 직접 할게요.** 이제 그건 신경 쓰지 마시고, **소프트웨어를 예정대로 준비하는 데 집중해 주세요.**

여 감사합니다, 휴 씨. 그렇게 하겠습니다.

어휘 development 개발 internal 내부의 come along 되어 가다 on schedule 정시에, 예정대로 a little behind 약간 뒤처진 run into a problem 문제가 생기다 priority 우선 사항 get back on track 정상으로 돌아오다 be supposed to + 동사원형 ~하기로 되어 있다 give a talk 강연하다 take over 인계받다 in fact 사실 focus on ~에 집중하다

Orientation Agenda

1. Welcome	Teri Duncan
2. Policies	Cindy Kim
3. Resources	Will Singleton
66 4. Systems	Ewa Kaminski

오리엔테이션 안건

1. 환영사	테리 던컨
2. 정책	신디 김
3. 자원	윌 싱글턴
4. 시스템	에바 카민스키

65

Why is the man speaking to the woman?

(A) To learn details about the orientation
(B) To receive an update on a project
(C) To request a special assignment
(D) To notify her of a revision to the agenda

남자가 여자에게 말을 건 이유는?

(A) 오리엔테이션 세부 사항에 대해 알아보기 위해
(B) 프로젝트의 최신 진행 상황을 듣기 위해
(C) 특별 임무를 요청하기 위해
(D) 여자에게 안건 변경을 알려주기 위해

어휘 request 요청하다 assignment 임무, 과제 notify 알리다 revision 변경, 수정

해설 세부 사항 관련 – 남자가 말을 건 이유

남자의 첫 번째 대사에서 내부 소프트웨어 플랫폼 개발이 예정대로 출시 준비가 되는지(how is the development ~ be ready for launch on schedule?) 물어보았으므로 정답은 (B)이다.

66

Look at the graphic. Who will the man replace as a speaker?

(A) Teri Duncan
(B) Cindy Kim
(C) Will Singleton
(D) Ewa Kaminski

시각 정보에 의하면, 남자는 누구를 대신해 연사로 나서겠는가?

(A) 테리 던컨
(B) 신디 김
(C) 윌 싱글턴
(D) 에바 카민스키

어휘 replace 대신하다

해설 시각 정보 문제 – 남자가 대신하는 연사

여자의 두 번째 대사에서 원래 본인이 내일 신입사원 오리엔테이션에서 시스템에 관한 강연을 하기로 되어 있다(I'm supposed to give a talk on our systems at the new employee orientation tomorrow.)고 했고 남자의 마지막 대사에서 자신이 하겠다(I'll do it myself.)고 했다. 표를 보면 시스템을 강연하는 사람은 에바 카민스키이므로 정답은 (D)이다.

Test 3

67

What does the man encourage the woman to do?

(A) Download some additional software
(B) Greet some new employees
(C) Negotiate a later deadline
(D) Concentrate on a development task

남자는 여자에게 무엇을 하라고 권하는가?

(A) 추가 소프트웨어 다운로드하기
(B) 신입사원 맞이하기
(C) 마감기한 연장 협상하기
(D) 개발 업무에 집중하기

어휘 encourage 장려하다 additional 추가의 greet 맞다, 환영하다 negotiate 협상하다 deadline 마감기한 concentrate on ~에 집중하다

해설 세부 사항 관련 - 남자가 권고하는 사항

남자의 마지막 대사에서 소프트웨어를 예정대로 준비하는 데 집중하라(You just focus on getting the software ready on time.)고 했으므로 정답은 (D)이다.

68-70 대화 + 메뉴

M-Au Ji-Young, [68]**I need you to inform the front counter staff we won't be able to serve any more watermelon juice today because we've run out of watermelons.**

W-Br We used them all?

M-Au Yes, so please tell the staff to apologize to our customers but to remind them we have many alternatives on the menu. [69]**Some, like the strawberry juice, are the same price as the watermelon juice.**

W-Br OK. [70]**I remember seeing some fruit as part of the delivery order tomorrow.** Will we get more then?

M-Au Yes. Oh, and [70] **when that delivery arrives, can you ask our supplier if he finally has more cooking oil in stock?** I want to order some soon.

W-Br No problem.

남: 지영, **수박이 다 떨어져서 오늘 수박 주스를 더 이상 제공할 수 없다고 앞 계산대 직원들에게 알려주세요.**

여: 전부 다 썼나요?

남: 네, 그러니 직원들에게 고객들에게 사과하고 대신 택할 수 있는 것들이 메뉴에 많이 있다는 점을 고객들에게 알려주라고 하세요. **딸기 주스 같은 것은 수박 주스와 가격이 같아요.**

여: 알겠어요. **내일 배달 주문에 과일이 약간 포함되어 있는 걸로 봤는데요.** 그때 더 받을까요?

남: 네. 아, 그리고 **배달품이 도착하면 우리 공급업자에게 이제는 식용유 재고가 더 있는지 물어보세요.** 곧 어느 정도 주문하고 싶거든요.

여: 걱정 마세요.

어휘 counter 계산대, 판매대 serve (음식을) 내다, 제공하다 watermelon 수박 run out of ~이 동이 나다, 다 써 버리다 apologize 사과하다 remind 상기시키다, 일깨우다 alternative 대안, 대체물 strawberry 딸기 supplier 공급업자 finally 드디어, 마침내 cooking oil 식용유 have ~ in stock ~의 재고가 있다

Juice	Price
Orange	$3.00
Mango	$3.50
[69]Strawberry	$4.00
Grapefruit	$4.50

주스	가격
오렌지	3달러
망고	3.5달러
딸기	4달러
포도	4.5달러

68

What problem are the speakers discussing?

(A) A product is not available.
(B) A shipment has been delayed.
(C) A machine is broken.
(D) A price has been miscalculated.

화자들이 어떤 문제를 논의하고 있는가?

(A) 한 제품은 구입할 수 없다.
(B) 배송이 지연되었다.
(C) 기계가 고장 났다.
(D) 가격이 잘못 계산되었다.

해설 세부 사항 관련 - 논의된 문제점

남자의 첫 번째 대사에서 여자에게 수박이 다 떨어져서 오늘 수박 주스를 더 이상 제공할 수 없다고 앞 계산대 직원들에게 알려 주라(I need you to inform the front counter staff ~ run out of watermelons.)고 했으므로 정답은 (A)이다.

▸▸ Paraphrasing 대화의 watermelon juice → 정답의 A product

69

Look at the graphic. How much does a watermelon juice cost?

(A) $3.00
(B) $3.50
(C) $4.00
(D) $4.50

시각 정보에 따르면, 수박 주스는 가격이 얼마인가?

(A) 3달러
(B) 3.5달러
(C) 4달러
(D) 4.5달러

해설 시각 정보 연계 – 수박 주스의 가격

남자의 두 번째 대사에서 딸기 주스 같은 것은 수박 주스와 가격이 같다(Some, like the strawberry juice, are the same price as the watermelon juice.)고 했다. 그리고 메뉴를 보면 딸기 주스의 가격이 4달러로 나와 있으므로 정답은 (C)이다.

70

What does the man ask the woman to do tomorrow?

(A) Attach a notice to a menu
(B) Unpack some boxes
(C) Wash some fruit
(D) Ask a question

남자가 여자에게 내일 하라고 요청하는 것은 무엇인가?

(A) 메뉴에 공지사항 붙이기
(B) 상자 포장 풀기
(C) 과일 씻기
(D) 문의하기

해설 세부 사항 관련 – 남자의 요청사항

여자의 두 번째 대사에서 내일 배달 주문에 과일이 약간 포함되어 있는 걸로 봤다(I remember seeing some fruit as part of the delivery order tomorrow.)고 했는데 남자가 배달품이 도착하면 공급업자에게 식용유 재고가 더 있는지 물어보라(when that delivery arrives ~ more cooking oil in stock?)고 했으므로 정답은 (D)이다.

PART 4

71-73 전화 메시지

M-Cn Hi, this is Lyle Mack. [71]**I'm calling about the checking account that I have at your institution.** Uh, [72]**I wanted to notify you that I'm heading overseas for a business trip next week.** The last time I did that, my debit card stopped working after one transaction because your system assumed that I wasn't the person using it. I don't want that to happen again. So [73]**I'd like you to temporarily change my account settings so that I'm allowed to use the card abroad.** I'll be away October eighth through twelfth. And please call me back to confirm that you did so. Thanks.

안녕하세요. 저는 라일 맥입니다. **귀사에 보유한 당좌예금 계좌에 관해 전화 드렸습니다. 다음 주에 출장으로 해외에 간다는 사실을 알려드리려고요.** 지난번 출장을 갔을 때 한 건 결제한 후 직불카드가 정지됐어요. 시스템 상에서 제가 카드를 쓰는 것이 아니라고 추정됐기 때문이죠. 그런 일이 다시는 없었으면 합니다. 그래서 **임시로 제 계좌 설정을 변경해 해외에서 카드를 사용하게 해 주셨으면 해요.** 10월 8일부터 12일까지 해외에 있을 겁니다. 그리고 조치하셨다는 확인 전화 부탁드립니다. 감사합니다.

어휘 checking account 당좌예금 계좌 institution 기관 notify 알리다 overseas 해외로 business trip 출장 debit card 직불카드, 현금카드 transaction 거래, 처리 assume 추정하다 temporarily 일시적으로, 임시로 setting 설정 abroad 해외에서 confirm 확인하다, 확정하다

71

What kind of business is the speaker calling?

(A) A magazine publisher
(B) A utility company
(C) A travel agency
(D) A bank

화자는 어떤 업체에 전화를 걸고 있는가?

(A) 잡지 출판사
(B) 공사
(C) 여행사
(D) 은행

어휘 publisher 출판사 utility company 공사(전기·수도·가스 등의 서비스를 제공하는 기업)

해설 세부 사항 관련 – 청자의 업체

지문의 초반부에서 화자는 귀사에 보유한 당좌예금 계좌에 관해 전화 드렸다(I'm calling about the checking account that I have at your institution.)고 했다. 그러므로 화자가 전화를 건 업체는 은행임을 알 수 있으므로 정답은 (D)이다.

72

What does the speaker say he will do next week?

(A) Make a large purchase
(B) Go to another country
(C) Start a new job
(D) Renew a membership

화자는 다음 주에 무엇을 할 것이라고 말하는가?

(A) 대량 구매하기
(B) 다른 나라에 가기
(C) 새로운 일 시작하기
(D) 멤버십 갱신하기

어휘 make a purchase 물건을 사다, 구매하다 renew 갱신하다, 연장하다

해설 세부 사항 관련 – 화자가 다음 주에 할 일

화자가 다음 주에 출장으로 해외에 간다는 사실을 알린다(I wanted to notify you that I'm heading overseas for a business trip next week.)고 했으므로 정답은 (B)이다.

73

What does the speaker want to change?

(A) A delivery method
(B) An account restriction
(C) Some reservation dates
(D) Part of an employment contract

화자는 무엇을 변경하고 싶어하는가?

(A) 배송 방법
(B) 계좌 이용 제한
(C) 예약일자
(D) 고용계약서 일부

어휘 restriction 제한, 규제 reservation 예약 employment contract 고용계약서

해설 세부 사항 관련 – 화자가 변경하고 싶어 하는 것

지문 후반부에서 화자가 임시로 자신의 계좌 설정을 변경해 해외에서 카드를 사용하게 해 줬으면 한다(I'd like you to temporarily change ~ to use the card abroad.)고 했으므로 정답은 (B)이다.

74-76 뉴스 보도

W-Am I'm Sue Planter, and this is the WPKK Radio morning news. [74] **The big story this week is that construction of the skyscraper on Fourth Avenue is finally underway.** The project was delayed due to the long rainy season we had this summer, but it seems the building crew is ready to start work. Once complete, the skyscraper will have two hundred floors and house dozens of large companies. Until then, [75]**there will be lots of dust along Fourth Avenue, so vehicles are urged to detour onto Mayberry Street instead.** On a similar note, I'll be back soon with your daily traffic report. [76]**But first, a quick commercial break.**

WPKK 라디오 아침 뉴스의 수 플랜터입니다. **이번 주 중대한 소식은 4번가의 초고층 건물 공사 작업이 마침내 진행되고 있다는 것입니다.** 이 사업은 올 여름 긴 장마 탓에 지연되었지만, 건설반원들이 작업을 시작할 준비가 된 것으로 보입니다. 이 초고층 건물은 일단 완공되면 200층 높이에 수십 개의 대기업을 수용할 예정입니다. 완공 시점까지 **4번가를 따라 먼지가 많이 날리겠으니 차량은 대신 메이베리 가로 돌아가시기 바랍니다.** 차량 말씀 드린 김에, 곧 다시 돌아와 오늘의 교통 정보를 전해 드리겠습니다. **하지만 먼저, 잠깐 광고를 들으시겠습니다.**

어휘 skyscraper 초고층 건물, 마천루 underway 진행 중인 be delayed 지연되다 due to ~ 때문에 complete 완성된, 완공된 house 수용하다 dozens of 수십 개의 dust 먼지, 분진 vehicle 차량 urge 충고하다 detour 돌아가다, 우회하다 instead 대신에 on a similar note 비슷한 논조의 이야기를 하자면 commercial break 광고 시간

74

What is the news report mainly about?

(A) An upcoming festival
(B) Some road maintenance
(C) A construction project
(D) Some weather conditions

뉴스 보도의 주된 내용은 무엇인가?

(A) 다가오는 축제
(B) 도로 보수공사
(C) 건설 사업
(D) 기상 여건

해설 전체 내용 관련 – 뉴스의 주된 내용

지문 초반부에 이번 주 주요 소식은 4번가의 초고층 건물에 대한 공사가 마침내 진행되고 있다는 것(The big story this week ~ is finally underway.)이라고 했으므로 정답은 (C)이다.

75

What are some listeners advised to do?

(A) Take a different driving route
(B) Obtain a neighborhood map
(C) Bring some waterproof materials
(D) Contact a city government office

일부 청자들은 무엇을 하라고 조언 받는가?

(A) 다른 운전 경로로 가기
(B) 동네 지도 구하기
(C) 방수 재료 가져오기
(D) 시 관공서에 연락하기

해설 세부 사항 관련 – 일부 청자들이 받은 조언

지문 후반부에 4번가를 따라 먼지가 많이 날릴 테니 차량은 대신 메이베리 가로 우회하기 바란다(there will be lots of dust ~ to detour onto Mayberry Street instead.)고 했으므로 정답은 (A)이다.

▸▸ **Paraphrasing** 대화의 detour → 정답의 Take a different driving route

76

What will the listeners hear next?

(A) A song
(B) A traffic report
(C) An interview
(D) An advertisement

청자들이 다음에 들을 것은 무엇인가?

(A) 노래
(B) 교통 정보
(C) 인터뷰
(D) 광고

해설 세부 사항 관련 - 청자들이 다음에 듣게 될 것

지문 맨 마지막에 화자가 청자들에게 먼저 잠깐 광고를 들을 것(But first, a quick commercial break.)이라고 했으므로 정답은 (D)이다.

▸▸ Paraphrasing 지문의 commercial → 정답의 advertisement

77-79 안내

M-Au [77]**Welcome to tonight's free performance, featuring jazz pianist Nick Patna.** This exciting event celebrates the completion of stage renovations made possible by generous support from Cultural Center members like you. Now, before we begin—[78]**I know some members have had issues accessing their membership accounts via our online system.** Well, it's a brand-new program. We ask for your patience as we resolve a few technical issues. Finally, [79]**we invite everyone to stay after tonight's show for a reception at which our volunteers will be passing out beverages and light snacks.** Simply come to the hall's lobby after the performance.

오늘 밤 재즈 피아니스트 닉 패트나와 함께하는 무료 공연에 오신 것을 환영합니다. 이 신나는 행사는 여러분 같은 문화센터 회원들의 아낌 없는 후원으로 이곳 무대를 새로 단장한 기념으로 열리고 있습니다. 자, 시작하기 전에, **일부 회원들께서 저희 온라인 시스템으로 회원 계정에 접속하시는 데 문제가 있다는 것을 알고 있습니다.** 음, 그게 아주 새로운 프로그램이라 그렇습니다. 몇몇 기술적 문제들을 해결하는 동안 인내심을 갖고 기다려 주시기를 당부 드립니다. 마지막으로 **오늘 저녁 공연이 끝난 후 모두들 남아 주시기 바랍니다. 환영회에서 자원봉사자 분들이 음료수와 가벼운 간식거리를 나눠드릴 예정입니다.** 공연이 끝난 후 공연장의 로비로 오시면 됩니다.

어휘 performance 공연 feature 출연시키다 celebrate 기념하다, 축하하다 renovation 개조[보수] generous support 아낌 없는 후원[지원] have issues -ing ~하는 데 문제를 겪다 access 접속하다, 접근하다 membership account 회원 계정 via ~을 통해 brand-new 아주 새로운 resolve 해결하다 technical 기술적 reception 환영회 volunteer 자원봉사자 pass out 나눠주다 beverage 음료수

77

Where most likely is the announcement being given?

(A) At a music concert
(B) At a film screening
(C) At a cooking demonstration
(D) At a fashion show

안내 방송이 나오는 장소는 어디겠는가?

(A) 음악회장
(B) 영화 상영회
(C) 요리 시연장
(D) 패션쇼

해설 전체 내용 관련 - 안내 방송이 나오는 장소

지문 맨 처음에 화자가 오늘 밤 재즈 피아니스 닉 패트나와 함께하는 무료 공연에 온 것을 환영한다(Welcome to tonight's free performance, featuring jazz pianist Nick Patna.)고 했다. 이를 통해 안내 방송이 음악 공연장에서 나오고 있음을 알 수 있으므로 정답은 (A)이다.

▸▸ Paraphrasing 지문의 performance → 정답의 music concert

78

Why does the speaker say, "it's a brand-new program"?

(A) To announce a schedule change
(B) To express excitement
(C) To encourage the listeners' participation
(D) To provide an excuse

화자가 "그게 아주 새로운 프로그램이라 그렇습니다"라고 말한 의도는?

(A) 일정 변경을 알리려고
(B) 흥분을 표현하려고
(C) 청자들의 참여를 장려하려고
(D) 변명을 하려고

어휘 excuse 변명, 핑계

해설 화자의 의도 파악 - 아주 새로운 프로그램이라고 말한 이유

인용문에 앞서 화자가 일부 회원들이 온라인 시스템으로 회원 계정에 접속하는 데 문제가 있는 걸 알고 있다(I know some members have had issues accessing their membership accounts via our online system.)고 했다. 인용문의 의도는 일부 회원들이 문제를 겪은 이유는 최신 프로그램이기 때문이라는 변명을 하기 위한 것이므로 정답은 (D)이다.

79

According to the speaker, what will happen after an event?

(A) Registrations will be accepted.
(B) Refreshments will be served.
(C) Photographs will be taken.
(D) Prizes will be awarded.

화자에 따르면, 행사 후에 무슨 일이 일어나겠는가?

(A) 등록을 받을 것이다.
(B) 다과가 제공될 것이다.
(C) 사진 촬영을 할 것이다.
(D) 상을 수여할 것이다.

어휘 refreshments 다과

해설 세부 사항 관련 - 행사 후 일정

지문 마지막에 화자가 청자들에게 공연이 끝난 후 모두 남아 주길 바라며 환영회에서 자원봉사자들이 음료수와 가벼운 간식거리를 나눠줄 것(we invite everyone to stay ~ passing out beverages and light snacks.)이라고 했으므로 정답은 (B)이다.

▸▸ **Paraphrasing** 지문의 **beverages and light snacks**
→ 정답의 **Refreshments** /
지문의 **passing out** → 정답의 **served**

80-82 회의 발췌

W-Br Good morning, everybody. [80]**I'm happy to inform you that all the managers of TMI Financial will be invited to a dinner this Friday to welcome our new CEO.** [81]**We're having it at Daniella's on Thornton Street, where we've reserved a private room for our group.** The first course will be served at 7:30 P.M., but please arrive early so that we're all present when the CEO arrives. Also, before we begin our meal, [82]**I want each of you to greet the CEO and let him know your name, which department you work in, and what project you're currently working on.** Any questions about that?

안녕하세요, 여러분. **이번 주 금요일 신임 최고경영자 환영 만찬에 TMI 파이낸셜의 모든 관리자들이 초대될 예정이라는 사실을 알려드리게 되어 기쁩니다. 장소는 손튼 가에 있는 대니엘라즈가 될 거고요 우리 그룹만을 위한 특실을 예약했습니다.** 첫째 코스는 오후 7시 30분에 나올 거지만 일찍 도착하셔서 최고경영자께서 오실 때 자리에 계시기를 바랍니다. 또 식사를 시작하기 전에 **여러분 각자가 최고경영자께 인사를 드리고 자신의 이름과 근무 부서, 그리고 현재 맡고 있는 프로젝트를 말씀해주시면 좋겠습니다.** 질문 있나요?

어휘 CEO 최고경영자(= chief executive officer) reserve 예약하다 present 참석한, 자리에 있는 work on ~을 작업하다

80

Why is the company organizing a special meal?

(A) To congratulate a manager on his retirement
(B) To reward some excellent workers
(C) To welcome a new executive
(D) To celebrate its corporate anniversary

회사가 특별 식사를 마련하는 이유는 무엇인가?

(A) 관리자의 은퇴를 축하하려고
(B) 몇몇 우수 사원들을 포상하려고
(C) 신임 임원을 환영하려고
(D) 회사 기념일을 축하하려고

어휘 reward 보답하다, 포상하다 executive 임원, 간부

해설 세부 사항 관련 - 특별 만찬의 이유

지문 초반부에 화자가 이번 주 금요일 신임 최고경영자 환영 만찬에 TMI 파이낸셜의 모든 관리자들이 초대될 예정임을 알리게 되어 기쁘다(I'm happy to inform you ~ this Friday to welcome our new CEO.)고 했으므로 정답은 (C)이다.

▸▸ **Paraphrasing** 지문의 **our new CEO**
→ 정답의 **a new executive**

81

What does the speaker mention about the site of the meal?

(A) Booking it was difficult.
(B) Only invited guests will be allowed into it.
(C) It has audiovisual capabilities.
(D) It is spacious.

화자는 식사 장소에 대해 무엇을 언급하는가?

(A) 예약하기 어려웠다.
(B) 초대받은 손님만 들어갈 수 있다.
(C) 시청각 시스템이 갖춰져 있다.
(D) 공간이 넓다.

어휘 booking 예약 spacious 널찍한

해설 세부 사항 관련 - 식사 장소의 특징

지문에서 화자가 장소는 손튼 가에 있는 대니엘라즈이고 화자의 그룹만을 위한 특실을 예약했다(We're having it at Daniella's ~ a private room for our group.)고 했으므로 정답은 (B)이다.

82

What does the speaker want the listeners to do after they arrive?

(A) Put up some decorations
(B) Sit with their department's employees
(C) Hand out party gifts
(D) Introduce themselves

화자는 청자들이 식당에 도착한 후 무엇을 하기를 바라는가?

(A) 장식 달기
(B) 자기 부서 직원들과 동석하기
(C) 파티 선물 분배
(D) 자기 소개

해설 세부 사항 관련 - 화자가 청자들에게 원하는 것

지문 후반부에 화자는 청자들에게 각자 최고경영자에게 인사를 하고 자신의 이름과 근무 부서, 그리고 현재 맡고 있는 프로젝트를 말씀드리면 좋겠다(I want each of you to greet the CEO ~ you're currently working on.)고 했으므로 정답은 (D)이다.

83-85 전화 메시지

W-Am Hi, Todd. I'm calling about the preparations for the Fitness Expo. I'm still gathering the samples we'll need—[83]**we'll be displaying every pro-athlete vitamin supplement and energy snack we market,** so there's quite a lot. [84]**Uh, our assigned booth is big enough, but... it's at the end of a long hallway. I'm going to call Pam, the organizer,** because I think we can do a little better. I'll let you know what she says. In the meantime, [85]**could you double-check the chart listing who's staffing the booth and when?** Just to make sure we're fully covered. I appreciate it!

안녕하세요, 토드. 피트니스 박람회 준비에 대해 전화했어요. 저는 아직도 저희가 필요로 할 견본품들을 모으고 있어요. **우리가 시판하는 프로 선수용 비타민 보충제와 에너지 보충용 간식을 모두 전시할 예정이니** 꽤 많아요. **우리가 배정받은 부스의 크기는 충분한데, 음… 긴 복도 끝에 있어요.** 제 생각엔 우리가 좀 더 잘해낼 수 있을 것 같아서 **주최자 팸에게 전화해보려고요.** 팸의 답변을 알려드릴게요. 그러는 동안 **당신은 부스를 지킬 직원들이 누구이고 시간은 언제인지 차트 목록을 다시 확인해 줄래요?** 부스가 잘 지켜지도록 확인하려는 거예요. 고마워요!

어휘 Fitness Expo 피트니스 박람회 gather 모으다 pro-athlete 프로 선수의 vitamin supplement 비타민 보충제 energy snack 에너지 보충용 간식 market 시판하다 assigned 할당된, 배정받은 hallway 복도 organizer 주최자 in the meantime 그동안에 double-check 재차 확인하다 staff 직원을 배치하다

83

What does the speaker's company most likely sell?

(A) Fitness clothing
(B) Sports nutrition products
(C) Home exercise equipment
(D) Stadium furnishings

화자의 회사는 무엇을 팔겠는가?

(A) 운동복
(B) 스포츠 영양제
(C) 가정용 운동 기구
(D) 경기장 비품

어휘 nutrition 영양 furnishing 비품, 가구

해설 세부 사항 관련 - 회사의 판매 상품

지문 초반부에 화자의 회사가 시판하는 프로 선수용 비타민 보충제와 에너지 보충용 간식을 모두 전시할 예정(we'll be displaying every pro-athlete vitamin supplement and energy snack we market)이라고 했으므로 정답은 (B)이다.

▸▸ **Paraphrasing** 지문의 **pro-athlete vitamin supplement and energy snack** → 정답의 **sports nutrition products**

84

What does the speaker mean when she says, "I think we can do a little better"?

(A) Her company's earnings are disappointing.
(B) Some preparations are progressing too slowly.
(C) She will inquire about other display options.
(D) She wants staff to attend skills workshops.

화자가 "제 생각엔 우리가 좀 더 잘해낼 수 있을 것 같아요"라고 말한 의도는 무엇인가?

(A) 회사의 소득이 실망스럽다.
(B) 몇 가지 준비가 너무 느리게 진행되고 있다.
(C) 다른 전시 옵션에 관해 문의할 것이다.
(D) 직원들이 기술 워크숍에 참석하기를 원한다.

해설 화자의 의도 파악 - 좀 더 잘할 수 있을 것이라는 말의 의미

인용문에 앞서 화자가 배정받은 부스의 크기는 충분한데, 긴 복도 끝에 있다(our assigned booth is big enough, but… it's at the end of a long hallway.)는 실망감을 나타냈다. 그리고 주최자인 팸에게 연락해보겠다(I'm going to call Pam, the organizer)고 했다. 즉, 다른 전시 옵션이 가능한지 팸에게 문의해 보겠다는 의미가 담겨 있으므로 정답은 (C)이다.

85

What does the speaker ask the listener to do?

(A) Proofread a press release
(B) Confirm a work schedule
(C) Clean a conference room
(D) Respond to a client's e-mail

화자는 청자에게 무엇을 요청하는가?

(A) 언론 보도 자료 교정
(B) 근무 일정표 확인
(C) 회의실 청소
(D) 고객 이메일에 답장

어휘 proofread 교정을 보다 press release 보도 자료 respond to ~에 답하다

해설 세부 사항 관련 - 화자의 요청사항

지문 후반부에 화자가 청자에게 부스에 나갈 직원들이 누구이고 시간은 언제인지 차트 목록을 다시 확인해 달라(could you double-check the chart listing for who's staffing the booth and when)는 부탁을 했으므로 정답은 (B)이다.

▸▸ **Paraphrasing** 지문의 **double-check** → 정답의 **Confirm**

86-88 소개

M-Cn Welcome to this year's Building Forward Association dinner. Before tonight's guest speaker joins me on stage, I'd like to briefly discuss his work. [86]**Gilbert Branson has designed fifteen of the most recognizable modern buildings in the United States,**

Test 3

including the Philadelphia location of the Seltino Hotel. He has truly made a huge contribution to our field. [87]**Although he plans to move to the United Kingdom early next year,** he still has several projects lined up in the United States. I'm sure some amazing structures will result from them. Now, we'll hear from Mr. Branson in a few minutes. [88]**But first, we'd like to show you a short film of his many wonderful designs.** Lights, please.

올해의 빌딩 포워드 협회 만찬에 오신 것을 환영합니다. 오늘 밤 초청 연사를 무대로 모시기 전에 그분의 업적에 관해 간단히 말씀드리고자 합니다. **길버트 브랜슨은 셀티노 호텔의 필라델피아 지점을 포함하여 미국 전역에서 가장 눈에 띄는 현대 건축물 15점을 설계했습니다.** 브랜슨 씨는 실로 건축 분야에 아주 큰 공헌을 했습니다. **비록 그분은 내년 초에 영국으로 이주할 계획이지만,** 미국에서 몇 건의 프로젝트가 대기 중입니다. 분명히 멋진 건축물들이 결과물로 나오겠지요. 잠시 후 브랜슨 씨의 말씀을 듣게 되실 텐데, **먼저 그분이 설계한 여러 훌륭한 디자인들을 다룬 짧은 영상을 보여드리겠습니다.** 소등해 주세요.

어휘 guest speaker 초청 연사 briefly 짧게, 간략히 recognizable 눈에 띄는, 알아볼 수 있는 make a contribution to ~에 공헌을 하다 line up 줄지어 세우다

86

What most likely is Mr. Branson's job?

(A) Web designer
(B) Hotel manager
(C) Architect
(D) Accountant

브랜슨 씨의 직업은 무엇이겠는가?

(A) 웹 디자이너
(B) 호텔 관리자
(C) 건축가
(D) 회계사

해설 전체 내용 관련 – 브랜슨 씨의 직업

지문 초반부에 길버트 브랜슨은 셀티노 호텔의 필라델피아 지점을 포함하여 미국 전역에서 가장 눈에 띄는 현대 건축물 15점을 설계했다(Gilbert Branson has designed ~ the Philadelphia location of the Seltino Hotel.)고 했다. 여기서 건축가임을 알 수 있으므로 정답은 (C)이다.

87

What does Mr. Branson intend to do next year?

(A) Teach a university course
(B) Remodel his office
(C) Relocate abroad
(D) Write a book

브랜슨 씨는 내년에 무엇을 하려고 하는가?

(A) 대학 과정 강의
(B) 사무실 개조
(C) 해외 이주
(D) 도서 집필

해설 세부 사항 관련 – 브랜슨 씨의 내년 계획

지문 중반부에 브랜슨 씨가 내년 초에 영국으로 이주할 계획(he plans to move to the United Kingdom early next year)이라고 언급했으므로 정답은 (C)이다.

▸▸ Paraphrasing 지문의 **move to the United Kingdom**
→ 정답의 **relocate abroad**

88

What will listeners most likely do next?

(A) Listen to a speech
(B) Enjoy a meal
(C) Watch a video
(D) Walk through a building

청자들은 다음에 무엇을 하겠는가?

(A) 연설 듣기
(B) 식사 즐기기
(C) 동영상 시청하기
(D) 건물 안 투어하기

해설 세부 사항 관련 – 청자들의 다음 행동

지문 맨 마지막에 화자가 청자들에게 브랜슨 씨가 설계한 여러 훌륭한 디자인들을 다룬 짧은 영상을 먼저 보여드리겠다(But first, we'd like to show you a short film of his many wonderful designs.)고 했으므로 정답은 (C)이다.

▸▸ Paraphrasing 지문의 **a short film** → 정답의 **a video**

89-91 광고

W-Br It's time to get fit at the newly renovated Arbax Fitness Club. [89]**Our workout rooms feature brand-new layouts**—we now have similar types of equipment conveniently grouped together. And did you know that our first personal training session is always free? [90]**Schedule a free, no-obligation consultation with a trainer today**—we can tailor a workout program to fit your needs. Now, we know what you're thinking. [91]**You're a busy professional with a full daily schedule.** Don't let that stop you! [91]**Arbax is available whenever you are.** Join us today!

새로 단장한 아르백스 피트니스 클럽에서 체력을 단련해 보세요. **저희 클럽 체력 단련실들의 배치를 전면 개편하여,** 이제 종류가 비슷한 기구들이 편리하게 한 데 모여 있습니다. 그리고 저희 개인 교습 시간이 처음 1회는 항상 무료라는 것을 알고 계셨나요? **꼭 등록하실 필요는 없으니 오늘 트레이너와 무료 상담 일정을 잡아 보세요.** 고객님의 필요에 맞는 운동 프로그램을 설계해 드릴 수 있습니다. 자, 저희는 고객님께서 지금 무슨 생각을 하고 계신지 압니다. **고객님은 매일 꽉 찬 일정을 소화해내야 하는 바쁜 전문 직업인이시죠.** 그렇다고 포기하지 마세요! **고객님께서 시간이 나실 때 아르백스는 열려 있습니다.** 오늘 저희 클럽에 등록하세요!

어휘 It's time to + 동사원형 ~할 시간이다 newly renovated 새롭게 단장한, 새로 보수한 workout 운동의 feature ~을 특징으로 하다 brand-new 아주 새로운, 신형의 layout 배치, 구조 conveniently grouped together 편리하게 한데 모여 있는 schedule 일정을 잡다 no-obligation 조건 없는, 부담이 없는 consultation 상담 tailor (특정한 목적, 사람 등에) 맞추다 fit one's needs ~의 필요에 맞추다 professional 전문 직업인

89

According to the speaker, what is new about Arbax Fitness Club?

(A) Its membership fees
(B) Its Web site
(C) Its floor plans
(D) Its range of classes

화자에 따르면 아르백스 피트니스 클럽은 무엇이 새로운가?

(A) 멤버십 비용
(B) 웹 사이트
(C) 공간 배치
(D) 다양한 종류의 수업

해설 세부 사항 관련 - 아르백스 피트니스 클럽의 새로운 점

지문 초반부에 클럽 체력 단련실들의 배치를 전면 개편하였다(Our workout rooms feature brand-new layouts)고 했으므로 정답은 (C)이다.

▸▸ Paraphrasing 지문의 **layouts** → 정답의 **floor plans**

90

What are listeners encouraged to do?

(A) Arrange a consultation
(B) Sign a long-term agreement
(C) Take an online survey
(D) Download a voucher

청자들은 무엇을 하도록 권고 받는가?

(A) 상담 예약
(B) 장기 계약서 서명
(C) 온라인 설문지 작성
(D) 쿠폰 다운로드

해설 세부 사항 관련 - 청자들에 대한 권장사항

지문 중반부에 꼭 등록하지 않아도 되니 오늘 트레이너와 무료 상담 일정을 잡아 보라(Schedule a free, no-obligation consultation with a trainer today)고 했으므로 정답은 (A)이다.

▸▸ Paraphrasing 지문의 **schedule** → 정답의 **Arrange**

91

What does the speaker imply when she says, "Don't let that stop you"?

(A) The club has long hours of operation.
(B) Club members can borrow workout clothes.
(C) There is a free trial period for new members.
(D) The club welcomes people of all fitness levels.

화자가 "그렇다고 포기하지 마세요"라고 말한 의도는 무엇인가?

(A) 클럽의 운영시간이 길다.
(B) 클럽 멤버들은 운동복을 대여할 수 있다.
(C) 새 멤버를 위한 무료 체험 기간이 있다.
(D) 클럽은 모든 체력 수준의 사람들을 환영한다.

해설 화자의 의도 파악 - 포기하지 말라고 말한 이유

인용문 앞에서 청자들은 매일 꽉 찬 일정을 소화해내야 하는 바쁜 전문 직업인(You're a busy professional with a full daily schedule.)이라고 했고, 인용문 바로 다음에 시간적 여유가 있을 때 아르백스는 열려 있다(Arbax is available whenever you are.)고 했다. 즉, 고객들에게 포기하지 말라는 인용문은 클럽의 운영 시간이 길기 때문에 포기할 필요가 없다는 뜻이므로 정답은 (A)이다.

Test 3

92-94 담화

M-Au [92]**It's nice to see so many people here for today's open house at 87 Grover Road.** This wonderful three-story home has already generated a lot of interest, so I don't expect it to stay on the market for very long. Today's event is a chance for you to take a look around the house and its pretty gardens, which are still maintained once a week. [93]**I'm afraid the power isn't on,** so it might be difficult to see in some of the upstairs rooms. You may have to use your mobile phone for light. Also, [94]**don't forget to pick up some brochures on your way out.** They contain information about this property and several other available homes in the area.

오늘 그로버 로드 87번지 주택 공개에 이렇게 많은 분들이 오신 것을 보니 기쁩니다. 이 근사한 3층짜리 주택은 진작부터 많은 관심을 불러일으켰기 때문에 이 집이 시장에 그리 오래 남아 있지 않을 거라고 예상합니다. 오늘의 이벤트를 기회로 삼아 이 집과 여전히 일주일에 한 번씩 관리되고 있는 예쁜 정원들을 한번 둘러보십시오. **유감스럽게도 전기가 들어오지 않아서** 몇몇 위층 방 안은 보시기 힘들 수도 있습니다. 휴대폰을 사용하여 빛을 비춰야 할 수도 있겠습니다. 그리고 **나가시는 길에 잊지 마시고 홍보 책자를 가져 가시기 바랍니다.** 이 집과 이 지역에서 매입할 수 있는 다른 주택 몇 채에 관한 정보가 담겨 있습니다.

어휘 open house (팔려고 내놓은 집을 둘러볼 수 있는) 주택 공개 three-story 3층짜리인 generate 만들어내다 expect 예상하다, 기대하다 stay on the market 시장에 매물로 남아 있다 take a look around ~을 둘러보다 power 전기, 전력 brochure 홍보 책자 contain 포함하다 property 부동산 available 구입[이용]할 수 있는

92

Who most likely are the listeners?

(A) Potential buyers
(B) Landscapers
(C) Journalists
(D) Paying tourists

청자들은 누구겠는가?
(A) 잠재적인 고객들
(B) 조경사들
(C) 기자들
(D) 돈을 지불하는 관광객들

해설 전체 내용 관련 - 청자들의 신분
지문 맨 처음에 화자가 청자들에게 오늘 그로버 로드 87번지 주택 공개에 많은 사람들이 온 것을 보니 기쁘다(It's nice to see so many people here for today's open house at 87 Grover Road.)고 했으므로 정답은 (A)이다.

93

What problem does the speaker mention?
(A) A garden is in poor condition.
(B) A set of stairs is steep.
(C) Many repairs are needed.
(D) There is no electricity.

화자는 어떤 문제점을 언급하는가?
(A) 정원 상태가 좋지 않다.
(B) 계단이 가파르다.
(C) 수리할 곳이 많다.
(D) 전기가 들어오지 않는다.

해설 세부 사항 관련 - 화자가 언급하는 문제점
지문 중반부에 화자가 유감스럽게도 전기가 들어오지 않는다(I'm afraid the power isn't on)고 했으므로 정답은 (D)이다.

▸▸ Paraphrasing 지문의 the power isn't on
→ 정답의 There is no electricity.

94

What are the listeners encouraged to do?
(A) Point out damage to a property
(B) Take some promotional materials
(C) Turn off their mobile phones
(D) Get some directions

청자들은 무엇을 하라고 권장 받는가?
(A) 건물의 훼손 부분 지적하기
(B) 홍보 자료 가져가기
(C) 휴대폰 끄기
(D) 길 안내 받기

해설 세부 사항 관련 - 청자들에 대한 권장사항
지문 후반부에서 화자가 청자들에게 나가는 길에 잊지 말고 홍보 책자를 가져가길 바란다(don't forget to pick up some brochures on your way out.)고 했으므로 정답은 (B)이다.

▸▸ Paraphrasing 지문의 pick up → 정답의 take

95-97 담화 + 목록

W-Br Hello, everyone. August was a busy month here at Al's Electronics Store. I've printed out a list of our best-selling items, which I'm handing out now. As you can see, [95]**the most popular item was our air conditioner, with six hundred twenty units sold.** [96]**I'm sure so many of these models were sold because it was so hot this summer.** Until it gets cooler, I want to keep selling as many of these air conditioners as possible. I think the usual method is to hold a sale, but I was wondering if there might be a more creative option. [97]**If you can think of any other ways to sell these products, please let me know.** Thanks.

안녕하세요, 여러분. 8월은 이곳 앨즈 전자제품 판매점이 바쁜 달이었습니다. 저희 매장에서 가장 잘 나가는 품목들의 목록을 뽑아 봤는데, 지금 나눠드리는 겁니다. 보시다시피 **가장 인기 있는 품목은 620대가 팔린 에어컨입니다. 이 모델이 이렇게 많이 팔린 이유는 올 여름 날씨가 몹시 더웠기 때문인 게 확실합니다.** 더 선선해지기 전까지 이 에어컨을 되도록 많이 팔고 싶습니다. 제 생각에 일반적인 방법은 할인 판매를 하는 것이겠지만, 혹시 보다 창의적인 방법이 있을까 했습니다. **달리 이 제품을 판매할 방법이 생각나면 제게 알려 주시기 바랍니다.** 감사합니다.

어휘 electronics 전자제품 best-selling items 가장 잘 팔리는 품목들 hand out 나눠주다 unit (상품의) 한 개 keep -ing 계속 ~하다 as ~ as possible 되도록, 가능한 한 usual method 평소의[일반적인] 방법 hold a sale 할인 판매를 하다 creative 창의적인, 기발한

Best-selling Items in August	
Product	**Units Sold**
[95]X190	620
Swiff B	455
Draco 1	390
BN237	110

8월 최다 판매 품목	
제품	판매 대수
X190	620
Swiff B	455
Draco 1	390
BN237	110

95

Look at the graphic. What product is the speaker talking about?

(A) X190
(B) Swiff B
(C) Draco 1
(D) BN237

시각 정보에 의하면, 화자는 어느 제품에 대해 말하고 있는가?

(A) X190
(B) Swiff B
(C) Draco 1
(D) BN237

해설 시각 정보 연계 - 화자가 가리키는 상품
지문 초반에 화자가 가장 인기 있는 품목은 620대가 팔린 에어컨(the most popular item was our air conditioner, with six hundred twenty units sold.)이라고 했다. 그리고 목록을 보면 X190의 판매 수량이 620대이므로 정답은 (A)이다.

96

According to the speaker, what has influenced the sales of air conditioners?

(A) A discount
(B) The weather
(C) A marketing campaign
(D) The release of a new model

화자에 따르면 에어컨 매출에 영향을 준 것은 무엇인가?

(A) 할인 판매
(B) 날씨
(C) 마케팅 캠페인
(D) 새로운 모델의 출시

해설 세부 사항 관련 - 에어컨 매출에 영향을 끼친 것
지문 중반에 화자가 에어컨이 이렇게 많이 팔린 이유는 올 여름 날씨가 몹시 더웠기 때문인 게 확실하다(I'm sure so many of these models were sold because it was so hot this summer.)고 했으므로 정답은 (B)이다.

97

What does the speaker ask the listeners to do?

(A) Install some equipment
(B) Keep a handout
(C) Enter data into a computer
(D) Share some ideas

화자는 청자들에게 무엇을 요청하는가?

(A) 장비 설치
(B) 유인물 보관
(C) 컴퓨터에 자료 입력
(D) 아이디어 공유

해설 세부 사항 관련 - 화자의 요청사항
지문 후반부에 화자가 청자들에게 이 제품을 판매할 방법이 생각나면 알려 달라(If you can think of any other ways to sell these products, please let me know.)고 했으므로 정답은 (D)이다.

98-100 전화 메시지 + 일정표

M-Cn Hi, Jacob. Can you help me? Mr. Chang, a buyer from Tep's Grocery Center, is meeting with me on Tuesday. [98]**He wants to learn more about the juice drinks and teas we make.** This isn't a formal meeting, but I'd like to hold it in meeting room B. It has the most comfortable seating. But [99]**it looks like you've booked the room for 2 P.M.—the time I would need it.** Could you make a switch with me? Room A is available for that time, and [100]**I'd be happy to set up that room beforehand for you.** Call me back and let me know. Thanks.

안녕하세요, 제이콥. 저 좀 도와주시겠어요? 텝스 식료품 센터의 구매 담당자 창 씨가 화요일에 저와 만나거든요. **그가 우리 회사에서 제조하는 주스와 차에 관해 더 알고 싶어 해요.** 공식적인 회의는 아니지만 B 회의실을 사용했으면 해서요. 거기 좌석이 가장 편하잖아요. 하지만 **제가 쓰려는 오후 2시에 당신이 그 회의실을 쓰려고 예약해 놓은 것 같더군요.** 저와 바꿔주실 수 있을까요? 그 시간에 A 회의실을 사용할 수 있으니까 **제가 당신을 위해 그 회의실을 사전에 준비해 드릴 수 있습니다.** 제게 전화해서 알려주세요. 고맙습니다.

어휘 buyer 구매 담당자 grocery 식료품 formal 공식적인
make a switch with ~와 맞바꾸다 set up 준비하다, 마련하다
beforehand 사전에, 미리

Meeting room B: Tuesday

Time	Event
1:00 P.M.	Software Training
[99]2:00 P.M.	Budget Discussion
3:00 P.M.	Focus Group Meeting
4:00 P.M.	Brainstorming Session

B 회의실: 화요일

시간	행사
오후 1:00	소프트웨어 교육
오후 2:00	**예산 논의**
오후 3:00	포커스 집단 회의
오후 4:00	브레인스토밍 회의

98

Where most likely does the speaker work?

(A) At a supermarket
(B) At an interior design firm
(C) At an advertising agency
(D) At a beverage company

화자는 어디에서 일할 것 같은가?

(A) 슈퍼마켓
(B) 실내 디자인 회사
(C) 광고 대행사
(D) 음료 회사

해설 전체 내용 관련 - 화자의 근무지

지문 초반부에 구매자인 창 씨가 화자의 회사가 만드는 주스 음료와 차에 대해 더 많이 알고 싶어 한다(He wants to learn ~ we make.)고 했다. 화자가 음료 회사에 근무한다는 것을 알 수 있으므로 정답은 (D)이다.

▸▸ **Paraphrasing** 지문의 juice drinks and teas
→ 정답의 beverage

99

Look at the graphic. What event did Jacob most likely reserve a room for?

(A) Software Training
(B) Budget Discussion
(C) Focus Group Meeting
(D) Brainstorming Session

시각 정보에 의하면, 제이콥은 어떤 행사를 위해 회의실을 예약했을 것 같은가?

(A) 소프트웨어 교육
(B) 예산 논의
(C) 포커스 집단 회의
(D) 브레인스토밍 회의

해설 시각 정보 연계 - 제이콥의 회의실 예약 용도

지문 중반부에 화자가 회의실이 필요한 시간인 오후 2시에 제이콥이 그 회의실을 예약해 놓은 것 같다(it looks like you've booked ~ I would need it.)고 했다. 그리고 일정표를 보면 오후 2시 회의는 예산 논의(Budget Discussion)로 명시되어 있으므로 정답은 (B)이다.

100

What does the speaker offer to do?

(A) Edit a report
(B) Update a Web site
(C) Prepare a meeting space
(D) Submit an invoice

화자는 무엇을 하겠다고 하는가?

(A) 보고서 편집
(B) 웹 사이트 업데이트
(C) 회의 공간 준비
(D) 청구서 제출

해설 세부 사항 관련 - 화자의 제안 사항

지문 후반부에 화자가 제이콥을 위해 A 회의실은 사전에 준비해 놓겠다(I'd be happy to ~ for you.)고 했으므로 정답은 (C)이다.

▸▸ **Paraphrasing** 지문의 set up that room
→ 정답의 Prepare a meeting space

TEST 4

01 (B)	**02** (B)	**03** (D)	**04** (C)	**05** (C)
06 (C)	**07** (C)	**08** (C)	**09** (B)	**10** (C)
11 (A)	**12** (C)	**13** (A)	**14** (B)	**15** (A)
16 (C)	**17** (C)	**18** (C)	**19** (A)	**20** (B)
21 (A)	**22** (A)	**23** (B)	**24** (C)	**25** (B)
26 (B)	**27** (B)	**28** (B)	**29** (A)	**30** (C)
31 (A)	**32** (B)	**33** (A)	**34** (B)	**35** (B)
36 (D)	**37** (A)	**38** (A)	**39** (B)	**40** (B)
41 (D)	**42** (B)	**43** (A)	**44** (D)	**45** (C)
46 (B)	**47** (A)	**48** (B)	**49** (A)	**50** (C)
51 (B)	**52** (B)	**53** (C)	**54** (B)	**55** (C)
56 (B)	**57** (C)	**58** (C)	**59** (A)	**60** (D)
61 (D)	**62** (B)	**63** (C)	**64** (C)	**65** (B)
66 (A)	**67** (C)	**68** (D)	**69** (D)	**70** (A)
71 (C)	**72** (B)	**73** (A)	**74** (D)	**75** (D)
76 (B)	**77** (B)	**78** (C)	**79** (A)	**80** (D)
81 (A)	**82** (C)	**83** (A)	**84** (C)	**85** (C)
86 (A)	**87** (A)	**88** (D)	**89** (C)	**90** (D)
91 (B)	**92** (C)	**93** (D)	**94** (D)	**95** (D)
96 (A)	**97** (B)	**98** (D)	**99** (C)	**100** (A)

PART 1

1 M-Au

(A) She's piling up some books.
(B) She's reading in an outdoor area.
(C) She's pouring a beverage.
(D) She's polishing her glasses.

(A) 여자가 책을 쌓고 있다.
(B) 여자가 실외에서 책을 읽고 있다.
(C) 여자가 음료를 따르고 있다.
(D) 여자가 안경을 닦고 있다.

어휘 pile up 쌓다 outdoor area 실외, 옥외 공간 pour 따르다, 붓다 beverage 음료 polish (윤이 나도록) 닦다

해설 1인 등장 사진 – 사람의 동작 묘사

(A) 여자가 책을 쌓는(is piling up) 모습이 아니므로 오답.

(B) 여자가 실외에서 책을 읽는(is reading) 모습이므로 정답.

(C) 사진에 음료수 컵이 보이지만 여자가 음료수를 따르는(is pouring) 모습이 아니므로 오답.

(D) 여자가 안경을 쓰고 있지 닦고 있는(is polishing) 모습이 아니므로 오답.

2 M-Cn

(A) A woman is folding a newspaper.
(B) Some people are gathered for a meeting.
(C) Some people are seated across from each other.
(D) One of the men is speaking into a telephone.

(A) 여자가 신문을 접고 있다.
(B) 몇몇 사람들이 회의를 위해 모여 있다.
(C) 몇몇 사람들이 서로 마주보고 앉아 있다.
(D) 남자 중 한 명이 전화기에 대고 말을 하고 있다.

어휘 fold 접다 gather 모으다, 모이다 be seated 앉아 있다 across from each other 서로 마주보고, 서로 반대편에

해설 2인 이상 등장 사진 – 사람의 상태 묘사

(A) 사진에 신문(newspaper)이 보이지 않으므로 오답.

(B) 세 사람이 회의를 위해 모여 있는(are gathered for a meeting) 모습이므로 정답.

(C) 사람들이 마주보고 앉아 있는(are seated across from each other) 모습은 아니므로 오답.

(D) 세 사람 중에 전화기에 대고 말을 하고 있는(is speaking into a telephone) 사람은 없으므로 오답.

3 W-Am

(A) He's arranging some merchandise.
(B) He's packing up some computers.
(C) He's strolling past a clothing shop.
(D) He's looking down at a laptop.

(A) 남자가 상품들을 정리하고 있다.
(B) 남자가 컴퓨터들을 포장하고 있다.
(C) 남자가 옷 가게를 걸어 지나가고 있다.
(D) 남자가 노트북 컴퓨터를 내려다보고 있다.

어휘 arrange 정리하다, 정돈하다 merchandise 상품 pack 포장하다 stroll 거닐다, 산책하다 look down at ~을 내려다보다 laptop 노트북 컴퓨터

해설 1인 등장 사진 – 사람의 동작 묘사

(A) 남자가 상품들을 정리하고 있는(is arranging some merchandise) 모습이 아니므로 오답.

(B) 남자가 컴퓨터들을 포장하고 있는(is packing up some computers) 모습이 아니므로 오답.

(C) 남자가 옷 가게를 걸어 지나가고 있는(is strolling past a clothing shop) 모습이 아니므로 오답.

(D) 남자가 자신 앞에 놓인 컴퓨터를 내려다보고 있는(is looking down at a laptop) 모습이므로 정답.

4 W-Br

(A) Passengers are waiting for a taxi to arrive.
(B) Some vehicles have arrived on a runway.
(C) Two taxis have been parked beside each other.
(D) A line of travelers leads into a terminal.

(A) 승객들이 택시가 도착하기를 기다리고 있다.
(B) 차량 몇 대가 활주로에 도착했다.
(C) 택시 두 대가 나란히 주차되어 있다.
(D) 여행객들의 줄이 터미널 안으로 이어져 있다.

어휘 wait for ~을 기다리다 vehicle 탈것, 차량 runway 활주로 park 주차하다 beside each other 서로 나란히

해설 실외 사물 사진 – 다양한 사물의 위치 묘사

(A) 사진에 승객들(passengers)이 보이지 않으므로 오답.

(B) 사진에 활주로(runway)가 보이지 않으므로 오답.

(C) 두 대의 택시가 나란히 주차되어 있는(have been parked beside each other) 모습이므로 정답.

(D) 사진에 여행자들(travelers)이 보이지 않으므로 오답.

5 M-Au

(A) Decorations are on display in a window.
(B) A waiter is distributing menus to some diners.
(C) Some people are preparing food on a large counter.
(D) There are several plates in a dish rack.

(A) 창문 안에 장식품들이 진열되어 있다.
(B) 웨이터가 식사 손님들에게 메뉴판을 나눠주고 있다.
(C) 사람들이 큰 조리대에서 음식을 준비하고 있다.
(D) 식기 선반에 접시가 몇 개 있다.

어휘 on display 전시된, 진열된 distribute 나눠주다 diner 식사하는 사람 counter 조리대 plate 접시 dish rack 식기 선반

해설 2인 이상 등장 사진 – 사람의 동작 묘사

(A) 사진에 창문(window)이 보이지 않으므로 오답.

(B) 메뉴판을 나눠주는(is distributing) 웨이터가 없으므로 오답.

(C) 사람들이 큰 조리대에서 음식을 준비하고(are preparing) 있으므로 정답.

(D) 접시가 조리대 위에 있지 식기 선반 안에(in a dish rack) 있지는 않으므로 오답.

6 W-Am

(A) A shopping basket has been filled with products.
(B) Workers in a store are hanging up a sign.
(C) A rolling ladder has been placed along some shelves.
(D) One of the men is loading some boxes onto a cart.

(A) 쇼핑 바구니에 상품이 가득 차 있다.
(B) 가게 안의 근로자들이 간판을 걸고 있다.
(C) 바퀴 달린 사다리가 선반들을 따라 놓여 있다.
(D) 남자들 중 한 명이 카트에 상자 몇 개를 싣고 있다.

어휘 basket 바구니 sign 간판 rolling ladder 바퀴 달린 사다리 shelf 선반, 서가 load (짐을) 싣다, 적재하다 cart 카트, 손수레

해설 2인 이상 등장 사진 – 다양한 사물의 위치 묘사

(A) 사진에 쇼핑 바구니(shopping basket)는 보이지만 상품으로 가득 차 있지(has been filled with products) 않으므로 오답.

(B) 근로자(Worker)로 보이는 사람 한 명과 간판(sign)이 보이지만 그것을 걸고 있는(hanging up) 상황이 아니므로 오답.

(C) 바퀴 달린 사다리가 선반들을 따라 놓여 있는(has been placed along some shelves) 상태이므로 정답.

(D) 사진에 카트(cart)가 보이지 않으므로 오답.

PART 2

7

W-Br Which film do you want to see?

M-Au (A) Some very talented actors.

(B) Sure—at the theater on Main Street?

(C) This action movie looks fun.

어떤 영화를 보고 싶으세요?

(A) 아주 재능 있는 배우들이요.

(B) 그럼요. 메인 가의 극장에서요?

(C) 이 액션 영화가 재미있어 보이네요.

어휘 film 영화 talented 재능 있는

해설 선택사항을 묻는 Which 의문문

(A) 연상 단어 오답. 질문의 film에서 연상 가능한 actors를 이용한 오답.

(B) 질문과 상관없는 오답. 영화를 보고 싶은지 묻는 질문에 어울리는 응답이므로 오답.

(C) 정답. 어느 영화를 보고 싶냐는 질문에 action movie라고 구체적인 정보로 응답하고 있으므로 정답.

8

W-Br Who's going to attend Ms. Lennon's retirement party?

W-Am (A) She doesn't seem tired.

(B) Let's get together again soon.

(C) Everyone except Bill.

레넌 씨의 퇴직 기념 파티에 누가 참석할 예정이죠?

(A) 그녀는 피곤한 것 같지 않아요.

(B) 곧 다시 만나요.

(C) 빌만 빼고 전원이요.

어휘 attend 참석하다 retirement 퇴직 except ~을 제외하고

해설 파티 참석자를 묻는 Who 의문문

(A) 유사 발음 오답. 질문의 retirement와 부분적으로 발음이 동일한 tired를 이용한 오답.

(B) 연상 단어 오답. 질문의 party에서 연상 가능한 get together를 이용한 오답.

(C) 정답. 퇴직 기념 파티(retirement party)의 참석자를 묻는 질문에 빌을 제외한 모든 사람(Everyone except Bill.)이라는 구체적인 대상으로 응답하고 있으므로 정답.

9

W-Am How long does it take to drive to New York from here?

M-Cn (A) Every other weekend.

(B) About five hours.

(C) It's a great place to visit.

여기서 뉴욕까지 차로 얼마나 걸리죠?

(A) 격주로 주말마다요.

(B) 대략 다섯 시간이요.

(C) 방문하기에 좋은 장소예요.

어휘 every other 하나 걸러 about 대략, 약

해설 운전 시간을 묻는 How long 의문문

(A) 질문과 상관없는 오답. 빈도를 묻는 How often에 대한 응답이므로 오답.

(B) 정답. 뉴욕까지 차로 얼마나 소요되는지 묻는 질문에, 대략 다섯 시간(About five hours.)이라는 구체적인 시간으로 응답하고 있으므로 정답.

(C) 연상 단어 오답. 질문의 New York에서 연상 가능한 a great place to visit를 이용한 오답.

10

M-Au Did you study computer science at university?

W-Br (A) An assistant professor.

(B) Yes, it's a published study.

(C) My degree was in finance.

대학에서 컴퓨터 공학을 공부하셨나요?

(A) 조교수요.

(B) 네, 그건 발표된 연구입니다.

(C) 재정 분야에서 학위를 받았습니다.

어휘 assistant professor 조교수 published 발표된 degree 학위 finance 재정

해설 대학에서의 전공을 묻는 일반 의문문

(A) 연상 단어 오답. 질문의 university에서 연상 가능한 professor를 이용한 오답.

(B) 단어 반복 오답. 질문에 나온 study를 반복한 오답.

(C) 정답. 대학 전공을 묻는 질문에 재정 분야 학위를 받았다고 답변을 하고 있으므로 정답.

11

M-Cn You work in the editing department, don't you?

W-Am (A) Yes, I've been there for ten years.

(B) The latest edition of the magazine.

(C) No, it departs at seven each day.

당신은 편집부에서 일하시죠, 그렇지 않나요?

(A) 네, 10년 동안 몸담아 왔어요.

(B) 잡지의 최신판이요.

(C) 아니요, 매일 7시에 출발해요.

어휘 editing 편집 latest edition 최신판 depart 떠나다, 출발하다

해설 편집부 소속인지 묻는 부가의문문

(A) 정답. 편집부에서 근무하는지에 대해 먼저 Yes로 긍정적 응답을 한 후, 10년 동안(for ten years) 근무했다고 부연 설명하고 있으므로 정답.

(B) 파생어 오답. 질문의 editing과 파생어 관계인 edition을 이용한 오답.

(C) 유사 발음 오답. 질문의 department와 부분적으로 발음이 동일한 departs를 이용한 오답.

Test 4

12

M-Au Can we postpone the sales meeting until Friday?

W-Br (A) The post office.

(B) Here are the final sales results.

(C) You'd better ask Ms. Garcia.

금요일까지 영업 회의를 연기할 수 있을까요?

(A) 우체국이요.

(B) 여기 최종 판매 결과가 있습니다.

(C) 가르시아 씨에게 물어보는 편이 좋겠어요.

어휘 postpone 연기하다 sales meeting 영업 회의 result 결과

해설 회의를 연기할 수 있는지 묻는 조동사(can) 제안/요청 의문문

(A) 유사 발음 오답. 질문의 postpone과 부분적으로 발음이 동일한 post office를 반복 이용한 오답.

(B) 단어 반복 오답. 질문의 sales를 반복 이용한 오답.

(C) 정답. 영업 회의를 연기할 수 있을지에 대해 즉각적인 답변을 피한 채, 가르시아 씨에게 물어보는 게 좋겠다(You'd better ask Ms. Garcia.)는 우회적 표현으로 응답하고 있으므로 정답.

13

W-Am When is your next business trip?

M-Cn (A) It depends on the company's needs.

(B) An orientation seminar.

(C) With several of my colleagues.

당신의 다음 출장은 언제예요?

(A) 회사의 필요에 달려 있어요.

(B) 오리엔테이션 세미나예요.

(C) 동료들 몇 명과 함께요.

어휘 business trip 출장 colleague 동료

해설 출장 시점을 묻는 When 의문문

(A) 정답. 다음 출장이 언제인지 묻는 질문에 대해 회사의 필요에 달려 있다(depends on the company's needs)는 불확실성 표현으로 응답하고 있으므로 정답.

(B) 연상 단어 오답. 질문의 business trip에서 연상 가능한 orientation seminar를 이용한 오답.

(C) 질문과 상관없는 오답. 동반자를 묻는 Who 의문문에 어울리는 응답이므로 오답.

14

M-Au Where is the printer paper we just bought?

W-Br (A) From an online store.

(B) Check the desk drawer.

(C) Do you have enough money?

우리가 방금 산 프린터 용지는 어디에 있어요?

(A) 온라인 상점에서요.

(B) 책상 서랍 안을 확인해보세요.

(C) 돈은 충분히 있으세요?

어휘 drawer 서랍

해설 프린터 용지의 위치를 묻는 Where 의문문

(A) 질문과 상관없는 오답. 프린터용 용지를 어디서 샀냐는 질문에 어울리는 응답이므로 오답.

(B) 정답. 프린터 용지가 어디에 있는지에 대해 책상 서랍 안을 확인해보라(Check the desk drawer.)는 구체적인 장소로 응답하고 있으므로 정답.

(C) 연상 단어 오답. 질문의 bought에서 연상 가능한 money를 이용한 오답.

15

W-Br How will we get back from the convention center?

M-Cn (A) We can take a taxi.

(B) A booth near the entrance.

(C) I got home at eight o'clock.

우리는 컨벤션 센터에서 어떻게 돌아오죠?

(A) 택시를 타면 돼요.

(B) 입구 근처의 부스요.

(C) 저는 8시에 집에 도착했어요.

어휘 entrance 입구

해설 이동 방법을 묻는 How 의문문

(A) 정답. 출발지로 다시 이동할 교통수단을 묻는 질문에 택시를 탈 수 있다(We can take a taxi.)는 구체적인 방법을 언급하고 있으므로 정답.

(B) 연상 단어 오답. 질문의 convention center에서 연상 가능한 booth를 이용한 오답.

(C) 연상 단어 오답. 질문의 get back에서 연상 가능한 got home을 이용한 오답.

16

W-Am Who's in charge of the safety training program?

M-Cn (A) For construction workers.

(B) I thought it was every six months.

(C) Ms. Boone has been running it for a while.

안전교육 프로그램 담당자가 누구지요?

(A) 건설 인부들을 위해서요.

(B) 6개월마다 한 번씩 있는 줄 알았어요.

(C) 분 씨가 한동안 담당해왔습니다.

어휘 in charge of ~을 맡아서, 담당해서 safety training 안전교육 run 운영[관리]하다

해설 담당자를 묻는 Who 의문문

(A) 연상 단어 오답. 질문의 safety training에서 연상 가능한 construction workers를 이용한 오답.

(B) 연상 단어 오답. 질문의 training program에서 연상 가능한 every six months를 이용한 오답.

(C) 정답. 담당자가 누구인지 묻는 질문에 사람 이름으로 답변을 하고 있으므로 정답.

17

M-Au Could you please tell me where the women's department is?

W-Am (A) Do you know her last name?

(B) It begins at three P.M.

(C) Take the elevator to the second floor.

여성용품 매장이 어디에 있는지 알려주시겠습니까?

(A) 그녀의 성(姓)을 혹시 아세요?

(B) 오후 3시에 시작해요.

(C) 엘리베이터를 타고 2층으로 가세요.

어휘 department 매장, 부서

해설 매장의 위치를 묻는 간접의문문

(A) 연상 단어 오답. 질문의 women's department를 잘못 이해했을 때 연상 가능한 her last name을 이용한 오답.

(B) 질문과 상관없는 오답. 시작 시점을 묻는 When 의문문에 어울리는 응답이므로 오답.

(C) 정답. 여성용품 매장의 위치를 묻는 질문에 엘리베이터를 타고 2층으로 가라(Take the elevator to the second floor.)는 구체적인 안내를 하고 있으므로 정답.

18

W-Br Why was your afternoon appointment canceled?

M-Cn (A) What an excellent suggestion!

(B) Through our scheduling system.

(C) The client had a personal issue.

당신의 오후 약속은 왜 취소됐어요?

(A) 훌륭한 제안이네요!

(B) 우리 일정 관리 시스템으로요.

(C) 고객에게 개인 사정이 있었거든요.

어휘 appointment 약속, (진료) 예약 cancel 취소하다 suggestion 제안

해설 약속이 취소된 이유를 묻는 Why 의문문

(A) 질문과 상관없는 오답. 뭔가를 제안하는 말에 어울릴 만한 응답이므로 오답.

(B) 연상 단어 오답. 질문의 appointment에서 연상 가능한 scheduling system을 이용한 오답.

(C) 정답. 오후 약속이 취소된 이유를 묻는 질문에 대해 그 고객에게 개인 사정이 있었다(The client had a personal issue.)는 구체적인 이유로 응답하고 있으므로 정답.

19

W-Br Is there any coffee in the employee lounge?

M-Au (A) Kazuki just made a fresh pot.

(B) Because it's the end of the day.

(C) Yes, I have an extra copy.

직원 라운지에 커피가 있나요?

(A) 카즈키 씨가 방금 새로 끓여 뒀어요.

(B) 오늘 하루가 다 갔으니까요.

(C) 네, 제게 여분의 복사본이 있어요.

어휘 make a fresh pot 커피를 새로 끓이다

해설 커피가 있는지를 묻는 be동사 Yes/No 의문문

(A) 정답. 커피가 있는지를 묻는 질문에 Yes를 생략한 채, 카즈키 씨가 방금 커피를 새로 끓였다(Kazuki just made a fresh pot.)고 응답하고 있으므로 정답.

(B) 질문과 상관없는 오답. 왜 직원 라운지에 커피가 없는지 이유를 묻는 질문에 어울리는 응답이므로 오답.

(C) 유사 발음 오답. 질문의 coffee와 발음이 유사한 copy를 이용한 오답.

20

W-Am What ideas do you have for this month's newsletter?

M-Cn (A) Once I finish reading it.

(B) I'd like to write about the internship program.

(C) Either one would be fine with me.

이번 달 회보와 관련해 어떤 아이디어가 있으세요?

(A) 일단 다 읽으면요.

(B) 인턴 프로그램에 관해 쓰고 싶어요.

(C) 둘 중 어느 것이든 좋습니다.

어휘 newsletter 회보, 사보 once 일단 ~하면 internship 인턴직, 인턴 과정

해설 어떤 아이디어가 있는지를 묻는 What 의문문

(A) 연상 단어 오답. 질문의 newsletter에서 연상 가능한 reading을 이용한 오답.

(B) 정답. 이번 달 회보 관련 아이디어를 묻는 질문에 인턴십 프로그램이라는 구체적인 답변을 하고 있으므로 정답.

(C) 연상 단어 오답. 질문의 ideas에서 연상 가능한 Either one would be fine을 이용한 오답.

21

M-Cn The hotel is near the airport, isn't it?

M-Au (A) I certainly hope so.

(B) The weeklong hotel stay.

(C) Flight V-Y-three-four, I think.

그 호텔은 공항 근처에 있죠, 그렇지 않나요?

(A) 그랬으면 정말 좋겠어요.

(B) 일주일간의 호텔 숙박이요.

(C) VY34 항공편인 것 같아요.

어휘 near ~에서 가까운 weeklong 일주일간의 flight 항공편

해설 호텔의 위치를 확인하는 부가의문문

(A) 정답. 호텔이 공항 근처에 있는지를 확인하는 질문에 그러길 정말 바란다(I certainly hope so.)는 불확실성 표현으로 응답하고 있으므로 정답.

(B) 단어 반복 오답. 질문의 hotel을 반복 이용한 오답.

(C) 연상 단어 오답. 질문의 airport에서 연상 가능한 flight를 이용한 오답.

22

M-Au Do you want to start working on the new project now or later?

W-Br (A) Actually, I started it this morning.

(B) To work late this week.

(C) The software development project.

새 프로젝트를 지금 시작하길 원해요, 아니면 나중에 시작하길 원해요?

(A) 사실 오늘 아침에 시작했어요.

(B) 이번 주에 늦게까지 일하려고요.

(C) 소프트웨어 개발 프로젝트요.

어휘 actually 사실 work late 늦게까지 일하다 development 개발

해설 단어를 연결한 선택의문문

(A) 정답. 새 프로젝트에 대한 작업 시작 시점으로 지금이 좋은지, 아니면 나중에 할 것인지에 대해 제시된 선택 사항이 아닌 오늘 아침에 벌써 시작했다(I started it this morning)는 제3의 답변으로 응답하고 있으므로 정답.

(B) 유사 발음 오답. 질문의 working과 later에 대해 각각 동사원형 work와 원급 late로 바꿔 이용한 오답.

(C) 단어 반복 오답. 질문의 project를 반복 이용한 오답.

23

M-Cn Where should I put this box of file folders?

W-Am (A) Save all files to your hard drive.

(B) Will it fit on the bottom shelf?

(C) They sell them at the local stationery store.

이 서류철 상자는 어디에 놓을까요?

(A) 모든 파일들을 하드 드라이브에 저장하세요.

(B) 맨 밑 선반에 들어갈까요?

(C) 지역 문구점에서 팔아요.

어휘 fit ~에 들어맞다 bottom 맨 아래의 local 지역의 stationery store 문구점

해설 상자를 놓을 위치를 묻는 Where 의문문

(A) 단어 반복 오답. 질문에 나온 file을 복수형 files로 바꿔 반복 이용한 오답.

(B) 정답. 서류철 상자를 어디에 두어야 할지에 대해 확정적 장소를 언급하는 대신 맨 밑 선반에 들어갈지(Will it fit on the bottom shelf?) 되묻는 우회적 표현으로 응답하고 있으므로 정답.

(C) 연상 단어 오답. 질문의 file folders에서 연상 가능한 local stationery store를 이용한 오답.

24

M-Cn Should we review the contract once more before signing it?

W-Br (A) Yes, I saw the sign by the door.

(B) No, I couldn't reach him.

(C) If you feel that it's necessary.

계약서에 서명하기 전에 한 번 더 검토해야 할까요?

(A) 네, 문 옆의 간판을 보았어요.

(B) 아니요, 그와 연락이 안 됐어요.

(C) 그럴 필요성을 느낀다면요.

어휘 review 검토하다 sign 서명하다; 부호, 표지 reach (전화로) 연락하다 necessary 필요한

해설 추가 검토 필요성을 묻는 조동사(should) Yes/No 의문문

(A) 파생어 오답. 질문의 signing과 파생어 관계인 sign을 이용한 오답.

(B) 유사 발음 오답. 질문의 contract를 contact로 잘못 이해했을 때 연상 가능한 reach를 이용한 오답.

(C) 정답. 서명 전에 계약서 검토를 한 번 더 해야 하는지에 대해 Yes를 생략한 채, 그게 필요하다고 생각하면 그러라(If you feel that it's necessary.)고 응답하고 있으므로 정답.

25

W-Am When is your office manager planning to relocate?

M-Au (A) We really need more space.

(B) As soon as she finds the right place.

(C) A companywide promotion.

당신의 부서장님은 언제 이전하실 계획인가요?

(A) 우리는 정말로 공간이 더 필요해요.

(B) 알맞은 곳을 찾으시는 대로요.

(C) 전사적인 승진이요.

어휘 relocate 이전하다 companywide 회사 전반에 걸친 promotion 승진

해설 이전 시점을 묻는 When 의문문

(A) 연상 단어 오답. 질문의 office와 relocate에서 연상 가능한 more space를 이용한 오답.

(B) 정답. 부서장이 언제 이전할 계획인지에 대해 알맞은 곳을 찾자마자(As soon as she finds the right place.)라고 시점으로 응답하고 있으므로 정답.

(C) 질문과 상관없는 오답. 질문에 나온 직위(office manager)에서 연상 가능한 promotion을 이용한 오답.

26

M-Au I have to call my building supervisor about the heating system.

W-Am (A) This month's rent increase.

(B) Oh, are you still having problems?

(C) The rainy weather.

난방 시스템 때문에 건물 관리자에게 전화해야 해요.

(A) 이번 달 월세 인상이요.

(B) 아, 아직도 문제가 있어요?

(C) 비 오는 날씨요.

어휘 supervisor 관리자 heating system 난방 시스템 rent 집세 increase 증가; 증가하다

해설 의지/계획의 평서문

(A) 연상 단어 오답. 평서문의 building supervisor에서 연상 가능한 rent를 이용한 오답.

(B) 정답. 난방 시스템에 대해 건물 관리자에게 전화해야 한다는 말에 난방 시스템에 여전히 문제가 있는지(are you still having problems?)를 되묻고 있으므로 정답.

(C) 질문과 상관없는 오답. 날씨를 묻는 의문문에 어울리는 응답이므로 오답.

27

M-Cn Do you plan to clean up the break room, or should I?

W-Br (A) I didn't know it was broken.

(B) It may be a job for two people.

(C) Two rooms on each floor.

휴게실을 청소하실 거예요, 아니면 내가 할까요?

(A) 그게 고장 난 줄 몰랐어요.

(B) 두 사람이 해야 할 일일 수도 있어요.

(C) 각 층에 방 두 개요.

어휘 break room 휴게실

해설 문장을 연결한 선택의문문

(A) 파생어 오답. 질문의 break와 파생어 관계인 broken을 이용한 오답.

(B) 정답. 질문의 선택사항으로 언급된 you나 I 대신, 제3의 선택사항을 제시한 것이므로 정답.

(C) 단어 반복 오답. 질문에 나온 room을 복수 형태인 rooms로 반복한 오답.

28

W-Br Why hasn't Tony arrived yet?

M-Cn (A) When was it shipped?

(B) He's probably stuck in traffic.

(C) At the address listed on the form.

토니는 왜 아직 도착을 못했죠?

(A) 언제 배송시켰어요?

(B) 아마 교통 체증에 갇힌 것 같아요.

(C) 양식에 적혀 있는 주소에요.

어휘 ship 배송시키다 probably 아마도 be stuck in traffic 교통 체증에 갇히다 list 목록에 언급하다 form 양식

해설 도착하지 않은 이유를 묻는 Why 부정의문문

(A) 연상 단어 오답. 질문의 arrived에서 연상 가능한 shipped를 이용한 오답.

(B) 정답. 토니 씨가 왜 도착하지 않았는지 묻는 질문에 대해 교통 체증에 갇혔을 것(He's probably stuck in traffic.) 같다고 자신이 생각하는 이유로 응답하고 있으므로 정답.

(C) 질문과 상관없는 오답. 장소를 묻는 Where 의문문에 어울리는 응답이므로 오답.

29

M-Au How about buying more plants for the waiting room?

W-Am (A) Patients do seem to like them.

(B) I haven't been waiting long.

(C) Great—we accept cash or credit.

대기실에 놓게 화초를 더 사는 게 어떨까요?

(A) 환자들이 그걸 좋아하는 거 같긴 해요.

(B) 오래 기다리진 않았어요.

(C) 좋아요. 현금이나 카드 다 받습니다.

어휘 plant 식물, 화초 patient 환자

해설 제안을 나타내는 How about 의문문

(A) 정답. 화초를 더 사자는 제안에 환자들도 좋아한다며 우회적으로 동의의 뜻을 나타내고 있으므로 정답.

(B) 단어 반복 오답. 질문에 나온 waiting을 반복한 오답.

(C) 연상 단어 오답. 질문에 나온 buying에서 연상 가능한 cash or credit을 이용한 오답.

30

W-Am Don't you need to set up the projector for your presentation?

M-Au (A) A few people were present.

(B) No, I'm going to wear a suit.

(C) Thanks, I almost forgot about that.

당신 발표를 위해 프로젝터를 설치해야 하지 않나요?

(A) 몇 명만 참석했어요.

(B) 아니요, 저는 정장을 입을 거예요.

(C) 고마워요, 잊어버릴 뻔했네요.

어휘 set up ~을 설치하다, 준비하다 present 참석한 suit 정장 almost 거의 forget 잊어버리다

해설 프로젝터 설치 필요성을 묻는 부정의문문

(A) 유사 발음 오답. 질문의 presentation과 부분적으로 발음이 유사한 present를 이용한 오답.

(B) 질문과 상관없는 오답. 프로젝터 설치 필요성을 묻는 질문에 정장을 입겠다(I'm going to wear a suit.)는 말은 맥락에서 벗어난 응답이므로 오답.

(C) 정답. 발표를 하는데 프로젝터를 설치해야 하지 않냐는 질문에 먼저 Thanks로 고마움을 표현한 후, 자신이 잊어버릴 뻔했다(I almost forgot about that)는 말로 고마워하는 이유를 언급하고 있으므로 정답.

31

M-Cn The Tokyo branch won the Customer Service Award this year.

W-Br (A) That's disappointing—I was sure we had a chance.

(B) Customers can vote on the company Web site.

(C) I've visited many of our Japanese locations.

도쿄 지사가 올해 고객 서비스 상을 받았어요.

(A) 그거 실망스럽네요. 우리한테 가망이 있다고 확신했는데.

(B) 고객들은 회사 웹 사이트에서 투표할 수 있어요.

(C) 저는 우리 일본 지사 여러 곳을 방문했어요.

어휘 branch 지사 disappointing 실망스러운 vote 투표하다 location 장소

해설 사실/정보 전달의 평서문

(A) 정답. 도쿄 지사 수상 소식에 실망을 나타내는 표현으로 응답을 하고 있으므로 정답.

(B) 단어 반복 오답. 질문의 customer를 복수 형태인 customers로 반복한 오답.

(C) 연상 단어 오답. 질문의 Tokyo branch에서 연상 가능한 Japanese locations를 이용한 오답.

32-34

M-Au Hi, Diana. [32]**It seems that some food orders aren't being processed properly and customers are being charged different prices than those printed on the menu.**

W-Br Actually, I've had a few difficulties using the cash register recently. [33]**Some of the buttons are stuck and it's affecting the input of orders.** Maybe we should get someone in here to fix it.

M-Au OK. [34]**I'll phone the supervisor and explain the situation to her.** It's important we don't mischarge customers.

남: 다이애나 씨, 안녕하세요. **음식 주문 일부가 제대로 처리되지 않아서 손님들에게 메뉴에 인쇄된 것과는 다른 가격이 청구되고 있는 것 같아요.**

여: 사실 최근에 금전등록기를 쓰는 데 문제가 좀 있더라고요. **버튼 몇 개가 꼭 끼어서 주문 입력에 영향을 주거든요.** 사람을 여기로 불러서 고쳐야 할 것 같아요.

남: 알겠어요. **관리자에게 전화해서 상황을 설명해드릴게요.** 손님들에게 가격을 잘못 청구하지 않는 것이 중요하죠.

어휘 process 처리하다 properly 제대로, 적절히 charge 청구하다 cash register 금전등록기 recently 최근에 stuck 꼼짝 못하는 affect 영향을 미치다 input 입력 supervisor 감독, 관리자 mischarge 요금을 잘못 청구하다

32

Where most likely do the speakers work?

(A) At a bookstore
(B) At a restaurant
(C) At a flower shop
(D) At a supermarket

화자들은 어디에서 일하겠는가?

(A) 서점
(B) 음식점
(C) 꽃집
(D) 슈퍼마켓

해설 전체 내용 관련 - 화자들의 근무지

남자의 첫 번째 대사에서 일부 음식 주문이 제대로 처리되지 않아서 손님들에게 메뉴에 인쇄된 것과는 다른 가격이 청구되고 있는 것 같다(It seems that some food orders aren't ~ on the menu.)고 했다. 이 문장에 쓰인 food orders, customers, menu를 통해 화자들이 식당에서 근무한다는 것을 알 수 있으므로 정답은 (B)이다.

33

According to the woman, what is the problem with the cash register?

(A) Some buttons are not working.
(B) Some money is missing.
(C) The screen has been broken.
(D) It does not open properly.

여자에 따르면, 금전등록기에 어떤 문제가 있는가?

(A) 몇 개의 버튼이 작동하지 않는다.
(B) 돈이 일부 없어졌다.
(C) 스크린이 고장 났다.
(D) 제대로 열리지 않는다.

해설 세부 사항 관련 - 금전등록기의 문제점

여자의 대사에서 금전등록기의 버튼 몇 개가 꼭 끼어서 주문 입력에 영향을 주고 있다(Some of the buttons are stuck and it's affecting the input of orders.)고 했으므로 정답은 (A)이다.

Paraphrasing 대화의 **are stuck**
→ 정답의 **are not working**

34

What will the man probably do next?

(A) Collect some receipts
(B) Call his manager
(C) Try to fix the cash register
(D) Give an explanation to customers

남자는 다음에 무엇을 하겠는가?

(A) 영수증 모으기
(B) 관리자에게 전화하기
(C) 금전등록기 수리 시도하기
(D) 손님들에게 설명하기

해설 세부 사항 관련 - 남자의 다음 행동

대화 맨 마지막에 남자가 관리자에게 전화해서 상황을 설명해드리겠다(I'll phone the supervisor and explain the situation to her.)고 했으므로 정답은 (B)이다.

Paraphrasing 대화의 **phone the supervisor**
→ 정답의 **call his manager**

35-37

M-Cn Good morning, this is Jeff Johns at RT Realty. We're currently in the process of expanding, and [35]**I was hoping your company could help us find some qualified candidates to fill several openings that have been created.**

W-Am Yes, of course. Please send me an e-mail including the positions you're hiring for and the requirements for each. [36]**I'll have to go over the details before we go any further.**

M-Cn OK. We'd really appreciate your services. We're a small company and have never gone through this process before.

W-Am In that case, I should let you know that [37]**it takes more time than you may think.** But we'll certainly do our best to ensure you succeed.

남: 안녕하세요. RT 부동산의 제프 존스입니다. 저희가 현재 회사를 확장하는 중이라 **새로 생긴 몇몇 직책을 맡을 유능한 직원 찾는 일을 귀사가 도와 주셨으면 하는데요.**

여: 네, 물론입니다. 채용하고자 하는 직책과 각 직책의 자격 요건을 포함해서 이메일을 보내주세요. **일을 더 진행하기 전에 세부 사항을 검토해야 할 것 같습니다.**

남: 네, 그래 주시면 너무 감사하겠습니다. 저희는 소규모 회사라 전에는 이런 과정을 거친 적이 없거든요.

여: 그렇다면, **생각하시는 것보다 과정이 더 오래 걸린다**는 것을 알려드려야 하겠군요. 하지만 일이 잘 진행되도록 저희는 물론 최선을 다하겠습니다.

어휘 realty 부동산 currently 현재 be in the process of ~하는 중이다 expand 확장하다 qualified 자격이 있는 candidate 후보자 opening 일자리 position 직책 hiring 채용 requirement 필요 조건, 자격 요건 go over ~을 검토하다 details 세부 사항 go any further 더 진전시키다 appreciate 고마워하다 go through ~을 겪다 certainly 분명히 ensure 반드시 ~하게 하다

35

What is the man calling about?

(A) Buying a house
(B) Hiring new employees
(C) Remodeling an office
(D) Delaying a delivery

남자는 무엇 때문에 전화하는가?

(A) 집 구매
(B) 신규 직원 채용
(C) 사무실 개조
(D) 배송 연기

해설 전체 내용 관련 – 전화 통화의 내용

남자의 첫 번째 대사에서 여자에게 새로 생긴 몇몇 직책을 맡을 유능한 직원 찾는 일을 도와주면 좋겠다(I was hoping your company could help ~ openings that have been created.)고 했으므로 정답은 (B)이다.

36

What does the woman say she has to do?

(A) Inspect some properties
(B) Order new products
(C) Meet with a consultant
(D) Review some written information

여자는 무엇을 해야 한다고 말하는가?

(A) 건물 검사
(B) 신제품 주문
(C) 컨설턴트 만나기
(D) 서면 자료 검토

어휘 inspect 점검하다 property 재산, 부동산

해설 세부 사항 관련 – 여자가 해야 할 일

여자의 첫 번째 대사에서 일을 더 진행하기 전에 세부 사항을 검토해야겠다(I'll have to go over the details before we go any further.)고 했으므로 정답은 (D)이다.

▸▸ **Paraphrasing** 대화의 **go over the details** → 정답의 **Review some written information**

37

What does the woman say about the process?

(A) It takes longer than expected.
(B) It is expensive.
(C) It is rarely successful.
(D) It has recently changed.

여자는 과정에 대해 뭐라고 말하는가?

(A) 예상보다 오래 걸린다.
(B) 가격이 비싸다.
(C) 성공하는 경우가 거의 없다.
(D) 최근 변경됐다.

어휘 expect 예상[기대]하다 rarely 좀처럼 ~ 않는

해설 세부 사항 관련 – 여자가 과정에 대해 하는 말

대화 마지막에 여자가 남자에게 생각보다 채용 과정이 더 오래 걸린다(it takes more time than you may think.)고 했으므로 정답은 (A)이다.

▸▸ **Paraphrasing** 대화의 **takes more time than you may think** → 정답의 **takes longer than expected**

38-40

M-Au Hi, can you help me, please? [38]**I was supposed to catch a connecting flight ten minutes ago, but my flight here to Frankfurt arrived late.**

W-Br Oh, that's terrible. Let's see... [39]**Your ticket says you came here from Toronto and you need to get to Moscow.** I can book you a flight for tomorrow morning. There's one at six-fifteen A.M.

M-Au Hmm, I'd really like to get there tonight. Is there anything else you can do?

W-Br The only earlier flight has a long stopover in Warsaw, so it would actually get you to Moscow later. I'm sorry. Luckily, our airline does offer compensation. [40]**You can stay at a hotel near the airport and get the expense reimbursed.**

남: 안녕하세요, 좀 도와주시겠어요? **제가 10분 전에 연결 항공편을 탔어야 했는데 이곳 프랑크푸르트로 오는 항공편이 늦게 도착했어요.**

Test 4

여: 아, 낭패군요. 어디 볼게요… **고객님 티켓을 보니 토론토에서 이곳으로 오셨고 모스크바로 가셔야 하네요.** 내일 아침 항공편을 예약해 드릴 수 있습니다. 아침 6시 15분에 모스크바행 비행기가 있습니다.

남: 음… 저는 꼭 오늘 밤 그곳에 도착했으면 하는데요. 도와 주실 다른 방법이 있을까요?

여: 유일하게 더 이른 항공편은 바르샤바에서 길게 기착하여 모스크바에 사실은 더 늦게 도착하게 될 거예요. 죄송합니다. 다행히 저희 항공사에서 보상을 해 드리고 있는데요. **공항 근처 호텔에 투숙하시고 비용을 환급받으실 수 있습니다.**

어휘 be supposed to + 동사원형 ~하기로 되어 있다 connecting flight 연결 항공편 terrible 끔찍한, 안 좋은 book a flight 항공편을 예약하다 stopover 기착 offer 제공하다 compensation 보상 expense 비용 reimburse (경비 등을) 변상하다, 환급하다

38

What does the man ask the woman for assistance?

(A) He missed a flight.
(B) His gate is far away.
(C) His bag was damaged.
(D) He misplaced his ticket.

남자는 왜 여자에게 도움을 요청하는가?

(A) 비행기를 놓쳤다.
(B) 탑승구가 멀다.
(C) 가방이 손상되었다.
(D) 항공권을 찾을 수가 없다.

어휘 misplace (~을 제자리에 두지 않아) 못 찾다

해설 세부 사항 관련 – 남자가 도움을 요청하는 이유

남자의 첫 번째 대사에서 10분 전에 연결 항공편을 탔어야 했는데 이곳 프랑크푸르트로 오는 항공편이 늦게 도착했다(I was supposed to catch a connecting flight ~ to Frankfurt arrived late.)고 했다. 이를 통해 남자가 연결 항공편을 놓쳤음을 알 수 있으므로 정답은 (A)이다.

39

What is the man's final destination?

(A) Toronto
(B) Moscow
(C) Frankfurt
(D) Warsaw

남자의 최종 목적지는 어디인가?

(A) 토론토
(B) 모스크바
(C) 프랑크푸르트
(D) 바르샤바

해설 세부 사항 관련 – 남자의 최종 목적지

여자의 첫 번째 대사에서 남자의 티켓을 보니 토론토에서 여기로 왔으며 모스크바로 가야 하는 걸로 되어 있다(Your ticket says you came here from Toronto and you need to get to Moscow.)고 했으므로 정답은 (B)이다.

40

What does the woman suggest the man do?

(A) Use a mobile app
(B) Obtain reimbursement
(C) Take an airport shuttle
(D) Submit feedback

여자는 남자에게 무엇을 하라고 제안하는가?

(A) 모바일 앱 사용
(B) 비용 환급받기
(C) 공항 셔틀버스 이용
(D) 피드백 제출

어휘 obtain 얻다, 획득하다 reimbursement 환급 submit 제출하다

해설 세부 사항 관련 – 여자의 제안 사항

대화 맨 마지막에 여자가 남자에게 공항 근처에 있는 호텔에 투숙하고 비용을 환급받을 수 있다(You can stay at a hotel near the airport and get the expense reimbursed.)고 했으므로 정답은 (B)이다.

▸▸ **Paraphrasing** 대화의 **get the expense reimbursed**
→ 정답의 **Obtain reimbursement**

41-43 3인 대화

W-Br Oscar, [41]**I just finished looking over the orientation manual you made for new laboratory technicians.**

M-Cn What did you think?

W-Br There's a lot about it that I like. You did a great job introducing our work culture.

M-Cn Thanks. But it sounds like there were some problems.

W-Br Well, [42]**some of the manual's instructions for using lab equipment weren't very specific.** Remember, it's better to give too much information than too little. So, let me introduce Odette from Accounting.

W-Am Hi, Oscar. [43]**Pauline has asked me to help by testing your instructions, since I don't know anything about lab procedures.**

M-Cn It's nice to meet you, Odette. OK. I'll revise the instructions so we can get started tomorrow.

여1: 오스카, **새로 들어온 실험실 기사들을 위해 만드신 오리엔테이션 안내서를 지금 막 다 검토했어요.**

남: 어떠세요?

여1: 맘에 드는 점이 많네요. 우리 작업 문화를 잘 소개하셨더라고요.

남: 고맙습니다. 그런데 무슨 문제가 있는 것처럼 들립니다.

여1: 음, **실험실 장비 사용에 대한 안내서의 일부 설명이 좀 구체적이지 않았어요.** 너무 적은 정보보다는 차라리 과한 정보를 주는 게 낫다는 걸 기억하세요. 그럼, 회계과의 오데트를 소개해 줄게요.

여2: 안녕하세요, 오스카. **폴린이 나한테 당신이 만든 설명서 테스트하는 걸 도와 주라고 부탁했어요. 난 실험실 절차에 관해서 아무것도 모르거든요.**

남: 만나서 반갑습니다, 오데트. 좋습니다. 우리가 내일 시작할 수 있게 제가 설명서를 수정하겠습니다.

어휘 look over 훑어보다 manual 안내서, 취급 설명서 laboratory 실험실(= lab) instructions 설명(서), 지시사항 specific 구체적인 procedure 절차 revise 수정하다

41

What is the conversation mainly about?

(A) A jobseeker's résumé
(B) A scientific report
(C) An employment contract
(D) A training manual

대화의 주된 내용은 무엇인가?

(A) 구직자의 이력서
(B) 과학 보고서
(C) 고용 계약서
(D) 교육 안내서

어휘 jobseeker 구직자 employment contract 고용 계약(서)

해설 전체 내용 관련 – 대화의 주제

첫 번째 여자가 첫 대사에서 새로 들어온 실험실 기사들을 위해 남자가 만든 오리엔테이션 안내서의 검토를 완료했다(I just finished looking over the orientation manual you made for new laboratory technicians.)고 했고 이와 관련된 대화가 이어지고 있으므로 정답은 (D)이다.

42

What is the problem with a document?

(A) It contains errors.
(B) It is not detailed enough.
(C) It has not been turned in yet.
(D) It is organized in a confusing way.

문서의 문제점은 무엇인가?

(A) 오류가 있다.
(B) 충분히 상세하지 않다.
(C) 아직 제출되지 않았다.
(D) 헷갈리게 정리되어 있다.

어휘 detailed 상세한 turn in 제출하다 organized 정리된, 정돈된

해설 세부 사항 관련 – 문서의 문제점

첫 번째 여자의 세 번째 대사에서 실험실 장비 사용에 대한 설명이 좀 구체적이지 않았다(some of the manual's instructions for using lab equipment weren't very specific.)고 했으므로 정답은 (B)이다.

43

What does Odette explain to the man?

(A) She is unfamiliar with some processes.
(B) She is concerned about a budget.
(C) She has tested some software.
(D) She has adjusted an estimate.

오데트는 남자에게 뭐라고 설명하는가?

(A) 어떤 절차를 잘 알지 못한다.
(B) 예산이 걱정된다.
(C) 소프트웨어를 테스트했다.
(D) 추정치를 조정했다.

어휘 be unfamiliar with ~을 잘 알지 못하다, ~에 익숙하지 않다 be concerned about ~을 염려하다 budget 예산 adjust 조정[조절]하다 estimate 추정치, 견적

해설 세부 사항 관련 – 남자가 들은 설명

두 번째 여자인 오데트가 폴린으로부터 부탁을 받았다(Pauline has asked me to help by testing your instructions)면서 실험실 절차에 관해 아무것도 모른다(I don't know anything about lab procedures.)고 했으므로 정답은 (A)이다.

44-46

W-Am Kirk, did you see this? It's an order we got from Bellardi's Best.

M-Au Bellardi's Best? [44]**That's the baked goods store on Colfax Street**—the small shop where all the pastries are made by hand. They're a steady client.

W-Am Right. This request is for one thousand two hundred ceramic coffee cups. Now, um... it's quite a large order. So...

M-Au Hmm... OK. [45]**I'd better call Phil Bellardi then. I'll let you know what I find out before we proceed.**

W-Am Sounds good. While I'm waiting, [46]**I think I'll post photos of our new products on our Web site—to keep us current.**

여: 커크 씨, 이거 봤어요? 벨라디즈 베스트에서 받은 주문 말이에요.

남: 벨라디즈 베스트요? **거기는 콜팩스 가에 있는 제과점이에요.** 모든 과자류를 수작업으로 만드는 작은 가게죠. 그 가게는 꾸준한 고객이에요.

여: 맞아요. 이번 요청은 1200개의 세라믹 커피잔이네요. 지금, 음… 꽤 큰 주문이에요. 그래서…

남: 음… 알겠어요. **그럼 제가 필 벨라디에게 전화해보는 게 좋겠어요. 진행하기 전에 확인해 보고 알려줄게요.**

여: 좋아요. 기다리는 동안 **저는 우리 회사의 최신 정보를 주기 위해 웹 사이트에 신제품 사진을 올릴까 봐요.**

어휘 baked goods store 제과점 pastry 가루 반죽 과자 by hand 손으로 steady 꾸준한 find out 알아내다 proceed 진행하다 post 게시하다 current 현재의

44

What kind of business is Bellardi's Best?

(A) An appliance retailer
(B) A furniture store
(C) A print shop
(D) A bakery

벨라디즈 베스트는 어떤 종류의 사업체인가?
(A) 가전제품 소매상
(B) 가구 매장
(C) 인쇄소
(D) 빵집

어휘 appliance 기기

해설 전체 내용 관련 - 벨라디즈 베스트의 업종
남자의 첫 번째 대사에서 벨라디즈 베스트는 콜팩스 가에 있는 제과점(That's the baked goods store on Colfax Street)이라고 했으므로 정답은 (D)이다.

▸▸ **Paraphrasing** 대화의 **the baked goods store**
→ 정답의 **a bakery**

45

What does the woman mean when she says, "it's quite a large order"?
(A) Additional workers should be hired.
(B) There may not be enough materials.
(C) She would like further confirmation.
(D) The order qualifies for a bulk discount.

여자가 "꽤 큰 주문이에요"라고 말한 의도는 무엇인가?
(A) 근로자를 추가로 고용해야 한다.
(B) 재료가 부족할 수도 있다.
(C) 추가 확인을 원한다.
(D) 대량 구입 할인을 받을 수 있는 주문이다.

어휘 material 재료 further 추가적인 qualify for ~에 자격이 있다 bulk 대량

해설 화자의 의도 파악 - 꽤 큰 주문이라는 말의 의도
남자의 두 번째 대사에서 자신이 필 벨라디에게 전화해보는 게 좋겠다고 하며 여자에게 일을 진행하기 전에 확인해 보고 알려 주겠다(I'd better call Phil Bellardi ~ before we proceed.)고 했는데, 주문에 대해 한 번 더 확인을 해 보자는 의미가 담겨 있는 것이므로 정답은 (C)이다.

46

What will the woman probably do next?
(A) Mail a package
(B) Update a Web site
(C) Post a sign-up sheet
(D) Search for a client file

여자는 다음에 무엇을 하겠는가?
(A) 소포 보내기
(B) 웹 사이트 업데이트하기
(C) 참가 신청서 게시하기
(D) 고객 파일 찾기

해설 세부 사항 관련 - 여자의 다음 행동
대화 맨 마지막에 여자가 회사의 최신 정보를 주기 위해 웹 사이트에 신제품 사진을 올리겠다(I think I'll post photos of our new products on our Web site—to keep us current.)고 했으므로 정답은 (B)이다.

47-49

W-Br Hi, Takumi. It's Bree in Public Relations. I'm making the agenda for my department's monthly training meeting. [47]**I know you're scheduled to give a presentation, and I was wondering what it will be about.**

M-Cn Oh. Actually, I had forgotten about that. Uh... it probably wouldn't be a good idea to try to decide right now. [48]**Could I think about it and get back to you?**

W-Br Sure. Let me know tomorrow.

M-Cn OK. Wait—could you tell me what these meetings are like?

W-Br Sorry, I don't really know. [49]**This is only the second one, and I missed the first one because I had to meet a deadline.** I can send you the agenda, though.

여: 안녕하세요, 타쿠미. 홍보부의 브리인데요. 우리 부서 월례 연수 회의를 위한 안건을 작성하고 있는 중이에요. **당신이 발표를 하기로 돼 있다고 알고 있는데, 무엇에 관한 건지 알고 싶어서요.**
남: 아, 사실은, 그걸 잊고 있었네요. 어… 지금 당장 결정하려고 하는 건 좋은 생각이 아닌 거 같고요. **생각해 본 다음에 다시 연락드려도 될까요?**
여: 그럼요. 내일 알려주세요.
남: 네, 잠깐만요. 이게 어떤 회의인지 알려주실 수 있습니까?
여: 죄송하지만, 저도 잘 모릅니다. **이제 겨우 두 번째이고, 첫 번째 회의는 제가 마감 일정을 맞추느라 참석하지 못했어요.** 하지만 의제는 보내드릴 수 있습니다.

어휘 public relations 홍보(부) agenda 안건, 의제 be scheduled to + **동사원형** ~하기로 일정이 잡혀 있다 wonder 궁금해하다 get back to ~에게 다시 연락하다 miss (참석하지 않아) 놓치다 meet a deadline 마감 일정을 맞추다

47

What does the woman ask about?
(A) A presentation topic
(B) The format of an agenda
(C) Some meeting invitations
(D) A venue reservation

여자는 무엇에 대해 물어보는가?
(A) 발표 주제
(B) 의제의 구성 방식
(C) 회의 초대
(D) 행사장 예약

어휘 format 포맷, 구성 방식 venue 행사장, 장소

해설 전체 내용 관련 - 여자의 질문
여자의 첫 번째 대사에서 남자의 발표 일정을 언급하며, 무엇에 관한 것인지 알고 싶다(I know you're scheduled to give a presentation, and I was wondering what it will be about.)고 했으므로 정답은 (A)이다.

48

What does the man ask permission to do?

(A) Download a document
(B) Delay a decision
(C) Notify other coworkers
(D) Return some equipment

남자는 무엇을 할 수 있게 해달라고 요청하는가?

(A) 서류 다운로드하기
(B) 결정 연기하기
(C) 다른 동료들에게 고지하기
(D) 장비 반환하기

어휘 permission 허가 notify 통지하다 coworker 동료

해설 세부 사항 관련 – 남자의 요청 사항

남자의 첫 번째 대사에서 생각한 후 연락해도 되는지(Could I think about it and get back to you?) 물어보고 있으므로 정답은 (B)이다.

49

Why was the woman unable to attend a previous meeting?

(A) She had to finish an assignment.
(B) She was on vacation.
(C) She was an intern.
(D) She did not know about it.

여자가 이전 회의에 참석하지 못한 이유는?

(A) 임무를 마쳐야 했다.
(B) 휴가 중이었다.
(C) 인턴사원이었다.
(D) 그것에 대해 모르고 있었다.

어휘 previous 이전의, 앞선 assignment 과제, 임무 intern 인턴사원

해설 세부 사항 관련 – 여자의 회의 불참석 이유

여자의 마지막 대사에서 이번이 두 번째이고 첫 번째 회의는 마감 일정을 맞추느라 참석하지 못했다(This is only the second one, and I missed the first one because I had to meet a deadline.)고 했으므로 정답은 (A)이다.

50-52 3인 대화

M-Cn OK, quick reminder... [50]**Please let our customers know that our entire store inventory—all our construction materials, paints, and hardware—will be on sale next week.**

W-Am Ah, right. Any updates on our other promotion—the do-it-yourself workshops?

M-Au Yes, about that... My "Smart Patio Design"class is already full.

M-Cn Can we open another section?

W-Am Oh! [51]**My friend, Lyle, is a landscaper and would like to lead a workshop. I'll call him today.**

M-Au Terrific. All right, then—[52]**let's all head to the cashier's stations.** I'll show you how to enter coupon codes when you're ringing up customers.

남 1: 좋아요, 빨리 상기시켜 드릴 게 있어요… **우리 매장 재고 일체, 즉 모든 건축 자재, 페인트, 철물을 다음 주에 할인한다고 고객들에게 알려주시기 바랍니다.**

여: 아, 알겠습니다. 다른 홍보 건인 DIY 워크숍에는 변동사항이 있나요?

남 2: 네, 그와 관련해서… 제 '스마트한 파티오 디자인' 강좌는 인원이 이미 다 찼어요.

남 1: 다른 강좌를 개설할 수 있을까요?

여: 아, **제 친구 라일이 조경사인데 워크숍을 진행하고 싶어 해요. 오늘 전화해 볼게요.**

남 2: 좋습니다. 자, 그럼… **지금은 다 같이 계산대로 갑시다.** 고객에게 계산해줄 때 쿠폰 코드 입력하는 법을 보여드릴게요.

어휘 reminder 상기시키는 것 entire 전체의 inventory 재고 목록 construction material 건축 자재 hardware 철물 be on sale 할인 판매 중이다 promotion 홍보 do-it-yourself 스스로 하는(= DIY) landscaper 조경사, 정원사 ring up 계산하다

50

Where most likely is the conversation taking place?

(A) At a safety training facility
(B) At a sporting goods store
(C) At a building supply store
(D) At an event planning agency

대화가 일어나는 곳은 어디겠는가?

(A) 안전 교육 시설
(B) 스포츠 용품점
(C) 건축 자재 상점
(D) 행사 기획 대행사

어휘 agency 대행사

해설 전체 내용 관련 – 대화 장소

대화 맨 처음에 남자가 매장에 있는 재고 일체, 즉 모든 건축 자재, 페인트, 철물 등을 다음 주에 할인한다는 점을 고객들에게 알려 주라(Please let our customers know that ~ will be on sale next week.)고 했다. 이 대사에 나온 construction materials, paints, hardware라는 단어를 통해 화자들이 건축 자재 상점에서 일하고 있음을 알 수 있으므로 정답은 (C)이다.

▸▸ **Paraphrasing** 대화의 **construction materials, paints, hardware** → 정답의 **building supply**

51

What does the woman offer to do?

(A) Install a phone system
(B) Recruit an instructor
(C) Rent a larger space
(D) Redesign a display

Test 4

여자는 무엇을 하겠다고 하는가?
(A) 전화 시스템 설치하기
(B) 강사 영입하기
(C) 더 넓은 공간 대여하기
(D) 전시물 다시 디자인하기

어휘 install 설치하다 recruit 채용하다 instructor 강사

해설 세부 사항 관련 - 여자가 하겠다고 하는 것
여자의 두 번째 대사에서 자신의 친구 라일이 조경사인데 워크숍을 진행하고 싶어 해서 오늘 전화해 보겠다(My friend, Lyle, is a landscaper and would like to ~ call him today.)고 했으므로 정답은 (B)이다.

▸▸ Paraphrasing 대화의 call → 정답의 Recruit

52
What will the speakers probably do next?
(A) Set up some shelving
(B) Go to a checkout area
(C) Discuss some job candidates
(D) Attend a product demonstration

화자들은 다음에 무엇을 하겠는가?
(A) 선반 설치하기
(B) 결제 구역으로 가기
(C) 지원자들에 대해 논의하기
(D) 제품 시연회 참석하기

어휘 candidate 후보자, 지원자 demonstration 시연

해설 세부 사항 관련 - 화자들의 다음 행동
대화 맨 마지막에 두 번째 남자가 다른 화자들에게 다 같이 계산대로 가자(let's all head to the cashier's stations.)고 했으므로 정답은 (B)이다.

▸▸ Paraphrasing 대화의 head to the cashier's stations
→ 정답의 Go to a checkout area

53-55

W-Br Hello. I'll be in town for business next month from the twelfth until the nineteenth. [53]**Do you have any rooms available then?**

M-Au Let me check for you. Sorry, I'm afraid we're fully booked on the twelfth. [54]**Why don't you come a day later?** We'll have a room available for you all week.

W-Br That doesn't work for me. I've already booked my flights.

M-Au OK. [55]**Would you like me to call our other location in town and see if they have anything for the twelfth?** Hopefully a room will be available there.

여: 안녕하세요. 제가 다음 달 12일부터 19일까지 일 때문에 그 지역에 갈 텐데요. **그때 이용 가능한 객실이 있나요?**

남: 확인해 드리겠습니다. 죄송합니다, 12일에는 이미 예약이 다 찼습니다. **하루 뒤에 오시면 어떨까요?** 일주일 내내 사용하실 수 있는 객실이 있는데요.

여: 제 일정과는 맞지 않네요. 이미 항공편을 예약했거든요.

남: 알겠습니다. **제가 시내에 있는 저희 다른 지점에 전화해서 12일에 방이 있는지 확인해드릴까요?** 그쪽에 객실이 있으면 좋겠네요.

어휘 available 이용 가능한 fully booked 예약이 꽉 찬 location 장소 hopefully 바라건대

53
Why is the woman calling?
(A) To request a transportation service
(B) To change some travel dates
(C) To book accommodations
(D) To ask about meal options

여자가 전화한 이유는?
(A) 교통편을 요청하기 위해
(B) 여행 날짜를 변경하기 위해
(C) 숙박 시설을 예약하기 위해
(D) 식사 선택 사항에 대해 문의하기 위해

어휘 transportation 차량, 운송 book 예약하다 accommodation 숙박

해설 전체 내용 관련 - 전화 통화의 이유
여자의 첫 번째 대사에서 남자에게 이용 가능한 객실이 있는지(Do you have any rooms available)를 물어보고 있으므로 정답은 (C)이다.

54
What does the man suggest the woman do?
(A) Visit a Web site
(B) Postpone her arrival
(C) Join a waiting list
(D) Upgrade her reservation

남자는 여자에게 무엇을 하라고 제안하는가?
(A) 웹 사이트 방문
(B) 도착 연기
(C) 대기자 명단에 이름 올리기
(D) 예약 업그레이드

해설 세부 사항 관련 - 남자의 제안 사항
남자의 첫 번째 대사에서 여자에게 하루 늦게 오는 것(Why don't you come a day later?)을 제안했으므로 정답은 (B)이다.

▸▸ Paraphrasing 대화의 come a day later
→ 정답의 Postpone her arrival

55
What does the man offer to do?
(A) Waive a fee
(B) Expedite some paperwork
(C) Contact another branch
(D) Refund a deposit

남자는 무엇을 해 주겠다고 하는가?
(A) 비용 면제
(B) 서류 작업의 신속한 처리
(C) 다른 지점에의 연락
(D) 보증금 환급

어휘 waive 면제하다 expedite 신속히 처리하다 deposit 보증금

해설 세부 사항 관련 – 남자의 제안
대화 맨 마지막에 남자가 여자에게 다른 지점에 전화해서 12일에 방이 있는지 확인하는 것(Would you like me to call our other location ~ for the twelfth?)을 제안했으므로 정답은 (C)이다.

▸▸ Paraphrasing 대화의 call our other location
→ 정답의 Contact another branch

56-58

M-Cn All right, here's the market research report from Marc-Dec Agency. [56]**It says our products, especially our T-shirts and jackets, are seen as rather old-fashioned.**

W-Am OK. So what did they recommend?

M-Cn [57]**They said we should market our products heavily on social media.** That will help us appeal to young consumers.

W-Am OK. And that reminds me of an idea I had... Our headquarters building is over a hundred years old. [58]**What about relocating to a more modern office?** It may better reflect our brand.

M-Cn Um... we just renovated the lobby here.

W-Am That's a good point. OK, then. I'll have my marketing team brainstorm some proposals this afternoon.

남: 좋아요, 여기 마크덱 대행사에서 온 시장조사 보고서가 있습니다. **우리 제품, 특히 티셔츠와 재킷이 좀 구식으로 보인다고 되어 있어요.**
여: 네. 그들은 무엇을 추천했어요?
남: **그들은 SNS 사이트들에서 적극적으로 제품을 마케팅해야 한다고 했습니다.** 그러면 젊은 소비자들에게 어필하는 데 도움이 될 거예요.
여: 네. 그래서 제가 가지고 있던 아이디어가 생각났는데요… 우리 본사 건물은 100년 이상 됐습니다. **좀 더 현대적인 사무실로 이전하는 건 어떨까요?** 브랜드를 더 잘 반영할 수 있을 텐데요.
남: 음… 이 건물 로비를 얼마 전 보수했잖아요.
여: 좋은 지적입니다. 그럼 알겠어요. 오늘 오후 우리 마케팅 팀이 다른 제안을 생각해 보도록 하겠어요.

어휘 market research 시장조사 rather 다소, 좀 old-fashioned 구식의 recommend 권하다 market 마케팅[홍보]하다 appeal to ~에게 호소하다 remind 상기시키다 headquarters 본사 relocate 이전하다 reflect 반영하다, 반향을 일으키다 renovate 보수하다 brainstorm 자유롭게 아이디어를 생각해 내다 proposal 제안

56

What kind of company do the speakers most likely work for?
(A) A software developer
(B) A clothing maker
(C) A magazine publisher
(D) A photography studio

화자들은 어떤 종류의 회사에서 근무하겠는가?
(A) 소프트웨어 개발 회사
(B) 의류 제조업체
(C) 잡지사
(D) 사진 스튜디오

해설 전체 내용 관련 – 화자들의 근무지
남자의 첫 번째 대사에서 시장조사 보고서에 화자들 회사의 제품, 특히 티셔츠와 재킷이 좀 구식으로 보이는 걸로 나와 있다(It says our products ~ as rather old-fashioned.)고 했다. 이 문장에 쓰인 T-shirts, jackets 등의 단어를 통해 화자들이 의류 제조업체에 근무한다는 것을 알 수 있으므로 정답은 (B)이다.

▸▸ Paraphrasing 대화의 T-shirts, jackets → 정답의 clothing

57

What did Marc-Dec Agency suggest the company do?
(A) Merge with another business
(B) Expand into overseas markets
(C) Advertise via social networking sites
(D) Discontinue several product lines

마크덱 대행사는 이 회사에 무엇을 하라고 제안했는가?
(A) 다른 사업체와 합병하기
(B) 해외 시장 진출
(C) SNS 사이트로 광고하기
(D) 몇 개 제품군의 생산을 중단하기

어휘 merge 합병하다 expand 확장하다 via ~을 통해 discontinue 중단하다

해설 세부 사항 관련 – 마크덱 대행사의 제안 사항
남자의 두 번째 대사에서 마크덱 대행사가 SNS 사이트들에서 적극적으로 제품을 마케팅하는 것을 권장한다(They said we should market our products heavily on social media.)고 했으므로 정답은 (C)이다.

58

What does the man imply when he says, "we just renovated the lobby here"?
(A) He recommends publicizing an enhancement.
(B) He wants suggestions for future design projects.
(C) The company does not need to move its headquarters.
(D) The company's recent sales have been strong.

Test 4

남자가 "이 건물 로비를 얼마 전 보수했잖아요"라고 말한 의도는 무엇인가?
(A) 그는 개선된 사항을 알리는 것을 추천한다.
(B) 추후 디자인 프로젝트를 위한 제안을 원한다.
(C) 회사는 본사를 이전할 필요가 없다.
(D) 회사는 최근 판매 호조를 보였다.

어휘 enhancement 향상, 증대 recent 최근의

해설 화자의 의도 파악 - 건물 로비를 얼마 전 개조했다는 말의 의미
여자의 두 번째 대사에서 남자에게 좀 더 현대적인 사무실로 이전하는 것이 어떨지(What about relocating to a more modern office?) 물어봤다. 이에 대해 남자가 긍정적 응답을 하지 않고 건물 로비를 얼마 전 보수했다(we just renovated the lobby here.)는 인용문을 언급했다. 즉, 본사 이전에 반대한다는 뜻을 간접적으로 나타낸 것이므로 정답은 (C)이다.

59-61

W-Br Edwin, [59]**I was looking over our mobile app release schedule, and I saw that the update to your card game app just became available for download.** How has it been doing?

M-Cn Well, [60]**the sales have held steady, but... some of the user comments in the online store have complaints.** People say the app has some bugs and its new layout is confusing.

W-Br Oh. You'd better get those problems taken care of quickly. Will that be difficult?

M-Cn I'm not sure—my team's still gathering information. [61]**I'm responding to the store reviews to ask for details.**

W-Br That's good. Let me know if there's anything I can do to help.

여: 에드윈, **우리 모바일 앱 출시 일정을 검토하고 있었는데요. 보니까 당신 카드 게임 앱 업데이트가 이제 막 다운로드할 수 있게 됐네요.** 어떻게 잘 되고 있나요?
남: 글쎄, **판매는 꾸준히 되고 있는데… 온라인 상점의 사용자 후기 중에 불만이 좀 있어요.** 사람들이 앱에 오류가 있고 바뀐 레이아웃이 혼동된다고 하네요.
여: 아. 그 문제들은 빨리 처리하는 게 좋겠네요. 어려울까요?
남: 잘 모르겠어요. 우리 팀에서 아직 정보를 모으고 있는 중입니다. **저는 구체적인 내용을 얻으려고 상점 후기에 응답하고 있고요.**
여: 좋습니다. 제가 도울 일이 있으면 알려 주세요.

어휘 look over 검토하다 release 출시; 출시하다 steady 꾸준한 user comment 사용자 후기 complaint 불평 bug (컴퓨터 프로그램의) 오류 layout 배치, 레이아웃 take care of ~을 처리하다 respond to ~에 대응하다 ask for (달라고) 요청하다

59

What does the woman say about a mobile app?
(A) A new version of it has been released.
(B) It won an industry competition.
(C) It can be downloaded for free.
(D) It conveniently stores business cards.

여자는 모바일 앱에 대해 무엇이라고 말하는가?
(A) 새 버전이 출시되었다.
(B) 업계 내 대회에서 우승했다.
(C) 무료로 다운로드할 수 있다.
(D) 명함을 편리하게 저장해 준다.

어휘 win a competition 경쟁에서 이기다 store 저장하다, 보관하다 business card 명함

해설 세부 사항 관련 - 여자의 앱에 대한 언급
여자의 첫 대사에서 모바일 앱 출시 일정을 검토하고 있었다(I was looking over our mobile app release schedule)면서 남자의 카드 게임 앱의 업데이트가 다운로드할 수 있게 됐다(the update to your card game app just became available for download)고 했으므로 정답은 (A)이다.

60

What problem does the man mention?
(A) A device has the wrong operating system.
(B) A screen layout cannot be customized.
(C) Some figures might not be accurate.
(D) Some customer reviews are negative.

남자는 어떤 문제를 언급하는가?
(A) 기기의 운영 체제가 잘못되었다.
(B) 화면 구성이 원하는 대로 조절되지 않는다.
(C) 일부 수치가 정확하지 않을 수 있다.
(D) 일부 고객의 평가가 부정적이다.

어휘 operating system 운영 체제 customize 개별 요구에 맞춰 만들다 figure 수치 accurate 정확한 negative 부정적인

해설 세부 사항 관련 - 남자가 언급하는 문제점
남자의 첫 번째 대사에서 판매는 꾸준하지만 온라인 상점의 사용자 후기 중 불만이 있다(the sales have held steady, but… some of the user comments in the online store have complaints.)고 했으므로 정답은 (D)이다.

61

What does the man say he is currently doing?
(A) Planning a team gathering
(B) Shopping for a new smartphone
(C) Reassigning some responsibilities
(D) Making some posts online

남자는 지금 무엇을 하고 있다고 말하는가?
(A) 팀 모임 기획
(B) 새 스마트폰 쇼핑
(C) 임무 재할당
(D) 온라인 게시 글 올리기

어휘 gathering 모임 reassign 다시 맡기다, 재할당하다 responsibility 책무 post (온라인) 게시, 게시 글

해설 세부 사항 관련 – 남자가 하고 있는 일

남자의 마지막 대사에서 구체적인 내용을 얻기 위해 상점 후기에 응답하고 있다(I'm responding to the store reviews to ask for details.)고, 즉 온라인 게시 글을 올리고 있다고 하므로 정답은 (D)이다.

62-64 대화 + 표지판

W-Am Hello. I have several hours before my train leaves for Paris, and I was wondering if you could recommend an activity I could do near this train station.

M-Au Yes, [62]**there's a nice public park with gardens and a fountain nearby. It's actually one of our city's most popular sightseeing destinations.** It's a five-minute walk from Exit Two.

W-Am That's perfect. Also, I wanted to store my luggage in a locker. But [63]**according to the sign, I need exactly nine euros.** I noticed the machine doesn't take banknotes. [64]**Where can I exchange my banknotes into coins?**

M-Au I could do that for you here.

여: 안녕하세요. 제가 탈 기차가 파리로 출발하기 전에 몇 시간이 남았는데요. 이 기차역 근처에서 할 만할 활동을 추천해 주실 수 있는지 궁금합니다.

남: 네, **근처에 정원과 분수가 있는 멋진 공원이 있습니다. 사실 저희 도시에서 가장 인기 있는 관광지 중 하나인데요.** 2번 출구에서 걸어서 5분 거리입니다.

여: 아주 좋네요. 그리고 제 짐을 물품 보관함에 두고 싶은데요. 하지만 **표지판에 따르면 정확히 9유로가 필요하네요.** 기계는 지폐를 받지 않던데, **어디서 지폐를 동전으로 바꿀 수 있나요?**

남: 제가 여기서 해드릴게요.

어휘 recommend 추천하다 fountain 분수 nearby 인근에 sightseeing destination 관광지 luggage 짐, 수하물 locker 물품 보관함 banknote 지폐 exchange 교환하다 coin 동전

Locker Size	Price
Small	€4
Medium	€7
[63]Large	€9
Extra Large	€12

물품 보관함 크기	가격
소	4유로
중	7유로
대	**9유로**
특대	12유로

62

What does the man recommend?

(A) Changing a departure time
(B) Visiting a tourist attraction
(C) Taking public transportation
(D) Purchasing items in the train station

남자는 무엇을 추천하는가?

(A) 출발시간 변경
(B) 관광 명소 방문
(C) 대중교통 이용
(D) 기차역 안에서 물품 구입

어휘 departure 출발 tourist attraction 관광 명소 public transportation 대중교통

해설 세부 사항 관련 – 남자의 추천 사항

남자의 첫 번째 대사에서 여자에게 근처에 정원과 분수가 있는 멋진 공원이 있는데 그곳은 사실 도시에서 가장 인기 있는 관광지 중 한 곳(there's a nice public park ~ our city's most popular sightseeing destinations.)이라고 했으므로 정답은 (B)이다.

▸▸ **Paraphrasing** 대화의 **one of our city's most popular sightseeing destinations**
→ 정답의 **a tourist attraction**

63

Look at the graphic. Which size locker will the woman use?

(A) Small
(B) Medium
(C) Large
(D) Extra large

시각 정보에 의하면, 여자는 어느 사이즈의 물품 보관함을 이용할 것인가?

(A) 소
(B) 중
(C) 대
(D) 특대

해설 시각 정보 연계 – 여자가 이용할 물품 보관함

여자의 두 번째 대사에서 표지판에 따르면 자신이 정확히 9유로가 필요하다고 했다. 표지판을 보면 대형 물품 보관함이 9유로로 나와 있으므로 정답은 (C)이다.

Test 4

64

What does the woman need to do?

(A) Remember a code
(B) Fill out a form
(C) Exchange some money
(D) Get some directions

여자는 무엇을 해야 하는가?

(A) 코드 기억하기
(B) 양식 작성하기
(C) 돈 교환하기
(D) 지시 받기

해설 세부 사항 관련 – 여자가 해야 할 일

여자의 두 번째 대사에서 남자에게 어디서 지폐를 동전으로 교환할 수 있는지(Where can I exchange my banknotes into coins?)를 물어봤으므로 정답은 (C)이다.

▸▸ **Paraphrasing** 대화의 **exchange my banknotes into coins**
→ 정답의 **Exchange some money**

65-67 대화 + 일정표

M-Au Hi, Camille. [65]**I called Gwen Porter yesterday, and she said she can come into the office tomorrow even on such short notice. I'm grateful we're working with such an accommodating author.**

W-Br Yes, me too. Also, did you contact the IT department? The schedule of upcoming book release dates on our Web site is still incorrect. [66]***Amazing Arizona* has been delayed three weeks, so it'll be released on the same day as *Up Kinabalu*.**

M-Au I did, but I guess they haven't had time to fix it yet. I'll call them.

W-Br We also need to inform the customers who have pre-ordered the book by sending out e-mails. [67]**Can you draft a message by tonight explaining the situation?**

M-Au Sure.

남: 안녕하세요, 카밀 씨. **어제 그웬 포터 씨에게 전화했는데요. 갑작스러운 연락을 받고도 내일 사무실로 올 수 있다고 합니다. 이렇게 협조적인 저자와 일할 수 있어 다행이에요.**

여: 네, 저도요. 그리고 IT 부서에도 연락하셨어요? 웹 사이트에 올려진 향후 발간될 책 출간 일자들이 아직도 틀려요. **〈어메이징 애리조나〉는 3주 연기돼서 〈업 키나발루〉와 같은 날 나올 겁니다.**

남: 연락했는데 아직 고칠 시간이 없었던 것 같아요. 전화해 볼게요.

여: 책을 선주문한 고객들에게도 이메일을 보내서 알려야 해요. **오늘 밤까지 상황을 설명하는 메시지 초안을 작성할 수 있겠어요?**

남: 물론입니다.

어휘 on short notice 갑작스러운 연락을 받고 grateful 고마워하는 accommodating 호의적인, 협조를 잘 하는 author 작가 upcoming 다가오는 release 출간 incorrect 부정확한 pre-order 선주문하다 draft 초안을 작성하다

Title	Release Date
[66]*Amazing Arizona*	April 3
Up Kinabalu	April 24
Cycling Spain	May 9
Tasmanian Lights	May 17

제목	출간 일자
어메이징 애리조나	4월 3일
업 키나발루	4월 24일
사이클링 스페인	5월 9일
태즈메이니안 라이츠	5월 17일

65

What did the man do yesterday?

(A) Read a manuscript
(B) Spoke to an author
(C) Returned from a trip
(D) Canceled a meeting

남자는 어제 무엇을 했는가?

(A) 원고 읽기
(B) 저자와 얘기하기
(C) 여행에서 돌아오기
(D) 회의 취소하기

어휘 manuscript 원고 cancel 취소하다

해설 세부 사항 관련 – 남자가 어제 한 일

남자의 첫 대사에서 어제 그웬 포터에게 전화했는데 그녀가 갑작스러운 연락을 받고도 내일 사무실로 올 수 있다고 했다(I called Gwen Porter yesterday, and ~ even on such short notice.)며 매우 협조적인 저자와 일할 수 있어 다행(I'm grateful we're working with such an accommodating author.)이라고 했다. 이를 통해 남자가 어제 저자와 얘기를 나눈 것을 알 수 있으므로 정답은 (B)이다.

▸▸ **Paraphrasing** 대화의 **called Gwen Porter**
→ 정답의 **Spoke to an author**

66

Look at the graphic. Which release date is no longer correct?

(A) April 3
(B) April 24
(C) May 9
(D) May 17

시각 정보에 의하면, 어느 출간 일자가 더 이상 옳지 않은가?

(A) 4월 3일
(B) 4월 24일
(C) 5월 9일
(D) 5월 17일

해설 시각 정보 연계 - 잘못된 출간 일자
여자의 첫 번째 대사에서 <어메이징 애리조나>는 3주 연기돼서 <업 키나발루>와 같은 날에 나올 것(*Amazing Arizona* has been delayed three weeks, so it'll be released on the same day as *Up Kinabalu*.)이라고 했다. 그리고 일정표를 보면 <업 키나발루>가 4월 24일에 출간될 예정으로 되어 있다. 즉, <어메이징 애리조나>도 4월 3일이 아닌 4월 24일에 출간될 것이므로 정답은 (A)이다.

67

What does the woman ask the man to do?

(A) Upload an e-book to a Web page
(B) Study some consumer research
(C) Write a notification e-mail
(D) Place an advance order

여자는 남자에게 무엇을 해달라고 요청하는가?

(A) 웹페이지에 전자책 업로드하기
(B) 소비자 조사 결과 연구하기
(C) 통지 이메일 쓰기
(D) 선주문하기

어휘 notification 통지 place an order 주문하다 advance 사전의

해설 세부 사항 관련 - 여자의 요청 사항
여자의 두 번째 대사에서 남자에게 오늘 밤까지 상황을 설명하는 메시지 초안을 작성해 달라(Can you draft a message by tonight explaining the situation?)는 요청을 했으므로 정답은 (C)이다.

▸▸ **Paraphrasing** 대화의 **draft** → 정답의 **Write**

68-70 대화 + 목록

M-Cn Danielle, what are you working on?

W-Am [68]**I'm fixing a notebook computer.** The owner spilled coffee on it, so I'm removing its internal parts to let them dry out.

M-Cn Oh, I see. [69]**I was asking because I'm a little concerned about how messy your work table is.** You know we have a rule about that.

W-Am Yes, I know. Well, these parts have to sit spread out like this, but I guess I could clean up some of the personal items I've left out.

M-Cn That would be great. When could you get to it?

W-Am [70]**I can do it after I finish taking this computer apart.** Just give me about twenty minutes.

남: 대니엘, 어떤 작업을 하고 있어요?
여: **노트북 컴퓨터를 고치는 중이에요.** 주인이 컴퓨터에 커피를 엎질러서, 말리려고 내부 부품들을 떼어내고 있습니다.
남: 아, 그렇군요. **난 당신 작업대가 지저분한 게 좀 걱정이 돼서 물어봤어요.** 관련 규칙이 있는 거 아시죠?
여: 네, 알아요. 음, 이 부품들은 이렇게 펼쳐 놓을 수밖에 없어요. 하지만 안 쓰는 개인 물건들을 치울 수는 있겠네요.
남: 그게 좋겠네요. 언제 시작할 수 있겠어요?
여: **이 컴퓨터 분해하는 걸 마친 후에 할 수 있어요.** 20분 정도만 주세요.

어휘 work on ~에 대해 작업하다[노력을 기울이다] spill 엎지르다 remove 떼어내다, 치우다 internal 내부의 parts 부품 dry out 마르다 messy 지저분한 spread out (여러 개의 물건을) 펼쳐 놓다 leave out 내어놓다 get to ~을 시작하다 take apart 분해하다 appropriate 적절한 eye protection 눈 보호대[안경] lift 들어 올리다 load 짐 maintain 유지하다 orderly 정돈된

Safety Rules

1. Wear appropriate eye protection.
2. Lift heavy loads safely.
3. Maintain the condition of your tools.
[69]4. Keep your work space orderly.

안전 수칙

1. 적절한 눈 보호대를 착용한다.
2. 무거운 짐은 안전하게 들어올린다.
3. 도구의 상태를 유지한다.
4. 작업 공간을 정돈한다.

68

What kind of device is the woman repairing?

(A) A hair dryer
(B) A coffee maker
(C) A digital camera
(D) A laptop computer

여자는 어떤 기기를 수리하고 있는가?

(A) 헤어 드라이기
(B) 커피 메이커
(C) 디지털 카메라
(D) 노트북 컴퓨터

어휘 laptop computer 노트북 컴퓨터

해설 세부 사항 관련 - 여자가 수리하는 기기
여자의 첫 번째 대사에서 노트북 컴퓨터를 고치고 있다(I'm fixing a notebook computer.)고 했으므로 정답은 (D)이다.

69

Look at the graphic. Which rule does the man refer to?

(A) Rule 1
(B) Rule 2
(C) Rule 3
(D) Rule 4

시각 정보에 의하면, 남자는 어떤 규칙을 언급하는가?

(A) 제1규칙
(B) 제2규칙
(C) 제3규칙
(D) 제4규칙

어휘 refer to ~을 언급하다

해설 시각 정보 연계 - 남자가 언급하는 규칙

남자의 두 번째 대사에서 여자의 작업대가 지저분한 게 걱정되어 물어보았다(I was asking because I'm a little concerned about how messy your work table is.)고 했다. 안전 수칙을 보면 해당하는 내용이 제4규칙이므로 정답은 (D)이다.

70

What does the woman say she will do next?

(A) Continue working on the device
(B) Check a cabinet for some safety gear
(C) Give a status report to a customer
(D) Remove some items from a table

여자는 다음에 무엇을 하겠다고 말하는가?

(A) 기기에 대한 작업 계속하기
(B) 안전 도구를 찾기 위해 캐비닛 확인하기
(C) 고객에게 현황 보고서 주기
(D) 테이블에서 일부 물건 치우기

어휘 safety gear 안전 도구 status report 현황 보고서

해설 세부 사항 관련 - 여자의 계획

여자의 마지막 대사에서 컴퓨터 분해를 먼저 마치고 치우겠다(I can do it after I finish taking this computer apart.)고 말하고 있어 여자는 기기에 대한 작업을 계속할 것임을 알 수 있으므로 정답은 (A)이다.

PART 4

71-73 담화

M-Cn [71]**I'd like to remind you all that we have a photographer coming in tomorrow to create individual and group portraits of the staff.** She'll be in the presentation room, because it has the best lighting. Uh, [72]**I'm going to send out an e-mail this afternoon with each of your names and the times you'll need to go in there.** Please check it today so that you know what to expect tomorrow. Oh, and remember, the portraits are going to be used in internal and external materials for at least the next year. So [73]**we hope you'll take care to wear neat, professional attire.** Any questions about that?

내일 사진사를 불러와서 개인 및 단체로 직원 사진을 찍는다는 것을 여러분 모두에게 다시 한 번 알려드립니다. 사진사는 프레젠테이션 방에 있을 거예요. 그곳이 조명이 가장 좋기 때문인데요. 어, **오늘 오후에 여러분 각자의 이름과 그곳에 가야 할 시간을 적은 이메일을 발송하겠습니다.** 내일 어떻게 할지 알 수 있도록 메일을 오늘 확인해 주시기 바랍니다. 아, 그리고 기억해 주세요, 사진들은 최소한 다음 해까지는 내외 자료로 사용될 예정입니다. 따라서 **여러분은 신경 써서 깔끔하고 전문가다운 복장을 갖추도록 해 주시기 바랍니다.** 이와 관련해 질문 있으세요?

어휘 remind 상기시키다 portrait (어깨 윗부분이 나오는) 인물 사진 lighting 조명 internal 내부의 external 외부의 material 자료 professional 전문직에 종사하는 attire 복장, 의복

71

What is the speaker mostly talking about?

(A) A group presentation
(B) A staff directory
(C) A photo shoot
(D) A travel policy

화자는 주로 무엇에 대해 말하는가?

(A) 그룹 프레젠테이션
(B) 직원 명부
(C) 사진 촬영
(D) 출장 규정

해설 전체 내용 관련 - 공지의 주제

지문 초반부에 화자가 청자들에게 알리는 사항으로 내일 사진사를 불러와 개인 및 단체로 직원 사진을 찍는다(we have a photographer coming in tomorrow to create individual and group portraits of the staff)고 했으므로 정답은 (C)이다.

72

What should the listeners do in the afternoon?

(A) Make a payment
(B) Consult a schedule
(C) Hold a practice session
(D) Send a text message

청자들은 오후에 무엇을 해야 하는가?

(A) 금액 납부
(B) 일정표 확인
(C) 연습 세션 실시
(D) 문자 메시지 발송

어휘 consult 참고하다, 찾아보다 practice session (체계적인)연습 세션

해설 세부 사항 관련 - 청자들이 오후에 할 일

지문 중반부에 화자가 청자들에게 오후에 각자의 이름과 프레젠테이션 방에 가야 할 시간을 적은 이메일을 발송하겠다(I'm going to send out an e-mail this afternoon ~ you'll need to go in there.)고 한 후 확인해달라고 했으므로 정답은 (B)이다.

73

What does the speaker ask the listeners to pay special attention to?

(A) Their clothing
(B) A time limit
(C) A file size
(D) Their noise level

화자는 청자들에게 무엇에 특별히 신경 쓰라고 요청하는가?

(A) 옷차림
(B) 시간 제한
(C) 파일 크기
(D) 소음 수준

어휘 clothing 옷 limit 제한

해설 세부 사항 관련 - 화자의 요청 사항

지문 후반부에 화자가 청자들에게 신경 써서 깔끔하고 전문가다운 복장을 갖추도록 해 주길 바란다(we hope you'll take care to wear neat, professional attire.)고 했으므로 정답은 (A)이다.

74-76 광고

W-Br Do your kitchen windows refuse to shine? Can you see your living room floor or is it covered in laundry? Contact the Wizards of Midtown for a free consultation. [74]**Our highly trained, full-time staff will take on even the most difficult household tasks and get any apartment or house tidy and ready for visitors.** This is why [75]**the local community has trusted us for fifty years to keep their spaces spotless.** Call us today and [76]**buy a cleaning package to get your first session for twenty-five percent off.** The Wizards of Midtown—for when your home needs a little magic.

주방 창문에서 좀처럼 빛이 안 나나요? 거실 바닥이 보이시나요, 아니면 세탁물로 뒤덮여 있나요? 미드타운의 마법사들에게 연락하셔서 무료 상담을 받아보세요. **잘 훈련된 정규직 직원들이 가장 어려운 집안일까지도 맡아 처리하며 어떠한 아파트나 주택이라도 깨끗이 싹 치워 손님 맞을 준비를 해 드립니다.** 그래서 **지역 사회에서는 지난 50년간 개인 공간을 티끌 하나 없이 청소하는 일에 대해 저희를 믿고 맡겨왔습니다.** 오늘 전화 주셔서 **청소 패키지를 구매하시면 처음 청소는 25% 할인해 드립니다.** 댁이 마술처럼 깨끗해지길 바라신다면 미드타운의 마법사들에게 연락주세요.

어휘 refuse to + 동사원형 ~하려 하지 않다 shine 빛나다 living room 거실 laundry 세탁물, 세탁 consultation 상담 highly trained 잘 훈련된 take on (일을) 맡다 household 가정 tidy 잘 정돈된 local community 지역 사회 spotless 티끌 하나 없는

74

What service is being advertised?

(A) Interior decorating
(B) Landscaping
(C) Plumbing
(D) Cleaning

어떤 서비스를 광고하고 있는가?

(A) 실내 장식
(B) 조경
(C) 배관
(D) 청소

해설 전체 내용 관련 - 광고 중인 서비스

지문 초반부에 화자가 잘 훈련된 정규직 직원들이 가장 어려운 집안일까지도 처리해 주며 어떠한 아파트나 주택이라도 깨끗이 치워 손님 맞을 준비를 해 준다(Our highly trained, full-time staff ~ ready for visitors.)고 했다. 청소 서비스를 광고하고 있으므로 정답은 (D)이다.

75

What is mentioned about the company?

(A) Its staff work part-time.
(B) It is located in a suburban area.
(C) It is owned by a local family.
(D) It has been in business for a long time.

이 회사에 대해 언급된 것은 무엇인가?

(A) 직원들은 파트타임직으로 일한다.
(B) 교외 지역에 위치해 있다.
(C) 현지에 거주하는 가족이 소유하고 있다.
(D) 오랫동안 영업해 왔다.

어휘 suburban 교외의 own 소유하다 local 지역의

해설 세부 사항 관련 - 회사와 관련된 언급

지문 중반부에 지역 사회에서는 지난 50년간 우리 회사를 신뢰해 왔다(the local community has trusted us for fifty years to keep their spaces spotless.)고 했다. 오랫동안 운영된 업체임을 알 수 있으므로 정답은 (D)이다.

76

According to the speaker, how can a listener receive a discount?

(A) By mentioning the advertisement
(B) By purchasing a package deal
(C) By referring a friend
(D) By paying with cash

화자에 따르면, 청자는 어떤 방법을 통해 할인을 받을 수 있는가?
(A) 광고 언급
(B) 패키지 상품 구매
(C) 친구 추천
(D) 현금 지불

어휘 refer 추천하다

해설 세부 사항 관련 - 할인을 받을 수 있는 방법
지문 후반부에 청소 패키지를 구매하면 첫 번째 청소에 대해 25퍼센트 할인을 해 준다(buy a cleaning package to get your first session for twenty-five percent off.)고 했으므로 정답은 (B)이다.

▸▸ **Paraphrasing** 지문의 **buy** → 정답의 **purchasing**

무엇이 특별 할인가에 제공되고 있는가?
(A) 인쇄 서비스
(B) 문구류
(C) 사무용 가구
(D) 제품 주문 제작

어휘 stationery 문구류 customization 주문 제작

해설 세부 사항 관련 - 특별 할인가에 제공되는 것
지문 초반부에 빅 숍 플러스는 공책, 달력식 수첩, 달력 등 가정용이나 사무용 종이 제품 일체에 대해 특별히 20퍼센트 할인을 제공한다(Big Shop Plus is offering a special twenty percent off deal on all its paper products ~ calendars, and more.)고 했으므로 정답은 (B)이다.

▸▸ **Paraphrasing** 지문의 **notebooks, planners, calendars** → 정답의 **stationery supplies**

77-79 안내

M-Au Ready to save money? [77]**Big Shop Plus is offering a special twenty percent off deal on all its paper products for the home or office—notebooks, planners, calendars, and more.** Visit Aisle 4 and stock up. Now... we have a lot of shoppers here today. [78]**Save yourself time in the cashier's lines by using our new automated checkout service.** Simply scan your items and swipe your credit card in the machine, and you're done. Shopping for the holiday weekend? [79]**We'll stay open an extra two hours on Thursday—until eleven P.M.** We hope you take advantage of this convenient service.

돈을 절약할 준비가 되셨습니까? **빅 숍 플러스는 공책, 달력식 수첩, 달력 등 가정용이나 사무용 종이 제품 일체에 대해 특별히 20% 할인을 제공합니다.** 4번 통로로 오셔서 제품을 많이 사 두세요. 지금… 오늘 이곳에 손님이 많은데요. **새로운 자동 결제 서비스를 이용하셔서 계산대에서 줄을 서는 시간을 아끼시기 바랍니다.** 간단히 제품을 스캔하고 기계에 신용카드를 긁으시기만 하면 됩니다. 연휴가 낀 주말에 쇼핑하십니까? **목요일에는 밤 11시까지, 두 시간 더 연장 운영합니다.** 이 편리한 서비스를 이용해 보시기 바랍니다.

어휘 planner 달력식 수첩 stock up 사서 비축하다 cashier's line 계산대에서 기다리는 줄 automated 자동화된 checkout 결제 swipe (신용카드를) 읽히다, 긁다 stay open until ~까지 영업하다 take advantage of ~를 이용하다 convenient 편리한

77

What is being offered at a special discount?
(A) Printing services
(B) Stationery supplies
(C) Office furniture
(D) Product customization

78

Why does the speaker say, "we have a lot of shoppers here today"?
(A) To confirm the success of a sales event
(B) To apologize for long waiting lines
(C) To promote a store's new feature
(D) To warn about merchandise being out of stock

화자가 "오늘 이곳에 손님이 많은데요"라고 말한 의도는 무엇인가?
(A) 할인 행사의 성공을 확인해 주기 위해
(B) 긴 대기 줄에 대해 사과하기 위해
(C) 매장의 새 기능을 홍보하기 위해
(D) 재고가 없는 상품에 대해 주의를 주기 위해

어휘 apologize for ~에 대해 사과하다 promote 홍보하다 feature (특징이 되는) 기능 out of stock 재고가 없는

해설 화자의 의도 파악 - 오늘 손님이 많다고 말한 이유
지문 중반부에 새로운 자동 결제 서비스를 이용해서 계산대에서 시간을 아끼길 바란다(Save yourself time in the cashier's lines by using our new automated checkout service.)고 했다. 즉, 오늘 이곳에 손님이 많다고 인용문을 말한 이유는 시간 절약을 위해 새로운 자동 결제 서비스를 이용해 보라는 의미를 전달하기 위한 것이므로 정답은 (C)이다.

▸▸ **Paraphrasing** 지문의 **our new automated checkout service** → 정답의 **a store's new feature**

79

According to the speaker, what will the store do on Thursday?
(A) Extend its operating hours
(B) Move to another location
(C) Start a loyalty card program
(D) Provide home deliveries

화자에 따르면, 상점은 목요일에 무엇을 할 것인가?
(A) 영업시간 연장
(B) 다른 곳으로 이전
(C) 포인트 적립 카드 프로그램 시작
(D) 가정 배달 서비스 제공

어휘 extend 늘이다, 연장하다 operations hours 영업시간

해설 세부 사항 관련 – 목요일의 상점 일정

지문 후반부에 목요일에는 밤 11시까지 두 시간 더 문을 열겠다(We'll stay open an extra two hours on Thursday-until eleven P.M.)고 했으므로 정답은 (A)이다.

▸▸ Paraphrasing 지문의 stay open an extra two hours
→ 정답의 extend its operating hours

80-82 회의 발췌

W-Br [80]**I've divided up the tasks that we need accomplished for our symposium on Friday.** Chen, please create and post signs to direct participants to the auditorium. Mark, you're in charge of meeting the audiovisual crew at eight A.M. to show them how we'd like the microphones and podium set up. [81]**Make sure they understand how the videotaping should proceed.** Sarah, you'll bring the, uh, nametags, symposium programs, and sign-in sheets, and staff the registration table to greet participants as they arrive. [82]**Min-Joon, you'll come to the reception area thirty minutes before each break to make sure that the catering services have prepared the coffee and tea.** Any questions?

금요일에 있을 토론회를 위해 처리해야 할 업무를 나눴습니다. 첸, 참석자들을 강당으로 안내할 표지판을 만들어서 붙여주세요. 마크, 아침 8시에 시청각 담당자들을 만나 마이크와 연단을 어떻게 설치해 주길 원하는지 알려주세요. **그들이 녹화 진행 방법을 이해하는지 확인해 주세요.** 세라, 이름표와 토론회 프로그램, 참가 신청서를 가져오고 참가자들이 도착했을 때 그들을 맞아줄 직원을 등록 테이블에 배치해 주세요. **민준, 휴식 시간마다 30분 전에 접수 구역으로 와서 출장 요리 업체가 커피와 차를 준비했는지 확인하세요.** 질문 있으신 분?

어휘 divide up 분담하다 accomplish 성취하다 symposium (공개) 토론회[좌담회], 심포지엄 post a sign 게시물을 내붙이다 participant 참석자 auditorium 강당 in charge of ~를 맡은 audiovisual 시청각의 podium 연단 videotaping 녹화 proceed 진행되다 sign-in sheet 참가 신청서 staff ~에 직원을 두다 catering service 출장 요리 업체

80

What will be held on Friday?

(A) A film screening
(B) A concert
(C) An awards banquet
(D) A symposium

금요일에는 무엇이 열릴 것인가?

(A) 영화 상영
(B) 콘서트
(C) 시상식 연회
(D) 토론회

해설 세부 사항 관련 – 금요일에 열릴 행사

지문 맨 처음에 화자가 금요일에 있을 토론회를 위해 처리해야 할 업무를 나누어 놓았다(I've divided up the tasks that we need accomplished for our symposium on Friday.)고 했으므로 정답은 (D)이다.

81

What is mentioned about the event?

(A) It will be recorded.
(B) It will be held outdoors.
(C) It will begin in the evening.
(D) It will have around 80 participants.

행사에 대해 언급된 것은 무엇인가?

(A) 녹화될 예정이다.
(B) 옥외에서 열릴 예정이다.
(C) 저녁에 시작할 것이다.
(D) 약 80명의 참석자가 올 것이다.

해설 세부 사항 관련 – 행사에 대한 언급된 내용

화자는 지문 중반부에 그들이 녹화 진행 방법을 이해하는지 확인하라(Make sure they understand how the videotaping should proceed.)고 했다. 이를 통해 행사가 녹화될 것이라는 점을 알 수 있으므로 정답은 (A)이다.

▸▸ Paraphrasing 지문의 videotaping → 정답의 recorded

82

What is mentioned as one of Min-Joon's duties?

(A) Designing handouts
(B) Monitoring electronics
(C) Checking on refreshments
(D) Ushering audience members

민준의 임무 중 하나로 언급된 것은 무엇인가?

(A) 인쇄물 디자인하기
(B) 전자제품 모니터하기
(C) 다과 확인하기
(D) 청중 안내하기

어휘 refreshment 다과 usher 안내하다; 안내인

해설 세부 사항 관련 – 민준의 임무 중 한 가지

지문 후반부에 화자가 민준에게 휴식 시간마다 30분 전에 접수 구역으로 와서 출장 요리 업체가 커피와 차를 준비했는지 확인하라(Min-Joon, you'll come to the reception area ~ coffee and tea.)고 했으므로 정답은 (C)이다.

▸▸ Paraphrasing 지문의 coffee and tea
→ 정답의 refreshments

83-85 방송

W-Am This is Hobart's Weather from 7KNF *The Scoop*. I hope you packed your sunscreen—you're going to need it. [83]**There's not a cloud in the sky, and without any wind, it's going to**

Test 4

be bright all day long. [84]This is good news for the charity swim race, Hobart Heroes, because it won't get rained out like last year. **[84]The fund-raiser always has a lot of spectators, so expect large crowds on Malton Beach.** And don't forget to bring a light coat if you do go out because temperatures might be a little cool, especially in the evening. **[85]Now, stay tuned to *The Scoop* for sports updates from Tim Herbert.** Tim?

7KNF 〈더 스쿱〉의 '호바트의 날씨' 코너입니다. 자외선 차단제를 챙겨 오셨길 바랍니다. 필요하실 거니까요. **하늘에는 구름 한 점 없고 바람도 없어서 종일 화창한 날씨가 될 것 같습니다. 자선 수영 경기 '호바트 히어로즈'에 좋은 소식이겠네요.** 지난해처럼 비 때문에 취소되지는 않을 테니까요. **이 기금 마련 행사에는 항상 관중이 많기 때문에 말턴 해변에 많은 인파가 모일 것으로 예상됩니다.** 특히 저녁에는 기온이 약간 쌀쌀할 수 있으니, 외출하실 경우 얇은 겉옷을 잊지 말고 챙기시기 바랍니다. **이제 팀 허버트가 전하는 스포츠 소식을 들으시기 위해 〈더 스쿱〉에 채널을 고정해 주세요.** 팀?

어휘 pack 싸다, 챙기다 sunscreen 자외선 차단제 bright (날씨가) 화창한 charity 자선 rain out 우천으로 연기하다, 중단하다 fundraiser 기금 모금 행사 spectator 관중 stay tuned to ~에 채널을 고정하다

83

What kind of weather does the speaker forecast?

(A) Clear
(B) Rainy
(C) Snowy
(D) Windy

화자는 어떤 날씨를 예보하는가?

(A) 맑음
(B) 비
(C) 눈
(D) 바람

해설 세부 사항 관련 - 화자가 예상하는 날씨

지문 초반부에 하늘에는 구름 한 점 없고 바람도 불지 않아 하루 종일 화창할 것(There's not a cloud in the sky, and without any wind, it's going to be bright all day long.)이라고 했으므로 정답은 (A)이다.

▸▸ **Paraphrasing** 지문의 not a cloud in the sky → 정답의 Clear

84

Why should listeners expect large crowds on Malton Beach?

(A) A sunset will be beautiful.
(B) A local celebrity will visit.
(C) There will be an athletic event.
(D) It is the last day of a festival.

청자들은 왜 말턴 해변에 많은 인파를 예상해야 하는가?

(A) 석양이 아름다울 것이다.
(B) 지역 출신 유명 인사가 올 것이다.
(C) 스포츠 행사가 있을 것이다.
(D) 축제 마지막 날이다.

어휘 celebrity 유명 인사 athletic 운동 경기의

해설 세부 사항 관련 - 많은 인파를 예상하는 이유

지문 중반부에 화창한 날씨가 '호바트 히어로즈'라는 자선 수영 경기에는 좋은 소식(This is good news for the charity swim race, Hobart Heroes)이라고 했다. 그리고 이 기금 마련 행사(자선 수영 경기)에는 항상 관중이 많기 때문에 말턴 해변에 많은 인파가 모일 것으로 예상된다(The fund-raiser always has ~ crowds on Malton Beach.)고 했으므로 정답은 (C)이다.

▸▸ **Paraphrasing** 지문의 the charity swim race
→ 정답의 an athletic event

85

What will listeners most likely hear next?

(A) A live music performance
(B) An update on traffic conditions
(C) A news report about sports
(D) A commercial for swimming gear

청자들은 다음에 무엇을 듣겠는가?

(A) 음악 공연 생중계
(B) 교통 상황 소식
(C) 스포츠 뉴스 보도
(D) 수영복 광고

어휘 commercial 광고; 상업적인 gear 복장, 장비

해설 세부 사항 관련 - 청자들이 다음에 들을 방송

지문 맨 마지막에 화자가 이제 팀 허버트가 전하는 스포츠 소식을 듣기 위해 〈더 스쿱〉에 채널을 고정해 달라(Now, stay tuned to *The Scoop* for sports updates from Tim Herbert.)고 했으므로 정답은 (C)이다.

▸▸ **Paraphrasing** 지문의 *The Scoop* for sports updates
→ 정답의 a news report about sports

86-88 전화 메시지

M-Au Ruth, it's Cecil. **[86]I'm sorry—I didn't see that you'd sent me an e-mail with new guidelines for the employee newsletter until just now.** Uh, but I wanted to let you know that **[87]I'll make sure to follow them for the upcoming issue.** Fortunately, I've only drafted a few articles so far. I'll get to work making them shorter and more informal. As for the article topic you suggested—I'd love to interview Ms. Abdi. But given her status as a company vice president, I feel a little nervous about approaching her.

[88]**Could you make the request for me, or at least let her know that I'll be contacting her?** I would really appreciate it.

루스, 세실인데요. **미안하지만 직원 회보에 대한 새 지침을 이메일로 보내셨던데 이제서야 알았어요.** 어, 하지만 **다음 호에서는 차질 없이 그 지침을 따를 것**이란 걸 알려 드립니다. 다행히, **지금까지 기사 몇 개의 초안밖에 안 썼어요.** 이제부터 더 간결하고 쉽게 만들도록 작업하겠습니다. 제안하신 기사 주제에 관해서는, 아브디 씨와 인터뷰를 하고 싶긴 해요. 하지만 회사 부사장이라는 그분의 지위를 고려하면 그분에게 다가가는 게 좀 떨립니다. **당신이 제 대신 요청해 주실 수 있을까요, 아니면 최소한 제가 연락드릴 거라는 걸 그분에게 알려 주실 수 있는지요?** 그렇게 해주시면 정말 감사하겠습니다.

어휘 guideline 지침 newsletter 회보 upcoming 다가오는 issue (정기 간행물의) 호 draft 초안을 작성하다 get to work 착수하다 informal 형식에 얽매이지 않는 as for ~에 대해 given ~을 고려할 때 status 지위 nervous 초조한, 겁을 먹은 approach 다가가다 appreciate 감사하다

86

Why does the speaker apologize to the listener?

(A) He failed to notice an e-mail from her.
(B) He misplaced some papers.
(C) He misunderstood some guidelines.
(D) He did not send her a copy of the newsletter.

화자가 청자에게 사과하는 이유는?

(A) 청자에게서 이메일이 온 것을 알지 못했다.
(B) 서류를 잃어버렸다.
(C) 지침을 잘못 이해했다.
(D) 청자에게 회보를 보내지 않았다.

어휘 notice 알아채다 misplace (잘못 두어) 잃어버리다 misunderstand 잘못 이해하다 copy (책 등의) 한 부

해설 세부 사항 관련 – 화자가 사과하는 이유

지문 초반부에 화자는 사과하며 청자가 직원 회보에 대한 새 지침을 이메일로 보낸 것을 이제야 알았다(I'm sorry—I didn't see ~ the employee newsletter until just now.)고 했으므로 정답은 (A)이다.

87

What does the speaker imply when he says, "I've only drafted a few articles so far"?

(A) It will be easy to make some revisions.
(B) Several potential topics have not been covered.
(C) An issue may be published late.
(D) He is not an experienced writer.

화자가 "지금까지 기사 몇 개의 초안밖에 안 썼어요"라고 말한 의도는 무엇인가?

(A) 수정하기가 쉬울 것이다.
(B) 몇몇 괜찮은 주제가 남아 있다.
(C) 한 호가 늦게 발행될 수도 있다.
(D) 자신은 경험이 풍부한 작가가 아니다.

어휘 revision 수정 potential 가능성이 있는 cover 다루다, 포함시키다 publish 발행하다, 출판하다 experienced 경험이 풍부한, 능숙한

해설 화자의 의도 파악 – 기사 몇 개의 초안밖에 안 썼다는 말의 의도

화자가 인용문 바로 앞 문장에서 다음 호에서는 차질 없이 지침을 따르겠다(I'll make sure to follow them for the upcoming issue)고 했다. 그런 다음 지금까지 기사 몇 개의 초안밖에 안 썼다고 했는데, 문맥상 인용문은 수정 작업이 비교적 쉬울 것이라는 의도를 나타낸 것이므로 정답은 (A)이다.

88

What does the speaker ask the listener to do?

(A) Write a short essay
(B) Grant a funding request
(C) Answer some questions
(D) Talk to an executive

화자는 청자에게 무엇을 해달라고 요청하는가?

(A) 짧은 에세이 작성
(B) 재정 지원 요청 승인
(C) 질문에 대답하기
(D) 중역에게 얘기하기

어휘 grant 승인하다 funding 재정 지원 executive 중역, 경영진

해설 세부 사항 관련 – 청자에게 요청하는 것

지문 후반부에 화자가 청자에게 대신 요청해주거나 화자가 연락할 것이라고 그분(회사 부사장)에게 알려 달라(Could you make the request for me, or at least let her know that I'll be contacting her?)고 했으므로 정답은 (D)이다.

89-91 녹음 메시지

W-Am You have reached the voice mail of Meryl Kennedy, programs supervisor at the Eastside Community Center. [89]**If you are calling to schedule a tour of the facilities, please contact the employee at our reception desk at extension 131.** For inquiries related to our regular courses and activities, however, you can reach me during my regular hours—Monday through Friday, eight A.M. to four P.M., and Saturdays from nine A.M. to twelve P.M. Again, [90]**I do not work past midday on Saturdays.** [91]**Please leave me a message that states your name, phone number, and the purpose of your call,** and I'll get back to you as soon as I can.

이스트사이드 커뮤니티 센터의 프로그램 감독관, 메릴 케네디의 음성 사서함입니다. **저희 시설 견학 일정을 잡기 위해 전화하신 분은 내선번호 131로 접수 데스크 직원에게 연락하십시오.** 그러나 저희 정기 강좌나 활동과 관련된 문의사항이 있으시면 정규 업무 시간, 즉 월요일에서 금요일까지는 오전 8시에서 오후 4시 사이, 토요일은 오전 9시에서 오후 12시 사이에 저에게 전화해 주십시오. 다시 말씀 드리지만, **저는 토요일에는 정오 이후에 근무하지 않습니다. 성함과 전화번호, 용건을 포함한 메시지를 남겨주시면** 가능한 한 빨리 연락 드리겠습니다.

Test 4

어휘 voice mail 음성 사서함 supervisor 감독관 extension 내선번호 inquiry 문의 activity 활동 regular hours 정규 업무 시간 midday 정오 state 말하다

89

Why should a listener contact the reception desk?

(A) To speak with Ms. Kennedy
(B) To hear a list of programs
(C) To set up a tour
(D) To obtain donation information

청자는 접수 데스크에 왜 연락해야 하는가?

(A) 케네디 씨와 통화하기 위해
(B) 프로그램 목록을 듣기 위해
(C) 견학 일정을 잡기 위해
(D) 기부 정보를 얻기 위해

해설 세부 사항 관련 - 접수 데스크에 연락해야 하는 이유

지문 초반부에 시설 견학 일정을 잡기 위해 전화를 했다면 내선번호 131로 접수 데스크 직원에게 연락하라(If you are calling to schedule a tour of ~ at extension 131.)고 했으므로 정답은 (C)이다.

▸▸ **Paraphrasing** 지문의 **schedule** → 정답의 **set up**

90

When does Ms. Kennedy say she is unavailable?

(A) On Monday mornings
(B) On Wednesday mornings
(C) On Friday afternoons
(D) On Saturday afternoons

케네디 씨는 언제 자신이 부재중이라고 말하는가?

(A) 매주 월요일 오전
(B) 매주 수요일 오전
(C) 매주 금요일 오후
(D) 매주 토요일 오후

해설 세부 사항 관련 - 케네디 씨가 부재중인 시간

지문 중후반부에 화자인 메릴 케네디는 토요일은 정오 이후로 근무하지 않는다(I do not work past midday on Saturdays.)고 했으므로 정답은 (D)이다.

91

What should a message for Ms. Kennedy include?

(A) The date and time
(B) The reason for contacting her
(C) A current course name
(D) A registration number

케네디 씨에게 남기는 메시지에 포함되어야 하는 내용은 무엇인가?

(A) 날짜와 시간
(B) 연락한 이유
(C) 현재 강좌명
(D) 등록번호

해설 세부 사항 관련 - 메시지에 포함시켜야 할 사항

지문 후반부에 성함, 전화번호, 용건을 포함한 메시지를 남겨 달라(Please leave me a message that states your name, phone number, and the purpose of your call)고 했으므로 정답은 (B)이다.

▸▸ **Paraphrasing** 지문의 **the purpose of your call**
→ 정답의 **The reason for contacting**

92-94 발표

M-Cn Before the meeting begins, I have an important announcement to make. [92]**As the head of this department, it's my pleasure to present the 'Sales Employee of the Quarter' award to Jung-Soon Hong.** Jung-Soon has been an effective employee ever since she was hired two years ago, but over the past few months she has really developed into a top performer. In that time, [93]**she formed contracts to sell Melving electronics to firms in Winnipeg and Montreal. And** don't forget about Vancouver! Impressive. [94]**Without employees like her, Melving Electronics wouldn't be able to maintain the steady expansion that has become our trademark.** Jung-Soon, please come up and accept this certificate.

회의를 시작하기 전에, 중대한 발표가 있습니다. **이 부서의 장으로서 '분기 최고 영업 사원' 상을 홍정순 씨에게 수여하게 되어 기쁩니다.** 정순 씨는 2년 전 고용된 이래로 항상 유능한 직원이었습니다만, 지난 몇 달간은 정말 최우수 직원으로 성장했습니다. 이 시기에 **그녀는 멜빙 전자제품들을 위니펙과 몬트리올에 있는 회사들에 판매하는 계약을 이루어 냈습니다.** 밴쿠버도 잊지 마세요! 훌륭합니다. **정순 씨 같은 직원들이 없다면 멜빙 전자는 우리의 트레이드마크가 된 그 지속적인 확장세를 유지해 나가지 못할 겁니다.** 정순 씨, 나오셔서 이 인증서를 받아 주십시오.

어휘 present 수여하다 quarter 분기 effective 유능한, 성공하는 ever since ~ 이래로 줄곧 hire 고용하다 top performer 최우수 직원 electronics 전자제품 form 형성시키다 firm 회사 impressive 감명 깊은 maintain 유지하다 expansion 확장 certificate 증명서

92

Who most likely is the speaker?

(A) An architect
(B) A travel agent
(C) A sales director
(D) A journalist

화자는 누구겠는가?
(A) 건축가
(B) 여행사 직원
(C) 영업 부장
(D) 기자

어휘 journalist 기자

해설 전체 내용 관련 – 화자의 신분
지문 초반부에 화자가 부서의 장으로서 '분기 최고 영업 사원'상을 홍정순 씨에게 수여하여 기쁘다(As the head of this department, it's my pleasure to present the "Sales Employee of the Quarter" award to Jung-Soon Hong.)고 했으므로 정답은 (C)이다.

93
Why does the speaker say, "don't forget about Vancouver"?
(A) To suggest an addition to an article
(B) To remind listeners of a venue option
(C) To show concern about a person's workload
(D) To emphasize a person's accomplishments

화자가 "밴쿠버도 잊지 마세요"라고 말한 이유는 무엇인가?
(A) 기사에 추가할 내용을 제안하려고
(B) 청자들에게 선택 가능한 장소를 상기시키려고
(C) 한 사람의 업무량에 우려를 표하려고
(D) 한 사람의 업적을 강조하려고

어휘 venue (행사 등의) 장소 option 선택, 선택권 concern 우려 workload 업무량 accomplishment 업적

해설 화자의 의도 파악 – 밴쿠버도 잊지 말라고 말하는 이유
인용문 바로 앞 문장에서 화자는 홍정순 씨가 멜빙 전자제품들을 위니펙과 몬트리올에 있는 회사들에 판매하는 계약을 따냈다(she formed contracts to sell Melving electronics to firms in Winnipeg and Montreal.)고 했다. 그런 다음 밴쿠버도 빼놓을 수 없다고 한 것은 밴쿠버에서도 계약을 따냈다는 의미이므로 정답은 (D)이다.

94
What does the speaker say the business is known for?
(A) Its technological innovations
(B) Its promotional campaigns
(C) Its corporate culture
(D) Its growth rate

화자는 이 업체가 무엇으로 유명하다고 말하는가?
(A) 기술 혁신
(B) 홍보 캠페인
(C) 기업 문화
(D) 성장률

어휘 be known for ~으로 유명하다 promotional 홍보의, 판촉의 corporate 기업(의)

해설 세부 사항 관련 – 업체가 유명한 이유
지문 후반부에 화자가 홍정순 씨와 같은 직원들이 없으면 멜빙 전자는 회사의 트레이드마크가 된 지속적인 확장세를 유지해 나가지 못할 것(Without employees like her, Melving Electronics wouldn't be able to maintain the steady expansion that has become our trademark.)이라고 말하여 이 업체는 성장률로 유명하다는 사실을 알 수 있으므로 정답은 (D)이다.

95-97 전화 메시지 + 지도

W-Am Hi, Brad. [95]**I'm calling to give you a couple of instructions regarding the booth we'll be operating at Corbin Arena for the art festival on Saturday.** All the paintings and drawings we're selling are in boxes in the storage room. [96]**What you need to do is pick up the boxes and unload them at our booth.** I've e-mailed you a map of the arena. [97]**Our booth will be located directly across from the entrance. So just walk straight after you pass through the gates. It's a great spot, right next to the gift shop,** so it'll be a busy area and good for business. OK, if you have any questions, give me a call. Thanks.

안녕하세요, 브래드. **토요일 미술 축제가 열리는 코빈 아레나에서 우리가 운영할 부스에 관해 두 가지 지시사항을 전달하고자 전화했습니다.** 우리가 판매할 그림과 소묘 일체는 창고의 상자 안에 있습니다. **브래드 씨가 하실 일은 그 상자를 우리 부스에 가져다 두는 것입니다.** 이메일로 경기장 지도를 보내드렸습니다. **우리 부스는 입구 바로 건너편에 위치해 있을 겁니다. 그래서 문을 통해 들어와서 곧장 걸어오시기만 하면 됩니다. 기념품점 바로 옆의 좋은 위치에 있으니** 이 구역이 붐벼서 영업하기에 좋을 것입니다. 질문이 있으시면 전화 주세요. 감사합니다.

어휘 instruction 지시사항 regarding ~에 관해 drawing 소묘 storage room 창고 unload (짐을) 내리다 arena 경기장 entrance 입구 walk straight 곧장 걸어가다 pass through ~를 통해 들어가다 next to ~ 옆에 lost and found 분실물 취급소

CORBIN ARENA

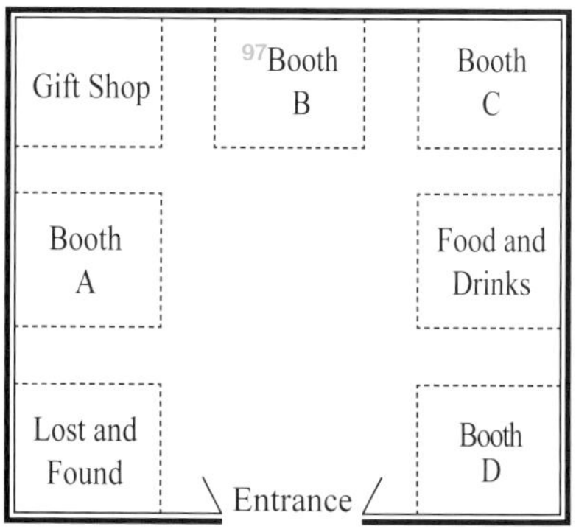

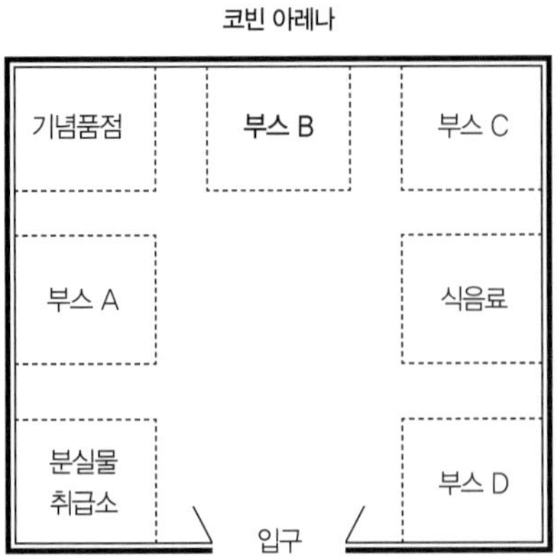

95

What event will take place at Corbin Arena on Saturday?

(A) A career fair
(B) A farmers market
(C) A hotel convention
(D) An art festival

토요일에 코빈 아레나에서 어떤 행사가 열릴 것인가?

(A) 직업 박람회
(B) 농산물 직거래 장터
(C) 호텔 컨벤션
(D) 미술 축제

해설 세부 사항 관련 - 토요일에 열릴 행사

지문 초반부에 화자가 토요일 미술 축제가 열리는 코빈 아레나에서 자신들이 운영할 운영할 부스에 관해 두 가지 지시사항을 전달하고자 전화했다(I'm calling to give you a couple of instructions regarding ~ on Saturday.)고 했으므로 정답은 (D)이다.

96

What does the speaker ask the listener to do?

(A) Transport some goods
(B) Organize a storage room
(C) E-mail a work schedule
(D) Meet near an entrance

화자는 청자에게 무엇을 해 달라고 요청하는가?

(A) 물건 운반하기
(B) 보관실 정리하기
(C) 업무 일정을 이메일로 보내기
(D) 입구 근처에서 만나기

어휘 transport 수송하다; 수송 organize 정리하다

해설 세부 사항 관련 - 화자의 요청 사항

지문 중반부에 청자가 할 일은 상자를 부스에 가져다 두는 것(What you need to do is pick up the boxes and unload them at our booth.)이라고 했으므로 정답은 (A)이다.

▸▸ Paraphrasing 지문의 pick up the boxes and unload them
→ 정답의 transport some goods

97

Look at the graphic. Which booth will the speaker occupy?

(A) Booth A
(B) Booth B
(C) Booth C
(D) Booth D

시각 정보에 의하면, 화자는 어느 부스를 차지할 것인가?

(A) 부스 A
(B) 부스 B
(C) 부스 C
(D) 부스 D

해설 시각 정보 연계 - 화자가 쓰게 될 부스

지문 후반부에 부스가 입구 바로 건너편에 위치해 있어서 문을 통해 들어와서 곧장 걸어오면 된다(Our booth will be located ~ after you pass through the gates.)고 했다. 또한 부스가 기념품점 바로 옆의 좋은 위치에 있다(It's a great spot, right next to the gift shop)고도 했다. 지도를 보면 입구 바로 건너편에 있으면서 기념품점 옆은 부스 B를 가리키므로 정답은 (B)이다.

98-100 회의 발췌 + 차트

M-Au Hello. I called this meeting to discuss the new membership level our fitness center is offering. As you can see on this chart, among our now four levels, [98]**this new level has the highest membership fee with no joining fee.** Each member who signs up for it is eligible to take group classes, use our saunas, and receive two free personal training sessions. And [99]**upon registration, we're handing out free towels featuring our fitness club logo.** The towels will be on display near the front water cooler. All right, [100]**I'm going to pass out some handouts now which highlight the benefits of this new level in more detail.** Please take a look.

안녕하세요. 우리 피트니스 센터가 제공하는 새로운 회원제 등급에 대해 말씀드리기 위해 회의를 소집했습니다. 차트에서 보시는 바와 같이 현재 네 등급 중 **이 새로운 등급은 가입비 없이 회비가 가장 비쌉니다.** 그 등급을 신청하시는 모든 회원들께는 단체 수업 등록, 사우나 이용, 두 번의 무료 개인 트레이닝을 받을 자격이 주어집니다. 그리고 **등록하면 우리 피트니스 센터 로고가 새겨진 무료 수건을 나눠 드립니다.** 수건은 앞쪽의 정수기 가까이 비치해 놓을 것입니다. 자, **이제 새 등급의 혜택을 더 자세히 강조한 인쇄물을 나눠 드릴 겁니다.** 한번 보세요.

어휘 call a meeting 회의를 소집하다 membership fee 회비 joining fee 가입비 sign up for ~에 등록하다 be eligible to + 동사원형 ~할 자격이 있다 hand out 나눠주다 pass out 배부하다 handout 인쇄물 highlight 강조하다 benefit 혜택 in more detail 더욱 자세하게

	Silver Membership	Titanium Membership	Gold Membership	98 Platinum Membership
Joining Fee	O	O	X	X
Membership Fee	$30	$45	$75	$100

	실버 회원	티타늄 회원	골드 회원	플래티넘 회원
가입비	O	O	X	X
회비	30달러	45달러	75달러	100달러

98

Look at the graphic. Which membership level did the fitness center recently add?

(A) Silver
(B) Titanium
(C) Gold
(D) Platinum

시각 정보에 의하면, 피트니스 센터는 최근에 어느 회원 등급을 추가했는가?

(A) 실버
(B) 티타늄
(C) 골드
(D) 플래티넘

해설 시각 정보 연계 - 최근에 추가한 회원 등급

지문 초반부에 화자가 새로 생긴 등급은 가입비 없이 회비가 가장 높다(this new level has the highest membership fee with no joining fee.)고 했다. 그리고 차트를 보면 플래티넘(Platinum) 등급이 가입비(Joining Fee) 없이 회비(Membership Fee)가 100달러로 가장 비싸므로 정답은 (D)이다.

99

What item will be given to new members?

(A) A T-shirt
(B) A bag
(C) A towel
(D) A water bottle

신규 회원들에게 어떤 물품이 지급될 것인가?

(A) 티셔츠
(B) 가방
(C) 수건
(D) 물병

해설 세부 사항 관련 - 신규 회원들에게 지급되는 물건

지문 중반부에 등록을 하면 피트니스 클럽 로고가 새겨진 무료 수건을 나눠 준다(upon registration, we're handing out free towels featuring our fitness club logo.)고 했으므로 정답은 (C)이다.

100

What will the speaker most likely do next?

(A) Distribute some documents
(B) Reveal a proposed logo
(C) Introduce a personal trainer
(D) Give an equipment demonstration

화자는 다음에 무엇을 하겠는가?

(A) 서류 배부
(B) 제안된 로고 공개
(C) 개인 트레이너 소개
(D) 장비 사용법 설명

어휘 distribute 배포하다 reveal 밝히다, 공개하다 equipment 장비

해설 세부 사항 관련 - 화자의 다음 행동

지문 후반부에 화자가 청자들에게 이제 새 등급의 혜택을 더 자세히 알려드리는 인쇄물을 배부하겠다(I'm going to pass out some handouts now which highlight the benefits of this new level in more detail.)고 했으므로 정답은 (A)이다.

▸▸ **Paraphrasing** 지문의 pass out some handouts
→ 정답의 distribute some documents

TEST 5

1 (D)	2 (C)	3 (C)	4 (A)	5 (A)
6 (D)	7 (A)	8 (B)	9 (A)	10 (C)
11 (B)	12 (B)	13 (B)	14 (C)	15 (A)
16 (C)	17 (A)	18 (C)	19 (A)	20 (A)
21 (B)	22 (A)	23 (B)	24 (C)	25 (C)
26 (C)	27 (C)	28 (A)	29 (B)	30 (C)
31 (C)	32 (C)	33 (A)	34 (B)	35 (B)
36 (B)	37 (C)	38 (D)	39 (A)	40 (D)
41 (C)	42 (D)	43 (C)	44 (A)	45 (C)
46 (D)	47 (B)	48 (A)	49 (C)	50 (A)
51 (A)	52 (B)	53 (C)	54 (D)	55 (B)
56 (C)	57 (B)	58 (B)	59 (B)	60 (A)
61 (D)	62 (C)	63 (C)	64 (B)	65 (A)
66 (A)	67 (D)	68 (B)	69 (A)	70 (A)
71 (A)	72 (B)	73 (B)	74 (D)	75 (A)
76 (C)	77 (B)	78 (D)	79 (C)	80 (D)
81 (D)	82 (B)	83 (C)	84 (C)	85 (A)
86 (D)	87 (C)	88 (B)	89 (B)	90 (B)
91 (B)	92 (A)	93 (D)	94 (D)	95 (C)
96 (D)	97 (A)	98 (C)	99 (A)	100 (A)

PART 1

1 M-Cn

(A) She's leaning on a counter.
(B) She's reaching for a telephone.
(C) She's putting files into a folder.
(D) She's operating a desktop computer.

(A) 여자가 카운터에 기대어 있다.
(B) 여자가 전화기에 손을 뻗고 있다.
(C) 여자가 서류철에 파일을 넣고 있다.
(D) 여자가 데스크톱 컴퓨터를 사용하고 있다.

어휘 lean on ~에 기대다 reach for ~을 잡으려고 손을 뻗다 operate 조작하다, 작동하다

해설 1인 등장 사진 - 사람의 동작 묘사

(A) 여자가 몸을 카운터에 기대고 있는(is leaning on a counter) 모습이 아니므로 오답.

(B) 사진에 전화기가 보이지만 여자가 전화기 쪽으로 손을 뻗고 있는(is reaching for a telephone) 모습이 아니므로 오답.

(C) 여자가 파일을 서류철에 넣고 있는(is putting files into a folder) 모습이 아니므로 오답.

(D) 여자가 책상에 앉아 데스크톱 컴퓨터를 사용하고 있는(is operating a desktop computer) 모습이므로 정답.

2 W-Am

(A) He's walking along a hallway.
(B) He's unzipping his jacket.
(C) He's holding onto a handrail.
(D) He's climbing some stairs.

(A) 남자가 복도를 따라 걷고 있다.
(B) 남자가 재킷의 지퍼를 열고 있다.
(C) 남자가 난간을 잡고 있다.
(D) 남자가 계단을 오르고 있다.

어휘 hallway 복도 unzip 지퍼를 열다 handrail 난간 climb 오르다 stairs 계단

해설 1인 등장 사진 - 사람의 동작 묘사

(A) 사진에 복도(hallway)가 보이지 않으므로 오답.

(B) 남자가 재킷의 지퍼를 열고 있는(is unzipping his jacket) 모습이 아니므로 오답.

(C) 남자가 한 손으로 난간을 잡고 있는(is holding onto a handrail) 모습이므로 정답.

(D) 남자가 계단을 오르고 있는(is climbing some stairs) 모습이 아니므로 오답.

3 M-Au

(A) Customers are paying for their purchases.
(B) A woman is searching in her purse.
(C) The door of a laundry machine has been opened.
(D) Clothing has been piled in a shopping cart.

(A) 고객들이 구입한 물건들의 값을 치르고 있다.
(B) 여자가 핸드백 안을 찾아보고 있다.
(C) 세탁기 문이 열려 있다.
(D) 옷이 쇼핑 카트 안에 쌓여 있다.

어휘 customer 고객 purchase 구매품; 구매하다 search 찾아보다 purse 핸드백, 지갑 laundry machine 세탁기 pile 쌓다, 포개다

해설 2인 이상 등장 사진 - 사람 또는 사물 중심 묘사

(A) 구입한 물건들의 값을 치르고 있는(are paying for their purchases) 사람은 없으므로 오답.

(B) 여자가 세탁기 안을 살펴보고 있는 중이지 핸드백 안을 찾아보고 있는(is searching in her purse) 모습이 아니므로 오답.

(C) 세탁기 문이 열려 있는(has been opened) 상태이므로 정답.

(D) 사진에 옷이 보이지만 쇼핑 카트 안에 쌓여 있는(has been piled in a shopping cart) 상태가 아니므로 오답.

4 W-Am

(A) They're carrying out some building maintenance.
(B) They're replacing the tires of a truck.
(C) A message is being painted on a window.
(D) Some ladders have been set up on the roof.

(A) 사람들이 건물을 보수하고 있다.
(B) 사람들이 트럭의 바퀴를 교체하고 있다.
(C) 창문에 메시지가 칠해지고 있다.
(D) 사다리 몇 개가 지붕 위에 세워져 있다.

어휘 carry out 실시하다, 시행하다 building maintenance 건물 정비, 건물 유지보수 replace 교체하다 ladder 사다리 set up 세우다 roof 지붕

해설 2인 이상 등장 사진 – 사람 또는 사물 중심 묘사

(A) 두 사람이 건물 정비 작업을 하고 있는(are carrying out some building maintenance) 모습이므로 정답.
(B) 사진에 트럭의 바퀴가 보이지만 두 사람이 바퀴를 교체하고 있지는(are replacing the tires of a truck) 않으므로 오답.
(C) 사진에 메시지가 보이지만 두 사람이 창문에 칠하고 있는(is being painted on a window) 모습은 아니므로 오답.
(D) 사다리들이 벽에 기대어 있는 상태이지 지붕 위에 세워져 있지는(have been set up on the roof) 않으므로 오답.

5 M-Au

(A) A customer is being served.
(B) A woman is washing her hands in a sink.
(C) Bottles are being placed in a cabinet.
(D) Some mirrors are packed in boxes.

(A) 고객이 관리를 받고 있다.
(B) 여자가 싱크대에서 손을 씻고 있다.
(C) 수납장 안에 병이 놓여지고 있다.
(D) 몇 개의 거울이 상자에 포장되어 있다.

어휘 cabinet 수납장 pack 싸다, 포장하다

해설 2인 이상 등장 사진 – 사람 또는 사물 중심 묘사

(A) 고객이 관리를 받고 있는(is being served) 모습이므로 정답.
(B) 여자가 싱크대에서 손을 씻고 있는(is washing her hands in a sink) 모습이 아니므로 오답.
(C) 수납장 안에 병이 놓여지고 (are being placed in a cabinet) 모습이 아니므로 오답.
(D) 사진에 거울은 보이지만 상자에 포장되어 있는(are packed in boxes) 모습이 아니므로 오답.

6 W-Br

(A) Cars have been parked along a road.
(B) A statue has been installed on a bridge.
(C) The sides of a river are lined with trees.
(D) Some park benches are empty.

(A) 차들이 길을 따라 주차되어 있다.
(B) 조각상이 다리 위에 설치되어 있다.
(C) 강의 양쪽으로 나무들이 줄지어 서 있다.
(D) 공원 벤치들이 비어 있다.

어휘 statue 조각상 install 설치하다 be lined with ~가 줄지어 있다 empty 비어 있는

해설 실외 사물/배경 묘사 사진 – 다양한 사물의 위치 묘사

(A) 사진에 차들(cars)이 보이지 않으므로 오답.
(B) 조각상이 공원에 설치되어 있지 다리 위에 설치되어 있는(has been installed on a bridge) 모습이 아니므로 오답.
(C) 사진에 강(river)이 보이지 않으므로 오답.
(D) 공원 벤치들이 비어 있는(are empty) 모습이므로 정답.

Test 5

PART 2

7

M-Cn When is the meeting with the client?

W-Am (A) At three o'clock.

(B) No, I don't think so.

(C) Because Adam is out of the office.

고객과의 회의가 언제인가요?

(A) 3시예요.

(B) 아뇨, 그렇게 생각하지 않아요.

(C) 애덤이 사무실을 비워서요.

어휘 client 고객

해설 회의 시간을 묻는 When 의문문

(A) 정답. 고객과의 회의가 언제인지를 묻는 질문에 3시(at three o'clock)라는 구체적인 시점으로 응답하고 있으므로 정답.

(B) Yes/No 불가 오답. 시점을 묻는 When 의문문에 Yes/No 응답이 불가능하기 때문에 오답.

(C) 질문과 상관없는 오답. 이유를 묻는 Why 의문문에 어울리는 응답이므로 오답.

8

W-Br Who's today's guest speaker?

M-Au (A) No, I couldn't see him.

(B) It's Ms. Paek.

(C) Right after lunch.

오늘 초청 연사는 누구인가요?

(A) 아니요, 그를 볼 수 없었어요.

(B) 백 씨예요.

(C) 점심 직후에요.

어휘 guest speaker 초청 연사

해설 초청 연사를 묻는 Who 의문문

(A) Yes/No 불가 오답. 인물을 묻는 Who 의문문에 Yes/No 응답이 불가능하기 때문에 오답.

(B) 정답. 오늘의 초청 연사(today's guest speaker)가 누구인지를 묻는 질문에 백 씨(Ms. Paek)라는 구체적인 인물로 응답하고 있으므로 정답.

(C) 질문과 상관없는 오답. 시점을 묻는 When 의문문에 어울리는 응답이므로 오답.

9

W-Am How would you like to pay for this?

M-Cn (A) With cash, please.

(B) Thanks, I appreciate it.

(C) Employees are paid monthly.

이것을 어떻게 지불하고 싶으세요?

(A) 현찰로요.

(B) 고맙습니다, 감사해요.

(C) 직원들은 월급으로 받습니다.

어휘 How would you like to+동사원형 ~? 어떻게 ~하고 싶으세요? with cash 현금으로 appreciate 고마워하다

해설 지불 방법을 묻는 How 의문문

(A) 정답. 어떻게 지불할 것인지에 대해 현금(with cash)이라는 구체적인 지불 수단을 언급하고 있으므로 정답.

(B) 질문과 상관없는 오답. 상대가 호의를 베풀었을 때 어울리는 응답이므로 오답.

(C) 단어 반복 오답. 질문의 pay를 과거분사형으로 바꿔 반복 이용한 오답.

10

W-Br How do I open this window?

M-Au (A) Oh, you can throw that away.

(B) Since the grand opening celebration.

(C) Push it up from the bottom.

이 창문은 어떻게 열죠?

(A) 아, 그거 버리시면 돼요.

(B) 개점 축하 행사 때부터요.

(C) 밑에서 밀어 올리세요.

어휘 grand opening 개점 celebration 축하 행사 bottom 밑, 바닥

해설 창문 여는 방법에 대한 How 의문문

(A) 질문과 상관없는 오답. 창문을 여는 방법을 묻는 질문에 그걸 버리면 된다(can throw that away)는 대답은 질문의 맥락에서 벗어난 응답이므로 오답.

(B) 파생어 오답. 질문의 open과 파생어 관계에 있는 opening을 이용한 오답.

(C) 정답. 창문을 어떻게 여는지 묻는 질문에 밑에서부터 밀어 올리라(Push it up from the bottom.)는 구체적인 방법을 알려 주고 있으므로 정답.

11

M-Cn Is the sales workshop today or tomorrow?

W-Am (A) The whole department.

(B) Actually, it's Tuesday.

(C) OK, I'll see you there.

영업 워크숍이 오늘인가요, 내일인가요?

(A) 부서 전체요.

(B) 실은 화요일이에요.

(C) 좋아요, 거기서 보죠.

어휘 department 부서 actually 사실은

해설 단어를 연결한 선택의문문

(A) 연상 단어 오답. 질문의 sales에서 연상 가능한 department를 이용한 오답.

(B) 정답. 워크숍이 오늘인지 내일인지를 묻는 질문에 오늘과 내일이 아니라 화요일(Tuesday)이라는 제3의 답변으로 응답하고 있으므로 정답.

(C) 질문과 상관없는 오답. 워크숍이 오늘인지 내일인지를 묻는 질문에 거기서 보자(see you there)는 대답은 질문의 맥락에서 벗어난 응답이므로 오답.

12

M-Au I need to buy a new mobile phone.

W-Br (A) At least fifty years old.

(B) Didn't you just get your current one?

(C) That's my extension number.

새로운 휴대폰을 사야 해요.

(A) 적어도 50세예요.

(B) 현재 사용 중인 걸 최근에 사지 않았나요?

(C) 그게 제 내선번호예요.

어휘 mobile phone 휴대폰 current 현재의 extension number 내선번호

해설 평서문

(A) 연상 단어 오답. 질문의 new에서 연상 가능한 old를 이용한 오답.

(B) 정답. 현재 사용 중인 걸 최근에 사지 않았는지(just get your current one) 물으며 놀라움을 나타내고 있으므로 정답.

(C) 연상 단어 오답. 질문의 phone에서 연상 가능한 extension number를 이용한 오답.

13

W-Am The train is going to be late because of heavy snow.

M-Cn (A) Let's weigh it now.

(B) When will it get here?

(C) The training was last week.

폭설 때문에 열차가 늦을 거예요.

(A) 지금 무게를 재 봅시다.

(B) 언제 이곳에 도착할까요?

(C) 교육은 지난주였어요.

어휘 heavy snow 폭설 weigh ~의 무게를 재다 training 훈련, 교육

해설 정보 제공의 평서문

(A) 연상 단어 오답. 기차의 연착에 대해 weigh를 wait로 잘못 들었을 때 기다리자는 의미로 이해하도록 유도한 오답.

(B) 정답. 폭설로(because of heavy snow) 기차가 연착할 것이라는 말에 대해 그럼 언제 도착할 것인지(When will it get here?) 되묻고 있으므로 정답.

(C) 유사 발음 오답. 질문의 train과 유사한 발음을 가진 training을 이용한 오답.

14

M-Cn Why don't you apply for travel insurance?

W-Am (A) The supplies by the entrance.

(B) To Hawaii, on vacation.

(C) That's not a bad suggestion.

여행자 보험에 가입하는 게 어때요?

(A) 출입구 옆의 자재요.

(B) 휴가차 하와이에요.

(C) 괜찮은 제안이군요.

어휘 Why don't you ~? ~하는 게 어때요? apply for ~을 신청하다, ~에 지원하다 insurance 보험 supply 자재 suggestion 제안

해설 보험 가입을 권하는 제안 의문문

(A) 질문과 상관없는 오답. 여행자 보험 가입을 제안하는 질문에 출입구 옆의 자재라는 대답은 질문의 맥락에서 벗어난 응답이므로 오답.

(B) 연상 단어 오답. 질문의 travel에서 연상 가능한 vacation을 이용한 오답.

(C) 정답. 보험 가입을 제의하는 질문에 괜찮은 제안(That's not a bad suggestion.)이라는 긍정적 표현으로 응답하고 있으므로 정답.

15

M-Au Where are the previous versions of these documents?

W-Br (A) I saved them on my computer.

(B) Which division is the largest?

(C) No, they're market research reports.

이 문서들의 이전 버전이 어디에 있지요?

(A) 제 컴퓨터에 저장해 뒀어요.

(B) 어느 부서가 가장 큰가요?

(C) 아니요, 그것들은 시장 조사 보고서입니다.

어휘 previous 이전의 save 저장하다 division 부서 report 보고서

해설 문서의 위치를 묻는 Where 의문문

(A) 정답. 문서들의 이전 버전이 어디에 있는지에 대해 컴퓨터에 저장해 두었다(saved them on my computer)는 말로 문서가 있는 구체적인 위치를 언급하고 있으므로 정답.

(B) 질문과 상관없는 오답. 문서들의 이전 버전이 어디에 있는지를 묻는 질문에 어느 부서가 가장 큰지를 묻고 있어 질문의 맥락에서 벗어났으므로 오답.

(C) Yes/No 불가 오답. 위치를 묻는 Where 의문문에 Yes/No 응답이 불가능하기 때문에 오답.

16

M-Cn Who left this letter on my desk?

W-Am (A) I edit those newsletters.

(B) No, a laptop computer.

(C) Probably the mail carrier.

누가 이 편지를 제 책상에 놔두었죠?

(A) 제가 그 소식지를 편집해요.

(B) 아니요, 노트북 컴퓨터요.

(C) 아마 집배원이겠죠.

어휘 leave 놔두다 newsletter 소식지 probably 아마, 십중팔구 mail carrier (우편) 집배원

해설 편지를 놔둔 사람을 묻는 Who 의문문

(A) 유사 발음 오답. 질문의 letter와 부분적으로 발음이 동일한 newsletters를 반복 이용한 오답.

(B) 연상 단어 오답. 질문의 desk에서 연상 가능한 laptop computer를 이용한 오답.

(C) 정답. 누가 편지를 책상 위에 놔뒀는지에 대해 집배원(mail carrier)이라는 구체적인 인물로 응답하고 있으므로 정답.

17

M-Au There's an umbrella on the floor in the waiting room.

W-Br (A) I'll put it in the lost and found.

(B) We're replacing it with carpet.

(C) My appointment at noon.

대기실 바닥에 우산이 있어요.

(A) 제가 분실물 보관소에 둘게요.

(B) 저희가 그것을 카펫으로 교체하고 있습니다.

(C) 정오의 제 약속이요.

어휘 floor 바닥 waiting room 대기실 lost and found 분실물 보관소 replace 교체하다 appointment 약속, 예약

해설 사실/정보 전달의 평서문

(A) 정답. 대기실(the waiting room)에 우산이 있다는 말에 분실물 보관소(the lost and found)에 두겠다는 응답을 하고 있으므로 정답.

(B) 연상 단어 오답. 질문의 floor에서 연상 가능한 carpet을 이용한 오답.

(C) 연상 단어 오답. 질문의 waiting room에서 연상 가능한 appointment를 이용한 오답.

18

M-Au Would you mind if I took a short break?

M-Cn (A) Sure, I'd love to.

(B) The repair manual.

(C) Not at all.

잠깐 쉬어도 될까요?

(A) 물론이죠, 그러고 싶어요.

(B) 수리 매뉴얼요.

(C) 그럼요.

어휘 mind 꺼리다 take a short break 잠깐 쉬다

해설 부탁/요청의 의문문

(A) 질문과 상관없는 오답. 잠깐 쉬어도 되는지 묻는 질문에 그러고 싶다(I'd love to)고 대답하는 것은 질문의 맥락에서 벗어난 응답이므로 오답.

(B) 연상 단어 오답. 질문의 break가 가진 다른 뜻(깨뜨리다)에서 연상 가능한 repair를 이용한 오답.

(C) 정답. 잠깐 쉬는 것을 꺼리는지에 대해 전혀 꺼리지 않는다(Not at all.)는 긍정적 응답을 하고 있으므로 정답.

19

M-Cn When can I announce that I'm transferring to the Milan branch?

W-Br (A) We're finalizing the paperwork now.

(B) How much money would he send?

(C) Through an official company memo.

제가 밀라노 지사로 전근을 간다는 걸 언제 알려도 되나요?

(A) 지금 서류 작업을 마무리하고 있습니다.

(B) 그가 돈을 얼마나 보낼까요?

(C) 회사 공식 메모를 통해서요.

어휘 announce 알리다, 공표하다 transfer 옮기다 branch 지점, 지사 finalize 마무리하다 paperwork 서류 작업 official 공식적인

해설 전근 발표 시점을 묻는 When 의문문

(A) 정답. 전근을 언제 알릴 수 있는지 묻는 질문에 서류 작업을 마무리하는 중(finalizing the paperwork now)이라는 불확실성 표현으로 응답하고 있으므로 정답.

(B) 연상 단어 오답. 질문의 transferring에서 연상 가능한 money를 이용한 오답.

(C) 질문과 상관없는 오답. 방법을 묻는 How 의문문에 어울리는 응답이므로 오답.

20

W-Am Should these brochures be done in color or black-and-white?

W-Br (A) I'll need them in color.

(B) Yes, and fold each one twice.

(C) There's an exhibition at the art museum.

이 소책자들을 컬러로 인쇄할까요, 흑백으로 인쇄할까요?

(A) 컬러본으로 필요해요.

(B) 네, 그리고 각각 두 번씩 접으세요.

(C) 미술관에서 전시회가 있어요.

어휘 brochure 소책자, 브로슈어 in black-and-white 흑백으로 fold 접다 exhibition 전시회 art museum 미술관

해설 구를 연결한 선택의문문

(A) 정답. 질문에서 인쇄 방법으로 제시된 컬러와 흑백, 두 가지 선택 사항 중에 컬러(in color)를 선택하고 있으므로 정답.

(B) 연상 단어 오답. 질문의 brochure에서 연상 가능한 fold를 이용한 오답.

(C) 연상 단어 오답. 질문의 in color or black-and-white에서 연상 가능한 art를 이용한 오답.

21

M-Au Was Vanessa's presentation on accounting interesting?

W-Am (A) Presents for the clients.

(B) That's what most people are saying.

(C) The professional conference in Hong Kong.

바네사 씨의 회계 관련 발표는 흥미로웠나요?

(A) 고객들을 위한 선물입니다.

(B) 사람들이 대부분 그렇게 얘기해요.

(C) 홍콩에서 열리는 전문가 회의요.

어휘 presentation 발표 accounting 회계 professional 전문적인; 전문가 conference 회의

해설 발표의 흥미 여부를 묻는 Be동사 Yes/No 의문문

(A) 유사 발음 오답. 질문의 presentation과 부분적으로 발음이 동일한 presents를 이용한 오답.

(B) 정답. 바네사 씨의 회계 관련 발표(presentation on accounting)가 흥미로웠는지 묻는 질문에 Yes를 생략하고 사람들이 대부분 그렇게 얘기한다(That's what most people are saying.)는 긍정적인 응답을 하고 있으므로 정답.

(C) 연상 단어 오답. 질문의 presentation에서 연상 가능한 conference를 이용한 오답.

22

M-Cn This is your coat, isn't it?

W-Br (A) Oh, thank you!

(B) Yes, the fresh paint.

(C) Maybe later, if there's time.

이것은 당신의 코트죠, 아닌가요?

(A) 오, 고마워요!

(B) 네, 새 페인트요.

(C) 시간이 있으면 나중에요.

어휘 paint 페인트, 물감

해설 코트 주인을 확인하는 부가의문문

(A) 정답. 코트의 주인을 확인하는 질문에 Yes라는 긍정적 대답을 생략한 채 고맙다(thank you)는 말로 자신의 것이 맞다는 응답을 하므로 정답.

(B) 연상 단어 오답. 질문의 coat를 '칠'로 잘못 이해했을 때 연상 가능한 paint를 이용한 오답.

(C) 질문과 상관없는 오답. 시점을 묻는 의문문에 대한 응답이므로 오답.

23

W-Am Why haven't you signed the lease agreement?

M-Au (A) Yes, I'm in agreement with his report.

(B) I still believe we can find a better property.

(C) An electronic image of my signature.

왜 임대 계약을 체결하지 않았나요?

(A) 네, 저는 그의 보고서에 동의합니다.

(B) 아직 더 나은 건물을 찾을 수 있다고 확신하거든요.

(C) 제 전자 서명입니다.

어휘 sign an agreement 계약을 체결하다 lease 임대, 대여 in agreement with ~와 일치하여, ~에 동의하여 property 재산, 부동산, 건물 electronic 전자의 signature 서명

해설 체결 거절 이유를 묻는 Why 의문문

(A) Yes/No 불가 오답. Why 의문문에 Yes/No 응답이 불가능하므로 오답.

(B) 정답. 임대 계약(the lease agreement)을 체결하지 않은 이유를 묻는 질문에 더 나은 건물을 찾을 수 있다(we can find a better property)고 생각한다는 구체적인 이유를 제시하고 있으므로 정답.

(C) 파생어 오답. 질문의 signed와 파생어 관계인 signature를 이용한 오답.

24

W-Br What's the password to this file?

M-Cn (A) Just a little past the bus stop.

(B) File it in the "Expenses" folder.

(C) It's written down somewhere.

이 파일의 비밀번호가 뭐지요?

(A) 버스 정류장을 조금만 더 지나서요.

(B) '비용' 폴더 안에 철해 두세요.

(C) 어딘가에 적혀 있어요.

어휘 file (컴퓨터) 파일; (서류를) 철하다 past ~을 지나서 expense 비용

해설 비밀번호를 묻는 What 의문문

(A) 유사 발음 오답. 질문의 password와 부분적으로 발음이 유사한 past를 이용한 오답.

(B) 단어 반복 오답. 질문의 file을 반복 이용한 오답.

(C) 정답. 비밀번호가 어디에 있는지에 대해 어딘가에 적혀 있다(written down somewhere)는 불확실성 표현으로 응답하고 있으므로 정답.

25

W-Am Do you think the cafeteria is open yet?

M-Cn (A) The updated menu online.

(B) Please close the door when you get out.

(C) It is supposed to start serving at nine.

구내 식당이 이미 열었을 거라 생각해요?

(A) 업데이트된 온라인 메뉴요.

(B) 나갈 때 문을 닫아 주세요.

(C) 9시에는 문을 열기로 되어 있어요.

어휘 cafeteria 구내 식당 be supposed to+동사원형 ~하기로 되어 있다 serve (식당 등에서 음식을) 제공하다

해설 구내 식당이 열렸을지 생각을 묻는 간접의문문

(A) 연상 단어 오답. 질문의 cafeteria에서 연상 가능한 menu를 이용한 오답.

(B) 연상 단어 오답. 질문의 open에서 연상 가능한 close를 이용한 오답.

(C) 정답. 구내 식당(cafeteria)이 문을 열었는지에 대해 확답을 피한 채 9시에는 열기로 되어 있다(It is supposed to start serving at nine.)는 말로 영업 시간에 대한 정보를 제공하고 있으므로 정답.

26

M-Au Haven't you already met Ms. Brown?

W-Br (A) Meeting Room B.

(B) A few minutes later.

(C) Yes, at the seminar in June.

브라운 씨를 벌써 만나지 않았나요?

(A) B 회의실요.

(B) 몇 분 후요.

(C) 예, 6월에 세미나에서요.

어휘 already (부정문) 벌써, 이미

해설 만남 여부를 확인하는 부정의문문

(A) 파생어 오답. 질문의 met를 명사로 바꿔 이용한 오답.

(B) 질문과 상관없는 오답. 시점을 묻는 When 의문문에 어울리는 응답이므로 오답.

(C) 정답. 브라운 씨를 벌써 만난 것은 아닌지에 대해 먼저 Yes로 긍정적 응답을 한 후, 6월에 세미나에서(at the seminar in June) 만났다는 구체적인 시점과 장소를 언급하고 있으므로 정답.

27

M-Cn Why are the lights still on in the lab?

W-Am (A) The electric bill for next month.

(B) Sometime earlier in the evening.

(C) Sorry, I forgot to turn them off.

왜 실험실 안의 불이 아직도 켜져 있죠?

(A) 다음 달 전기요금 고지서요.

(B) 아까 저녁쯤이요.

(C) 미안해요, 끄는 걸 잊었어요.

어휘 be on 켜져 있다 lab 실험실 electric bill 전기요금 고지서

해설 조명이 켜진 이유를 묻는 Why 의문문

(A) 연상 단어 오답. 질문의 lights에서 연상 가능한 electric을 이용한 오답.

(B) 질문과 상관없는 오답. 시점을 묻는 의문문에 대한 응답이므로 오답.

(C) 정답. 불이 왜 아직도 켜져 있는지에 대해 먼저 Sorry로 죄송함을 나타낸 후, 끄는 것을 잊어버렸다(I forgot to turn them off)는 구체적인 이유를 언급하고 있으므로 정답.

28

W-Br Which candidates do you want to invite for an interview?

M-Au (A) Let me see that first résumé again.

(B) To discuss the receptionist position.

(C) I'm usually free on Wednesday mornings.

인터뷰에 어떤 지원자를 부르고 싶으세요?

(A) 첫 번째 이력서를 다시 한 번 봅시다.

(B) 접수원직에 대해 논의하기 위해서요.

(C) 저는 보통 수요일 오전에 다른 일이 없습니다.

어휘 candidate 지원자, 후보자 résumé 이력서 receptionist 접수원 usually 대개 free 다른 계획(약속)이 없는

해설 인터뷰할 지원자를 묻는 Which 의문문

(A) 정답. 어떤 지원자를 인터뷰할지 묻는 질문에 첫 번째 이력서를 다시 보자(Let me see that first résumé again.)는 우회적 표현으로 응답하고 있으므로 정답.

(B) 연상 단어 오답. 질문의 candidates에서 연상 가능한 receptionist position을 이용한 오답.

(C) 질문과 상관없는 오답. When 의문문에 어울리는 응답이므로 오답.

29

W-Br Do you want Indian food, or should we try somewhere new?

M-Cn (A) They already tried that.

(B) I don't have a preference.

(C) Ask the server what he recommends.

인도 음식을 드실래요, 아니면 새로운 곳에 가 보실래요?

(A) 그들은 그걸 벌써 해봤어요.

(B) 저는 뭐든 좋아요.

(C) 웨이터가 뭘 추천하는지 물어봐요.

어휘 somewhere new 어딘가 새로운 곳 preference 선호하는 것 server 웨이터 recommend 추천하다

해설 문장을 연결한 선택의문문

(A) 질문과 상관없는 오답. They가 가리키는 대상이 질문에 없으므로 오답.

(B) 정답. 인도 음식을 먹고 싶은지, 아니면 새로운 곳(somewhere new)으로 갈지에 대해 뭐든 좋다(don't have a preference)고 응답하고 있으므로 정답.

(C) 질문과 상관없는 오답. 음식점을 정한 후 메뉴판에서 음식을 정할 때 할 수 있는 말이므로 오답.

30

M-Au You'll e-mail us copies of the handouts, won't you?

W-Am (A) The copy machine is down right now.

(B) All the meals will be provided.

(C) If you give me your e-mail addresses.

그 유인물 사본을 우리에게 이메일로 보내 주실 거죠, 아닌가요?

(A) 복사기가 현재 다운됐어요.

(B) 모든 식사가 제공될 거예요.

(C) 제게 이메일 주소를 알려 주시면요.

어휘 copy 사본 handout 유인물 meal 식사, 끼니

해설 유인물의 이메일 전송에 대한 부가의문문

(A) 질문과 상관없는 오답. 유인물을 이메일로 보내 줄 것인지에 대해 복사기가 현재 고장 났다는 대답은 질문의 맥락에서 벗어난 응답이므로 오답.

(B) 유사 발음 오답. 질문의 e-mail과 부분적으로 발음이 유사한 meals를 이용한 오답.

(C) 정답. 유인물을 이메일로 보내 줄 것인지에 대해 이메일 주소(your e-mail addresses)를 알려 주면 보내 주겠다는 조건을 제시하고 있으므로 정답.

31

W-Am Did you hear that Dylan's speech won third place?

M-Au (A) Noise from the traffic downstairs.

(B) September third of last year.

(C) Was it the one about leadership?

딜런의 연설이 3등을 차지했다는 소식 들었나요?

(A) 아래층의 차량으로 인한 소음요.

(B) 지난해 9월 3일요.

(C) 리더십에 관한 연설 말인가요?

어휘 speech 연설 win third place 3등을 하다 noise 소음 traffic 차량들 leadership 지도력, 리더십

해설 조동사(do) Yes/No 의문문

(A) 연상 단어 오답. 질문의 hear에서 연상 가능한 noise를 이용한 오답.

(B) 단어 반복 오답. 질문의 third를 반복 이용한 오답.

(C) 정답. 딜런의 연설(Dylan's speech)이 3등을 했다는 소식을 들었는지에 대해 긍정, 부정의 답변을 생략한 채 리더십에 관한 그 연설이 맞는지 되묻고 있으므로 정답.

PART 3

32-34

W-Am Hello. [32]**I'd like a ticket for the express bus to Copenhagen,** please.

M-Au Do you have a transit pass? They're accepted everywhere in Denmark now. You can also use your, uh, credit card, provided it's from a domestic bank.

W-Am Well, [33]**I don't have an account here, so that won't work.** But I'll be staying here for a while. Now that I think about it, a transit pass would be useful.

M-Au Great. [34]**You'll have to buy it from one of the vending machines at the entrance to the platform,** though. We don't sell passes here at the ticket windows anymore.

여: 안녕하세요. **코펜하겐으로 가는 고속버스 표 한 장 주세요.**
남: 교통카드를 가지고 계신가요? 현재 덴마크 전역에서 받아줍니다. 또 국내 은행에서 발행한 것이면, 음, 신용카드도 사용하실 수 있어요.
여: 음, **저는 이곳에 계좌가 없어서 안 될 거예요.** 하지만 당분간 여기 머물 예정이거든요. 다시 생각해 보니 교통카드가 유용하겠네요.
남: 네. 하지만 **승강장 입구에 있는 자동발매기에서 구입하셔야 할 거예요.** 여기 매표소에서는 더 이상 교통카드를 팔지 않습니다.

어휘 I'd like ~ 주세요 transit pass 교통카드 accept 받아주다, 수락[허용]하다 provided 만약 ~라면(= if) domestic 국내의 account 계좌 work (계획 등이) 잘 되어 가다 for a while 한동안, 당분간 now that ~이니까(= since) vending machine 자동발매기, 자판기 entrance 입구 platform 승강장, 플랫폼

32

Where is the conversation taking place?

(A) At a car rental agency
(B) At a train terminal
(C) At a bus station
(D) At an airport

어디에서 나누는 대화인가?

(A) 렌터카 업체
(B) 기차 터미널
(C) 버스 터미널
(D) 공항

해설 전체 내용 관련 – 대화의 장소
대화 맨 처음에 여자가 코펜하겐으로 가는 버스표 한 장을 달라(I'd like a bus ticket to Copenhagen)고 했다. 버스표를 구입할 수 있는 곳은 버스 터미널이므로 정답은 (C)이다.

33

Why is the woman unable to use her credit card?

(A) It is not from a local bank.
(B) She has lost it.
(C) Its credit limit is too low.
(D) It has been damaged.

여자가 자신의 신용카드를 사용하지 못하는 이유는?

(A) 현지 은행에서 발급된 것이 아니다.
(B) 카드를 잃어버렸다.
(C) 신용 한도가 너무 낮다.
(D) 손상되었다.

어휘 local 현지의 credit limit 신용 한도(액) damage 손상시키다

해설 세부 사항 관련 – 신용카드를 쓸 수 없는 이유
여자의 두 번째 대사에서 이곳에 계좌가 없어서 안 될 것(I don't have an account here, so that won't work.)이라고 했다. 즉, 덴마크 현지 은행을 이용하지 않아서 자신의 신용카드를 쓸 수 없다는 뜻이므로 정답은 (A)이다.

34

What will the woman probably do next?

(A) Exchange a ticket
(B) Locate a machine
(C) Buy a road map
(D) Make a phone call

여자는 다음에 무엇을 하겠는가?

(A) 승차권 교환
(B) 기계 위치 파악
(C) 도로 지도 구입
(D) 전화 통화

어휘 locate ~의 위치를 찾아내다

해설 세부 사항 관련 – 여자의 다음 행동
대화 맨 마지막에 남자가 여자에게 승강장 입구에 있는 자동발매기에서 교통카드를 구입해야 한다(You'll have to buy it from one of the vending machines at the entrance to the platform)고 했다. 따라서 여자는 승강장 입구로 가서 교통카드 발매기를 찾아볼 것이므로 정답은 (B)이다.

35-37

M-Cn [35]**I see that you presently work for Fun Hour Media. Could you please describe some of the key responsibilities of your position there?**

W-Br Certainly. [36]**I lead a team of six graphic designers and oversee the development of all digital artwork.** I make sure everything is completed according to specifications.

M-Cn OK. Now, if you were hired here at Anderton Communications Online, [37]**the team you'd lead in our news department works in a fast-paced environment. The job comes with a lot of demands.**

Test 5

W-Br That's not a problem. In my current role, I'm under considerable pressure to meet deadlines, and I consistently rise to the challenge.

남: **현재 펀 아워 미디어에서 근무하시는군요. 그곳에서 맡은 핵심 직무 몇 가지를 설명해 주시겠어요?**

여: 물론입니다. **그래픽 디자이너 6명으로 구성된 팀을 이끌고 모든 디지털 미술 작품의 개발을 감독하고 있습니다.** 모든 일이 세부 사항에 맞게 완료되도록 확인합니다.

남: 좋습니다. 이곳 앤더튼 커뮤니케이션즈 온라인에 채용되면 **우리 뉴스부에서 당신이 이끌게 될 팀은 업무 진행이 빠른 환경에서 일합니다. 이 일에는 힘든 점이 많아요.**

여: 문제 없습니다. 현재 제 역할에서도 저는 심한 압박을 받으며 마감 시한을 맞추고 있고 어려움에 꾸준히 잘 대처하고 있으니까요.

어휘 presently 현재, 지금 describe 설명하다, 서술[묘사]하다 key 핵심적인, 주요한 responsibility 책임 position 직위 lead a team 팀을 이끌다 oversee 감독하다 development 개발, 발전 make sure 확실히 하다 complete 완료하다, 완성하다 according to ~에 따라 specifications 세부 사항 hire 고용[채용]하다 fast-paced 업무 진행이 빠른[빨리 돌아가는] demands (어렵거나 힘든) 일, 요구(되는 일) under considerable pressure 심한 압박을 받는 meet deadlines 마감 시한을 맞추다 consistently 꾸준히, 일관되게 rise to the challenge 어려움[난관]에 잘 대처하다

35

Who most likely is the man?

(A) A production intern
(B) A human resources manager
(C) A business consultant
(D) A job applicant

남자는 누구겠는가?

(A) 생산부 인턴 사원
(B) 인사부장
(C) 사업 컨설턴트
(D) 구직자

해설 전체 내용 관련 - 남자의 신분

대화 맨 처음에 남자가 여자에게 현재 펀 아워 미디어에서 근무하고 있는데 그곳에서 맡은 핵심 직무 몇 가지를 설명해 달라(I see that you presently work for ~ your position there?)고 했다. 채용 면접 상황임을 알 수 있으며, 회사에서 면접을 담당하는 사람은 인사부장이므로 정답은 (B)이다.

36

What skill does the woman mention?

(A) Restoring antique art
(B) Supervising a team of people
(C) Analyzing survey results
(D) Recruiting staff from overseas

여자는 어떤 직무 기술을 언급하는가?

(A) 고미술품 복원
(B) 직원들로 이루어진 팀 관리
(C) 설문 결과 분석
(D) 해외 직원 모집

어휘 restore (예술 작품을) 복원하다 antique art 고미술품 supervise 감독하다 analyze 분석하다 recruit 채용하다

해설 세부 사항 관련 - 여자가 언급한 기술

여자의 첫 번째 대사에서 그래픽 디자이너 6명으로 구성된 팀을 이끌고 모든 디지털 미술 작품의 개발을 감독하고 있다(I lead a team ~ digital artwork.)고 했으므로 정답은 (B)이다.

▸▸ **Paraphrasing** 대화의 **lead a team of six graphic designers** → 정답의 **Supervising a team of people**

37

What does the man say about a job?

(A) It is well-paid.
(B) It is in a new department.
(C) It can be stressful.
(D) It may be done from home.

남자는 일에 관해 뭐라고 말하는가?

(A) 봉급이 많다.
(B) 새로운 부서에 있다.
(C) 스트레스가 심할 수 있다.
(D) 재택 근무로 일할 수 있다.

어휘 well-paid 급료가 좋은

해설 세부 사항 관련 - 일에 대한 남자의 언급

남자의 두 번째 대사에서 여자가 뉴스부에서 이끌게 될 팀은 업무 진행이 빠른 환경에서 근무를 하며 그런 업무에는 힘든 점이 많다(the team you'd lead in our ~ a lot of demands.)고 했다. 즉, 업무 스트레스가 심할 수도 있다는 말이므로 정답은 (C)이다.

38-40

W-Am Glen, could you help me? [38]**My account worked fine before my meeting this morning, but now I receive an error notification when I enter my password.**

M-Au Oh, the computer maintenance personnel visited the office during your meeting. They updated the software on each computer and restarted the system. In doing so, [39]**they accidentally deleted our passwords.**

W-Am I see. Well, is there a temporary password I can use to get in for now?

M-Au Yes, it's the name of the company written entirely in lowercase letters. And [40]**it's probably best to change it as soon as you can.**

여: 글렌, 저를 좀 도와 줄 수 있어요? **회의 전에 오늘 아침에는 내 계정이 괜찮았는데, 지금 제가 비밀번호를 입력하니까 오류 메시지가 뜨네요.**

남: 아, 회의 중에 컴퓨터 관리부 직원들이 사무실에 왔었어요. 컴퓨터마다 소프트웨어를 업데이트하고 시스템을 다시 시작했어요. 그러다가 **잘못해서 우리의 비밀번호를 지워버렸지 뭐예요.**

여: 그렇군요. 어, 제가 일단 사용할 수 있는 임시 비밀번호가 있을까요?

남: 네, 우리 회사 이름을 전부 소문자로 치세요. 그리고 **가능한 한 빨리 비밀번호를 변경하는 게 아마 가장 좋을 거예요.**

어휘 work fine 제대로 작동하다 error notification 오류 메시지 maintenance personnel 관리 직원 accidentally 잘못해서, 우연히 delete 지우다 temporary 임시의 entirely 전부 in lowercase letters 소문자로 as soon as one can 가능한 한 빨리

38

What is the woman unable to do?

(A) Turn on her laptop
(B) Find some files
(C) Upload some documents
(D) Log in to her account

여자는 무슨 일을 못하고 있는가?

(A) 노트북 컴퓨터 켜기
(B) 몇몇 파일 찾기
(C) 몇몇 문서 업로드하기
(D) 자신의 계정에 접속하기

해설 세부 사항 관련 - 여자의 문제점

여자의 첫 번째 대사에서 회의 전에는 자신의 계정이 괜찮았는데, 지금은 비밀번호를 입력하면 오류 메시지가 뜬다(My account worked fine before my meeting ~ when I enter my password.)고 했으므로 정답은 (D)이다.

39

What does the man say has caused the problem?

(A) An error made by staff
(B) A computer virus
(C) A power outage
(D) An increase in network users

남자는 무엇 때문에 문제가 생겼다고 말하는가?

(A) 직원의 실수
(B) 컴퓨터 바이러스
(C) 정전
(D) 네트워크 사용자 증가

해설 세부 사항 관련 - 남자가 말하는 문제의 원인

남자의 첫 번째 대사에서 컴퓨터 관리부 직원들이 작업을 하다가 잘못해서 비밀번호를 지워버렸다(they accidentally deleted our passwords.)고 했으므로 정답은 (A)이다.

40

What does the man suggest?

(A) Verifying the spelling of a name
(B) Contacting technical support
(C) Removing some software
(D) Updating a password

남자는 무엇을 하라고 권하는가?

(A) 이름의 철자를 확인할 것
(B) 기술 지원부에 연락할 것
(C) 소프트웨어를 제거할 것
(D) 비밀번호를 갱신할 것

어휘 verify 확인하다

해설 세부 사항 관련 - 남자의 권고 사항

대화 맨 마지막에 남자가 여자에게 가능하면 빨리 비밀번호를 변경하는 게 가장 좋을 것(it's probably best to change it as soon as you can)이라고 했으므로 정답은 (D)이다.

▸▸ **Paraphrasing** 대화의 **change** → 정답의 **Updating**

41-43

W-Br [41]**I just heard that the marketing department has decided to hire a famous person to promote our products.** Isn't that exciting? I guess [42]**it's because we have some additional funds for advertisements this year.**

M-Cn Great. It seems like many successful device manufacturers use celebrities for endorsements these days. Have they chosen anyone yet?

W-Br Yes, but they're having a problem with the contract negotiations. It seems that the celebrity has agreed to the endorsement fee, but [43]**she'll only sign for one year and we want her for a minimum of two.** We're waiting to hear back from her agent.

여: **마케팅부에서 유명인을 고용해 우리 제품들을 홍보하기로 했다는 소식을 방금 들었어요.** 흥미롭지 않아요? **올해는 우리가 광고에 쓸 추가 자금이 생겨서 그럴 거예요.**

남: 잘됐군요. 잘나가는 기기 제조업체 다수가 요즘에 유명인들을 써서 제품 홍보를 하는 것 같아요. 사람은 벌써 결정됐나요?

여: 네, 하지만 계약 협상에 문제가 있어요. 그 유명인이 광고료에는 합의한 것 같은데 **그 사람은 1년 계약만 하려 하고, 우리는 적어도 2년 계약을 원하고요.** 우리 회사에서는 그 사람의 에이전트로부터 회신이 오기를 기다리는 중이래요.

어휘 famous 유명한 additional 추가의, 부가적인 fund 자금, 재원 it seems like ~인 것 같다 device manufacturer 기기 제조업체 celebrity 유명인사 endorsement (유명인이 광고에 나와서 하는) 보증, 홍보 contract negotiations 계약 협상 a minimum of 최소한의 agent (문화·체육 부문의) 에이전트, 대리인

Test 5

41

What are the speakers mainly discussing?

(A) A new executive
(B) A defective product
(C) An advertising campaign
(D) Some hiring policies

화자들은 주로 무엇에 관해 논의하고 있는가?

(A) 신임 이사
(B) 불량 제품
(C) 광고 캠페인
(D) 몇몇 채용 방침

어휘 defective 결함이 있는

해설 전체 내용 관련 – 대화의 주제

대화 맨 처음에 여자가 마케팅부에서 유명인을 고용해 회사 제품들을 홍보하기로 결정했다는 소식을 들었다(I just heard that the marketing department ~ to promote our products.)고 했다. 화자들이 회사의 광고 캠페인에 대해 얘기하고 있으므로 정답은 (C)이다.

42

Why does the woman say a change is being made?

(A) An expert recommended it.
(B) Customers have asked for it.
(C) Technology has advanced.
(D) Extra funding is available.

여자는 변화가 시도되는 이유가 무엇이라고 말하는가?

(A) 전문가가 추천했다.
(B) 고객들이 요청했다.
(C) 기술이 발달했다.
(D) 여유 자금이 생겼다.

어휘 expert 전문가

해설 세부 사항 관련 – 변화를 시도하는 이유

여자의 첫 번째 대사에서 유명인을 고용해 광고를 하려는 이유에 대해 올해는 광고에 쓸 추가 자금이 생겨서 그럴 것(it's because we have some additional funds for advertisements this year.)이라고 했으므로 정답은 (D)이다.

▸▸ **Paraphrasing** 대화의 additional funds
→ 정답의 Extra funding

43

According to the woman, what part of an agreement has not been decided?

(A) A start date
(B) A location
(C) A duration
(D) A fee

여자에 따르면, 계약 내용 중 어떤 부분이 결정되지 않았는가?

(A) 시작 날짜
(B) 위치
(C) 기간
(D) 보수

해설 세부 사항 관련 – 계약의 미결정 부분

여자의 두 번째 대사에서 유명인은 1년 계약만 하려 하고, 회사는 적어도 2년 계약을 원한다(she'll only sign for one year and we want her for a minimum of two.)고 했다. 즉, 계약 기간이 아직 결정되지 않은 것을 알 수 있으므로 정답은 (C)이다.

44-46 3인 대화

M-Au Mallory, you look frustrated. Is everything OK?

W-Am Hi, Graham. I'm fine. It's just that [44]**I'm going to the fitness center this evening after work,** and I can't figure out how to set up the workout tracking app on my new smartwatch.

M-Au Well, I would help if I could. [45]**Why don't you ask Yoon-Hee about it? She has a smartwatch.** And here she comes now.

W-Am Oh, does she? Thanks. Hi, Yoon-Hee. Could you help me with an app on my smartwatch?

W-Br Let me see... Oh sorry, Mallory, but mine has a different operating system. [46]**Have you looked online for instructions?**

W-Am Not yet. [46]**I'll try that now.**

남: 맬러리, 낙담한 것처럼 보여요. 괜찮아요?
여1: 안녕하세요, 그레이엄. 괜찮아요. **오늘 저녁 퇴근 후에 피트니스 센터에 가려고 하는데** 새 스마트워치에 운동량 추적 앱을 설치하는 방법을 알 수가 없네요.
남: 음, 내가 할 수 있다면 도와 드릴 텐데요. **윤희에게 물어보지 그러세요? 스마트워치를 갖고 있거든요.** 지금 오네요.
여1: 아, 그래요? 고맙습니다. 윤희, 안녕하세요. 제 스마트워치에 앱 설치하는 것 좀 도와주시겠어요?
여2: 어디 한번 보죠. 맬러리, 죄송하지만 제 것은 운영체제가 달라요. **온라인에서 설명서를 찾아보셨나요?**
여1: 아직요. **지금 찾아볼게요.**

어휘 frustrated 좌절한, 낙담한 after work 퇴근 후에 figure out 알아내다, 이해하다 set up 설치하다 workout 운동 tracking 추적 let me see 글쎄, 어디 보자 operating system 운영체제 instructions 설명(서)

44

What will Mallory most likely do this evening?

(A) Exercise
(B) Go shopping
(C) Work overtime
(D) Make vacation plans

맬러리는 오늘 저녁 무엇을 하겠는가?

(A) 운동
(B) 쇼핑
(C) 연장 근무
(D) 휴가 계획 짜기

어휘 overtime 연장 근무, 시간 외 근무

해설 세부 사항 관련 - 맬러리의 저녁 계획

남자의 첫 대사를 통해 대화하는 상대방 여자가 맬러리라는 것을 알 수 있다. 첫 번째 여자인 맬러리의 첫 대사에서 저녁 퇴근 후에 피트니스 센터에 갈 예정(I'm going to the fitness center this evening after work)이라고 했으므로 정답은 (A)이다.

45

Why does the man recommend asking Yoon-Hee for help?

(A) She has a lot of free time.
(B) She often visits a site.
(C) She owns a certain device.
(D) She has completed a course.

남자가 윤희에게 도움을 요청할 것을 권하는 이유는 무엇인가?

(A) 그녀는 시간이 많다.
(B) 그녀는 현장을 자주 방문한다.
(C) 그녀는 특정 기기를 갖고 있다.
(D) 그녀는 과정을 완료했다.

어휘 site 현장, 장소 certain 특정한

해설 세부 사항 관련 - 도움 요청을 권한 이유

남자의 두 번째 대사에서 스마트워치가 있는 윤희에게 물어보라(Why don't you ask Yoon-Hee about it? She has a smartwatch.)고 했으므로 정답은 (C)이다.

46

What does Mallory say she will do next?

(A) Photocopy some instructions
(B) Upgrade an operating system
(C) Send a group text message
(D) Conduct an Internet search

맬러리는 다음에 무엇을 할 것이라고 말하는가?

(A) 사용 설명서 복사하기
(B) 운영 체제 업그레이드하기
(C) 단체 문자 메시지 보내기
(D) 인터넷 검색하기

어휘 photocopy 복사하다 conduct 수행하다 search 검색

해설 세부 사항 관련 - 맬러리가 다음에 할 일

두 번째 여자가 맬러리에게 온라인에서 설명서를 찾아보았는지(Have you looked online for instructions?) 물어봤는데 지금 찾아보겠다(I'll try that now.)고 대답했으므로 정답은 (D)이다.

47-49

M-Cn Good morning, Amber. I was thinking—[47]**I really like how you make designs on the surface of some of our coffee drinks.**

W-Am Thanks, Raul. That's called latte art. I learned it in my barista training program.

M-Cn Ah, I see. [48]**If we have a slow hour this afternoon, could you show me how to do it too?**

W-Am Oh, the store next door is starting a big sale today. But are you working on Monday? Things will have calmed down by then.

M-Cn Monday would be perfect. Thanks. OK, [47, 49]**I'm going to go get my cap and apron.** I'll see you at the counter in a minute.

남: 안녕하세요, 앰버. 제가 요즘 드는 생각이, **당신이 몇몇 커피 음료 위에 무늬를 넣으시는 방식이 참 맘에 드네요.**

여: 고마워요, 라울. 라떼 아트라고 해요. 바리스타 교육 프로그램에서 배웠어요.

남: 아, 그렇군요. **오늘 오후에 좀 한가한 때가 있으면 어떻게 하는지도 보여줄 수 있나요?**

여: 아, 오늘은 옆 가게에서 큰 할인 행사를 시작해요. 하지만 월요일에 근무하세요? 그때쯤에는 잠잠해져 있을 거예요.

남: 월요일이면 딱 좋겠네요. 고마워요. **저는 모자와 앞치마를 가지러 갑니다.** 곧 카운터에서 봐요.

어휘 make designs 무늬를 넣다 surface 표면 training 교육, 훈련 slow 한산한 calm down 진정되다 by then 그때쯤에는 apron 앞치마 in a minute 곧

47

Where do the speakers most likely work?

(A) At a bookstore
(B) At a café
(C) At a hotel
(D) At a supermarket

화자들은 어디에서 일하겠는가?

(A) 서점
(B) 카페
(C) 호텔
(D) 슈퍼마켓

해설 전체 내용 관련 - 화자들의 근무지

남자가 첫 대사에서 여자가 커피 음료 위에 무늬를 넣는 방식이 맘에 든다(I really like how you make designs ~ our coffee drinks.)고 언급했다. 이후 관련된 내용이 이어지다가 마지막에 남자가 모자와 앞치마를 가지러 간다고 하는 것으로 보아 화자들은 카페 직원임을 알 수 있으므로 정답은 (B)이다.

48

What does the woman mean when she says, "the store next door is starting a big sale today"?

(A) She will not be able to fulfill a request.
(B) She is unhappy about some competition.
(C) She suggests visiting a neighboring business.
(D) She wants the man to do a task quickly.

Test 5

여자가 "오늘은 옆 가게에서 큰 할인 행사를 시작해요"라고 말한 의도는?

(A) 요청받은 것을 해 주지 못할 것이다.
(B) 경쟁에 대해 기분이 좋지 않다.
(C) 이웃 업체 방문을 제안한다.
(D) 남자가 일을 빨리 완수하길 바란다.

어휘 fulfill 이행하다 request 요청 competition 경쟁 neighboring 이웃의, 인근의 do a task 일을 완수하다

해설 화자의 의도 파악 - 오늘 옆 가게에서 큰 할인 행사를 시작한다는 말의 의미

인용문 바로 전 대사에서 남자가 오늘 오후 한가한 때에 라떼 아트를 좀 보여줄 수 있는지(If we have a slow hour ~ how to do it too?) 물어봤다. 이에 여자가 오늘 옆 가게에서 큰 할인 행사를 시작한다고 했으므로, 그 때문에 손님이 많아 바빠서 남자가 요청한 것을 해 주지 못할 것이라는 의미가 내포되어 있음을 알 수 있어 정답은 (A)이다.

49

What will the man most likely do next?

(A) Clear off a counter
(B) Assist a customer
(C) Put on a work uniform
(D) Set up a window display

남자는 다음으로 무엇을 하겠는가?

(A) 카운터를 깨끗이 치우기
(B) 고객 응대하기
(C) 근무복 입기
(D) 쇼윈도 상품 진열하기

어휘 clear off 치우다 assist 돕다 put on 입다 set up 설치하다

해설 세부 사항 관련 - 남자가 다음에 할 일

남자의 마지막 대사에서 모자와 앞치마를 가지러 간다(I'm going to go get my cap and apron.)고 했다. 따라서 카페에서 근무하기 위한 유니폼을 입을 것임을 알 수 있으므로 정답은 (C)이다.

50-52

W-Br Our new work space is great, isn't it? I like how the designers styled it with sofas and tables instead of cubicles and desks. [50]**The open concept encourages us to walk around here in the office and talk to one another.**

M-Au Right. [51]**It promotes cooperation among employees.** And I really like the bright, open spaces. The new windows give us great views of the outside garden. Looking out the window for a few minutes is so refreshing.

W-Br Actually, [52]**I just heard that pictures of our office will be posted on the *Fontaine Urban Interiors* Web site next month.** They're going to focus on the balance of art and functionality. They might even feature our meeting table!

여: 새로운 업무 공간이 아주 멋지지 않아요? 디자이너들이 칸막이와 책상 대신에 소파와 탁자로 꾸민 게 마음에 들어요. **개방성 개념으로 구성된 공간이라 우리가 여기 사무실을 돌아다니면서 서로 얘기할 마음이 생기잖아요.**

남: 맞아요. **직원들 간의 협력을 증진시키죠.** 그리고 저는 공간이 환하고 탁 트여 있어서 정말 마음에 들어요. 새로운 창문으로 옥외 정원이 아주 잘 보이잖아요. 몇 분 동안 창밖을 내다보면 아주 상쾌해요.

여: 실은, **우리 사무실을 찍은 사진들이 다음 달에 〈폰테인 어번 인테리어스〉 웹 사이트에 실린다는 소식을 방금 들었어요.** 예술과 기능성의 조화에 초점을 맞출 예정이래요. 우리 회의 탁자도 들어갈지 몰라요!

어휘 style 꾸미다, 모양을 내다 cubicle 칸막이 open concept 개방형 콘셉트 encourage 격려하다, 촉진하다 one another 서로 cooperation 협동, 협력 give A(사람) great views of ~이 A에게 아주 잘 보이게 하다 refreshing 상쾌한, 기분을 전환시키는 post 싣다 focus on ~에 초점을 맞추다 functionality 기능성 feature 특집으로 싣다, 특별히 포함하다

50

Where most likely are the speakers?

(A) In an office
(B) In a house
(C) In a library
(D) In a museum

화자들이 있는 곳은 어디겠는가?

(A) 사무실
(B) 주택
(C) 도서관
(D) 박물관

해설 전체 내용 관련 - 화자들의 위치

여자의 첫 번째 대사에서 개방성 개념으로 구성된 공간이라 이 사무실을 돌아다니면서 서로 얘기할 마음이 생긴다(The open concept encourages us to walk around here in the office and talk to one another.)고 했으므로 정답은 (A)이다.

51

What do the speakers say about the new layout?

(A) It encourages collaboration.
(B) It provides greater privacy.
(C) It enhances security.
(D) It conserves energy.

화자들은 새로운 배치에 관해 뭐라고 말하는가?

(A) 협력을 촉진한다.
(B) 사생활을 더 많이 보장한다.
(C) 보안을 향상시킨다.
(D) 에너지를 절약한다.

어휘 collaboration 협력, 공동 작업 privacy 사생활 enhance 향상시키다, 강화하다 conserve 아끼다

해설 세부 사항 관련 – 새로운 배치에 대한 화자들의 의견
남자의 첫 번째 대사에서 개방형 배치가 직원들 간의 협력을 증진시킨다(It promotes cooperation among employees.)고 했으므로 정답은 (A)이다.

▸▸ Paraphrasing 대화의 promote cooperation among employees → 정답의 encourage collaboration

52

According to the woman, what will happen next month?

(A) Another space will be rearranged.
(B) Some photographs will appear online.
(C) A commercial will be filmed.
(D) Some signs will be put up.

여자에 따르면, 다음 달에 무슨 일이 있을 것인가?
(A) 다른 공간이 재배치될 것이다.
(B) 사진 몇 장이 온라인상에 게재될 것이다.
(C) 광고 영상을 찍을 것이다.
(D) 표지판이 몇 개 설치될 것이다.

어휘 appear 나타나다 commercial 광고; 상업적인

해설 세부 사항 관련 – 다음 달에 발생할 일
여자의 두 번째 대사에서 사무실 사진들이 다음 달에 〈폰테인 어번 인테리어스〉 웹 사이트에 실린다는 소식을 방금 들었다(I just heard that pictures of our office ~ Web site next month.)고 했으므로 정답은 (B)이다.

▸▸ Paraphrasing 대화의 pictures → 정답의 photographs

53-55 3인 대화

W-Am Hi, all. We have a problem. [53]**The control system for Loading Dock Six isn't working properly, so that door won't close.**

M-Cn I noticed that. I'll have the delivery drivers use other docks until it's fixed.

M-Au Oh, also... [54]**my shipping crew mentioned that their work areas are rather dark. They've requested putting in bright lights.**

M-Cn Ah, my crew made the same suggestion. [54]**Can we talk about it in our all-staff meeting?**

W-Am [54]**Absolutely**. And one more thing... [55]**Tomorrow afternoon I'm showing a vendor around the complex**, so I won't be in the office. Call me at my mobile phone if you need me.

여: 다들 안녕하세요. 문제가 생겼습니다. **6번 하역장의 제어 시스템이 제대로 작동하지 않아서 문이 닫히질 않아요.**
남1: 그렇더라고요. 그게 고쳐질 때까지 배달 기사들에게 다른 하역장들을 이용하라고 할게요.
남2: 아, 그리고… **제 배송 직원들이 작업장이 다소 어둡다고 하더라고요. 밝은 전등을 설치해달라고 요청했어요.**
남1: 아, 제 직원들도 같은 제안을 했어요. **전체 직원 회의에서 그에 관해 얘기할 수 있을까요?**
여: **물론이죠.** 그리고 한 가지 더요… **내일 오후에는 제가 판매 업체에 회사 단지를 구경시킬 예정이라** 사무실에 없을 거예요. 필요하시면 제 휴대폰으로 전화하세요.

어휘 control system 제어 시스템 loading dock 하역장 properly 제대로 notice 알아채다 rather 얼마간, 다소 put in 설치하다 vendor 판매상, 판매회사 complex 단지

53

What problem does the woman mention?

(A) A loading area is disorganized.
(B) A shipment is missing.
(C) A door control is out of order.
(D) A delivery vehicle has been delayed.

여자는 어떤 문제를 언급하는가?
(A) 적하 구역이 정리되어 있지 않다.
(B) 배송물이 없어졌다.
(C) 문 제어 장치가 망가졌다.
(D) 배송 차량이 늦고 있다.

해설 세부 사항 관련 – 여자가 언급하는 문제점
대화 맨 처음에서 여자가 6번 하역장의 제어 시스템이 제대로 작동하지 않아서 문이 닫히질 않는다(The control system for Loading Dock Six ~ door won't close.)고 했으므로 정답은 (C)이다.

▸▸ Paraphrasing 대화의 not work properly → 정답의 out of order

54

What will the speakers most likely discuss at a meeting?

(A) Recruiting more part-time workers
(B) Starting a mentorship program
(C) Renting some industrial machinery
(D) Installing better lighting in a workplace

화자들은 회의에서 무엇을 논의하겠는가?
(A) 더 많은 시간제 직원 채용
(B) 멘토 프로그램 시작
(C) 산업용 기계 대여
(D) 작업장에 개선된 전등 설치

어휘 industrial 산업의

해설 세부 사항 관련 – 화자들이 회의 때 논의할 사항
두 번째 남자가 배송 직원들이 작업장이 좀 어둡다고 하면서 밝은 전등 설치를 요청했다(my shipping crew mentioned ~ requested putting in bright lights.)고 하자 첫 번째 남자가 자신의 직원들도 같은 제안을 했다고 하면서 전체 직원 회의에서 이 문제를 얘기할 수 있을지(Can we talk about it in our all-staff meeting?) 여자에게 물어봤다. 여자가 물론이라고 대답했으므로 정답은 (D)이다.

▸▸ Paraphrasing 대화의 putting in bright lights → 정답의 Installing better lighting

55

What does the woman say she will do tomorrow?

(A) Train a technician
(B) Give a facility tour
(C) Extend a meal break
(D) Create a slide show

여자는 내일 무엇을 할 것이라고 말하는가?

(A) 기술자 교육
(B) 시설 견학 인솔
(C) 식사 시간 연장
(D) 슬라이드 쇼 제작

어휘 extend 연장하다

해설 세부 사항 관련 - 여자가 내일 할 일

대화 맨 마지막에서 여자가 내일 오후에 판매 업체에 회사 단지를 구경시켜 줄 것(Tomorrow afternoon I'm showing a vendor around the complex)이라고 했으므로 정답은 (B)이다.

▸▸ **Paraphrasing** 대화의 **showing a vendor around the complex** → 정답의 **Give a facility tour**

56-58

M-Cn Hi, Jessica. Well, our shop floor's upgraded signs look great...

W-Br I'll say. [56]**Customers have been commenting on the store's new look since the remodeling work was finished last week.** I'm sure Kevin and Yolanda will enjoy their visit next Thursday too.

M-Cn Kevin... Yolanda... Oh, the district managers. Uh... what brings them here?

W-Br [57]**It's a routine visit—not a site inspection. We're fine.**

M-Cn Oh, OK. Can we talk to them about our inventory needs?

W-Br Sure. When we meet, [58]**I'm going to recommend that we stock a wider selection of locally grown food products.** We've had requests for that.

남: 안녕하세요, 제시카. 음, 우리 매장의 개선된 표지판들이 아주 좋아 보여요…

여: 그러게요. **지난주 리모델링 작업이 끝난 이후 고객들이 점포의 새로워진 모습에 대해 한 마디씩 하세요.** 케빈과 욜란다도 다음 주 목요일에 방문하면 분명히 기분이 좋을 거예요.

남: 케빈… 욜란다… 아, 지역 관리자들 말이군요. 음… 그들이 여기에 무슨 일로 오는 거죠?

여: **통상적인 방문이에요. 현장 시찰이 아니고요. 우린 괜찮아요.**

남: 오, 그렇군요. 그들에게 우리의 재고 필요성에 관해 얘기해도 되나요?

여: 물론이죠. 우리가 만나면 **이 지역에서 재배한 식품들을 더 다양하게 구비해 놓자고 제안할 거예요.** 그런 요청들을 받아왔거든요.

어휘 sign 표지(판), 표시 I'll say. (상대의 말에 맞장구 치며) 그러게요. 그럼요. remodeling 리모델링, 개조 district manager 지역 관리자 routine 통상적인, 일상적인 site inspection 현장 시찰 inventory needs 재고 필요성 stock 비축하다, 갖추다 a wider selection of 더 다양하게 구비된 ~ locally grown 현지에서 재배한

56

According to the woman, what happened recently?

(A) A Web site was launched.
(B) A survey was administered.
(C) Renovations were completed.
(D) Contracts with suppliers were signed.

여자에 따르면, 최근에 무슨 일이 있었는가?

(A) 웹 사이트가 개설되었다.
(B) 설문 조사가 실시됐다.
(C) 개조 작업이 끝났다.
(D) 공급자들과의 계약이 성사되었다.

어휘 launch 시작하다 administer 운영하다, 집행하다

해설 세부 사항 관련 - 최근에 발생한 일

여자가 첫 번째 대사에서 지난주 리모델링 작업이 끝난 이후 고객들이 점포의 새로워진 모습에 대해 한 마디씩 한다(Customers have been commenting ~ the remodeling work was finished last week.)고 했으므로 정답은 (C)이다.

57

Why does the man say, "what brings them here"?

(A) He is excited.
(B) He is worried.
(C) He is frustrated.
(D) He is relieved.

남자가 "그들이 여기에 무슨 일로 오는 거죠?"라고 말한 이유는 무엇인가?

(A) 신이 난다.
(B) 걱정된다.
(C) 좌절했다.
(D) 안심이 된다.

해설 화자의 의도 파악 - 그들이 오는 이유를 물어보는 의도

여자의 두 번째 대사에서 지역 관리자들의 방문이 통상적인 것이지 현장 시찰은 아니기 때문에 괜찮다(It's a routine visit ~ We're fine.)고 하면서 남자를 안심시켰다. 즉, 남자가 그들이 여기에 왜 오는지를 물어본 인용문은 지역 관리자들의 방문에 대한 염려를 나타낸 것이므로 정답은 (B)이다.

58

What will the woman suggest at a meeting?

(A) Stocking more items in large sizes
(B) Selling more local produce
(C) Redesigning the store's logo
(D) Changing the store's hours

여자는 회의에서 무엇을 제안할 것인가?
(A) 큰 사이즈 물품들을 더 많이 비축할 것
(B) 현지 농산물을 더 많이 판매할 것
(C) 매장의 로고를 다시 디자인할 것
(D) 매장 영업시간을 변경할 것

어휘 stock 비축하다 produce 농산물

해설 세부 사항 관련 - 회의 때 여자가 할 제안
대화 맨 마지막에 여자가 현지에서 재배된 식품들을 더 다양하게 구비해 놓을 것을 제안하겠다(I'm going to recommend ~ locally grown food products.)고 했으므로 정답은 (B)이다.

▸▸ **Paraphrasing** 대화의 **stock a wider selection of locally grown food products**
→ 정답의 **Selling more local produce**

59-61

M-Au Did you see the newspaper today? [59]**There was a story about a proposed merger between our firm and, um, South Stark Industries.**

W-Am Yes, I read it. I also received an e-mail from headquarters. [60]**Management is asking us not to comment publicly on the subject, so you should be careful not to talk about it outside of the office.** They plan to release a statement about it to the press tomorrow.

M-Au Oh, OK. But we two can talk about it, right? This is exciting news! Do you think it will be a positive move for our company?

W-Am Yes, I do. [61]**South Stark does business in multiple countries.** This could help us expand into some new markets.

남: 오늘 신문 봤어요? **우리 회사와, 음, 사우스 스타크 인더스트리즈 간 합병 제의에 관한 기사가 났어요.**

여: 네, 읽었어요. 본사에서 온 이메일도 받았어요. **경영진이 우리에게 그 문제를 공개적으로 거론하지 말라고 하고 있으니, 당신도 사무실 밖에서 얘기하지 않도록 조심해야 해요.** 경영진에서 내일 언론에 합병에 관한 성명을 발표할 계획이에요.

남: 아, 알았어요. 하지만 우리 둘이서는 얘기해도 되죠? 신나는 소식이잖아요! 당신은 이것이 우리 회사에 긍정적인 움직임이라고 생각해요?

여: 네. **사우스 스타크는 여러 나라에서 사업을 하잖아요.** 우리가 몇몇 새로운 시장으로 진출하는 데 도움이 될 수 있을 거예요.

어휘 merger 합병 comment on ~에 관해 논평하다, ~을 거론하다 publicly 공개적으로 subject 화제, 주제 be careful not to + 동사원형 ~하지 않도록 조심하다 release a statement 성명을 발표하다 the press 언론 a positive move 긍정적인 조처[움직임] multiple 여럿의 expand into new markets 새로운 시장으로 확장[진출]하다

59

What is the conversation mainly about?
(A) A proposed law
(B) A company merger
(C) A trade show
(D) A current market trend

대화는 주로 무엇에 관한 내용인가?
(A) 상정된 법안
(B) 기업 합병
(C) 무역 박람회
(D) 현재의 시장 동향

해설 전체 내용 관련 - 대화의 주제
남자의 첫 번째 대사에서 화자들의 회사와 사우스 스타크 인더스트리즈 간 합병 제의에 관한 기사가 났다(There was a story about a proposed merger ~ South Stark Industries.)고 하면서 이와 관련된 내용이 이어지고 있으므로 정답은 (B)이다.

60

What does the woman advise the man to do?
(A) Avoid discussing an issue openly
(B) Decline an invitation politely
(C) Do further research
(D) Reply to an e-mail

여자는 남자에게 무엇을 하라고 권하는가?
(A) 문제를 공개적으로 논의하지 않기
(B) 초청을 정중히 거절하기
(C) 더 조사하기
(D) 이메일에 답장하기

어휘 avoid -ing ~하지 않도록 하다 decline 거절하다

해설 세부 사항 관련 - 여자의 제안 사항
여자의 첫 번째 대사에서 남자에게 경영진이 그 문제를 공개적으로 거론하지 말라고 하고 있으니 사무실 밖에서 얘기하지 않도록 조심해야 한다(Management is asking us not to ~ of the office.)고 했으므로 정답은 (A)이다.

▸▸ **Paraphrasing** 대화의 **not to comment publicly on the subject** → 정답의 **Avoid discussing an issue openly**

61

What does the woman say about South Stark Industries?
(A) It has a long history.
(B) It sponsored an event.
(C) It recently expanded.
(D) It operates internationally.

여자는 사우스 스타크 인더스트리즈에 관해 뭐라고 말하는가?
(A) 역사가 오래 되었다.
(B) 한 행사를 후원했다.
(C) 최근 사업을 확장했다.
(D) 세계적으로 사업한다.

Test 5

어휘 sponsor 후원하다 expand 확장하다 operate 운영하다

해설 세부 사항 관련 - 사우스 스타크 인더스트리즈에 관한 여자의 언급
여자의 두 번째 대사에서 사우스 스타크는 여러 나라에서 사업을 한다(South Stark does business in multiple countries.)고 했으므로 정답은 (D)이다.

▸▸ Paraphrasing do business in multiple countries
→ 정답의 operates internationally

62-64 대화 + 차트

W-Br Nigel, have you seen this magazine article? It has a chart that shows which major clothing companies a group of shoppers were most satisfied with.

M-Cn Hmm... [62]**I see we've come in second. We're only five percent behind Hatnex.**

W-Br Yes. The article stated shoppers were most pleased with our personal styling consultations, but [63]**didn't like how we don't have an alteration service. We need to offer this like Hatnex does so customers can get their clothes fixed at our stores.**

M-Cn [64]**Why don't you mention this during our weekly meeting on Monday?** I think it would be a good idea to discuss it and get other people's opinions.

여: 나이젤, 이 잡지 기사 봤어요? 여기 이 도표를 보면 쇼핑객들이 어떤 주요 의류 업체들에 가장 만족했는지 나와 있어요.

남: 흠… **우리가 2등이군요. 햇넥스에 겨우 5퍼센트 뒤져 있어요.**

여: 그래요. 이 기사에는 쇼핑객들이 우리의 개인 스타일링 상담은 아주 좋아하지만, **수선 서비스가 없다는 것은 마음에 들어 하지 않는다고 나오네요. 우리도 햇넥스처럼 수선 서비스를 제공해서 고객들이 우리 매장에서 옷을 고칠 수 있도록 해야 해요.**

남: **월요일 주간 회의 때 이 문제를 거론하지 그래요?** 이 점을 논의하고 다른 사람들의 의견을 들어 보면 좋을 것 같네요.

어휘 be satisfied with ~에 만족하다 come in second 2등을 하다 state 진술하다 be pleased with ~을 마음에 들어 하다 consultation 상담 alteration 수선 clothes 옷, 의류

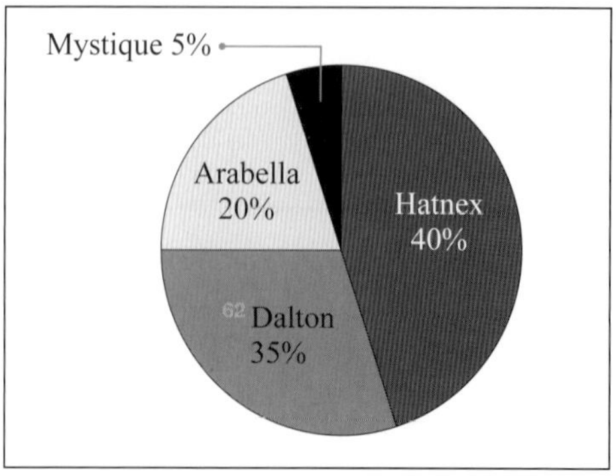

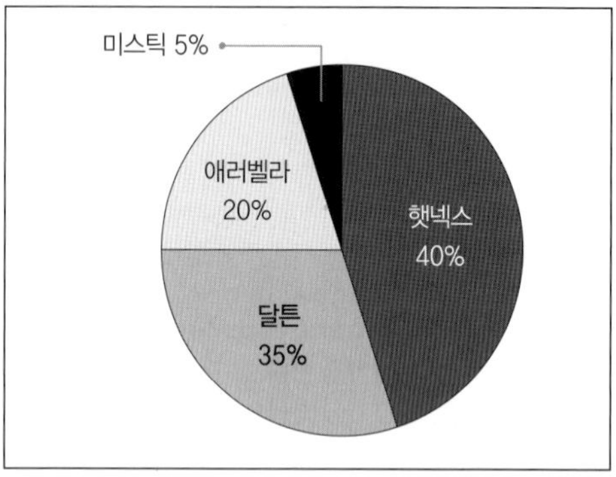

62

Look at the graphic. Which company do the speakers work for?

(A) Mystique
(B) Arabella
(C) Dalton
(D) Hatnex

시각 정보에 의하면, 화자들은 어느 회사에 근무하는가?
(A) 미스틱
(B) 애러벨라
(C) 달튼
(D) 햇넥스

해설 시각 정보 연계 - 화자들의 근무지
남자의 첫 번째 대사에서 화자들의 회사가 2등을 했으며 햇넥스에 겨우 5% 뒤져 있다(I see we've come in second. We're only five percent behind Hatnex.)고 했다. 차트를 보면 달튼이 35퍼센트로 햇넥스에 5퍼센트 뒤져 있으므로 정답은 (C)이다.

63

What service does the woman want to start offering to customers?

(A) Styling consultations
(B) Expedited deliveries
(C) Clothing alterations
(D) Electronic catalogs

여자는 고객들에게 어떤 서비스의 제공을 시작하고 싶어 하는가?
(A) 스타일링 상담
(B) 신속 배송
(C) 의류 수선
(D) 전자 카탈로그

해설 세부 사항 관련 – 여자가 원하는 고객 서비스
여자의 두 번째 대사에서 고객들이 수선 서비스가 없다는 점은 마음에 들어 하지 않는다고 하면서 햇넥스처럼 수선 서비스를 제공해서 고객들이 매장에서 옷을 고칠 수 있도록 해야 한다(didn't like how we don't have an alteration service ~ get their clothes fixed at our stores.)고 했으므로 정답은 (C)이다.

64

What does the man suggest the woman do on Monday?
(A) Temporarily suspend a project
(B) Introduce a topic during a meeting
(C) Hand out copies of a magazine article
(D) Look for unnecessary expenses in a budget

남자는 여자에게 월요일에 무엇을 할 것을 제안하는가?
(A) 프로젝트의 일시적 연기
(B) 회의 때 안건 제기
(C) 잡지 기사의 복사본 나눠 주기
(D) 예산에서 불필요한 비용 찾기

어휘 temporarily 임시로 suspend 연기하다 expense 비용 budget 예산

해설 세부 사항 관련 – 남자의 제안 사항
남자의 두 번째 대사에서 여자에게 월요일 주간 회의 때 수선 문제를 거론해 보라(Why don't you mention this during our weekly meeting on Monday?)고 했으므로 정답은 (B)이다.

▸▸ **Paraphrasing** 대화의 mention → 정답의 Introduce

65-67 대화 + 영수증

W-Am Hello, Bernard. It's Cheryl. [65]**I'm outside of Ivory Office Max right now, and I was wondering if we needed any office supplies.** I forgot to check before I left. I remember we ran out of tape, but do we need anything else?

M-Au Yes, we might need some cash register receipt paper. While [66]**I was fixing one of the broken cash registers with the new employee this morning,** I noticed we were running low on it. Could you buy a few rolls?

W-Am No problem. [67]**I'm going to return the printer paper I purchased yesterday.** So I'll buy that with the money I'll be refunded. I'll see you back at the office soon.

여: 안녕하세요, 버나드. 셰릴이에요. **제가 지금 아이보리 오피스 맥스 밖에 있는데, 우리에게 필요한 사무용품이 있는지 궁금해서요.** 제가 나오기 전에 확인한다는 걸 깜빡했어요. 테이프를 다 쓴 걸로 기억하는데, 다른 필요한 것들이 있나요?
남: 네, 현금등록기 영수증 용지가 좀 필요할 거예요. **오늘 아침에 제가 신입사원과 고장 난 현금등록기들 중 하나를 고치면서** 보니 영수증 용지가 떨어져 가더라고요. 몇 롤만 사올 수 있어요?
여: 그럼요. **제가 어제 산 프린터 용지를 반품할 거예요.** 그러니 환불 받을 돈으로 영수증 용지를 살게요. 곧 사무실에서 봐요.

어휘 wonder if ~인지 궁금하다 office supplies 사무용품 run out of ~을 다 써버리다 cash register 현금등록기 receipt paper 영수증 용지 run low on ~이 적어지다

Ivory Office Max

Item	Price
Clipboard	$9
Envelope	$13
Folder	$17
[67]Printer paper	$48
Total:	$87

아이보리 오피스 맥스

품목	가격
클립보드	9달러
봉투	13달러
폴더	17달러
프린터 용지	48달러
합계:	87달러

65

Why did the woman call the man?
(A) To check some inventory
(B) To revise an order
(C) To negotiate a price
(D) To ask about a misplaced item

여자가 남자에게 전화한 이유는?
(A) 물품 재고를 확인하려고
(B) 주문을 수정하려고
(C) 가격을 협상하려고
(D) 제자리에 없는 물건에 대해 물으려고

Test 5

어휘 inventory 재고, 물품 목록 negotiate 협상하다

해설 전체 내용 관련 - 여자가 전화한 이유

여자의 첫 대사에서 자신이 지금 아이보리 오피스 맥스 밖에 있는데 필요한 사무용품이 있는지 궁금하다(I'm outside of Ivory Office ~ office supplies.)고 하는 것으로 보아 물품 재고를 확인하기 위해 남자에게 전화를 한 것이므로 정답은 (A)이다.

66

What did the man do this morning?

(A) Repaired some equipment
(B) Made a cash deposit
(C) Hired a new employee
(D) Posted some sale signs

남자는 오늘 아침에 무엇을 했는가?

(A) 장비 수리
(B) 현금 예금
(C) 신입 사원 채용
(D) 할인행사 안내문 게시

해설 세부 사항 관련 - 남자가 아침에 한 일

남자의 첫 번째 대사에서 오늘 아침에 신입 사원과 고장 난 현금등록기를 고쳤다(I was fixing one of the broken cash registers with the new employee this morning)고 했으므로 정답은 (A)이다.

▸▸ **Paraphrasing** 대화의 fixing one of the broken cash registers → 정답의 Repaired some equipment

67

Look at the graphic. How much will the woman be refunded?

(A) $9
(B) $13
(C) $17
(D) $48

시각 정보에 의하면, 여자는 얼마를 환불받을 것인가?

(A) 9달러
(B) 13달러
(C) 17달러
(D) 48달러

해설 시각 정보 연계 - 여자가 환불받을 금액

여자의 두 번째 대사에서 어제 산 프린터 용지를 반품하겠다(I'm going to return the printer paper I purchased yesterday.)고 했다. 그리고 영수증을 보면 프린터 용지(Printer paper)의 가격이 48달러로 명시되어 있으므로 정답은 (D)이다.

68-70 대화 + 강의실 배정표

W-Br Hi. [68]**I registered online to start one of your group Spanish classes this evening, and I came in early to buy the textbook.** Where can I do that?

M-Cn You can do that here at the front desk, actually. [69]**What level are you taking?**

W-Br [69]**Beginner.**

M-Cn OK. This is the beginner-level book. It's eighteen dollars.

W-Br Here you are. Well, that didn't take as long as I'd expected. [69]**Is it all right if I wait in the classroom until my class starts at 7:30?**

M-Cn Oh, there's an intermediate class in there right now. But it'll just be a few minutes. [70]**Why don't you have a seat at one of the tables here?**

W-Br OK. Thanks.

여: 안녕하세요. **오늘 저녁에 스페인어 그룹 강좌 중 하나를 시작하려고 온라인으로 신청했어요. 교재를 사려고 일찍 왔습니다.** 어디서 살 수 있나요?

남: 실은 이곳 접수처에서 구입하실 수 있습니다. **어떤 단계를 들으시죠?**

여: **초급 단계요.**

남: 네. 이게 초급 단계 책입니다. 18달러고요.

여: 여기 있어요. 뭐, 예상만큼 오래 걸리진 않았네요. **7시 30분에 강좌가 시작될 때까지 강의실에서 기다려도 되나요?**

남: 아, 지금은 강의실에서 중급 강좌가 진행되고 있습니다. 하지만 몇 분이면 끝날 거예요. **여기 테이블 중에 앉아 계시면 어때요?**

여 네. 감사합니다.

어휘 register 등록하다 textbook 교재 intermediate 중급의 have a seat 앉다 assignment 배정 advanced 고급의, 상급의

Room Assignments
Evening Group Classes

	6:00 - 7:20	7:30 - 8:50
Beginner	Classroom C	[69]Classroom A
Intermediate 1	Classroom A	Classroom B
Intermediate 2	Classroom D	
Advanced	Classroom B	

강의실 배정
저녁 그룹 강좌

	6:00 - 7:20	7:30 - 8:50
초급	C 강의실	**A 강의실**
중급 1	A 강의실	B 강의실
중급 2	D 강의실	
고급	B 강의실	

68

Why has the woman arrived early at the language institute?

(A) She needs to take a level test.
(B) She has to purchase class materials.
(C) A trip took less time than expected.
(D) She misunderstood a schedule.

여자가 어학원에 일찍 도착한 이유는?

(A) 레벨 테스트를 받아야 한다.
(B) 수업 자료를 사야 한다.
(C) 오는 데 예상보다 시간이 적게 걸렸다.
(D) 시간표를 잘못 알았다.

어휘 take a test 시험을 치르다 purchase 구입하다 class material 수업 자료 misunderstand 오해하다

해설 세부 사항 관련 – 여자가 일찍 도착한 이유

여자의 첫 대사에서 스페인어 그룹 강좌를 시작하려고 온라인으로 신청했고 교재를 사려고 일찍 왔다(I registered online to start ~ I came in early to buy the textbook.)고 밝혔으므로 정답은 (B)이다.

69

Look at the graphic. Which room is the woman's class most likely held in?

(A) Classroom A
(B) Classroom B
(C) Classroom C
(D) Classroom D

시각 정보에 의하면, 여자의 강좌는 어떤 강의실에서 이뤄지겠는가?

(A) A 강의실
(B) B 강의실
(C) C 강의실
(D) D 강의실

어휘 be held 개최되다, 열리다

해설 시각 정보 연계 – 여자의 강의실

남자의 첫 번째 대사에서 여자가 어떤 단계를 듣는지(What level are you taking?) 묻자 초급 단계(Beginner.)라고 대답했다. 이후 여자의 세 번째 대사에서 7시 30분 강좌가 시작될 때까지 교실에서 기다려도 되는지 물었고(Is it all right if I wait in the classroom until my class starts at 7:30?), 강의실 배정표를 보면 7시 30분에 시작하는 초급 수업은 A 강의실에서 진행되므로 정답은 (A)이다.

70

What does the man suggest that the woman do?

(A) Wait in the reception area
(B) Keep a registration receipt
(C) Sit in the front part of the classroom
(D) Leave a message for an instructor

남자는 여자에게 무엇을 할 것을 제안하는가?

(A) 접수처에서 기다리기
(B) 등록 영수증 보관하기
(C) 강의실 앞쪽에 앉기
(D) 강사에게 메시지 남기기

어휘 reception 접수처 registration 등록 receipt 영수증 instructor 강사

해설 세부 사항 관련 – 남자의 제안 사항

대화 후반부에 남자가 여자에게 여기(접수처 구역)에서 기다리라(Why don't you have a seat at one of the tables here?)고 제안했으므로 정답은 (A)이다.

PART 4

71-73 안내

M-Au Attention, shoppers. [71]**Our store is closing in thirty minutes.** Please finish gathering your groceries and make your way to the checkout counter. If you don't have time to get everything you need, you can come back in the morning when we open at eight A.M.[72]**You can also order most groceries anytime through our mobile app** and pick them up at our customer service counter. Finally, please remember that [73]**you can also receive a five-cent discount on top of all other coupons every time you bring your own reusable bags to carry your groceries.** Thank you, and drive home safely.

쇼핑객 여러분, 안내 말씀 드립니다. **저희 매장은 30분 후에 영업을 종료합니다.** 식료품 구입을 끝내시고 계산대로 와 주시기 바랍니다. 시간이 없어서 원하시는 것을 전부 구입하지 못하셨으면, 내일 아침 8시에 개점하오니 그때 다시 와 주십시오. **또한 고객님은 대부분의 식료품을 저희 휴대폰 앱으로 언제든지 주문하시고** 저희 고객 서비스 카운터에서 찾아가실 수 있습니다. 마지막으로 **식료품을 담아갈 재사용 가능한 가방을 직접 가져오실 때마다 모든 다른 쿠폰과 함께 5센트 추가 할인을 받으실 수 있다**는 점을 알려 드립니다. 감사합니다. 댁까지 안전 운전하시기 바랍니다.

어휘 gather 모으다 groceries 식료품 make one's way to ~로 가다 checkout counter 계산대 mobile application 휴대폰 앱 pick up ~을 찾다, 수령하다 on top of ~에 더하여 reusable bag 재사용 가방(재사용할 수 있는 가방이나 봉투, 장바구니) carry 나르다, 운반하다

71

What is the reason for the announcement?

(A) A store is closing.
(B) There is a traffic problem.
(C) There is a special sale.
(D) A new service is available.

안내 방송을 하는 이유는 무엇인가?

(A) 매장이 문을 닫는다.
(B) 교통 문제가 있다.
(C) 특별 할인 행사가 있다.
(D) 새로운 서비스를 이용할 수 있다.

해설 전체 내용 관련 - 안내 방송의 이유

지문 맨 처음에 화자가 쇼핑객들에게 매장이 30분 후에 영업을 종료한다(Our store is closing in thirty minutes.)며 식료품 구입을 끝내고 계산대로 와 달라고 했으므로 정답은 (A)이다.

72

What does the speaker say a customer can do with a mobile app?

(A) Download a voucher
(B) Order some goods
(C) Compare some prices
(D) Access a floor plan

화자는 고객이 휴대폰 앱으로 무엇을 할 수 있다고 말하는가?

(A) 상품권 다운로드
(B) 상품 주문
(C) 가격 비교
(D) 평면도확인

어휘 voucher 상품권 compare 비교 floor plan 평면도

해설 세부 사항 관련 - 휴대폰 앱으로 할 수 있는 일

지문 중반부에 대부분의 식료품을 휴대폰 앱으로 언제든지 주문할 수 있다(You can also order most groceries anytime through our mobile app)고 했으므로 정답은 (B)이다.

73

What can customers do to receive an additional discount?

(A) Use a self-checkout machine
(B) Supply their own bags
(C) Fill out a questionnaire
(D) Show a membership card

손님들은 어떻게 하면 추가 할인을 받을 수 있는가?

(A) 셀프 계산대를 이용함으로써
(B) 자신의 장바구니를 가져옴으로써
(C) 설문지를 작성함으로써
(D) 회원카드를 보여 줌으로써

해설 세부 사항 관련 - 고객들이 할인을 받을 수 있는 방법

지문 후반부에 고객이 식료품을 담아갈 재사용 가능한 가방을 직접 가져올 때마다 모든 다른 쿠폰과 함께 5센트를 추가로 할인받을 수 있다(you can also receive a five percent ~ groceries.)고 했으므로 정답은 (B)이다.

74-76 전화 메시지

W-Am Hi, Hinata. It's Joyce. [74]**I just let the IT worker into your office to look at your printer. Bad news—he says it can't be fixed.** Apparently several of the components have been damaged too badly. He left a note with a detailed explanation, so you can look at that when you get back. Anyway, this means a request will need to be made for a new printer. [75]**You can try doing it yourself, but** it's a complicated process. And I think you may have an especially hard time because of [76]**the company budget cuts that were announced last week.** So I'll be standing by. OK, see you soon.

안녕하세요, 히나타. 조이스입니다. **방금 프린터 확인을 위해 IT 작업자를 사무실로 들여보냈습니다. 안 좋은 소식인데, 프린터를 고칠 수 없다고 합니다.** 들어보니 부품 몇 개가 너무 많이 손상됐다고 해요. 자세한 설명이 있는 메모를 남겼으니 돌아오시면 보실 수 있어요. 어쨌든 새 프린터를 요청해야 한다는 건데요. **직접 해보실 수 있지만** 절차가 복잡해요. 그리고 **지난주 발표된 회사 예산 삭감** 때문에 특히 힘드실 것 같아요. 그러니 제가 대기하고 있겠습니다. 곧 뵙겠습니다.

어휘 apparently 듣자 하니, 보아하니 several 몇 개 component 부품 detailed 자세한 explanation 설명 complicated 복잡한 process 과정, 절차 especially 특히 budget cut 예산 삭감 stand by 대기하다

74

What is the message mainly about?

(A) A departmental restructuring
(B) A recent publication
(C) An office party
(D) A broken device

메시지는 주로 무엇에 관한 것인가?

(A) 부서 구조조정
(B) 최근 발행물
(C) 사무실 파티
(D) 고장 난 기기

어휘 departmental 부서의 restructuring 구조조정 recent 최근의 publication 출판물 device 기기

해설 전체 내용 관련 - 전화 메시지의 주제

지문 초반부에 화자는 IT작업자가 프린터를 확인하도록 사무실로 들여보냈는데 수리가 안 된다(I just let the IT worker into your office ~ he says it can't be fixed.)고 하면서 이와 관련된 내용을 전하고 있으므로 정답은 (D)이다.

▸▸ Paraphrasing 지문의 printer → 정답의 device

75

What does the speaker imply when she says, "it's a complicated process"?

(A) The listener will probably need help.
(B) The listener should provide some instructions.
(C) She should not be blamed for a mistake.
(D) She might miss a due date.

화자가 "절차가 복잡해요"라고 말한 의도는 무엇인가?

(A) 청자는 아마 도움을 필요로 할 것이다.
(B) 청자는 설명서를 제공해야 한다.
(C) 화자는 실수로 비난을 받아서는 안 된다.
(D) 화자는 만기일을 넘길지도 모른다.

어휘 instructions 설명서 be blamed for ~ 때문에 비난 받다 due date 만기일

해설 화자의 의도 파악 - 절차가 복잡하다는 말의 의도

인용문의 앞부분에서 화자는 청자가 직접 해볼 수 있지만(You can try doing it yourself, but) 절차가 복잡하다고 했는데, 문맥상 청자가 도움을 필요로 할 것이라는 의도를 나타낸 것이므로 정답은 (A)이다.

76

According to the speaker, what happened last week?

(A) The listener left for a business trip.
(B) The speaker's job transfer was announced.
(C) Changes to a financial plan were revealed.
(D) A company facility was sold.

화자에 따르면, 지난주에 무슨 일이 있었는가?

(A) 청자가 출장을 떠났다.
(B) 화자의 전근이 발표됐다.
(C) 재무 계획 변경 사항이 공개되었다.
(D) 회사 시설이 팔렸다.

어휘 job transfer 전근, 이직 financial 금융의, 재정의 reveal 밝히다, 공개하다

해설 세부 사항 관련 - 지난주에 있었던 일

지문 후반부에 화자는 청자가 지난주 발표된 회사 예산 삭감(the company budget cuts that were announced last week) 때문에 특히 힘들 것 같다고 했으므로 정답은 (C)이다.

▸▸ **Paraphrasing** 지문의 **budget cuts**
→ 정답의 **Changes to a financial plan**

77-79 회의 발췌

M-Cn As you may know, [77]**Phillips & Ackerman Law Firm is hosting a charity banquet later this year** to promote safe driving practices. [78]**They were so pleased with the advertising campaign we did for their dinner series last year that they'd like to use our publicity services again this year.** However, there is a difference from last time. [79]**We're only promoting a single event, so the fee we're receiving is lower.** Now, although we're receiving less, I think it's important to maintain a good relationship with Phillips & Ackerman, so let's put our best effort into it.

아시겠지만, **필립스 앤 애커맨 법률 사무소는 올해 말에** 안전 운행을 홍보하기 위한 **자선 연회 행사를 열려고 합니다. 그 회사는 우리가 지난해 그들의 저녁 만찬 시리즈를 위해 마련했던 광고 캠페인이 매우 마음에 들어 올해도 우리 회사의 홍보 서비스를 쓰고 싶어 합니다.** 하지만 지난번과 다른 점이 있습니다. **우리가 하나의 행사만 홍보하기 때문에 우리가 받게 되는 수수료가 더 적을 것이라는 점입니다.** 자, 우리가 보수는 더 적게 받지만 필립스 앤 애커맨과 좋은 관계를 유지하는 게 중요하다는 게 내 생각입니다. 그러니 이 일에 최선을 다합시다.

어휘 charity banquet 자선 연회 promote 홍보하다, 증진하다 safe driving practices 안전 운행 fee 비용, 수수료 maintain 유지하다 put one's best effort into ~에 최선의 노력을 다하다

77

What type of event will a law firm host?

(A) A lecture
(B) A fund-raiser
(C) A retirement banquet
(D) A job fair

법률 회사는 어떤 행사를 주최할 것인가?

(A) 강의
(B) 모금 행사
(C) 퇴직 기념 만찬
(D) 취업 박람회

해설 세부 사항 관련 - 행사의 종류

지문 초반부에 필립스 앤 애커맨 법률 사무소가 올해 말에 자선 연회 행사를 열려고 한다(Phillips & Ackerman Law Firm is hosting a charity banquet later this year)고 했으므로 정답은 (B)이다.

▸▸ **Paraphrasing** 지문의 **a charity banquet**
→ 정답의 **A fund-raiser**

Test 5

78

Who most likely are the listeners?

(A) Tour organizers
(B) New lawyers
(C) Catering chefs
(D) Marketing employees

청자들은 누구겠는가?

(A) 투어 주최자들
(B) 신입 변호사들
(C) 연회 업체 요리사들
(D) 마케팅 직원들

해설 전체 내용 관련 - 청자들의 신분

지문 초반부에 필립스 앤 애커맨 법률 사무소가 지난해 저녁 만찬 시리즈를 위해 마련했던 광고 캠페인이 매우 마음에 들어 올해도 다시 청자들의 회사를 고용하고 싶어 한다(They were so pleased with the advertising campaign ~ our publicity services again this year.)고 했다. 이를 통해 청자들은 타 회사의 광고 캠페인을 해 주는 마케팅 직원임을 알 수 있으므로 정답은 (D)이다.

79

What difference from last year's project does the speaker mention?

(A) The client representative is new.
(B) The work will take longer.
(C) The payment is smaller.
(D) More paperwork will be required.

화자는 지난해 프로젝트와 다른 점으로 무엇을 언급하는가?

(A) 고객 담당자가 새로운 사람이다.
(B) 일이 더 오래 걸릴 것이다.
(C) 지불액이 더 적다.
(D) 서류 작업이 더 많이 필요하다.

어휘 client representative 고객[영업] 담당자

해설 세부 사항 관련 - 지난해 계약과 다른 점

지문 후반부에 한 가지 행사만을 홍보하기 때문에 우리가 받게 되는 수수료가 더 적을 것(We're only promoting a single event ~ is lower.)이라고 했으므로 정답은 (C)이다.

▸▸ **Paraphrasing** 지문의 **the fee** → 정답의 **payment**

80-82 전화 메시지

M-Au Hi, Chris. This is Dwain Wilson from Elegant Executive. I'm calling regarding your recent order. As we promised, [80]**the couches and coffee tables for your office will be available for delivery on Thursday, as will the conference table.** However, there will be a brief delay in delivering the six chairs. [81]**We have completely run out of the fabric that you selected for them,** but we expect to have more of it by the end of the week, and will finish the chairs as soon as possible. We should have them on your doorstep in exactly two weeks. [82]**I am very sorry for the delay.** Please don't hesitate to contact us with any questions.

안녕하세요, 크리스. 엘리건트 이그제큐티브의 드웨인 윌슨입니다. 최근 주문하신 것과 관련해 전화드렸습니다. 약속드린 대로, **사무실에서 쓰실 소파와 커피 탁자들은 목요일에 배송해 드릴 수 있고, 회의 탁자도 마찬가지입니다.** 하지만 의자 여섯 개는 배송이 조금 지연될 겁니다. **고르신 의자에 쓰이는 천이 다 동이 났거든요.** 하지만 주말까지는 더 들어올 것으로 예상되니 가능한 한 빨리 의자 제조 작업을 끝내겠습니다. 정확히 2주 후에는 고객님 사무실 문 앞에 갖다 드리겠습니다. **일이 지연되어 대단히 죄송합니다.** 궁금하신 점이 있으시면 망설이지 마시고 연락 주십시오.

어휘 regarding ~에 관하여 couch 소파 available for delivery 배달할 수 있는 conference table 회의 탁자 brief 짧은 delay 지연, 지체 completely 완전히 run out of ~이 다 떨어지다, 동이 나다 fabric 천 by the end of the week 주말까지 doorstep 문간, 현관 hesitate 망설이다

80

What did the listener order?

(A) Curtains
(B) Coffee
(C) Clothing
(D) Furniture

청자는 무엇을 주문했는가?

(A) 커튼
(B) 커피
(C) 의류
(D) 가구

해설 세부 사항 관련 - 청자의 주문품

지문 초반부에 화자가 청자에게 사무실용 소파와 커피 탁자들은 목요일에 배송 가능하고 회의 탁자도 마찬가지(the couches and coffee tables ~ conference table.)라고 했다. 청자가 가구를 주문했음을 알 수 있으므로 정답은 (D)이다.

▸▸ **Paraphrasing** 대화의 **couches, coffee tables, conference table** → 정답의 **furniture**

81

What has caused a delay?

(A) A payment was not received.
(B) A warehouse was damaged.
(C) A highway is undergoing roadwork.
(D) A material is out of stock.

지연되는 이유는 무엇인가?
(A) 대금을 받지 못했다.
(B) 창고가 파손되었다.
(C) 고속도로가 공사 중이다.
(D) 재료가 떨어졌다.

해설 세부 사항 관련 – 지연된 이유
지문 중반부에 의자 여섯 개는 배송이 조금 지연될 텐데 그 이유는 고객이 의자용으로 고른 천이 완전히 떨어졌기 때문(We have completely run out of the fabric that you selected for them)이라고 했으므로 정답은 (D)이다.

▸▸ **Paraphrasing** 지문의 **completely run out of the fabric**
→ 정답의 **A material is out of stock.**

82
What does the speaker give the listener?
(A) A partial refund
(B) An apology
(C) A phone number
(D) A choice of options

화자는 청자에게 무엇을 전하는가?
(A) 부분적 환불
(B) 사과
(C) 전화 번호
(D) 몇 가지 선택 안

해설 세부 사항 관련 – 화자가 청자에게 전하는 것
지문 후반부에 일이 지연되어 대단히 죄송하다(I am very sorry for the delay.)고 했으므로 정답은 (B)이다.

▸▸ **Paraphrasing** 지문의 **sorry** → 정답의 **apology**

83-85 담화

W-Br You're all here today because we've been receiving complaints about the cleanliness of our facility. Customers say that the floors are sticky and covered with popcorn. So for the last few days [83, 84]**I've been tracking the time that employees spend on cleaning between films, and—I'm disappointed.** Sometimes these sessions are over within five minutes. [83]**You all do an excellent job serving customers at the snack bar and the box office**, but that's not your only duty. Now, I've put all of your cleaning tasks in the chart on these laminated cards. [85]**Please start taking a card with you when you clean and mark the box next to each task after you complete it.** Thanks.

여러분은 오늘 시설 청결에 관한 불만사항 접수 건들로 이 자리에 모였습니다. 고객들은 바닥이 끈적끈적하고 팝콘으로 뒤덮여 있다고 이야기합니다. 그래서 지난 며칠간 **영화 상영 사이에 직원들이 청소하는 데 들이는 시간을 추적해 봤는데 실망스러웠습니다.** 때로는 청소 시간이 5분 안에 끝났습니다. **여러분 모두 스낵바와 매표소에서 고객들을 응대하는 일은 훌륭히 수행하고 있지만** 여러분의 임무는 그것만이 아닙니다. 자, 제가 여러분의 청소 업무를 이 코팅된 카드의 차트에 모두 적어 두었습니다. **청소하실 때 카드를 가져가셔서, 완료한 후 각 업무 옆에 있는 박스에 체크해주세요.** 감사합니다.

어휘 complaint 불만 cleanliness 청결 sticky 끈적끈적한 be covered with ~로 덮이다 track 추적하다 spend 보내다, 소비하다 disappointed 실망한 box office 매표소 duty 의무 laminated 보호용 포장막을 입힌 mark 표시하다 complete 완료하다

83
Who is the talk intended for?
(A) Store clerks
(B) Cafeteria servers
(C) Movie theater staff
(D) Postal workers

담화는 누구를 대상으로 한 것인가?
(A) 가게 점원
(B) 카페 종업원
(C) 영화관 직원
(D) 우체부

어휘 clerk 점원, 사무원 postal 우편의

해설 전체 내용 관련 – 청자의 신분
지문 중반에 화자가 영화 상영 사이에 직원들이 청소하는 데 들이는 시간을 추적해 봤는데 실망했다(I've been tracking the time ~ I'm disappointed.)고 말한 후에, 스낵바와 매표소에서 고객들을 응대하는 업무는 훌륭히 수행하고 있다(You all do an excellent job ~ the box office)고 하는 것으로 보아 정답은 (C)이다.

84
Why does the speaker say, "Sometimes these sessions are over within five minutes"?
(A) To praise the listeners for their efficiency
(B) To reassure the listeners about an assignment
(C) To criticize the listeners for being careless
(D) To alert the listeners to a possible difficulty

화자가 "때로는 청소 시간이 5분 안에 끝났습니다"라고 말한 이유는 무엇인가?
(A) 청자들의 효율성에 대해 칭찬하기 위해
(B) 청자들에게 임무에 대해 안심시키기 위해
(C) 청자들의 부주의함을 지적하기 위해
(D) 청자들에게 어려움이 있을 수 있다는 점을 경고하기 위해

Test 5

어휘 praise 칭찬하다 efficiency 효율성 reassure 안심시키다 assignment 임무 criticize 지적하다, 비판하다 careless 부주의한 alert 알리다, 경고하다

해설 화자의 의도 파악 – 때로는 청소 시간이 5분 안에 끝났다는 말의 의도

인용문 바로 앞 문장에서 영화 상영 사이에 직원들이 청소하는 데 들이는 시간을 추적해 봤는데 실망했다(I've been tracking the time ~ I'm disappointed.)고 한 뒤 청소 시간이 5분 안에 끝났다고 했으므로 정답은 (C)이다.

85

What does the speaker instruct the listeners to do?

(A) Use a checklist
(B) Move some boxes
(C) Take some business cards
(D) Watch a video

화자는 청자들에게 무엇을 하라고 지시하는가?

(A) 체크리스트 활용하기
(B) 상자 옮기기
(C) 명함 가져가기
(D) 동영상 시청하기

어휘 business card 명함

해설 세부 사항 관련 – 청자들이 해야 할 일

지문 후반부에 화자가 청자들에게 청소할 때 카드를 가져가서, 완료한 후 각 업무 옆 박스에 체크하라(Please start taking a card with you ~ after you complete it.)고 했으므로 정답은 (A)이다.

86-88 광고

W-Am [86]**Wearing headphones for longer than a quick jog or airplane ride is uncomfortable, but professionals that work with audio technology don't have a choice.** That's why Surefoot Acoustics' new headphones are made just for them. [87]**The Surefoot XL22 headphones are extremely comfortable no matter how long you wear them.** They gently rest on your ears with ear cups made out of ultra-light padding, and the band that connects the ear cups evenly spreads the weight of the headphones over the listener's head. Visit our Web site to see how cheap it is to outfit your entire workplace with [88]**our great discounts on bulk orders** too. Get your pair of Surefoot XL22s today to enjoy real comfort.

단시간의 조깅이나 비행기 탑승 시간보다 더 오래 헤드폰을 착용하는 것은 불편하지만, 오디오 기술로 작업하는 전문직 종사자들은 어쩔 수가 없습니다. 그래서 슈어풋 어쿠스틱스의 신형 헤드폰은 그들에게 안성맞춤입니다. **슈어풋 XL22 헤드폰은 아무리 오래 착용해도 매우 편안합니다.** 초경량 완충재로 만든 귀덮개가 귀를 부드럽게 감싸주며, 귀덮개와 연결된 밴드가 헤드폰의 무게를 청취자의 머리에 골고루 분산시킵니다. 저희 웹 사이트에 방문하셔서, **대량 주문으로 가격을 대폭 할인받아** 직장 전체에 얼마나 저렴하게 장비를 갖출 수 있는지도 살펴보세요. 오늘 슈어풋 XL22를 구입하셔서 진정한 편안함을 즐겨 보세요.

어휘 uncomfortable 불편한 professional 전문직 종사자 no matter how long 아무리 오래 ~해도 gently 부드럽게 rest on ~에 얹히다 ear cup (헤드폰의) 귀덮개 made out of ~로 만들어진 ultralight 초경량의 padding 완충재 evenly 균일하게, 고르게 spread 퍼뜨리다 outfit (장비를) 갖추다, 장착하다 bulk 대량의 comfort 편안함

86

What does the speaker say about the intended users of the product?

(A) They travel frequently.
(B) They manufacture computers.
(C) They exercise with headphones.
(D) They wear headphones for long periods.

화자는 상품이 대상으로 하는 사용자에 대해 뭐라고 말하는가?

(A) 그들은 여행을 자주 한다.
(B) 그들은 컴퓨터를 제조한다.
(C) 그들은 헤드폰을 쓰고 운동한다.
(D) 그들은 장시간 헤드폰을 착용한다.

어휘 frequently 자주 manufacture 제조하다

해설 전체 내용 관련 – 상품이 대상으로 하는 사용자

지문 맨 처음에 단시간의 조깅이나 비행기 탑승 시간보다 더 오래 헤드폰을 착용하는 것은 불편하지만 오디오 기술을 가지고 작업하는 전문직 종사자들은 어쩔 수가 없다(Wearing headphones for longer ~ don't have a choice.)고 했다. 이 말을 통해 광고의 대상이 장시간 헤드폰을 착용하는 사람임을 알 수 있으므로 정답은 (D)이다.

87

According to the speaker, what is special about the product?

(A) It produces a loud sound.
(B) It does not break easily.
(C) It is very comfortable.
(D) It has a built-in microphone.

화자에 따르면, 이 제품의 특별한 점은 무엇인가?

(A) 큰 음향을 재생해 낸다.
(B) 잘 고장 나지 않는다.
(C) 매우 편안하다.
(D) 내장 마이크가 있다.

해설 세부 사항 관련 – 제품의 특별한 점

지문 초반부에 슈어풋 XL22 헤드폰은 아무리 오래 착용해도 매우 편안하다(The Surefoot XL22 headphones ~ you wear them.)고 했으므로 정답은 (C)이다.

▸▸ **Paraphrasing** 지문의 **extremely** → 정답의 **very**

88

How can customers get a discount?

(A) By making a referral
(B) By buying many pairs of the product
(C) By using a coupon code
(D) By purchasing the product soon

고객들은 어떻게 할인을 받을 수 있는가?

(A) 지인을 소개해서
(B) 다량 구매해서
(C) 쿠폰 코드를 사용해서
(D) 제품을 빨리 구매해서

어휘 make a referral 소개하다

해설 세부 사항 관련 – 할인을 받을 수 있는 방법

지문 후반부에 대량 주문으로 가격을 대폭 할인받으라(our great discounts on bulk orders)고 했으므로 정답은 (B)이다.

▸▸ **Paraphrasing** 지문의 **bulk orders**
→ 정답의 **buying many pairs**

89-91 회의 발췌

M-Au OK. [89]**With the opening of our company's Mumbai branch office last month,** I've instructed the budget committee to purchase a new videoconferencing system. It's a Telephonik Plus premium model, with large screens and powerful microphones. [90]**Now, there have been questions about its cost.** Seven thousand dollars is a lot of money. But note that just a few international plane trips will add up to that amount, so the system pays for itself. [91]**A company representative is scheduled to visit us next Thursday at two P.M. and give us hands-on training using the system.** Please plan to attend.

좋아요. **지난달에 우리 회사의 뭄바이 지사가 개설되면서,** 저는 예산위원회에 새로운 화상회의 시스템을 구매하라고 지시했습니다. 그것은 대형 스크린과 성능 좋은 마이크를 갖춘 텔레포닉 플러스 최고급 모델입니다. **그런데 그 구입 비용을 놓고 의문 제기가 있었습니다.** 7000달러는 큰돈입니다. 하지만 국제선 항공기를 몇 번만 타도 그 정도 금액이 되니 이 시스템으로 본전은 뽑는다는 점을 유념해 주십시오. **회사 직원이 다음 주 목요일 오후 2시에 우리를 방문해서 시스템 사용 실습을 진행할 예정이니** 참석해 주시기 바랍니다.

어휘 branch office 지사 instruct 지시하다 budget committee 예산위원회 videoconferencing system 화상회의 시스템 premium model 최고급 모델 international plane trip 국제선 항공기 여행 add up to ~ 합계 ~가 되다 amount 액수, 금액 pay for itself 본전을 뽑다, 비용만큼 절약이 되다 hands-on training 실습

89

What does the speaker say happened at his company recently?

(A) A product line was launched.
(B) A branch office was opened.
(C) A press conference was held.
(D) A sales trip was canceled.

화자는 최근 자신의 회사에서 무슨 일이 일어났다고 말하는가?

(A) 제품군이 출시되었다.
(B) 지사가 문을 열었다.
(C) 기자회견이 열렸다.
(D) 영업 출장이 취소되었다.

어휘 press conference 기자회견

해설 세부 사항 관련 – 최근에 회사에 발생한 일

지문 맨 처음에 회사의 뭄바이 지사가 지난달에 개설되었다(With the opening of our company's Mumbai branch office last month)고 했으므로 정답은 (B)이다.

90

What does the speaker imply when he says, "Seven thousand dollars is a lot of money"?

(A) He is disappointed with a negotiation's results.
(B) He understands other people's concerns.
(C) He will need to reduce operating costs.
(D) He is having doubts about a proposal.

화자가 "7000달러는 큰돈입니다"라고 말한 의도는 무엇인가?

(A) 그는 협상의 결과에 실망했다.
(B) 그는 다른 사람들이 염려하는 바를 이해한다.
(C) 그는 운영비를 줄여야 할 것이다.
(D) 그는 제안에 대하여 의구심을 가지고 있다.

어휘 negotiation 협상 concern 염려 reduce 줄이다, 낮추다 operating cost 운영비 doubt 의구심

해설 화자의 의도 파악 – 7000달러는 큰돈이라는 말의 의도

지문 중반부에 텔레포닉 플러스 최고급 모델의 가격을 놓고 여러 가지 의문이 제기되었다(Now, there have been questions about its cost.)고 했다. 그러고 나서 7000달러는 큰돈이라는 인용문을 언급했다. 즉, 텔레포닉 플러스의 구매가 이례적으로 비용이 많이 드는 것임을 화자도 알고 있다는 의미를 내포하고 있는 것이므로 정답은 (B)이다.

91

What is scheduled for next Thursday?

(A) A factory inspection
(B) A training session
(C) A welcome reception
(D) A shareholders' meeting

다음 주 목요일에 예정되어 있는 것은?

(A) 공장 시찰
(B) 교육 과정
(C) 환영회
(D) 주주 총회

어휘 shareholder 주주

해설 세부 사항 관련 – 다음 주 목요일에 예정된 일

지문 후반부에 회사 직원이 다음 주 목요일 오후 2시에 방문해서 시스템 사용 실습을 진행할 예정(A company representative is scheduled to visit us next ~ using the system.)이라고 했으므로 정답은 (B)이다.

▸▸ **Paraphrasing** 지문의 **hands-on training**
→ 정답의 **A training session**

92-94 소개

W-Br All right, [92]**now that the waitstaff have cleared the dishes away, it's time for our main event.** We're gathered here tonight to celebrate Ernest Woodruff. Ernest joined Willotte Electronics nearly thirty years ago, soon after graduating from Tansley University with a degree in electrical engineering. In addition to earning frequent promotions, he worked in two different divisions and three locations of Willotte, including our Tokyo branch. Now, as [93]**he concludes this long and successful career and leaves the workforce,** I'm sure I speak for all of us when I say he'll be missed. [94]**It is rare to find such a patient, helpful, and friendly coworker and boss.** Ladies and gentlemen, Ernest Woodruff.

자, 종업원들이 접시를 다 치웠으니 주요 행사 시간입니다. 오늘 밤 우리는 어니스트 우드러프 씨를 축하하기 위해 이곳에 모였습니다. 어니스트 씨는 거의 30년 전, 탠즐리 대학교에서 전기공학 학위를 받아 졸업하시고 윌럿 일렉트로닉스에 바로 입사하셨습니다. 빠른 승진을 거듭하며 윌럿의 두 개 부서와 동경 지부를 포함한 세 곳의 지부에서 근무하셨습니다. 이제 **그가 성공적인 오랜 직장 생활을 마감하고 회사를 떠나시니** 어니스트 씨가 그리울 거라고 말씀드리는 게 우리 모두의 마음을 대변하는 것이라 확신합니다. **이토록 인내심 강하고 언제나 도움을 주시며 친절한 동료이자 리더는 만나보기 힘들 것입니다.** 여러분, 어니스트 우드러프 씨를 맞아주십시오.

어휘 waitstaff 종업원들 gather 모이다 celebrate 축하하다 nearly 거의 graduate from ~를 졸업하다 degree 학위 electrical engineering 전기공학 in addition to ~에 덧붙여 frequent 잦은 promotion 승진 division 부서 branch 지부, 지점 conclude 끝내다, 마치다 workforce 노동력, 직원 speak for ~를 대변하다 rare 드문 patient 참을성 있는 coworker 동료

92

Where most likely is the introduction taking place?

(A) In a restaurant
(B) In a park
(C) In an auditorium
(D) In a radio station

소개는 어디서 이루어지고 있겠는가?

(A) 식당
(B) 공원
(C) 강당
(D) 라디오 방송국

어휘 auditorium 강당 radio station 라디오 방송국

해설 전체 내용 관련 – 소개가 이뤄지는 장소

지문 초반부에 화자가 청자들에게 종업원들이 접시를 다 치웠으니 주요 행사 시간이다(now that the waitstaff have cleared ~ for our main event.)라고 했으므로 정답은 (A)이다.

93

Why most likely is Mr. Woodruff being introduced?

(A) He recently returned from abroad.
(B) He has won an award.
(C) He is being promoted.
(D) He is retiring.

우드러프 씨를 소개하는 이유는 무엇이겠는가?

(A) 최근 해외에서 돌아왔다.
(B) 상을 받았다.
(C) 승진했다.
(D) 은퇴한다.

어휘 abroad 해외에 win an award 상을 받다

해설 전체 내용 관련 – 우드러프 씨를 소개하는 이유

지문 중반부에 화자는 우드러프 씨가 성공적인 오랜 직장 생활을 마감하고 회사를 떠난다(he concludes this long and successful career and leaves the workforce)고 했으므로 정답은 (D)이다.

94

What does the speaker emphasize about Mr. Woodruff?

(A) His leadership
(B) His creativity
(C) His honesty
(D) His kindness

화자가 우드러프 씨에 대해 강조하는 것은 무엇인가?
(A) 리더십
(B) 창의성
(C) 정직성
(D) 친절함

어휘 creativity 창의성 honesty 정직성

해설 세부 사항 관련 – 우드러프 씨에 대해 강조하는 점
지문 후반부에 화자는 우드러프 씨처럼 인내심 강하고 언제나 도움을 주며 친절한 동료이자 리더는 만나보기 힘들 것이다(It is rare to find such a patient, helpful, and friendly coworker and boss.)라고 했으므로 정답은 (D)이다.

▸▸ Paraphrasing 지문의 **helpful and friendly**
→ 정답의 **kindness**

95-97 관광 정보 + 일정표

M-Cn Welcome to the Mirasora Estate tour. I'm David Daniels, your guide. [95]**We're going to be taking a tour of the grounds owned by the famous novelist Ellen Mirasora.** She lived on this beautiful estate in the nineteenth century. Visitors will clearly see this time period's style and architecture, especially in the Main House. Now, unfortunately, [96]**Gertie Gardens is currently closed for renovations. Instead, we'll be visiting Stables Swimming Pool during that time on our tour.** I apologize for any disappointment this may cause. However, [97]**visitors rarely get to see Stables Swimming Pool as it's not part of any tour,** so I hope you'll consider it a special treat. All right, let's begin.

미라소라 사유지 투어에 오신 것을 환영합니다. 저는 여러분의 가이드인 데이비드 대니얼스입니다. **우리는 유명 소설가인 엘렌 미라소라 소유의 땅을 둘러볼 것입니다.** 그녀는 19세기에 이 아름다운 사유지에서 살았습니다. 방문객들께서는 특히 본관에서 이 시대의 양식과 건축을 확실히 보실 수 있을 겁니다. 그런데 안타깝게도 **거티 정원은 현재 새 단장을 하느라 폐쇄되어 있습니다. 대신에 우리는 그 시간 동안 스테이블즈 수영장을 둘러볼 예정입니다.** 이것 때문에 실망하셨다면 사과 드립니다. 하지만 **스테이블즈 수영장은 어떤 투어에도 포함되지 않은, 방문객들이 좀처럼 볼 수 없는 곳이니** 여러분 모두 특별 대접을 받는다고 생각해주시기 바랍니다. 자, 이제 갑시다.

어휘 estate 사유지, 토지 novelist 소설가 time period 시대 architecture 건축(술) currently 현재 disappointment 실망 rarely 드물게, 좀처럼 ~하지 않는 treat 특별한 것, 대접 pavilion 가설 건축물, 전시관 mulberry 뽕나무

Tour Schedule

Location	Time
Main House	10:45 A.M. – 11:45 A.M.
Roy Pavilion	11:45 A.M. – 12:00 P.M.
Mulberry Row	12:00 P.M. – 12:30 P.M.
[96]Gertie Gardens	12:30 P.M. – 12:45 P.M.

투어 일정

장소	시간
본관	오전 10:45~오전 11:45
로이 파빌리온	오전 11:45~오후 12:00
멀베리 길	오후 12:00~오후 12:30
거티 정원	오후 12:30~오후 12:45

95

Who was Ms. Mirasora?
(A) A painter
(B) A scientist
(C) A writer
(D) An architect

미라소라 씨의 직업은 무엇이었는가?
(A) 화가
(B) 과학자
(C) 작가
(D) 건축가

해설 전체 내용 관련 – 엘렌 미라소라의 신분
지문 초반부에 화자가 청자들에게 유명한 소설가인 엘렌 미라소라 소유의 땅을 둘러볼 예정(We're going to ~ novelist Ellen Mirasora.)이라고 했으므로 정답은 (C)이다.

▸▸ Paraphrasing 지문의 **the famous novelist**
→ 정답의 **writer**

96

Look at the graphic. When will the listeners begin touring Stables Swimming Pool?
(A) At 10:45 A.M.
(B) At 11:45 A.M.
(C) At 12:00 P.M.
(D) At 12:30 P.M.

시각 정보에 의하면, 청자들은 스테이블즈 수영장을 언제 둘러보기 시작하겠는가?
(A) 오전 10:45에
(B) 오전 11:45에
(C) 오후 12:00에
(D) 오후 12:30에

Test 5

해설 시각 정보 연계 - 청자들의 스테이블즈 수영장 방문 시간

지문 중반부에 거티 정원이 현재 새 단장을 하느라 폐쇄되어서 대신 그 시간 동안 스테이블즈 수영장을 둘러볼 예정(Gertie Gardens is currently closed ~ on our tour.)이라고 했다. 그리고 일정표를 보면 거티 정원 방문 시간이 오후 12시 30분에서 12시 45분으로 나와 있다. 즉, 이 시간에 청자들은 스테이블즈 수영장에 갈 것이므로 정답은 (D)이다.

97

What does the speaker mention about Stables Swimming Pool?

(A) It is usually closed to the public.
(B) It has recently been renovated.
(C) It was expensive to build.
(D) It is cleaned twice a week.

화자가 스테이블즈 수영장에 관해 언급한 것은?

(A) 평소에는 일반인이 출입할 수 없다.
(B) 최근에 새 단장을 했다.
(C) 짓는 데 비용이 많이 들었다.
(D) 일주일에 두 번 청소한다.

해설 세부 사항 관련 - 스테이블즈 수영장에 대한 언급

지문 후반부에 스테이블즈 수영장은 어떤 투어에도 포함된 곳이 아니라서 방문객들이 좀처럼 볼 수 없다(visitors rarely get to ~ not part of any tour)고 했으므로 정답은 (A)이다.

98-100 뉴스 보도 + 표지판

W-Br This is Rosa Velez from Channel 9 News. [98]**I'm standing on Lyon Boulevard where preparations are underway for the city's annual marathon this Saturday, April ninth.** This year, there will be over one thousand athletes competing, the biggest turnout in the event's history. The city will be blocking many major roads and putting up "No Parking" signs on others. Some streets will be no-parking zones for a couple hours. These include Maple Road and Durden Lane. [99]**Other streets, such as Carson Avenue, will ban parking all day.** If you plan on traveling around the city this Saturday, [100]**please go to the city's official Web site and get detailed information about all road closures and changes.**

채널 9 뉴스의 로자 벨레즈입니다. **저는 지금 이번 주 토요일인 4월 9일에 있을, 시 연례 마라톤 경기 준비가 한창인 라이온 대로에 서 있습니다.** 올해에는 1000명이 넘는 선수들이 경쟁을 벌이게 되는데요, 이는 행사 역사상 가장 많은 참가 인원입니다. 시는 여러 주요 도로를 차단하고 다른 도로들에는 '주차 금지' 표지판을 설치할 예정입니다. 메이플 로드와 더든 레인을 포함한 일부 거리들은 두 시간 동안 주차 금지 구역이 됩니다. **카슨 애비뉴 같은 다른 거리들에서는 하루 종일 주차가 금지될 예정입니다. 이번 주 토요일에 시내를 돌아다니실 계획이라면 시의 공식 웹 사이트에 가셔서 도로 폐쇄와 변경 사항에 관한 자세한 정보를 얻으시기 바랍니다.**

어휘 boulevard 대로 underway 진행 중인 athlete 운동선수 compete 겨루다 turnout 참가 인원, 참가자 수 block 차단하다 put up signs 표지판을 설치하다[세우다] no-parking zone 주차 금지 구역 ban 금지하다 road closure 도로 폐쇄 by order of ~의 명령으로

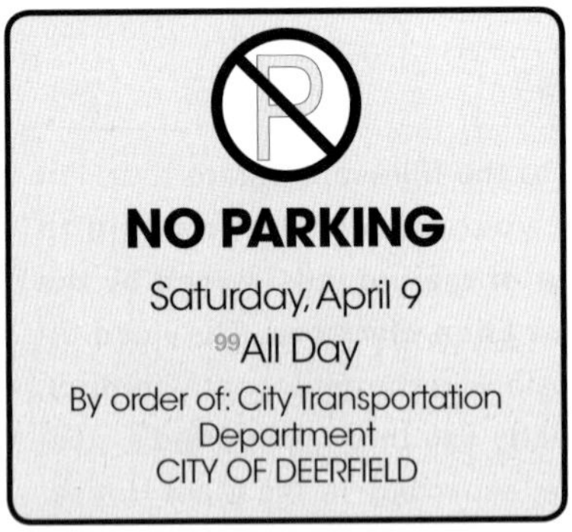

NO PARKING
Saturday, April 9
[99]All Day
By order of: City Transportation Department
CITY OF DEERFIELD

4월 9일, 토요일

시 교통과의 명에 의해
디어필드 시

98

What is happening in the city this Saturday?

(A) A holiday parade
(B) An automobile exposition
(C) An athletic event
(D) A music festival

시에서 이번 주 토요일에 무슨 일이 일어날 것인가?

(A) 공휴일 퍼레이드
(B) 자동차 박람회
(C) 체육 행사
(D) 음악 축제

해설 세부 사항 관련 – 이번 주 토요일 시 행사

지문 초반부에 화자가 지금 4월 9일, 이번 주 토요일에 있을 시 연례 마라톤 경기 준비가 한창인 라이온 대로에 서 있다(I'm standing on ~ April ninth.)고 했으므로 정답은 (C)이다.

▸▸ **Paraphrasing** 지문의 **the city's annual marathon**
→ 정답의 **athletic event**

99

Look at the graphic. On which street will the sign most likely be posted?

(A) Carson Avenue
(B) Maple Road
(C) Durden Lane
(D) Lyon Boulevard

시각 정보에 의하면, 어느 거리에 이 표지판이 설치되겠는가?

(A) 카슨 애비뉴
(B) 메이플 로드
(C) 더든 레인
(D) 라이온 대로

해설 시각 정보 연계 – 표지판이 설치될 거리

지문 후반부에 카슨 애비뉴 같은 다른 거리에는 하루 종일 주차가 금지될 예정(Other streets, such as Carson Avenue, will ban parking all day.)이라고 했다. 그리고 표지판을 보면 종일(All Day) 주차 금지(NO PARKING)로 표시되어 있으므로 정답은 (A)이다.

100

What does the speaker encourage the listeners to do?

(A) Visit a Web site
(B) Call a city official
(C) Join an activity
(D) Use a residential road

화자는 청자들에게 무엇을 할 것을 권하는가?

(A) 웹 사이트 방문
(B) 시 공무원에게 전화
(C) 활동에 참가
(D) 주거지 도로 사용

어휘 city official 시 공무원 residential 주거지의

해설 세부 사항 관련 – 화자의 권장 사항

지문 맨 마지막에 화자가 청자들에게 시 공식 웹 사이트에 들어가서 도로 폐쇄와 변경 사항에 관한 자세한 정보를 얻으라(please go to the city's official Web site and ~ road closures and changes.)고 했으므로 정답은 (A)이다.

▸▸ **Paraphrasing** 지문의 **go to the city's official Web site**
→ 정답의 **visit a Web site**

TEST 6

1 (A)	2 (D)	3 (A)	4 (C)	5 (D)
6 (C)	7 (B)	8 (C)	9 (A)	10 (C)
11 (B)	12 (A)	13 (C)	14 (A)	15 (C)
16 (C)	17 (A)	18 (B)	19 (A)	20 (B)
21 (C)	22 (B)	23 (C)	24 (B)	25 (B)
26 (C)	27 (A)	28 (A)	29 (A)	30 (C)
31 (B)	32 (D)	33 (B)	34 (B)	35 (B)
36 (B)	37 (B)	38 (C)	39 (C)	40 (D)
41 (A)	42 (D)	43 (D)	44 (C)	45 (A)
46 (B)	47 (B)	48 (B)	49 (B)	50 (A)
51 (D)	52 (B)	53 (A)	54 (C)	55 (C)
56 (A)	57 (C)	58 (A)	59 (A)	60 (B)
61 (B)	62 (D)	63 (A)	64 (A)	65 (C)
66 (B)	67 (A)	68 (C)	69 (B)	70 (D)
71 (A)	72 (D)	73 (D)	74 (B)	75 (D)
76 (A)	77 (C)	78 (A)	79 (C)	80 (C)
81 (B)	82 (B)	83 (C)	84 (D)	85 (A)
86 (A)	87 (D)	88 (B)	89 (A)	90 (C)
91 (D)	92 (D)	93 (A)	94 (B)	95 (A)
96 (C)	97 (D)	98 (B)	99 (A)	100 (C)

PART 1

1 W-Br

(A) A man is using a shovel.
(B) A man is cutting some grass.
(C) A woman is kneeling by a tree.
(D) A woman is putting on work gloves.

(A) 남자가 삽을 사용하고 있다.
(B) 남자가 잔디를 깎고 있다.
(C) 여자가 나무 옆에서 무릎을 꿇고 있다.
(D) 여자가 작업용 장갑을 끼는 중이다.

어휘 shovel 삽 grass 잔디 kneel 무릎을 꿇다 glove 장갑

해설 2인 이상 등장 사진 – 사람의 동작 묘사

(A) 남자가 삽을 사용하고 있는(is using a shovel) 모습이므로 정답.

(B) 남자가 잔디 위에 서서 작업하고 있지, 깎고 있는(is cutting some grass) 모습은 아니므로 오답.

(C) 사진에 나무가 있지만 여자가 그 옆에 무릎을 꿇고 있는(is kneeling by a tree) 모습이 아니므로 오답.

(D) 여자가 작업용 장갑을 이미 착용하고 있지, 끼는 중(is putting on work gloves)이 아니므로 오답

2 M-Cn

(A) A floor is being swept.
(B) A refrigerator is being cleaned out.
(C) A fan is hanging from the ceiling.
(D) A kitchen is unoccupied.

(A) 바닥이 쓸리고 있다.
(B) 냉장고 안이 치워지고 있다.
(C) 선풍기가 천장에 매달려 있다.
(D) 주방이 비어 있다.

어휘 sweep 쓸다, 청소하다 fan 선풍기 ceiling 천장 unoccupied 비어 있는

해설 사물/배경 사진 – 다양한 사물의 상태 묘사

(A) 바닥이 누군가에 의해 쓸리고 있는(is being swept) 중이 아니므로 오답.

(B) 냉장고 안이 누군가에 의해 치워지고 있는(is being cleaned out) 중이 아니므로 오답.

(C) 선풍기가 천장에 매달려 있는(is hanging from the ceiling) 모습이 아니므로 오답.

(D) 주방을 쓰고 있는 사람이 없는(is unoccupied) 상태이므로 정답.

3 M-Au

(A) She's shopping for groceries.
(B) She's entering a grocery store.
(C) She's opening a product's packaging.
(D) She's stocking some shelves.

(A) 여자가 식료품 쇼핑을 하고 있다.
(B) 여자가 식료품점에 들어서고 있다.
(C) 여자가 한 제품의 포장재를 열고 있다.
(D) 여자가 선반들을 채우고 있다.

어휘 groceries 식료품류 packaging 포장재 stock 채우다, (판매할 상품을) 갖춰두다

해설 1인 등장 사진 – 사람의 동작 묘사

(A) 여자가 식료품 쇼핑을 하고 있는(is shopping for groceries) 모습이므로 정답.

(B) 여자가 이미 식료품 가게에 들어와 있는 상태이지 지금 들어가고 있는(is entering a grocery store) 모습이 아니므로 오답.

(C) 여자가 제품을 손으로 잡고 있는 상태이지, 제품의 포장재를 열고 있는(is opening a product's packaging) 모습은 아니므로 오답.

(D) 여자가 선반들을 물품으로 채우고 있는(is stocking some shelves) 모습이 아니므로 오답.

4 W-Am

(A) One of the men is writing notes.
(B) One of the men is handing out pencils.
(C) Two men are shaking hands.
(D) Two men are wearing headphones.

(A) 남자 중 한 명이 메모를 하고 있다.
(B) 남자 중 한 명이 연필을 나누어 주고 있다.
(C) 남자 두 명이 악수를 하고 있다.
(D) 남자 두 명이 헤드폰을 쓰고 있다.

어휘 write a note 메모하다, 짧은 글을 적다 hand out 나누어 주다 shake hands 악수하다

해설 2인 이상 등장 사진 – 사람의 동작 묘사
(A) 남자들 중에 메모를 하는 중인(is writing notes) 사람은 없으므로 오답.
(B) 남자들 중에 연필을 나누어 주고 있는(is handing out pencils) 사람은 없으므로 오답.
(C) 세 남자 중 두 명이 서로 악수하고 있는(are shaking hands) 모습이므로 정답.
(D) 책상 위에 이어폰은 보이지만, 헤드폰을 착용하고 있는 사람은 없으므로 오답.

5 M-Cn

(A) A car is being driven through a parking area.
(B) Water is being sprayed from a hose.
(C) A front tire is being removed.
(D) A vehicle is being washed by hand.

(A) 차가 주차 구역에서 주행 중이다.
(B) 호스에서 물이 분사되고 있다.
(C) 앞 타이어가 제거되고 있다.
(D) 차량이 손으로 세차되고 있다.

어휘 parking area 주차 구역, 주차장 spray 뿌리다 remove 치우다, 제거하다 vehicle 차량

해설 1인 등장 사진 – 사람 또는 사물 중심 묘사
(A) 차가 정차되어 있는 중이지 주행 중(is being driven)인 모습이 아니므로 오답.
(B) 물이 분사되고 있는(is being sprayed) 호스가 없으므로 오답.
(C) 사진에 앞 타이어가 보이지만, 타이어를 빼내고 있는(is being removed) 상황이 아니므로 오답.
(D) 남자가 차를 손으로 세차하고 있는(is being washed by hand) 모습이므로 정답.

6 W-Br

(A) An umbrella is leaning against a wall.
(B) A woman is folding her coat.
(C) Some people are reading.
(D) A briefcase is stored in an overhead rack.

(A) 우산 하나가 벽에 기대어 놓여 있다.
(B) 여자가 자신의 코트를 접고 있다.
(C) 몇몇 사람이 독서를 하고 있다.
(D) 서류가방 하나가 머리 위 선반에 보관되어 있다.

어휘 lean against ~에 기대다 fold 접다 overhead rack(좌석 위에 있는) 짐 놓는 선반

해설 2인 이상 등장 사진 – 사람 또는 사물 중심 묘사
(A) 한 남자가 우산을 다리에 끼고 있는 모습은 보이지만, 우산이 벽에 기대어 놓여 있는(is leaning against a wall) 상태가 아니므로 오답.
(B) 사진 속 여자들 중에 코트를 접고 있는(is folding her coat) 사람은 아무도 없으므로 오답.
(C) 몇몇 사람들이 독서를 하고 있는(are reading) 모습이므로 정답.
(D) 사진에 짐 놓는 선반(overhead rack)은 보이지 않으므로 오답.

Test 6

PART 2

7

W-Br What time is the electrician scheduled to come?

M-Cn (A) Invoices are sent out once a month.

(B) Between nine A.M. and one P.M.

(C) To install new electric lines.

전기 기사가 몇 시에 오기로 되어 있나요?

(A) 송장은 한 달에 한 번 보내요.

(B) 오전 9시에서 오후 1시 사이에요.

(C) 새 전기선을 설치하기 위해서요.

어휘 electrician 전기 기술자 install 설치하다 electric line 전기선

해설 도착 시간을 묻는 What time 의문문

(A) 연상 단어 오답. 질문의 electrician에서 연상 가능한 invoices를 이용한 오답.

(B) 정답. 전기 기사(electrician)의 도착 예정 시간을 묻는 질문에 9시와 1시 사이(Between nine A.M. and one P.M.)라는 구체적인 시간대로 응답하고 있으므로 정답.

(C) 연상 단어 오답. 질문의 electrician에서 연상 가능한 electric lines를 이용한 오답.

8

W-Am Where's the nearest bus stop?

M-Cn (A) Some downtown routes.

(B) What they want to shop for.

(C) I have no idea.

가장 가까운 버스 정류장이 어디죠?

(A) 몇몇 시내 노선들요.

(B) 그들이 사고 싶어 하는 거요.

(C) 모르겠어요.

어휘 near 가까운 downtown 시내에(로) route 노선

해설 버스 정류장의 위치를 묻는 Where 의문문

(A) 연상 단어 오답. 질문의 bus에서 연상 가능한 routes를 이용한 오답.

(B) 유사 발음 오답. 질문의 stop과 발음이 유사한 shop을 이용한 오답.

(C) 정답. 가장 가까운 버스 정류장(the nearest bus stop)의 위치를 묻는 질문에 자신은 모른다(I have no idea.)는 불확실성 표현으로 응답하고 있으므로 정답.

9

W-Br Who's in charge of catering?

M-Au (A) That would be Maria.

(B) Lunch for four people.

(C) It should be fully charged now.

음식 공급 담당자는 누구죠?

(A) 마리아일 거예요.

(B) 4인분의 점심요.

(C) 이제 완전히 충전됐을 거예요.

어휘 be in charge of ~을 담당하다, 맡다 catering 음식 공급, 출장 연회 charge 책임; (전자 기기를) 충전하다

해설 음식 공급 담당자를 묻는 Who 의문문

(A) 정답. 음식 공급(catering)을 담당하는 사람이 누구인지 묻는 질문에 마리아일 것(That would be Maria.)이라고 구체적인 인물을 언급하고 있으므로 정답.

(B) 연상 단어 오답. 질문의 catering에서 연상 가능한 lunch를 이용한 오답.

(C) 단어 반복 오답. 질문의 charge에 -(e)d를 붙여 반복 이용한 오답. 여기서 charge는 '충전하다'의 의미로 쓰였다.

10

M-Cn Would you rather sit by the window or in the aisle seat?

W-Br (A) Oh, I'll close it if you're cold.

(B) We don't need another chair.

(C) Either one is fine.

창가에 앉는 편이 좋습니까, 아니면 통로 쪽 좌석이 좋습니까?

(A) 아, 당신이 춥다면 닫을게요.

(B) 우리는 다른 의자가 필요하지 않아요.

(C) 어느 쪽이든 상관없어요.

어휘 would rather+동사원형 (차라리) ~하고 싶다 aisle 통로

해설 구를 연결한 선택의문문

(A) 연상 단어 오답. 질문의 window에서 연상 가능한 close를 이용한 오답.

(B) 연상 단어 오답. 질문의 sit에서 연상 가능한 chair를 이용한 오답.

(C) 정답. 창가와 통로 쪽 좌석 중 어디에 앉고 싶은지를 묻는 선택의문문에 대해 제시된 선택 사항이 아닌, 어느 쪽이든 상관없다(Either one is fine.)는 제3의 답변으로 응답하고 있으므로 정답.

11

W-Am When did you receive the achievement award?

M-Cn (A) For improving our efficiency.

(B) Last week at the banquet.

(C) I don't have my receipt.

공로상을 언제 받았나요?

(A) 저희 효율성을 증진시켜서요.

(B) 지난주 연회에서요.

(C) 저는 영수증이 없어요.

어휘 achievement award 공로상 improve 개선하다 efficiency 효율성 banquet 연회 receipt 영수증

해설 수상 시점을 묻는 When 의문문

(A) 질문과 상관없는 오답. 이유를 묻는 Why 의문문에 어울리는 응답이므로 오답.

(B) 정답. 공로상(achievement award)을 언제 받았는지에 대해 지난주 연회 때(Last week at the banquet.)라는 구체적인 시점으로 응답하고 있으므로 정답.

(C) 파생어 오답. 질문의 receive와 파생어 관계인 receipt를 이용한 오답.

12

M-Au Why don't we ask Donna to lead the museum tour?

W-Am (A) Do you think she'd do a good job?

(B) Just a few minutes ago.

(C) No, I'm a tourist here myself.

도나에게 박물관 견학을 안내해 달라고 요청해 보면 어떨까요?

(A) 그녀가 잘할 거라고 생각하나요?

(B) 불과 몇 분 전에요.

(C) 아니요, 저도 여기 관광객입니다.

어휘 lead 안내하다, 이끌다 do a good job (일을) 잘하다

해설 안내원을 제안하는 Why don't we 제안 의문문

(A) 정답. 도나에게 박물관 견학을 안내해 달라고(lead the museum tours) 부탁해 보자는 제안에 대해, 확답을 피한 채 도나가 잘할지(she'd do a good job)를 되묻고 있으므로 정답.

(B) 질문과 상관없는 오답. 시점을 묻는 When 의문문에 어울리는 응답이므로 오답.

(C) 파생어 오답. 질문의 tour와 파생어 관계인 tourist를 이용한 오답.

13

M-Cn Who's working the late shift tonight?

M-Au (A) Because of the factory inspection.

(B) You have a good night, too.

(C) Hyun-Gi might know.

오늘 밤 야간 근무 때 누가 일합니까?

(A) 공장 시찰 때문에요.

(B) 당신도 편안한 밤 되세요.

(C) 현기가 알 수도 있어요.

어휘 late shift 야간 교대근무 factory inspection 공장 시찰

해설 야간 근무자를 묻는 Who 의문문

(A) 연상 단어 오답. 질문의 late shift에서 연상 가능한 factory를 이용한 오답.

(B) 유사 발음 오답. 질문의 tonight과 부분적으로 발음이 동일한 night를 이용한 오답.

(C) 정답. 누가 오늘 밤 야간 근무(the late shift)를 하는지에 대해 누가 일할지 현기가 알 수 있다고 응답하고 있으므로 정답.

14

M-Cn Are you going to pick the consultant up at the airport?

W-Am (A) No, my assistant will do it.

(B) He already picked up his flight ticket.

(C) It looks too heavy for me.

당신이 공항에서 컨설턴트를 태워 오실 건가요?

(A) 아니요, 제 비서가 할 겁니다.

(B) 그는 이미 자신의 항공권을 찾아 갔어요.

(C) 저한테는 너무 무거워 보이네요.

어휘 pick up (차량 따위로) [사람·물건 등]을 도중에서 태우다[마중 나가다]; ~을 집어 올리다, 찾다 assistant 비서, 조수 flight ticket 항공권

해설 컨설턴트를 픽업할 것인지 여부를 묻는 be동사 Yes/No 의문문

(A) 정답. 공항에서 컨설턴트를 태워 올 것(pick the consultant up)인지를 묻는 질문에 먼저 No로 부정의 응답을 한 후, 자신의 비서가 할 것(my assistant will do it)이라고 제3자를 언급하고 있으므로 정답.

(B) 단어 반복 오답. 질문의 pick up을 과거동사로 바꿔 반복 이용한 오답.

(C) 연상 단어 오답. 질문의 pick up을 '(물건을) 집어 들다'로 잘못 이해했을 때 연상 가능한 too heavy를 이용한 오답.

15

M-Au How many interviews have you conducted today?

W-Am (A) About an hour per applicant.

(B) The view is great from here.

(C) Only two so far.

오늘 채용 면접을 몇 번 진행했나요?

(A) 각 지원자당 약 한 시간씩요.

(B) 여기서 보니 경치가 멋지군요.

(C) 지금까지 두 번밖에 안 돼요.

어휘 interview 채용 면접 conduct 수행하다 applicant 지원자 view 전망 so far 지금까지

해설 면접 횟수를 묻는 How many 의문문

(A) 연상 단어 오답. 질문의 interviews에서 연상 가능한 applicant를 이용한 오답.

(B) 유사 발음 오답. 질문의 interviews와 부분적으로 발음이 동일한 view를 이용한 오답.

(C) 정답. 오늘 채용 면접을 몇 번이나 진행했는지에 대해 지금까지 단지 두 번(Only two)이라는 구체적인 횟수로 응답하고 있으므로 정답.

16

M-Cn Let's go to the concert in City Park this weekend.

W-Br (A) I'm glad you enjoyed it.

(B) I parked down the road.

(C) That sounds like fun.

이번 주말에 시립 공원에서 하는 콘서트에 갑시다.

(A) 좋았다고 하시니 다행입니다.

(B) 길 아래쪽에 주차했어요.

(C) 재미있겠네요.

어휘 down the road 길 아래에

해설 제안/권유의 평서문

(A) 연상 단어 오답. 질문의 concert에서 연상 가능한 enjoyed를 이용한 오답.

(B) 단어 반복 오답. 질문의 Park를 동사 park(주차하다)의 과거형으로 바꿔 반복 이용한 오답.

(C) 정답. 콘서트에 같이 가자는 제안에 대해 재미있겠다(That sounds like fun.)는 표현으로 긍정적 응답을 하고 있으므로 정답.

17

W-Br Where is your business located?

M-Au (A) Third Avenue and Main Street.

(B) Retail accounting, mostly.

(C) We keep them in the filing cabinet.

당신의 회사 위치는 어디인가요?

(A) 3번 애비뉴와 메인 가의 모퉁이에 있어요.

(B) 주로 소매 업체 회계 일이요.

(C) 우리는 그것들을 서류 캐비닛에 보관해요.

어휘 be located 위치하다 retail 소매의 accounting 회계 filing cabinet 서류 캐비닛

해설 사무실 위치를 묻는 Where 의문문

(A) 정답. 사무실 위치를 묻는 질문에 Third Avenue and Main Street라는 구체적인 장소를 언급하고 있으므로 정답.

(B) 질문과 상관없는 오답. 어떤 종류의 사업을 하는지 묻는 What 의문문에 어울리는 응답이므로 오답.

(C) Where is ~ located?로 어떤 서류나 물건의 위치를 물었을 때 응답 가능한 filing cabinet을 이용한 오답.

18

W-Am Why did you return the desk lamp?

M-Cn (A) Not until this morning.

(B) Its cord was damaged.

(C) Turn left at the light.

탁상용 램프를 왜 반품했나요?

(A) 오늘 아침에서야 했어요.

(B) 코드가 파손되었어요.

(C) 신호등에서 좌회전하세요.

어휘 return 반품하다 damage 손상시키다, 파손시키다

해설 반품 이유를 묻는 Why 의문문

(A) 질문과 상관없는 오답. 시점을 묻는 When 의문문에 어울리는 응답이므로 오답.

(B) 정답. 탁상용 램프(desk lamp)를 왜 반품했는지 묻는 질문에 코드가 파손(Its cord was damaged.)되었기 때문이라고 구체적인 이유로 응답하고 있으므로 정답.

(C) 유사 발음 오답. 질문의 return과 부분적으로 발음이 동일한 turn을 이용한 오답.

19

W-Br Mr. Wong called twice while you were in the meeting.

M-Au (A) Did he leave a message?

(B) Try it once to see if it works.

(C) Some potential clients.

회의하시는 동안 왕 씨가 두 번 전화했어요.

(A) 그가 메시지를 남겼나요?

(B) 한 번 해 봐서 잘 되는지 보세요.

(C) 잠재 고객 몇 명이요.

어휘 twice 두 번, 2회 leave a message 메시지를 남기다 once 한 번 potential 잠재적인, 가능성이 있는

해설 정보 제공의 평서문

(A) 정답. 왕 씨가 두 번 전화했었다(called twice)는 말에 추가 정보를 얻기 위해 그가 메시지를 남겼는지 되묻고 있으므로 정답.

(B) 연상 단어 오답. 질문의 twice에서 연상 가능한 once를 이용한 오답.

(C) 연상 단어 오답. 질문의 meeting에서 연상 가능한 clients를 이용한 오답.

20

W-Am Can I bring you a dessert menu?

W-Br (A) Sure, here you go.

(B) No, thanks—just the bill, please.

(C) There's a recipe in the cookbook.

후식 메뉴를 가져다 드릴까요?

(A) 물론이죠, 여기 있습니다.

(B) 괜찮습니다. 계산서만 주세요.

(C) 요리책에 조리법이 있어요.

어휘 dessert 디저트, 후식 bill 계산서 recipe 조리법

해설 제안 의문문

(A) 질문과 상관없는, 상대방에게 어떤 물건을 내줄 때 쓰는 말이므로 오답.

(B) 정답. 디저트 메뉴를 갖다 주겠다는 제안에 먼저 No, thanks로 거절한 후, 계산서만 달라(just the bill, please)는 말로 자신이 원하는 것을 명확히 전달하고 있으므로 정답.

(C) 연상 단어 오답. 질문의 dessert에서 연상 가능한 recipe와 cookbook을 이용한 오답.

21

M-Au Which supplier should we order the building materials from?

W-Am (A) There's room in the warehouse.

(B) One thousand kilograms of steel.

(C) We need to set the construction budget first.

건축 자재를 어떤 납품업자에게 주문해야 할까요?

(A) 창고에 공간이 있어요.

(B) 강철 천 킬로그램이요.

(C) 건설 예산부터 세워야 해요.

어휘 supplier 공급자, 납품업자 building materials 건축 자재 warehouse 창고 steel 강철 budget 예산

해설 주문할 납품업자를 묻는 Which 의문문

(A) 연상 단어 오답. 질문의 building materials에서 연상 가능한 warehouse를 이용한 오답.

(B) 연상 단어 오답. 질문의 building materials에서 연상 가능한 steel을 이용한 오답.

(C) 정답. 어떤 납품업자에게 주문할지 묻는 질문에 대해 건설 예산부터 세워야 한다(We need to set the construction budget first.)는 말로 차후 결정을 제안하고 있으므로 정답.

22

M-Au Aren't the computers on sale right now?

W-Br (A) No, but I do have time tomorrow.

(B) That's what the sign says.

(C) Tech support is on the second floor.

그 컴퓨터들은 지금 할인 중이지 않아요?

(A) 아니요, 하지만 내일은 시간이 돼요.

(B) 표지판에는 그렇게 쓰여 있네요.

(C) 기술 지원팀은 2층에 있어요.

어휘 be on sale 할인 중이다 tech support 기술 지원팀

해설 컴퓨터의 할인 여부를 확인하는 부정의문문

(A) 질문을 지금(right now) 시간이 있는지 묻는 것으로 잘못 이해했을 때 나올 수 있는 응답으로 오답.

(B) 정답. 지금 컴퓨터가 할인되는지에 대해 표지판에는 그렇게 쓰여 있다(That's what the sign says.)는 우회적 표현으로 응답하고 있으므로 정답.

(C) 연상 단어 오답. 질문의 computers에서 연상 가능한 Tech support를 이용한 오답.

23

M-Cn Do you have a twelve-month or an eighteen-month service contract?

W-Br (A) At least forty-five dollars a month.

(B) Yes, he served our table already.

(C) I chose the one-year option.

서비스 계약을 12개월로 하셨어요, 18개월로 하셨어요?

(A) 한 달에 최소한 45달러입니다.

(B) 네, 그는 우리 테이블에 이미 서빙을 했습니다.

(C) 1년짜리를 선택했습니다.

어휘 contract 계약 serve 음식을 내다, 시중을 들다

해설 단어를 연결한 선택의문문

(A) 연상 표현 오답. 질문의 service contract에서 연상 가능한 forty-five dollars a month를 이용한 오답.

(B) Yes/No 불가 오답. 단어를 연결한 선택의문문에 Yes/No 응답이 불가능하므로 오답.

(C) 정답. 질문에서 선택 사항으로 언급된 12개월(twelve-month)과 18개월 계약 중 12개월짜리(one-year option)를 선택한 것이므로 정답.

24

W-Am Do you know if Bob is going to submit a proposal for funding?

M-Au (A) Yes, it was a fun time.

(B) He hasn't decided yet.

(C) The necessary forms.

밥이 자금 지원을 위한 제안서를 제출할 건지 아세요?

(A) 네, 정말로 즐거운 시간이었어요.

(B) 그는 아직 결정하지 못했어요.

(C) 필요한 양식요.

어휘 submit 제출하다 proposal 제안서 funding 자금 지원

해설 다른 사람이 제안서를 제출할 것인지 묻는 간접의문문

(A) 유사 발음 오답. 질문의 funding과 부분적으로 발음이 동일한 fun을 이용한 오답.

(B) 정답. 밥이 자금 지원 제안서를 제출할 것인지에 대해 그가 아직 결정을 못 내렸다(He hasn't decided yet.)는 불확실성 표현으로 응답하고 있으므로 정답.

(C) 연상 단어 오답. 질문의 submit에서 연상 가능한 forms를 이용한 오답.

25

M-Au Where do you want to go on Saturday?

W-Br (A) Oh, I hadn't heard about that.

(B) Anywhere you'd like.

(C) Every Sunday afternoon.

토요일에 어디에 가고 싶어요?

(A) 아, 그 얘기는 못 들었어요.

(B) 당신이 원하는 곳 어디든지요.

(C) 매주 일요일 오후에요.

해설 가고 싶은 장소를 묻는 Where 의문문

(A) 질문과 상관없는 오답. 어디에 가고 싶은지 묻는 질문에 그 소식은 못 들었다는 말은 질문의 맥락에서 벗어난 응답이므로 오답.

(B) 정답. 토요일에 가고 싶은 장소를 묻는 질문에 상대방이 원하는 곳이면 어디라도 좋다(Anywhere you'd like.)는 포괄적 표현으로 응답하고 있으므로 정답.

(C) 연상 단어 오답. 질문의 Saturday에서 연상 가능한 주말 요일인 Sunday를 이용한 오답.

26

W-Br I think the courtyard should be the location for the photo shoot, don't you?

M-Cn (A) I must have left mine at home—sorry.

(B) A professional photographer.

(C) As long as it's not too windy.

안뜰이 사진 촬영 장소로 좋다고 생각하는데, 그렇지 않나요?

(A) 내 건 집에 놓고 온 거 같아요. 죄송합니다.

(B) 전문 사진사요.

(C) 바람이 너무 불지만 않으면요.

어휘 courtyard 안뜰 photo shoot 사진 촬영 leave 두고 오다 as long as ~인 한

해설 촬영 장소 선호 여부를 확인하는 부가의문문

(A) 질문과 상관없는 오답. mine이 가리키는 대상이 질문에 없으므로 오답.

(B) 연상 단어 오답. 질문의 photo에서 연상 가능한 photographer를 이용한 오답.

(C) 정답. 안뜰이 촬영 장소로 좋은지에 대한 질문에 Yes를 생략하고, 바람이 너무 불지 않으면(As long as it's not too windy.) 좋겠다는 조건을 제시한 우회적인 응답이므로 정답.

27

M-Cn When will the brochures be ready for distribution?

W-Am (A) Well, there's been a delay at the printer's.
(B) No, but we could hand out some flyers.
(C) That page features a different product.

안내 책자는 언제 배부 준비가 될까요?
(A) 음, 인쇄소에서 지체되었어요.
(B) 아니요, 하지만 전단지를 좀 배포할 수도 있어요.
(C) 그 페이지에는 다른 제품이 나옵니다.

어휘 brochure (얇은) 안내 책자, 브로슈어 distribution 배부, 배포 printer's 인쇄소 hand out 배포하다 flyer (안내용) 전단지 feature (특징적으로) 등장시키다

해설 배부 가능 시점을 묻는 When 의문문

(A) 정답. 안내 책자 배부 가능 시점을 묻는 질문에 인쇄소에서 지체되었다(there's been a delay at the printer's.)는 불확실성 표현으로 응답하고 있으므로 정답.

(B) Yes/No 불가 오답. When 의문문에 Yes/No 응답이 불가능하므로 오답.

(C) 연상 단어 오답. 질문의 brochures에서 연상 가능한 page, product를 이용한 오답.

28

W-Am Why wasn't Eva in the office yesterday?

M-Au (A) She's still out of town.
(B) She forgot to turn it off.
(C) The break room on the 3rd floor?

에바는 왜 어제 사무실에 없었나요?
(A) 그녀는 아직 타지에 있어요.
(B) 그녀가 끄는 것을 깜박했어요.
(C) 3층의 휴게실요?

어휘 out of town 도시를 떠나 있는 forget 잊어버리다 turn off ~을 끄다 break room 휴게실

해설 사무실에 없었던 이유를 묻는 Why 부정의문문

(A) 정답. 어제 에바가 왜 사무실에 나오지 않았는지 묻는 질문에 대해 그녀가 아직도 타지에 있다(She's still out of town.)는 구체적인 이유를 언급하고 있으므로 정답.

(B) 질문과 상관없는 오답. 그녀가 그것을 끄는 것(turn it off)을 잊었다는 말은 질문의 맥락에서 벗어난 응답이므로 오답.

(C) 연상 단어 오답. 질문의 office에서 연상 가능한 break room을 이용한 오답.

29

W-Br You're going to hire someone to do the painting, aren't you?

M-Cn (A) Doing it ourselves would be cheaper.
(B) Hang it a little higher, please.
(C) I'm definitely going—I'm a fan of that artist.

페인트칠을 할 사람을 고용할 거죠, 그렇지 않나요?
(A) 우리가 직접 하는 게 더 저렴할 거예요.
(B) 조금 더 높은 곳에 걸어 주세요.
(C) 저는 꼭 갈 거예요. 그 화가의 팬이거든요.

어휘 hire 고용하다 hang 걸다, 매달다 definitely 분명히, 틀림없이

해설 페인트칠을 할 인부 고용 여부를 묻는 부가의문문

(A) 정답. 페인트칠을 할 사람(someone to do the painting)을 고용할 것인지 묻는 질문에 대해 우리가 직접 하는 게 더 저렴할 거(Doing it ourselves would be cheaper.)라는 우회적인 부정 응답을 하고 있으므로 정답.

(B) 동일 발음 오답. 질문의 hire와 발음이 동일한 higher를 이용한 오답.

(C) 연상 단어 오답. 질문의 painting에서 연상 가능한 artist를 이용한 오답.

30

W-Am I've learned so much during my internship at your lab.

M-Au (A) We'll focus on medical science.
(B) Yes, we're looking for some student interns.
(C) We've appreciated your hard work.

귀하의 실험실 인턴 과정에서 정말 많은 걸 배웠습니다.
(A) 우리는 의학에 초점을 맞출 거예요.
(B) 네, 우리는 학생 인턴들을 찾고 있습니다.
(C) 열심히 일해 주어서 고맙습니다.

어휘 internship 인턴직, 인턴 과정 lab 실험실(= laboratory) appreciate 감사하다

해설 소감을 밝히는 평서문

(A) 연상 표현 오답. 질문의 lab에서 연상 가능한 medical science를 이용한 오답.

(B) 유사 발음 오답. 질문의 internship과 부분적으로 발음이 같은 interns를 이용한 오답.

(C) 정답. 실험실 인턴 과정(internship)에서 많은 것을 배웠다는 말에 열심히 일해 주어 고맙다(We've appreciated your hard work.)는 응답을 하고 있으므로 정답.

31

M-Cn Didn't one of the store managers take inventory recently?

W-Am (A) Maybe we could rent a storage unit.
(B) There's no record of that in the system.
(C) A big shipment of merchandise.

매장 관리자 중 한 명이 최근에 재고 조사를 하지 않았나요?
(A) 어쩌면 보관 칸을 임대할 수도 있을 거예요.
(B) 시스템 상에는 그런 기록이 없는데요.
(C) 대량의 수송 상품이요.

어휘 take inventory 재고 조사를 하다 storage 보관 shipment 수송, 적하물 merchandise 상품, 물품

해설 재고 조사 여부를 묻는 부정의문문

(A) 파생어 오답. 질문의 store와 파생어 관계인 storage를 이용한 오답.

(B) 정답. 매장 관리자 중 한 명이 재고 조사를 했는지 묻는 질문에 그런 기록이 없다(There's no record of that)는 말로 부정적 응답을 하고 있으므로 정답.

(C) 연상 단어 오답. 질문의 inventory에서 연상 가능한 merchandise를 이용한 오답.

PART 3

32-34

W-Br Hi, [32]**I'm bringing back the car that I rented at a different branch a few days ago.**

M-Au I'd be happy to assist you with that. [33]**I'll just need to see your driver's license.**

W-Br Here you go. Also, I have to say that the car I was given was quite uncomfortable. The fabric on the seats was scratchy, and the heater broke on the second day.

M-Au I'm very sorry to hear that. [34]**Let me get my manager.** It's his policy to apologize himself whenever there's a problem with any of our vehicles.

여: 안녕하세요. **제가 며칠 전 다른 지점에서 대여한 차량을 반납하려고 가져왔어요.**
남: 기꺼이 도와 드리겠습니다. **운전 면허증 좀 보여주세요.**
여: 여기 있어요. 그리고 제가 받았던 차량은 꽤 불편했어요. 좌석 천은 따끔거리고 히터는 둘째 날 고장 났어요.
남: 정말 죄송합니다. **관리자를 불러 드리겠습니다.** 저희 차량에 문제가 발생했을 때마다 직접 사과드리는 것이 그의 방침이어서요.

어휘 assist 돕다, 거들다 driver's license 운전 면허증 fabric 직물, 천 scratchy 따끔거리는 break 고장 나다 apologize 사과하다 vehicle 차량

32

What does the woman want to do?

(A) Sell her personal vehicle
(B) Take driving lessons
(C) Arrange some repairs
(D) Return a rental vehicle

여자는 무엇을 하고 싶어 하는가?

(A) 개인 차량 판매
(B) 운전 교습 수강
(C) 수리 주선
(D) 렌터카 반납

해설 세부 사항 관련 – 여자가 원하는 것

대화 맨 처음에 여자가 며칠 전 다른 지점에서 빌린 차량을 반납하려고 가져왔다(I'm bringing back the car ~ a few days ago.)고 했으므로 정답은 (D)이다.

▸▸ **Paraphrasing** 대화의 **the car that I rented**
→ 정답의 **a rental vehicle**

33

What does the man ask for?

(A) A payment
(B) Some identification
(C) Operating instructions
(D) A price quote

남자는 무엇을 요청하는가?

(A) 요금 지불
(B) 신분증
(C) 운영 지침
(D) 가격 견적

어휘 quote 견적액

해설 세부 사항 관련 – 남자가 요청하는 것

남자의 첫 번째 대사에서 여자에게 운전 면허증을 보여달라(I'll just need to see your driver's license.)고 했으므로 정답은 (B)이다.

▸▸ **Paraphrasing** 대화의 **driver's license**
→ 정답의 **identification**

34

What does the man say he will do?

(A) Print a policy statement
(B) Bring out a supervisor
(C) Call a different branch
(D) Conduct an inspection

남자는 무엇을 하겠다고 얘기하는가?

(A) 정책 설명서 출력하기
(B) 관리자 데려오기
(C) 다른 지점에 전화하기
(D) 점검하기

어휘 policy statement 정책 설명서 supervisor 상사, 관리자 conduct 실시하다 inspection 검사

해설 세부 사항 관련 – 남자의 다음 행동

남자의 두 번째 대사에서 관리자를 불러오겠다(Let me get my manager.)고 했으므로 정답은 (B)이다.

▸▸ **Paraphrasing** 대화의 **get my manager**
→ 정답의 **Bring out a supervisor**

35-37

M-Au Hi, I'm interested in your health club's Basic Membership Package, but I have a question. [35]**Can I put my membership on hold if I'm going to be away?**

W-Br Sure. We can suspend it for up to three months with advance notice. The service charge is twenty-five dollars a month.

M-Au [36]**That sounds reasonable.** Here is the signed contract.

Test 6

W-Br Let me just look over this... OK! Now, I'll just need your credit card to set up automatic payments.

M-Au Here you go.

W-Br Congratulations on joining Poppie Fitness! [37]**Let's take a picture for your membership card.** Can you step over here and look at the camera?

남: 안녕하세요. 이 헬스클럽의 기본 회원 패키지에 관심이 있는데요. 질문이 있어요. **제가 타지에 있게 되면 회원권을 일시 중지시킬 수 있나요?**

여: 물론이죠. 미리 말씀해 주시면 저희가 최대 3개월까지 회원권을 중지해 드릴 겁니다. 서비스 비용은 한 달에 25달러입니다.

남: **합리적인 것 같네요.** 여기 서명한 계약서가 있습니다.

여: 한번 살펴볼게요… 됐습니다! 이제 자동결제를 위해 신용카드를 주셔야 합니다.

남: 여기 있습니다.

여: 포피 피트니스에 등록하신 것을 축하합니다. **회원 카드용으로 사진을 찍으시죠.** 이쪽으로 오셔서 카메라를 봐 주시겠어요?

어휘 put ~ on hold ~을 보류[연기]하다 suspend 중단하다, 유예하다 up to 최대 ~까지 advance notice 사전 고지 reasonable 합당한, 사리에 맞는 look over 살펴보다 automatic 자동의

35

What does the man ask about?

(A) Upgrading a service package
(B) Suspending a membership
(C) Inviting guests to a club
(D) Beginning a trial period

남자는 무엇에 대해 질문하는가?

(A) 서비스 패키지 상품 업그레이드
(B) 회원권 일시 중지
(C) 클럽에 손님 초대
(D) 무료 체험 기간 시작

어휘 trial (최종 결정을 내리기 전의) 시험

해설 세부 사항 관련 - 남자의 문의 사항

남자의 첫 번째 대사에서 타지에 있을 경우 회원권을 일시 중지시킬 수 있는지(Can I put my membership on hold if I'm going to be away?) 물었으므로 정답은 (B)이다.

36

What does the man imply when he says, "Here is the signed contract"?

(A) He thinks the woman is misinformed.
(B) He would like to join an organization.
(C) He cannot understand some rules.
(D) He has found a lost document.

남자가 "여기 서명한 계약서가 있습니다"라고 말한 의도는 무엇인가?

(A) 그는 여자가 뭔가 잘못 알고 있다고 생각한다.
(B) 그는 단체에 가입하고 싶다.
(C) 그는 몇몇 규정을 이해하지 못한다.
(D) 그는 분실된 서류를 찾았다.

해설 화자의 의도 파악 - 여기 서명한 계약서가 있다고 말한 의도

남자는 회원권 중지에 대한 수수료 얘기를 듣고 합리적인 것 같다(That sounds reasonable.)고 했고 이어서 여자에게 서명한 계약서를 제시했다. 인용문은 헬스클럽에 가입하고 싶다는 의도로 말한 것이므로 정답은 (B)이다.

37

What will the woman most likely do next?

(A) Shred some papers
(B) Take a photo
(C) Examine a credit card
(D) Issue a refund

여자는 다음에 무엇을 하겠는가?

(A) 서류 파쇄
(B) 사진 촬영
(C) 신용카드 검사
(D) 환불 처리

어휘 shred (갈가리) 자르다, 찢다 examine 검사하다, 조사하다 issue 지급하다, 발행하다

해설 세부 사항 관련 - 여자의 다음 행동

대화 마지막에 여자가 남자에게 회원 카드에 들어갈 사진을 찍자(Let's take a picture for your membership card.)고 했으므로 정답은 (B)이다.

▸▸ **Paraphrasing** 대화의 **take a picture** → 정답의 **take a photo**

38-40

M-Cn Hello. This is Tony at Doctor Bayer's office. [38]**Our clinic was damaged by last night's storm, and we can't see patients here until it's cleaned up.** I'm sorry, but we'll have to cancel your appointment tomorrow.

W-Am Oh, that's disappointing. [39]**I've been hired at Fenley Industries, and I need to get a health check before I begin work.** I wonder if this will delay my start date.

M-Cn Well, I know that Blue Lakes Health Center also does occupational health checks. [40]**Why don't you call and see if they have any openings tomorrow?**

W-Am Yes, I guess that's worth a try. Thanks for the suggestion.

남: 안녕하세요. 바이에르 병원의 토니입니다. **어젯밤 폭풍 때문에 저희 병원이 파손됐어요. 정돈될 때까지 여기서는 환자를 볼 수가 없습니다.** 죄송하지만, 고객님의 내일 진료 예약을 취소해야겠는데요.

여: 아, 실망스럽네요. **제가 펜리 인더스트리즈에 채용돼서 근무를 시작하기**

전에 건강 검진을 받아야 하거든요. 이것 때문에 근무 시작일이 연기되지 않을까 모르겠네요.

남: 음, 블루 레이크스 헬스 센터에서도 직업 관련 건강 검진을 하는 것으로 알고 있습니다. 그곳에 전화하셔서 내일 빈자리가 있는지 확인해 보시면 어떨까요?

여: 네, 그렇게 해보는 게 좋겠네요. 제안해 주셔서 감사합니다.

어휘 doctor's office 병원, 의원 clinic 병원 storm 폭풍 cancel 취소하다 appointment (업무상의) 약속 disappointing 실망스러운 hire 고용하다 health check 건강 검진 occupational 직업과 관련된 worth a try 시도해 볼 가치가 있는 suggestion 제안, 의견

38

What problem does the man describe?

(A) A medical professional is unavailable.
(B) A receptionist has made a mistake.
(C) A facility is temporarily unusable.
(D) A medication is out of stock.

남자는 어떤 문제에 대해 말하는가?

(A) 전문 의료진을 만날 수 없다.
(B) 접수 담당자가 실수를 했다.
(C) 시설을 당분간 사용할 수 없다.
(D) 약이 재고가 없다.

어휘 medical professional 의료 전문가 unavailable 만날 수 없는, 이용할 수 없는 receptionist 접수 담당자 medication 약 out of stock 재고가 없는

해설 전체 내용 관련 – 남자가 언급하는 문제

남자의 첫 번째 대사에서 어젯밤 폭풍 때문에 병원이 파손되어 정돈될 때까지 환자를 볼 수 없다(Our clinic was damaged by last night's storm ~ until it's cleaned up.)고 밝히고 있어 남자가 병원 시설을 당분간 사용할 수 없는 문제를 말하고 있음을 알 수 있으므로 정답은 (C)이다.

39

Why does the woman need to see a doctor?

(A) An illness requires treatment.
(B) It is time for her regular checkup.
(C) She is about to start a new job.
(D) She has to travel overseas.

여자가 진찰을 받아야 하는 이유는 무엇인가?

(A) 질환을 치료해야 한다.
(B) 정기 검진을 받아야 할 때다.
(C) 새로운 일을 시작하려는 참이다.
(D) 해외 여행을 해야 한다.

어휘 illness 병 treatment 치료 regular checkup 정기 검진 be about to+동사원형 막 ~하려는 참이다 overseas 해외로

해설 세부 사항 관련 – 여자가 진찰을 받아야 하는 이유

여자의 첫 번째 대사에서 펜리 인더스트리즈에 채용되어 근무 시작 전에 건강 검진을 받아야 한다(I've been hired at Fenley Industries ~ before I begin work.)고 했으므로 정답은 (C)이다.

40

What does the man suggest doing?

(A) Resting at home
(B) Changing an appointment time
(C) Speaking to a doctor by phone
(D) Trying another clinic

남자는 무엇을 하라고 제안하는가?

(A) 집에서 쉬기
(B) 예약 시간 변경하기
(C) 전화로 의사와 얘기하기
(D) 다른 병원에 가 보기

어휘 rest 쉬다

해설 세부 사항 관련 – 남자의 제안

남자의 마지막 대사에 다른 병원인 블루 레이크스 헬스 센터로 전화해서 내일 빈자리가 있는지 확인해 보라(Why don't you call and see if they have any openings tomorrow?)고 했으므로 정답은 (D)이다.

41-43 3인 대화

W-Br Wow, [41]**I had no idea that chemistry could be so interesting.**

W-Am [41]**Yes, the exhibits here are really fun and educational.** Oh, what's that? Let's check it out.

W-Br OK. Hmm... [42]**I can't figure out what this thing is supposed to do.** Do you see a sign for it, Kyoko?

W-Am No. But there's a staff member. [42]**Let's ask him.** Excuse me—could you tell us what this is?

M-Cn It's a sound mirror. [43]**There's another one on the opposite wall. See it? If you each stand in front of one, you'll be able to hear each other talking,** even though you're far away.

W-Am Oh, [43]**let's try it out! You stay here,** Elaine.

여1: 와, **화학이 이렇게 재미있는지 몰랐어요.**

여2: **네, 여기 전시물이 정말 재미있으면서도 교육적이네요.** 어, 저게 뭐죠? 가서 봅시다.

여1: 좋아요. 음… **이게 뭘 하는 건지 모르겠는데.** 안내판 보여요, 쿄코?

여2: 아니요, 근데 저기 직원이 있어요. **물어봅시다.** 실례합니다만, 이게 뭔지 알려 주실 수 있을까요?

남: 사운드 미러예요. **맞은편 벽에 또 하나가 있어요. 보이시죠? 각자 하나씩 앞에 서 계시면 서로 얘기하는 게 들립니다.** 설사 멀리 떨어져 있어도요.

여2: 아, **우리도 한번 해 봐요! 여기 서 있어요,** 일레인.

어휘 chemistry 화학 exhibit 전시품 educational 교육적인 check out 확인하다 figure out 이해하다, 파악하다 sign 표지, 안내판 opposite 맞은편의

Test 6

41

Where most likely are the speakers?

(A) At a science museum
(B) At a hardware store
(C) At a photography studio
(D) At a research laboratory

화자들이 있는 곳은 어디겠는가?

(A) 과학 박물관
(B) 철물점
(C) 사진관
(D) 연구소

어휘 hardware store 철물점 research laboratory 연구소

해설 전체 내용 관련 - 화자들이 있는 장소

첫 번째 여자가 첫 대사에서 화학이 이렇게 재미있는지 몰랐다(I had no idea that chemistry could be so interesting.)고 언급했고, 이에 대해 두 번째 여자가 여기 전시물이 재미있고 교육적(Yes, the exhibits here are really fun and educational.)이라고 했다. 화학 관련물이 전시될 수 있는 장소는 과학 박물관이므로 정답은 (A)이다.

42

What problem do the women have?

(A) They are not permitted to operate a machine.
(B) The cost of a service has increased.
(C) There is an error in a printed sign.
(D) An object's purpose is unclear.

여자들에게 무슨 문제가 있는가?

(A) 기계를 조작하도록 허용되지 않는다.
(B) 서비스 비용이 올라갔다.
(C) 인쇄된 간판에 오류가 있다.
(D) 어떤 물건의 용도가 명확하지 않다.

어휘 permit 허락하다 operate (기계를) 조작하다 object 물건 unclear 분명하지 않은

해설 세부 사항 관련 - 여자들이 직면한 문제

첫 번째 여자의 두 번째 대사에서 이게 뭘 하는 건지 모르겠다(I can't figure out what this thing is supposed to do.)고 했고 이에 대해 두 번째 여자도 직원에게 물어보자(Let's ask him.)고 했으므로 정답은 (D)이다.

43

What will Kyoko most likely do next?

(A) Read the results of a test
(B) Place an item back on a shelf
(C) Listen to an audio recording
(D) Go to the other side of the room

코코는 다음에 무엇을 하겠는가?

(A) 테스트 결과 읽기
(B) 물건을 선반에 되돌려 놓기
(C) 녹음 음원 듣기
(D) 방의 반대편으로 가기

어휘 place ~ back ~을 원래 있던 곳에 놓다

해설 세부 사항 관련 - 쿄코가 다음에 할 일

남자의 대사에서 사운드 미러가 맞은편 벽에 또 하나가 있는데 각자 하나씩 앞에 서 있으면 상대방의 소리를 들을 수 있다(There's another one on the opposite wall ~ you'll be able to hear each other talking)고 했다. 이에 두 번째 여자인 쿄코가 첫 번째 여자인 Elaine에게 한번 해 보자며 여기 서 있으라(let's try it out! You stay here)고 했고, 이는 쿄코가 방의 반대편으로 갈 것이라는 의미이므로 정답은 (D)이다.

44-46

M-Au Louise, [44]**your team is trying to come up with ideas for new cosmetics goods, right?** How's it going?

W-Br Not great. We've had trouble deciding on what direction to take. After several brainstorming sessions, we're still not sure what kind of products consumers would be interested in.

M-Au [45]**Why don't you bring in a consultant to do some market research?** That's what we did at my previous company. Then you'd have some, uh... data to work with.

W-Br We considered that, but unfortunately, [46]**our budget is too small.** We'll have to find a different way.

남: 루이즈, **당신 팀에서 새로운 화장품에 대한 아이디어를 내려고 하는 중이지요?** 어떻게 되어갑니까?

여: 쉽지 않네요. 어떤 방향을 취할지 결정하는 데 어려움을 겪었어요. 아이디어 회의를 몇 차례 했지만 소비자가 어떤 종류의 제품에 관심이 있는지 아직도 확신할 수가 없어요.

남: **시장 조사를 담당할 컨설턴트를 데려오지 그래요?** 제가 있던 전 회사에서는 그렇게 했는데요. 그러면 일할 때 활용할… 자료를 보유하게 되죠.

여: 저희도 고려해 봤지만 안타깝게도 **우리 예산이 너무 적어요.** 다른 방법을 찾아야 할 거예요.

어휘 come up with (아이디어 등을) 내놓다, 찾아내다 cosmetics 화장품 decide on ~으로 결정하다 brainstorming 브레인스토밍(자유롭게 생각을 제시하는 것) session 모임, 시간 market research 시장 조사 previous 이전의 consider 고려하다 budget 예산

44

What does the man ask the woman about?

(A) Employee training
(B) A security procedure
(C) Product development
(D) An advertising campaign

남자는 여자에게 무엇에 대해 질문하는가?

(A) 직원 교육
(B) 보안 절차
(C) 제품 개발
(D) 광고 캠페인

어휘 procedure 절차

해설 세부 사항 관련 – 남자의 질문

대화 맨 처음에 남자가 여자의 팀에서 새로운 화장품에 대한 아이디어를 내는 중인지(your team is trying to come up with ideas for new cosmetics goods, right?)에 대해 물어봤으므로 정답은 (C)이다.

45

What does the man suggest the woman's team do?

(A) Hire a special advisor
(B) Change a timeline
(C) Create some guidelines
(D) Limit access to some data

남자는 여자의 팀이 무엇을 할 것을 제안하는가?

(A) 특별 고문 고용
(B) 일정 변경
(C) 지침 작성
(D) 일부 자료에 대한 접근권 제한

어휘 advisor 고문 timeline 일정 guideline 지침 limit 제한하다 access 접근권

해설 세부 사항 관련 – 남자의 제안 사항

남자의 두 번째 대사에서 여자에게 시장 조사를 담당할 컨설턴트 고용을 제안(Why don't you ~ market research?)하고 있으므로 정답은 (A)이다.

▸▸ **Paraphrasing** 대화의 bring in a consultant
→ 정답의 Hire a special advisor

46

What does the woman say about the man's suggestion?

(A) There is not enough time for it.
(B) There is not enough money for it.
(C) She will mention it to her team.
(D) It would probably not be effective.

여자는 남자의 제안에 대해 뭐라고 말하는가?

(A) 그럴 만한 시간이 충분치 않다.
(B) 그럴 만한 자금이 충분치 않다.
(C) 자신의 팀에 이야기할 것이다.
(D) 아마 효율적이지 않을 것이다.

어휘 mention 언급하다 effective 효율적인

해설 세부 사항 관련 – 남자의 제안에 대한 여자의 반응

대화 맨 마지막에 여자가 예산이 너무 적다(our budget is too small)고 했다. 즉, 시장 조사를 담당할 컨설턴트를 고용하기에는 돈이 충분하지 않다는 의미이므로 정답은 (B)이다.

▸▸ **Paraphrasing** 대화의 our budget is too small
→ 정답의 There is not enough money for it.

47-49

M-Cn You've reached Han's Aroma Emporium's customer service line. [47]**Please visit our Web site to see up-to-date prices for all of our candles.** Now, what can I do for you?

W-Am Actually, I'm trying to place an order on your Web site, but I think there is an error in calculating the shipping cost. [48]**You're offering a fifty-percent shipping discount, but when I try to check out, it shows the full shipping cost.**

M-Cn Where are you placing the order from? Our shipping discounts only apply to domestic orders.

W-Am Oh, really? [49]**I'm working overseas long-term now,** so that must be the problem. I'll just pay the full price for shipping, then.

남: 한스 아로마 엠포리엄의 고객 서비스 전화입니다. **저희가 보유한 모든 양초의 최신 가격을 확인하시려면 웹 사이트를 방문해 주세요.** 자, 무엇을 도와드릴까요?

여: 사실 제가 온라인으로 주문을 하려고 하는데 배송비가 잘못 계산된 것 같아요. **그쪽에서는 50%의 배송비 할인을 제공하는데 제가 결제하려고 하니 배송비 전액이 표시되네요.**

남: 어디서 주문을 하셨나요? 저희 배송료 할인은 국내 주문에만 적용됩니다.

여: 아, 그래요? **저는 지금 해외에서 장기 근무 중이거든요.** 틀림없이 그게 문제였겠네요. 그럼 그냥 배송비 전액을 낼게요.

어휘 aroma 향기, 향내 emporium 가게 up-to-date 최신의 candle 양초 place an order 주문하다 calculate 계산하다 shipping cost 배송비 check out 계산하다 apply to ~에 적용되다 domestic 국내의 overseas 해외에서

47

What does the man say can be found on a Web site?

(A) Customer reviews
(B) Product prices
(C) Branch locations
(D) Business hours

남자는 웹 사이트에서 무엇을 찾을 수 있다고 말하는가?

(A) 고객 리뷰
(B) 제품 가격
(C) 지점 위치
(D) 영업 시간

해설 세부 사항 관련 – 웹 사이트에서 볼 수 있는 정보

남자의 첫 번째 대사에서 상점이 보유한 모든 양초의 최신 가격을 확인하려면 웹 사이트를 방문해 달라(Please visit our Web site to see up-to-date prices for all of our candles.)고 했으므로 정답은 (B)이다.

Test 6

48

Why is the woman calling?

(A) To track a shipment
(B) To verify a discount
(C) To request an exchange
(D) To cancel an order

여자가 전화한 이유는 무엇인가?

(A) 물품 배송을 추적하기 위해
(B) 할인을 확인하기 위해
(C) 교환을 요청하기 위해
(D) 주문을 취소하기 위해

어휘 track 추적하다 shipment 선적물 verify 확인하다 exchange 교환

해설 전체 내용 관련 - 전화 통화의 이유

여자의 첫 번째 대사에서 회사가 50퍼센트 배송비 할인을 제공하는데 자신이 결제하려고 하니 배송비 전액이 표시된다(You're offering a fifty-percent shipping discount ~ the full shipping cost.)고 했으므로 정답은 (B)이다.

49

What does the woman say about herself?

(A) Her company needs some supplies.
(B) She lives outside the country.
(C) Her computer is malfunctioning.
(D) She has shopped at the store before.

여자는 자신에 대해 뭐라고 언급하는가?

(A) 그녀의 회사는 자재를 필요로 한다.
(B) 그녀는 외국에 산다.
(C) 그녀의 컴퓨터가 오작동한다.
(D) 그녀는 그 상점에서 쇼핑한 적이 있다.

어휘 supply 자재 malfunction (기계나 장치가) 오작동하다

해설 세부 사항 관련 - 여자와 관련된 언급

대화 마지막에 여자가 자신이 지금 해외에서 장기 근무하고 있다(I'm working overseas long-term now)고 했으므로 정답은 (B)이다.

▸▸ **Paraphrasing** 대화의 work overseas
→ 정답의 lives outside the country

50-52 3인 대화

W-Am This painting is beautiful! [50]**I really love the texture that the mixed media adds to the canvas.** Don't you, Mark?

M-Cn Yes. In fact, I'd like to buy it for my waiting room. Excuse me—how much is this painting?

M-Au Unfortunately, that one is already sold. But [51]**the artist, Bianca, is having a solo show at the Oak Street Gallery soon.** She should have many new works for sale there, including some glazed ceramics.

W-Am When will that be?

M-Au [52]**July first to July twentieth.**

M-Cn Oh, I'll make sure to visit it.

M-Au [52]**She's having a reception on opening night, with a local string quartet and catering from Viva.** It should be really fun.

여: 이 그림은 아름답네요! **혼합된 매체가 캔버스에 주는 질감이 정말 좋아요.** 안 그래요, 마크?

남1: 네, 사실 저는 대기실에 걸 용도로 그 그림을 사고 싶어요. 실례합니다, 이 그림은 얼마인가요?

남2: 안타깝지만 그 그림은 이미 팔렸습니다. 하지만 **화가인 비앙카 씨가 곧 오크 스트리트 갤러리에서 개인전을 엽니다.** 거기서 새 작품을 많이 판매할 겁니다, 유약 처리된 도자기를 비롯해서요.

여: 그게 언제인가요?

남2: **7월 1일부터 20일까지입니다.**

남1: 아, 꼭 방문해야겠어요.

남2: **개장일 밤에는 지역의 현악 4중주단과 비바의 음식 제공 서비스가 마련된 환영 연회가 있습니다.** 정말 재미있을 겁니다.

어휘 mixed media 혼합 매체 texture 감촉, 질감 gallery 미술관, 화랑 glazed 유약을 바른 ceramic 도자기 reception 리셉션, 환영 연회 string quartet 현악 4중주단 catering 음식 제공(업)

50

What does the woman emphasize about a painting?

(A) Its texture
(B) Its colors
(C) Its subjects
(D) Its frame

여자가 그림에 대해 강조하는 것은 무엇인가?

(A) 질감
(B) 색상
(C) 소재
(D) 액자

해설 세부 사항 관련 - 여자가 그림에서 강조하는 것

여자의 첫 번째 대사에서 혼합된 매체가 캔버스에 주는 질감이 정말 좋다(I really love the texture that the mixed media adds to the canvas.)고 했으므로 정답은 (A)이다.

51

What is mentioned about an art show?

(A) It will be publicized online.
(B) It will include a demonstration.
(C) It will take place outdoors.
(D) It will feature only one artist's work.

미술전에 대해 언급된 내용은 무엇인가?

(A) 온라인에서 홍보될 것이다.
(B) 시연이 포함될 것이다.
(C) 실외에서 열릴 것이다.
(D) 한 화가만의 작품들이 전시될 것이다.

어휘 publicize 홍보하다 demonstration 시연 feature 포함하다, 전시하다

해설 세부 사항 관련 – 미술 전시회에 대해 언급된 내용

두 번째 남자의 첫 번째 대사에서 작가인 비앙카가 곧 오크 스트리트 갤러리에서 개인전을 연다(the artist, Bianca, is having a solo show at the Oak Street Gallery soon.)고 했으므로 정답은 (D)이다.

52

What will happen on July 1?

(A) The art show will end.
(B) A party will be held.
(C) Purchases will be delivered.
(D) A date will be announced.

7월 1일에 무슨 일이 있을 것인가?

(A) 미술전이 막을 내릴 것이다.
(B) 파티가 있을 것이다.
(C) 구매한 물건이 배송될 것이다.
(D) 날짜가 공지될 것이다.

어휘 purchase 구매품 deliver 배달하다 announce 공지하다

해설 세부 사항 관련 – 7월 1일에 발생할 일

두 번째 남자의 두 번째 대사에서 비앙카의 개인전이 7월 1일부터 7월 20일까지 열린다(July first to July twentieth.)고 했고, 대화 맨 마지막에 개장일 밤에는 지역의 현악 4중주단과 비바의 음식 제공 서비스가 마련된 환영 연회가 있다(She's having a reception ~ and catering from Viva.)고 했으므로 정답은 (B)이다.

▸▸ Paraphrasing 대화의 **a reception** → 정답의 **a party**

53-55

W-Br Now, [53]**if you're hired, you'll start out by operating one of these machines here on the main production floor.** [54]**Have you used industrial sewing machines professionally before?**

M-Au Yes, at my last job I ran an embroidery machine. I've also been trained on hemming machines, although I haven't spent much time operating one.

W-Br Then [55]**you might be a good candidate for promotion to a position at a specialized station—but we require all new hires to work on the standard machines for at least six months first.** We expect even the floor managers to have hands-on experience with all parts of the production process.

여: 자, **입사가 결정되면 여기 중앙 생산 작업장에서 이 기계들 중 하나를 조작하는 것부터 시작할 거예요. 전문적으로 공업용 재봉틀을 사용해 본 적이 있나요?**

남: 네, 제 마지막 직장에서 자수 기계를 돌렸습니다. 또한 단처리 기계 교육도 받았습니다. 비록 오래 조작해 보지는 못했지만요.

여: 그럼 **전문 부서 자리로 승진하기에 적합한 지원자일 수도 있겠군요. 하지만 저희는 모든 신규 채용자가 우선은 최소 6개월간 표준 기계로 작업하도록 하고 있습니다.** 심지어 현장 관리자까지도 생산 공정의 모든 부분에 실제 경험을 갖기를 원하거든요.

어휘 start out 시작하다 production floor 생산 작업장 industrial 공업용의, 산업의 sewing machine 재봉틀 embroidery 자수 hemming 단접기 candidate 지원자 promotion 승진 specialized 전문화된, 특수화된 station 담당 장소, 부서 new hire 신규 채용자 at least 최소한 hands-on experience 직접적인 경험

53

Where is the conversation taking place?

(A) In a factory
(B) In a warehouse
(C) On a farm
(D) At a construction site

대화가 일어나는 곳은 어디인가?

(A) 공장
(B) 창고
(C) 농장
(D) 건설 현장

해설 전체 내용 관련 – 대화 장소

여자의 첫 번째 대사에서 남자가 고용되면 여기 주요 생산 작업장에서 기계들을 조작하는 것부터 시작할 것(if you're hired ~ here on the main production floor.)이라고 했으므로 정답은 (A)이다.

▸▸ Paraphrasing 대화의 **on the main production floor** → 정답의 **In a factory**

54

What does the woman ask the man about?

(A) His education
(B) His expected salary
(C) His work experience
(D) His career goals

여자는 남자에게 무엇을 물어보는가?

(A) 학력
(B) 희망 급여
(C) 경력
(D) 직업적 목표

어휘 salary 급여

해설 세부 사항 관련 – 여자의 질문

여자의 첫 번째 대사에서 남자에게 전문적으로 공업용 재봉틀을 다뤄 본 적이 있는지(Have you used industrial sewing machines professionally before?) 물어봤으므로 정답은 (C)이다.

55

What does the woman tell the man about a special position?

(A) It comes with a pay raise after six months.
(B) She is not certain that it is vacant.
(C) He is not yet eligible for it.
(D) It involves working at night.

여자는 남자에게 특수 보직에 대해 뭐라고 말하는가?

(A) 6개월 뒤에는 급여 인상이 있다.
(B) 공석인지 확실치 않다.
(C) 그는 아직 자격이 안 된다.
(D) 야간 근무를 요한다.

어휘 certain 확실한 vacant 비어 있는 be eligible for ~에 자격이 있다 involve ~을 수반하다

해설 세부 사항 관련 – 여자가 남자에게 특수 보직에 대해 하는 말

여자의 두 번째 대사에서 남자에게 전문 부서 자리로 승진하기에 적합한 지원자일 수 있지만 모든 신규 채용자가 우선은 최소 6개월간 표준 기계로 작업하도록 요구하고 있다(you might be a good candidate for ~ at least six months first.)고 했으므로 정답은 (C)이다.

▸▸ **Paraphrasing** 대화의 **a position at a specialized station**
→ 정답의 **a special position**

56-58

M-Cn Hi, Corinne. [56]**This is Jamal from Copies and More calling to tell you that your pamphlets are ready for pick-up.**

W-Am Thank you. How late are you open today? I'm not sure I'll be there in time to pick them up.

M-Cn [57]**We close in thirty minutes.**

W-Am Oh... I'm an hour away. Uh, would you mind holding the order for me overnight?

M-Cn No problem. We open again tomorrow morning at seven-thirty.

W-Am That's a relief. [58]**The roads are so busy right now that it's already taken me an hour just to drive a few blocks!** I'll see you tomorrow morning, then.

남: 안녕하세요, 코린 씨. **카피스 앤 모어의 자말입니다. 주문하신 팸플릿이 찾아가실 수 있게 준비가 되어 전화 드렸습니다.**
여: 감사합니다. 오늘 얼마나 늦게까지 여나요? 제가 제시간에 가지러 갈 수 있을지 잘 모르겠어요.
남: **저희는 30분 후에 문을 닫습니다.**
여: 아… 저는 한 시간 떨어진 곳에 있어요. 하룻밤 동안 주문품을 보관해 주실 수 있을까요?
남: 물론이죠. 내일 아침 7시 30분에 다시 문을 엽니다.
여: 그렇다면 안심이네요. **지금 교통이 너무 막혀서 차로 몇 블록을 지나가는 데 벌써 한 시간이나 걸렸거든요.** 그럼 내일 아침에 뵐게요.

어휘 in time 시간 맞춰, 늦지 않게 overnight 하룻밤 동안 relief 안도, 안심

56

Why is the man calling the woman?

(A) An order has been fulfilled.
(B) An event is about to begin.
(C) He wants some information.
(D) He received a text message from her.

남자가 여자에게 전화를 건 이유는 무엇인가?

(A) 주문한 물건이 준비되어 있다.
(B) 행사가 시작하려고 한다.
(C) 자료를 좀 원한다.
(D) 그녀에게 문자 메시지를 받았다.

어휘 fulfill 이행하다, 충족시키다 be about to+동사원형 막 ~하려고 하다

해설 전체 내용 관련 – 남자가 전화를 건 이유

대화 맨 처음에 남자가 여자에게 자신은 카피스 앤 모어의 자말이며 여자가 주문한 팸플릿이 찾아갈 수 있게 준비가 되어서 전화한다(This is Jamal from Copies and More ~ ready for pick-up.)고 했으므로 정답은 (A)이다.

57

What does the woman mean when she says, "I'm an hour away"?

(A) The man has misunderstood an itinerary.
(B) The man should handle a problem by himself.
(C) She cannot arrive before a store closes.
(D) She will have to communicate electronically.

여자가 "저는 한 시간 떨어진 곳에 있어요"라고 말한 의도는 무엇인가?

(A) 남자는 여행 일정을 잘못 이해했다.
(B) 남자는 문제를 스스로 해결해야 한다.
(C) 여자는 매장이 문을 닫기 전에 도착할 수 없다.
(D) 여자는 온라인으로 의사소통해야 할 것이다.

어휘 itinerary 여행 일정 communicate 의사소통하다

해설 화자의 의도 파악 – 한 시간 떨어진 곳에 있다고 말한 의도

남자의 두 번째 대사에서 30분 후에 문을 닫는다(We close in thirty minutes.)고 했더니 이 말을 듣고 여자가 한 시간 떨어진 곳에 있다는 인용문을 말했다. 즉, 여자의 말은 상점이 문을 닫기 전에 도착할 수 없다는 뜻이므로 정답은 (C)이다.

58

What does the woman say is causing a delay?

(A) Heavy traffic
(B) Unreliable navigation
(C) Bad weather
(D) Car trouble

여자는 무엇 때문에 늦고 있다고 말하는가?

(A) 교통체증
(B) 신뢰할 수 없는 네비게이션
(C) 악천후
(D) 차량 문제

어휘 delay 지연, 연기 unreliable 신뢰할 수 없는

해설 세부 사항 관련 – 여자가 늦는 이유

대화 맨 마지막에 여자가 지금 교통이 너무 막혀서 몇 블록을 차로 가는 데 벌써 한 시간이 걸렸다(The roads are so busy ~ a few blocks!)고 했으므로 정답은 (A)이다.

59-61

M-Cn Hello. [59]**I'm calling because I'm interested in having the exterior of my home repainted, and I've noticed your signs around our neighborhood here in the Forest Acres area.** The houses you've worked on look beautiful!

W-Am Thanks. Yes, we do a lot of work there. In fact, we'll be out there later today and could come take a look so I can give you a quote. Let me ask you a quick question—[60]**how big is your place?**

M-Cn It's fifteen hundred square feet, and we have mostly wood siding. But [61]**you'll see that we have some uneven stone surfaces too, so even though the house is small, it's a complex job.**

W-Am OK, I'll keep that in mind.

남: 안녕하세요. **저희 집 외관 페인트칠을 다시 하고 싶은데, 여기 집 근처의 포레스트 에이커스 지역에서 간판을 보고 전화 드렸습니다.** 작업하신 집들이 보기 좋더군요.

여: 고맙습니다. 네, 그 지역에서 일을 많이 합니다. 사실 오늘 이따가 그쪽에 가는데 가서 보고 견적을 내 드릴 수 있습니다. 간단한 질문 하나 드릴게요. **집이 얼마나 큰가요?**

남: 1500평방 피트이고, 외장이 주로 목재로 되어 있어요. 하지만 **울퉁불퉁한 석재 표면도 있는 걸 보실 텐데요, 그래서 집은 작지만 작업이 복잡합니다.**

여: 네, 유념하겠습니다.

어휘 exterior 외면, 외관 quote 견적액 siding 벽널, 외장용 자재 uneven 울퉁불퉁한 surface 표면

59

Who most likely is the woman?

(A) A house painter
(B) A landscaper
(C) A real estate agent
(D) An event planner

여자는 누구이겠는가?

(A) 집 페인트공
(B) 조경사
(C) 부동산 중개인
(D) 행사 기획자

해설 전체 내용 관련 – 여자의 직업

대화 맨 처음에 남자가 여자에게 집 외관 페인트칠을 다시 하고 싶어서 집 근처 포레스트 에이커스 지역의 간판을 보고 전화했다(I'm calling because I'm interested ~ here in the Forest Acres area.)고 했다. 이를 통해 여자가 페인트공임을 알 수 있으므로 정답은 (A)이다.

60

What does the woman ask about?

(A) The availability of parking
(B) The size of a structure
(C) The budget for a project
(D) The address of a property

여자는 무엇에 대해 물어보는가?

(A) 주차장 유무
(B) 건축물의 크기
(C) 프로젝트 예산
(D) 집 주소

해설 세부 사항 관련 – 여자의 문의 사항

여자의 첫 번째 대사에서 남자에게 집이 얼마나 큰지(how big is your place?)를 물어봤으므로 정답은 (B)이다.

▸▸ **Paraphrasing** 대화의 **place** → 정답의 **structure**

61

Why will the job be difficult?

(A) Some materials are rare.
(B) Some surfaces are rough.
(C) A deadline cannot be changed.
(D) A location is inconvenient.

작업이 왜 어렵겠는가?

(A) 특정 자재는 구하기 힘들다.
(B) 거친 표면이 있다.
(C) 마감 시한을 변경할 수 없다.
(D) 교통이 불편한 곳에 있다.

어휘 rare 희귀한, 드문 surface 표면 rough 거친 inconvenient 불편한

해설 세부 사항 관련 – 작업이 어려운 이유

남자의 두 번째 대사에서 울퉁불퉁한 석재 표면이 있어서 집은 작지만 작업이 복잡하다(you'll see that ~ a complex job.)고 했으므로 정답은 (B)이다.

▸▸ **Paraphrasing** 대화의 **some uneven stone surfaces**
→ 정답의 **Some surfaces are rough.**

62-64 대화 + 일기 예보

M-Au Rebecca, can I talk to you for a second? [62]**It's about the game of outdoor tennis that we had scheduled for Saturday.** It looks like it's going to rain that day.

Test 6

W-Br Let me check the forecast. Oh yes, I see. And I'm sure the court will be wet the next day. How about a weekday evening, then? [63]**It looks like the weather will be warm and clear on this day.**

M-Au That works for me. [64]**Would you like to drive to the sports complex together after work? There's plenty of room for both of our equipment bags in my car.**

W-Br Sure, that would be great.

남: 레베카, 잠시 얘기 좀 할 수 있을까요? **토요일로 잡혀 있는 야외 테니스 게임에 관한 건데요.** 그날 비가 올 거 같네요.

여: 예보를 확인해 볼게요. 아 그러네요, 알겠어요. 코트가 그 다음 날도 분명히 젖어 있을 텐데. 그럼 평일 저녁엔 어떨까요? **이 날엔 날씨가 따뜻하고 맑을 거 같아요.**

남: 저는 좋아요. **퇴근 후에 같은 차로 종합운동장에 갈까요?** 내 차 안에 우리 둘의 용품 가방을 넣을 공간이 충분히 있어요.

여: 네, 그거 좋겠네요.

어휘 court (테니스 등을 하는) 코트 wet 젖은 weekday 평일 sports complex 종합운동장 room 공간 equipment 용품, 장비

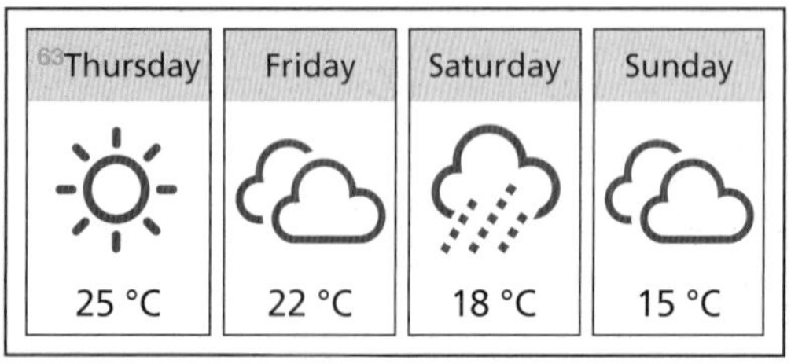

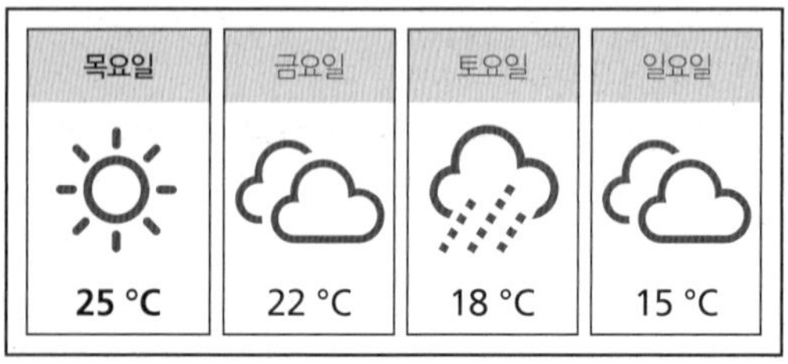

62

What are the speakers planning to do together?

(A) Visit a market
(B) Take a walking tour
(C) Clean up an outdoor space
(D) Play a competitive sport

화자들은 함께 무엇을 할 계획인가?

(A) 시장 방문
(B) 도보 여행
(C) 옥외 공간 청소
(D) 스포츠 경기

어휘 outdoor space 옥외[야외] 공간 competitive sport 스포츠 경기(어느 쪽이 이길지 겨루는 스포츠)

해설 전체 내용 관련 – 화자들의 계획

남자의 첫 대사에서 토요일로 잡힌 야외 테니스 게임에 관한 것(It's about the game of outdoor tennis that we had scheduled for Saturday.)을 얘기하자고 했으므로 정답은 (D)이다.

63

Look at the graphic. Which day do the speakers select?

(A) Thursday
(B) Friday
(C) Saturday
(D) Sunday

시각정보에 의하면, 화자들은 무슨 요일을 선택하는가?

(A) 목요일
(B) 금요일
(C) 토요일
(D) 일요일

해설 시각 정보 연계 – 화자들이 선택한 요일

여자의 첫 번째 대사에서 이 날 날씨가 따뜻하고 맑을 것(It looks like the weather will be warm and clear on this day.)이라고 했다. 일기 예보표를 보면 기온이 가장 높으면서 맑은 날은 목요일이므로 정답은 (A)이다.

64

What does the man offer the woman?

(A) Transportation to a location
(B) Assistance with a work duty
(C) Some used equipment
(D) The key to a storage room

남자는 여자에게 무엇을 제공하는가?

(A) 어떤 장소로 가는 교통편
(B) 업무 지원
(C) 중고 장비
(D) 창고 열쇠

어휘 transportation 교통 수단, 차편 assistance 도움, 보조 used 중고의

해설 세부 사항 관련 – 남자가 여자에게 제공하는 것

남자의 마지막 대사에서 퇴근 후에 같은 차로 종합운동장에 가겠는지 물어보면서 자신의 차에 용품 가방을 넣을 공간이 충분하다(Would you like to drive ~ our equipment bags in my car.)고 했으므로 정답은 (A)이다

65-67 대화+그래픽

W-Br Excuse me. I'm looking for the book *Achieving Career Success*. It's not on the shelf even though the library's online system says it's checked in.

M-Au Let me help you. [65]**It's supposed to be on the "General Business" shelf, but uh... there it is on the shelf below that.**

W-Br Ah, thank you!

M-Au You're welcome. You know, you're lucky to find this in stock! [66]**It's been loaned out almost continually since we got it in.**

W-Br It was on a newspaper's "Best Books of the Year" list—that's probably why. [67]**Its author, John Haskins, will speak at a conference I'm attending,** and I wanted to get some background on him. Thanks again for your help.

여: 실례합니다. 〈직업적으로 성공하기〉라는 책을 찾고 있어요. 도서관 온라인 시스템에서는 반납됐다고 하는데 책장에는 없네요.

남: 도와드리겠습니다. **그 책은 '일반 비즈니스' 칸에 있어야 하는데요, 어… 저기 그 아래 칸에 있군요.**

여: 아, 감사합니다!

남: 네. 이 책이 들어와 있을 때 찾으시다니 운이 좋으시네요! **들여왔을 때부터 거의 계속해서 대출되고 있어요.**

여: 아마도 어느 신문에서 선정한 '올해 최고의 책' 목록에 올라서일 거예요. **저자인 존 해스킨스 씨가 제가 참석하는 컨퍼런스에서 연설을 하거든요.** 그래서 그에 대한 배경지식을 좀 얻고 싶었어요. 도와주셔서 정말 감사합니다.

어휘 look for ~를 찾다 achieve 성취하다 check in (도서관에서 책을) 반납하다 loan out 빌려주다 continually 계속해서 author 저자 background 배경 stack 서가 arrival 도착한 것 finance 금융 management 경영, 관리

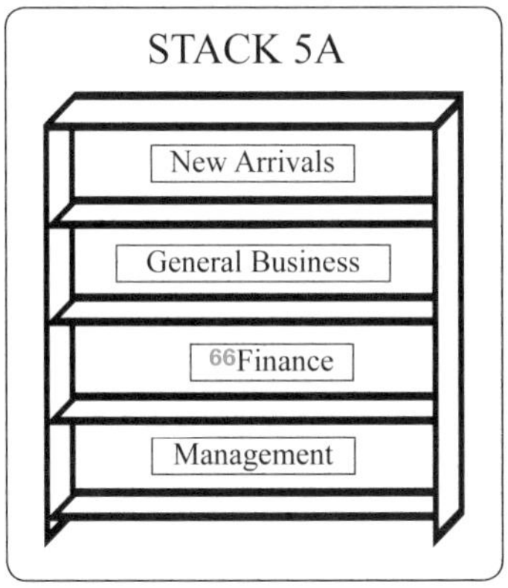

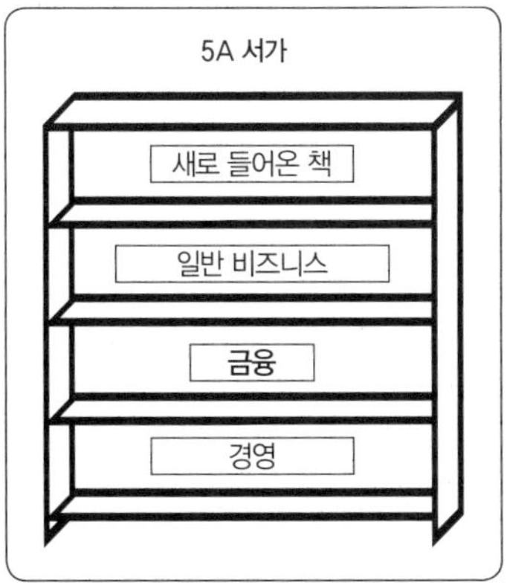

65

Look at the graphic. On which shelf does the man find the book?

(A) New Arrivals
(B) General Business
(C) Finance
(D) Management

시각 정보에 의하면, 남자는 어느 칸에서 책을 찾았는가?

(A) 새로 들어온 책
(B) 일반 비즈니스
(C) 금융
(D) 경영

해설 시각 정보 연계 - 책을 찾은 칸

남자의 첫 번째 대사에서 여자가 찾는 책이 '일반 비즈니스' 칸에 있어야 하는데 그 아래 칸에 있다(It's supposed to be ~ below that.)고 했다. 그리고 5A 서가를 보면 '일반 비즈니스' 칸 밑에 '금융' 칸으로 나와 있으므로 정답은 (C)이다.

66

What does the man say about the book?

(A) Its category was difficult to determine.
(B) It is popular with library patrons.
(C) It is unusually large.
(D) Its loan period cannot be extended.

남자는 책에 대해 뭐라고 말하는가?

(A) 카테고리를 정하기 어려웠다.
(B) 도서관 이용자들에게 인기가 많다.
(C) 비정상적으로 크다.
(D) 대여 기간을 연장할 수 없다.

어휘 determine 결정하다 patron 고객, 이용자 extend 연장하다

해설 세부 내용 관련 - 책에 관한 사항

남자의 두 번째 대사에서 들여왔을 때부터 거의 계속해서 대출되고 있다(It's been loaned out almost continually since we got it in.)고 했으므로 정답은 (B)이다.

67

Who most likely is Mr. Haskins?

(A) A writer of a book
(B) A librarian
(C) A newspaper reporter
(D) An organizer of a conference

해스킨스 씨는 누구겠는가?

(A) 책의 저자
(B) 도서관 사서
(C) 신문 기자
(D) 컨퍼런스 담당자

해설 세부 사항 관련 – 해스킨스 씨의 신분

여자의 세 번째 대사에서 책의 저자인 존 해스킨스가 여자가 참석하는 컨퍼런스에서 연설을 한다(Its author, John Haskins, will speak at a conference I'm attending)고 했으므로 정답은 (A)이다.

▸▸ **Paragraphing** 대화의 **author** → 정답의 **writer of a book**

68-70 대화 + 일정표

W-Am Devin, your presentation on the marketing strategy for our new software program was terrific.

M-Cn Thank you. I worked hard on it.

W-Am [68]**Would you like to help me prepare a presentation for the investors' meeting in July?**

M-Cn I'd be glad to. That's the meeting that takes place right after the quarterly reports are released, right?

W-Am That's right. Now, [69]**I see you still have a time slot open Wednesday morning. Let's meet up then and go over a basic outline.** Then we can check in weekly until the job is done.

M-Cn Sounds good. [70]**Why don't you send me the slides from last year's meeting so I can start generating some ideas?**

여: 데빈, 새 소프트웨어 프로그램을 위한 마케팅 전략 발표는 정말 훌륭했어요.

남: 감사합니다. 발표 준비를 열심히 했습니다.

여: **제가 7월에 있을 투자자 회의 발표를 준비하는 데 도와줄 수 있나요?**

남: 물론입니다. 분기 보고서가 나온 직후에 열리는 회의죠?

여: 맞아요. **지금 보니 당신은 수요일 아침에 아직 빈 시간대가 있군요. 그때 만나서 기본 개요를 검토하기로 해요.** 그리고 일이 마무리될 때까지 매주 확인하면 돼요.

남: 좋습니다. **제가 아이디어를 낼 수 있도록 작년 회의 때 슬라이드를 좀 제게 보내 주시겠어요?**

어휘 presentation 발표 strategy 전략 terrific 훌륭한, 멋진 prepare 준비하다 investor 투자자 take place 열리다 quarterly 분기의 release 공개하다, 발표하다 time slot 시간대 go over ~을 검토하다 outline 개요 generate 만들어 내다

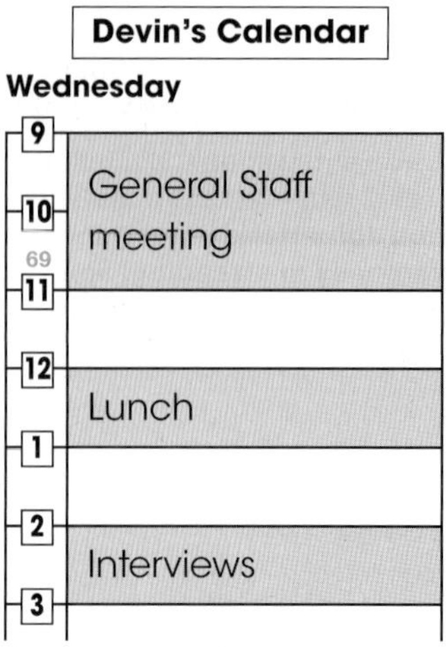
Devin's Calendar
Wednesday
9
10
69
11
12
1
2
3
General Staff meeting
Lunch
Interviews

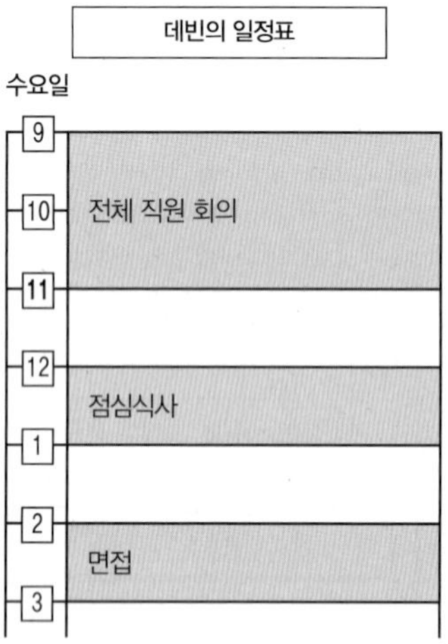
데빈의 일정표
수요일
9
10
11
12
1
2
3
전체 직원 회의
점심식사
면접

68

What does the woman ask for help with?

(A) Preparing quarterly reports

(B) Scheduling a meeting

(C) Creating a presentation

(D) Reserving a venue

여자는 무엇에 대해 도움을 요청하는가?

(A) 분기 보고서 준비

(B) 회의 일정 잡기

(C) 발표 자료 만들기

(D) 장소 예약

어휘 venue 장소

해설 세부 사항 관련 – 여자의 요청 사항

여자의 두 번째 대사에서 남자에게 7월에 있을 투자자 회의 발표를 준비하는 데 도움을 줄 수 있는지(Would you like to ~ meeting in July?) 물어봤으므로 정답은 (C)이다.

▸▸ **Paraphrasing** 대화의 **prepare a presentation**
→ 정답의 **Creating a presentation**

69

Look at the graphic. When will the speakers most likely meet?

(A) At 10:00 A.M.
(B) At 11:00 A.M.
(C) At 1:00 P.M.
(D) At 2:00 P.M.

시각 정보에 의하면, 화자들은 언제 만나겠는가?

(A) 오전 10시
(B) 오전 11시
(C) 오후 1시
(D) 오후 2시

해설 시각 정보 연계 - 화자들이 만날 시간

여자의 세 번째 대사에서 남자가 수요일 아침에 빈 시간대가 있으니 그때 만나서 기본적인 개요를 검토하자(I see you still have ~ a basic outline.)고 했다. 그리고 남자의 일정표를 보면 아침에는 11시에서 12시까지의 일정이 비어 있는 걸로 되어 있으므로 정답은 (B)이다.

70

What will the woman probably send the man?

(A) A press release
(B) A software update
(C) Some contact information
(D) Some visual materials

여자는 남자에게 무엇을 보내겠는가?

(A) 보도 자료
(B) 소프트웨어 업데이트
(C) 연락처 정보
(D) 시각 자료

해설 세부 사항 관련 - 여자가 남자에게 보낼 자료

대화 맨 마지막에 남자가 여자에게 아이디어를 낼 수 있도록 작년 회의 때의 슬라이드를 보내 달라(Why don't you send me ~ generating some ideas?)고 했으므로 정답은 (D)이다.

▸▸ **Paraphrasing** 대화의 **slides** → 정답의 **visual materials**

PART 4

71-73 전화 메시지

M-Cn Hi, this is Felix Russell from the Pellson Foundation calling for Lois Graves. According to the information we've been given, [71]**you're the current supervisor of a teacher named Jeannette Collier.** If that's correct, we'd like your assistance. [72]**Ms. Collier has been nominated for the foundation's "Excellence in Teaching Prize".** It's an honor that comes with both a financial reward and professional development opportunities. [72]**To help me and the rest of the judges' committee determine if Ms. Collier deserves to win,** [73]**we would like you to write a letter describing her achievements as an educator.** If you can, please call me back at 555-0136 for details. Thanks.

안녕하세요. 저는 펠슨 재단의 펠릭스 러셀로, 로이스 그레이브즈 님께 전화드립니다. 저희가 받은 정보에 따르면, **귀하가 지네트 콜리어라는 교사의 현 상사로 되어 있습니다.** 그것이 맞다면, 귀하의 도움이 필요합니다. **콜리어 씨는 저희 재단이 수여하는 '우수 교사상' 후보로 지명되었습니다.** 이 상은 금전적 보상과 직업 능력 개발 기회의 영예가 주어집니다. **저와 나머지 심사위원들이 콜리어 씨의 수상 자격 여부를 결정할 수 있도록 도움을 주시려면, 콜리어 씨가 교육자로서 이뤄낸 성과를 설명하는 편지를 써주시기 바랍니다.** 가능하신 경우, 555-0136 번으로 제게 전화 주시면 자세한 사항을 알려드리겠습니다. 고맙습니다.

어휘 foundation 재단 supervisor 상사, 감독자 named ~라 불리는, 이름이 ~인 be nominated for ~의 후보로 지명되다 excellence 우수함 honor 명예, 영예 financial 재정적인 reward 보상 professional development 직업 능력 개발 rest 나머지 judges' committee 심사 위원회 determine 결정하다 deserve to + 동사원형 ~할 가치가 있다 win (상을) 받다 achievement 업적, 성취한 것 educator 교육자

71

Who most likely is the listener?

(A) A school administrator
(B) A bank supervisor
(C) A magazine editor
(D) A restaurant owner

청자는 누구겠는가?

(A) 학교 관리자
(B) 은행 감독자
(C) 잡지 편집자
(D) 레스토랑 주인

어휘 administrator (행정) 관리자 editor 편집자

해설 전체 내용 관련 - 청자의 신분

지문 초반부에 화자가 청자에게 지네트 콜리어라는 교사의 현 상사로 되어 있다(you're the current supervisor of a teacher named Jeannette Collier.)고 말하고 있어 청자가 학교 관리자라는 사실을 알 수 있으므로 정답은 (A)이다.

72

What project is the speaker working on?

(A) Publishing an article
(B) Filling a job opening
(C) Conducting a survey
(D) Giving out an award

Test 6

화자는 어떤 일을 하는 중인가?
(A) 기사 발표
(B) 공석에 직원 채용
(C) 설문 조사 실시
(D) 상 수여

어휘 work on ~에 관한 일을 하다[애쓰다] publish 발표하다, 출판하다 fill (빈 자리에 사람을) 채우다 job opening (직장의) 공석 conduct a survey 설문조사를 하다

해설 세부 사항 관련 - 화자가 하고 있는 일
지문 중반부에 콜리어 씨가 화자의 재단이 수여하는 '우수 교사상' 후보로 지명되었다(Ms. Collier has been nominated ~ Teaching Prize".)면서 심사위원들이 콜리어 씨의 수상 자격 여부를 결정할 수 있도록 도움을 줄 수 있는지(To help me and the ~ Ms. Collier deserves to win) 확인하는 것으로 보아, 화자는 상을 수여하는 일을 하는 중임을 알 수 있으므로 정답은 (D)이다.

73

What does the speaker want to know about?
(A) An educational opportunity
(B) A marketing technique
(C) An organization's reputation
(D) A person's accomplishments

화자는 무엇에 대해 알고 싶어 하는가?
(A) 교육 받을 기회
(B) 마케팅 기술
(C) 한 조직의 평판
(D) 한 개인의 업적

어휘 opportunity 기회 organization 조직, 기관 reputation 평판, 소문 accomplishment 업적, 성취

해설 세부 사항 관련 - 화자가 알고 싶어 하는 것
지문 후반부에 화자가 청자에게 콜리어 씨가 교육자로서 이뤄낸 성과를 설명하는 편지를 써주기 바란다(we would like you to write a letter describing her achievements as an educator.)고 했으므로 정답은 (D)이다.

▸▸ **Paraphrasing** 지문의 achievements
→ 정답의 accomplishments

74-76 회의 발췌

W-Br Moving on, I've received a request regarding the new Client Services Department. It's going to be made up of four new hires, and [74]**management has asked Human Resources to send someone from our team to help put together the listings for the new positions.** I guess [75]**Mario Ramos, the head of the new department,** hasn't been in charge of a hiring process before. We're supposed to make sure the postings contain all of the necessary information and will attract good candidates. So, [76]**could one of you offer to help Mr. Ramos?** He'll do all of the preparation, so you'd just need to give him some advice and review his writing. Who's interested?

다음 주제로 넘어가서요, 제가 새로 생긴 고객 서비스 부서와 관련해 한 가지 요청을 받았습니다. 이 부서는 신입사원 4명으로 구성될 예정인데, **경영진이 우리 팀에서 사람을 보내 신규 직책 업무 내용을 목록화하는 걸 도와주라고 인사부에 요청을 했습니다. 새 부서의 수장 마리오 라모스 씨는** 채용 과정을 담당했던 적이 없는 것 같습니다. 우리는 반드시 게시글에 필요한 정보가 빠짐없이 담기도록 해야 하고, 또 이것이 훌륭한 지원자들을 끌어들일 수 있도록 해야 합니다. 그래서, **여러분 중 라모스 씨를 도와주실 분 있습니까?** 라모스 씨가 모든 준비를 할 거라서 여러분은 조언을 해 주고 그가 작성한 걸 검토만 해 주면 됩니다. 관심 있는 분 계신가요?

어휘 move on (다음 주제로) 넘어가다 regarding ~에 관한 be made up of ~으로 이루어지다 management 경영진 Human Resources 인사부 put together (취합해서) 만들다 listing 목록의 내용 be in charge of ~을 담당하다[책임지다] posting (인터넷 상의) 공지, 게시

74

What is the speaker mainly discussing?
(A) Planning an orientation session
(B) Writing some employment advertisements
(C) Negotiating the terms of a contract
(D) Interviewing some candidates

화자는 주로 무엇을 논의하고 있는가?
(A) 오리엔테이션 기획
(B) 채용 공고 작성
(C) 계약 조건 협상
(D) 지원자 면접

어휘 employment 취업, 채용 negotiate 협상하다 terms of a contract 계약 조건

해설 전체 내용 관련 - 논의의 주제
지문 초반부에 경영진이 화자의 팀에서 사람을 보내 신규 직책 업무 내용을 목록화하는 걸 도와주라고 인사부에 요청을 했다(management has asked Human Resources ~ the listings for the new positions.)면서 이와 관련된 내용이 이어지고 있으므로 정답은 (B)이다.

75

Who most likely is Mr. Ramos?
(A) A client
(B) A job applicant
(C) An intern
(D) A department manager

라모스 씨는 누구겠는가?
(A) 고객
(B) 구직자
(C) 인턴 사원
(D) 부서장

어휘 job applicant 구직자 department manager 부서장, 부장

해설 전체 내용 관련 – 라모스 씨의 신분

지문 중반부에 새 부서의 수장이 마리오 라모스 씨(Mario Ramos, the head of the new department)라고 했으므로 정답은 (D)이다.

76

What are the listeners asked to do?

(A) Volunteer for a task
(B) Shorten a list of names
(C) Review some feedback
(D) Prepare for a seminar

청자들은 무엇을 하라고 요청 받는가?

(A) 업무에 지원하기
(B) 명단 줄이기
(C) 피드백 검토하기
(D) 세미나 준비하기

어휘 volunteer for ~에 지원하다[자청하다] shorten 짧게 하다

해설 세부 사항 관련 – 청자들이 받은 요청

지문 후반부에 화자가 청자들 중 라모스 씨를 도와줄 사람이 있는지(could one of you offer to help Mr. Ramos?) 묻고 있으므로 정답은 (A)이다.

77-79 전화 메시지

M-Cn Hi, Evelyn. It's Hee-Oh. [77]**I'm calling to talk to you about the lab's new digital incubator machine.** Remember how you said it would be useful for my experiment? Well, [78]**I tried to operate it today, but I couldn't figure it out.** And you know, I'm usually good at that sort of thing! Anyway, so I was wondering if you had time to meet tomorrow. The incubator isn't available, but [79]**I'd like to look over the manual together.** I think understanding that may be enough to teach me how to use the incubator. So call me back. Thanks.

안녕하세요, 에블린. 희오입니다. **실험실에 있는 새 디지털 배양기에 관해 얘기하려고 전화했습니다.** 제 실험에 유용할 거라고 말하신 거 기억나죠? 음, **오늘 작동을 시도해 봤는데, 기계를 파악하지 못하겠더라고요.** 당신도 알듯이 **전 보통 그런 것에 능숙하잖아요!** 아무튼, 그래서 내일 저와 만날 시간이 있으신지 알고 싶었어요. 배양기를 써 볼 수는 없더라도 **설명서를 같이 검토하고 싶습니다.** 설명서를 이해만 하면 배양기를 어떻게 사용하는지 제가 알 수 있을 거예요. 그러니까 전화주세요. 고맙습니다.

어휘 lab 실험실(= laboratory) incubator machine 부화기, 배양기 experiment 실험 operate (기계를) 조작하다 figure out 이해하다, 파악하다 be good at ~에 능숙하다 sort 종류 manual 설명서

77

What is the speaker calling about?

(A) A laboratory policy
(B) A research experiment
(C) A piece of equipment
(D) A communication method

화자는 무엇에 대해 전화하고 있는가?

(A) 실험실 방침
(B) 연구 실험
(C) 장비
(D) 의사소통 방식

어휘 policy 정책, 방침 method 방법

해설 전체 내용 관련 – 전화 메시지의 주제

지문 초반부에 화자가 실험실에 있는 새 디지털 배양기에 관해 얘기하려고 전화했다(I'm calling to talk to you about the lab's new digital incubator machine.)고 했으므로 정답은 (C)이다.

▸▸ Paraphrasing 지문의 **new digital incubator machine**
→ 정답의 **equipment**

78

Why does the speaker say, "I'm usually good at that sort of thing"?

(A) To express surprise at a failure
(B) To show interest in a project
(C) To refuse an offer of help
(D) To provide a reason for a choice

화자가 "전 보통 그런 것에 능숙하잖아요"라고 한 이유는 무엇인가?

(A) 실패에 대한 당혹감을 표현하려고
(B) 프로젝트에 관심을 보이려고
(C) 도와주겠다는 제안을 거절하려고
(D) 선택한 이유를 알려주려고

어휘 express 표현하다 failure 실패 refuse 거절하다

해설 화자의 의도 파악

인용문 바로 앞 문장에서 오늘 작동하려고 해 봤는데, 기계를 파악하지 못하겠다(I tried to operate it today, but I couldn't figure it out)고 했다. 그런 다음 자신은 보통 그런 것에 능숙하다고 했는데, 문맥상 인용문은 기계를 파악하지 못한 것에 대한 당혹감을 표현하기 위한 것이므로 정답은 (A)이다.

79

Why does the speaker want to meet?

(A) To look for a missing item
(B) To make some plans
(C) To study a document
(D) To reorganize a room's layout

화자가 만나고 싶어 하는 이유는 무엇인가?

(A) 분실물을 찾으려고
(B) 계획을 세우려고
(C) 문서를 살펴보려고
(D) 방 안을 재배치하려고

Test 6

어휘 missing 분실한 reorganize 재정비하다 layout 배치, 레이아웃

해설 세부 사항 관련 - 화자가 만나고 싶어 하는 이유

지문 후반부에 화자가 청자에게 설명서를 같이 검토하고 싶다(I'd like to look over the manual together.)고 했으므로 정답은 (C)이다.

▸▸ Paraphrasing 지문의 look over the manual
→ 정답의 study a document

80-82 안내

W-Br Good afternoon, Lockhart shoppers. It's winter season, and [80]**Lockhart has a great selection of winter athletic gear such as ice skates, hockey sticks, and more.** In five minutes, we'll even be teaching our valued customers all about snowboarding boots. [81]**Sit down with one of our professionals and get an individual assessment, recommendation, and fitting.** If you're interested, stop by the snowboarding section near the back of the store. And [82]**don't forget we're also offering a special deal on personalizing any small accessory that you purchase in the store, such as a hat or gloves.** Whether it's your initials or a team name, you can add letters at no extra cost. So take advantage of this service today!

안녕하세요, 록하트 손님 여러분. 이 겨울 시즌에 **록하트에서는 스케이트화, 하키 스틱 등 멋진 동계 운동 장비 특선을 준비했습니다.** 5분 뒤 저희 귀중한 고객 여러분께 스노보드용 부츠에 대한 모든 것도 알려드립니다. **저희 전문가 한 명과 함께 앉으셔서 개인 평가와 추천을 받고 착용도 해보시기 바랍니다.** 관심이 있으시면 매장 뒤편 근처에 있는 스노보드 섹션에 들러 보세요. 아울러 **모자나 장갑 등 매장에서 구매하시는 모든 작은 액세서리에 이름을 새겨 드리는 특별 판매 서비스도 하고 있다는 것을 기억해 주세요.** 이름 머리글자든 팀 이름이든 별도의 비용 없이 글자를 더할 수 있습니다. 오늘 이 서비스를 이용해 보시기 바랍니다!

어휘 a selection of ~ 모음 athletic gear 운동 장비 valued 귀중한 individual 개인의 assessment 평가 recommendation 추천 fitting 착용 stop by ~에 들르다 personalize (개인 소유를 나타내는) 표시를 하다 at no extra cost 별도[추가] 비용 없이

80

Where most likely is the announcement being made?

(A) At a fitness center
(B) At a television station
(C) At a sporting goods store
(D) At a stadium

안내 방송은 어디서 나오고 있겠는가?

(A) 피트니스 센터
(B) 텔레비전 방송국
(C) 스포츠용품 매장
(D) 경기장

해설 전체 내용 관련 - 안내 방송이 나오는 장소

지문 맨 처음에 록하트에서는 스케이트화, 하키 스틱 등 멋진 동계 운동장비 특선을 준비했다(Lockhart has a great selection of winter athletic gear such as ice skates, hockey sticks, and more.)고 했다. 이 문장에 쓰인 athletic gear를 통해 안내 방송이 나오는 장소가 스포츠용품 매장임을 알 수 있으므로 정답은 (C)이다.

▸▸ Paraphrasing 지문의 athletic gear
→ 정답의 sporting goods

81

What can listeners do today?

(A) Join a loyalty program
(B) Receive a consultation
(C) Use a promotional coupon
(D) Enter a trivia contest

청자들은 오늘 무엇을 할 수 있는가?

(A) 회원 우대 프로그램에 가입
(B) 상담 받기
(C) 홍보용 쿠폰 사용
(D) 퀴즈 대회 참여

해설 세부 사항 관련 - 청자들이 할 수 있는 것

지문 중반에 화자가 손님들에게 전문가 한 명과 같이 앉아서 개인 평가와 추천을 받고 착용도 해보라(Sit down with one of our professionals ~ and fitting.)고 했다. 결국 전문가의 상담을 받는다는 의미이므로 정답은 (B)이다.

▸▸ Paraphrasing 지문의 get an individual assessment, recommendation
→ 정답의 Receive a consultation

82

What special offer is currently available?

(A) Free samples
(B) A customization service
(C) An online discount
(D) Ticket upgrades

현재 어떤 특별 서비스가 이용 가능한가?

(A) 무료 샘플
(B) 고객 맞춤 서비스
(C) 온라인 할인
(D) 표 업그레이드

어휘 customization 맞춤 제작

해설 세부 사항 관련 - 이용 가능한 특별 서비스

지문 후반부에 모자나 장갑 등 매장에서 구매하는 모든 작은 액세서리에 이름을 새겨 주는 특별 판매 서비스도 하고 있다(don't forget we're also offering a special deal on ~ a hat or gloves.)고 했다. 즉, 고객이 구매한 액세서리에 이름을 새겨 주는 것은 고객 맞춤 서비스에 해당하므로 정답은 정답은 (B)이다.

▸▸ **Paraphrasing** 지문의 **personalizing any small accessory**
→ 정답의 **A customization service**

83-85 팟캐스트

W-Am Welcome to *Travel Tips*. I'm your host, Helen Mathis. [83]**On today's episode, I'm discussing Mexico City, a place that drew millions of sightseers last year.** But first, let's talk briefly about Hentman Travel Insurance, one of this podcast's wonderful advertisers. Hentman's insurance plans are flexible and convenient. [84]**Are you worried that they won't provide coverage for all of your adventurous travel activities? Don't be.** I'm looking at their plans right now. I can't recommend Hentman Travel Insurance enough. If you want to know more about them, [85]**please visit www.ttpodcast.com/partners and click on "Hentman Travel Insurance" to go to their site.** OK, on with the show.

〈트래블 팁스〉에 오신 걸 환영합니다. 저는 진행자 헬렌 매티스입니다. **오늘 방송에서는 작년에 수백만 명의 관광객을 끌어들였던 멕시코 시티 얘기를 해보겠습니다.** 하지만 우선, 이 팟캐스트의 멋진 광고주 중 하나인 헨트먼 여행 보험에 대해 간단히 얘기하겠습니다. 헨트먼 보험 상품들은 융통성 있고 편리합니다. **이 상품들이 새로운 경험으로 가득 찬 여러분의 여행 활동 전부에 대해 보상을 제공하지 않을까 봐 걱정이 되시나요? 걱정하실 필요 없습니다.** 제가 지금 그 상품들을 보고 있는데요. 헨트먼 여행 보험은 정말 추천 드리고 싶습니다. 상품에 대해 자세히 알고 싶으시면 **www.ttpodcast.com/partners를 방문해 '헨트먼 여행 보험'을 클릭하시면 회사 웹 사이트로 연결됩니다.** 자, 프로그램을 시작하겠습니다.

어휘 host 진행자 draw (사람의 마음, 관객 등을) 끌다 sightseer 관광객 travel insurance 여행 보험 advertiser 광고주 flexible 융통성 있는 convenient 편리한 coverage (보험의) 보장, 보장 범위 adventurous 모험적인 can't ~ enough 아무리 ~해도 지나치지 않다

83

What is the main topic of this episode of the podcast?

(A) Luggage brands
(B) Travel photography
(C) A tourist destination
(D) A mobile app

이번 회차의 팟캐스트 주제는 무엇인가?

(A) 여행용 가방 상표들
(B) 여행 사진 촬영
(C) 관광지
(D) 모바일 앱

어휘 luggage 여행용 짐 가방 photography 사진 촬영 (기술) tourist destination 관광지

해설 전체 내용 관련 - 팟캐스트의 주제

지문 초반부에 화자가 오늘 방송에서는 작년에 수백만 명의 관광객을 끌어들였던 멕시코 시티 얘기를 해 보겠다(On today's episode, I'm discussing Mexico City, a place that drew millions of sightseers last year.)고 했으므로 정답은 (C)이다.

84

What does the speaker imply when she says, "I'm looking at their plans right now"?

(A) An itinerary lists some exciting activities.
(B) A tourist has new goals for the future.
(C) A facility will make use of modern technology.
(D) A company's offerings are comprehensive.

화자가 "제가 지금 그 상품들을 보고 있는데요"라고 말한 의도는 무엇인가?

(A) 여행 일정표에 흥미로운 활동들이 나와 있다.
(B) 한 관광객이 새로운 미래의 목표를 가지고 있다.
(C) 한 시설이 현대적인 기술을 활용할 것이다.
(D) 한 회사에서 제공하는 상품들이 포괄적이다.

어휘 itinerary 여행 일정표 offering (팔기 위해 생산한) 상품 comprehensive 포괄적인

해설 화자의 의도 파악 - 지금 그 상품들을 보고 있다는 말의 의도

인용문 바로 앞에서 화자는 보험 상품들이 새로운 경험으로 가득 찬 청자들의 여행 활동 전부에 대해 보상을 제공하지 않을까 봐 걱정이 되는지(Are you worried ~ your adventurous travel activities?) 묻고, 바로 걱정할 필요 없다(Don't be.)고 했다. 문맥상 인용문은 한 회사가 제공하는 상품들이 포괄적임을 의미하는 것이므로 정답은 (D)이다.

85

What are listeners encouraged to do on the podcast's Web site?

(A) Follow a link
(B) Download a file
(C) Leave a comment
(D) Enter a code

청자들은 팟캐스트 웹 사이트에서 무엇을 하도록 권유 받는가?

(A) 링크 따라가기
(B) 파일 다운로드하기
(C) 의견 남기기
(D) 코드 입력하기

어휘 enter 적어 놓다, 입력하다

해설 세부 사항 관련 - 청자들이 권유 받는 사항

지문 후반부에 화자가 청자들에게 팟캐스트 웹 사이트에서 '헨트먼 여행 보험'을 클릭하면 사이트로 연결된다(please visit ~ to go to their site.)고 말하고 있으므로 정답은 (A)이다.

Test 6

86-88 담화

W-Am Good morning, everyone. We'll be upgrading the store's point-of-sale system on Friday, March thirtieth, and [86]**you'll need to attend an hour-long training session on the system on March fifteenth.** There will be three sessions that day to accommodate everyone's schedules—one at six A.M., one at noon, and one at nine P.M. [87]**If you absolutely cannot make one of these sessions, please speak with me after this meeting and we'll try to work out an alternate time.** The new system is similar to the old one, but [88]**you'll notice that the interface has been simplified to make it more user-friendly.** We expect everyone to master the new system by the beginning of April.

여러분, 안녕하십니까? 저희는 3월 30일 금요일에 포스(POS) 시스템 업그레이드를 하는 관계로, **여러분은 3월 15일에 새 시스템에 대해 한 시간 동안 교육을 받아야 합니다.** 3월 15일에는 모든 직원의 일정에 맞추기 위해 오전 6시, 낮 12시, 밤 9시, 이렇게 3회의 교육 시간이 마련됩니다. **이 중 어느 교육에도 참석하실 수 없는 분은 이 회의가 끝나고 저에게 말씀해 주시면 대체 시간을 잡아 보겠습니다.** 새 시스템은 기존 시스템과 유사하지만 **사용 편의성을 위해 인터페이스가 간결해졌음을 보시게 될 것입니다.** 모든 직원이 4월 초까지 신규 시스템을 완전히 익히시기를 바랍니다.

어휘 point-of-sale[POS] system 판매 시점 정보를 기록하는 시스템 accommodate 맞추다 absolutely 전혀, 전적으로 make (장소나 행사 등에) 가다 work out 생각해 내다, 알아내다 alternate 대체의 be similar to ~와 유사하다 simplify 간결화하다 user-friendly 사용하기 쉬운 master 익히다

86

What information does the speaker provide about the training sessions?

(A) How long they will last
(B) Where they will be held
(C) Who will lead them
(D) What participants should bring to them

화자는 교육 시간에 대해 어떤 정보를 제공하는가?

(A) 지속 시간
(B) 장소
(C) 교육 강사
(D) 참가자들의 준비물

어휘 last 지속되다 participant 참가자

해설 세부 사항 관련 - 교육에 대해 제공한 정보

지문 초반부에 직원들이 3월 15일에 새 시스템에 대해서 한 시간 동안 교육을 받아야 한다(you'll need to attend an hour-long training session on the system on March fifteenth.)고 했으므로 정답은 (A)이다.

87

Why should the listeners contact the speaker?

(A) To offer to assist with the upgrade
(B) To vote for one of three options
(C) To get a manual for the new system
(D) To schedule a separate training session

청자들이 화자에게 연락해야 하는 이유는 무엇인가?

(A) 업그레이드를 위한 도움을 주기 위해
(B) 세 가지 선택 사항 중 하나를 투표하기 위해
(C) 신규 시스템 사용 설명서를 받기 위해
(D) 별도의 교육 시간 일정을 잡기 위해

어휘 assist 돕다 separate 별도의

해설 세부 사항 관련 - 화자에게 연락해야 하는 이유

지문 중반부에 화자가 청자들에게 세 번의 교육 중 하나도 들을 수 없는 직원은 회의가 끝나고 청자에게 얘기하면 대체 시간을 잡아 보겠다(If you absolutely cannot make ~ an alternate time.)고 했다. 즉, 대체 교육 시간을 정해야 할 직원이라면 화자에게 연락해야 하므로 정답은 (D)이다.

▸▸ **Paraphrasing** 지문의 **work out an alternate time**
→ 정답의 **schedule a separate training session**

88

According to the speaker, what is better about the new system?

(A) It has more features.
(B) It is easier to use.
(C) It is less expensive.
(D) It requires less counter space.

화자에 따르면, 새 시스템의 향상된 점은 무엇인가?

(A) 기능이 더 많다.
(B) 사용하기가 더 쉽다.
(C) 더 저렴하다.
(D) 계산대 공간을 덜 차지한다.

어휘 feature 기능

해설 세부 사항 관련 - 신규 시스템의 개선된 점

지문 후반부에 사용의 편의성을 위해 인터페이스가 간결해졌다(you'll notice that the interface has been simplified to make it more user-friendly.)고 했으므로 정답은 (B)이다.

89-91 전화 메시지

M-Au Hi, this is Tim Anderson. [89]**I came to your store last Tuesday to get some running shoes, but you didn't have my size in stock. So, with the help of your salesperson Marcie, I placed a special order.** She said she would call when they came in. [90]**The problem is that they were**

supposed to have arrived by now, but I haven't heard from her, and there's a race on Saturday. [91]**I would really appreciate it if Marcie would call me back as soon as possible to resolve this.** Oh, and my order number was 8152, if that helps. Thank you.

안녕하세요, 저는 팀 앤더슨입니다. **지난 화요일에 운동화를 사러 귀사의 매장에 갔는데요, 제게 맞는 사이즈가 없었습니다. 그래서 점원 마시의 도움을 받아, 저는 특별 주문을 넣었습니다.** 그 점원은 제품이 들어오면 전화해 주겠다고 했습니다. **문제는 제품이 지금쯤 도착했어야 하는데 아직 아무 연락을 받지 못했고,** 토요일에 달리기 시합이 있습니다. **마시가 최대한 빨리 제게 답신 전화를 주셔서 이 문제를 해결해주시면 고맙겠습니다.** 아, 혹시 도움이 될지 모르겠는데요, 제 주문 번호는 8152입니다. 감사합니다.

어휘 running shoes 운동화 have ~ in stock ~의 재고가 있다 salesperson 판매원 by now 지금쯤은 race 달리기 시합, 경주 appreciate 감사하다 resolve 해결하다

89

How most likely did the speaker previously place an order?

(A) In person
(B) By phone
(C) Online
(D) By mail

화자는 이전에 주문을 어떤 방법으로 했겠는가?

(A) 직접 방문하여
(B) 전화로
(C) 온라인으로
(D) 우편으로

해설 세부 사항 관련 - 화자가 주문한 방법

지문 초반부에 화자가 지난 화요일에 운동화를 사러 매장에 갔는데 자신에게 맞는 사이즈가 없었지만 점원이 특별 주문하는 것을 도와주었다(I came to your store ~ a special order.)고 했다. 즉, 화자가 직접 매장에 가서 점원의 도움을 받아 주문을 한 것이므로 정답은 (A)이다.

90

What does the speaker imply when he says, "there's a race on Saturday"?

(A) He would like to invite the listener to an event.
(B) He is alerting the listener to a sponsorship opportunity.
(C) He needs some goods before the weekend.
(D) He would like to cancel an appointment.

화자가 "토요일에 달리기 시합이 있습니다"라고 말한 의도는 무엇인가?

(A) 청자를 행사에 초대하고 싶다.
(B) 청자에게 후원의 기회를 알려 주고 있다.
(C) 주말 전에 상품이 필요하다.
(D) 예약을 취소하고 싶다.

어휘 alert 주의를 환기시키다, 경보를 울리다

해설 화자의 의도 파악 - 토요일에 경주가 있다는 말의 의도

지문 중반부에 화자가 제품이 지금쯤 도착했어야 하는데 직원으로부터 아직 연락을 받지 못했다(The problem is that ~ haven't heard from her)고 했고 이어서 토요일에 달리기 시합이 있다고 했다. 즉, 인용문은 토요일 경주가 있기 전에 제품을 받아야 한다는 뜻이므로 정답은 (C)이다.

91

What does the speaker request that Marcie do?

(A) Visit a Web site
(B) Confirm his new address
(C) Make a reservation
(D) Return his call

화자는 마시가 무엇을 해 줄 것을 요청하는가?

(A) 웹 사이트 방문하기
(B) 새 주소 확인하기
(C) 예약하기
(D) 답신 전화하기

해설 세부 사항 관련 - 화자의 요청 사항

지문 후반부에 화자가 문제 해결을 위해 마시가 최대한 빨리 자신에게 답신 전화를 해 주면 고맙겠다(I would really appreciate it if Marcie ~ to resolve this.)고 했으므로 정답은 (D)이다.

▸▸ **Paraphrasing** 지문의 **call me back** → 정답의 **return his call**

Test 6

92-94 소개

M-Au It's my pleasure to introduce today's guest speaker, Professor Linda Nomura. [92]**Professor Nomura teaches courses in organizational psychology at the University of Crider.** [93]**She'll be speaking today about strategies for leading mid-sized teams,** introducing the latest research on employee satisfaction and productivity. You won't find a more knowledgeable authority on these topics. Her lecture is based on research she conducted for her upcoming book, *Improving the Way We Work*, which will be released by Navid Publishing this fall. [94]**Afterwards, she will take questions for half an hour.** Please give Professor Nomura a warm welcome!

오늘의 초청 연사이신 린다 노무라 교수님을 소개해 드리게 되어 기쁩니다. **노무라 교수님께서는 크라이더 대학교에서 조직심리학 강의를 하고 계십니다. 오늘은 중간 규모의 팀을 이끄는 전략에 대해 강의하실 예정이며,** 직원 만족과 생산성에 관한 최근 연구를 소개하실 겁니다. 이런 주제에 대해 더 박식한 권위자는 찾지 못하실 겁니다. 교수님의 강의는 곧 발간될 저서 〈일하는 법 향상시키기〉를 위해 수행한 조사에 근거를 두고 있으며, 책은 올 가을 나비드 출판사에서 출간될 예정입니다. **강의 후에 교수님은 30분간 질문을 받으실 겁니다.** 노무라 교수님을 따뜻하게 맞아 주십시오!

어휘 guest speaker 초청 연사 organizational psychology 조직심리학 latest 최신의 satisfaction 만족 productivity 생산성 lecture 강의 knowledgeable 박식한 authority 권위자 be based on ~에 토대를 두다 release 발간하다

92

What field does Ms. Nomura most likely work in?

(A) Law
(B) Hospitality
(C) Technology
(D) Education

노무라 씨는 어떤 분야에서 일하겠는가?

(A) 법률
(B) 서비스업
(C) 과학 기술
(D) 교육

해설 세부 사항 관련 – 노무라 씨의 강의 주제

지문 초반부에 노무라 교수는 크라이더 대학교에서 조직심리학 강의를 하고 있다(Professor Nomura teaches courses in organizational psychology at the University of Crider.)고 했다. 즉, 대학교에서 강의를 하고 있으므로 정답은 (D)이다.

93

What will Ms. Nomura's lecture be about?

(A) Management techniques
(B) Customer satisfaction
(C) Workplace design
(D) Financial investing

노무라 씨의 강의는 무엇에 관한 것이겠는가?

(A) 관리 기술
(B) 고객 만족
(C) 작업 공간 설계
(D) 투자 금융

해설 세부 사항 관련 – 노무라 씨의 강의 주제

지문 초중반부에 노무라 교수가 오늘 중간 규모의 팀을 이끄는 전략에 대해 강의할 예정(She'll be speaking today about strategies for leading mid-sized teams)이라고 했으므로 정답은 (A)이다.

94

What will Ms. Nomura do after her lecture?

(A) Attend a formal dinner
(B) Answer audience questions
(C) Lead some role-play exercises
(D) Read from her new book

노무라 씨는 강의 후 무엇을 할 것인가?

(A) 공식 만찬에 참석
(B) 청중의 질문에 답변
(C) 역할극 연습 인솔
(D) 출간된 새 책 낭독

어휘 attend 참석하다 formal 공식적인

해설 세부 사항 관련 – 노무라 씨가 강의 후 할 일

지문 후반부에 강의 후 노무라 박사가 30분간 질문을 받을 것(Afterwards, she will take questions for half an hour.)이라고 했으므로 정답은 (B)이다.

▸▸ **Paraphrasing** 지문의 **take questions**
→ 정답의 **answer audience questions**

95-97 회의 발췌 + 차트

M-Cn The consumer survey results are in, and there's great news for us here at Tasteen Snacks. Our Healthy Crisps snack got a positive rating of eighty-nine percent! And [95]**they earned the highest satisfaction ratings in a key area—that of flavor.** All right, moving on... Oh, this chart compares the offerings of our company and those of Sandac Foods, our main competitor. Now, [96]**Sandac Foods offers the public one thing that we don't—see that on the chart? I'll actually discuss that area more in our afternoon meeting.** Right now, though, [97]**let me turn off the projector screen and pass out these outlines of the survey results** so we can review the major points together.

소비자 조사 결과가 나왔고, 우리 테이스틴 스낵에 좋은 소식이 있습니다. 우리의 헬시 크리습스 과자가 만족도 89%라는 긍정적인 평가를 얻었습니다! 그리고 **주요 영역인 맛 부문에서 가장 높은 만족도를 얻었습니다.** 좋아요, 다음으로… 이 차트는 우리 회사가 제공하는 것과 주요 경쟁사인 샌댁 푸드가 제공하는 것을 비교한 것인데요. 자, **샌댁 푸드는 우리가 제공하지 못하는 것 하나를 대중에게 제공합니다. 차트에서 알아보시겠습니까? 오후 회의에서 이 부분을 더 자세히 논의하죠.** 하지만 지금은 **프로젝터 화면을 끄고 이번 조사 결과의 요약본을 나눠 드려** 주요 사안을 함께 검토하실 수 있도록 하겠습니다.

어휘 consumer survey 소비자 조사 positive 긍정적인 rating 평가, 지지도 satisfaction ratings 만족도 key 주요한 offering 제공물 competitor 경쟁자, 경쟁사 outline 개요, 요약

Comparison of Company offerings

	Tasteen Snacks	Sandac Foods
Wholesale bulk ordering	✓	✓
Online shopping	✓	
[96]Collectible gift boxes		✓
Seasonal promotions	✓	✓

회사들이 제공하는 것 비교

	테이스틴 스낵	샌댁 푸드
대량 도매 주문	✓	✓
온라인 쇼핑	✓	
수집용 선물 상자		**✓**
계절에 따른 홍보	✓	✓

95

According to the speaker, what did consumers like best about Healthy Crisps?

(A) Their taste
(B) Their packaging
(C) Their healthiness
(D) Their cost

화자에 따르면, 헬시 크리습스에 대해 소비자들이 가장 좋아한 점은 무엇인가?

(A) 맛
(B) 포장
(C) 건강 지향성
(D) 가격

해설 세부 사항 관련 – 헬시 크리습스에 대해 가장 좋아한 것

지문 초반부에 헬시 크리습스는 주요 영역인 맛에서 가장 높은 만족도를 얻었다(they earned the highest satisfaction ratings in a key area—that of flavor.)고 했다. 정답은 (A)이다.

▸▸ **Paraphrasing** 지문의 **flavor** → 정답의 **taste**

96

Look at the graphic. Which area will the speaker discuss in the afternoon?

(A) Wholesale bulk ordering
(B) Online shopping
(C) Collectible gift boxes
(D) Seasonal promotions

시각 정보에 의하면, 화자는 오후에 어느 부분에 대해 얘기할 것인가?

(A) 대량 도매 주문
(B) 온라인 쇼핑
(C) 수집용 선물 상자
(D) 계절에 따른 홍보

어휘 wholesale 도매 collectible 모을 수 있는, 수집용의

해설 시각 정보 연계 – 화자의 오후 논의 내용

지문 중반부에 샌댁 푸드는 화자의 회사에서 제공하지 못하는 것 하나를 대중에게 제공하고 있는데 오후 회의에서 그 부분을 자세히 논의할 것(Sandac Foods offers the public ~ afternoon meeting.)이라고 했다. 그리고 차트를 보면 테이스틴 스낵에서는 수집용 선물 상자(Collectible gift boxes) 부분에만 체크 표시가 없으므로 정답은 (C)이다.

97

What will the speaker probably do next?

(A) Take a lunch break
(B) Begin a videoconference
(C) Show a competitor's commercial
(D) Distribute some summaries

화자는 다음에 무엇을 하겠는가?

(A) 점심 식사를 한다.
(B) 화상 회의를 시작한다.
(C) 경쟁사의 광고를 보여준다.
(D) 요약본을 배부한다.

어휘 commercial 광고; 상업적인 distribute 배포하다 summary 요약(본)

해설 세부 사항 관련 – 화자의 다음 행동

지문 맨 마지막에 화자가 이번 조사 결과의 요약본을 나눠주겠다(let me ~ pass out these outlines of the survey results)고 했으므로 정답은 (D)이다.

▸▸ **Paraphrasing** 지문의 **pass out these outlines**
→ 정답의 **distribute some summaries**

98-100 안내 + 표

W-Br Attention, passengers. [98]**This is a gate change announcement. Flight 3759 continuing on to Chicago will be arriving at Gate A-21, not C-13.** Again, the new gate will be A-21. [99]**In order to reach Area A, you will have to take a shuttle bus from the central exit,** just past the taxi stands. The flight is delayed by forty minutes, so you should have enough time to reach Gate A-21. When you arrive, [100]**please have your flight ticket ready to show to the staff at the gate.** You may speak to me or another agent if you have any questions or need special assistance.

Test 6

승객 여러분께 알려드립니다. **게이트 변경 안내입니다. 시카고행 3759 항공편은 C-13 게이트가 아닌 A-21 게이트에 도착할 예정입니다.** 다시 알려드립니다. 바뀐 게이트는 A-21입니다. **A 구역으로 가시려면** 택시 승강장 바로 지나서 있는 **중앙 출구에서 셔틀버스를 타셔야 합니다.** 비행기가 40분 연착되었으니 게이트 A-21까지 가실 시간이 충분할 겁니다. 도착하시면 **게이트에 있는 직원에게 보여줄 수 있도록 항공권을 준비해 주십시오.** 질문이 있으시거나 특별한 도움이 필요하시면 저나 다른 직원에게 말씀하십시오.

어휘 reach ~에 도달하다 taxi stand 택시 승강장 be delayed by ~만큼 지연되다 special assistance 특별한 도움

Area served	Bus color
99 A	Red
B	Yellow
C	Green
D	Blue

운행 구역	버스 색상
A	빨강
B	노랑
C	녹색
D	파랑

98

Where is the announcement taking place?

(A) In a subway station
(B) In an airport
(C) At a bus station
(D) On a train platform

이 안내 방송은 어디에서 나오고 있는가?

(A) 지하철 역
(B) 공항
(C) 버스 정류장
(D) 기차 플랫폼

해설 전체 내용 관련 - 안내 방송이 나오는 장소

지문 초반부에 게이트 변경을 알리며 시카고행 3759 항공편은 게이트 C-13이 아닌 A-21에 도착할 예정(This is a gate change announcement ~ not C-13.)이라고 했다. 공항이라는 것을 알 수 있으므로 정답은 (B)이다.

99

Look at the graphic. What color is the bus that the affected passengers should take?

(A) Red
(B) Yellow
(C) Green
(D) Blue

시각 정보에 의하면, 안내 방송에 해당하는 승객들이 타야 하는 버스의 색상은 무엇인가?

(A) 빨강
(B) 노랑
(C) 녹색
(D) 파랑

해설 시각 정보 연계 - 관련 승객들이 탑승해야 할 버스의 색깔

지문 초반부에 A 구역으로 가려면 중앙 출구에서 셔틀버스를 타야 한다(In order to reach Area A ~ the central exit)고 했는데 표를 보면 운행 구역(Area served) A로 가는 버스는 빨강(Red)으로 나와 있으므로 정답은 (A)이다.

100

According to the speaker, what should passengers show to a staff member?

(A) Meal receipts
(B) Completed forms
(C) Transportation passes
(D) Baggage claim tickets

화자에 따르면, 승객들이 직원에게 보여주어야 하는 것은 무엇인가?

(A) 식사 영수증
(B) 작성한 양식
(C) 교통편 티켓
(D) 수하물 표

어휘 baggage claim tickets 수하물 보관표

해설 세부 사항 관련 - 승객들이 제시해야 할 것

지문 후반부에 청자인 승객들에게 게이트에서 제시할 수 있도록 항공권을 준비해 두라(please have your flight ticket ready to show to the staff at the gate.)고 했으므로 정답은 (C)이다.

▸▸ **Paraphrasing** 지문의 **your flight ticket**
→ 정답의 **transportation passes**

TEST 7

1 (A)	2 (D)	3 (D)	4 (C)	5 (D)
6 (B)	7 (B)	8 (C)	9 (C)	10 (B)
11 (A)	12 (B)	13 (B)	14 (C)	15 (A)
16 (B)	17 (A)	18 (C)	19 (B)	20 (A)
21 (C)	22 (A)	23 (B)	24 (A)	25 (B)
26 (C)	27 (C)	28 (A)	29 (C)	30 (B)
31 (A)	32 (A)	33 (D)	34 (C)	35 (D)
36 (C)	37 (B)	38 (D)	39 (D)	40 (B)
41 (B)	42 (A)	43 (A)	44 (C)	45 (B)
46 (B)	47 (A)	48 (C)	49 (A)	50 (B)
51 (A)	52 (B)	53 (D)	54 (A)	55 (B)
56 (C)	57 (D)	58 (A)	59 (B)	60 (A)
61 (C)	62 (C)	63 (D)	64 (C)	65 (D)
66 (A)	67 (D)	68 (A)	69 (B)	70 (B)
71 (D)	72 (B)	73 (A)	74 (B)	75 (C)
76 (C)	77 (D)	78 (B)	79 (D)	80 (C)
81 (B)	82 (A)	83 (C)	84 (B)	85 (D)
86 (D)	87 (B)	88 (A)	89 (B)	90 (D)
91 (C)	92 (A)	93 (D)	94 (C)	95 (C)
96 (A)	97 (A)	98 (C)	99 (C)	100 (D)

PART 1

1 M-Au

(A) They're riding bicycles.
(B) They're hiking in a forest.
(C) They're driving on a street.
(D) They're swimming in the water.

(A) 사람들이 자전거를 타고 있다.
(B) 사람들이 숲에서 하이킹을 하고 있다.
(C) 사람들이 도로에서 차를 몰고 있다.
(D) 사람들이 물속에서 수영을 하고 있다.

어휘 ride a bicycle 자전거를 타다 forest 숲

해설 2인 이상 등장 사진 – 사람의 동작 묘사

(A) 남녀 한 쌍이 나란히 자전거를 타고 있는(riding bicycles) 모습이므로 정답.

(B) 두 사람이 숲에서 하이킹을 하고 있는(hiking in a forest) 모습은 아니므로 오답.

(C) 두 사람이 자전거를 타고 있는 중이지 차를 몰고 있는(driving on a street) 모습이 아니므로 오답.

(D) 사진에 물은 보이지만 두 사람이 수영을 하고 있는(swimming in the water) 모습은 아니므로 오답.

2 W-Am

(A) A man is looking out a window.
(B) A man is reaching for a mug.
(C) A bookcase is being built.
(D) Some papers are on the floor.

(A) 남자가 창밖을 내다보고 있다.
(B) 남자가 머그잔을 집으려고 손을 뻗고 있다.
(C) 책장이 만들어지고 있다.
(D) 종이 몇 장이 바닥에 놓여 있다.

어휘 look out 밖을 내다보다 reach for ~을 집으려고 손을 뻗다 bookcase 책장, 책꽂이 floor 바닥, 마루

해설 1인 등장 사진 – 사람 또는 사물 중심 묘사

(A) 사진에 창문이 보이지만 남자가 창밖을 내다보고 있는(is looking out a window) 모습은 아니므로 오답.

(B) 사진에 머그잔이 보이지만 머그잔을 집으려고 손을 뻗고 있는(is reaching for a mug) 모습은 아니므로 오답.

(C) 사진에 책장이 보이지만 현재 남자가 책장을 만들고 있는(is being built) 모습은 아니므로 오답.

(D) 바닥에 종이 몇 장이 놓여 있는(are on the floor) 상태이므로 정답.

3 W-Br

(A) Tourists are browsing in an outdoor market.
(B) A woman is waving to some friends.
(C) Some people are taking a picture.
(D) Two men are holding a map.

(A) 관광객들이 노천 시장에서 구경을 하고 있다.
(B) 한 여자가 친구들에게 손을 흔들고 있다.
(C) 몇몇 사람들이 사진을 찍고 있다.
(D) 두 남자가 지도 하나를 들고 있다.

어휘 tourist 관광객 browse 구경하다, (대충) 훑어보다 outdoor market 노천 시장 wave 손을 흔들다, 손을 흔들어 인사하다 take a picture 사진을 찍다 map 지도

해설 2인 이상 등장 사진 – 사람의 동작 묘사

(A) 사진에 노천 시장(an outdoor market)이 보이지 않으므로 오답.

(B) 여자는 무언가를 가리키고 있지(is pointing) 친구들에게 손을 흔들고 있지(is waving to some friends) 않으므로 오답.

(C) 사진에 몇몇 사람들이 보이지만 사람들이 사진을 찍고 있는(taking a picture) 모습은 아니므로 오답.

(D) 두 남자가 지도 하나를 함께 들고 있는(are holding a map) 모습이므로 정답.

Test 7

4 M-Au

(A) Safety helmets have been left on a container.
(B) One of the men is lifting up a stepladder.
(C) One of the men is working with a wired object.
(D) Workers are reading the text on a spray bottle.

(A) 안전모들이 컨테이너 위에 놓여 있다.
(B) 남자들 중 한 명이 발판 사다리를 들어올리고 있다.
(C) 남자들 중 한 명이 전선으로 연결된 물체의 작업을 하고 있다.
(D) 인부들이 분무기 병에 쓰인 글을 읽고 있다.

어휘 safety helmet 안전모 lift up 들어올리다 stepladder 발판 사다리 wire 전선으로 연결하다 object 물건, 물체

해설 2인 이상 등장 사진 - 사람의 동작 묘사
(A) 사진에 안전모들이 컨테이너 위에(on a container) 있지 않으므로 오답.
(B) 발판 사다리를 들어올리는(is lifting up) 남자가 없으므로 오답.
(C) 남자들 중 한 명이 전선으로 연결된 물체(a wired object)의 작업을 하고 있으므로 정답.
(D) 사진에 분무기(spray bottle)가 보이지 않으므로 오답.

5 M-Cn

(A) Plates are displayed in a cabinet.
(B) Bread is being put into an oven.
(C) Drinks are being made at café.
(D) Food has been placed on a table.

(A) 접시들이 수납장 안에 진열되어 있다.
(B) 빵이 오븐에 넣어지고 있다.
(C) 음료수들이 카페에서 만들어지고 있다.
(D) 음식이 식탁에 놓여 있다.

어휘 plate 접시 display 진열하다, 전시하다 cabinet 수납장, 캐비닛 put A into B A를 B에 넣다 drink 음료수 place 놓다

해설 사물 사진 - 다양한 사물 묘사
(A) 사진에 수납장(cabinet)이 보이지 않으므로 오답.
(B) 사진에 오븐(oven)이 보이지 않으므로 오답.
(C) 현재 누군가에 의해 음료수가 만들어지고 있는(are being made) 모습이 아니므로 오답.
(D) 여러 가지 음식이 식탁에 차려져 있는(has been placed on a table) 상태이므로 정답.

6 W-Am

(A) A forklift is being driven through a warehouse.
(B) Some goods have been arranged on shelves.
(C) Some people are turning on a row of lights.
(D) Labels have been attached to a wall.

(A) 지게차가 창고에서 주행 중이다.
(B) 상품들이 선반 위에 정리되어 있다.
(C) 사람들이 줄지어 있는 조명을 켜고 있다.
(D) 라벨들이 벽에 붙어 있다.

어휘 forklift 지게차 warehouse 창고 arrange 정리하다, 배열하다 shelf 선반 a row of 일렬로 늘어선, 줄지어 있는 attach 붙이다

해설 2인 이상 등장 사진 - 사람 또는 사물 중심 묘사
(A) 사진에 지게차(forklift)가 보이지 않으므로 오답.
(B) 상품들이 선반 위에 정리되어 있는(have been arranged on shelves) 상태이므로 정답.
(C) 줄지어 있는 조명이 켜져 있지 사람들이 켜고 있는(are turning on) 모습은 아니므로 오답.
(D) 사진에 라벨들이 벽에(to a wall) 붙어 있지 않으므로 오답.

PART 2

7

M-Au How long will the workshop last?

W-Am (A) No, it's my first.

(B) Only an hour.

(C) Five miles or so.

워크숍이 얼마나 오래 계속할까요?

(A) 아뇨, 저는 처음이에요.

(B) 한 시간 동안만요.

(C) 5마일 정도요.

어휘 workshop 워크숍, 연수, 교육 last 지속[계속]되다

해설 지속 시간을 묻는 How long 의문문

(A) Yes/No 불가 오답. 지속 시간을 묻는 How long 의문문에 Yes/No 응답이 불가능하기 때문에 오답.

(B) 정답. 워크숍이 얼마나 오래 진행되는지를 묻는 질문에 단지 한 시간(Only an hour.)이라는 구체적인 지속 시간으로 응답하고 있으므로 정답.

(C) 연상 단어 오답. 질문의 How long에서 연상 가능한 miles를 이용한 오답.

8

W-Br Which day do we have scheduled for the building inspection?

M-Cn (A) How many did you expect?

(B) On the fourth floor.

(C) I believe it's Monday.

우리가 건물 준공 검사를 무슨 요일로 잡았나요?

(A) 얼마나 많이 예상했어요?

(B) 4층에서요.

(C) 월요일일 거예요.

어휘 schedule 일정을 잡다 building inspection 건물 준공 검사 expect 기대하다, 예상하다

해설 건물 검사 요일을 묻는 Which 의문문

(A) 유사 발음 오답. 질문의 inspection과 부분적으로 발음이 유사한 expect를 이용한 오답.

(B) 연상 단어 오답. 질문의 building에서 연상 가능한 the fourth floor를 이용한 오답.

(C) 정답. 건물 검사가 무슨 요일로 예정되어 있는지에 대해 월요일(Monday)이라는 구체적인 시점으로 응답하고 있으므로 정답.

9

M-Au When did the shipment leave the warehouse?

W-Br (A) I didn't know what to wear.

(B) At the boat dock.

(C) Just a short while ago.

배송품이 언제 창고에서 떠났나요?

(A) 무엇을 입어야 할지 몰랐어요.

(B) 보트 선착장에서요.

(C) 조금 전에요.

어휘 shipment 배송품, 운송품 warehouse 창고 dock 선착장 a short while ago 조금 전에

해설 출고 시점을 묻는 When 의문문

(A) 유사 발음 오답. 질문의 warehouse와 부분적으로 발음이 동일한 wear를 이용한 오답.

(B) 연상 단어 오답. 질문의 shipment를 ship으로 잘못 들었을 때 정박 위치 측면에서 연상 가능한 boat dock을 이용한 오답.

(C) 정답. 배송품이 언제 출고되었는지에 대해 조금 전(Just a short while ago.)이라는 시점으로 응답하고 있으므로 정답.

10

W-Am Who's going to assist you with the research project?

M-Cn (A) Yes, she's my assistant.

(B) I'm considering a few people.

(C) After I finish my current study.

그 조사 프로젝트에서 누가 당신을 도울 건가요?

(A) 네, 그녀는 제 비서예요.

(B) 몇 사람을 고려 중이에요.

(C) 현재의 연구를 끝낸 후에요.

어휘 assist 돕다 research project 조사[연구] 프로젝트 assistant 비서, 조수 current 현재의

해설 도와 줄 사람을 묻는 Who 의문문

(A) Yes/No 불가 오답. 인물을 묻는 Who 의문문에 Yes/No 응답이 불가능하므로 오답.

(B) 정답. 도와줄 사람을 몇 사람 고려 중이라(I'm considering a few people.)는 불확실성 표현으로 응답하므로 정답.

(C) 연상 단어 오답. 질문의 research에서 연상 가능한 study를 이용한 오답

11

W-Br Where did you work before joining our firm?

W-Am (A) At a small company in Atlanta.

(B) I'd love to join you.

(C) A retail salesperson.

우리 회사에 입사하기 전에 어디에서 일했지요?

(A) 애틀랜타에 있는 작은 회사에서요.

(B) 당신과 함께하고 싶어요.

(C) 소매점 판매원이요.

어휘 join 입사하다, 함께하다 firm 회사 would love to + 동사원형 ~하고 싶다 retail 소매의; 소매 salesperson 판매원, 영업 사원

해설 전 근무지를 묻는 Where 의문문

(A) 정답. 이전 근무지를 묻는 질문에 애틀랜타에 있는 작은 회사(At a small company in Atlanta.)라는 구체적인 장소로 응답하고 있으므로 정답.

(B) 파생어 오답. 질문의 joining과 파생어 관계인 join을 이용한 오답.

(C) 연상 단어 오답. 질문의 work와 firm에서 연상 가능한 retail salesperson을 이용한 오답.

12

W-Br Are you going to ride with us to the gallery, or would you rather walk?

M-Au (A) The pleasant weather.

(B) Oh, is there room in the van?

(C) Ruriko is a better writer than I am.

우리와 함께 차를 타고 화랑에 가실래요, 아니면 그냥 걸어가실래요?

(A) 좋은 날씨요.

(B) 오, 승합차에 탈 공간이 있나요?

(C) 루리코가 지 보다 더 나은 작가예요.

어휘 ride 차를 타고 가다 would rather+동사원형 차라리 ~하다 room 여유 공간 van 승합차

해설 문장을 연결한 선택의문문

(A) 유사 발음 오답. 질문의 rather와 부분적으로 발음이 유사한 weather를 반복 이용한 오답.

(B) 정답. 화랑에 차로 같이 갈 것인지 아니면 걸어갈 것인지를 묻는 질문에 승합차에 자리가 있는지(Is there room in the van?)를 되물음으로써 자리가 있으면 차로 같이 가겠다는 의사를 전달한 것이므로 정답.

(C) 유사 발음 오답. 질문의 ride와 부분적으로 발음이 유사한 writer를 반복 이용한 오답.

13

M-Cn Why was the manager looking for me?

W-Am (A) In the hallway.

(B) She didn't say.

(C) I looked everywhere.

매니저가 왜 저를 찾던가요?

(A) 복도에서요.

(B) 그녀가 말 안 했어요.

(C) 제가 사방을 찾아다녔어요.

어휘 look for ~을 찾다 hallway 복도 look everywhere 사방을 찾다, 샅샅이 찾다

해설 찾는 이유를 묻는 Why 의문문

(A) 질문과 상관없는 오답. 장소를 묻는 Where 의문문에 어울리는 응답이므로 오답.

(B) 정답. 매니저가 찾는 이유를 묻자 그녀가 이유에 대해서는 말을 안 했다(She didn't say.)는 불확실성 표현으로 응답하고 있으므로 정답.

(C) 파생어 오답. 질문의 looking과 파생어 관계인 looked를 이용한 오답.

14

W-Am How about ordering new uniforms for the employees?

M-Cn (A) Application forms.

(B) OK, hand me the menu.

(C) Our budget won't allow it.

새로운 직원 유니폼을 주문하는 게 어떨까요?

(A) 지원서 양식이요.

(B) 좋아요, 내게 메뉴판을 건네주세요.

(C) 우리 예산으로는 안 될 거예요.

어휘 uniform 유니폼, 제복 employee 직원 application form 지원서 양식 hand 건네주다, 주다 budget 예산 allow 허락[허용]하다, 가능하게 하다

해설 새 유니폼을 주문하자는 제안 의문문

(A) 유사 발음 오답. 질문의 uniforms와 부분적으로 발음이 동일한 forms를 이용한 오답.

(B) 연상 단어 오답. 질문의 ordering에서 연상 가능한 menu를 이용한 오답.

(C) 정답. 새로운 직원 유니폼을 주문하자는 제안에 대해 우리 예산으로는 안 될 것(Our budget won't allow it.)이라고 우회적으로 응답을 하고 있으므로 정답.

15

W-Br Which sofa do you think we should buy for the reception area?

M-Au (A) The blue one matches the carpet.

(B) It's very comfortable.

(C) The space under the windows.

응접실용으로 어떤 소파를 사야 사야 한다고 생각하세요?

(A) 파란색 소파가 카펫과 어울리네요.

(B) 그것은 아주 편안해요.

(C) 창문 아래 자리요.

어휘 reception area 로비, 응접실, 접수처 match 어울리다 comfortable 편안한, 안락한 space 공간, 자리

해설 구매할 소파의 종류를 묻는 Which 의문문

(A) 정답. 어떤 소파를 구매할지에 대해 파란색 소파(The blue one)가 카펫과 어울린다는 말로 파란색 소파를 구매하자는 우회적 응답을 하고 있으므로 정답.

(B) 연상 단어 오답. 질문의 sofa에서 연상 가능한 very comfortable을 이용한 오답.

(C) 연상 단어 오답. 질문의 sofa나 reception area에서 연상 가능한 space under the windows를 이용한 오답.

16

W-Br Aren't we supposed to start updating our online catalog today?

M-Cn (A) Yes, I'm on the mailing list.

(B) Mr. Blake's team is working on it.

(C) My appointment date isn't decided yet.

온라인 카탈로그 업데이트를 오늘 시작하기로 하지 않았나요?

(A) 네, 저는 메일 수신자 명단에 있어요.

(B) 블레이크 씨의 팀이 작업하고 있어요.

(C) 약속 날짜는 아직 확실하지 않아요.

어휘 be supposed to+동사원형 ~하기로 되어 있다 catalog 카탈로그, 상품 목록 mailing list 우편[이메일] 수신자 명단 appointment 약속 decided 확실한, 결정적인

해설 업데이트를 하기로 하지 않았는지 묻는 부정의문문

(A) 연상 단어 오답. 질문의 catalog에서 연상 가능한 mailing list를 이용한 오답.

(B) 정답. 오늘 온라인 카탈로그 업데이트를 시작해야 하지 않느냐는 질문에 블레이크 씨 팀(Mr. Blake's team)이 그 작업을 하고 있다는 말로 구체적인 업무 담당자를 밝히고 있으므로 정답.

(C) 유사 발음 오답. 질문의 updating과 부분적으로 발음이 유사한 date를 이용한 오답.

17

M-Cn Would you like me to drive you to the airport?

W-Am (A) That won't be necessary.

(B) I'd prefer a direct flight.

(C) You can review my copy.

제가 공항까지 차로 모셔다 드릴까요?

(A) 그러실 필요 없어요.

(B) 저는 직항편이 더 좋아요.

(C) 제 것을 검토해 보세요.

어휘 drive A(사람) to B(장소) A를 B까지 차로 데려다 주다 necessary 필요한 direct flight (비행기의) 직항편 review 검토하다

해설 차로 데려다 주겠다는 제안 의문문

(A) 정답. 공항까지 차로 데려다 주겠다는 제안에 대해 그럴 필요 없다(That won't be necessary.)는 말로 거절 의사를 전달하고 있으므로 정답.

(B) 연상 단어 오답. 질문의 airport에서 연상 가능한 direct flight를 이용한 오답.

(C) 질문과 상관없는 오답. 공항까지 차로 데려다 주겠다는 제안에 자신의 것을 검토해 보라는 것은 맥락에서 벗어난 응답이므로 오답.

18

M-Au There's a charge for ten computers on this invoice.

W-Br (A) Sorry, I'll try to speak more quietly.

(B) I don't have any change.

(C) That can't be right.

이 송장에 컴퓨터 10대에 대한 대금이 청구되었어요.

(A) 미안해요, 더 조용히 말해 볼게요.

(B) 저는 거스름돈이 없어요.

(C) 그게 맞을 리가 없어요.

어휘 charge 대금, 청구 금액 invoice 송장, 청구서 quietly 조용히 change 거스름돈 can't be ~일리가 없다

해설 정보 전달의 평서문

(A) 연상 단어 오답. 평서문의 invoice를 voice로 잘못 들었을 때 목소리 크기 측면에서 연상 가능한 speak more quietly를 이용한 오답.

(B) 유사 발음 오답. 질문의 charge와 발음이 유사한 change를 이용한 오답.

(C) 정답. 10대의 컴퓨터에 대해 대금이 청구되었다는 말에 그게 맞을 리가 없다(That can't be right.)는 말로 의구심을 나타내고 있으므로 정답.

19

M-Cn When will you be available to tour the construction site?

M-Au (A) An apartment complex.

(B) I'll let you know tomorrow.

(C) On the north side of town.

언제쯤 건설 현장을 둘러볼 시간이 날 것 같아요?

(A) 아파트 단지요.

(B) 내일 알려드릴게요.

(C) 마을의 북쪽 편에요.

어휘 available 시간이 있는 construction site 건설[공사] 현장 apartment complex 아파트 단지

해설 견학 가능 시간을 물어보는 When 의문문

(A) 연상 단어 오답. 질문의 construction에서 연상 가능한 apartment complex를 이용한 오답.

(B) 정답. 언제 공사장을 둘러볼 시간이 되는지에 대해 확답을 피한 채 내일 알려주겠다(I'll let you know tomorrow.)는 불확실성 표현으로 응답하고 있으므로 정답.

(C) 유사 발음 오답. 질문의 site와 발음이 유사한 side를 이용한 오답.

20

M-Cn The shuttle bus to the hotel is free, isn't it?

W-Am (A) There might be a small fee.

(B) Maybe two or three minutes.

(C) Check the back row of seats.

호텔로 가는 셔틀버스는 무료죠, 아닌가요?

(A) 요금이 조금 있을 거예요.

(B) 아마 2~3분 정도요.

(C) 뒷좌석을 확인해 보세요.

어휘 fee 수수료, 요금 back row 뒷줄

해설 셔틀버스가 무료인지를 확인하는 부가의문문

(A) 정답. 호텔 셔틀버스가 무료인지를 확인하는 질문에 대해 약간의 요금(a small fee)을 낼 수도 있다는 정보를 주고 있으므로 정답.

(B) 연상 단어 오답. 질문의 shuttle bus to the hotel에 대해 이동 시간 측면에서 연상 가능한 two or three minutes를 이용한 오답.

(C) 연상 단어 오답. 질문의 shuttle bus에서 연상 가능한 the back row of seats을 이용한 오답.

21

W-Au Does your magazine offer any discount subscriptions?

M-Br (A) A coupon for an online shopping mall.

(B) I enjoy entertainment magazines.

(C) Are you a student, or over the age of sixty?

귀사의 잡지는 구독료를 할인해주나요?

(A) 온라인 쇼핑몰 쿠폰입니다.

(B) 저는 연예 잡지를 즐겨 봐요.

(C) 학생이시거나 아니면 60세를 넘으셨습니까?

어휘 magazine 잡지 subscription 구독료, 구독 entertainment 연예, 오락

해설 구독료 할인 여부를 묻는 일반 의문문

(A) 연상 단어 오답. 질문의 discount에서 연상 가능한 coupon을 이용한 오답.

(B) 단어 반복 오답. 질문의 magazine을 복수 형태인 magazines로 변형해 반복 이용한 오답.

(C) 정답. 구독료 할인 여부를 묻는 질문에 학생이거나 60세를 넘었는지(a student, or over the age of sixty) 자격 요건을 되묻고 있으므로 정답.

22

W-Br I hope to see you at the grand opening of our store.

M-Cn (A) Don't worry, I'll be there.

(B) From nine A.M. to six P.M.

(C) Unfortunately, that opening has been filled.

저희 점포 개업식에서 뵙기를 바랍니다.

(A) 염려 마세요. 참석할게요.

(B) 오전 9시부터 오후 6시까지요.

(C) 안타깝지만, 그 자리는 충원되었어요.

어휘 grand opening 개업식 opening 공석, 빈자리 fill 충원하다, 빈자리를 채우다

해설 제안/초청의 평서문

(A) 정답. 새 점포의 개업식에서 보기를 소망한다는 말에 그 자리에 가겠다(I'll be there.)는 긍정적 응답을 하고 있으므로 정답.

(B) 연상 단어 오답. 평서문의 opening과 store에 대해 영업 시간 측면에서 연상 가능한 From nine to six를 이용한 오답.

(C) 단어 반복 오답. 평서문의 opening을 반복 이용한 오답. 평서문에서는 '개업'의 의미로 쓰였으나, 여기에서는 '공석, 빈자리'의 의미로 쓰임.

23

M-Au Do you think we should switch to a new brand of motor oil?

W-Am (A) The truck that broke down this morning.

(B) Tell me about some of the options.

(C) Sung-Yoon is in a band.

우리가 새로운 브랜드의 엔진 오일로 바꿔야 한다고 생각하세요?

(A) 오늘 아침에 고장 난 트럭이요.

(B) 선택 가능한 것들에 대해 말씀해 주세요.

(C) 성윤 씨는 악단에 속해 있어요.

어휘 switch to ~로 바꾸다 motor oil 엔진 오일 break down 고장 나다 option 선택

해설 오일 교체에 대한 의견을 묻는 일반 의문문

(A) 연상 단어 오답. 질문의 motor oil에서 연상 가능한 truck을 이용한 오답.

(B) 정답. 엔진 오일을 교체해야 하는지 묻는 질문에 선택 가능한 것들을 말해 달라(Tell me about some of the options.)는 우회적 표현으로 응답하고 있으므로 정답.

(C) 유사 발음 오답. 질문의 brand와 발음이 비슷한 band를 이용한 오답.

24

M-Au Do you want to hold the meeting in Mr. Lee's office or yours?

W-Br (A) Well, my office is bigger.

(B) Just put it on that desk.

(C) About the Jefferson account.

이 씨의 사무실에서 회의하고 싶으세요, 당신 사무실에서 하고 싶으세요?

(A) 글쎄요, 내 사무실이 더 크죠.

(B) 그냥 그 책상 위에 두세요.

(C) 제퍼슨 계정에 관해서요.

어휘 hold a meeting 회의를 하다 account 계정, 계좌, 고객, 거래 (관계)

해설 단어를 연결한 선택의문문

(A) 정답. 이 씨의 사무실과 당신의 사무실 중 어디에서 회의를 하고 싶은지에 대해 자신의 사무실이 더 크다(my office is bigger)는 우회적 응답으로 자신의 사무실을 선택하고 있으므로 정답.

(B) 연상 단어 오답. 질문의 office에서 연상 가능한 desk를 이용한 오답. 장소를 묻는 Where 의문문에 가능한 응답.

(C) 연상 단어 오답. 질문의 meeting에서 연상 가능한 About the Jefferson account.를 이용한 오답.

25

W-Am Didn't you get reimbursed for your last business trip?

M-Cn (A) To visit our overseas location.

(B) No, I'm still waiting.

(C) Yes, I brought the receipt for my new purse.

지난번 출장 경비를 환급 받지 않았나요?

(A) 우리 해외 지점을 방문하기 위해서요.

(B) 아뇨, 아직 기다리고 있어요.

(C) 네, 새 핸드백을 산 영수증을 가져왔어요.

어휘 get reimbursed 비용을 환급 받다 business trip 출장 overseas location 해외 사무소[지점]

해설 비용 환급 여부를 묻는 부정의문문

(A) 연상 단어 오답. 질문의 business trip에 대해 장소 측면에서 연상 가능한 our overseas location을 이용한 오답.

(B) 정답. 지난번 출장 비용을 환급 받지 않았는지 묻는 질문에 먼저 No로 부정적 응답을 한 후, 아직 기다리고 있다(I'm still waiting.)는 말로 아직 환급 받지 못했음을 확인시켜주고 있으므로 정답.

(C) 연상 단어 오답. 질문의 get reimbursed에서 연상 가능한 receipt를 이용한 오답.

26

M-Cn Could I make some suggestions for the merger negotiation?

W-Br (A) The press conference.

(B) Let me find the list of ingredients.

(C) We've already reached an agreement.

합병 협상에 관해 제안을 몇 가지 해도 됩니까?
(A) 기자 회견요.
(B) 재료 목록을 찾아볼게요.
(C) 우린 이미 합의에 도달했어요.

어휘 make a suggestion 제안하다, 의견을 말하다 merger 합병 negotiation 협상, 교섭 press conference 기자 회견 ingredient 재료, 성분

해설 제안/권유의 의문문
(A) 연상 표현 오답. 질문의 merger에서 연상 가능한 press conference를 이용한 오답.
(B) 연상 단어 오답. 질문의 negotiation에서 연상 가능한 list를 이용한 오답.
(C) 정답. 협상에 관해 제안을 해도 되는지 묻는 질문에 이미 합의에 도달했다(already reached an agreement)며 우회적으로 거절을 표현하고 있으므로 정답.

27

W-Am Why isn't the radio station broadcasting our advertisement?
M-Au (A) Television advertising is more expensive.
(B) Would you prefer to listen to classical music?
(C) Leslie heard it aired yesterday, actually.

라디오 방송국은 왜 우리 광고를 내보내지 않는 건가요?
(A) TV 광고가 돈이 더 많이 듭니다.
(B) 클래식 음악 듣는 것을 선호하시나요?
(C) 사실 레슬리 씨가 어제 방송된 걸 들었어요.

어휘 radio station 라디오 방송국 broadcast 방송하다 advertisement 광고 expensive 비싼 prefer 좋아하다, 원하다 air 방송하다, 방송되다 actually 사실

해설 광고를 안 내보내는 이유를 묻는 Why 의문문
(A) 파생어 오답. 질문의 advertisement와 파생어 관계인 advertising을 이용한 오답.
(B) 연상 단어 오답. 질문의 radio에서 연상 가능한 music을 이용한 오답.
(C) 정답. 방송국이 광고(advertisement)를 왜 안 내보내는지를 묻는 질문에 레슬리 씨가 어제 방송된 걸 들었다(Leslie heard it aired yesterday)며 우회적인 표현으로 잘못 알고 있는 사실을 정정하고 있으므로 정답.

28

M-Cn Who was chosen to be keynote speaker at the awards ceremony?
W-Am (A) No one yet.
(B) That key is for a different door.
(C) I recommend the Lambrett Auditorium.

시상식의 기조 연설자로 누가 선정되었나요?
(A) 아직 아무도 선정되지 않았어요.
(B) 그 열쇠는 다른 문 열쇠예요.
(C) 저는 람브레트 강당을 추천해요.

어휘 keynote speaker 기조 연설자 awards ceremony 시상식 auditorium 강당

해설 기조 연설자로 선정된 사람을 묻는 Who 의문문
(A) 정답. 누가 기조 연설자로 선정되었는지 묻는 질문에 대해 아직 아무도 선정되지 않았다(No one yet.)고 부정적 응답을 하고 있으므로 정답.
(B) 유사 발음 오답. 질문의 keynote와 부분적으로 발음이 동일한 key를 이용한 오답.
(C) 연상 단어 오답. 질문의 awards ceremony에서 연상 가능한 Auditorium을 이용한 오답.

29

W-Br Is there a manual for the department's new printer?
M-Cn (A) Here's the company directory.
(B) Yes, he's the painter.
(C) There should be.

부서의 새 프린터에 대한 사용설명서가 있나요?
(A) 회사 인명부가 여기 있어요.
(B) 네, 그는 화가예요.
(C) 있을 거예요.

어휘 manual 사용설명서 directory 주소 성명록, 인명부

해설 사용설명서 유무를 묻는 be동사 Yes/No 의문문
(A) 연상 단어 오답. 질문의 department에서 연상 가능한 company directory를 이용한 오답.
(B) 유사 발음 오답. 질문의 printer와 발음이 유사한 painter를 이용한 오답.
(C) 정답. 새로 산 프린터의 사용설명서가 있는지에 대해 있을 것(There should be.)이라는 긍정적인 추측으로 응답하고 있으므로 정답.

30

M-Au I gave you my business card, didn't I?
W-Br (A) It's a beautifully designed car.
(B) I seem to have misplaced it.
(C) No, I'm not too busy.

제 명함을 당신에게 드렸죠, 안 드렸나요?
(A) 디자인이 멋진 자동차네요.
(B) 어디에 잘못 둔 거 같은데요.
(C) 아뇨, 저는 그다지 바쁘지 않아요.

어휘 business card 명함 misplace 잘못 두다, 둔 곳을 잊다

해설 명함 제공 여부를 묻는 부가의문문
(A) 유사 발음 오답. 질문의 card와 발음이 유사한 car를 이용한 오답.
(B) 정답. 명함을 주었는지를 확인하는 질문에 어디에 잘못 둔 거 같다(I seem to have misplaced it.)는 말로 이미 받았지만 다시 달라는 의미를 우회적으로 표현한 것이므로 정답.
(C) 유사 발음 오답. 질문의 business와 부분적으로 발음이 유사한 busy를 이용한 오답.

31

W-Am Aren't you going to mark your vacation on the calendar?

M-Au (A) My request for time off was denied.

(B) Somewhere in Southeast Asia.

(C) Fifteen days per year.

달력에 휴가를 표시하지 않을 건가요?

(A) 제 휴가 요청이 반려되었어요.

(B) 동남아시아의 어느 지역이요.

(C) 1년에 15일입니다.

어휘 request 요청 time off 휴식, 휴가 deny 받아들이지 않다

해설 휴가 표시 여부에 대한 부정의문문

(A) 정답. 달력에 휴가를 표시하지 않을 거냐는 질문에 휴가 요청이 반려되어서(My request for time off was denied.) 휴가 표시를 하지 않는다는 의미를 전달한 것이므로 정답.

(B) 연상 표현 오답. 질문의 vacation에서 연상 가능한 Southeast Asia를 이용한 오답.

(C) 연상 표현 오답. 질문의 vacation에서 연상 가능한 Fifteen days per year를 이용한 오답.

PART 3

32-34

M-Cn [32]**Welcome to Millman Park Inn.** Do you have a reservation?

W-Am Yes, I do. My booking should be under the name Irina Morozova.

M-Cn I see it. Great. But you're early. Our check-in time is two P.M., and we've just adopted a new policy against early check-ins. In the past, we had no clear policy. So [33]**some guests could check in early at the clerk's discretion, but others couldn't. This inconsistency led to dissatisfaction and negative feedback.**

W-Am Oh. I understand, but that gives me a whole hour of time. Are there any coffee shops or stores nearby?

M-Cn Well, this is a nice neighborhood to take a walk in. [34]**If you'd like to do that, I could put your baggage here behind the desk.**

남: **밀맨 파크 인에 오신 것을 환영합니다.** 예약하셨나요?

여: 네. 예약은 이리나 모로조바라는 이름으로 되어 있을 거예요.

남: 여기 있네요. 좋습니다. 근데 일찍 오셨네요. 저희 체크인 시간은 오후 2시인데, 조기 체크인을 금지하는 새 정책이 이제 막 채택됐거든요. 예전에는 뚜렷한 정책이 없었어요. 그래서 **일부 투숙객들은 접수 직원의 재량에 따라 일찍 체크인할 수 있었고, 일부는 못 했죠. 이렇게 일관성이 없어서 손님들이 불만스러워하고 부정적인 피드백을 주게 됐어요.**

여: 아. 이해합니다만, 한 시간이 족히 남아 있네요. 근처에 커피숍이나 상점이 있나요?

남: 음, 이 곳은 산책하시기에 좋은 지역입니다. **산책하고 싶으시면 짐을 여기 책상 뒤에 두겠습니다.**

어휘 inn (작은) 호텔 reservation 예약 adopt 채택하다 policy against ~를 금지하는 정책 at ~'s discretion ~의 재량에 따라 inconsistency 불일치 dissatisfaction 불만 negative 부정적인 nearby 근처에 neighborhood 지역, 근방 take a walk 산책하다 baggage 짐

32

Where does the man work?

(A) At a hotel

(B) At an airport

(C) At a hospital

(D) At a bookstore

남자는 어디에서 일하는가?

(A) 호텔

(B) 공항

(C) 병원

(D) 서점

해설 전체 내용 관련 - 남자의 근무지

남자의 첫 대사에서 밀맨 파크 인에 온 것을 환영한다(Welcome to Millman Park Inn.)고 한 후, 예약했는지 묻고 있어 남자가 호텔 직원임을 알 수 있으므로 정답은 (A)이다.

33

Why most likely was a new policy introduced?

(A) To save money

(B) To satisfy a regulation

(C) To guarantee employees' safety

(D) To prevent customer complaints

새 정책은 왜 도입됐겠는가?

(A) 비용 절감을 위해

(B) 규정에 맞추기 위해

(C) 직원 안전을 보장하기 위해

(D) 고객 불만을 방지하기 위해

어휘 introduce 도입하다 satisfy 충족시키다 regulation 규정 guarantee 보장하다 safety 안전 prevent 막다, 방지하다 complaint 불만

해설 세부 사항 관련 - 새 정책의 도입 이유

남자의 두 번째 대사에서 일부 투숙객들은 접수 직원의 재량에 따라 일찍 체크인할 수 있었는데 일관성이 없어서 손님들이 불만스러워하고 부정적인 피드백을 주었다(some guests could check in early ~ dissatisfaction and negative feedback.)고 했으므로 정답은 (D)이다.

34

What does the man offer to do?

(A) Call a service desk
(B) Supply reading materials
(C) Store the woman's belongings
(D) Cancel a reservation

남자는 무엇을 하겠다고 제안하는가?

(A) 서비스 데스크에 전화하기
(B) 읽을거리 제공하기
(C) 여자의 소지품 보관하기
(D) 예약 취소하기

어휘 reading material 읽을거리 store 보관하다 belongings 소지품 cancel 취소하다

해설 세부 사항 관련 – 남자의 제안 사항

남자의 마지막 대사에서 여자가 산책을 원한다면 짐을 여기 책상 뒤에 두겠다(If you'd like to do that, I could put your baggage here behind the desk.)고 했으므로 정답은 (C)이다.

35-37

M-Au Kayla, you're a very organized person. How do you do it? [35]**I'm always late to appointments, if I even remember them in the first place.**

W-Br I use a calendar app on my mobile phone. You just enter your appointments and assignments into it, and it reminds you about them.

M-Au That's such a good idea! [36]**I often leave my paper notepad behind**, but I never forget to carry my phone. Can you show me how to install the app?

W-Br Oh, it's easy. [37]**Just visit www.minicalendarplus.com on your phone's Web browser.** You can download it for free there.

남: 케일라, 당신은 아주 체계적인 사람이군요. 어떻게 그렇게 하죠? **나는 약속에 맨날 늦는데 말이죠. 우선 그조차 기억을 할 경우에 말이에요.**

여: 저는 휴대폰에 있는 달력 앱을 사용해요. 약속과 업무를 앱에 입력하기만 하면, 휴대폰이 그것들에 관해 상기시켜 주죠.

남: 참 좋은 생각이군요! **제가 메모장은 자주 놓고 나오지만** 휴대폰은 절대로 잊지 않고 갖고 다니거든요. 그 앱을 어떻게 설치하는지 알려줄 수 있어요?

여: 오, 쉬워요. **휴대폰 웹 브라우저로 www.minicalendarplus.com을 방문하기만 하면 돼요.** 거기서 그 앱을 무료로 다운로드할 수 있어요.

어휘 organized 체계적인, 정리된 appointment 약속 in the first place 우선, 애초에 application 앱, 어플리케이션, 응용 프로그램 assignment 임무, 업무 remind 상기시키다 leave ~ behind ~을 두고 가다, 뒤에 남기다 notepad 메모장 install 설치하다

35

What is the man concerned about?

(A) Keeping some costs low
(B) Keeping a workstation organized
(C) Keeping records of accomplishments
(D) Keeping track of appointments

남자는 무엇에 관해 걱정하는가?

(A) 비용을 절감하는 것
(B) 자리를 정리하는 것
(C) 성과를 기록하는 것
(D) 약속을 기억하는 것

어휘 accomplishment 성과, 업적 keep track of ~에 대해 계속 알고 있다

해설 세부 사항 관련 – 남자의 걱정거리

남자의 첫 번째 대사에서 여자에게 어떻게 체계적인 사람이 될 수 있는지를 물으면서, 자신은 기억을 하더라도 약속에 맨날 늦는다(I'm always late to appointments, if I even remember them in the first place.)고 했다. 즉 남자는 약속을 어떻게 관리하는지에 대해 걱정하고 있음을 알 수 있으므로, 정답은 (D)이다.

36

According to the man, what is the problem with a notepad?

(A) It has been damaged.
(B) It is heavy to carry.
(C) It is easy to forget.
(D) It is almost full.

남자에 따르면, 메모장의 문제는 무엇인가?

(A) 파손되었다.
(B) 가지고 다니기 무겁다.
(C) 잊어버리기 쉽다.
(D) 거의 다 썼다.

해설 세부 사항 관련 – 남자의 메모장에 대한 문제점

남자의 두 번째 대사에서 자신은 메모장을 자주 놓고 나온다(I often leave my paper notepad behind)고 했으므로 정답은 (C)이다.

37

What does the woman tell the man to do?

(A) Visit her office
(B) Go to a Web site
(C) Post a reminder sign
(D) Change his daily schedule

여자는 남자에게 무엇을 하라고 말하는가?

(A) 그녀의 사무실 방문
(B) 웹 사이트 방문
(C) 상기시켜 주는 표지판 게시
(D) 그의 일과표 변경

해설 세부 사항 관련 - 여자가 남자에게 하는 말

대화 마지막에 여자가 남자에게 휴대폰 웹 브라우저로 사이트에 방문해서 해당 앱을 무료로 다운 받으라(Just visit www.minicalendarplus.com on your phone's Web browser.)고 했으므로 정답은 (B)이다.

▸▸ **Paraphrasing** 대화의 **visit www. minicalendarplus.com**
→ 정답의 **go to a Web site**

38-40

W-Br	Mr. Jenkins? If you have a moment, [38]**could you take a look at the revisions I made to this document? It includes that additional clause to our steel supply agreement.**
M-Cn	Sure, Deborah, I've got time. Hmm... this is our supply contract for Katerina Titanium, correct? Uh, is there a problem?
W-Br	Well, you've been working on that account since before I started working here. And [39]**since you're the district manager,** I just want to make sure that you think it looks OK before I submit it for review by the head office.
M-Cn	Let me see. Oh, here's something! [40]**The company owner's name starts with a K, not a C.** Fix that and then I'll take another look at it.

여: 젠킨스 씨? 잠시 시간 있으시면 **제가 이 문서에 수정한 것 좀 봐주실래요? 우리의 강철 공급 계약서에 추가 조항을 포함시켰어요.**
남: 물론이죠, 데보라, 시간 있어요. 음… 이건 카테리나 타이타늄에 대한 우리의 공급 계약서죠, 그렇죠? 어, 무슨 문제가 있나요?
여: 음, 제가 여기서 근무를 시작하기 전부터 그 거래처 일을 해오셨잖아요. 그리고 **지역 관리자시니까** 제가 본사의 검토를 받기 위해 그 계약서를 보내기 전에 괜찮다고 생각하시는지 확인하고 싶어서요.
남: 어디 봅시다. 아, 여기 뭔가 있네요! **그 회사의 소유주 이름은 C가 아니라 K로 시작해요.** 그거 수정하시고요, 전 다른 걸 찾아볼게요.

어휘 take a look at ~을 (한 번) 살펴보다 make a revision 수정[개정]하다 additional clause 추가 조항 steel 강철 supply agreement 공급 계약(서) account (신용 거래를 하는) 거래처 district manager 지역 관리자 make sure 확인하다 submit 제출하다 review 검토 head office 본사

38

What type of document has the woman created?

(A) A recommendation letter
(B) A training manual
(C) A press release
(D) A business document

여자는 어떤 종류의 문서를 작성했는가?

(A) 추천서
(B) 교육 안내책자
(C) 보도 자료
(D) 업무 문서

해설 세부 사항 관련 – 여자가 작성한 문서의 종류

여자의 첫 번째 대사에서 수정한 문서를 검토해 달라면서 강철 공급 계약서에 추가 조항을 포함시켰다(could you take a look at the revisions ~ to our steel supply agreement.)고 했으므로 정답은 (D)이다.

▸▸ **Paraphrasing** 대화의 **our steel supply agreement**
→ 정답의 **A business document**

39

Who is the man?

(A) A visiting researcher
(B) An outside vendor
(C) A prospective client
(D) A regional supervisor

남자는 누구인가?

(A) 객원 연구원
(B) 외부 업체
(C) 잠재 고객
(D) 지역 관리자

해설 세부 사항 관련 - 남자의 신분

여자의 두 번째 대사에서 남자가 지역 관리자(since you're the district manager)라고 했으므로 정답은 (D)이다.

▸▸ **Paraphrasing** 대화의 **the district manager**
→ 정답의 **A regional supervisor**

40

What mistake did the woman make?

(A) She submitted a draft too early.
(B) She spelled a name incorrectly.
(C) She forgot to add her signature.
(D) She used the wrong date.

여자는 어떤 실수를 했는가?

(A) 초안을 너무 일찍 제출했다.
(B) 이름의 철자를 잘못 표기했다.
(C) 서명하는 것을 잊어버렸다.
(D) 틀린 날짜를 사용했다.

어휘 draft 초안 spell 철자를 쓰다 incorrectly 부정확하게, 틀리게

해설 세부 사항 관련 - 여자의 문제점

대화 마지막에 남자가 여자에게 회사 소유주 이름은 C가 아니라 K로 시작한다(The company owner's name starts with a K, not a C.)고 했으므로 정답은 (B)이다.

41-43

W-Am Hi, Mr. Delaney. This is Jen Landegren, your landlord. [41]**I received your e-mail stating you're moving out of your apartment.**

M-Au Hi, Ms. Landegren. Yes, I'm being transferred to a different city.

W-Am I see. Well, [42]**I'd like to take a look at your place to check that it's in good enough condition to show to potential new tenants.** Would that be all right with you?

M-Au Sure. But I'm out of the apartment most of the day, so if it's OK with you, [43]**I'll leave the keys with Ms. Jacobson next door.** That way, you can come anytime while I'm gone.

여: 안녕하세요, 델레이니 씨. 저는 집주인인 젠 랜디그렌이에요. **아파트에서 이사를 나가실 거라는 당신의 이메일을 받았어요.**

남: 안녕하세요, 랜디그렌 씨. 네, 다른 도시로 도시로 전근을 가서요.

여: 그렇군요. 음, **장래 신규 세입자들에게 보여 줄 수 있을 정도로 상태가 좋은지 확인하기 위해 당신 집을 좀 보고 싶은데요.** 괜찮으세요?

남: 물론이죠. 하지만 제가 하루 중 아파트에 있는 시간이 별로 없어요. 괜찮으시면 **옆집에 사는 제이컵슨 씨에게 열쇠를 맡겨 둘게요.** 그러니 제가 없는 동안 아무 때나 오세요.

어휘 landlord 집주인 state 언급하다, 밝히다 move out of ~에서 이사를 나가다 transfer 전근시키다 check 점검하다 potential 잠재적인, 가능성이 있는 tenant 세입자

41

What did the man let the woman know by e-mail?

(A) He is unhappy with a fee increase.
(B) He plans to move away.
(C) He would like to carry out renovations.
(D) He discovered a problem with his apartment.

남자는 이메일로 여자에게 무엇을 알려 주었는가?

(A) 요금 인상에 불만이 있다.
(B) 이사를 나갈 계획이다.
(C) 보수 공사를 하고 싶다.
(D) 아파트에 문제가 있다는 것을 발견했다.

해설 세부 사항 관련 – 남자가 여자에게 알린 것

여자의 첫 번째 대사에서 아파트에서 이사를 나갈 것이라는 남자의 이메일을 받았다(I received your e-mail stating you're moving out of your apartment.)고 했으므로, 정답은 (B)이다.

▸▸ **Paraphrasing** 대화의 **you're moving out of your apartment** → 정답의 **He plans to move away.**

42

What does the woman want to do?

(A) Inspect a living space
(B) Notify a building's residents
(C) Check some paperwork
(D) Speak with a contractor

여자는 무엇을 하고 싶어 하는가?

(A) 사는 공간 점검
(B) 건물 주민들에게 통지
(C) 서류 작업 확인
(D) 계약자와 논의

어휘 inspect 점검하다 notify 통지하다

해설 세부 사항 관련 – 여자가 원하는 것

여자의 두 번째 대사에서 장래 신규 세입자들에게 보여 줄 수 있을 정도로 상태가 좋은지 확인하기 위해 집을 보고 싶다(I'd like to take a look at your place to check that it's in good enough condition to show to potential new tenants.)고 했으므로 정답은 (A)이다.

▸▸ **Paraphrasing** 대화의 **take a look at your place** → 정답의 **Inspect a living space**

43

What will the man leave for the woman?

(A) Some keys
(B) A payment
(C) A container
(D) Some blueprints

남자는 여자를 위해 무엇을 남겨둘 것인가?

(A) 열쇠
(B) 지불금
(C) 용기
(D) 청사진

해설 세부 사항 관련 – 남자가 남겨둘 것

대화 마지막에 남자가 옆집에 사는 제이컵슨 씨에게 열쇠를 맡기겠다(I'll leave the keys with Ms. Jacobson next door.)고 했으므로 정답은 (A)이다.

44-46

W-Am Hey, Mike. [44]**You know how I've been looking over the responses to the customer satisfaction surveys. Well, I just finished that up.** [45]**Have you gone through them yet?**

M-Cn [45]**Sorry.** Uh... I've been pretty busy with billing work. Did you note any recurring comments?

W-Am Yes, some customers said that our Web site is too complicated, with too many features.

M-Cn Oh, really? Well then, [46]**we'd better try to simplify it.**

W-Am I agree. [46]**I'll recommend that when I present the survey findings at our weekly meeting.** Talk later, then.

여: 안녕하세요, 마이크. **제가 고객 만족도 조사의 응답을 살펴보고 있었잖아요. 음, 방금 다 봤어요. 당신도 살펴봤나요?**

남: **미안해요.** 어… 제가 청구서 작업 때문에 몹시 바빴어요. 반복되는 의견들이 있던가요?

여: 네, 일부 고객들이 우리 웹 사이트가 너무 복잡하고 기능들이 너무 많다고 하더군요.

남: 오, 정말요? 음, 그러면 **웹 사이트를 간소화해야겠군요.**

여: 제 생각도 같아요. **주간회의에서 설문조사 결과를 발표할 때 그렇게 하자고 할게요.** 그럼 나중에 얘기해요.

어휘 look over 살펴보다, 훑어보다 response 응답, 반응 customer satisfaction 고객 만족도 finish up 다 끝내다 go through ~을 살펴보다, 검토하다 billing work 청구서 작업 note ~을 알아채다, ~에 주목하다 recurring 되풀이되는, 거듭 발생하는 comment 의견 complicated 복잡한 feature 기능 simplify 간소화하다 present 발표[설명]하다 survey findings 설문조사 결과

44

What did the woman recently do?

(A) She spoke at a conference.
(B) She designed a brochure.
(C) She reviewed survey results.
(D) She responded to e-mail inquiries.

여자는 최근에 무슨 일을 했는가?

(A) 회의에서 연설했다.
(B) 안내 책자를 디자인했다.
(C) 설문조사 결과를 검토했다.
(D) 이메일 문의에 응답했다.

해설 세부 사항 관련 – 여자가 최근에 한 일

대화 맨 처음에 여자가 고객 만족도 조사의 응답을 살펴보고 있었고 방금 다 봤다(You know how I've been looking over the responses ~ finished that up.) 고 했으므로 정답은 (C)이다.

▸▸ **Paraphrasing** 대화의 **looking over the responses to the customer satisfaction surveys**
→ 정답의 **reviewed survey results**

45

Why does the man say, "I've been pretty busy with billing work"?

(A) To request extra help
(B) To provide an excuse
(C) To decline invitation
(D) To correct an error

남자가 "제가 청구서 작업 때문에 몹시 바빴어요"라고 말한 이유는 무엇인가?

(A) 추가로 도움을 요청하려고
(B) 변명을 하려고
(C) 초대를 거절하려고
(D) 실수를 바로잡으려고

해설 화자의 의도 파악 – 청구서 작업으로 몹시 바빴다고 말한 이유

여자의 첫 번째 대사에서 남자에게 설문조사 결과를 살펴봤는지(Have you gone through them yet?) 물어봤다. 이에 대해 남자가 미안하다(Sorry.)고 하면서 청구서 작업 때문에 몹시 바빴다고 했다. 즉, 인용문은 설문조사 결과를 검토하지 못한 것에 대한 변명으로 청구서 작업 얘기를 한 것이므로 정답은 (B)이다.

46

What will the woman suggest at a weekly meeting?

(A) Extending business hours
(B) Modifying a Web site
(C) Simplifying a hiring process
(D) Postponing an announcement

여자는 주간회의에서 어떤 제안을 할 것인가?

(A) 영업 시간 연장
(B) 웹 사이트 수정
(C) 채용 과정 단순화
(D) 발표 연기

어휘 extend 연장하다 modify 수정하다

해설 세부 사항 관련 – 여자의 제안 사항

남자의 두 번째 대사에서 웹 사이트를 간소화해야겠다(we'd better try to simplify it.)고 하자, 이에 대해 여자가 주간회의에서 설문조사 결과를 발표할 때 그 점을 제안하겠다(I'll recommend ~ at our weekly meeting.)고 했으므로 정답은 (B)이다.

▸▸ **Paraphrasing** 대화의 **simplify it**
→ 정답의 **Modifying a Web site**

47-49 3인 대화

M-Au That concludes the first part of our tour, a look at the work of Lars Aalders. [47]**Does anyone have any final questions about Mr. Aalders or his photographs?**

M-Cn Elton, I was looking for Aalders' famous work, *Lilac*, but I didn't see it anywhere.

M-Au Ah, [48]**that photograph is now on display at the Larkin Museum.** We have the work out on loan to them, and it's not scheduled to return to this gallery for another year. Yes, another question?

W-Br I really liked the artwork *Yellow Field*. Are there any postcards of *Yellow Field* that I can buy?

M-Au Of course, we have some in the gift shop. [49]**I'd be happy to locate them for you when we stop by later.** All right, let's continue our tour.

남1: 지금까지 관람의 1부인 라스 알더스 씨의 작품을 봤습니다. **마지막으로 알더스 씨나 그의 사진 작품들에 관해 질문 있으신 분 계신가요?**
남2: 엘튼, 저는 알더스의 유명한 작품인 〈라일락〉을 찾고 있었는데 어디에도 보이지 않았어요.
남1: 아, **그 사진 작품은 현재 라킨 미술관에 전시 중입니다.** 저희는 그 작품을 라킨 미술관에 대여 중이며, 이 화랑에 반환되려면 1년 더 있어야 합니다. 네, 다른 질문 있나요?
여: 저는 〈노란 들판〉이라는 작품이 정말 좋았습니다. 〈노란 들판〉이 담긴 엽서를 살 수 있나요?
남1: 물론이죠. 저희 기념품 가게에 좀 있습니다. **우리가 나중에 그곳에 들를 때 제가 기꺼이 위치를 알려 드릴게요.** 좋습니다, 계속해서 다음 관람을 합시다.

어휘 conclude 끝나다, 결론짓다 tour (미술관·박물관) 관람 look for ~을 찾다 on display 전시 중인 on loan 대여 중인 postcard 엽서 locate 위치를 찾다

47

Who most likely is Mr. Aalders?

(A) A photographer
(B) A painter
(C) A fashion designer
(D) A sculptor

라스 알더스는 누구인가?

(A) 사진작가
(B) 화가
(C) 패션 디자이너
(D) 조각가

해설 세부 사항 관련 – 알더스 씨의 신분
첫 번째 남자의 첫 번째 대사에서 라스 알더스 씨의 작품을 관람했는데, 알더스 씨나 그의 사진 작품들에 관한 질문이 있는지(Does anyone have any final questions about Mr. Aalders or his photographs?) 물어봤다. 따라서 라스 알더스 씨는 사진작가임을 알 수 있으므로 정답은 (A)이다.

48

What does Elton mention about *Lilac*?

(A) It is very small in size.
(B) It is undergoing restoration.
(C) It is being shown at another institution.
(D) It is displayed in the main gallery.

엘튼은 〈라일락〉에 관해 뭐라고 하는가?

(A) 크기가 아주 작다.
(B) 복원 작업을 하고 있다.
(C) 현재 다른 미술관에 전시 중이다.
(D) 주 전시실에 진열되어 있다.

어휘 undergo ~을 받다, 겪다 restoration (원래 상태로의) 복원, 복구

해설 세부 사항 관련 – 〈라일락〉에 대한 엘튼의 언급
첫 번째 남자(엘튼)의 두 번째 대사에서 그 사진 작품은 현재 라킨 미술관에 전시 중(that photograph is now on display at the Larkin Museum.)이라고 했으므로 정답은 (C)이다.

▸▸ **Paraphrasing** 대화의 **that photograph is now on display at the Larkin Museum** → 정답의 **It is being shown at another institution.**

49

What does Elton say he will do for the woman?

(A) Find some items
(B) Issue a refund
(C) Get an audio guide
(D) Explain an artistic technique

엘튼은 여자에게 무엇을 해 주겠다고 말하는가?

(A) 물품 찾기
(B) 환불해주기
(C) 음성 안내기 구해주기
(D) 예술적 기술 설명하기

해설 세부 사항 관련 – 엘튼이 여자를 위해 할 일
대화 맨 마지막에 엘튼이 여자에게 나중에 같이 기념품 가게에 들를 때 엽서가 있는 곳을 알려주겠다(I'd be happy to locate them for you when we stop by later.)고 했으므로 정답은 (A)이다.

▸▸ **Paraphrasing** 대화의 **locate** → 정답의 **find**

Test 7

50-52

M-Au Deedee, do you want to come with me to the lobby? I'm going to get a snack. [50]**I promise that we'll be back in our seats before the second act starts.**

W-Br Sure—I'd like to get up and walk around a little. So, [50]**what do you think of the play so far?** I'm really enjoying it. [51]**I can see why it has gotten such positive reviews in the local newspapers.**

M-Au Me too. The acting is especially good, in my opinion. [52]**In fact—did you happen to bring your copy of the program?** I'd like to find out some of the actors' names and what other plays they've appeared in.

남: 디디 씨, 저랑 같이 로비에 가실래요? 간식을 사려고요. **2막이 시작하기 전에는 자리에 확실히 돌아올 수 있어요.**
여: 좋아요. 일어나서 좀 걷고 싶네요. **지금까지 연극은 어떠셨나요?** 저는 정말 재미있게 봤어요. **지역 신문에서 그렇게 호평을 받은 이유를 알겠어요.**
남: 저도요. 제 생각엔 연기력이 특히 뛰어나네요. **그런데 혹시 프로그램북을 가져오셨나요?** 배우들의 이름과 그들이 출연한 다른 연극들을 알아보고 싶어서요.

어휘 promise 약속하다 act (연극, 공연 등의) 막 so far 지금까지 positive 긍정적인 review 평가 local 지역의 in fact 실은, 사실은 happen to 우연히 ~ 하다 appear 출연하다

50

Who most likely are the speakers?

(A) Ushers
(B) Theater patrons
(C) Professional actors
(D) Backstage crew members

화자들은 누구겠는가?

(A) 좌석 안내원
(B) 극장 관객
(C) 전문 배우
(D) 공연 보조 직원

어휘 usher 좌석 안내원 patron 고객, 후원자 professional 전문적인 backstage 무대 뒤

해설 전체 내용 관련 – 화자들의 신분

남자가 여자에게 간식을 사러 가자고 하면서 2막 시작 전에는 자리에 확실히 돌아올 수 있다(I promise ~ before the second act starts.)고 했다. 이에 여자가 동의하며 연극이 지금까지 어땠는지(what do you think of the play so far) 물어보고 있으므로 정답은 (B)이다.

51

What does the woman mention about the play?

(A) It has been praised by critics.
(B) Its characters are interesting.
(C) Tickets for it have sold out.
(D) It has a positive theme.

여자가 연극에 대해 언급한 것은 무엇인가?

(A) 비평가들에게 호평을 받았다.
(B) 등장인물들이 흥미롭다.
(C) 연극 티켓이 매진됐다.
(D) 주제가 긍정적이다.

어휘 praise 칭찬하다 critic 비평가 be sold out 다 팔리다, 매진되다 theme 주제

해설 세부 사항 관련 – 연극에 대한 언급 사항

여자의 첫 번째 대사에서 연극에 대해 언급하며 지역 신문에서 호평을 받은 이유를 알겠다(I can see why it has gotten such positive reviews in the local newspapers.)고 했으므로 정답은 (A)이다.

▸▸ **Paraphrasing** 대화의 **gotten such positive reviews**
→ 정답의 **been praised by critics**

52

What does the man want to see?

(A) Some sales figures
(B) A play program
(C) Some newspaper articles
(D) A copy of a script

남자는 무엇을 보고 싶어하는가?

(A) 매출액
(B) 연극 프로그램북
(C) 신문 기사
(D) 대본

어휘 sales figures 매출액 article 기사 script 대본

해설 세부 사항 관련 – 남자가 보고 싶어하는 것

남자의 마지막 대사에서 프로그램북을 가져왔는지(In fact—did you happen to bring your copy of the program?) 여자에게 묻고 있으므로 정답은 (B)이다.

53-55

M-Cn Thanks for calling Janet's Cooking Supplies Catalog. This is Carl.

W-Am Hi, this is Abby from Timeless Terracotta. [53]**We make clay pots called Multi-Pots that are great for storage or cooking,** and I think they would fit well in your catalog.

M-Cn We already sell a lot of cookware, but none of it is clay, so you might be right. Tell me more.

W-Am Well, [54]**the best thing about the Multi-Pot is its range of uses. It can do anything from making delicious loaves of bread to storing potatoes.**

M-Cn Hmm... that could be a good addition to our catalog. [55]**Can you send us a sample?**

W-Am Sure thing.

남: 재닛의 조리용품 카탈로그에 전화해 주셔서 감사합니다. 저는 칼입니다.

여: 안녕하세요. 저는 타임리스 테라코타의 애비라고 해요. **저희는 저장용이나 요리용으로 아주 좋은 멀티포트라는 도기 냄비를 만들고 있는데,** 그 제품이 귀사의 카탈로그와 잘 맞을 것 같아요.

남: 저희는 이미 많은 조리 기구를 판매하고 있기는 하지만, 도기는 하나도 없으니 그럴 수도 있겠군요. 더 말씀해 보세요.

여: 글쎄요. **멀티포트의 가장 큰 장점은 용도가 다양하다는 거예요. 맛있는 빵을 만들거나 감자를 보관하는 것에 이르기까지 뭐든 할 수 있어요.**

남: 음… 저희 카탈로그에 그걸 추가하면 좋겠군요. **저희에게 견본품을 하나 보내주시겠어요?**

여: 물론이죠.

어휘 cooking supplies 조리용품 catalog 카탈로그, (물품 등의) 목록 clay pot 도기 냄비 storage 저장 fit well 잘 맞다[어울리다] cookware 조리 기구 a loaf of bread 빵 한 덩이 store 보관하다, 저장하다 addition 추가, 첨가

53

What kind of business does the woman work for?

(A) A restaurant
(B) A food industry magazine
(C) A cooking school
(D) A kitchenware manufacturer

여자는 어떤 종류의 업체에서 일하는가?
(A) 식당
(B) 식품업계 잡지
(C) 요리 학교
(D) 주방용품 제조업체

해설 전체 내용 관련 - 여자의 근무지
여자의 첫 번째 대사에서 저장용이나 요리용으로 아주 좋은 멀티포트라는 도기 냄비를 만들고 있다(We make clay pots called Multi-Pots that are great for storage or cooking)고 했다. 여자가 주방용품 제조업체에 근무한다는 것을 알 수 있으므로 정답은 (D)이다.

▶▶ **Paraphrasing** 대화의 clay pots → 정답의 kitchenware

54
What does the woman highlight about the Multi-Pot?
(A) Its functions
(B) Its weight
(C) Its popularity
(D) Its available colors

여자는 멀티포트에 관해 무엇을 강조하는가?
(A) 기능
(B) 무게
(C) 인기도
(D) 구입 가능한 색상

해설 세부 사항 관련 - 멀티포트에 대해 강조한 것
여자의 두 번째 대사에서 멀티포트의 가장 큰 장점은 용도가 다양하다는 것인데, 맛있는 빵을 만들거나 감자를 보관하는 등 뭐든 할 수 있다(the best thing about the Multi-Pot is its range of uses. It can do anything from making delicious loaves of bread to storing potatoes.)고 했으므로 정답은 (A)이다.

55
What does the man ask the woman for?
(A) A promotional code
(B) A product sample
(C) A contact number
(D) A catalog

남자는 여자에게 무엇을 요청하는가?
(A) 판촉 쿠폰 번호
(B) 제품의 견본
(C) 연락 가능한 전화번호
(D) 카탈로그

해설 세부 사항 관련 - 남자의 요청 사항
남자의 세 번째 대사에서 여자에게 견본품을 하나 보내 달라고(Can you send us a sample?) 요청했으므로 정답은 (B)이다.

56-58

W-Br Good evening, Mr. Irwin. [56]**Before you begin your workout, can I tell you about a special deal our gym is running?**

M-Au Sure. I'm not in a hurry.

W-Br Great. You know how we hold exercise classes for certain purposes, like "flexibility" or "stress relief"? Well, [57]**we just opened a new class designed to boost energy levels, and it's free for members all this month.**

M-Au Oh, I have been feeling tired lately. Hmm... Is there a class tonight?

W-Br There is, but it's already halfway over. But if you'd like, [58]**I could put your name on the list for an upcoming session.** When do you plan to come in next?

여: 안녕하세요, 어윈 씨. **운동을 시작하시기 전에 저희 헬스클럽에서 진행 중인 특별 할인에 대해 말씀드려도 될까요?**
남: 좋습니다. 바쁘지 않아요.
여: 잘됐네요. 저희가 "유연성"이나 "스트레스 해소" 등 특정 목적으로 운동 강좌를 개설하는 것은 알고 계시죠? **저희가 에너지 레벨을 높이기 위해 고안된 새 강좌를 마침 열었는데, 이번 달 내내 전 회원에게 무료입니다.**
남: 아, 최근 피로를 느끼긴 했어요. 음… 오늘 저녁에 강좌가 있나요?
여: 있지만 이미 절반쯤 진행됐어요. 하지만 원하신다면 **앞으로 있을 강좌 목록에 성함을 적어드릴게요.** 다음엔 언제 오실 계획이시죠?

어휘 workout 운동 special deal 특가 상품 in a hurry 서둘러, 바쁜 certain 특정한 purpose 목적, 의도 flexibility 유연성 relief 완화, 제거 boost 신장시키다, 북돋우다 lately 최근 halfway 중간쯤에 upcoming 다가오는, 곧 있을

56
Where most likely are the speakers?
(A) At a medical clinic
(B) At a pharmacy
(C) At a fitness center
(D) At a health food store

화자들은 어디에 있겠는가?
(A) 병원
(B) 약국
(C) 피트니스 센터
(D) 건강식품 매장

어휘 pharmacy 약국

해설 전체 내용 관련 - 대화 장소
여자의 첫 번째 대사에서 남자가 운동을 시작하기 전에 여자의 헬스클럽에서 진행하는 특별 할인에 대해 말해도 되는지(Before you begin your workout ~ our gym is running?) 물어보고 있으므로 정답은 (C)이다.

57
Why does the man say, "I have been feeling tired lately"?
(A) To explain the reason for his visit
(B) To agree with the woman's analysis
(C) To apologize for a misunderstanding
(D) To indicate that an offer is attractive

Test 7

남자가 "최근 피로를 느끼긴 했어요"라고 말한 이유는 무엇인가?
(A) 방문한 까닭을 설명하기 위해
(B) 여자의 분석에 동의하기 위해
(C) 오해한 것에 대해 사과하기 위해
(D) 제안이 마음에 든다는 것을 나타내기 위해

어휘 analysis 분석 apologize for ~에 대해 사과하다 misunderstanding 오해 attractive 매력적인, 마음을 끄는

해설 화자의 의도 파악 – 최근 피로를 느낀다고 말한 이유

인용문 바로 전 대사에서 여자가 헬스클럽에서 에너지 레벨을 높이기 위해 고안된 새 강좌를 열었고 이번 달 내내 회원들에게 무료(we just opened a new class ~ free for members all this month.)라고 했다. 이에 남자가 최근 피로를 느끼긴 했다고 했으므로, 여자의 새 강좌 제안이 마음에 든다는 것을 나타내기 위해 말했음을 알 수 있어 정답은 (D)이다.

58

What does the woman say she can do?

(A) Sign the man up for a class
(B) Give the man some free goods
(C) Demonstrate some exercises
(D) Search for a pamphlet

여자는 무엇을 할 수 있다고 말하는가?
(A) 남자의 강좌 신청하기
(B) 남자에게 무료 상품 주기
(C) 운동 시범 보여주기
(D) 팜플렛 찾기

어휘 sign up for ~를 신청하다 demonstrate 보여주다, 시연하다

해설 세부 사항 관련 – 여자가 할 수 있는 것

여자의 마지막 대사에서 앞으로 있을 강좌 목록에 이름을 적어주겠다(I could put your name on the list for an upcoming session.)고 했으므로 정답은 (A)이다.

▸▸ **Paraphrasing** 대화의 put your name on the list
→ 정답의 Sign the man up for a class

59-61 3인 대화

W-Br Excuse me? Can you tell me the price of this vacuum? It doesn't have a price tag on it.

M-Au Hmm... I'm not sure. Let me check with a colleague. [59]**Marissa, do you know how much this vacuum is?**

W-Am It's ninety pounds.

W-Br Oh, OK. Do you have anything cheaper?

W-Am Yes, we have a lot, but I'd recommend the Cleanster J9. [60]**Its original price is over one hundred pounds, but it's currently being sold at just seventy pounds.**

W-Br That could work...

M-Au Great. The Cleanster and our other vacuums are in aisle four. [61]**I'd be happy to take you over there and help you with your selection.**

W-Br I'd appreciate it.

여1: 실례합니다. 이 진공청소기의 가격을 알려 주실 수 있나요? 가격표가 붙어 있지 않네요.
남: 음… 잘 모르겠습니다. 동료한테 확인해 보겠습니다. **마리사, 이 진공청소기 얼마인지 알아요?**
여2: 90파운드예요.
여1: 오, 알겠습니다. 더 싼 물건도 있나요?
여2: 네, 많이 있습니다만 저는 클린스터 J9을 권해 드리고 싶네요. **원래 정가는 100파운드가 넘지만, 현재는 단돈 70파운드에 판매되고 있습니다.**
여1: 그러면 괜찮을 수도 …
남: 좋아요. 4번 통로에 클린스터와 저희의 다른 진공청소기가 있습니다. **제가 그쪽으로 모시고 가서 선택하시는 걸 도와드리겠습니다.**
여1: 그렇게 해 주시면 고맙죠.

어휘 vacuum 진공청소기 price tag 가격표 colleague 동료 original price (원래) 정가 aisle 통로 selection 선택

59

Why does the man ask Marissa for assistance?

(A) He is unable to operate a machine.
(B) He wants information about a product.
(C) He is confused about a policy.
(D) He does not know where a manager is.

남자는 왜 마리사에게 도움을 청하는가?
(A) 기계를 작동할 수 없어서
(B) 제품에 대한 정보를 알고 싶어서
(C) 방침이 헷갈려서
(D) 매니저가 어디에 있는지 몰라서

해설 세부 사항 관련 – 남자가 마리사에게 도움을 청하는 이유

남자는 마리사에게 진공청소기가 얼마인지(Marissa, do you know how much this vacuum is?) 물어봤는데, 제품의 가격은 제품에 대한 정보에 해당하므로 정답은 (B)이다.

60

What does Marissa mention about the Cleanster J9?

(A) It is being sold at a discount.
(B) It can be gift-wrapped at no additional cost.
(C) It is the store's best-selling vacuum.
(D) It is a relatively new model.

마리사는 클린스터 J9에 관해 무슨 말을 하는가?
(A) 할인가에 판매되고 있다.
(B) 추가 비용 없이 선물 포장이 된다.
(C) 매장에서 가장 잘 팔리는 진공청소기이다.
(D) 비교적 최신 모델이다.

해설 세부 사항 관련 – 클린스터 J9에 대해 마리사가 한 말

마리사의 두 번째 대사에서 클린스터 J9의 원래 가격은 100파운드가 넘지만, 현재는 단돈 70파운드에 판매되고 있다(Its original price is over one hundred pounds ~ seventy pounds.)고 했으므로 정답은 (A)이다.

61

What will the man most likely do next?

(A) Help a customer carry a device
(B) Stock some shelves
(C) Guide a customer to another area
(D) Take some measurements

남자는 다음에 무엇을 하겠는가?

(A) 고객이 장치를 운반하는 걸 돕기
(B) 선반에 상품을 쌓아 두기
(C) 고객을 다른 구역으로 안내하기
(D) 치수 재기

해설 세부 사항 관련 – 남자가 할 일

남자의 두 번째 대사에서 여자에게 4번 통로에 클린스터와 다른 진공청소기가 있다면서 그쪽으로 안내해서 선택하는 걸 도와주겠다(I'd be happy to take you over there and help you with your selection.)고 했으므로 정답은 (C)이다.

▸▸ **Paraphrasing** 대화의 **take you over there**
→ 정답의 **Guide a customer to another area**

62-64 대화 + 주문서

M-Cn Judy, [62]**I have an idea for the employee appreciation picnic we're putting together.** Let's order our snacks and beverages from Delmat Foods.

W-Am Hmm... [63]**Could Delmat bring the items to our venue in the park—the pavilion?**

M-Cn [63]**Yes, that's the reason I'd like to order from them.** Their Web site lists the park as a delivery area—see? And here's a possible order for our group.

W-Am Looks great. But Sue's team will bring baked treats for all of us. So [64]**we don't need the dessert package.**

M-Cn OK. I'll take it off the order. Everything else is good, then?

W-Am Yes, let's try Delmat.

남: 주디, **우리가 준비 중인 직원 감사 야유회에 관해 좋은 생각이 있어요.** 간식과 음료를 델맷 식품에서 주문합시다.

여: 음… **공원에서 우리가 쉼터에 있을 건데 그곳으로 델맷이 물품을 가져올 수 있을까요?**

남: **네, 그래서 제가 거기에 주문을 하자는 거예요.** 웹 사이트에 있는 배달 장소 목록에 그 공원도 있어요, 보이죠? 그리고 우리가 주문할 만한 것들이 여기 있어요.

여: 아주 좋아 보이는데요. 하지만 수의 팀이 우리 모두를 위해 과자를 구워 오기로 했어요. 그러니 **후식 패키지는 필요하지 않아요.**

남: 알겠어요. 그것은 주문에서 삭제할게요. 그럼 다른 것은 모두 괜찮죠?

여: 네, 델맷을 이용해 보죠.

어휘 appreciation 감사 picnic 야유회 order 주문하다; 주문품 snack 간식 beverage 음료수 venue 장소 pavilion 파빌리언, 쉼터, 정자 list 목록에 포함하다, 열거하다 baked treats 구운 과자나 케이크 따위 dessert 후식 try 시험 삼아 (이용)해보다 pizza slice sampler 모듬 조각 피자 platter 큰 접시(에 담은 요리)

Your Order:

Item	Quantity	Total
Juice (large bottles)	25	$45
Pizza slice sampler	30	$80
[64]Dessert package	50	$110
Sandwich platter	50	$135

귀하의 주문 내역:

품목	수량	합계
주스 (큰 병)	25	45달러
모듬 조각 피자	30	80달러
후식 패키지	**50**	**110달러**
샌드위치 플래터	50	135달러

62

What kind of event are the speakers planning?

(A) A store opening
(B) A music festival
(C) A staff picnic
(D) A charity fund-raiser

화자들은 어떤 종류의 행사를 계획하고 있는가?

(A) 매장 개점
(B) 음악 축제
(C) 직원 야유회
(D) 자선 모금 행사

해설 세부 사항 관련 – 계획 중인 행사

대화 맨 처음에 남자가 자신들이 준비하고 있는 직원 감사 야유회에 대해 좋은 생각이 있다(I have an idea for ~ putting together.)고 했으므로 정답은 (C)이다.

▸▸ **Paraphrasing** 대화의 **the employee appreciation picnic**
→ 정답의 **a staff picnic**

63

Why most likely does the man want to use Delmat Foods?

(A) They use high-quality ingredients.
(B) They offer reduced prices on large orders.
(C) They have a convenient parking facility.
(D) They provide a delivery service.

남자는 왜 델맷 식품을 이용하고 싶어 하겠는가?
(A) 질 좋은 재료를 사용한다.
(B) 대량 주문 시 가격을 할인해 준다.
(C) 주차 시설이 편리하다.
(D) 배달 서비스를 제공한다.

해설 세부 사항 관련 – 남자가 델맷 식품을 이용하고 싶은 이유

여자의 첫 번째 대사에서 남자에게 야유회 장소가 공원 쉼터인데 그곳으로 델맷이 물품을 가져올 수 있는지(Could Delmat bring the items to our venue in the park—the pavilion?)를 물어봤다. 이에 대해 남자가 그렇다고 하면서 바로 그런 이유로 그곳에 주문하고 싶다(Yes, that's the reason I'd like to order from them.)고 했으므로 정답은 (D)이다.

64

Look at the graphic. Which amount will be removed from the order?

(A) $45
(B) $80
(C) $110
(D) $135

시각 정보에 의하면, 주문서에서 얼마의 비용이 빠질 것인가?
(A) 45달러
(B) 80달러
(C) 110달러
(D) 135달러

해설 시각 정보 연계 – 주문서에서 빠지는 비용

여자의 두 번째 대사에서 후식 패키지는 필요하지 않다(we don't need the dessert package.)고 했다. 그리고 주문서를 보면 후식 패키지의 가격이 110달러로 나와 있으므로 정답은 (C)이다.

65-67 대화 + 쿠폰

M-Au So, Quinn, do you have any plans for the weekend?

W-Br I do, actually. [65]**A friend of mine just moved into a new house, and she's having a get-together there to celebrate.**

M-Au Sounds fun!

W-Br Yes, I'm looking forward to it. I haven't figured out what to get her for a housewarming gift, though.

M-Au Hmm... how about a nice bouquet of roses? [66]**I just saw that Ladden Supermarket is having a sale that includes its in-store florist shop.**

W-Br Oh, what a good idea, Derek! I could stop by there on my way to her house. Do I need a coupon?

M-Au Yes, but [67]**you can download it from Ladden's Web site. I can show you how.** Do you have time now?

남: 퀸 씨, 주말 계획 있으세요?
여: 네, 있어요. **친구 중 한 명이 새 집으로 이제 막 이사했는데, 거기서 축하 파티를 열거든요.**
남: 재미있겠네요!
여: 네, 기대하고 있어요. 그런데 집들이 선물로 무엇을 줄지 아직 결정하지 못했어요.
남: 음… 근사한 장미 꽃다발은 어때요? **래든 슈퍼마켓에서 매장 내 꽃집을 포함해 할인하는 걸 방금 봤어요.**
여: 아, 좋은 생각이네요, 데릭! 친구 집에 가는 길에 들를 수 있겠어요. 쿠폰이 필요한가요?
남: 네, 근데 **래든 웹 사이트에서 다운로드할 수 있어요. 방법을 알려드릴게요.** 지금 시간 되세요?

어휘 actually 실은, 사실은 get-together 모임, 파티 celebrate 축하하다 look forward to ~를 고대하다 figure out 생각해 내다 housewarming 집들이 bouquet 꽃다발 in-store 매장 내의 stop by 잠시 들르다

☆ Ladden Supermarket ☆

Weeklong sale on select items!

[66]**5% off**	flowers
10% off	cosmetics
15% off	baked goods
20% off	produce

☆ 래든 슈퍼마켓 ☆

엄선된 상품을 1주일간 할인 판매합니다!

5% 할인	꽃
10% 할인	화장품
15% 할인	제과
20% 할인	농산물

65

What does the woman say will happen this weekend?

(A) Her friend will go out of town.
(B) Her hobby club will have a gathering.
(C) A movie will be broadcast on television.
(D) A housewarming party will take place.

여자는 이번 주말에 무슨 일이 있을 것이라고 말하는가?
(A) 친구가 그 지역을 떠날 것이다.
(B) 동호회에서 모임이 있을 것이다.
(C) 영화가 TV에서 방영될 것이다.
(D) 집들이 파티가 열릴 것이다.

어휘 gathering 모임 broadcast 방송하다 take place 개최되다

해설 전체 내용 관련 – 주말에 있을 일

주말 계획을 묻는 남자의 물음에 여자가 첫 번째 대사에서 친구가 이사해서 축하 파티를 연다(A friend of mine just moved into a new house, and she's having a get-together there to celebrate.)고 했으므로 정답은 (D)이다.

66

Look at the graphic. Which price reduction will the woman try to receive?

(A) 5%
(B) 10%
(C) 15%
(D) 20%

시각 정보에 의하면, 여자는 얼마의 가격 할인을 받으려 할 것인가?

(A) 5%
(B) 10%
(C) 15%
(D) 20%

어휘 reduction 감소, 할인

해설 시각 정보 연계 – 여자가 받을 할인 가격

남자의 세 번째 대사에서 집들이 선물로 꽃다발을 추천하며 래든 슈퍼마켓에서 매장 내 꽃집을 포함해 할인하는 걸 보았다(I just saw that Ladden Supermarket is having a sale that includes its in-store florist shop.)고 했다. 이에 여자도 좋은 생각이라고 동의했으므로 여자는 꽃을 살 것임을 알 수 있다. 슈퍼마켓 할인표를 보면 꽃은 5퍼센트 할인이라고 되어 있으므로 정답은 (A)이다.

67

What does the man offer to do for the woman?

(A) Write down a recipe
(B) Download a street map
(C) Lend her his loyalty card
(D) Assist with obtaining a coupon

남자는 여자에게 무엇을 해 주겠다고 제안하는가?

(A) 조리법 적어주기
(B) 약도 다운로드해주기
(C) 고객 카드 빌려주기
(D) 쿠폰 받는 것 도와주기

어휘 recipe 조리법 loyalty card 고객 (포인트 적립) 카드 obtain 얻다, 구하다

해설 세부 사항 관련 – 남자의 제안 사항

여자의 마지막 대사에서 쿠폰이 필요한지 물었고 이에 남자가 래든 웹 사이트에서 다운로드 받을 수 있다며 방법을 알려주겠다(you can download it from Ladden's Web site. I can show you how.)고 했으므로 정답은 (D)이다.

▸▸ **Paraphrasing** 대화의 **download it**
→ 정답의 **obtaining a coupon**

68-70 대화 + 스크린샷

M-Cn Gloria, could you help me? I can't get into my company e-mail account.

W-Am Did you reset your password? The old ones expired Friday, when you were away on business.

M-Cn [68]**I made a reset request, but I have to wait another hour to get assigned a new password.** So, I want to check... [69]**Did the e-mail with the sales projections come through?**

W-Am Sure, I have it here. If you'd like, [70]**I'll print out the summary of the key figures from my computer.**

M-Cn Thanks, but that won't be necessary. I just needed to confirm that it had been sent. I can review the file in time for the afternoon meeting.

남: 글로리아, 저 좀 도와주시겠어요? 제 회사 이메일 계정에 들어갈 수가 없네요.

여: 비밀번호를 재설정하셨어요? 옛날 번호는 금요일에 만료되었는데, 그때 출장을 가서 자리를 비우셨잖아요.

남: **재설정을 요청했는데, 새 비밀번호를 배정받으려면 한 시간을 더 기다려야 해요.** 그래서 확인해 보고 싶어요··· **예상 매출 자료가 이메일로 들어왔나요?**

여: 물론이죠, 여기 있어요. 원하시면 **제 컴퓨터에서 핵심 수치 요약본을 출력해 드릴게요.**

남: 고맙지만 그럴 필요는 없어요. 자료가 발송되었는지 확인해야 했거든요. 제가 오후 회의 시간에 맞춰서 파일을 검토할 수 있어요.

어휘 e-mail account 이메일 계정 reset 재설정하다; 재설정 expire 만료되다 be away 자리를 비우다 on business 출장으로 make a request 요청하다 get assigned ~을 배정[할당]받다 sales projection 예상 매출 summary 요약본 figure 수치 confirm 확인[확정]하다 in time for ~할 시간에 맞춰

FROM:	SUBJECT:
Mai Okazaki	Facility Tour Schedule
[69]Sung-Chul Oh	ATTACHED: Sales Projections
Drew Langpro	Conference Planning Checklist
Hyun-Jin Seo	CANCELED: Computer Workshop

발신:	제목:
오카자키 마이	시설 견학 일정
오성철	**첨부: 예상 매출 자료**
드루 랭프로	회의 기획 점검표
서현진	취소: 컴퓨터 교육

Test 7

68

Why is the man unable to access an e-mail account?

(A) He does not have a valid password.
(B) His account's storage is full.
(C) He cannot get an Internet connection.
(D) He needs to install some new software.

남자가 이메일 계정에 접속하지 못하는 이유는?

(A) 유효한 비밀번호가 없다.
(B) 계정의 저장 용량이 가득 찼다.
(C) 인터넷에 접속할 수 없다.
(D) 새 소프트웨어 프로그램을 설치해야 한다.

해설 세부 사항 관련 - 남자의 이메일 접속 불가 이유

남자의 두 번째 대사에서 비밀번호 재설정을 요청했는데 새 비밀번호를 배정받으려면 한 시간을 더 기다려야 한다(I made a reset request, but I have to wait another hour to get assigned a new password.)고 했으므로 정답은 (A)이다.

69

Look at the graphic. Who sent the e-mail the speakers are discussing?

(A) Ms. Okazaki
(B) Mr. Oh
(C) Mr. Langpro
(D) Ms. Seo

시각 정보에 의하면, 화자들이 얘기하고 있는 이메일은 누가 보냈는가?

(A) 오카자키 씨
(B) 오 씨
(C) 랭프로 씨
(D) 서 씨

해설 시각 정보 연계 - 화자들이 말하는 이메일의 발송자

남자의 두 번째 대사에서 여자에게 예상 매출 자료가 이메일로 들어왔는지(Did the e-mail with the sales projections come through?) 물어봤고 여자는 그렇다고 대답했다. 그리고 목록을 보면 첨부파일로 예상 매출 자료(ATTACHED: Sales Projections)를 보낸 사람은 오성철이므로 정답은 (B)이다.

70

What does the woman offer to do?

(A) Revise a document
(B) Print a data summary
(C) Arrange a team meeting
(D) Reply to a written request

여자는 무엇을 하겠다고 하는가?

(A) 서류 수정
(B) 자료 요약본 출력
(C) 팀 회의 준비
(D) 서면 요청서에 응답

어휘 revise 수정하다

해설 세부 사항 관련 - 여자의 제안 사항

여자의 두 번째 대사에서 자신의 컴퓨터에서 핵심 수치 요약본을 출력해 주겠다(I'll print out the summary of the key figures from my computer.)고 했으므로 정답은 (B)이다.

▸▸ **Paraphrasing** 대화의 **the summary of the key figures**
→ 정답의 **a data summary**

PART 4

71-73 전화 메시지

M-Cn Hello, Ms. Lowe. This is Matt from Ivanek's, and I'm calling about your order. [71]**The sofa and bookcase will be shipped shortly.** However, [72]**I regret to inform you that item 09102, the side table, is permanently out of stock.** We've issued a store credit, in the amount matching the cost of the item, to your account. While you can have it refunded to your credit card, we hope you'll use it to order a replacement item from our Web site. We're actually having a sale right now, so I think you'll be able to find something you like. [73]**Please visit your account page to view the amount of credit you have available.** Again, we are very sorry for the inconvenience.

안녕하세요, 로우 씨. 저는 이바넥스의 매트입니다. 고객님의 주문과 관련해 전화 드립니다. **소파와 책장은 곧 배송될 예정입니다.** 하지만 **품목 번호 09102, 보조 탁자는 완전히 품절되었음을 알려 드리게 되어 유감입니다.** 저희는 그 품목의 가격에 상응하는 금액을 고객님 계정으로 스토어 크레디트를 발급해 드렸습니다. 고객님 신용카드로 환불받으실 수도 있지만, 저희는 고객님께서 그것으로 저희 웹 사이트에서 대용품을 주문해 주셨으면 합니다. 사실 저희가 지금 할인 판매를 하고 있으니 마음에 드시는 물건을 찾으실 수 있을 겁니다. **저희 계정 페이지를 방문하셔서 이용 가능한 크레디트 잔고를 확인해 보세요.** 불편을 끼쳐 드려 다시 한번 대단히 죄송하다는 말씀드립니다.

어휘 ship 배송하다, 발송하다 shortly 곧 regret 유감이다 inform 알리다 permanently 영구적으로 out of stock 품절된 store credit 스토어 크레디트(환불한 물건의 값을 나중에 그 상점에서 다른 물건을 살 수 있도록 처리하는 것, 또는 가격을 적어 놓은 표) matching 상응하는 account 계정, 계좌 refund 환불하다 replacement (item) 교체품, 대용품 actually 실은, 실제로 have a sale 세일[할인 판매]하다 available 이용 가능한 inconvenience 불편

71
What does the speaker's business sell?

(A) Clothing
(B) Appliances
(C) Books
(D) Furniture

화자의 사업체는 무엇을 판매하는가?

(A) 의류
(B) 가전제품
(C) 도서
(D) 가구

해설 전체 내용 관련 - 화자 사업체의 판매 물품

지문 초반부에 화자가 청자에게 소파와 책장은 곧 배송될 예정(The sofa and bookcase will be shipped shortly.)이라고 했으므로 정답은 (D)이다.

▸▸ **Paraphrasing** 지문의 **the sofa and bookcase** → 정답의 **Furniture**

72
What is the problem?

(A) An address is incorrect.
(B) An item is unavailable.
(C) A price was misquoted.
(D) An invoice was not paid.

무엇이 문제인가?

(A) 주소가 틀리다.
(B) 물건을 구할 수 없다.
(C) 가격이 잘못 기재되었다.
(D) 청구 대금이 지불되지 않았다.

어휘 misquote 잘못 인용하다

해설 세부 사항 관련 - 문제점

지문 초반부에 화자가 청자에게 품목번호 09102, 보조 탁자가 완전히 품절되었다는 점을 알리게 되어 유감(I regret to inform you ~ permanently out of stock.)이라고 했으므로 정답은 (B)이다.

▸▸ **Paraphrasing** 지문의 **permanently out of stock** → 정답의 **unavailable**

73
What does the speaker say the listener can see on her account page?

(A) Her balance of store credit
(B) Her contact preferences
(C) A set of instructions
(D) A shipping update

화자는 청자가 계정 페이지에서 무엇을 볼 수 있다고 말하는가?

(A) 스토어 크레디트 잔액
(B) 선호하는 연락처
(C) 일련의 설명서
(D) 최신 배송 현황

해설 세부 사항 관련 - 청자가 계정 페이지에서 볼 수 있는 것

지문 후반부에서 화자는 청자에게 계정 페이지를 방문해서 이용 가능한 크레디트 잔고를 확인해 보라(Please visit your account page to view the amount of credit you have available.)고 했으므로, 정답은 (A)이다.

▸▸ **Paraphrasing** 지문의 **the amount of credit you have available** → 정답의 **Her balance of store credit**

74-76 회의 발췌

W-Am The status report for my department this week is the same as last week—we're understaffed. [74]**My employees are working**

double shifts to keep the company's appliances working and to make sure the building is clean. [75]I've posted job ads on all the major Web sites, but considering the number and quality of responses I've received... we need a new strategy. I think the problem is that our wages are too low to attract skilled workers. Can we raise them? **[76]I wanted to use this weekly management meeting to bring up the issue. What do you all think?**

이번 주 저희 부서 현황 보고서는 지난주와 같습니다. 인원이 부족합니다. **저희 직원들은 회사 기기들을 계속 가동하고 건물을 깨끗하게 유지하기 위해 밤낮으로 일하고 있습니다. 주요 웹 사이트들에 전부 구인 공고를 게시했습니다만, 제가 받은 회신의 개수와 질을 고려해 볼 때…** 새로운 전략이 필요합니다. 숙련된 작업자를 데려오기에 저희 임금이 너무 낮은 것이 문제라고 봅니다. 급여를 올릴 수 있을까요? **이번 주간 관리자 회의 때 이 문제를 제기하고 싶었습니다. 모두 어떻게 생각하십니까?**

어휘 status report 현황 보고서 understaffed 인원이 부족한 work double shifts 밤낮으로 일하다 appliance 가전제품 post 게시하다 response 응답, 회신 strategy 전략 wage 임금 skilled 숙련된 raise 올리다 bring up an issue 문제를 제기하다

74
What department does the speaker most likely manage?

(A) Shipping and Receiving
(B) Maintenance
(C) Parking
(D) Security

화자는 어떤 부서를 관리하고 있겠는가?

(A) 배송 및 수령
(B) 유지 보수
(C) 주차
(D) 보안

어휘 shipping 배송 maintenance 유지 보수 security 보안

해설 전체 내용 관련 - 화자가 관리하는 부서

지문 초반부에 화자가 자신의 부서 직원들은 회사 기기들을 계속 가동하고 건물을 깨끗하게 유지하기 위해 밤낮으로 일하고 있다(My employees are working double shifts ~ the building is clean.)고 했으므로 정답은 (B)이다.

75
What does the speaker imply when she says, "we need a new strategy"?

(A) A budget limit has been exceeded.
(B) A training program has received poor feedback.
(C) A recruiting attempt has not been successful.
(D) A technology is no longer free.

화자가 "새로운 전략이 필요합니다"라고 말한 의도는 무엇인가?

(A) 예산 한도액을 초과했다.
(B) 교육 프로그램에 대한 피드백이 좋지 않았다.
(C) 채용 시도가 성공적이지 못했다.
(D) 기술이 더 이상 무료가 아니다.

어휘 budget 예산 exceed 초과하다 recruiting 채용 attempt 시도

해설 화자의 의도 파악 - 새로운 전략이 필요하다는 말의 의도

인용문 바로 앞 부분에서 화자는 주요 웹 사이트들에 전부 구인 공고를 게시했지만, 자신이 받은 회신의 개수와 질을 고려해 볼 때(I've posted job ads ~ quality of responses I've received) 새로운 전략이 필요하다고 했는데, 문맥상 인용문은 원하는 직원을 채용하려는 시도가 성공적이지 못했다는 것을 의미하므로 정답은 (C)이다.

76
What will the listeners most likely do next?

(A) Greet a visitor
(B) Fill out a form
(C) Discuss a problem
(D) Conclude a meeting

청자들은 다음에 무엇을 하겠는가?

(A) 방문객 맞이하기
(B) 양식 작성하기
(C) 문제에 대해 토의하기
(D) 회의 마무리하기

어휘 fill out a form 양식을 작성하다 conclude 끝내다

해설 세부 사항 관련 - 청자들이 다음으로 할 일

지문 마지막에 화자가 이번 주간 관리자 회의 때 이 문제를 제기하고 싶다(I wanted to use this weekly management meeting to bring up the issue.)며, 청자들이 어떻게 생각하는지 묻고 있어 청자들이 문제에 대해 토의할 것임을 알 수 있으므로 정답은 (C)이다.

▸▸ **Paraphrasing** 지문의 **bring up the issue**
→ 정답의 **Discuss a problem**

77-79 광고

M-Au **[77]Are you interested in how computer systems are built?** Then you should apply for Byrom Academy's Hardware Engineering Program today. **[77]Our courses teach students how to work with circuits, systems, and devices,** and give them the skills they need to work in corporate research, manufacturing, and government agencies. **[78]We even offer many of our classes over the Internet for busy students.** If you'd like to get qualified for one of the most in-demand careers in the IT industry, **[79]visit our Web site, www.byromacademy.edu, to register and to find detailed explanations of courses that will be taught in the upcoming session.**

컴퓨터 시스템이 어떻게 구축되는지 관심이 있습니까? 그렇다면 오늘 바이롬 아카데미의 하드웨어 엔지니어링 프로그램에 등록하십시오. **저희 강좌들은 학생**

들에게 회로와 시스템, 장치를 어떻게 다루는지 가르치고, 학생들이 기업의 연구소나 제조업체, 그리고 정부 기관에서 일하는 데 필요한 기술들을 알려 줍니다. **저희는 바쁜 학생들을 위해 다수의 강좌를 인터넷으로도 제공합니다.** IT 업계에서 가장 수요가 많은 직종 중 하나에 자격을 갖추시려면 **저희 웹 사이트 www.byromacademy.edu를 방문하셔서 다가오는 학기의 강좌들에 관한 자세한 설명을 찾아보시고 등록하시기 바랍니다.**

어휘 be interested in ~에 관심[흥미]이 있다 apply for ~을 신청하다 course 강좌, 과정 circuit 회로 corporate 기업의, 회사의 manufacturing 제조업 government agency 정부 기관 get qualified for ~에 필요한 자격을 얻다 in-demand 수요가 많은 career 직업 register 등록하다

77

What does the advertised program most likely teach?

(A) Graphic design
(B) Tax preparation
(C) Business management
(D) Computer engineering

광고하는 프로그램은 무엇을 가르칠 것 같은가?

(A) 그래픽 디자인
(B) 세금 준비
(C) 기업 경영
(D) 컴퓨터 공학

해설 세부 사항 관련 - 프로그램이 가르치는 것

지문 맨 처음에 청자들에게 컴퓨터 시스템 구축 방법에 관심이 있는지(Are you interested in how computer systems are built?)를 묻고 나서 자신들이 제공하는 강좌들은 학생들에게 회로와 시스템, 장치를 어떻게 다루는지를 가르친다(Our courses teach students how to work with circuits, systems, and devices)고 했다. 즉, 컴퓨터 공학을 가르친다는 걸 알 수 있으므로 정답은 (D)이다.

78

What is mentioned about the program?

(A) It lasts more than one year.
(B) It offers some classes online.
(C) It includes career planning services.
(D) Its graduates receive a university degree.

프로그램에 관해 언급된 것은 무엇인가?

(A) 1년 넘게 계속된다.
(B) 일부 강좌를 인터넷으로 제공한다.
(C) 진로 계획 서비스를 포함한다.
(D) 수료생들은 대학 학위를 받는다.

해설 세부 사항 관련 - 프로그램에 대한 언급

지문 중반부에 바쁜 학생들을 위해 다수의 강좌를 인터넷으로도 제공한다(We even offer many of our classes over the Internet for busy students.)고 했으므로 정답은 (B)이다.

▸▸ **Paraphrasing** 지문의 **offer many of our classes over the Internet** → 정답의 **offer some classes online**

79

What does the speaker say visitors to a Web site can do?

(A) Download an online course book
(B) Chat with academy staff
(C) Watch some videos
(D) Read course descriptions

화자는 웹 사이트 방문자들이 무엇을 할 수 있다고 말하는가?

(A) 온라인 강좌 교재 다운받기
(B) 아카데미 직원과 대화하기
(C) 동영상 시청하기
(D) 강좌 설명문 읽기

해설 세부 사항 관련 - 웹 사이트 방문자들이 할 수 있는 것

지문 맨 마지막에 청자들에게 웹 사이트를 방문해서 다가오는 학기의 강좌들에 관한 자세한 설명을 찾아보고 등록하라(visit our Web site ~ in the upcoming session.)고 했으므로 정답은 (D)이다.

▸▸ **Paraphrasing** 지문의 **detailed explanations of courses** → 정답의 **course descriptions**

80-82 전화 메시지

W-Br Hi, Robert. This is Beverly Hopkins. [80]**Unfortunately, we're having heavy showers and fog here in London and all flights have been postponed.** This means I won't be able to get to the conference on time. I'm really sorry to ask this, but [81]**since you're already there, you'll have to do the presentation.** [82]**I've uploaded the presentation file to the company's online drive.** If you look in the "RWSO Conference" folder, you'll see two folders. The file you want is in the one labeled "Final." Just use that, and I know you'll do a fantastic job.

안녕하세요, 로버트. 비벌리 홉킨스예요. **유감스럽게도, 이곳 런던에 폭우가 내리고 안개가 짙어 모든 항공편이 지연되었어요.** 그래서 제가 컨퍼런스에 시간에 맞춰 가지 못할 것 같아요. 이런 부탁을 해서 정말 미안하지만, **당신은 이미 거기에 가 있으니 당신이 발표를 해주셔야겠어요. 발표용 파일은 제가 사내 온라인 드라이브에 올려놨어요.** 'RWSO 컨퍼런스' 폴더 안을 보시면 두 개의 하위 폴더가 보일 거예요. 당신이 원하는 파일은 '최종'이라고 적힌 폴더 안에 있어요. 그것만 사용해 주시고, 당신이 아주 잘 해낼 거라 믿어요.

어휘 shower 소나기 fog 안개 flight 항공편 postpone 연기하다 on time 정각에 upload (자료를) 올리다, 업로드하다 label 라벨을 붙여 분류하다, 꼬리표를 달다 do a fantastic job 훌륭하게 해내다

Test 7

80

What problem does the speaker describe?

(A) A presentation is not ready.
(B) A document is missing.
(C) A trip is delayed by weather.
(D) An itinerary contains an error.

화자가 설명하는 문제는 무엇인가?

(A) 발표 준비가 되지 않았다.
(B) 서류 하나가 빠졌다.
(C) 날씨 때문에 여행이 지연되고 있다.
(D) 일정표에 오류가 있다.

해설 세부 사항 관련 - 화자가 언급하는 문제점

지문 초반부에 화자가 유감스럽게도 이곳 런던에 폭우가 내리고 안개가 짙어 모든 항공편이 지연되었다(Unfortunately, we're having ~ have been postponed.)고 했으므로 정답은 (C)이다.

▸▸ **Paraphrasing** 지문의 **heavy showers and fog**
→ 정답의 **weather**

81

What does the speaker ask the listener to do?

(A) Register for a conference
(B) Give a public talk
(C) Print out some graphs
(D) Modify a reservation

화자는 청자에게 무엇을 해달라고 요청하는가?

(A) 회의 등록
(B) 발표
(C) 도표들 출력
(D) 예약 변경

해설 세부 사항 관련 - 화자의 요청 사항

지문 중반부에 화자는 청자가 이미 거기에 가 있으니 발표를 해달라(since you're already there, you'll have to do the presentation.)고 했으므로 정답은 (B)이다.

▸▸ **Paraphrasing** 지문의 **do the presentation**
→ 정답의 **give a public talk**

82

How can the listener get a file?

(A) By accessing it online
(B) By meeting the speaker
(C) By going to the post office
(D) By using a delivery service

청자는 파일을 어떻게 받을 수 있는가?

(A) 온라인으로 접속해서
(B) 화자를 만나서
(C) 우체국에 가서
(D) 배달 서비스를 이용해서

해설 세부 사항 관련 - 파일을 받을 수 있는 방법

지문 중반부에 발표용 파일을 회사 온라인 드라이브에 올려놓았다(I've uploaded ~ online drive.)고 했다. 청자는 온라인 파일에 접속해 파일을 받을 수 있으므로 정답은 (A)이다.

83-85 담화

M-Cn Good morning, everyone. I'd like to introduce you to Keith Stone. [83]**Mr. Stone is one of the best IT consultants available**, and he has advised many of the leading companies of our industry. [84]**He'll be working with us for the next few weeks to help the company adjust to the changing work environment.** He's going to show each department how to integrate new technologies to make our day-to-day tasks go a little smoother. We are excited to have him here and [85]**we ask that you'll give him whatever time or assistance he asks of you.** Now, without further delay, let's give Mr. Stone a warm welcome.

여러분, 안녕하세요. 여러분에게 키스 스톤 씨를 소개하려고 합니다. **스톤 씨는 우리가 구할 수 있는 최고의 IT 컨설턴트 중 한 명이며,** 우리 업계의 많은 선도기업들에 자문을 제공해 왔습니다. **그는 앞으로 몇 주 동안 우리와 함께 근무하며 회사가 변화하는 근무 환경에 적응하도록 도움을 줄 것입니다.** 그는 각 부서에 일상 업무가 좀 더 매끄럽게 진행되도록 새로운 기술들을 통합하는 방법을 보여줄 예정입니다. 우리는 그가 이곳에 있어서 기대가 크며, **그가 여러분에게 요청하면 시간이나 도움을 아끼지 말고 제공해 주길 부탁합니다.** 자, 더 이상 지체하지 말고 스톤 씨를 따뜻하게 맞이합시다.

어휘 IT 정보기술(= information technology) consultant 컨설턴트, 상담역, 고문 leading company 선도기업 adjust to ~에 적응하다 work environment 근무 환경 integrate 통합하다 technology 기술 day-to-day task 일상 업무 smooth 매끄러운 assistance 도움, 지원 without further delay 더 이상 지체하지 않고 give a warm welcome 따뜻하게 맞이하다

83

Who most likely is Mr. Stone?

(A) A financial advisor
(B) A legal expert
(C) A technical consultant
(D) A marketing specialist

스톤 씨는 누구일 것 같은가?

(A) 재정 고문
(B) 법률 전문가
(C) 기술 컨설턴트
(D) 마케팅 전문가

해설 전체 내용 관련 - 스톤 씨의 신분

지문 초반부에 화자가 스톤 씨는 우리가 구할 수 있는 최고의 IT 컨설턴트 중 한 명(Mr. Stone is one of the best IT consultants available)이라고 소개했으므로 정답은 (C)이다.

▸▸ Paraphrasing 지문의 **one of the best IT consultants**
→ 정답의 **a technical consultant**

84

Why does the speaker say Mr. Stone has been hired?

(A) To assist with a difficult decision
(B) To keep the company up-to-date
(C) To comply with environmental regulations
(D) To network with outside organizations

화자는 스톤 씨가 왜 고용되었다고 말하는가?

(A) 어려운 결정을 내리는 것을 돕기 위해
(B) 회사를 첨단으로 유지하기 위해
(C) 환경 법규를 준수하기 위해
(D) 외부 조직들과 연계하기 위해

어휘 up-to-date 최신(식)의 network 업무상의 관계를 구축하다

해설 세부 사항 관련 – 스톤 씨가 고용된 이유

지문 중반부에 스톤 씨는 앞으로 몇 주 동안 함께 근무하며 회사가 변화하는 근무 환경에 적응하도록 도움을 줄 것(He'll be working ~ changing work environment.)이라고 했다. 이 말은 곧 회사가 최신 업무 환경을 갖추도록 도움을 줄 것이라는 의미이므로 정답은 (B)이다.

85

What are the listeners asked to do?

(A) Review some guidelines
(B) Gather again tomorrow
(C) Submit proposals for change
(D) Cooperate with Mr. Stone

청자들은 무엇을 하라는 요청을 받는가?

(A) 일부 지침을 살펴볼 것
(B) 내일 다시 모일 것
(C) 변화를 위한 제안서를 제출할 것
(D) 스톤 씨에게 협력할 것

어휘 guideline 지침 gather 모이다 cooperate 협조하다

해설 세부 사항 관련 – 청자들이 요청 받은 사항

지문 후반부에 화자가 청자들에게 스톤 씨가 요청할 경우 시간이나 도움을 아끼지 말고 제공해 주길 바란다(we ask that you'll ~ he asks of you.)고 했으므로 정답은 (D)이다.

▸▸ Paraphrasing 지문의 **give him whatever time or assistance he asks of you**
→ 정답의 **cooperate with Mr. Stone**

86-88 회의 발췌

M-Au OK. A few quick things. First, when you get a chance, [86]**I'd like you all to check on your levels of office supplies.** We want to make sure we don't run out of shipping labels or anything else during this new product release season. Also, I just got back from the loading docks, and... have you seen all the trucks? [87]**I think I'll need to call a staffing agency to arrange for extra help.** For now, [88]**I'm going to create a list of available overtime slots for those who wish to work more hours.** Thanks.

자, 몇 가지만 빨리 얘기하죠. 첫 번째, 기회가 있을 때 **여러분 모두 자신의 사무용품이 얼마나 있는지 확인해 보기 바랍니다.** 이번 신제품 출시 기간 동안 배송 라벨이나 그 밖의 물품들이 떨어지지 않게끔 확실히 하려고 합니다. 그리고 방금 선적장에서 돌아왔는데… **그 모든 트럭들을 보셨나요?** **제가 인력 알선업체에 전화해서 추가로 도움을 받아야 할 것 같습니다.** 우선은, **연장 근무를 원하는 직원들의 초과근무 가능 시간대 목록을 만들려고 합니다.** 고맙습니다.

어휘 get a chance 기회를 얻다 run out of ~을 다 쓰다, ~이 동나다 shipping label 배송 라벨 loading dock 선적장 staffing agency 인력 알선업체 arrange for ~을 마련하다 extra help 추가 도움 slot 시간대

86

What does the speaker ask the listeners to do?

(A) Arrange some boxes
(B) Collect some receipts
(C) Repair some equipment
(D) Check some inventories

화자는 청자들에게 무엇을 하라고 요청하는가?

(A) 상자 정리
(B) 영수증 모으기
(C) 장비 수리
(D) 재고 확인

어휘 inventory 재고

해설 세부 사항 관련 – 화자의 요청 사항

지문 초반부에 화자가 청자들에게 자신의 사무용품이 얼마나 있는지 확인해 달라(I'd like you all to check on your levels of office supplies.)고 했으므로 정답은 (D)이다.

87

What does the speaker mean when he says, "have you seen all the trucks"?

(A) He had to park his car far from a work site.
(B) He thinks that a work area is especially busy.
(C) He wants advice on purchasing new vehicles.
(D) He is concerned about some drivers' safety.

화자가 "그 모든 트럭들을 보셨나요?"라고 말한 의도는 무엇인가?

(A) 작업장에서 멀리 떨어진 곳에 주차를 해야 했다.
(B) 작업 구역이 특히 분주하다고 생각한다.
(C) 새 차량을 구입하는 것에 대한 조언을 원한다.
(D) 몇몇 운전자들의 안전에 대해 걱정한다.

Test 7

해설 화자의 의도 파악 - 모든 트럭들을 봤는지를 물어본 의도

지문 중반부에 화자는 청자들에게 그 모든 트럭들을 봤는지 물어본 다음, 인력 알선업체에 전화해서 추가로 도움을 받아야 할 것 같다(I think I'll need to call a staffing agency to arrange for extra help.)고 했다. 즉, 인용문은 많은 트럭들로 인해 작업 구역이 매우 분주해서 추가 인력이 필요하다는 의도를 나타낸 것이므로 정답은 (B)이다.

88

What will the speaker probably do next?

(A) Make a list
(B) Reschedule an appointment
(C) Clean a workstation
(D) Update a product description

화자는 다음에 무엇을 하겠는가?

(A) 명단 작성
(B) 약속 변경
(C) 사무용 책상 청소
(D) 제품 설명서 갱신

해설 세부 사항 관련 - 화자의 다음 행동

지문 후반부에 화자는 연장 근무를 원하는 직원들의 초과근무 가능 시간대 목록을 만들겠다(I'm going to create ~ more hours.)고 했으므로 정답은 (A)이다.

▸▸ **Paraphrasing** 지문의 **create a list** → 정답의 **make a list**

89-91 방송

W-Am As we continue today's show, [89]**I'd like to talk about smartphones. These gadgets are meant to make our lives more efficient. But a recent study showed that an increase in phone usage at home is contributing to employee exhaustion.** People spend more time checking work-related e-mails before going to bed and this makes them anxious and disrupts their sleep. So, they come to work feeling less engaged and less productive. [90]**Clearly, we need to put our phones down at night.** [91]**Researcher Ann Crouch recently gave an interesting lecture about this subject, and I'd like to play some of it for you.** Here's a short clip.

계속해서 오늘 방송에서는 **스마트폰에 관해 말씀드리겠습니다. 이 기기는 우리 삶을 더 효율적으로 만들어 주기 위한 것입니다. 그러나 최근의 연구에 따르면 가정 내 휴대폰 사용의 증가로 인해 직원들이 피곤해 하고 있습니다.** 사람들이 잠자리에 들기 전에 업무 관련 이메일을 확인하느라 더 많은 시간을 보내는 바람에 불안을 느끼고 수면에 지장을 받습니다. 그래서 집중력과 생산성이 떨어진 채로 회사에 옵니다. **분명 우리는 밤에는 휴대폰을 내려놓아야 합니다. 연구자인 앤 크라우치가 최근 이 주제로 흥미로운 강연을 했는데, 그중 일부를 여러분에게 보여주고 싶습니다.** 여기 짧은 영상을 하나 보시겠습니다.

어휘 gadget 기기, 장치 efficient 효율적인, 능률적인 contribute to ~에 기여하다 exhaustion 피로, 피곤, 기진맥진 spend + 시간 + -ing ~하느라 시간을 보내다 work-related 일[업무]과 관련된 anxious 불안한, 근심스러운 disrupt 방해하다 engaged 몰두한 productive 생산적인 put down 내려놓다 researcher 연구자 give a lecture 강의[강연]하다 short clip 짧은 동영상

89

What is the main topic of the broadcast?

(A) The advantages of public transportation
(B) The effects of personal electronics
(C) A new form of outdoor exercise
(D) Home improvement methods

방송의 주제는 무엇인가?

(A) 대중교통의 이점
(B) 개인용 전자제품의 영향
(C) 새로운 종류의 야외 운동
(D) 주택 개량 방법들

해설 전체 내용 관련 - 방송 주제

지문 초반부에 화자가 스마트폰에 관해 얘기하겠다면서 이 기기는 우리 삶을 더 효율적으로 만들기 위한 것이지만 최근의 연구를 보면 가정 내 휴대폰 사용 증가로 인해 직원들이 피곤해 하고 있다(I'd like to talk ~ contributing to employee exhaustion.)고 했다. 이를 통해 방송의 주제는 스마트폰이 우리 삶에 미치는 영향이라는 것을 알 수 있으므로 정답은 (B)이다.

▸▸ **Paraphrasing** 지문의 **smartphones**
→ 정답의 **personal electronics**

90

According to the speaker, when should an activity be avoided?

(A) In the morning
(B) During lunch breaks
(C) In the afternoon
(D) At night

화자에 따르면, 언제 특정 활동을 피해야 하는가?

(A) 아침
(B) 점심 시간
(C) 오후
(D) 밤

해설 세부 사항 관련 - 활동을 피해야 할 시간

지문 후반부에 우리는 분명 밤에 휴대폰을 내려놓아야 한다(Clearly, we need to put our phones down at night.)고 했는데 이는 밤에 휴대폰을 보는 활동을 피하라는 뜻이므로 정답은 (D)이다.

91

What will listeners probably hear next?

(A) An advertisement
(B) An interview
(C) A speech
(D) A song

청자들은 다음에 무슨 내용을 듣게 될 것인가?

(A) 광고
(B) 인터뷰
(C) 강연
(D) 노래

해설 세부 사항 관련 - 청자들이 듣게 될 내용

지문 후반부에 화자가 청자들에게 연구자 앤 크라우치가 최근 이런 주제로 흥미로운 강연을 했는데, 그것의 일부를 보여주고 싶다(Researcher Ann Crouch recently ~ for you.)고 했으므로 정답은 (C)이다.

▸▸ **Paraphrasing** 지문의 **an interesting lecture**
→ 정답의 **a speech**

92-94 회의 발췌

M-Cn OK, [92]**you should now have a good understanding of conservation programs, recycling initiatives, and other sustainable business practices, and how to adopt them at your business.** During the final part of the workshop, we'll talk about advertising them. Of course, [93]**the fundamental purpose of these programs should be to preserve our planet for future generations. But there's a secondary benefit to them in regards to your corporate image.** And your customers will want to know about this kind of thing. Now, there are several approaches to this. I've collected some real advertisements to give you an idea of each. [94]**Please look at the first page of the packet I'm passing out now.**

자, **여러분께서는 이제 환경 보호 프로그램, 재활용 운동, 기타 지속 가능한 사업 관행과 이를 귀사에서 활용하는 방법을 모두 아시고 계실 겁니다.** 워크숍 마지막 부분에서는 이를 알리는 것에 대해 이야기할 것입니다. 물론 **해당 프로그램의 기본 목적은 후손들을 위해 지구를 보호하는 것이겠지요. 하지만 기업 이미지와 관련해 부수적인 이점도 있습니다.** 그리고 **고객들은 이런 종류의 일에 대해 알고 싶어할 것입니다.** 여러 가지 접근 방식이 있는데요. 여러분께서 이해하실 수 있도록 실제 광고 몇 개를 모아봤습니다. **지금 나눠드릴 모음집의 첫 번째 페이지를 봐주십시오.**

어휘 have a good understanding of ~를 잘 이해하고 있다 conservation 보존, 보호 recycling 재활용 initiative (특정한 문제 해결을 위한) 계획, 운동 sustainable 지속 가능한 practice 관행 adopt 택하다, 취하다 advertise 알리다, 광고하다 fundamental 기본적인 preserve 보호하다, 지키다 generation 세대 secondary 이차적인, 부수적인 in regards to ~에 관해서 corporate 회사의 approach 접근법 pass out 나눠주다

92

What is the workshop mainly about?

(A) Environmental initiatives
(B) Business expansions
(C) Employee benefits
(D) Customer loyalty programs

워크숍은 주로 무엇에 관한 것인가?

(A) 환경 운동
(B) 사업 확장
(C) 직원 혜택
(D) 고객 로열티 프로그램

어휘 environmental 환경의 expansion 확장, 확대 customer loyalty program 충성고객을 위한 포인트 적립 등의 제도

해설 전체 내용 관련 - 워크숍의 주제

지문 초반부에 화자가 청자들이 이제 환경 보호 프로그램, 재활용 운동, 기타 지속 가능한 사업 관행과 이를 청자들의 회사에서 활용하는 방법을 알고 있을 것(you should now have a good understanding ~ how to adopt them at your business.)이라고 했으므로 정답은 (A)이다.

93

What does the speaker imply when he says, "your customers will want to know about this kind of thing?"

(A) Some mistakes should be admitted.
(B) Some instructions should be clarified.
(C) Some achievements should be celebrated.
(D) Some positive efforts should be publicized.

화자가 "고객들은 이런 종류의 일에 대해 알고 싶어할 것입니다"라고 말한 의도는 무엇인가?

(A) 실수를 인정해야 한다.
(B) 지시 사항을 명확히 해야 한다.
(C) 업적을 축하해야 한다.
(D) 긍정적인 노력이 알려져야 한다.

어휘 admit 인정하다, 시인하다 instructions 설명, 지시 clarify 명확하게 하다 achievement 업적 publicize 알리다, 홍보하다

해설 화자의 의도 파악 - 고객들은 이런 종류의 일에 대해 알고 싶어할 것이라는 말의 의도

인용문 앞에서 해당 프로그램의 기본 목적은 후손들을 위해 지구를 보호하는 것이지만 기업 이미지와 관련해 부수적인 이점이 있다(the fundamental purpose of these programs ~ in regards to your corporate image.)고 한 것으로 보아, 문맥상 인용문은 환경 계획에 대한 긍정적인 노력이 알려져야 한다는 의도를 나타낸 것이므로 정답은 (D)이다.

94

What are the listeners asked to look at?

(A) A whiteboard
(B) A poster
(C) A handout
(D) A projector screen

Test 7

청자들은 무엇을 보라고 요청 받았는가?

(A) 화이트보드
(B) 포스터
(C) 유인물
(D) 프로젝터 스크린

어휘 handout 유인물, 인쇄물

해설 세부 사항 관련 – 청자들이 받은 요청

지문 마지막에 화자가 청자들에게 지금 나눠 줄 모음집의 첫 번째 페이지를 봐달라(Please look at the first page of the packet I'm passing out now.)고 했으므로 정답은 (C)이다.

95-97 안내 + 일정표

W-Br [95]**This is a travel reminder for ticketed passengers waiting for the departure of the 2:25 bus to Dahlview.** Don't forget that bus is set to depart on schedule from Gate 13 on the left side of the terminal. Also, [96]**the management at Central Bus Terminal encourages all travelers to purchase tickets from our automated vending machines** to save time and avoid long lines. Finally, [97]**waiting passengers are invited to enjoy complimentary bottled water and lemonade available this week only in our brand new passenger lounge.** Thank you.

2시 25분발 달뷰행 버스의 출발을 기다리고 계시는 승차권 소지 승객 여러분께 다시 한 번 알려 드립니다. 버스가 터미널 왼편에 있는 13번 탑승구에서 예정대로 출발하오니 잊지 마시기 바랍니다. 또한, **센트럴 버스터미널 운영진은 모든 여행객들이 저희 자동 발매기에서 승차권을 구입하시어** 시간을 절약하시고 길게 줄 서는 일을 피하시길 권장합니다. 마지막으로, **대기 중인 승객들께서는 이번 주에 한해 새로운 승객 휴게실에서 무료 생수와 레모네이드를 즐기시기 바랍니다.** 감사합니다.

어휘 reminder 상기시키는 것 ticketed 차표를 지닌 departure 출발 be set to + 동사원형 ~할 예정이다 on schedule 예정대로 management 운영진, 관리소 encourage 장려[권장]하다 automated 자동화된 vending machine 자동 발매기 avoid 피하다 complimentary 무료의, 공짜의 brand new 아주 새로운

Central Bus Terminal (departures)

Route	Destination	Departure time	Status
104	Trillburgh	1:55 P.M.	DEPARTED
312	Matford	2:10 P.M.	ON TIME
[95]165	Dahlview	2:25 P.M.	ON TIME
981	Ledhurst	3:00 P.M.	DELAYED

센트럴 버스터미널 (출발)

노선	목적지	출발 시각	(출발) 상황
104번	트릴버그	오후 1:55	출발
312번	맷포드	오후 2:10	정시
165번	**달뷰**	**오후 2:25**	**정시**
981번	레드허스트	오후 3:00	연착

95

Look at the graphic. Which bus route is the announcement for?

(A) 104
(B) 312
(C) 165
(D) 981

시각 정보에 의하면, 안내 방송은 어떤 버스 노선을 위한 것인가?

(A) 104번
(B) 312번
(C) 165번
(D) 981번

해설 시각 정보 연계 – 해당하는 버스 노선

지문 맨 처음에 안내 방송이 2시 25분발 달뷰행 버스 승차권을 가지고 있는 승객들을 위한 것(This is a travel reminder ~ 2:25 bus to Dahlview.)이라고 했는데 시간표를 보면 출발 시간이 오후 2시 25분인 달뷰행 버스는 165번 노선이므로 정답은 (C)이다.

96

What are all travelers encouraged to do?

(A) Use vending machines
(B) Form lines in front of gates
(C) Buy tickets through a mobile app
(D) Complete a feedback survey

모든 여행객에게 무엇을 하라고 권하는가?

(A) 자동 발매기 이용
(B) 게이트 앞에서 줄서기
(C) 모바일 앱을 통한 승차권 구입
(D) 평가 설문지 작성

해설 세부 사항 관련 – 여행객들에 대한 권장 사항

지문 중반부에 센트럴 버스터미널 운영진은 모든 여행객들이 자동 발매기에서 승차권을 구입하길 권장한다(the management ~ from our automated vending machines)고 했으므로 정답은 (A)이다.

▸▸ Paraphrasing 지문의 purchase tickets from our automated vending machines
→ 정답의 use vending machines

97

According to the speaker, what is temporarily available for free?

(A) Some refreshments
(B) Wireless Internet access
(C) Use of a storage locker
(D) Seating upgrades

화자에 따르면, 무엇을 일시적으로 무료로 이용할 수 있는가?

(A) 가벼운 음료
(B) 무선 인터넷
(C) 물품 보관함 이용
(D) 좌석 업그레이드

해설 세부 사항 관련 – 무료로 이용할 수 있는 것

지문 맨 마지막에 대기 중인 승객들은 이번 주에 한해 새로운 승객 휴게실에서 편히 쉬면서 무료 생수와 레모네이드를 즐기길 바란다(waiting passengers are invited to enjoy ~ brand new passenger lounge.)고 했으므로 정답은 (A)이다.

▸▸ **Paraphrasing** 지문의 bottled water and lemonade
→ 정답의 Some refreshments

98-100 담화 + 지도

W-Am Everyone, thanks for coming in early today. I'd like to go over our preparations for the Shunders Beach Volleyball Tournament. [98]**This is Marv's Beach Gear's first year as an official, paid sponsor of the competition,** so it's an important chance to make a good impression. Now, judging from last year, a lot of the visitors will be staying at Rannod Hotel—but [99]**the biggest rush of customers will be at our location closest to the volleyball courts.** So, [100]**we're going to shift about ten percent of the rental inventory from our northern locations to that store before the competition starts.** All right? Now, let's talk about promotional activities.

여러분, 오늘 일찍 와 주셔서 감사합니다. 션더즈 비치 발리볼 토너먼트 대회 준비 상황을 검토하고자 합니다. **마브즈 비치 기어가 대회의 공식 유료 후원자 가 된 첫 해이므로** 좋은 인상을 심어줄 중요한 기회입니다. 작년 기준으로 판단하건대, 많은 방문객이 래너드 호텔에 투숙할 것입니다. 하지만 **손님들이 발리볼 코트와 가장 가까운 지점에 제일 많이 몰려들 것입니다.** 따라서 **대회 시작에 앞서 북부 지점들의 대여 물품 중 약 10퍼센트를 해당 매장으로 옮길 예정입니다.** 문제 없죠? 그럼 이제 홍보 활동에 대해 얘기해 보죠.

어휘 go over 검토하다 preparation 준비 official 공식적인 paid 유급의 competition 대회 make a good impression 좋은 인상을 주다 judging from ~으로 판단하건대 shift 옮기다 inventory 재고 목록 promotional 홍보의 activity 활동

Marv's Beach Gear Locations on Shunders Beach

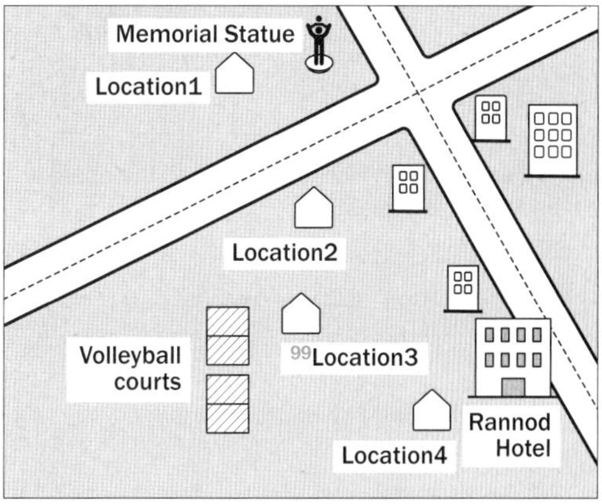

션더즈 비치상의 마브즈 비치 기어의 지점 위치도

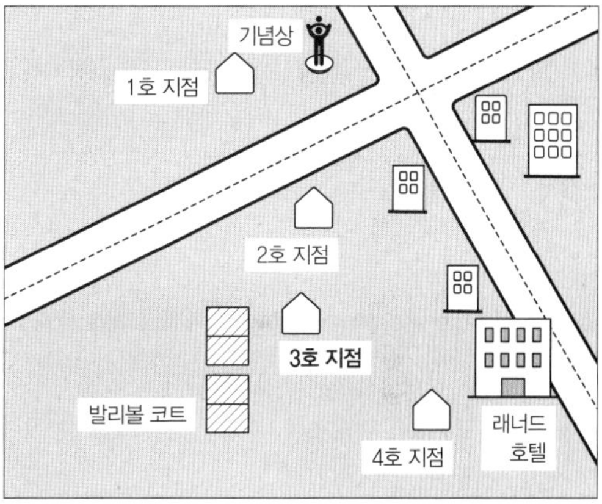

98

What does the speaker say about the upcoming event?

(A) This is the first year it has been held.
(B) It will be attended by a top city official.
(C) Marv's Beach Gear is supporting it financially.
(D) Some of Marv's Beach Gear's staff are participating in it.

화자가 다가오는 행사에 대해 뭐라고 말하는가?

(A) 개최 첫 해를 맞는다.
(B) 시의 고위 의원이 참석할 것이다.
(C) 마브즈 비치 기어가 재정적인 후원을 한다.
(D) 마브즈 비치 기어 직원 일부가 참여한다.

Test 7

어휘 attend 참석하다 city official 시 공무원 financially 재정적으로, 금전적으로 participate in ~에 참여하다

해설 세부 사항 관련 – 행사에 대해 언급된 사항

지문 초반부에 화자가 마브즈 비치 기어가 대회의 공식 유료 후원자가 된 첫 해(This is Marv's Beach Gear's first year as an official, paid sponsor of the competition)라고 했으므로 정답은 (C)이다.

▸▸ **Paraphrasing** 지문의 **an official, paid sponsor**
→ 정답의 **supporting it financially**

99

Look at the graphic. Which location does the speaker believe will be the busiest?

(A) Location 1
(B) Location 2
(C) Location 3
(D) Location 4

시각 정보에 의하면 화자는 어느 지점이 가장 붐빌 것으로 생각하는가?

(A) 1호 지점
(B) 2호 지점
(C) 3호 지점
(D) 4호 지점

해설 시각 정보 연계 – 가장 붐빌 지점

지문 중반부에 화자는 손님들이 발리볼 코트와 가장 가까운 지점에 제일 많이 몰려들 것(the biggest rush of customers will be at our location closest to the volleyball courts)이라고 했다. 지도를 보면 발리볼 코트와 가장 가까운 지점은 3호 지점이므로 정답은 (C)이다.

100

According to the speaker, what will the listeners do before the event?

(A) Exchange shifts with each other
(B) Rehearse a performance
(C) Hang up some banners
(D) Move some stock

화자에 따르면 청자들은 행사에 앞서 무엇을 할 것인가?

(A) 서로 교대근무 시간 바꾸기
(B) 공연 리허설하기
(C) 현수막 내걸기
(D) 재고 이동시키기

어휘 exchange 교환하다 shift 교대근무 시간 performance 공연 banner 현수막 stock 비축품, 재고

해설 세부 사항 관련 – 청자들이 행사 전에 할 일

지문 후반부에 화자가 청자들에게 대회 시작에 앞서 북부 지점들의 대여 물품 중 약 10퍼센트를 해당 매장으로 옮길 예정(we're going to shift about ten percent ~ before the competition starts.)이라고 했으므로 정답은 (D)이다.

▸▸ **Paraphrasing** 지문의 **shift about ten percent of the rental inventory**
→ 정답의 **Move some stock**

TEST 8

1 (C)	2 (A)	3 (B)	4 (C)	5 (A)
6 (B)	7 (C)	8 (A)	9 (C)	10 (A)
11 (C)	12 (B)	13 (B)	14 (B)	15 (A)
16 (A)	17 (C)	18 (A)	19 (B)	20 (A)
21 (C)	22 (B)	23 (A)	24 (B)	25 (C)
26 (A)	27 (B)	28 (A)	29 (C)	30 (B)
31 (B)	32 (D)	33 (A)	34 (C)	35 (D)
36 (A)	37 (A)	38 (C)	39 (B)	40 (A)
41 (C)	42 (B)	43 (D)	44 (A)	45 (D)
46 (C)	47 (A)	48 (B)	49 (B)	50 (B)
51 (D)	52 (D)	53 (B)	54 (A)	55 (D)
56 (B)	57 (D)	58 (D)	59 (A)	60 (C)
61 (B)	62 (D)	63 (B)	64 (C)	65 (B)
66 (C)	67 (C)	68 (C)	69 (B)	70 (A)
71 (C)	72 (C)	73 (B)	74 (A)	75 (B)
76 (D)	77 (C)	78 (A)	79 (C)	80 (A)
81 (D)	82 (B)	83 (B)	84 (C)	85 (A)
86 (A)	87 (D)	88 (C)	89 (C)	90 (B)
91 (D)	92 (D)	93 (A)	94 (B)	95 (B)
96 (D)	97 (C)	98 (D)	99 (D)	100 (A)

PART 1

1 M-Cn

(A) He's going ice skating.
(B) He's raking some leaves.
(C) He's shoveling snow.
(D) He's cutting tree branches.

(A) 남자가 스케이트를 타러 가고 있다.
(B) 남자가 갈퀴로 낙엽을 모으고 있다.
(C) 남자가 삽으로 눈을 치우고 있다.
(D) 남자가 나뭇가지를 자르고 있다.

어휘 rake 갈퀴로 모으다 shovel 삽으로 파다 tree branch 나뭇가지

해설 1인 등장 사진 - 사람의 동작 묘사

(A) 남자가 스케이트를 타러 가는(going ice skating) 모습이 아니므로 오답.

(B) 남자가 갈퀴로 낙엽을 모으고 있는(raking some leaves) 모습이 아니므로 오답.

(C) 남자가 삽으로 눈을 치우고 있는(shoveling snow) 모습이므로 정답.

(D) 사진에 나뭇가지가 보이지만 남자가 나뭇가지를 자르고 있는(cutting tree branches) 모습은 아니므로 오답.

2 W-Am

(A) Some people are boarding an airplane.
(B) Some passengers are waiting for a train.
(C) Some steps lead up to a street.
(D) Some tickets are being collected at a gate.

(A) 몇몇 사람들이 비행기에 탑승하고 있다.
(B) 몇몇 승객들이 기차를 기다리고 있다.
(C) 몇몇 계단들이 도로까지 이어져 있다.
(D) 게이트에서 표를 걷고 있다.

어휘 board 탑승하다 airplane 비행기(= plane) passenger 승객 steps 계단 lead up to ~로 이어지다, ~로 통하다

해설 2인 이상 등장 사진 - 사람의 동작 묘사

(A) 승객 몇 명이 비행기에 탑승하고 있는(are boarding an airplane) 모습이므로 정답.

(B) 승객들이 비행기에 탑승 중이지 기차를 기다리고 있는(are waiting for a train) 모습이 아니므로 오답.

(C) 사진에 계단이 보이기는 하지만 도로로 이어져 있지(lead up to a street) 않으므로 오답.

(D) 사진에 표(tickets)를 걷는 모습은 보이지 않으므로 오답.

3 M-Cn

(A) A woman is assembling a rack.
(B) A woman is examining a piece of clothing.
(C) A woman is sewing a shirt.
(D) A woman is using a laundry machine.

(A) 여자가 선반을 조립하고 있다.
(B) 여자가 옷 한 벌을 살펴보고 있다.
(C) 여자가 셔츠를 바느질하고 있다.
(D) 여자가 세탁기를 사용하고 있다.

어휘 assemble 조립하다 rack 선반, 걸이 examine 살펴보다, 조사하다 sew 바느질하다 laundry machine 세탁기

해설 1인 등장 사진 - 사람의 동작 묘사

(A) 사진에 선반이 보이지만 여자가 선반을 조립하고 있는(is assembling a rack) 모습은 아니므로 오답.

(B) 여자가 옷 한 벌을 살펴보고 있는(is examining a piece of clothing) 모습이므로 정답.

(C) 여자가 셔츠를 바느질하고 있는(is sewing a shirt) 모습이 아니므로 오답.

(D) 사진에 세탁기(laundry machine)가 보이지 않으므로 오답.

Test 8

4 W-Br

(A) They're inspecting some equipment.
(B) A safety vest is hanging from a hook.
(C) One of the men is pointing at a clipboard.
(D) A notebook computer has been set on a railing.

(A) 사람들이 장비를 검사하고 있다.
(B) 안전 조끼가 걸이에 걸려 있다.
(C) 남자들 중 한 명이 클립보드를 가리키고 있다.
(D) 노트북 컴퓨터가 난간에 놓여 있다.

어휘 inspect 검사하다 equipment 장비 safety vest 안전 조끼 hang 걸리다 hook 걸이, 고리 point at ~을 가리키다 clipboard 클립보드 set 놓다 railing 난간

해설 2인 이상 등장 사진 - 사람의 동작 묘사
(A) 장비를 검사하고 있는(are inspecting some equipment) 사람들은 없으므로 오답.
(B) 안전 조끼는 남자 한 명이 착용한 상태지 걸이에 걸려 있는(is hanging from a hook) 모습이 아니므로 오답.
(C) 남자들 중 한 명이 클립보드를 가리키고 있는(is pointing at a clipboard) 모습이므로 정답.
(D) 사진에 노트북 컴퓨터가 난간에(on a railing) 놓여 있지 않으므로 오답.

5 M-Au

(A) There is a set of stairs in front of a window.
(B) A dinner table has been placed on a rug.
(C) There are lamps on both sides of a bookcase.
(D) A rolling chair stands in the corner of a room.

(A) 창문 앞에 계단이 있다.
(B) 식탁이 깔개 위에 놓여 있다.
(C) 책장 양 옆에 램프들이 있다.
(D) 바퀴 달린 의자가 방 구석에 있다.

어휘 (a set of) stairs (층과 층 사이의) 계단 place 놓다 rug 깔개 bookcase 책장 rolling chair 바퀴 달린 의자 corner 구석

해설 실내 사물/배경 묘사 사진 - 다양한 사물의 위치 묘사
(A) 창문 앞에(in front of a window) 계단이 있으므로 정답.
(B) 사진에 책상이 있지 식탁(a dinner table)은 보이지 않으므로 오답.
(C) 책장 양 옆에(on both sides of a bookcase) 램프가 없으므로 오답.
(D) 바퀴 달린 의자가 방 가운데에 있지 방 구석에(in the corner of a room) 있지는 않으므로 오답.

6 W-Br

(A) One of the men is measuring a desk.
(B) Some pieces of paper have been rolled up.
(C) A woman is picking up a coffee cup.
(D) A clock has been mounted on a wall.

(A) 남자들 중 한 명이 책상을 재고 있다.
(B) 종이 몇 장이 말려 있다.
(C) 여자가 커피 컵을 들어올리고 있다.
(D) 시계가 벽면에 고정되어 있다.

어휘 measure (치수를) 재다 roll up 말다 pick up 집어 올리다 mount on ~에 고정시키다

해설 2인 이상 등장 사진 – 사람 또는 사물 중심 묘사
(A) 책상을 재는(is measuring) 남자는 없으므로 오답.
(B) 종이 몇 장이 말려(have been rolled up) 있으므로 정답.
(C) 여자가 커피 컵을 들어올리고(is picking up) 있지 않으므로 오답.
(D) 시계가 책장에 있지 벽면에(on a wall) 있지는 않으므로 오답.

PART 2

7

W-Br When does the warranty on this computer expire?

M-Au (A) Yes, I took care of it.

(B) A detailed protection plan.

(C) A year from now.

이 컴퓨터의 품질 보증 기간은 언제 만료되나요?

(A) 네, 내가 처리했어요.
(B) 상세한 보호 계획이요.
(C) 지금부터 1년 후에요.

어휘 warranty 품질 보증 기간 take care of ~을 처리하다, 돌보다 detailed 상세한, 자세한 protection 보호

해설 보증서의 만료 시점을 묻는 When 의문문

(A) Yes/No 불가 오답. 시점을 묻는 When 의문문에 Yes/No 응답이 불가능하기 때문에 오답.

(B) 연상 단어 오답. 질문의 warranty에서 연상 가능한 detailed protection을 이용한 오답.

(C) 정답. 컴퓨터 품질 보증 기간이 언제 만료되는지 묻는 질문에 지금부터 1년 후(A year from now.)라는 구체적인 시점으로 응답하므로 정답.

8

W-Am Where can I buy stamps around here?

W-Br (A) The shop next door sells them.

(B) I'll lend you some money.

(C) There's a mailbox on the corner.

이 근처 어디에서 우표를 살 수 있어요?

(A) 옆 가게에서 팔아요.
(B) 내가 돈을 좀 빌려 줄게요.
(C) 모퉁이에 우편함이 있어요.

어휘 stamp 우표 next door 옆집에, 이웃에 lend 빌려주다

해설 우표 구입처를 묻는 Where 의문문

(A) 정답. 우표 구입처를 묻는 질문에 옆 가게(The shop next door)라는 구체적인 장소로 응답하고 있으므로 정답.

(B) 연상 단어 오답. 질문의 buy에 대해 지불 측면에서 연상 가능한 some money를 이용한 오답.

(C) 연상 단어 오답. 질문의 stamps에 대해 우편물 측면에서 연상 가능한 mailbox를 이용한 오답.

9

M-Cn How long have you been working in the Beijing office?

W-Am (A) Because I speak Chinese.

(B) Employee recruitment, mostly.

(C) I transferred there six months ago.

베이징 사무실에서 얼마나 오래 일해 왔습니까?

(A) 제가 중국어를 하니까요.
(B) 대개는 직원 채용이요.
(C) 6개월 전에 그곳으로 옮겼어요.

어휘 recruitment 채용, 구인 mostly 대개, 대부분 transfer 전근하다

해설 근무 기간을 묻는 How long 의문문

(A) 연상 단어 오답. 질문의 Beijing에 대해 언어 측면에서 연상 가능한 Chinese를 이용한 오답.

(B) 연상 단어 오답. 질문의 working이나 Beijing office에서 연상 가능한 Employee recruitment를 이용한 오답.

(C) 정답. 베이징 사무실에서의 근무 기간을 묻는 질문에 6개월 전(six months ago)에 그곳으로 옮겼다는 말로 근무 기간이 6개월이라는 응답을 하고 있으므로 정답.

10

W-Am Which hotel should we use to book a room for our overseas client?

M-Au (A) One that isn't too far from our office.

(B) It's the client's book.

(C) The room has a view of the ocean.

해외 고객을 위해 어느 호텔의 객실을 예약해야 하죠?

(A) 우리 사무실에서 너무 멀지 않은 곳이요.
(B) 그것은 고객의 책입니다.
(C) 그 객실에서는 바다가 보입니다.

어휘 book 예약하다 overseas 해외의 view 전망

해설 호텔 선택을 묻는 Which 의문문

(A) 정답. 어느 호텔을 예약해야 할지에 대해 사무실에서 너무 멀지 않는 곳(One that isn't too far from our office.)이라는 위치 관련 구체적인 지침을 주고 있으므로 정답.

(B) 단어 반복 오답. 질문의 client와 book을 반복 이용한 오답.

(C) 단어 반복 오답. 질문의 room을 반복 이용한 오답.

11

M-Au Weren't you supposed to close the windows last night?

W-Am (A) They do seem a little closer.

(B) No, the aisle seat.

(C) I thought I did.

어젯밤 당신이 창문을 닫기로 하지 않았어요?

(A) 정말로 좀 가까워 보여요.
(B) 아니오, 통로 쪽 좌석이요.
(C) 닫았다고 생각했어요.

어휘 be supposed to+동사원형 ~하기로 되어 있다 aisle seat 통로 쪽 좌석

해설 창문 닫기 여부에 대한 부정의문문

(A) 파생어 오답. 질문의 close에 대해 비교급 형용사인 closer를 이용한 오답. 질문에서 close는 '닫다'라는 의미의 동사로 쓰였으나, 여기에서 close는 '가까운'이라는 의미의 형용사로 쓰임.

(B) 연상 단어 오답. 질문의 windows에 대해 좌석 측면에서 연상 가능한 aisle seat를 이용한 오답.

(C) 정답. 어젯밤에 창문을 닫았어야 하지 않았냐는 질문에 그렇게 한 줄 알았다(I thought I did.)는 말로 자신의 착각을 시인한 응답이므로 정답.

12

W-Br Could you make me a copy of that article?

M-Cn (A) Would you like milk or sugar?

(B) Sure, I'll do that right away.

(C) Thomas already agreed to write it.

그 기사를 한 부 복사해 주시겠어요?

(A) 우유나 설탕을 넣을까요?

(B) 물론이죠. 바로 해드릴게요.

(C) 이미 토마스가 쓰기로 했어요.

어휘 make a copy of ~를 한 부 복사하다 article 기사, 글 right away 곧바로, 즉각

해설 제안/요청의 의문문

(A) 연상 단어 오답. 질문의 copy를 coffee로 오해한 경우 연상 가능한 milk or sugar를 이용한 오답.

(B) 정답. 기사를 복사해 달라는 요청에 대해 먼저 Sure로 긍정적 응답을 한 후, 즉시 하겠다(I'll do that right away)는 말로 복사 시점을 구체적으로 알려주고 있으므로 정답.

(C) 연상 단어 오답. 질문의 article에 대해 작성 측면에서 연상 가능한 write를 이용한 오답.

13

W-Am Should I set up the projector for the slideshow?

M-Au (A) Did you like the movie?

(B) That would be great.

(C) The project report is complete.

슬라이드 쇼를 위해 제가 프로젝터를 설치할까요?

(A) 그 영화 좋았어요?

(B) 그렇게 해주면 좋겠어요.

(C) 프로젝트 보고서가 완성됐어요.

어휘 set up 설치하다 projector 프로젝터, 영사기 complete 완료된

해설 프로젝터를 설치할지 묻는 제안 의문문

(A) 연상 단어 오답. 질문의 projector에서 연상 가능한 movie를 이용한 오답.

(B) 정답. 슬라이드 쇼를 위해 프로젝터를 설치해야 하는지에 대해 그게 좋겠다(That would be great.)는 긍정적 응답을 하고 있으므로 정답.

(C) 파생어 오답. 질문의 projector와 파생어 관계인 project를 이용한 오답.

14

M-Au Do you know where Mr. Peterson's office is?

W-Br (A) The marketing director.

(B) It's just down the hall in Room C.

(C) No, he isn't.

피터슨 씨의 사무실이 어딘지 아세요?

(A) 마케팅 이사요.

(B) 복도 저쪽의 C번 방이에요.

(C) 아니요, 그는 아닙니다.

어휘 director 이사, 책임자

해설 사무실 위치를 묻는 간접의문문

(A) 연상 단어 오답. 질문의 Mr. Peterson에 대해 직책 측면에서 연상 가능한 marketing director를 이용한 오답.

(B) 정답. 피터슨의 사무실이 어디에 있는지 묻는 질문에 대해 복도 저쪽의 C번 방(down the hall in Room C)이라는 위치로 응답하므로 정답.

(C) 질문과 상관없는 오답. 질문에 부정 응답을 하려면 No, I don't.라고 해야 하므로 오답.

15

W-Am This new packaging machine works better than our old one, doesn't it?

M-Cn (A) Yes, it's much more efficient.

(B) I can send that for you.

(C) A couple more repairmen.

이 새 포장 기계는 예전 것보다 더 잘 작동하죠, 아닌가요?

(A) 네, 훨씬 더 효율적이에요.

(B) 내가 당신에게 그걸 보낼 수 있어요.

(C) 수리 기사 두 명 더요.

어휘 packaging 포장 efficient 효율적인, 능률적인 couple 두 사람, 두 개 repairman 수리 기사, 수리공

해설 새 포장 기계의 성능을 확인하는 부가의문문

(A) 정답. 새 프린터의 성능을 확인하는 질문에 Yes로 긍정적 응답을 한 후, 훨씬 더 효율적(much more efficient)이라는 부연 설명을 하므로 정답.

(B) 연상 단어 오답. 질문의 packaging에서 연상 가능한 send를 이용한 오답.

(C) 연상 단어 오답. 질문의 machine에 대해 수리 측면에서 연상 가능한 repairmen을 이용한 오답.

16

M-Au Where in Brazil is the new employee from?

W-Br (A) He didn't say.

(B) It's a company policy.

(C) The finance department.

신입 직원은 브라질의 어디 출신인가요?

(A) 그는 얘기하지 않았어요.

(B) 그게 회사 방침이에요.

(C) 경리부요.

어휘 policy 방침, 규정 finance department 경리부, 회계부

해설 출신 지역을 묻는 Where 의문문

(A) 정답. 신입 직원의 출신 지역을 묻는 질문에 그가 얘기하지 않았다(He didn't say.)는 불확실성 표현으로 응답하고 있으므로 정답.

(B) 연상 단어 오답. 질문의 new employee에서 연상 가능한 company policy를 이용한 오답.

(C) 연상 단어 오답. 질문의 employee에서 연상 가능한 finance department를 이용한 오답.

17

M-Cn Don't you think we should take an umbrella?

W-Am (A) That would be faster.

(B) The black one in the catalog.

(C) Is it supposed to rain?

우리가 우산을 가져가야 한다고 생각하지 않아요?

(A) 그게 더 빠를 거예요.

(B) 카탈로그에 있는 검은 거요.

(C) 비가 올 예정인가요?

어휘 catalog 카탈로그, 목록

해설 우산 필요 관련 부정의문문

(A) 질문과 상관없는 오답. 우산을 가져가야 하는지를 묻는 질문에 그게 더 빠를 것이라는 답변은 질문의 맥락에서 벗어난 것이므로 오답

(B) 연상 단어 오답. 질문의 umbrella에 대해 우산 색깔 측면에서 연상 가능한 black one을 이용한 오답.

(C) 정답. 우산을 가져가야 하지 않느냐는 질문에 비가 올 예정인지(Is it supposed to rain?)를 되물으며 추가 정보를 요청하고 있으므로 정답.

18

W-Am How much is a train ticket to Central Station?

M-Au (A) Ask the ticket agent.

(B) From Platform D.

(C) OK—please help me with my luggage.

센트럴 역까지 기차표는 얼마죠?

(A) 매표원에게 물어보세요.

(B) 플랫폼 D에서요.

(C) 좋아요. 제 수화물 옮기는 것 좀 도와 주세요.

어휘 ticket agent 매표원 stop 정거장 luggage 수화물, 짐

해설 기차표 요금을 묻는 How much 의문문

(A) 정답. 기차 요금이 얼마인지 묻는 질문에 대해 매표원에게 물어보라(Ask the ticket agent.)는 우회적 표현으로 응답하고 있으므로 정답.

(B) 연상 단어 오답. 질문의 train에 대해 탑승 장소 측면에서 연상 가능한 Platform D를 이용한 오답.

(C) 연상 단어 오답. 질문의 train에 대해 휴대용 짐 측면에서 연상 가능한 luggage를 이용한 오답.

19

W-Br Who was responsible for organizing the welcome reception?

M-Cn (A) My phone is getting good reception.

(B) Jordan arranged everything.

(C) We're so glad you could come.

누가 환영회 준비를 맡았죠?

(A) 내 전화기 수신이 좋아지고 있어요.

(B) 조던이 모든 것을 준비했어요.

(C) 당신이 올 수 있다니 우리는 아주 기뻐요.

어휘 be responsible for ~에 책임이 있다 organize 준비하다, 조직하다 welcome reception 환영회 reception 수신(율) arrange 마련하다

해설 환영회 준비 책임자를 묻는 Who 의문문

(A) 단어 반복 오답. 질문의 reception을 반복 이용한 오답. 질문에서 reception은 '리셉션, 환영회'의 의미로 쓰였으나 여기서는 '수신, 수신율'의 의미로 의미로 쓰임.

(B) 정답. 연회 준비 책임자가 누구였는지에 대해 조던(Jordan)이라는 구체적인 인물로 응답하고 있으므로 정답.

(C) 연상 단어 오답. 질문의 welcome에서 연상 가능한 glad나 come을 이용한 오답.

20

M-Au Should we paint the lobby blue or green?

W-Am (A) The CEO said she prefers green.

(B) Well, I don't mind doing it.

(C) The paint is dry now.

로비를 파란색으로 칠할까요, 아니면 녹색으로 칠할까요?

(A) 최고 경영자가 녹색이 좋다고 했어요.

(B) 글쎄요, 제가 그걸 해도 좋아요.

(C) 페인트가 이제 다 말랐어요.

어휘 CEO 최고 경영자 (= Chief Executive Officer) mind ~을 싫어하다 dry 건조한, 마른

해설 단어를 연결한 선택의문문

(A) 정답. 로비를 파란색과 녹색 중 어떤 색으로 칠해야 할지에 대해 최고 경영자가 녹색이 좋다고 했다(The CEO said she prefers green.)면서 녹색으로 칠하자는 우회적 표현으로 응답하고 있으므로 정답.

(B) 연상 단어 오답. 질문의 paint the lobby에 대해 작업 측면에서 연상 가능한 doing it을 이용한 오답.

(C) 단어 반복 오답. 질문의 paint를 반복 이용한 오답.

21

W-Br We should get a vending machine for the cafeteria.

M-Cn (A) I'm not hungry right now.

(B) Oh, did it arrive already?

(C) Let's suggest it at the meeting.

구내식당에 자판기를 놓아야 해요.

(A) 지금은 배고프지 않아요.

(B) 오, 벌써 도착했어요?

(C) 회의 때 제안해 보죠.

어휘 vending machine 자판기 cafeteria 카페테리아, 구내식당

해설 의견 제시의 평서문

(A) 연상 단어 오답. 질문의 cafeteria에서 연상 가능한 hungry를 이용한 오답.

(B) 질문과 상관없는 오답. 구내식당에 자판기가 필요하다는 의견에 대해 벌써 도착했는지(did it arrive already?)를 묻는 것은 맥락에서 벗어난 응답이므로 오답.

(C) 정답. 구내식당에 자판기를 놓자는 의견에 회의 때 제안해 보자(Let's suggest it at the meeting.)고 답변했으므로 정답.

22

M-Au Have you visited our dental clinic before?

W-Br (A) Toothpaste is in Aisle Four.

(B) I just moved to this city in January.

(C) Doctor Hayashi is available.

전에 저희 치과 방문한 적 있으세요?

(A) 치약은 네 번째 통로에 있어요.

(B) 이제 막 1월에 이 도시로 이사 왔어요.

(C) 하야시 선생님께서 계십니다.

어휘 dental clinic 치과 toothpaste 치약 aisle 통로 available 만날 수 있는, 이용할 수 있는

해설 치과 방문 경험을 묻는 일반 의문문

(A) 연상 단어 오답. 질문의 dental clinic에서 연상 가능한 Toothpaste를 이용한 오답.

(B) 정답. 치과를 방문한 적 있는지 묻는 질문에 이제 막 1월에 이 도시로 이사 왔다는 우회적인 답변을 하고 있으므로 정답.

(C) 연상 단어 오답. 질문의 dental clinic에서 연상 가능한 Doctor를 이용한 오답.

23

M-Cn You have to wear a safety helmet on the factory floor.

M-Au (A) Where can I get one?

(B) On the list of guidelines.

(C) These floors are hard to damage.

공장의 작업 현장에서는 안전모를 착용해야 해요.

(A) 어디서 하나 받을 수 있죠?

(B) 지침 목록에요.

(C) 이 바닥들은 잘 손상되지 않아요.

어휘 safety helmet 안전모 factory floor (공장의) 작업 현장 guideline 지침, 수칙, 가이드라인 floor 바닥, 마루 damage 손상시키다

해설 요청/정보 전달의 평서문

(A) 정답. 안전모를 착용해야 한다는 말에 대해 어디서 안전모를 하나 받을 수 있는지(Where can I get one?) 되묻고 있으므로 정답.

(B) 연상 단어 오답. 평서문의 wear a safety helmet에서 연상 가능한 guidelines를 이용한 오답.

(C) 단어 반복 오답. 질문의 floor를 반복 이용한 오답.

24

W-Am Do you want to water the plants or empty the trash bins?

M-Cn (A) The container behind the building.

(B) I was going to clean the counters.

(C) That's very kind of you.

화초에 물 줄래요, 쓰레기통 비울래요?

(A) 건물 뒤에 있는 통이요.

(B) 조리대를 닦으려고 했는데요.

(C) 정말 친절하십니다.

어휘 water 물을 주다 plant 식물, 화초 empty 비우다 trash bin 쓰레기통 container 그릇, 용기, 통 counter 조리대

해설 구를 연결한 선택의문문

(A) 연상 단어 오답. 질문의 empty에 대해 비우는 대상 측면에서 연상 가능한 container를 이용한 오답.

(B) 정답. 질문의 선택사항으로 언급된 water the plants나 empty the trash bins 대신, 제3의 선택사항을 제시한 것이므로 정답.

(C) 질문과 상관없는 오답. 누군가 친절을 베풀었을 때 어울리는 응답이므로 오답.

25

W-Br Why don't we hire a graphic designer to create the logo?

M-Au (A) It's a beautiful design.

(B) A chart might be better than a graph.

(C) How much would that cost?

로고를 만들 그래픽 디자이너를 고용하는 게 어때요?

(A) 아름다운 디자인이군요.

(B) 그래프보다는 도표가 더 나을 것 같아요.

(C) 그러면 비용이 얼마나 들까요?

어휘 hire 고용하다 logo (상품명·회사명의) 로고 chart 차트, 도표 cost (돈·시간·노력 등이) 들다

해설 그래픽 디자이너 고용 관련 제안 의문문

(A) 파생어 오답. 질문의 designer와 파생어 관계에 있는 명사 design을 이용한 오답.

(B) 연상 단어 오답. 질문의 graphic에서 연상 가능한 chart와 graph를 이용한 오답.

(C) 정답. 실내 디자이너를 고용하자는 제안에 대해 동의나 반대를 유보한 채 비용이 얼마나 들지(How much would that cost)를 되물으며 질문자에게 추가 정보를 요청하고 있으므로 정답.

26

M-Cn Why is the project so far behind schedule?

W-Am (A) Shipping issues, I think.

(B) Next week works for me.

(C) It's not too far from here.

그 프로젝트는 일정보다 왜 그렇게나 많이 늦나요?

(A) 운송 문제 때문인 것 같아요.

(B) 저는 다음 주가 좋아요.

(C) 여기서 그다지 멀지 않아요.

어휘 far 멀리, 훨씬 behind schedule 일정에 뒤처진 shipping 운송, 선적

해설 프로젝트가 지연되는 이유를 묻는 Why 의문문

(A) 정답. 프로젝트가 왜 일정보다 많이 늦어지는지에 대해 운송 문제인 것 같다(Shipping issues, I think.)는 이유를 제시하므로 정답.

(B) 연상 단어 오답. 질문의 schedule에서 연상 가능한 Next week를 이용한 오답.

(C) 단어 반복 오답. 질문의 far를 반복 이용한 오답.

27

M-Au The advertisement for the sales position has been posted, right?

M-Br (A) Some nice discounts on sportswear.

(B) Applications started coming in this morning.

(C) Yes, they're filming it at the Rinksville store.

판매직 구인 광고 게시됐지요?

(A) 운동복에 대한 괜찮은 할인이요.

(B) 오늘 아침에 지원서가 들어오기 시작했어요.

(C) 네, 링크스빌 상점에서 그걸 촬영하고 있어요.

어휘 sales position 판매직 post 게시하다 sportswear 운동복 application 지원, 지원서 film 촬영하다

해설 광고 게시 여부를 확인하는 부가의문문

(A) 연상 단어 오답. 질문의 sales에서 연상 가능한 discounts를 이용한 오답.

(B) 정답. 구인 광고 게시를 확인하는 질문에 오늘 아침에 지원서가 들어오기 시작했다는 우회적인 답변을 하고 있으므로 정답.

(C) 연상 단어 오답. 질문의 advertisement에서 연상 가능한 filming을 이용한 오답.

28

M-Cn I'd also like to book a hotel room and rental car with my flight.

W-Br (A) OK, we have a great package deal for you.

(B) Sorry, that flight is full.

(C) I always read on the plane, too.

제 항공편과 함께 호텔 객실과 렌터카도 예약하고 싶습니다.

(A) 네, 고객님을 위한 좋은 패키지 상품이 있습니다.

(B) 죄송합니다만 그 항공편은 만석입니다.

(C) 저도 비행기에서는 항상 책을 읽어요.

어휘 book 예약하다 package deal 일괄 계약 상품

해설 문의/요청의 평서문

(A) 정답. 항공편과 함께 호텔방과 렌터카를 예약하고 싶다는 요청에 대해 먼저 OK로 긍정적 응답을 한 후, 좋은 패키지 상품이 있다(we have a great package deal for you.)는 말로 답변하므로 정답.

(B) 단어 반복 오답. 질문의 flight를 반복 이용한 오답.

(C) 연상 단어 오답. 질문의 book을 '책'으로 잘못 이해했을 때 독서 측면에서 연상 가능한 read를 이용한 오답.

29

W-Am Can we play music at the company picnic?

M-Cn (A) He's a local jazz musician.

(B) We're planning to serve sandwiches.

(C) The park has rules about making noise.

우리 회사 야유회 때 음악을 연주해도 될까요?

(A) 그는 이 지역 재즈 음악가예요.

(B) 우리는 샌드위치를 제공할 계획이에요.

(C) 그 공원에는 소음 관련 규정이 있어요.

어휘 local 지역의 serve (음식을) 차려 내다 rule 규칙, 규정 make noise 소음을 내다

해설 부탁/요청의 의문문

(A) 파생어 오답. 질문의 music과 파생어 관계인 musician을 이용한 오답.

(B) 연상 단어 오답. 질문의 picnic에서 연상 가능한 sandwiches를 이용한 오답.

(C) 정답. 회사 야유회 때 음악을 연주해도 되는지 묻는 질문에 공원에는 소음 관련 규정(rules about making noise)이 있다는 우회적인 답변으로 부정적인 응답을 하고 있으므로 정답.

30

M-Au When does this report need to be finished?

W-Br (A) No more than five pages.

(B) There's no hurry.

(C) That's what Audrey told me.

이 보고서는 언제까지 완료되어야 하죠?

(A) 5페이지를 넘지 않아요.

(B) 급한 건 아니에요.

(C) 오드리가 내게 그렇게 말했어요.

어휘 no more than ~가 넘지 않게, 딱 ~ 정도 hurry 매우 급함

해설 보고서 완료 시점을 묻는 When 의문문

(A) 연상 단어 오답. 질문의 report에 대해 분량 측면에서 연상 가능한 five pages를 이용한 오답.

(B) 정답. 보고서 완료 시점을 묻는 질문에 대해 정확한 시점을 피한 채 급한 건 아니다(There's no hurry.)라는 불확실성 표현으로 응답하므로 정답.

(C) 질문과 상관없는 오답. 보고서 완료 시점을 묻는 질문에 오드리가 그렇게 말했다는 답변은 질문의 맥락에서 벗어난 것이므로 오답.

31

M-Cn What will the president's press conference be about?

W-Am (A) This conference center is usually quite busy.

(B) The topic hasn't been announced yet.

(C) I'll start practicing my speech.

대통령의 기자 회견은 무엇에 관한 걸까요?

(A) 회의 센터는 대개 아주 붐벼요.

(B) 주제가 아직 발표되지 않았어요.

(C) 난 연설 연습을 시작할 거예요.

어휘 press conference 기자 회견 conference 회의, 학회 announce 발표하다 practice 연습하다

해설 기자 회견 주제를 묻는 What 의문문

(A) 단어 반복 오답. 질문에 나온 conference를 반복한 오답.

(B) 정답. 기자 회견(press conference)이 무엇에 관한 것인지 묻는 질문에 주제가 아직 발표되지 않았다는 불확실성 표현으로 응답하고 있으므로 정답.

(C) 연상 단어 오답. 질문의 conference에서 연상 가능한 speech를 이용한 오답.

PART 3

32-34

M-Au Hi, Carla. It's Sanjay in the research department. [32]**Do you remember how all the employees received new business cards after our company moved to the new offices last month?**

W-Br Yes, they should've arrived last week. Did you not receive yours?

M-Au Actually, I got them, but there was an error on my cards. The new address is correct, but [33]**my office extension number should be ninety-two, not seventy-two.**

W-Br Oh, I'm sorry about that, Sanjay. You can request new cards through the company's online system. If you have some time now, [34]**why don't you sign in and I can take you through the instructions?** The steps can be a bit confusing.

남: 칼라 씨, 안녕하세요. 연구부의 산제이입니다. **우리 회사가 지난달 새 사무실로 이사한 후 모든 직원이 새 명함을 받은 거 기억하세요?**

여: 네, 명함이 지난주에 도착했어야 하는데요. 못 받으셨어요?

남: 사실 받았는데 내 명함에 오류가 있어요. 새 주소는 맞는데 **내 내선번호는 72가 아니라 92여야 해요.**

여: 아, 죄송해요, 산제이 씨. 회사의 온라인 시스템을 통해 새 명함을 요청하실 수 있어요. 지금 시간이 되시면 **로그인하셔서 제가 설명대로 하실 수 있게 도와드리면 어때요?** 절차가 약간 헷갈리기 쉬워서요.

어휘 business card 명함 correct 정확한 extension 내선 전화 take A(사람) through B A가 B를 통과하도록 하다 instructions 지시, 설명 step 단계 confusing 혼란시키는

32

What did the speakers' company do last month?

(A) It redecorated its offices.
(B) It recruited new researchers.
(C) It merged some departments.
(D) It moved to a new location.

화자들의 회사는 지난달에 무엇을 했는가?

(A) 사무실을 개조했다.
(B) 새 연구원들을 채용했다.
(C) 일부 부서를 통합했다.
(D) 새로운 곳으로 이전했다.

해설 세부 사항 관련 – 회사가 지난달에 한 일

남자의 첫 번째 대사에서 회사가 지난달 새 사무실로 이사한 후 모든 직원이 새 명함을 받았다(Do you remember ~ last month?)고 했으므로 정답은 (D)이다.

▸▸ **Paraphrasing** 대화의 **moved to the new offices**
→ 정답의 **moved to a new location**

33

What information is incorrect on the man's business cards?

(A) A phone number
(B) An address
(C) A name
(D) A job title

남자의 명함에 어떤 정보가 잘못되었는가?

(A) 전화번호
(B) 주소
(C) 이름
(D) 직책

해설 세부 사항 관련 – 명함에서 잘못된 정보

남자의 두 번째 대사에서 사무실 내선번호가 72가 아니라 92여야 한다(my office extension number should be ninety-two, not seventy-two)고 했으므로 정답은 (A)이다.

▸▸ **Paraphrasing** 대화의 **my office extension number**
→ 정답의 **a phone number**

34

What does the woman suggest the man do next?

(A) Read an instruction manual
(B) Write a note on a business card
(C) Log in to a computer system
(D) Call a technical support team

여자는 남자에게 다음에 무엇을 하라고 제안하는가?

(A) 사용설명서 읽기
(B) 명함에 메모하기
(C) 컴퓨터 시스템에 로그인하기
(D) 기술지원팀에 전화하기

어휘 obtain 얻다, 획득하다

해설 세부 사항 관련 – 여자의 제안 사항

여자의 두 번째 대사에서 남자에게 지금 시간이 되면 로그인해서 설명대로 하도록 도와주겠다(why don't you sign in and I can take you through the instructions?)는 제안을 했으므로 정답은 (C)이다.

▸▸ **Paraphrasing** 대화의 **sign in** → 정답의 **log in to a computer system**

35-37

M-Au Excuse me, [35]**I bought a Maximus 94 video camera at this store last week, but I just saw the price has dropped by twenty euros.**

W-Am Yes, that camera started being sold at a cheaper price on Monday. Fortunately, our store offers a product price match for thirty days. So just bring in proof of purchase and we'll refund you the difference between your purchase price and the current sales price.

M-Au Hmm... [36]**I don't remember where my receipt is.**

W-Am Well, we don't have any other way of confirming the price at which you bought the item. But [37]**let me check with my manager to see if there's anything else we can do.**

남: 실례합니다. **지난주에 이 가게에서 막시무스 94 비디오 카메라를 구매했는데요, 방금 가격이 20유로 내린 걸 봤어요.**

여: 네, 그 카메라는 월요일부터 더 저렴한 가격으로 판매되기 시작했어요. 다행히 저희 가게는 30일간 제품 최저가 보상을 제공합니다. 구매 증거만 가져오시면 구매하신 금액과 현재 할인 가격의 차액만큼 저희가 환불해 드리겠습니다.

남: 흠… **영수증이 어디 있는지 모르겠어요.**

여: 음, 제품을 구매하신 가격을 확인할 다른 방법이 없습니다. 하지만 **저희가 달리 할 수 있는 게 있는지 관리자에게 확인해 볼게요.**

어휘 drop 떨어지다 fortunately 다행히도 price match 최저가 보상제 proof of purchase 구매 증거 (구매자 이름이나 판매 일자 등을 증명할 수 있는 것) refund 환불하다 confirm 확인해 주다, 확정하다

35

What did the man notice about the Maximus 94?

(A) A new version
(B) A recall announcement
(C) An additional color option
(D) A price decrease

남자는 막시무스 94에 대해 무엇을 알아냈는가?

(A) 새 버전
(B) 리콜 공표
(C) 추가 색상 옵션
(D) 가격 인하

어휘 recall (결함 상품의) 회수, 리콜

해설 세부 사항 관련 – 남자가 막시무스 94에 대해 발견한 점

대화 맨 처음에 남자가 지난주에 여자의 가게에서 막시무스 94 비디오 카메라를 구입했는데 방금 가격이 20유로 내린 걸 봤다(I bought a Maximus 94 ~ by twenty euros.)고 했으므로 정답은 (D)이다.

▸▸ **Paraphrasing** 대화의 **the price has dropped**
→ 정답의 **a price decrease**

36

What problem does the man have?

(A) He has misplaced a receipt.
(B) He forgot to bring a coupon.
(C) He cut a tag off a product.
(D) He does not have cash.

남자는 어떤 문제가 있다고 언급하는가?

(A) 영수증을 어디에 두었는지 잊어버렸다.
(B) 쿠폰을 가져오는 걸 잊어 버렸다.
(C) 물건에서 가격표를 떼어냈다.
(D) 현금이 없다.

어휘 misplace ~을 놓고 잊어버리다 tag 꼬리표

해설 세부 사항 관련 – 남자가 언급하는 문제점

남자의 두 번째 대사에서 영수증이 어디 있는지 모르겠다(I don't remember where my receipt is.)고 했으므로 정답은 (A)이다.

37

What does the woman say she will do next?

(A) Speak to a supervisor
(B) Exchange an item
(C) Check some inventory
(D) Give the man some paperwork

여자는 다음에 무엇을 하겠다고 말하는가

(A) 상사에게 이야기하기
(B) 물품 교환하기
(C) 재고 확인하기
(D) 남자에게 서류 업무 주기

해설 세부 사항 관련 – 여자의 다음 행동

대화 맨 마지막에 여자가 달리 할 수 있는 게 있는지 관리자에게 확인해 보겠다(let me check with my manager to see if there's anything else we can do.)고 했으므로 정답은 (A)이다.

▸▸ **Paraphrasing** 대화의 **check with my manager**
→ 정답의 **speak to a supervisor**

38-40

M-Cn Darland Rental Cars. How may I help you?

W-Br Hi. If I'm riding the Northern Line train, which one of your locations should I rent a car from to visit Sparret Castle? [38]**The train doesn't go there.**

M-Cn Let me check... It looks like our Nellshire location is the closest one on the Northern Line.

W-Br Great. Can I make a reservation now? It's for June fourth, and I'd like a Grenzel Motors sedan. Oh, and with a navigation system, because [39]**I don't want to spend the day getting lost.**

M-Cn Hmm... [40]**we don't have any Grenzel Motors sedans available on that day.** But the Grenzel compact car has a navigation system.

W-Br Well, I guess that would be all right.

남: 달란드 렌탈 카즈입니다. 무엇을 도와드릴까요?
여: 안녕하세요. 제가 노던 라인 열차를 타고 갈 경우, 스패럿 성을 방문하려면 그 회사 사무소 중 어느 지점에서 차를 빌려야 할까요? **기차가 거기까지 안 가거든요.**
남: 확인해 볼게요… 저희 넬셔 사무소가 노던 라인에서 가장 가까운 곳인 것 같네요.
여: 좋습니다. 지금 예약을 할 수 있을까요? 6월 4일이고요, 그렌젤 모터스 세단을 원합니다. 아, 네비게이션이 달린 거로요. **길을 잃고 하루 종일 시간을 허비하고 싶지는 않거든요.**
남: 음… **그날은 이용할 수 있는 그렌젤 모터스 세단이 없네요.** 하지만 그렌젤 소형차에 네비게이션이 달려 있습니다.
여: 음, 그것도 괜찮을 거 같네요.

어휘 location 지점, 지사 rent (집, 차를) 임차하다, 빌리다 make a reservation 예약을 하다 sedan 세단형 자동차 get lost 길을 잃다 compact car 소형 승용차

38

What does the woman say about a train?

(A) Its seats are uncomfortable.
(B) Its tickets are difficult to obtain.
(C) It does not serve a certain destination.
(D) It does not run frequently.

여자는 기차에 대해 무슨 얘기를 하는가?

(A) 좌석이 불편하다.
(B) 승차권을 구하기 힘들다.
(C) 특정 목적지까지는 차편이 없다.
(D) 자주 운행하지 않는다.

어휘 seat 좌석 uncomfortable 불편한 obtain 입수하다 serve (교통 서비스를) 제공하다 destination 목적지, 행선지 run (정기 노선이) 운행하다 frequently 자주

해설 세부 사항 관련 – 기차에 대해 언급된 사항

여자의 첫 번째 대사에서 스패럿 성을 방문하려는 계획을 언급하며 기차가 거기까지 안 간다(The train doesn't go there.)고 했으므로 정답은 (C)이다.

39

What does the woman want to avoid doing?

(A) Losing her luggage
(B) Using her time poorly
(C) Spending a lot of money
(D) Driving on narrow roads

여자는 무엇을 피하고 싶어 하는가?

(A) 수하물 분실
(B) 시간 낭비
(C) 과다 지출
(D) 좁은 도로 운전

어휘 avoid 피하다 luggage 짐, 수하물 poorly 좋지 못하게, 형편없이 narrow 좁은

해설 세부 사항 관련 – 여자가 피하고 싶은 것

여자의 두 번째 대사에서 길을 잃고 하루 종일 시간을 허비하고 싶지 않다(I don't want to spend the day getting lost.)고 했으므로 정답은 (B)이다.

40

Why does the man say, "the Grenzel compact car has a navigation system"?

(A) To suggest an alternative vehicle
(B) To explain a high rental fee
(C) To correct an inaccurate description
(D) To reassure the woman about a trip

남자가 "그렌젤 소형차에 네비게이션이 달려 있습니다"라고 말한 이유는 무엇인가?

(A) 대안 차량을 제안하려고
(B) 비싼 대여료를 해명하려고
(C) 잘못된 묘사를 바로잡으려고
(D) 여자에게 여행에 대해 안심시키려고

어휘 suggest 제안하다 alternative 대안의 vehicle 차량 rental fee 대여료 correct 바로잡다 inaccurate 부정확한, 틀린 description 서술, 묘사, 표현 reassure 안심시키다

해설 화자의 의도 파악 – 그렌젤 소형 승용차에도 네비게이션이 있다고 말한 이유

인용문 바로 앞 문장에서 남자는 그날은 이용할 수 있는 그렌젤 모터스 세단이 없다(we don't have any Grenzel Motors sedans available on that day)고 했다. 그러나 이어서 그렌젤 소형차에 네비게이션이 달려 있다고 했으므로, 대안 차량을 제안하기 위해 말했음을 알 수 있어 정답은 (A)이다.

41-43

M-Cn Amber, I heard your team's research is going well.
W-Am Yeah, [41]**we finished collecting all of our samples yesterday and took them down to the laboratory for testing.** I saw some of the data, and it looks really promising.
M-Cn That's great. Speaking of data... [42]**I was trying to input some information into our database, but I ran into some problems. Do you think you could help me with that?** My supervisor's out today.
W-Am Sure. [43]**I'm planning on stepping outside and resting for a bit right now, but I could drop by your desk afterwards.** Uh... let's say at four o'clock.

남: 앰버 씨, 당신 팀의 연구가 잘 진행되고 있다고 들었어요.
여: 네, **어제 전체 샘플 수집을 완료했고 검사를 위해 실험실로 가져갔어요.** 데이터를 일부 봤는데 조짐이 무척 좋아요.
남: 그거 잘됐군요. 데이터에 대해 말인데… **저는 데이터베이스에 일부 정보를 입력하려고 했지만 몇 가지 문제에 부딪혔어요. 이 부분을 도와주실 수 있나요?** 제 상사분이 오늘 없거든요.
여: 물론이죠. **지금 당장은 밖에 나가서 잠시 휴식을 취하려고 하고요, 나중에 당신 자리에 들를게요.** 어… 일단 4시로 하죠.

어휘 research 연구, 조사 go well 잘되다 sample 샘플, 표본 laboratory 실험실 promising 유망한, 조짐이 좋은 speaking of ~에 관해 말한다면 input 입력하다 run into ~와 충돌하다, 우연히 만나다 step outside 밖으로 나가다 drop by ~에 잠깐 들르다

41

Who most likely is the woman?

(A) A lawyer
(B) A reporter
(C) A scientist
(D) An architect

여자는 누구일 것 같은가?

(A) 변호사
(B) 리포터
(C) 과학자
(D) 건축가

해설 전체 내용 관련 – 여자의 신분

여자의 첫 번째 대사에서 어제 전체 샘플 수집을 완료했고 검사를 위해 실험실로 가져갔다(we finished collecting all ~ for testing.)고 했으므로 정답은 (C)이다.

42

What does the man ask the woman to do?

(A) Consult with a manager
(B) Assist with a task
(C) Present some statistics
(D) Postpone a deadline

남자는 여자에게 무엇을 해달라고 요청하는가?

(A) 관리자와 협의하기
(B) 업무 도와주기
(C) 통계 보여주기
(D) 마감일 연기하기

어휘 present 보이다 statistics 통계 자료 postpone 연기하다, 미루다 deadline 마감(일), 최종 기한

해설 세부 사항 관련 – 남자의 요청 사항

남자의 두 번째 대사에서 데이터베이스에 일부 정보를 입력하려고 했지만 몇 가지 문제에 부딪혔는데 이 부분을 도와줄 수 있는지(I was trying to input some information ~ with that?) 여자에게 물어봤으므로 정답은 (B)이다.

▸▸ **Paraphrasing** 대화의 **help** → 정답의 **assist**

43

What will the woman most likely do next?

(A) Install a computer program
(B) Look through a database
(C) Send a package
(D) Take a break

여자는 다음에 무엇을 할 것 같은가?

(A) 컴퓨터 프로그램 설치하기
(B) 데이터베이스 훑어보기
(C) 소포 보내기
(D) 휴식 취하기

해설 세부 사항 관련 – 여자의 다음 행동

여자의 두 번째 대사에서 지금 당장은 밖에 나가서 잠시 휴식을 취할 거고 나중에 자리에 들르겠다(I'm planning on ~ drop by your desk afterwards.)고 했으므로 정답은 (D)이다.

▸▸ **Paraphrasing** 대화의 **resting** → 정답의 **take a break**

44-46 3인 대화

W-Am [44]**Welcome to Ganswell Financial.** How can I help you today?

M-Au [44,45]**I read about your special savings accounts for aspiring homeowners, and I like that they have a high rate of return. So I want to start one.**

W-Am Wonderful! It looks like one of our specialist representatives is free now, so please follow me to her desk. Ms. Jung, this gentleman would like to sign up for a New Home Saver.

W-Br Thank you, Luanne. Have a seat, sir. Now, before we start any paperwork, let me ask you about your situation.

M-Au Sure.

W-Br First, [46]**how much do you have saved already?**

M-Au About twenty thousand dollars.

W-Br OK, that's good. You'll qualify for some favorable terms.

여1: **갠즈웰 파이낸셜에 오신 걸 환영합니다.** 오늘은 무엇을 도와드릴까요?

남: **향후 주택 소유를 목표로 하는 사람들을 위한 특별한 저축 예금에 관해 읽었는데요, 수익률이 높은 게 마음에 들었습니다. 그래서 하나 개설하고 싶어요.**

여1: 좋습니다! 우리 전문 직원 하나가 지금 짬이 나는 것 같으니 제가 그쪽 책상으로 안내해드리겠습니다. 정 씨, 이 분께서 뉴 홈 세이버를 신청하고 싶어 하십니다.

여2: 감사합니다, 루앤. 앉으세요, 선생님. 자, 서류 작성을 시작하기 전에, 선생님 조건에 대해 질문드리겠습니다.

남: 네.

여2: 우선, **지금까지 얼마나 저축을 하셨습니까?**

남: 2만 달러 정도요.

여2: 네, 좋습니다. 선생님은 유리한 조건을 적용받을 자격이 되실 거예요.

어휘 savings account 저축 예금 aspiring 장차 ~가 되려는, 야망[포부] 있는 homeowner 주택 소유자 rate of return 수익률 specialist 전문가 representative (회사, 기관을 대표하는) 직원 sign up for ~을 신청하다 have a seat 앉다 paperwork 서류 작업 situation 상황 save 저축하다 qualify for ~을 가질 자격이 있다 favorable terms 유리한 조건

Test 8

44

Where does the conversation take place?

(A) At a bank
(B) At a real estate agency
(C) At a utility company
(D) At a newspaper office

대화는 어디에서 일어나는가?

(A) 은행
(B) 부동산 중개소
(C) 공익 기업
(D) 신문사

어휘 real estate agency 부동산 중개소 utility company (전기, 가스, 전화 등의) 공익 기업

해설 전체 내용 관련 – 대화 장소

첫 번째 여자가 첫 대사에서 갠즈웰 파이낸셜에 온 것을 환영한다(Welcome to Ganswell Financial.)고 했고, 이어서 남자가 이곳의 특별 저축 예금에 관해 읽었다(I read about your special savings accounts)고 했으므로 정답은 (A)이다.

45

What is the purpose of the man's visit?

(A) To propose a partnership
(B) To file a complaint
(C) To make an inquiry
(D) To open an account

남자가 방문한 목적은 무엇인가?

(A) 동업을 제안하려고
(B) 불만을 제기하려고
(C) 문의하려고
(D) 계좌를 개설하려고

어휘 propose 제안하다 partnership 동업 file a complaint 불만을 제기하다 inquiry 질문, 문의 open an account 계좌를 개설하다

해설 세부 사항 관련 – 남자의 방문 목적

남자의 첫 번째 대사에서 향후 주택 소유를 목표로 하는 사람들을 위한 특별한 저축 예금에 관해 읽었는데 수익률이 높은 게 마음에 든다며 하나 개설하고 싶다(I read about your special savings ~ I want to start one.)고 했으므로 정답은 (D)이다.

46

What information does Ms. Jung ask the man for?

(A) A business's name
(B) A starting date
(C) An amount of money
(D) A property's location

정 씨는 남자에게 어떤 정보를 문의하는가?

(A) 사업장 이름
(B) 시작일
(C) 돈의 액수
(D) 부동산의 위치

어휘 amount 총액, 액수 property 부동산, 건물 location 위치

해설 세부 사항 관련 – 남자에게 문의하는 정보

첫 번째 여자의 두 번째 대사를 통해 두 번째 여자가 정 씨임을 알 수 있다. 두 번째 여자의 두 번째 대사에서 지금까지 얼마나 저축했는지(how much do you have saved already?) 물어보고 있으므로 정답은 (C)이다.

47-49

W-Br Hi. I need to set up a beverage refrigerator in my restaurant. [47]**I want it to be easy for customers to see what type of drinks we sell and grab them from the refrigerator themselves.** Could you recommend a good one to me?

M-Cn Of course. The G4 is the best one on the market right now. [48]**It has five removable shelves. And you can change the height of each shelf according to the size of your bottles or cans.** It holds up to two hundred beverages.

W-Br Hmm... If you don't mind, [49]**I'd like you to show me how that works.** Is there one in the store?

여: 안녕하세요. 제 식당에 음료용 냉장고를 설치해야 해서요. **고객들이 저희가 어떤 종류의 음료를 판매하는지 보고 냉장고에서 직접 꺼내기에 쉬웠으면 좋겠어요.** 좋은 냉장고를 추천해 주실 수 있나요?

남: 물론입니다. 지금 시장에선 G4가 가장 좋습니다. **떼어낼 수 있는 선반이 다섯 개 있어요. 그리고 병이나 캔의 크기에 따라 각 선반의 높이를 조정할 수 있고요.** 음료수가 최고 200개까지 들어갑니다.

여: 음… 괜찮으시다면 **그것이 어떻게 작동하는지 제게 보여 주셨으면 합니다.** 이 매장에 있나요?

어휘 set up 설치하다 beverage 음료수 refrigerator 냉장고 grab 잡다 recommend 추천하다 removable 떼어낼 수 있는 height 높이 according to ~에 따라

47

What does the woman want to do in her restaurant?

(A) Increase convenience
(B) Reduce expenses
(C) Improve security
(D) Provide entertainment

여자는 자신의 식당에 무엇을 하고 싶어하는가?

(A) 편의성 증진
(B) 비용 절감
(C) 보안 강화
(D) 여흥 제공

해설 세부 사항 관련 – 여자가 자신의 식당에 하고 싶은 일

대화 초반에 여자가 자신의 식당에서 고객들이 어떤 종류의 음료를 판매하는지 보고 냉장고에서 직접 꺼내기에 쉬웠으면 좋겠다(I want it to be easy ~ from the refrigerator themselves.)고 했으므로 정답은 (A)이다.

48

What does the man mention about the G4?

(A) It is a wireless device.
(B) It has adjustable components.
(C) It is energy efficient.
(D) It comes in five colors.

남자는 G4에 대해 뭐라고 말하는가?

(A) 무선 기기이다.
(B) 조절 가능한 부품이 있다.
(C) 에너지 효율적이다.
(D) 다섯 가지 색상이 있다.

어휘 wireless 무선의 adjustable 조절할 수 있는 component 부품, 구성요소 energy efficient 에너지 효율적인

해설 세부 사항 관련 - G4에 대한 남자의 언급

남자의 첫 번째 대사에서 G4에는 떼어낼 수 있는 선반 다섯 개가 있으며 병이나 캔의 크기에 따라 각 선반의 높이를 조정할 수 있다(It has five removable ~ bottles or cans.)고 했으므로 정답은 (B)이다.

▸▸ **Paraphrasing** 대화의 **change the height of each shelf**
→ 정답의 **has adjustable components**

49

What does the woman ask the man to do?

(A) Replace a machine part
(B) Give a demonstration
(C) Confirm a model number
(D) Arrange a shipment

여자는 남자에게 무엇을 하라고 요청하는가?

(A) 기계 부품 교체
(B) 시연
(C) 모델 번호 확인
(D) 배송 처리

해설 세부 사항 관련 - 여자의 요청 사항

대화 맨 마지막에 여자가 남자에게 어떻게 작동하는지 보여달라고 요청(I'd like you to show me how that works.)했으므로 정답은 (B)이다.

▸▸ **Paraphrasing** 대화의 **show me how that works**
→ 정답의 **give a demonstration**

50-52

W-Am Hello again. [50]**I finished my job interview with Mr. Goldberg at Plath Corporation,** so I came to return the visitor's badge to you.

M-Au Oh, thank you. I hope your interview went well.

W-Am It did, thanks. Uh, [51]**I parked my car in the parking garage, and I was told I wouldn't have to pay if I get a validation ticket.** Mr. Goldberg mentioned I could ask you...

M-Au Yeah... OK, here you go. Just insert this ticket into the machine when you exit the parking garage and the gate should open. Also, [52]**Piven Road is currently under construction, so you must use Maple Street instead when you drive out of the area.**

여: 다시 뵙네요. **플라스 주식회사에서 골드버그 씨와의 면접을 마쳤고요,** 방문자용 배지를 돌려드리려고 왔어요.

남: 아, 감사합니다. 면접이 잘 진행됐기를 바랍니다.

여: 잘 진행됐어요. 고맙습니다. 어, **제가 주차장에 차를 세웠는데 확인증이 있으면 주차비를 내지 않아도 된다고 들었어요.** 골드버그 씨가 당신에게 요청하라고 하셨는데…

남: 네… 자, 여기 있습니다. 주차장에서 나가실 때 이 표를 기계에 넣으면 문이 열릴 겁니다. 그리고 **피벤 로드는 지금 공사 중이라 이 지역을 빠져 나갈 때는 대신 메이플 가를 이용해야 합니다.**

어휘 job interview 채용 면접 parking garage 주차장 mention 언급하다 validation 확인 insert 집어넣다 under construction 공사 중인

50

Why did the woman visit Plath Corporation?

(A) To meet a former colleague
(B) To have an interview
(C) To deliver a package
(D) To speak with a client

여자는 왜 플라스 주식회사를 방문했는가?

(A) 이전 직장 동료를 만나기 위해
(B) 면접을 보기 위해
(C) 소포를 배송하기 위해
(D) 고객과 면담하기 위해

어휘 former 이전의, 과거의 colleague 동료

해설 세부 사항 관련 - 여자의 방문 이유

여자의 첫 번째 대사에서 자신이 플라스 주식회사에서 골드버그 씨와의 면접을 마쳤다(I finished my job interview with Mr. Goldberg at Plath Corporation)고 했으므로 정답은 (B)이다.

51

What does the woman ask the man for?

(A) Some coins
(B) His signature
(C) Directions to a building
(D) Validation for parking

여자는 남자에게 무엇을 요청하는가?

(A) 동전
(B) 남자의 서명
(C) 건물로 가는 길
(D) 주차 확인

해설 세부 사항 관련 - 여자의 요청 사항

여자의 두 번째 대사에서 확인증이 있으면 주차비를 내지 않아도 된다는 얘기를 들었다(I parked my car ~ if I get a validation ticket.)고 했으므로 정답은 (D)이다.

▸▸ **Paraphrasing** 대화의 **a validation ticket**
→ 정답의 **validation for parking**

52

What problem does the man mention?

(A) A broken gate
(B) A slow machine
(C) A narrow exit path
(D) A road closure

남자는 어떤 문제를 언급하는가?

(A) 고장난 문
(B) 느린 기계
(C) 좁은 출구 길
(D) 도로 폐쇄

어휘 closure 폐쇄

해설 세부 사항 관련 - 남자가 언급하는 문제점

대화 맨 마지막에 남자가 피벤 로드는 지금 공사 중이라 지금 있는 지역을 빠져나갈 때는 대신 메이플 가를 이용해야 한다(Piven Road is currently under construction ~ out of the area.)고 했으므로 정답은 (D)이다.

▸▸ **Paraphrasing** 대화의 **Piven Road is currently under construction** → 정답의 **a road closure**

53-55

M-Cn Hello. 53**I'd like fifteen tickets for the seven o'clock performance of Fordham's Ballet on September fourth.**

W-Am Sure. 54**Since you have a group of ten or more, you're eligible to receive a discount.** If you're a member of our theater, you can receive an additional five percent off all tickets. Would you like to sign up?

M-Cn Hmm... no, thank you.

W-Am OK. 55**Do you like to sit close to the stage?** I have seats in the seventh row, where you can see all the dancers up close. 55**Or would you prefer a view of the entire stage?** I also have seats up in the balcony.

남: 안녕하세요. **9월 4일 7시에 있을 포드햄 발레 공연 표 15장을 사려고요.**

여: 네. **10인 이상의 단체 고객이시기 때문에 할인 받으실 수 있습니다.** 저희 극장 회원이 되시면 모든 표에 대해 추가로 5% 할인을 받으실 수 있고요. 가입하시겠어요?

남: 음, 아니요. 괜찮습니다.

여: 알겠습니다. **무대 가까이에 앉고 싶으신가요?** 모든 무희들을 바로 가까이에서 보실 수 있는 7열에 좌석이 있습니다. **아니면 전체 무대가 보이는 곳을 선호하세요?** 위쪽 발코니 좌석도 있어요.

어휘 performance 공연 be eligible to + 동사원형 ~할 자격이 있다 additional 추가의 sign up 가입하다, 등록하다 prefer 선호하다 entire 전체의 stage 무대

53

What type of performance is the man interested in?

(A) Comedy
(B) Dance
(C) Acting
(D) Singing

남자는 어떤 종류의 공연에 관심이 있는가?

(A) 코미디
(B) 춤
(C) 연기
(D) 노래

해설 세부 사항 관련 - 남자가 관심 갖는 공연

대화 맨 처음에 남자가 9월 4일 7시에 있을 포드햄 발레 공연 표 15장을 사겠다(I'd like fifteen tickets ~ performance of Fordham's Ballet on September fourth.)고 했으므로 정답은 (B)이다.

54

Why does the man qualify for a discount?

(A) He is purchasing more than ten tickets.
(B) He has a membership card.
(C) He is attending a show in the daytime.
(D) He is buying tickets on the day of the performance.

남자는 왜 할인 받을 자격이 되는가?

(A) 열 장 이상의 표를 구매해서
(B) 회원 카드를 소지하고 있어서
(C) 낮 시간대에 공연을 보러 가서
(D) 공연 당일에 티켓을 구매해서

해설 세부 사항 관련 - 남자가 할인을 받을 수 있는 이유

여자의 첫 번째 대사에서 남자의 단체가 10인 이상이기 때문에 할인을 받을 수 있다(Since you have ~ a discount.)고 했으므로 정답은 (A)이다.

▸▸ **Paraphrasing** 대화의 **are eligible to receive a discount**
→ 질문의 **qualify for a discount**

55

What information does the woman ask the man for?

(A) A card number
(B) An e-mail address
(C) A pick-up time
(D) A seating preference

여자는 남자에게 어떤 정보를 요청하는가?
(A) 카드 번호
(B) 이메일 주소
(C) 픽업 시간
(D) 선호하는 좌석

해설 세부 사항 관련 - 여자가 요청하는 정보
여자의 두 번째 대사에서 남자에게 무대 가까이 앉고 싶은지(Do you like to sit close to the stage?), 아니면 전체 무대가 보이는 곳을 선호하는지(Or would you prefer a view of the entire stage?)를 물어봤는데 이것은 선호하는 좌석에 대한 정보를 요청하는 것이므로 정답은 (D)이다.

56-58 3인 대화

M-Cn The last item on today's agenda is our upcoming feature in *Mighty Eats* magazine. [56]**A representative will come by our eatery next Thursday to take pictures of our dishes for it.** Does anyone have any suggestions for what to make?

W-Br How about our risotto, Miguel? It's our restaurant's signature dish.

M-Cn Well, [57]**we made that for the newspaper article a few months ago.**

M-Au Perhaps we should present something from our fall menu? After all, those are the dishes that'll be available when the magazine's published in October.

M-Cn Yes, I like that idea. [58]**Stephano, since you're in charge of that, let's get together after this meeting so I can get more information about the menu.**

남1: 오늘의 마지막 안건은 〈마이티 잇츠〉 잡지에 실릴 우리 업체의 특집기사입니다. **한 직원이 특집 기사에 실릴 우리 요리 사진을 찍기 위해 다음 주 목요일에 식당으로 올 겁니다.** 무엇을 만들어야 할지 제안하실 분 있나요?
여: 리소토가 어때요, 미겔 씨? 우리 레스토랑에서 가장 유명한 요리잖아요.
남1: 글쎄요, **그건 몇 달 전 신문 기사를 위해 만들었잖아요.**
남2: 아마도 우리 가을 메뉴 중에서 무언가를 보여줘야 하지 않나요? 결국, 그 메뉴들이 10월에 잡지가 발간될 때 판매할 요리들이잖아요.
남1: 네, 그거 좋네요. **스테파노 씨, 그 책임을 맡았으니 이 회의 후에 모입시다. 제가 메뉴에 대한 정보를 더 얻을 수 있도록요.**

어휘 agenda 안건 upcoming 다가오는 feature (신문, TV 등의) 특집 (기사, 방송); 특별히 포함하다 eatery 식당 suggestion 제안 risotto 리소토(이탈리아식 볶음밥) signature dish 요리사의 가장 유명한 요리 present 보여주다, 공개하다 available 이용 가능한 publish 출판하다 in charge of ~를 맡고 있는

56

Who will visit the restaurant on Thursday?
(A) A food critic
(B) A photographer
(C) A television producer
(D) A politician

누가 목요일에 음식점을 방문할 것인가?
(A) 음식 비평가
(B) 사진작가
(C) TV 프로듀서
(D) 정치인

해설 세부 사항 관련 - 목요일에 음식점에 올 사람
첫 번째 남자의 첫 번째 대사에서 한 직원이 다음 특집 기사에 실릴 요리 사진을 찍기 위해 다음 주 목요일에 식당으로 온다(A representative will come by our eatery ~ our dishes for it.)고 했으므로 정답은 (B)이다.

57

What concern does Miguel have about the signature dish?
(A) It must be prepared by the head chef.
(B) It takes too long to cook.
(C) It requires too many ingredients.
(D) It was already featured in a publication.

미겔은 식당의 가장 유명한 요리에 대해 무엇을 걱정하는가?
(A) 수석 주방장이 준비해야 한다.
(B) 조리에 시간이 너무 오래 걸린다.
(C) 너무 많은 재료가 필요하다.
(D) 이미 출판물에 실렸다.

해설 세부 사항 관련 - 가장 유명한 요리에 대한 미겔의 걱정
첫 번째 남자(미겔)의 두 번째 대사에서 그 리조토는 몇 달 전 어느 신문 기사를 위해 만들었다(we made that ~ a few months ago.)고 했으므로 정답은 (D)이다.

▸▸ **Paraphrasing** 대화의 **the newspaper article**
→ 정답의 **a publication**

Test 8

58

What will the men most likely do after the meeting?
(A) Inspect a kitchen
(B) Plan a business trip
(C) Review an advertisement
(D) Discuss a menu

남자들은 회의 후에 무엇을 할 것 같은가?
(A) 주방 점검하기
(B) 출장 계획하기
(C) 광고 검토하기
(D) 메뉴 상의하기

해설 세부 사항 관련 - 회의 후 남자들이 할 일
첫 번째 남자의 세 번째 대사에서 스테파노가 그 책임을 맡았으니 회의 후에 모여서 메뉴에 대한 더 많은 정보를 알려 달라(Stephano, since you're in charge of ~ about the menu.)고 했으므로 정답은 (D)이다.

59-61

W-Am Isaac, our shelves here at the front of the store look a little empty. [59]**If you'd like, I can fill them back up with some merchandise from the stockroom.**

M-Au That would be great, yes. In fact, [60]**I phoned our natural food supplier this morning to order more products**—just so we don't run out.

W-Am Great. And that reminds me—I heard we're exhibiting at this summer's food festival. [61]**Have you booked a booth yet?**

M-Au [61]**No, not yet.**

W-Am Well, I know the festival is several weeks away, but... it's going to be a really big event.

M-Au Hmm... OK. [61]**I'll check out the online booking form later today.**

여: 아이작, 가게 앞쪽에 있는 여기 선반들이 좀 비어 보이네요. **괜찮으시면 제가 창고의 물품을 가져다 다시 채워 넣을게요.**

남: 네, 그렇게 해주면 좋겠네요. 사실 **오늘 아침에 제품을 더 주문하기 위해 자연식품 공급업자에게 전화했어요.** 다 떨어지지 않게 하려고요.

여: 잘했네요. 그러고 보니, 우리 이번 여름 음식 축제 때 전시를 할 거라고 들었어요. **벌써 부스를 예약했나요?**

남: **아니요, 아직이요.**

여: 음, 축제 전까지 몇 주 남은 건 알지만… 정말 큰 행사가 될 거예요.

남: 음… 알았어요. **이따가 온라인 예약 신청 양식을 확인할게요.**

어휘 stockroom 물품 보관소, 창고 supplier 공급업자 run out 다 떨어지다 remind 상기시키다 exhibit 전시하다 booth (전시회장 등의) 전시 공간, 부스

59

What does the woman offer to do?

(A) Stock some shelves
(B) Clean a loading area
(C) Refill some cash registers
(D) Lead a store tour

여자는 무엇을 하겠다고 하는가?

(A) 선반 채우기
(B) 적하 구역 청소하기
(C) 계산대 다시 채우기
(D) 매장 견학 진행하기

어휘 stock (상품으로) 채우다

해설 세부 사항 관련 - 여자의 제안 사항

여자의 첫 번째 대사에서 남자에게 괜찮다면 창고의 물품을 가져다 다시 채워 넣겠다(If you'd like, I can fill them back up with some merchandise from the stockroom.)는 제안을 했으므로 정답은 (A)이다.

▸▸ **Paraphrasing** 대화의 **fill them back up**
→ 정답의 **stock some shelves**

60

What does the man say he did this morning?

(A) He assembled a display cabinet.
(B) He repaired some equipment.
(C) He placed a supply order.
(D) He visited a warehouse.

남자는 오늘 아침에 무엇을 했다고 하는가?

(A) 진열 캐비닛을 조립했다.
(B) 장비를 수리했다.
(C) 물품을 주문했다.
(D) 창고에 갔다.

어휘 place an order 주문하다

해설 세부 사항 관련 - 남자가 아침에 한 일

남자의 첫 번째 대사에서 오늘 아침에 제품을 더 주문하기 위해 자연식품 공급업자에게 전화를 했다(I phoned our natural food supplier this morning to order more products)고 했으므로 정답은 (C)이다.

▸▸ **Paraphrasing** 대화의 **order more products**
→ 정답의 **placed a supply order**

61

What does the woman imply when she says, "it's going to be a really big event"?

(A) The man will need several people to work in a booth.
(B) The man should make a reservation soon.
(C) She wants to help design an exhibit.
(D) She intends to request vacation time.

여자가 "정말 큰 행사가 될 거예요"라고 말한 의도는 무엇인가?

(A) 남자는 부스에서 일 할 사람이 몇 명 필요할 것이다.
(B) 남자가 곧 예약을 해야 한다.
(C) 여자는 전시회 기획을 도와주길 원한다.
(D) 여자가 휴가를 요청할 의도이다.

해설 화자의 의도 파악 - 정말 큰 행사가 될 거라는 말의 의도

여자가 남자에게 부스 예약을 했는지(Have you booked a booth yet?) 물어봤는데, 아직 안 했다고 했고 여자가 이 말을 한 후에 남자는 이따가 온라인 예약 신청 양식을 확인하겠다(I'll check out the online booking form later today.)고 했다. 즉, 예약을 하지 않았다는 남자의 말에 정말 큰 행사가 될 것이라고 여자가 응답한 것은 남자에게 서둘러 행사 부스를 예약하라는 의도를 전달했기 때문이므로 정답은 (B)이다.

62-64 대화+목차

W-Am Kyung-Soo, [62]**I'm struggling with the wording of a news release I've been assigned to write.** Do you have some time this afternoon to look over it?

M-Cn I'm sorry, but I'm really busy today. Have you checked *The Oliver Writing Handbook*? That always helps me. And [63]**it's our company's recommended**

writing guide for employees, which means that it won't give you any advice that management wouldn't like.

W-Am Oh, I don't know why I didn't think of that. Thanks!

M-Cn No problem. What do you have to write about, anyway?

W-Am [64]**You know how we're going to begin selling a new type of standing lamp next month?** I'm writing the announcement for that.

여: 경수 씨, **제가 작성을 맡은 보도 자료의 단어 선택 때문에 애를 먹고 있어요.** 오늘 오후에 검토 좀 해 주실 시간이 있는지요?

남: 죄송한데, 오늘은 정말 바빠요. 〈올리버 작문 안내서〉 보셨어요? 저는 그게 항상 도움이 되더라고요. 게다가 **그게 우리 회사에서 직원들에게 추천하는 작문 안내서니까** 경영진이 싫어할 만한 도움말은 없을 거예요.

여: 아, 왜 그 생각을 못했는지 모르겠네요. 고마워요!

남: 뭘요. 그런데 뭐에 관해 쓰셔야 하는데요?

여: **다음 달에 새로운 종류의 스탠딩 램프를 출시하게 되는 거 아시죠?** 그거 발표 내용을 쓰고 있어요.

어휘 struggle with ~로 고심하다 wording 단어 선택 news release 보도 자료(= press release) assign (과제를) 부과하다 look over 검토하다 handbook 안내서, 핸드북 recommend 추천하다 guide 안내서, 지침 management 경영진 anyway 그런데, 그건 그렇고 standing lamp 스탠딩 램프(사람 키만큼 높은 램프) announcement 발표 (내용) table of contents 목차

Table of Contents

1. E-mails and memos
2. Letters
3. Reports
[62]4. Press releases

목차

1. 이메일과 메모
2. 편지
3. 보고서
4. **보도 자료**

62

Look at the graphic. Which chapter will the woman most likely consult?

(A) Chapter 1
(B) Chapter 2
(C) Chapter 3
(D) Chapter 4

시각 정보에 의하면, 여자는 어느 장을 참고하겠는가?

(A) 제1장
(B) 제2장
(C) 제3장
(D) 제4장

어휘 consult (참고하기 위해) 찾아보다

해설 시각 정보 연계 - 여자가 참고할 장

여자의 첫 번째 대사에서 여자가 작성을 맡은 보도 자료의 단어 선택 때문에 애를 먹고 있다(I'm struggling with the wording of a news release I've been assigned to write.)고 했는데 목차를 보면 보도 자료는 제4장이므로 정답은 (D)이다.

63

What does the man say is an advantage of *The Oliver Writing Handbook*?

(A) Its explanations are easy to understand.
(B) Its contents are approved by the company.
(C) It comes with membership in an online forum.
(D) It is available to employees for free.

남자는 〈올리버 작문 안내서〉의 장점이 무엇이라고 말하는가?

(A) 설명이 이해하기 쉽다.
(B) 회사가 내용을 인정한다.
(C) 온라인 포럼에 가입하면 딸려온다.
(D) 직원들이 무료로 얻을 수 있다.

어휘 advantage 이점 explanation 설명 contents 내용 approve 승인하다, 인정하다 membership 회원 자격 available 손에 넣을 수 있는 for free 무료로

해설 세부 사항 관련 - 〈올리버 작문 안내서〉의 장점

남자의 첫 번째 대사에서 〈올리버 작문 안내서〉를 보았는지 물어보며 그것이 화자들 회사에서 직원들에게 추천하는 작문 안내서(it's our company's recommended writing guide for employees)라고 했으므로 정답은 (B)이다.

64

What will the speakers' company do next month?

(A) Revise a personnel policy
(B) Negotiate a contract
(C) Launch a new product
(D) Stop offering a service

Test 8

화자들의 회사는 다음 달에 무엇을 할 것인가?
(A) 인사 규정 개정
(B) 계약 협상
(C) 신제품 출시
(D) 서비스 제공 중단

어휘 revise 개정하다 personnel policy 인사 규정 negotiate 협상하다 contract 계약 launch 출시하다, 출간하다

해설 세부 사항 관련 – 회사가 다음 달에 할 일
여자의 마지막 대사에서 다음 달에 새로운 종류의 스탠딩 램프를 출시한다(You know how ~ standing lamp next month?)고 했으므로 정답은 (C)이다.

▸▸ **Paraphrasing** 대화의 **begin selling a new type of standing lamp**
→ 정답의 **Launch a new product**

65-67 대화 + 일정표

W-Br Hi, Fred. Everything is set for Mary Soto's customer service training. [65]**If you'd like, I'll start setting up her workstation in the office**—to save you some time.

M-Cn Terrific. Thanks! And, just want to note—[66]**I still plan to sit in on the two o'clock training session.** I can play the role of the customer.

W-Br Sounds great. I'll keep that in mind.

M-Cn All right, then. [67]**For now, I'll get back to the sales report. I'm checking it for errors before I submit it this afternoon.**

여: 안녕하세요, 프레드. 메리 소토의 고객 서비스 교육을 위한 모든 준비가 끝났습니다. **원하시면 제가 사무실에 그녀의 업무 공간을 마련하기 시작할게요.** 시간을 아껴드리기 위해서요.
남: 아주 좋아요. 고맙습니다. 그리고 말씀 드리고 싶은 것은, **저는 여전히 2시에 있을 교육 시간에 참석하려고 해요.** 제가 고객 역할을 할 수 있을 테니까요.
여: 그거 좋겠네요. 명심할게요.
남: 그럼 좋아요. **지금은 저는 다시 판매 보고서 업무로 돌아갈게요. 오늘 오후에 제출하기 전에 오류가 있는지 확인하고 있어요.**

어휘 be set for ~를 위한 준비가 되다 workstation 작업 공간 terrific 아주 좋은, 훌륭한 note 언급하다 sit in on ~에 참석하다 play the role of ~의 역할을 하다 keep ~ in mind ~을 명심하다, 유념하다 submit 제출하다 take an order 주문을 받다 handle 처리하다, 다루다 complaint 불만 process 처리하다

Training schedule for: *Mary Soto*	
Time	**Session title**
10:00 A.M.	Describing Products
1:00 P.M.	Taking Orders
[66]2:00 P.M.	Handling Complaints
4:00 P.M.	Processing Refunds

교육 일정표: 메리 소토	
시간	교육명
오전 10:00	제품 설명하기
오후 1:00	주문 받기
오후 2:00	**불만사항 처리하기**
오후 4:00	환불 처리하기

65
What does the woman offer to do for the man?
(A) Record a presentation
(B) Prepare a work area
(C) Photocopy a manual
(D) Mail some invoices

여자는 남자를 위해 무엇을 해주겠다고 제안하는가?
(A) 프레젠테이션 녹화하기
(B) 업무 공간 준비하기
(C) 설명서 복사하기
(D) 송장 발송하기

해설 세부 사항 관련 – 여자의 제안 사항
여자의 첫 번째 대사에서 남자가 원하면 지금 사무실에 메리 소토의 업무 공간을 마련하기 시작하겠다(If you'd like, I'll start setting up her workstation in the office)고 했으므로 정답은 (B)이다.

▸▸ **Paraphrasing** 대화의 **setting up her workstation**
→ 정답의 **prepare a work area**

66
Look at the graphic. Which session does the man plan to attend?
(A) Describing Products
(B) Taking Orders
(C) Handling Complaints
(D) Processing Refunds

시각 정보에 의하면, 남자는 어떤 시간에 참석할 계획인가?
(A) 제품 설명하기
(B) 주문 받기
(C) 불만사항 처리하기
(D) 환불 처리하기

해설 시각 정보 연계 – 남자가 참석할 교육 시간

남자의 첫 번째 대사에서 2시에 있을 교육 시간에 참석할 계획(I still plan to sit in on the two o'clock training session.)이라고 했다. 교육 일정표를 보면 2시의 교육은 불만사항 처리하기(Handling Complaints)이므로 정답은 (C)이다.

67

What will the man probably do next?

(A) Gather some training materials
(B) Contact a sales representative
(C) Proofread a report
(D) Make some graphs

남자는 다음에 무엇을 할 것 같은가?

(A) 교육 자료 모으기
(B) 판매 직원에게 연락하기
(C) 보고서 교정하기
(D) 그래프 만들기

어휘 gather 모으다 sales representative 판매 직원, 영업 사원

해설 세부 사항 관련 – 남자의 다음 행동

남자의 두 번째 대사에서 지금은 다시 판매 보고서 업무로 돌아가서 오늘 오후에 제출하기 전에 오류가 있는지 확인하겠다(For now, I'll get back ~ before I submit it this afternoon.)고 했으므로 정답은 (C)이다.

▸▸ **Paraphrasing** 대화의 **checking it for errors**
→ 정답의 **proofread a report**

68-70 대화 + 공지

M-Au Hi, Janice. Sorry for calling so early. But I just saw a local traffic notice, and... [68]**the street we always travel on to get to work is closed due to construction.**

W-Br Oh, I hadn't heard about that... Thanks for the heads-up.

M-Au Sure. We can take alternate routes.

W-Br That's right. [69]**The videoconference I'm leading is scheduled to start at 10 A.M.**, so I'll be on time for that.

M-Au Ah, right... That'll involve everyone, so I'll call Ralph Davidson to remind him—[70]**he's just started managing our newest branch office.** OK. See you soon.

남: 안녕하세요, 재니스. 너무 일찍 전화드려 죄송합니다. 하지만 방금 지역 교통 안내를 봤는데··· **우리가 사무실에 갈 때 항상 이용하는 길이 공사 때문에 폐쇄됐어요.**

여: 아, 저는 못 들었어요··· 알려주셔서 고마워요.

남: 네. 다른 길로 갈 수 있어요.

여: 맞아요. **제가 주재하는 화상회의가 오전 10시에 시작될 예정인데** 제시간에 도착할 수 있겠군요.

남: 아, 그래요··· 회의에 모두가 들어가니 제가 랠프 데이비드슨에게 전화해서 알려줄게요. **그가 우리 신규 지점을 관리하기 시작했거든요.** 그래요. 이따 봐요.

어휘 traffic notice 교통 안내 get to work 일하러 가다 due to ~ 때문에 construction 공사 heads-up 주의, 경계 alternate 대체 가능한 route 경로 videoconference 화상회의 be on time 제시간에 가다 involve 포함하다 branch office 지점, 지사

Notice—street closures

Street name	Reason for closing
Bay Avenue	Fallen tree
Tilden Drive	Parade
[68]Dee Road	Construction
Nelson Way	Sign painting

안내 – 도로 폐쇄

도로명	폐쇄 사유
베이 애비뉴	나무가 쓰러짐
틸든 드라이브	가두 행진
디 로드	공사
넬슨 웨이	안내판 페인트칠

68

Look at the graphic. Which street do the speakers most likely use to go to work?

(A) Bay Avenue
(B) Tilden Drive
(C) Dee Road
(D) Nelson Way

시각 정보에 의하면, 화자들은 출근할 때 어떤 길을 이용하는 것 같은가?

(A) 배이 애비뉴
(B) 틸든 드라이브
(C) 디 로드
(D) 넬슨 웨이

해설 시각 정보 연계 – 화자들이 이용할 길

남자의 첫 번째 대사에서 화자들이 사무실에 갈 때 항상 이용하는 길이 공사로 폐쇄됐다(the street we always travel on to get to work is closed due to construction.)고 했다. 그리고 안내문을 보면 디 로드(Dee Road)의 폐쇄 이유가 공사(Construction)로 명시되어 있다. 즉, 화자들이 평상 시 출근할 때 이용하는 길은 디 로드이므로 정답은 (C)이다.

69

What does the woman say she will do this morning?

(A) Deliver some packages
(B) Host a videoconference
(C) Interview job applicants
(D) Purchase new furniture

Test 8

여자는 오늘 아침 무엇을 할 것인가?
(A) 소포 배송
(B) 화상회의 주재
(C) 입사 지원자 면접
(D) 새 가구 구입

해설 세부 사항 관련 - 여자가 아침에 할 일
여자의 두 번째 대사에서 자신이 주재하는 화상회의가 오전 10시에 시작될 예정(The videoconference ~ at 10 A.M.)이라고 했으므로 정답은 (B)이다.

▸▸ **Paraphrasing** 대화의 **lead** → 정답의 **host**

70

Who most likely is Mr. Davidson?

(A) A branch manager
(B) A potential client
(C) An incoming intern
(D) A guest lecturer

데이비드슨 씨는 누구일 것 같은가?
(A) 지점장
(B) 잠재 고객
(C) 새로 들어올 인턴
(D) 객원 강사

해설 세부 사항 관련 - 데이비드슨 씨의 신분
대화 맨 마지막에 남자는 데이비드슨이 가장 최근에 생긴 지점을 관리하기 시작했다(he's just started managing our newest branch office.)고 했다. 그러므로 정답은 (A)이다.

PART 4

71-73 담화

M-Au [71]**Welcome to the Boragon City Music Museum, the region's only home of rare musical instruments from around the world.** Your tour today is self-guided, so feel free to view our exhibits at your own pace. Before you start, though, [72]**I want to give each of you a paper ticket that will allow you reentry to the museum all day.** This will be useful if you need a snack break at the café next door. Also, [73]**at two o'clock our staff will perform some traditional guitar playing techniques, and give hands-on practice to some members of the audience too.** That will be in the Main Hall.

전 세계 희귀 악기를 소장하고 있는 이 지역 유일의 시설인 보라건 시 음악 박물관에 오신 것을 환영합니다. 오늘 여러분의 관람은 셀프 가이드 방식이니 본인의 속도에 맞춰 전시물을 스스로 자유롭게 둘러보십시오. 관람을 시작하시기 전에 **여러분 모두에게 하루 종일 박물관에 재입장하실 수 있는 종이 표를 드리려고 합니다.** 옆 건물 카페에서 간식을 드시며 쉴 때 유용할 것입니다. 아울러 **2시에는 저희 직원이 전통 기타 연주 기법으로 공연을 하고 관람객 가운데 몇 분이 직접 연주해 보시도록 해드릴 것입니다.** 이건 메인 홀에서 열릴 예정입니다.

어휘 region 지역 musical instrument 악기 exhibit 전시 at one's own pace 자신만의 속도로 reentry 재입장 perform 공연하다, 연주하다 traditional 전통적인 hands-on 직접 해 보는 audience 청중

71

Where is the talk being given?

(A) In a store showroom
(B) On a factory floor
(C) At a museum
(D) In a recording studio

이 담화가 이루어지고 있는 장소는?
(A) 매장 전시실
(B) 공장 작업장
(C) 박물관
(D) 녹음 스튜디오

해설 전체 내용 관련 - 담화의 장소
지문 맨 처음에 화자가 청자들에게 전 세계 희귀 악기를 상설 전시하는 지역 유일의 보라건 시 음악 박물관에 온 것을 환영한다(Welcome to the Boragon City Music Museum ~ around the world.)고 했다. 즉, 박물관 가이드의 설명이므로 정답은 (C)이다.

72

What will the speaker distribute to the listeners?

(A) Bags of snacks
(B) Audio devices
(C) Reusable passes
(D) Guide maps

화자는 청자들에게 무엇을 나누어 줄 것인가?

(A) 간식 봉지
(B) 오디오 기기
(C) 재사용 가능한 티켓
(D) 안내도

해설 세부 사항 관련 - 청자들에게 나눠 줄 것

지문 중반부에 화자가 청자들에게 하루 종일 박물관에 재입장할 수 있는 종이 표를 드리려 한다(I want to give each of you ~ all day.)고 했으므로 정답은 (C)이다.

73

According to the speaker, what will happen at two o'clock?

(A) A fund-raising auction
(B) An interactive performance
(C) A contest announcement
(D) A staff appreciation event

화자에 따르면, 2시에 무슨 일이 있을 것인가?

(A) 기금 마련 경매
(B) 참여 방식의 공연
(C) 대회 발표
(D) 직원 감사 행사

해설 세부 사항 관련 - 2시에 있을 일

지문 맨 마지막에 두 시에 직원이 전통 기타 연주 기법으로 공연을 하고 관람객 몇 명도 직접 연주해 보도록 할 것(at two o'clock ~ of the audience too.)이라고 했다. 즉, 참여 방식의 공연을 진행한다는 것이므로 정답은 (B)이다.

▸▸ **Paraphrasing** 지문의 **hands-on practice**
→ 정답의 **an interactive performance**

74-76 전화 메시지

W-Am Hello, this message is for Henry Meyer. [74]**This is Jill, the volunteer coordinator here at the South Branch Public Library.** [75]**I just got your e-mail expressing interest in helping out at our used book sale this weekend.** Actually, the registration period for new volunteers ended in June. But I'd like to place you on a list for upcoming volunteer projects. [76]**If you could, please fill out the "Volunteer Information" form on our Web site and then turn it in electronically.** That way, my office can contact you when future opportunities arise. Thank you so much.

안녕하세요. 헨리 메이어 씨께 남기는 메시지입니다. **저는 이곳 사우스 브랜치 공립 도서관에서 코디네이터 자원봉사를 하는 질이라고 합니다. 이번 주말에 있을 중고 도서 판매 때 돕고 싶다는 관심을 나타내신 귀하의 이메일을 방금 받았습니다.** 사실 신규 자원봉사자 등록 기간은 6월에 끝났습니다. 하지만 앞으로 있을 자원봉사 프로젝트를 위해 귀하를 명단에 올려놓으려 합니다. **가능하시면 저희 웹 사이트에서 '자원봉사자 정보' 양식을 기입하셔서 온라인으로 제출해 주시기 바랍니다.** 그러면 향후 기회가 생길 때 저희 사무실에서 연락을 드릴 수 있습니다. 대단히 감사합니다.

어휘 volunteer 자원봉사자 express interest in ~에 관심을 표하다 registration period 등록 기간 fill out a form 서식에 기입하다 turn in ~을 제출하다 electronically 전자적으로 opportunity 기회 arise 생기다, 발생하다

74

Where does the speaker work?

(A) At a public library
(B) At a community center
(C) At a nature reserve
(D) At a school

화자는 어디서 일하는가?

(A) 공립 도서관
(B) 커뮤니티 센터
(C) 자연 보호 구역
(D) 학교

해설 전체 내용 관련 - 화자의 근무지

지문 초반부에 화자가 자신을 사우스 브랜치 공립 도서관에서 코디네이터 자원봉사를 하는 질(This is Jill, the volunteer coordinator here at the South Branch Public Library.)이라고 소개했으므로 정답은 (A)이다.

75

Why does the speaker say, "the registration period for new volunteers ended in June"?

(A) To express concern about a program
(B) To highlight a missed deadline
(C) To accept an invitation
(D) To justify a proposal

화자가 "신규 자원봉사자 등록 기간은 6월에 끝났습니다"라고 말한 이유는 무엇인가?

(A) 프로그램에 대한 우려를 표하기 위해
(B) 등록 기간이 지난 것을 강조하기 위해
(C) 초대를 수락하기 위해
(D) 제안의 타당성을 증명하기 위해

어휘 highlight 강조하다 justify 타당함을 증명하다

해설 화자의 의도 파악 - 신규 자원봉사자 등록 기간을 언급한 의도

지문 초반부에 화자가 이번 주말에 있을 중고 도서 판매 때 돕고 싶다는 관심을 나타낸 이메일을 방금 받았다(I just got your e-mail expressing ~ sale this weekend.)고 했다. 그런 다음에 신규 자원봉사자 등록 기간은 6월에 끝났다고 인용문을 말했는데 이는 청자가 등록 기간을 놓쳤음을 알리기 위한 의도를 담은 것이므로 정답은 (B)이다.

Test 8

76
What does the speaker ask the listener to do?

(A) Take some photographs
(B) Revise a budget
(C) Come to her office
(D) Submit an online form

화자가 청자에게 요청하는 것은 무엇인가?

(A) 사진 찍기
(B) 예산 수정하기
(C) 사무실 방문하기
(D) 온라인 양식 제출하기

해설 세부 사항 관련 – 화자의 요청 사항

지문 후반부에 화자가 가능하면 웹 사이트에서 '자원봉사자 정보' 양식을 기입한 다음 온라인으로 제출해 달라(If you could, please fill out ~ electronically.)고 요청했으므로 정답은 (D)이다.

77-79 광고

W-Br [77]**As an independent retailer, it can be difficult to manage your business's expenses and earnings.** To meet this challenge, many business operators have turned to Trakk-Plus. [78]**It's a powerful software program that helps you track costs, schedule supply orders, create reports, and much more.** Best of all, Trakk-Plus is affordable and easy to use. Want to learn more about it? [79]**Go to www.trakkplus.com today and register to test out a trial version**—you'll be able to use all its features for free. That's how confident we are that Trakk-Plus will meet all of your needs.

독립적인 소매상으로, 여러분 매장의 지출과 수입을 파악하시느라 힘드실 겁니다. 이러한 어려움에 대처하기 위해 많은 사업자들이 트랙플러스의 도움을 받아 왔습니다. **트랙플러스는 비용을 추적하고, 물품 주문 일정을 잡고, 보고서를 작성하는 등의 업무를 돕는 매우 유용한 소프트웨어 프로그램입니다.** 무엇보다도 트랙플러스는 가격이 적당하고 사용하기가 쉽습니다. 더 자세히 알고 싶으신가요? **오늘 www.trakkplus.com에 가셔서 등록하시고 시험용 버전을 써 보세요.** 모든 기능을 무료로 사용해 보실 수 있습니다. 저희는 트랙스플러스가 여러분의 모든 요구를 충족시킬 것임을 확신합니다.

어휘 retailer 소매상 expense 비용, 경비 earnings 수입, 소득 meet the challenge 어려움에 대처하다 turn to ~에 의지하다 track 추적하다 affordable 가격이 적당한 register 등록하다 test out 시험해 보다 trial version 시험해 보는 버전 feature 기능 confident 확신하는, 자신 만만한

77
Who is the advertisement most likely intended for?

(A) Marketing specialists
(B) Property managers
(C) Store owners
(D) Jobseekers

광고는 누구를 대상으로 하겠는가?

(A) 마케팅 전문가
(B) 부동산 관리자
(C) 매장 소유주
(D) 구직자

해설 전체 내용 관련 – 광고의 대상

지문 맨 처음에 독립적인 소매상으로 매장의 지출과 수입을 파악하는 데 어려움이 있을 것(As an independent retailer, ~ earnings.)이라고 했다. 광고의 대상이 독립적인 소매상임을 알 수 있으므로 정답은 (C)이다.

78
What is the speaker mainly describing?

(A) A software program
(B) A series of workshops
(C) A security system
(D) A clothing line

화자는 주로 무엇에 대해 설명하고 있는가?

(A) 소프트웨어 프로그램
(B) 워크숍 시리즈
(C) 보안 시스템
(D) 의상 라인

해설 전체 내용 관련 – 화자의 설명 내용

지문 중반부에 이 상품은 비용을 추적하고, 물품 주문 일정을 잡고, 보고서를 작성하는 등의 업무를 돕는 매우 유용한 소프트웨어 프로그램(It's a powerful software ~ and much more.)이라고 했다. 즉, 매장 운영에 도움을 주는 소프트웨어 프로그램에 대해 설명하고 있으므로 정답은 (A)이다.

79
What are listeners encouraged to do?

(A) Register for a trade show
(B) Make a phone call
(C) Visit a Web site
(D) Use a discount voucher

청자들에게 무엇을 하라고 권하는가?

(A) 무역 박람회 등록
(B) 전화하기
(C) 웹 사이트 방문
(D) 할인 쿠폰 사용

해설 세부 사항 관련 – 청자들에 대한 권장 사항

지문 맨 마지막에 청자들에게 웹 사이트에 가서 등록하고 트랙플러스 시험용 버전을 써 보라(Go to www.trakkplus.com today and register to test out a trial version)고 했으므로 정답은 (C)이다.

▸▸ **Paraphrasing** 지문의 **Go to www.trakkplus.com**
→ 정답의 **Visit a Web site**

80-82 안내

M-Cn Good morning, shoppers! [80]**As the region's top seller of new and used furnishings**, we are the place to come when you want to set up a beautiful home on a budget. And our stock changes all the time. So browse around—[81]**you might spot a great piece you didn't see before.** Want to spend less? [82]**Come to our service desk and pick up a "Save More" packet—it's filled with discount coupons for great in-store savings.** The packets are free to take. No purchase is necessary.

안녕하세요, 손님 여러분! 저희는 **새 가구 및 중고 가구를 판매하는 지역 최고의 판매상으로서,** 한정된 예산으로 아름다운 집을 만들기를 원할 때 방문해야 할 곳입니다. 그리고 저희의 재고는 항시 변경됩니다. 그러니 맘껏 둘러보십시오. **전에 본 적 없는 좋은 것을 발견할 수도 있습니다.** 돈을 절약하고 싶으신가요? **안내 데스크로 오셔서 '세이브 모어' 쿠폰집을 가져가세요. 매장 내에서 돈을 많이 절약할 수 있는 할인 쿠폰들입니다.** 쿠폰 묶음은 무료입니다. 가구를 구매하지 않으셔도 받으실 수 있습니다.

어휘 furnishing 가구 설비, 비품 on a budget 한정된 예산으로 stock 재고 browse around ~를 둘러보다 spot a great piece 좋은 것을 찾다 less 더 적게 packet 다발, 묶음 be filled with ~으로 가득 차다 in-store 매장 내의 purchase 구매

80

What does the speaker's store sell?

(A) Furniture
(B) Art supplies
(C) Hardware
(D) Plants

화자의 가게는 무엇을 판매하는가?

(A) 가구
(B) 미술용품
(C) 철물
(D) 식물

해설 세부 사항 관련 – 판매하는 제품

지문 초반부에 새 가구 및 중고 가구를 판매하는 지역 최고의 판매상(As the region's top seller of new and used furnishings)이라고 했으므로 정답은 (A)이다.

▸▸ **Paraphrasing** 지문의 **furnishings** → 정답의 **furniture**

81

What does the speaker imply when he says, "our stock changes all the time"?

(A) He is proud of the staff's hard work.
(B) Some prices may not be marked accurately.
(C) Some of the store's aisles may be blocked.
(D) He wants to encourage repeat visits.

화자가 "저희의 재고는 항시 변경됩니다"라고 말한 의도는 무엇인가?

(A) 직원들의 노고를 자랑스러워한다.
(B) 일부 가격이 정확히 찍혀 있지 않을 수도 있다.
(C) 매장의 일부 통로는 폐쇄될 수도 있다.
(D) 재차 방문하도록 권하고 있다.

해설 화자의 의도 파악 – 저희의 재고는 항시 변경된다는 말의 의도

지문 중반부에 청자들에게 전에 본 적 없던 좋은 물건을 발견할 수도 있다(you might spot a great piece you didn't see before)고 했다. 즉, 재고는 항시 변경된다는 인용문은 청자들에게 매장을 여러 번 방문해서 좋은 가구를 찾아보라는 의도를 담은 것이므로 정답은 (D)이다.

82

According to the speaker, what can customers obtain at the service desk?

(A) Sample goods
(B) Store coupons
(C) Order forms
(D) Job applications

화자에 따르면, 고객들이 안내 데스크에서 얻을 수 있는 것은?

(A) 제품 견본
(B) 매장 쿠폰
(C) 주문 양식
(D) 입사 지원서

해설 세부 사항 관련 – 안내 데스크에서 받을 수 있는 것

지문 후반부에 청자들에게 안내 데스크로 와서 '세이브 모어' 쿠폰집을 가져가라고 했으며 매장 내에서 돈을 많이 절약할 수 있는 할인 쿠폰들(Come to our service desk ~ in-store savings.)이라고 했으므로 정답은 (B)이다.

▸▸ **Paraphrasing** 지문의 **discount coupons for great in-store savings**
→ 정답의 **store coupons**

83-85 전화 메시지

M-Au Hi. [83]**This is Byung-Gwan Joon, the manager at Belplex Fitness Center.** I just want to let you know that we've completed our facility improvements and are running our individual and group exercise classes on normal schedules again. [84]**The upgrades involved the installation of new, heavy-duty flooring material in our weight room,** which should enhance your workout experience. Now, to help us offer even better service, [85]**we'd like you to fill out a brief feedback survey on your next visit.** Look for it at the front desk. Thank you.

안녕하세요. **벨플렉스 피트니스 센터의 매니저인 병관 준입니다.** 저희 클럽의 시설 개선을 완료해서 현재 개인 및 단체 운동 수업이 다시 정상적인 일정으로 진행되고 있음을 알려 드립니다. **시설 개선 작업에는 웨이트 실에 튼튼한 새 바닥**

Test 8

재 설치가 포함되었으며, 이는 귀하의 운동 경험을 향상시킬 것입니다. 저희가 더 나은 서비스를 제공할 수 있도록, **다음에 방문하실 때 간단한 피드백 설문지를 작성해 주셨으면 합니다.** 설문지는 프런트에서 찾으세요. 감사합니다.

어휘 complete 완료하다 improvement 개선, 향상 individual 개인의 installation 설치 heavy-duty 튼튼한 flooring material 바닥재 enhance 향상시키다 workout 운동 fill out a survey 설문조사를 작성하다

83

Where most likely does the speaker work?

(A) At a convention center
(B) At a fitness club
(C) At a medical clinic
(D) At an interior design firm

화자는 어디에서 일할 것 같은가?

(A) 컨벤션 센터
(B) 피트니스 클럽
(C) 병원
(D) 실내 디자인 회사

해설 전체 내용 관련 - 화자의 근무지

지문 맨 처음에 화자가 자신을 벨플렉스 피트니스 센터의 매니저인 병관 준(This is Byung-Gwan Joon, the manager at Belplex Fitness Center.)이라고 소개했으므로 정답은 (B)이다.

▸▸ Paraphrasing 지문의 Belplex Fitness Center
→ 정답의 a fitness club

84

What does the speaker say was upgraded?

(A) A parking area
(B) An audio system
(C) A floor surface
(D) A passenger elevator

화자는 무엇이 개선되었다고 말하는가?

(A) 주차 구역
(B) 오디오 시스템
(C) 바닥 표면
(D) 승객용 엘리베이터

해설 세부 사항 관련 - 개선된 점

지문 중반에 이번 개선 작업에는 웨이트 실에 튼튼한 새 바닥재 설치도 포함되었다(The upgrades involved ~ in our weight room)고 했으므로 정답은 (C)이다.

85

What does the speaker encourage the listener to do?

(A) Complete questionnaire
(B) Postpone an appointment
(C) Register for e-mail updates
(D) Go to an upcoming party

화자는 청자에게 무엇을 할 것을 권하는가?

(A) 설문지 작성하기
(B) 약속 연기하기
(C) 이메일 소식 신청하기
(D) 다가오는 파티에 가기

어휘 postpone 연기하다, 미루다

해설 세부 사항 관련 - 화자의 권장 사항

지문 맨 마지막에 화자가 청자에게 다음 방문 때 간단한 피드백 설문지를 작성해 주면 좋겠다(we'd like you to fill out a brief feedback survey on your next visit)고 했으므로 정답은 (A)이다.

▸▸ Paraphrasing 지문의 fill out a brief feedback survey
→ 정답의 complete a questionnaire

86-88 담화

W-Am Hello, and welcome to today's session. My name is Akari Furuta, and I'm a consultant with more than twenty years of experience in helping businesses and employees become the best they can be. [86]**Your management brought me in here today to help your department improve its teamwork.** [87]**I've been told that much of the staff is new, and you're finding it hard to share information and ideas because you're not close yet.** Today we'll do some exercises that will address this problem. Let's start by getting to know each other. [88]**I'd like you to say your name, job title, and one fun fact about yourself.** Can someone volunteer to go first?

안녕하세요. 오늘 교육에 참여하신 걸 환영합니다. 제 이름은 아카리 후루타고요, 업체와 직원들이 능력을 최대한 발휘할 수 있도록 돕는 일에 20여 년간 종사해 온 컨설턴트입니다. **이곳 경영진 분들이 여러분 부서가 팀워크를 향상시킬 수 있게 도움을 주라고 오늘 저를 이곳으로 불렀습니다. 여기 직원들 다수가 신입이고, 아직 친하지 않아서 정보나 아이디어를 공유하는 걸 어려워한다고 들었어요.** 오늘 우리는 이 문제를 다루기 위한 활동을 할 겁니다. 서로를 알아가는 것부터 시작해봅시다. **여러분 이름, 직책, 그리고 자신에 관해 재미있는 사실 하나씩을 얘기해 주시면 좋겠네요.** 누구 제일 먼저 하실 분?

어휘 session (회의, 교육 등의) 시간 consultant 자문위원, 컨설턴트 management 경영진 bring in (도움, 조언 등을 얻기 위해) 불러들이다, 관여시키다 department 부서 improve 향상시키다 share 나누다, 공유하다 close 친한 exercise 활동 address (문제를) 다루다 get to know 알게 되다 job title 직책

86

Where is the talk taking place?

(A) At a training seminar
(B) At a product demonstration
(C) At a focus group session
(D) At a board meeting

담화는 어디에서 일어나는가?
(A) 교육 세미나
(B) 제품 설명회
(C) 포커스 그룹 세션
(D) 이사회

어휘 training 훈련, 교육 demonstration (시범을 보이며 하는) 설명 focus group 포커스 그룹(시장 조사나 여론 조사를 위해 각 계층을 대표하도록 뽑은 소수의 사람들로 이뤄진 그룹) board meeting 이사회

해설 전체 내용 관련 – 담화 장소
지문 초반부에 화자가 자신을 컨설턴트라고 소개한 후, 청자들의 경영진이 부서 팀워크 향상에 도움을 주라고 자신을 이곳으로 불렀다(Your management brought me in here today to help your department improve its teamwork.)고 했으므로 정답은 (A)이다.

87

What problem does the speaker mention?
(A) Unnecessary information in some documents
(B) The large distance between two buildings in a complex
(C) The difficulty of maintaining healthy exercise habits
(D) A lack of communication between workers

화자는 어떤 문제점을 언급하는가?
(A) 일부 문서에 담긴 불필요한 정보
(B) 단지 내 두 건물 사이의 먼 거리
(C) 건강한 운동 습관 유지의 어려움
(D) 직원들 간의 의사소통 부족

어휘 document 문서 complex 단지, 복합 건물 maintain 유지하다 healthy 건강한, 건강에 좋은 lack 부족, 결여

해설 세부 사항 관련 – 화자가 언급하는 문제점
지문 중반부에 화자가 직원들 다수가 신입이고, 아직 친하지 않아서 정보나 아이디어 공유를 어려워하는 것으로 들었다(I've been told that much of the staff ~ because you're not close yet.)고 했으므로 정답은 (D)이다.

▸▸ Paraphrasing 지문의 share information and ideas
→ 정답의 communication

88

What are the listeners asked to do?
(A) Take detailed notes
(B) Look at some charts
(C) Introduce themselves
(D) Volunteer for a committee

청자들은 무엇을 하라고 요청받았는가?
(A) 상세한 메모하기
(B) 도표 보기
(C) 자기 소개하기
(D) 위원회에 자원하기

어휘 take notes 메모하다 detailed 상세한 introduce oneself 자신을 소개하다 committee 위원회

해설 세부 사항 관련 – 청자들이 받은 요청
지문 후반부에 화자가 청자들에게 이름, 직책, 그리고 자신들에 관해 재미있는 사실 하나씩 얘기해 주면 좋겠다(I'd like you to say your name, job title, and one fun fact about yourself.)고 했으므로 정답은 (C)이다.

89-91 방송

M-Au It's time for your one P.M. local news update here on KYPP Radio. This week, [89]**the remodeled Starburst Motel, located in the Davis Gardens neighborhood, will welcome its first guests in over six months.** The motel's new owners have upgraded its interior and added several bicycle-related amenities to take advantage of its proximity to a popular bike path. [90]**Other businesses and residents in the neighborhood say they are pleased by the motel's renewal, but not surprised.** Davis Gardens underwent extensive roadwork in May. It seems that expectations are high for the neighborhood's future. Now, [91]**Shelby Rawlings will tell us about current conditions on the city's roads.** Shelby?

KYPP 라디오에서 오후 1시 최신 지역 소식을 전할 시간입니다. 이번 주에 **데이비스 가든즈 지역에 위치하는, 리모델링된 스타버스트 모텔이 6개월여 만에 첫 손님들을 맞이합니다.** 모텔 새 주인들은 내부를 개선하고, 인기 있는 자전거 도로와 가깝다는 점을 활용하기 위해 자전거 관련 편의시설 몇 곳을 추가했습니다. **이 지역의 다른 업체와 주민들은 모텔이 개선되어 기쁘다면서, 놀랄 일은 아니라고 말합니다.** 데이비스 가든즈는 5월에 대규모 도로 공사를 했는데요. 그 지역 미래에 대한 기대가 높아진 것으로 보입니다. 이제, **쉘비 롤링스가 우리 도시의 현재 도로 상황을 전해 주겠습니다.** 쉘비?

어휘 remodel 리모델링하다 located in ~에 위치한 neighborhood 동네, 지역 upgrade 개선하다 interior 내부 amenities 편의시설, 오락시설 take advantage of ~을 이용하다 proximity to ~에 근접함 bike path 자전거 도로 resident 주민 pleased 기뻐하는, 만족하는 renewal 재개발, 개선 surprised 놀란 undergo 겪다 extensive 대규모의, 광범위한 roadwork 도로 공사 expectation 기대 conditions 상황

89

What is the broadcast mainly about?
(A) Upgrades to bicycle paths
(B) Tours of a neighborhood
(C) A business's reopening
(D) A sporting event

방송은 주로 무엇에 대한 것인가?
(A) 자전거 도로 개선
(B) 지역 투어
(C) 한 업체의 재개장
(D) 스포츠 행사

Test 8

어휘 broadcast 방송 reopening 재개장

해설 전체 내용 관련 - 방송의 주제

지문 초반부에 화자가 최신 지역 소식으로 데이비스 가든즈 지역에 위치하는, 리모델링된 스타버스트 모텔이 6개월여 만에 첫 손님들을 맞이한다(the remodeled Starburst Motel ~ its first guests in over six months.)고 했으므로 정답은 (C)이다.

90

What does the speaker mean when he says, "Davis Gardens underwent extensive roadwork in May"?

(A) Some funds have already been spent.
(B) An improvement project is not unique.
(C) Some retailers were inconvenienced.
(D) A delay was unavoidable.

화자가 "데이비스 가든즈는 5월에 대규모 도로 공사를 했는데요"라고 말한 의도는 무엇인가?

(A) 자금을 이미 다 써 버렸다.
(B) 개선 사업이 특별할 것은 없다.
(C) 몇몇 소매업자들이 불편해했다.
(D) 지체가 불가피했다.

어휘 fund 자금 unique 독특한, 특별한 retailer 소매상 inconvenience 불편하게 하다 delay 지체 unavoidable 피할 수 없는

해설 화자의 의도 파악 - 데이비스 가든즈는 5월에 대규모 도로 공사를 했다는 말의 의도

인용문 바로 앞 문장에서 화자는 지역 내 다른 업체와 주민들은 모텔 개선에 기뻐하지만 놀랄 일은 아니라고 말한다(Other businesses and residents ~ but not surprised.)고 했다. 그런 다음 데이비스 가든즈는 5월에 대규모 도로 공사를 했다고 했는데, 문맥상 이 인용문은 지역의 개선 사업이 특별할 것은 없다는 의미이므로 정답은 (B)이다.

91

What will most likely happen next?

(A) Some songs will be played.
(B) Some advertisements will air.
(C) A telephone interview will begin.
(D) A traffic report will be given.

다음에 어떤 일이 일어나겠는가?

(A) 노래가 나올 것이다.
(B) 광고 방송이 나올 것이다.
(C) 전화 인터뷰가 시작될 것이다.
(D) 교통 정보가 제공될 것이다.

어휘 advertisement 광고 air 방송되다 traffic report 교통 정보

해설 세부 사항 관련 - 다음에 일어날 일

지문 후반부에 화자는 쉘비 롤링스가 도시의 현재 도로 상황을 전해 주겠다(Shelby Rawlings will tell us about current conditions on the city's roads.)고 했으므로 정답은 (D)이다.

92-94 공지

W-Br Now, I'm pleased to end today's meeting with an exciting announcement. [92]**Tellenk Associates is going to start a mentorship program. Junior employees like you will have the chance to develop your leadership skills and industry expertise by meeting one-on-one with executives.** Doesn't that sound great? [93]**I'd like to thank our team member Francisco for proposing it.** And I hope you all know that Tellenk Associates would welcome other good ideas that any of you may have. Uh, [94]**if you'd like to take part in the mentorship program, there will be an information session in Conference Room A on Friday at eleven A.M.** OK, that's all for today.

이제, 흥미로운 공지를 전하면서 오늘 회의를 마치게 되어 기쁩니다. **텔렌크 어소시에이츠가 멘토 프로그램을 시작할 예정입니다. 여러분 같은 평사원들이 중역들과 일대일 만남을 통해 지도력과 업계 전문 지식을 쌓을 수 있는 기회를 갖게 될 텐데요.** 굉장하지 않아요? **이를 제안해 주신 우리 팀원 프란시스코에게 감사하고 싶습니다.** 그리고 여러분 모두 텔렌크 어소시에이츠가 여기 계신 분 누구든 가지고 있을지 모르는 또 다른 좋은 아이디어를 환영한다는 걸 알길 바랍니다. 어, **멘토 프로그램에 참여하고 싶으시면 금요일, 오전 11시 A회의실에서 설명회가 있을 예정입니다.** 자, 오늘은 이상입니다.

어휘 end 끝마치다 announcement 발표 junior employee 평사원, 하위직 사원 leadership skill 지도력 expertise 전문 지식 one-on-one 일대일로 executive 중역 propose 제안하다 take part in ~에 참석하다 information session 설명회

92

What will the listeners have the opportunity to do?

(A) Compete for an industry award
(B) Develop foreign language skills
(C) Influence hiring decisions
(D) Learn from senior employees

청자들은 무엇을 할 기회를 갖게 될 것인가?

(A) 업계 상을 받기 위한 경쟁
(B) 외국어 사용 능력 개발
(C) 고용 결정에 영향력 행사
(D) 고위 직원들로부터 배우기

어휘 compete for ~을 얻기 위해 경쟁하다 influence 영향을 미치다 hire 고용하다 senior employee 고참 사원, 고위 임직원

해설 세부 사항 관련 - 청자들이 갖게 될 기회

지문 초반부에 화자가 청자들에게 텔렌크 어소시에이츠가 멘토 프로그램을 시작할 예정이며, 중역들과 일대일 만남을 통해 지도력과 업계 전문 지식을 쌓을 수 있는 기회를 갖게 될 것(Tellenk Associates is going to start ~ one-on-one with executives.)이라고 했으므로 정답은 (D)이다.

▸▸ Paraphrasing 지문의 executives
→ 정답의 senior employees

93

What does the speaker thank Francisco for?

(A) Making a suggestion
(B) Conducting some research
(C) Leading a special team
(D) Following some rules

화자가 프란시스코에게 감사하는 이유는 무엇인가?

(A) 제안을 해서
(B) 조사를 해서
(C) 특별한 팀을 이끌어서
(D) 규칙을 따라서

어휘 make a suggestion 제안하다 conduct 수행하다 follow (지시를) 따르다 rule 규칙

해설 세부 사항 관련 - 프란시스코에게 감사하는 이유

지문 중반부에 화자가 이를 제안해 준 팀원 프란시스코에게 감사하고 싶다(I'd like to thank our team member Francisco for proposing it.)고 했으므로 정답은 (A)이다.

94

What should interested listeners do?

(A) Submit an application
(B) Attend another meeting
(C) Talk to Francisco
(D) Read a memo

관심 있는 청자들은 무엇을 해야 하는가?

(A) 신청서 제출
(B) 다른 모임 참가
(C) 프란시스코와 얘기하기
(D) 메모 읽기

어휘 interested 관심 있는 submit 제출하다 application 신청서 attend 참가하다

해설 세부 사항 관련 - 청자들이 해야 할 일

지문 후반부에 화자가 청자들에게 멘토 프로그램에 참여하고 싶으면 금요일, 오전 11시 A회의실에서 설명회가 있을 예정(if you'd like to take part ~ on Friday at eleven A.M.)이라고 말하여 관심 있는 청자들은 이 모임에 참가해야 한다는 사실을 알 수 있으므로 정답은 (B)이다.

Paraphrasing 지문의 **information session**
→ 정답의 **another meeting**

95-97 회의 발췌 + 쿠폰

M-Cn OK, all. To start, [95]**I want to discuss our plans for the party to mark our firm's third year in operation.** It'll be a big event! At least forty-five people plan to attend, and [96]**the date is set for July nineteenth. Uh, it looks like I can't use that special coupon for Dardano's Inn.** So I'm looking into booking the event somewhere else—we still have many options. In fact, I'm finding the range of choices to be a little overwhelming. [97]**If anyone can suggest a particular venue that you think would fit our needs, please do so after the meeting.** Thanks.

좋습니다, 여러분. 우선 **우리 회사의 영업 3주년 기념 파티 계획에 대해 논의하고자 합니다.** 이번엔 큰 행사가 될 겁니다! 최소 45명이 참석할 계획이며 **날짜는 7월 19일로 정해졌습니다. 어, 다르다노스 호텔의 그 특별 쿠폰은 사용할 수 없을 것 같아요.** 그래서 저는 다른 곳에 예약을 할까 살펴보는 중입니다. 아직 선택할 수 있는 곳이 많습니다. 실은, 선택권이 다양해서 좀 힘들어요. **우리의 필요에 적합하다고 생각되는 특정 장소를 제안하실 수 있다면, 회의 후에 그렇게 해 주세요.** 감사합니다.

어휘 mark 기념하다 in operation 운영[가동] 중인 look into ~를 자세히 살펴보다 overwhelming 압도적인, 대응하기 힘든 particular 특정한 venue 장소, 개최지 fit 어울리다, 맞다

Coupon

Dardano's Inn

10% off banquet room rental

—For groups of 30^+ guests
—Rent a private room for three hours!

[96]Expires: July 1

쿠폰

다르다노스 호텔

연회장 대여 10% 할인

–30인 이상의 단체
–3시간 동안 전용 객실을 대관하세요!

만료: 7월 1일

95

According to the speaker, why is the event being held?

(A) To recognize a staff member's retirement
(B) To celebrate a business anniversary
(C) To host some potential clients
(D) To promote new merchandise

화자에 따르면, 행사는 왜 열리는가?

(A) 직원의 퇴직을 기리기 위해
(B) 회사 기념일을 경축하기 위해
(C) 잠재 고객을 접대하기 위해
(D) 신제품을 홍보하기 위해

해설 세부 사항 관련 - 행사가 열리는 이유

지문 맨 처음에 화자가 우리 회사의 영업 3주년 기념 파티 계획에 대해 다시 말하고자 한다(I want to discuss ~ third year in operations.)고 했으므로 정답은 (B)이다.

▸▸ **Paraphrasing** 지문의 mark our firm's third year in operation → 정답의 celebrate a business anniversary

96

Look at the graphic. Why will the speaker be unable to use the coupon?

(A) His group's size is too small.
(B) His group will require buffet service.
(C) The event is expected to last too long.
(D) The event will happen after an expiration date.

시각 정보에 의하면, 화자는 왜 쿠폰을 사용하지 못하는가?

(A) 그의 단체 규모가 너무 작다.
(B) 그의 단체가 뷔페 서비스를 요청할 것이다.
(C) 행사가 너무 길게 계속될 것으로 예상된다.
(D) 행사가 만료일 이후에 열릴 것이다.

해설 시각 정보 연계 - 쿠폰을 사용할 수 없는 이유

지문 중반부에 행사 날짜가 7월 19일로 정해져서 다르다노스 호텔 특별 쿠폰을 사용할 수 없을 것 같다(the date is set for ~ coupon for Dardano's Inn.)고 했다. 그리고 쿠폰을 보면 만료 날짜가 7월 1일(Expires: July 1)로 되어 있다. 쿠폰을 사용할 수 없는 이유는 회사 행사가 쿠폰의 유효 기간 이후에 열리기 때문이므로 정답은 (D)이다.

97

What does the speaker ask the listeners for?

(A) A cost estimate
(B) Some instructions
(C) A recommendation
(D) Some donations

화자는 청자들에게 무엇을 요청하는가?

(A) 견적가
(B) 사용 설명서
(C) 추천
(D) 기부

해설 세부 사항 관련 - 화자의 요청 사항

우리의 필요에 적합하다고 생각되는 특정 장소를 제안할 수 있으면 회의 후에 제안해 달라(If anyone can suggest ~ please do so after the meeting.)고 했으므로, 정답은 (C)이다.

▸▸ **Paraphrasing** 지문의 suggest → 정답의 a recommendation

98-100 안내 + 좌석 배치도

W-Am Hello, all. [98]**Thank you for volunteering to check tickets and show patrons to their seats during tonight's musical.** Right now, I just want to give you some special instructions. Once the show starts, [99]**please take a seat in the seating zone closest to the exit.** That way, you can minimize disturbance to others as you assist guests who come late. Also, [100]**when the show concludes, please stay a little longer to help us put on a special recognition ceremony for Donna Park, our theater's Employee of the Year.** She was chosen via positive patron feedback, and we'd really appreciate your assistance in celebrating her contributions. It should only take about fifteen minutes.

안녕하세요, 여러분. **오늘 밤 뮤지컬 공연 동안에 티켓을 확인하고 공연 관람객들에게 좌석을 안내하는 자원봉사에 응해 주셔서 감사합니다.** 지금 여러분께 특별 지시를 드립니다. 일단 공연이 시작되면 **출구에서 가장 가까운 좌석 구역에 앉으십시오.** 그렇게 하면 늦게 도착하신 관람객분들을 도와드릴 때 다른 분들을 방해하는 것을 최소화할 수 있습니다. 아울러 **공연이 끝나면 조금 더 기다리셔서 우리 극장의 올해 최우수 직원으로 뽑힌 도나 파크를 위한 특별 표창식 거행에 함께 해 주시기 바랍니다.** 그녀는 관람객들의 좋은 평가를 받아서 선정됐으며, 그녀의 공헌을 축하할 수 있도록 도와주신다면 정말 감사하겠습니다. 15분 정도 밖에 걸리지 않을 것입니다.

어휘 volunteer 자원봉사하다; 자원봉사자 patron (단골) 고객 once 일단 ~하면 take a seat 앉다 seating 좌석 zone 구역(= section) exit 출구 minimize 최소화하다 disturbance 방해 assist 돕다 conclude 끝내다, 마치다 via ~를 통해서 positive 긍정적인 contribution 공헌, 기여

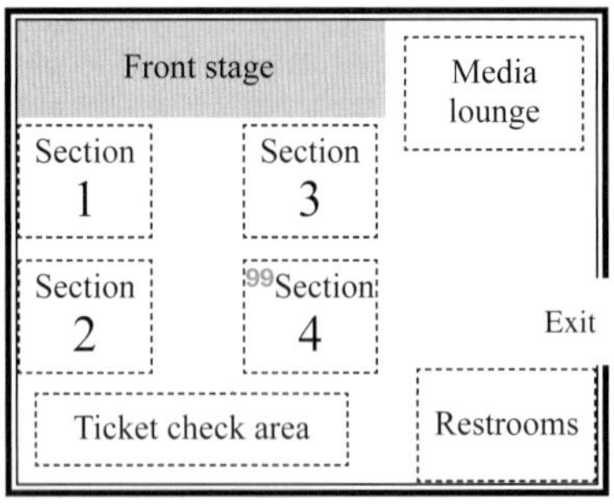

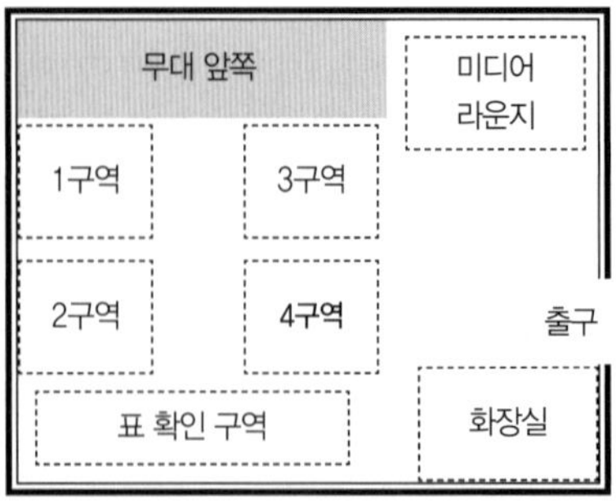

98

Who most likely are the listeners?

(A) Lighting technicians
(B) Music journalists
(C) Performers
(D) Ushers

청자들은 누구일 것 같은가?

(A) 조명 기사
(B) 음악 저널리스트
(C) 연기자
(D) 안내원

해설 전체 내용 관련 - 청자들의 신분

지문 맨 처음에 화자가 오늘 밤 뮤지컬 공연 동안에 티켓을 확인하고 공연 관람객들에게 좌석을 안내하는 자원봉사에 응해 줘서 고맙다(Thank you for volunteering to check tickets and show patrons to their seats during tonight's musical.)고 했으므로, 청자들은 자원봉사를 하는 안내원들임을 알 수 있다. 따라서 정답은 (D)이다.

99

Look at the graphic. What section does the speaker tell the listeners to sit in?

(A) Section 1
(B) Section 2
(C) Section 3
(D) Section 4

시각 정보에 의하면, 화자는 청자들에게 어느 구역에 앉으라고 하는가?

(A) 1구역
(B) 2구역
(C) 3구역
(D) 4구역

해설 시각 정보 연계 - 청자들이 앉아야 할 구역

지문 중반부에 화자가 청자들에게 일단 오늘 저녁 공연이 시작되면 출구와 가장 가까운 좌석 구역에 앉으라(please take a seat in the seating zone closest to the exit.)고 했다. 좌석 배치도를 보면 출구(Exit)와 가장 가까운 구역이 Section 4이므로 정답은 (D)이다.

100

What are the listeners asked to do after the show ends?

(A) Participate in a ceremony
(B) Share some feedback
(C) Return some equipment
(D) View an updated schedule

청자들은 공연이 끝난 후 무엇을 하도록 요청받는가?

(A) 기념식 참석
(B) 피드백 공유
(C) 장비 반환
(D) 업데이트된 일정 보기

어휘 participate in ~에 참여하다 return 돌려주다, 반환하다

해설 세부 사항 관련 - 청자들에 대한 요청 사항

지문 후반부에 청자들에게 공연이 끝나면 조금 더 기다렸다가 극장의 올해 최우수 직원인 도나 파크를 위한 특별 표창식 거행에 함께해달라(when the show concludes ~ our theater's Employee of the Year.)고 요청했으므로 정답은 (A)이다.

Test 8

TEST 9

1 (D)	**2** (A)	**3** (A)	**4** (D)	**5** (B)
6 (B)	**7** (B)	**8** (C)	**9** (C)	**10** (A)
11 (B)	**12** (C)	**13** (B)	**14** (C)	**15** (A)
16 (A)	**17** (A)	**18** (B)	**19** (C)	**20** (A)
21 (C)	**22** (A)	**23** (B)	**24** (C)	**25** (C)
26 (B)	**27** (B)	**28** (A)	**29** (B)	**30** (C)
31 (C)	**32** (B)	**33** (D)	**34** (A)	**35** (D)
36 (D)	**37** (B)	**38** (A)	**39** (B)	**40** (C)
41 (B)	**42** (B)	**43** (B)	**44** (A)	**45** (C)
46 (B)	**47** (C)	**48** (B)	**49** (C)	**50** (D)
51 (D)	**52** (B)	**53** (C)	**54** (A)	**55** (C)
56 (D)	**57** (A)	**58** (D)	**59** (D)	**60** (C)
61 (A)	**62** (D)	**63** (A)	**64** (A)	**65** (C)
66 (B)	**67** (C)	**68** (A)	**69** (B)	**70** (D)
71 (D)	**72** (A)	**73** (A)	**74** (C)	**75** (C)
76 (D)	**77** (A)	**78** (C)	**79** (A)	**80** (C)
81 (D)	**82** (B)	**83** (C)	**84** (C)	**85** (A)
86 (A)	**87** (D)	**88** (D)	**89** (B)	**90** (D)
91 (A)	**92** (C)	**93** (B)	**94** (C)	**95** (D)
96 (A)	**97** (B)	**98** (B)	**99** (B)	**100** (C)

PART 1

1 W-Am

(A) She's driving a car.
(B) She's replacing a tire.
(C) She's polishing a side-view mirror.
(D) She's wiping a windshield.

(A) 여자가 자동차를 운전하고 있다.
(B) 여자가 자동차 바퀴를 갈고 있다.
(C) 여자가 측면 거울을 닦고 있다.
(D) 여자가 자동차 앞 유리를 닦고 있다.

어휘 replace 교체하다, 갈다 polish (윤이 나게) 닦다, 광[윤]을 내다 side-view mirror 측면 거울 windshield (자동차의) 앞 유리

해설 1인 등장 사진 - 사람의 동작 묘사

(A) 동사 오답. 여자가 차를 운전하고 있는(driving a car) 모습이 아니므로 오답.

(B) 사진에 없는 명사를 이용한 오답. 사진에 타이어(tire)가 보이지 않으므로 오답.

(C) 명사 오답. 사진에 자동차의 측면 거울이 보이지만 여자가 측면 거울을 닦고 있는(polishing a side-view mirror) 모습은 아니므로 오답.

(D) 정답. 여자가 자동차의 앞 유리를 닦고 있는(wiping a windshield) 모습이므로 정답.

2 M-Au

(A) They're wearing safety helmets.
(B) They're building a house.
(C) One of the men is kneeling on the ground.
(D) One of the men is pointing to some machinery.

(A) 사람들이 안전모를 착용한 상태이다.
(B) 사람들이 집을 짓고 있다.
(C) 남자들 중 한 명이 바닥에 무릎을 꿇고 있다.
(D) 남자들 중 한 명이 기계를 가리키고 있다.

어휘 wear 입다, 착용하다 safety helmet 안전모 kneel 무릎을 꿇다 machinery 기계류, 기계장치

해설 2인 이상 등장 사진 - 사람의 상태 묘사

(A) 남자 네 명이 모두 안전모를 착용한(wearing safety helmets) 상태이므로 정답.

(B) 건설 인부들은 보이지만 사진에 집(house)이 보이지 않으므로 오답.

(C) 남자가 바닥에 무릎을 꿇고 있는(kneeling on the ground) 모습이 아니므로 오답.

(D) 사진에 기계(some machinery)가 보이지 않으므로 오답.

3 M-Cn

(A) Two men are talking to each other.
(B) A document is attached to a desk.
(C) A phone call is being made.
(D) A vehicle is stopped at an intersection.

(A) 두 남자가 대화를 나누고 있다.
(B) 문서가 책상에 부착되어 있다.
(C) 전화 통화를 하고 있다.
(D) 자동차 한 대가 교차로에 서 있다.

어휘 document 문서, 서류 attach 붙이다, 첨부하다 vehicle 탈것, 자동차 intersection 교차로, 사거리

해설 2인 이상 등장 사진 - 사람 또는 사물 중심 묘사

(A) 두 남자가 대화를 나누고 있는(are talking to each other) 모습이므로 정답.

(B) 책상 위에 문서가 보이지만 책상에 부착되어 있는(is attached to a desk) 상태가 아니므로 오답.

(C) 사진에 전화기는 하나 있지만 전화 통화를 하고 있는(is being made) 사람은 없으므로 오답.

(D) 사진에 자동차 한 대가 보이지만 교차로에 정차해 있는(is stopped at an intersection) 상태가 아니므로 오답.

4 W-Br

(A) A table is being assembled.
(B) A sofa is being moved into a room.
(C) Some curtains are pulled closed.
(D) Armchairs have been placed on a floor.

(A) 탁자가 조립되고 있다.
(B) 소파가 방 안으로 옮겨지고 있다.
(C) 커튼들이 닫혀져 있다.
(D) 안락의자들이 바닥에 놓여 있다.

어휘 assemble 조립하다 pull 당기다 closed 닫힌, 폐쇄된 armchair 안락의자 place 놓다

해설 실내 사물 사진 – 다양한 사물의 상태 묘사

(A) 탁자가 조립되고 있는(is being assembled) 모습이 아니므로 오답.
(B) 소파가 방 안으로 옮겨지고 있는(is being moved) 모습이 아니므로 오답.
(C) 커튼이 열려 있는 상태이지 닫혀 있는(are pulled closed) 모습이 아니므로 오답.
(D) 안락의자들이 바닥에 놓여 있는(have been placed on a floor) 상태이므로 정답.

5 W-Am

(A) Some grass is being planted.
(B) A lawn mower is being operated.
(C) Some bricks are piled next to a low wall.
(D) A man is pushing a wheelbarrow.

(A) 잔디가 심어지고 있다.
(B) 잔디 깎는 기계가 작동되고 있다.
(C) 낮은 담 옆에 벽돌이 쌓여 있다.
(D) 남자가 손수레를 밀고 있다.

어휘 plant 심다 lawn mower 잔디 깎는 기계 operate 가동하다, 조작하다 pile 쌓다, 포개다 wheelbarrow 손수레

해설 사물/배경 사진 –사물의 위치 및 상태 묘사

(A) 사진에 잔디가 보이지만 현재 심어지고 있는(is being planted) 상황이 아니므로 오답.
(B) 잔디 깎는 기계가 남자에 의해 작동되는(is being operated) 모습이므로 정답.
(C) 사진에 벽돌(bricks)이 보이지 않으므로 오답.
(D) 남자가 기계를 작동하고 있는 중이지 손수레를 밀고 있는(is pushing a wheelbarrow) 모습은 아니므로 오답.

6 M-Au

(A) Meals are being cooked by chefs.
(B) Lamps are hanging above a counter.
(C) A cashier is handing a receipt to a woman.
(D) A menu is being shown to customers.

(A) 식사가 요리사들에 의해 조리되고 있다.
(B) 조리대 위에 전등들이 달려 있다.
(C) 계산원이 여자에게 영수증을 하나 건네고 있다.
(D) 메뉴가 손님들에게 보여지고 있다.

어휘 meal 식사 cook 조리[요리]하다 chef 요리사 lamp 전등 hang 매달리다 counter 조리대, 카운터 cashier 계산원 hand 건네다 receipt 영수증 customer 고객, 손님

해설 2인 이상 등장 사진 – 사람 또는 사물 중심 묘사

(A) 요리사들에 의해 식사가 조리되고 있는(are being cooked) 모습이 아니므로 오답.
(B) 여러 개의 전등이 조리대 위에 달려 있는(are hanging above a counter) 모습이므로 정답.
(C) 계산원이 영수증을 건네는(is handing a receipt) 모습이 아니므로 오답.
(D) 사진에 메뉴(menu)가 보이지 않고, 고객 중 한 명은 종업원과 이야기하고 있으므로 오답.

PART 2

7

M-Cn Who placed the lunch order?

W-Am (A) It's on the table.

(B) The office manager.

(C) In alphabetical order.

누가 점심을 주문했죠?

(A) 식탁 위에 있어요.

(B) 사무장님이요.

(C) 알파벳순으로요.

어휘 place an order 주문하다 in alphabetical order 알파벳순으로

해설 주문자를 묻는 Who 의문문

(A) 연상 단어 오답. 질문의 place를 '(물건을) 두다'로 잘못 이해했을 때 위치 측면에서 연상 가능한 on the table을 이용한 오답.

(B) 정답. 점심 주문자를 묻는 질문에 사무장(office manager)이라는 구체적인 인물로 응답하고 있으므로 정답.

(C) 단어 반복 오답. 질문의 order를 반복 이용한 오답. 질문에서 order는 '주문'의 의미로 쓰였으나 여기서는 '순서'의 의미로 쓰임.

8

W-Br Could I borrow your phone?

M-Au (A) It's written on my business card.

(B) A call in the afternoon.

(C) Sure, when it finishes charging.

당신 전화기 좀 빌릴 수 있을까요?

(A) 내 명함에 적혀 있어요.

(B) 오후에 전화요.

(C) 물론이죠, 충전이 끝나면요.

어휘 borrow 빌리다 business card 명함 charge 충전하다

해설 부탁/요청의 의문문

(A) 연상 단어 오답. 질문의 phone에 대해 전화 번호 출처 측면에서 연상 가능한 business card를 이용한 오답.

(B) 연상 단어 오답. 질문의 phone에서 연상 가능한 call을 이용한 오답.

(C) 정답. 전화기를 빌려달라는 요청을 수락한(Sure) 후, 충전이 끝나면(when it finishes charging) 빌려주겠다고 응답하고 있으므로 정답.

9

W-Am Where is the registration desk?

M-Cn (A) In his briefcase.

(B) I need more chairs.

(C) Down the hall and to the left.

등록 데스크가 어디에 있나요?

(A) 그의 서류가방 안에요.

(B) 의자가 더 필요해요.

(C) 복도 저쪽으로 가시면 왼편에 있어요.

어휘 registration desk 등록 데스크 briefcase 서류가방 down the hall 복도를 따라 쭉 가서, 복도 저쪽에 to the left 왼편으로

해설 등록 데스크의 위치를 묻는 Where 의문문

(A) 질문과 상관없는 오답. 등록 데스크가 서류가방 안에 있을 수는 없으므로 오답.

(B) 연상 단어 오답. 질문의 desk에서 연상 가능한 chairs를 이용한 오답.

(C) 정답. 등록 데스크가 어디에 있는지 묻는 질문에 대해 복도를 따라가다 왼쪽에 있다(Down the hall and to the left.)는 구체적인 길 안내로 응답하고 있으므로 정답.

10

W-Cn When will the air conditioning be turned on?

W-Am (A) That's Ms. Ingram's decision.

(B) They're in pretty good condition.

(C) The red button at the top.

에어컨은 언제 켜지나요?

(A) 잉그램 씨가 결정합니다.

(B) 상태가 꽤 좋아요.

(C) 상단에 있는 빨간 버튼요.

어휘 decision 결정 in good condition 상태가 좋은

해설 에어컨 작동 시점을 묻는 When 의문문

(A) 정답. 에어컨 작동 시점을 묻는 질문에 잉그램 씨가 결정한다(Ms. Ingram's decision)고 응답하고 있으므로 정답.

(B) 유사 발음 오답. 질문의 conditioning과 부분적으로 발음이 동일한 condition을 이용한 오답.

(C) 연상 단어 오답. 질문의 air conditioning에서 연상 가능한 button을 이용한 오답.

11

M-Au Do you need help with that stack of boxes?

W-Br (A) The information on our stock.

(B) No, they're not as heavy as they look.

(C) Hugh in General Affairs.

그 상자 더미들에 대해 도움이 필요하신가요?

(A) 저희 재고에 관한 정보요.

(B) 아니요, 보이는 것만큼 무겁지는 않아요.

(C) 총무부의 휴요.

어휘 stack 더미 stock 재고 general affairs 총무, 서무

해설 도움 필요 여부를 묻는 일반 의문문

(A) 유사 발음 오답. 질문의 stack과 발음이 유사한 stock을 이용한 오답.

(B) 정답. 도움 필요 여부에 대해 먼저 No라고 부정적 응답을 한 후, 보이는 것만큼 무겁지 않다(they're not as heavy as they look)는 부연 설명을 하고 있으므로 정답.

(C) 질문과 상관없는 오답. Who 의문문에 어울리는 응답이므로 오답.

12

W-Br How did you learn about this exhibition?

M-Cn (A) There will be several kinds of art on display.

(B) Yes, let's go to the gift shop.

(C) A coworker recommended it.

이 전시회에 대해 어떻게 알게 되셨어요?
(A) 여러 종류의 예술품이 전시될 겁니다.
(B) 네, 기념품점으로 가시죠.
(C) 동료가 추천해 줬어요.

어휘 exhibition 전시, 전시회 on display 전시된 coworker 동료 recommend 추천하다

해설 정보 습득 경로를 묻는 How 의문문

(A) 연상 단어 오답. 질문의 exhibition에서 연상 가능한 display를 이용한 오답.

(B) Yes/No 불가 오답. How 의문문에 Yes/No 응답이 불가능하므로 오답.

(C) 정답. 전시회에 대해 어떻게 알게 되었는지 묻는 질문에 동료가 추천했다(A coworker recommended it.)는 구체적인 경로를 제시하고 있으므로 정답.

13

M-Au Would you like me to take your baggage to your room?

W-Am (A) The train left at one.

(B) I'd appreciate it.

(C) Enough for a sweater.

짐을 방으로 옮겨 드릴까요?
(A) 기차는 1시에 떠났어요.
(B) 그래 주면 고맙겠어요.
(C) 스웨터를 넣기에는 충분해요.

어휘 baggage 짐, 수화물 appreciate 고마워하다

해설 제안/권유의 의문문

(A) 연상 단어 오답. 질문의 baggage에 대해 운송 수단 측면에서 연상 가능한 train을 이용한 오답.

(B) 정답. 짐을 방으로 옮겨주겠다는 제안에 대해 그렇게 해 주면 고맙겠다(I'd appreciate it.)라는 표현으로 응답하고 있으므로 정답.

(C) 연상 단어 오답. 질문의 baggage에 대해 크기 면에서 연상 가능한 Enough를 이용한 오답.

14

M-Au Albert's stuck in traffic at the moment.

W-Br (A) Try restarting it.

(B) The high taxi fee.

(C) How late will he be?

앨버트는 지금 교통체증으로 막혀 있대요.
(A) 재시동 해 보세요.
(B) 비싼 택시 요금이요.
(C) 그가 얼마나 늦을까요?

어휘 be stuck in traffic 교통체증으로 꼼짝 못하다 restart 재시동시키다 taxi fee 택시 요금

해설 사실/정보 전달의 평서문

(A) 연상 단어 오답. 평서문의 stuck에 대해 자동차 고장 측면에서 연상 가능한 restarting을 이용한 오답.

(B) 연상 단어 오답. 평서문의 traffic에 대해 교통비 측면에서 연상 가능한 high taxi fee를 이용한 오답.

(C) 정답. 그가 교통체증에 걸렸다는 말을 듣고 그가 얼마나 늦을 건지(How late will he be?)를 되물으며 추가 정보를 요청하므로 정답.

15

W-Am Where will you take your next vacation?

W-Br (A) Somewhere warm, preferably.

(B) Isn't she off-duty now?

(C) At the end of the month.

다음 휴가는 어디에서 보낼 건가요?
(A) 가급적 어딘가 따뜻한 곳이요.
(B) 그녀는 지금 비번 아닌가요?
(C) 이 달 말에요.

어휘 vacation 휴가 preferably 가급적, 이왕이면 off-duty 비번의, 쉬는

해설 휴가지를 묻는 Where 의문문

(A) 정답. 다음 휴가지를 묻는 질문에 구체적인 장소를 언급하는 대신 어딘가 따뜻한 곳(somewhere warm)이라는 불확실성 표현으로 응답하고 있으므로 정답.

(B) 질문과 상관없는 오답. she가 가리키는 대상이 질문에 없으므로 오답.

(C) 연상 단어 오답. 질문의 Where를 시점을 묻는 When으로 잘못 들은 경우 시점 측면에서 연상 가능한 At the end of the month를 이용한 응답.

16

M-Au The painters will be here tomorrow morning.

M-Cn (A) We'd better move some of this furniture.

(B) No, the brochures should be printed in color.

(C) I don't hear anything.

페인트공들이 내일 아침에 여기 올 거예요.
(A) 이 가구 중 일부를 좀 옮기는 게 좋겠어요.
(B) 아뇨, 그 소책자들은 컬러로 인쇄해야 해요.
(C) 아무것도 들리지 않아요.

어휘 painter 페인트공, 화가 had better+동사원형 ~하는 게 낫다 brochure 팸플릿, 소책자 print ~ in color ~을 컬러로 인쇄하다

해설 사실/정보 전달의 평서문

(A) 정답. 페인트칠하는 사람들이 내일 아침에 온다는 말에 가구 중 일부를 옮기는 게(move some of this furniture) 낫겠다는 응답으로 사전 준비 작업을 제안하고 있으므로 정답.

(B) 연상 단어 오답. 평서문의 painters에 대해 색깔 측면에서 연상 가능한 in color를 이용한 오답.

(C) 유사 발음 오답. 평서문의 here와 부분적으로 발음이 동일한 hear를 이용한 오답.

Test 9

17

M-Au Which flight will you take to the biotech conference?

W-Br (A) Probably the 10 A.M. one.

(B) The match on channel eleven.

(C) That's a long layover.

생물공학 회의에 어떤 항공편을 타고 갈 건가요?
(A) 아마 오전 10시 비행기요.
(B) 채널 11에서 하는 경기요.
(C) 기착 시간이 길군요.

어휘 flight 항공편 biotech 생물공학, 바이오테크놀러지 match 경기, 시합 layover 기착, 도중하차(= stopover)

해설 항공편을 묻는 Which 의문문

(A) 정답. 회의에 어떤 항공편을 타고 가는지에 대해 오전 10시 비행기(the 10 A.M. one)라는 구체적인 시간의 항공편을 언급하고 있으므로 정답.

(B) 연상 단어 오답. 질문의 flight에 대해 시간 측면에서 연상 가능한 eleven을 이용한 오답.

(C) 연상 단어 오답. 질문의 flight에서 연상 가능한 layover를 이용한 오답.

18

M-Cn Weren't you looking for the information booth earlier?

W-Am (A) A question about the organization.

(B) Yes, but Lauren gave me a map.

(C) I can help you set it up.

아까 안내소를 찾고 있지 않았나요?

(A) 그 기관에 대한 질문이요.

(B) 네, 하지만 로렌이 내게 지도를 줬어요.

(C) 내가 당신이 그걸 설치하는 걸 도와줄 수 있어요.

어휘 look for ~을 찾다 information booth 안내소 organization 기관, 기구 set up 설치하다

해설 안내소를 찾고 있었는지를 확인하는 부정의문문

(A) 연상 단어 오답. 질문의 information에 대해 문의 사항 측면에서 연상 가능한 question을 이용한 오답.

(B) 정답. 아까 안내소를 찾고 있지 않았냐는 질문에 먼저 Yes로 긍정적 응답을 한 후, 로렌이 지도를 줬다(Lauren gave me a map)는 부연 설명을 하고 있으므로 정답.

(C) 연상 단어 오답. 질문의 booth에 대해 설치 측면에서 연상 가능한 set it up을 이용한 오답.

19

W-Am The building offers parking passes, doesn't it?

M-Au (A) It usually passes inspections.

(B) Let's make our best offer.

(C) They cost forty-five dollars a month.

그 건물은 주차권을 제공하죠, 아닌가요?

(A) 그건 대개 검사에 합격해요.

(B) 우리가 낼 수 있는 가장 좋은 금액을 제시합시다.

(C) 한 달에 45달러예요.

어휘 offer 제공하다; 호가 parking pass 주차권 pass 통과하다, 합격하다 inspection 점검, 검사 make one's best offer 가장 좋은 가격을 제시하다

해설 주차권 제공 여부를 묻는 부가의문문

(A) 단어 반복 오답. 질문의 passes를 반복 이용한 오답. 질문에서 pass는 '통행증'의 의미로 쓰였으나 여기서는 '합격하다, 통과하다'의 의미로 쓰였음.

(B) 단어 반복 오답. 질문의 offers에서 s를 빼고 반복 이용한 오답.

(C) 정답. 건물에서 주차권을 제공하는지에 대해 Yes를 생략한 채 한 달에 45달러(forty-five dollars a month)라는 구체적인 주차권 가격을 언급하고 있으므로 정답.

20

M-Cn Why are we leaving at four on Friday?

W-Br (A) Mr. Choi is letting us go early for the holiday.

(B) After the training session.

(C) Leave them on my desk, please.

우리가 왜 금요일에 4시에 퇴근하는 건가요?

(A) 우리가 휴일을 보내도록 최 씨가 일찍 보내 주는 거예요.

(B) 교육 과정 후에요.

(C) 그것들을 제 책상 위에 두세요.

어휘 leave 떠나다, 퇴근하다; 놔두다 holiday 휴일, 휴가 training session 교육 (과정), 훈련

해설 4시에 퇴근하는 이유를 묻는 Why 의문문

(A) 정답. 금요일에 왜 4시에 퇴근하는지를 묻는 질문에 휴일을 보내도록 최 씨가 일찍 보내주는 것(letting us go early for the holiday)이라는 구체적인 이유를 언급하고 있으므로 정답.

(B) 질문과 상관없는 오답. 시점을 묻는 When 의문문에 어울리는 응답이므로 오답.

(C) 파생어 오답. 질문의 leaving과 파생어 관계인 leave를 이용한 오답.

21

W-Br Who will supervise the interns this year?

M-Au (A) Because of budget cuts.

(B) No, I wasn't surprised.

(C) Who did it last year?

올해는 누가 인턴 사원들을 관리하게 되나요?

(A) 예산 삭감 때문에요.

(B) 아니오, 놀라지 않았어요.

(C) 작년에는 누가 했죠?

어휘 supervise 감독하다, 관리하다 intern 인턴 사원 budget cut 예산 삭감[감축]

해설 인턴 관리자를 묻는 Who 의문문

(A) 질문과 상관없는 오답. 이유를 묻는 Why 의문문에 어울리는 응답이므로 오답.

(B) Yes/No 불가 오답. 인턴 관리자를 묻는 Who 의문문에 Yes/No 응답이 불가능하기 때문에 오답.

(C) 정답. 올해 인턴 관리자를 묻는 질문에, 작년 관리자는 누구였는지(Who did it last year?)를 되묻고 있으므로 정답.

22

W-Br Have you run across any tips for handling e-mails?

M-Au (A) There was a helpful article last month.

(B) The review had tips on jogging.

(C) The engine's not running.

이메일 관리에 관한 조언을 본 적 있나요?

(A) 지난달에 유용한 기사가 하나 있었어요.

(B) 그 논평에 조깅에 관한 조언들이 있었어요.

(C) 엔진이 작동을 하지 않아요.

어휘 run across 우연히 발견하다 tip 조언 handle 다루다, 처리하다 review 논평, 평가 run (기계 등이) 작동하다, 움직이다

해설 조언을 봤는지를 묻는 조동사(have) Yes/No 의문문

(A) 정답. 이메일 관리에 관한 조언을 봤는지에 대해 Yes를 생략한 채 지난달에 유용한 기사(a helpful article)가 하나 있었다는 우회적 응답을 하고 있으므로 정답.

(B) 단어 반복 오답. 질문의 tips를 반복 이용한 오답.

(C) 파생어 오답. 질문의 run과 파생어 관계인 running을 이용한 오답.

23

M-Au Dae-Hyun won the design contest, didn't he?

W-Am (A) Check the contest instructions first.

(B) He bought a computer with the prize money.

(C) In the lobby of Parseman Associates.

대현 씨가 디자인 대회에서 우승했죠, 그렇지 않나요?

(A) 대회 안내문을 먼저 확인하세요.

(B) 그는 상금으로 컴퓨터를 샀어요.

(C) 파스먼 어소시에이츠의 로비에서요.

어휘 instructions 지시, 설명 prize money 상금

해설 우승 여부를 확인하는 부가의문문

(A) 단어 반복 오답. 질문에 나온 contest를 반복한 오답.

(B) 정답. 대현 씨가 디자인 대회에서 우승했는지에 대한 질문에 상금으로 컴퓨터를 샀다(He bought a computer with the prize money.)는 우회적 표현으로 응답하고 있으므로 정답.

(C) 질문과 상관없는 오답. 장소를 묻는 Where 의문문에 어울리는 응답이므로 오답.

24

W-Br Why is Sandra handing out those blue envelopes?

M-Cn (A) By the elevators on this floor.

(B) We could use handheld devices, too.

(C) They're invitations to the staff banquet.

샌드라는 왜 저 파란 봉투들을 나눠주고 있나요?

(A) 이 층에 있는 엘리베이터들 옆에요.

(B) 우리는 휴대용 장치도 필요해요.

(C) 직원 연회 초대장이에요.

어휘 hand out 나눠주다, 배포하다 handheld 손으로 들고 다니는 device 장치 invitation 초대 banquet 연회

해설 봉투를 나눠주는 이유를 묻는 Why 의문문

(A) 질문과 상관없는 오답. 장소를 묻는 Where 의문문에 어울리는 응답이므로 오답.

(B) 유사 발음 오답. 질문의 handing과 부분적으로 발음이 동일한 handheld를 이용한 오답.

(C) 정답. 샌드라 씨가 파란 봉투를 나눠주는 이유를 묻는 질문에 봉투는 직원 연회 초대장(They're invitations to the staff banquet.)이라는 우회적 표현으로 응답하고 있으므로 정답.

25

W-Am When is Maki Sakurai's next book going to be published?

M-Au (A) Better reviews than her last one.

(B) I haven't read either of them.

(C) Should be early next year.

마키 사쿠라이의 다음 책은 언제 출간될 예정인가요?

(A) 지난번 것보다 평가들이 좋아요.

(B) 저는 둘 다 읽어 본 적이 없어요.

(C) 아마 내년 초일 거예요.

어휘 be published 출간[출판]되다 not ~ either 둘 다 ~ 아닌

해설 출간 시점을 묻는 When 의문문

(A) 연상 작용 오답. 질문의 next book에 대해 순서 측면에서 연상 가능한 last one을 이용한 오답.

(B) 연상 작용 오답. 질문의 book에서 연상 가능한 read를 이용한 오답.

(C) 정답. 마키 사쿠라이의 다음 책이 언제 출간될 것인지에 대해 내년 초쯤(Should be early next year.)이라는 대략의 시점으로 응답하고 있으므로 정답.

26

M-Au Ava's traveled thirty-two weeks out of the past year.

W-Br (A) Her assistant came in late today.

(B) What a busy schedule!

(C) It's a two-week-long course.

애바는 작년에 32주 동안 여행을 다녔어요.

(A) 그녀의 비서가 오늘 지각했어요.

(B) 정말 바쁜 일정이었군요!

(C) 그건 2주짜리 과정이에요.

어휘 travel 여행하다, 이동하다 out of ~ 중에 assistant 조수, 비서 come in late 지각하다

해설 사실/정보 전달의 평서문

(A) 질문과 상관없는 오답. 애바가 작년에 32주간 여행을 다녔다는 말에 그녀의 비서(Her assistant)가 오늘 지각을 했다는 응답은 맥락에서 벗어난 것이므로 오답.

(B) 정답. 애바가 작년에 32주 동안 여행을 다녔다는 말에 정말 바쁜 일정이었군요!(What a busy schedule!) 하고 감탄문으로 응답을 하고 있으므로 정답.

(C) 단어 반복 오답. 평서문의 weeks에서 s를 빼고 반복 이용한 오답.

27

M-Cn Shall we bring her in for an interview?

W-Am (A) When did you bring that?

(B) Yes, she was my favorite candidate.

(C) Who will view the interim results?

그녀를 면접에 부를까요?

(A) 그걸 언제 가져왔어요?

(B) 네, 가장 내 마음에 드는 지원자였어요.

(C) 누가 중간 결과를 살펴볼 건가요?

어휘 bring+사람+in ~를 불러들이다 bring 가져오다 interview 채용 면접, 인터뷰 candidate 지원자, 후보 view 주의 깊게 보다[살피다] interim results 중간 결과

해설 제안/권유의 의문문

(A) 단어 반복 오답. 질문의 bring을 반복 이용한 오답.

(B) 정답. 그녀를 면접에 부르자는 제안에 대해 먼저 Yes로 긍정적 응답을 한 후, 그녀가 가장 마음에 드는 지원자(my favorite candidate)였다고 호평을 하고 있으므로 정답.

(C) 유사 발음 오답. 질문의 interview와 부분적으로 발음이 동일한 interim을 이용한 오답.

28

W-Br Are you going to hang this safety sign on the door or higher up?

M-Au (A) There may be guidelines about that.

(B) A lot of people have signed up.

(C) To keep visitors out of the warehouse.

이 안전 표지판을 문에 걸 건가요, 아니면 더 높이 달 건가요?

(A) 그것에 대한 지침이 있을 거예요.

(B) 많은 사람들이 신청했어요.

(C) 방문객들이 창고에 들어가지 않게 하려고요.

어휘 safety 안전 guideline 지침 sign up 신청하다, 등록하다 keep ~ out of … ~를 …에 들이지 않다 warehouse 창고

해설 구를 연결한 선택의문문

(A) 정답. 질문의 선택사항으로 언급된 on the door나 higher up 대신, 제3의 선택사항을 제시한 것이므로 정답.

(B) 파생어 오답. 질문의 sign과 파생어 관계인 signed를 이용한 오답.

(C) 질문과 상관없는 오답. 이유를 묻는 Why 의문문에 어울리는 응답이므로 오답.

29

W-Am I can't find my company ID card.

M-Cn (A) Just place it on the scanner.

(B) You'll have to notify Security.

(C) There's another page on the back.

회사 신분증을 못 찾겠어요.

(A) 그냥 스캐너 위에 두세요.

(B) 보안팀에 알려야 할 거예요.

(C) 뒤에 페이지가 또 하나 있어요.

어휘 place 놓다, 두다 notify 알리다, 통고하다 security 보안

해설 사실/정보 전달의 평서문

(A) 연상 단어 오답. ID card에서 연상 가능한 scanner를 이용한 오답.

(B) 정답. 회사 신분증을 못 찾겠다는 말에 보안팀에 알려야 한다(You'll have to notify Security.)는 대처 방안을 제시한 것이므로 정답.

(C) 연상 단어 오답. can't find에서 연상 가능한 another page on the back을 이용한 오답.

30

W-Br Can we discuss the focus group findings at Monday's meeting?

M-Cn (A) We've recruited thirty customers.

(B) Monthly project updates.

(C) The agenda has already been set.

월요일 회의에서 포커스 그룹 조사 결과를 논의할 수 있을까요?

(A) 저희는 30명의 고객을 모집했어요.

(B) 월별 프로젝트 업데이트요.

(C) 회의 안건은 이미 정해졌어요.

어휘 focus group 포커스 그룹, 초점집단 findings 조사[연구] 결과 recruit 모집하다, 뽑다 agenda 의제, 안건

해설 부탁/요청의 의문문

(A) 연상 단어 오답. 질문의 focus group에서 연상 가능한 customers를 이용한 오답.

(B) 연상 단어 오답. 질문의 meeting에서 연상 가능한 Monthly project를 이용한 오답.

(C) 정답. 회의 안건이 이미 정해졌다(The agenda has already been set.)면서 포커스 그룹 조사 결과를 논의할 수 없음을 우회적으로 표현하고 있으므로 정답.

31

W-Am Don't you have to finish building the prototype tonight?

M-Au (A) An award nomination.

(B) Color ink from the office supplies store.

(C) The deadline was extended to tomorrow.

견본 제작을 오늘 저녁에 끝내야 하지 않나요?

(A) 수상 후보 지명이요.

(B) 사무용품점에서 구입한 칼라 잉크요.

(C) 마감일이 내일로 연장됐어요.

어휘 prototype 견본, 원형 award 상 nomination 지명, 임명 office supplies 사무용품 deadline 마감일 extend 연장하다

해설 제작 완료 여부를 묻는 부정의문문

(A) 질문과 상관없는 오답. 견본 제작을 오늘 저녁까지 마쳐야 하는지에 대해 수상 후보지명(An award nomination)이라는 답변은 질문의 맥락에서 벗어난 것이므로 오답.

(B) 질문과 상관없는 오답. What 의문문에 어울리는 응답이므로 오답.

(C) 정답. 제작을 오늘 저녁까지 마쳐야 하는지 묻는 질문에 마감일이 내일로 연장되었다(The deadline was extended to tomorrow.)는 응답을 하고 있으므로 정답.

PART 3

32-34

M-Cn [32]**Reilly Air, Joe speaking.** How can I help you today?

W-Am Hello. I'm calling to make a change to a reservation. You see, [33]**I booked a flight for a coworker without realizing that he's a vegetarian. I need to make sure he gets the appropriate lunch option.**

M-Cn That shouldn't be a problem. [34]**Could you tell me the confirmation number for the booking?** It should be right at the top of your confirmation e-mail.

W-Am Sure. It's 045581. And my coworker's name is Luther Webb.

남: **라일리 에어의 조입니다.** 오늘은 무엇을 도와드릴까요?

여: 안녕하세요. 예약을 변경하려고 전화했어요. 글쎄, **동료가 채식주의자라는 사실을 모르고 그의 항공편을 예약했어요. 그가 적절한 점심 식사를 받도록 해야 해요.**

남: 문제 없을 겁니다. **예약 확정 번호를 말씀해 주시겠어요?** 확정 이메일 바로 위에 있을 겁니다.

여: 네. 045581입니다. 동료의 이름은 루터 웹이고요.

어휘 make a change to ~를 변경하다 reservation 예약 book 예약하다 coworker 동료 realize 인식하다, 깨닫다 vegetarian 채식주의자 appropriate 적절한 confirmation 확정

32

Who most likely is the man?

(A) A hotel clerk
(B) An airline employee
(C) A restaurant manager
(D) A rental car agent

남자는 누구겠는가?

(A) 호텔 직원
(B) 항공사 직원
(C) 식당 관리자
(D) 렌터카 업체 직원

어휘 clerk 직원, 사무원 agent 대리인, 중개인

해설 전체 내용 관련 – 남자의 신분

남자의 첫 대사에서 라일리 에어의 조(Reilly Air, Jeo speaking.)라고 한 후, 여자에게 도와줄 사항이 무엇인지 물어보는 것으로 보아 남자는 항공사 직원이라는 사실을 알 수 있으므로 정답은 (B)이다.

33

Why is the woman calling?

(A) To cancel a reservation
(B) To complain about a policy
(C) To ask about a misplaced item
(D) To request a special meal

여자가 전화를 건 목적은 무엇인가?

(A) 예약을 취소하기 위해
(B) 정책에 관한 불만을 제기하기 위해
(C) 제자리에 없는 물건에 대해 물어보기 위해
(D) 특별식을 요청하기 위해

어휘 complain 불평하다 policy 정책 misplace 제자리에 두지 않다

해설 세부 사항 관련 – 전화를 건 목적

여자의 첫 대사에서 동료가 채식주의자인지 모르고 그의 항공편을 예약했다(I booked a flight ~ that he's a vegetarian.)면서 그가 적절한 점심 식사를 받도록 해야 한다(I need to make sure he gets the appropriate lunch option.)고 했으므로 정답은 (D)이다.

34

What does the man ask the woman to do?

(A) Provide a code
(B) Wait for a moment
(C) Send an e-mail
(D) Confirm an address

남자는 여자에게 무엇을 해달라고 요청하는가?

(A) 코드 알려주기
(B) 잠시 기다리기
(C) 이메일 전송하기
(D) 주소 확인해 주기

어휘 confirm 확인하다

해설 세부 사항 관련 – 여자가 받은 요청

남자의 마지막 대사에서 예약 확정 번호를 말해달라(Could you tell me the confirmation number for the booking?)고 요청했으므로 정답은 (A)이다.

▸▸ **Paraphrasing** 대화의 **tell me the confirmation number**
→ 정답의 **Provide a code**

35-37

M-Cn Yoon-Ji, I've been getting a lot of complaints about the pens that we ordered recently. [35]**Many employees say when they write with the pens, they feel rough and rub against their fingers in a painful way.** Is it possible to return them?

W-Br Oh, [36]**I don't think we can, because the office supply company has a policy of not accepting returns after the product boxes have been opened.**

M-Cn Well, I don't want our staff to continue using these pens. [37]**Can you please look online for some similar pens in the same price range?** I want to order some by the end of the day.

W-Br [37]**Sure, I'll do that right now.**

남: 윤지, 우리가 최근에 주문한 펜들에 대해 불만들이 많아요. **많은 직원이 펜으로 쓸 때 감촉이 거칠고 손가락이 쓸려서 아프대요.** 펜들을 반품할 수 있을까요?

여: 아, **할 수 없을 거예요. 제품 상자가 개봉된 다음에는 반품을 받지 않는 게 사무용품 회사의 방침이라서요.**

남: 음, 우리 직원들에게 이 펜을 계속 쓰게 하고 싶지 않네요. **같은 가격대에 비슷한 펜들이 있는지 인터넷으로 찾아봐 줄래요?** 오늘 안에 주문을 하면 좋겠어요.

여: **물론이죠, 지금 당장 찾아볼게요.**

어휘 complaint 불만, 불평 feel rough 거칠게 느껴지다 rub against ~에 대고 비비다 in a painful way 아프게 return 반품하다; 반품 accept 받아주다 similar 비슷한 price range 가격대 by the end of the day 오늘 안에

35

What does the man mention about the pens?

(A) They are too expensive.
(B) Their ink dries too slowly.
(C) Their design is unattractive.
(D) Using them is uncomfortable.

남자는 펜들에 대해 뭐라고 말하는가?

(A) 너무 비싸다.
(B) 잉크가 너무 느리게 마른다.
(C) 디자인이 볼품 없다.
(D) 사용하기에 불편하다.

어휘 unattractive 매력적이지 않은, 볼품이 없는

해설 세부 사항 관련 – 펜에 대한 남자의 언급

남자의 첫 번째 대사에서 많은 직원에 따르면 펜으로 쓸 때 감촉이 거칠고 손가락이 쓸려서 아프다(Many employees say ~ in a painful way.)고 했으므로 정답은 (D)이다.

▸▸ **Paraphrasing** 대화의 **rough ~ in a painful way**
→ 정답의 **uncomfortable**

36

Why is the woman unable to return the pens?

(A) She cannot find a receipt.
(B) She lost one of them.
(C) The return period has ended.
(D) Their packaging has been opened.

여자는 왜 펜들을 반품할 수 없는가?

(A) 영수증을 찾지 못한다.
(B) 펜 한 자루를 잃어버렸다.
(C) 반품 기간이 끝났다.
(D) 포장이 개봉되었다.

어휘 receipt 영수증 packaging 포장

해설 세부 사항 관련 – 반품할 수 없는 이유

여자의 첫 번째 대사에서 제품 상자가 개봉된 다음에는 반품을 받지 않는 게 사무용품 회사의 방침이기 때문에 반품을 할 수가 없을 것(I don't think we can ~ been opened.)이라고 했다. 즉, 포장이 개봉되어 반품을 할 수 없다는 의미이므로 정답은 (D)이다.

▸▸ **Paraphrasing** 대화의 **the product boxes**
→ 정답의 **Their packaging**

37

What will the woman most likely do next?

(A) Rearrange a storage room
(B) Search for replacements
(C) Collect some boxes
(D) Write an online review

여자는 다음에 무엇을 할 것 같은가?

(A) 보관 창고 재정리
(B) 대체품 조사
(C) 상자들 수거
(D) 온라인 이용 후기 작성

해설 세부 사항 관련 – 여자의 다음 행동

남자의 두 번째 대사에서 여자에게 같은 가격대의 비슷한 펜들이 있는지 인터넷에서 찾아봐 달라(Can you please look ~ price range?)고 부탁했고 이에 대해 여자가 지금 당장 찾아보겠다(Sure, I'll do that right now.)고 했으므로 정답은 (B)이다.

▸▸ **Paraphrasing** 대화의 **some similar pens in the same price range** → 정답의 **replacements**

38-40

M-Au Good afternoon. [38]**You've reached Tailored Cleaners, where we offer the best cleaning and ironing services in town.** How may I help you?

W-Am Hi. My name's Joanna Hardwick. [39]**I dropped off two rugs to be cleaned two weeks ago.** I've already paid for them. [39]**I just wanted to know if they're ready to be picked up.**

M-Au Oh, Ms. Hardwick. [40]**I tried to reach you on your mobile phone yesterday.** Yes, your rugs are ready. The clothes you brought in this week have also been dry-cleaned, so you can pick everything up at your earliest convenience.

남: 안녕하세요, **테일러드 세탁소입니다. 저희는 시내에서 가장 훌륭한 세탁 및 다림질 서비스를 제공합니다.** 무엇을 도와드릴까요?

여: 안녕하세요. 제 이름은 조애너 하드윅입니다. **제가 2주 전에 양탄자 두 장을 세탁 맡겼어요.** 계산은 이미 했고요. **그것을 찾으러 가도 되는지 알고 싶어요.**

남: 아, 하드윅 씨. **어제 휴대폰으로 전화드렸었는데요.** 네, 양탄자들이 준비되어 있습니다. 이번 주에 가져오신 옷도 드라이클리닝해 두었으니 되도록 빠른 시일에 오셔서 모두 찾아가시면 됩니다.

어휘 reach 연락하다, 도달하다 cleaning 세탁 ironing 다림질 drop off 갖다 놓다 rug 깔개, 양탄자 pay for ~의 비용을 지불하다 pick up ~을 찾다 clothes 옷, 의류 at one's earliest convenience 되도록 빠른 시일에, 형편이 닿는 대로

38

Where most likely does the man work?

(A) At a dry cleaner
(B) At a home appliance store
(C) At a fabric manufacturing company
(D) At a shoe shop

남자는 어디에서 일할 것 같은가?

(A) 세탁소
(B) 가전제품 판매점
(C) 방직 회사
(D) 신발 가게

해설 전체 내용 관련 – 남자의 근무지
대화 맨 처음에 남자가 전화를 받으며 테일러드 세탁소이며 시내에서 가장 훌륭한 세탁 및 다림질 서비스를 제공한다(You've reached Tailored Cleaners ~ in town.)고 했으므로 정답은 (A)이다.

▸▸ **Paraphrasing** 대화의 **Tailored Cleaners** → 정답의 **a dry cleaner**

39

What is the purpose of the woman's call?

(A) To report a problem
(B) To inquire about the status of an order
(C) To verify some business hours
(D) To find out a price

여자가 전화한 목적은 무엇인가?

(A) 문제를 알리려고
(B) 주문 상태에 관해 문의하려고
(C) 영업시간을 확인하려고
(D) 가격을 알아보려고

어휘 inquire 문의하다 status 상태, 사정 verify 확인하다, 입증하다

해설 전체 내용 관련 – 여자가 전화를 건 목적
여자의 대사에서 2주 전에 양탄자 두 장을 세탁 맡겼다(I dropped off two rugs to be cleaned two weeks ago.)면서 그 양탄자들을 찾으러 가도 되는지 알고 싶다(I just wanted to know ~ picked up.)고 했다. 여자는 세탁 주문한 물품의 상태에 관해 문의하려고 전화를 한 것이므로 정답은 (B)이다.

40

What did the man do yesterday?

(A) Worked overtime
(B) Fixed a machine
(C) Called a customer
(D) Picked up some files

남자는 어제 무엇을 했는가?

(A) 야근을 했다.
(B) 기계를 수리했다.
(C) 손님에게 전화했다.
(D) 서류철을 몇 개 가져갔다.

해설 세부 사항 관련 – 남자가 어제 한 일
남자의 두 번째 대사에서 어제 여자에게 휴대폰으로 전화를 했었다(I tried to reach you on your mobile phone yesterday)고 했으므로 정답은 (C)이다.

▸▸ **Paraphrasing** 대화의 **tried to reach you on your mobile phone** → 정답의 **Called a customer**

41-43

W-Br Hi, Jason. I just read over your market research report. [41]**I really like the way its charts provide side-by-side comparisons of customer satisfaction ratings.**

M-Cn Thank you. I wanted to make sure the data was presented efficiently.

W-Br Yes, and [42]**the last section summarizes the findings well. Just one thing...** most reports end with a list of recommendations.

M-Cn OK, I'll work on that then. I have until Friday morning to submit it, right?

W-Br Yes, but [43]**I'll be away that entire day to host the grand opening celebration of our new branch office.** So please turn it in to Kevin.

여: 안녕하세요, 제이슨. 방금 당신의 시장조사 보고서를 다 읽었어요. **고객 만족도 순위를 도표로 나란히 비교한 것이 정말 마음에 들어요.**
남: 고맙습니다. 자료를 효율적으로 제시하고 싶었습니다.
여: **네, 그리고 마지막 부분에서 결과를 잘 요약하고 있더군요. 다만 한 가지...** 대부분의 보고서는 끝에 건의사항을 제시하지요.
남: 그렇군요. 그럼 그 부분을 손보도록 하겠습니다. 금요일 아침까지 제출하면 되지요?
여: **네, 하지만 제가 그날은 신규 지점 개업 축하 행사를 주최하러 하루 종일 나가 있을 거예요.** 그러니 케빈에게 제출해 주세요.

어휘 market research 시장조사 chart 도표 provide 제공하다 side-by-side comparison 나란히 놓고 하는 비교 customer satisfaction ratings 고객 만족도 순위 make sure 꼭 ~하다 present 제시하다 efficiently 효율적으로 summarize 요약하다 findings 결과 end with ~로 끝나다 recommendation 건의사항 work on ~을 손보다 submit 제출하다(= turn in) be away 출타[부재] 중이다 entire day 하루 종일 host 주최하다 grand opening 개업, 개점 celebration 축하 행사 branch office 지점

41

What does the woman say about the man's report?

(A) It covers one year of research.
(B) It includes some graphics.
(C) It will be released to the public.
(D) It was completed after a due date.

Test 9

여자는 남자의 보고서에 관해 무슨 말을 하는가?

(A) 1년 동안의 연구를 다루고 있다.
(B) 그래픽을 포함하고 있다.
(C) 일반인들에게 공개될 것이다.
(D) 제출일 이후에 완성되었다.

해설 세부 사항 관련 - 남자의 보고서에 대한 여자의 언급

여자의 첫 번째 대사에서 남자의 보고서에 대해 고객 만족도 순위를 도표로 나란히 비교한 것이 정말 마음에 든다(I really like the way ~ satisfaction ratings.)고 했으므로 정답은 (B)이다.

▸▸ **Paraphrasing** 대화의 **charts** → 정답의 **some graphics**

42

What does the woman most likely mean when she says, "most reports end with a list of recommendations"?

(A) She did not finish reading a report.
(B) She is suggesting a revision.
(C) She is confused by some results.
(D) She appreciates the man's creativity.

여자가 "대부분의 보고서는 끝에 건의사항을 제시하지요"라고 말한 의도는 무엇인가?

(A) 보고서를 다 읽지 않았다.
(B) 수정을 제안하고 있다.
(C) 일부 결과들을 보고 혼란스러워한다.
(D) 남자의 창의성을 인정한다.

어휘 revision 수정 appreciate 진가를 인정하다[알아보다]

해설 화자의 의도 파악 - 대부분의 보고서에 대한 언급

여자의 두 번째 대사에서 보고서 마지막 부분에서 결과를 잘 요약하고 있지만 그런데 한 가지.. (the last section summarizes the findings well. Just one thing…)라고 말을 했다. 그러고 나서 대부분의 보고서는 끝에 건의사항을 제시한다는 말을 했으므로 정답은 (B)이다.

43

What will the woman most likely do on Friday?

(A) Proofread a document
(B) Host an event
(C) Move her office
(D) Issue some invoices

여자는 금요일에 무엇을 할 것 같은가?

(A) 문서 교정
(B) 행사 주최
(C) 사무실 이전
(D) 청구서 발행

해설 세부 사항 관련 - 여자가 금요일에 할 일

대화 맨 마지막에 여자가 그날(금요일)은 신규 지점 개업 축하 행사를 주최하러 하루 종일 자리를 비울 것(I'll be away ~ branch office.)이라고 했으므로 정답은 (B)이다.

▸▸ **Paraphrasing** 대화의 **the grand opening celebration**
→ 정답의 **an event**

44-46

W-Am [44]**Hideki, how was your trip to Madrid?**

M-Au [44]**I had a wonderful holiday.** The hotel I was staying at was hosting a workshop, so it was crowded, but my trip was great overall. Did anything exciting happen at the office while I was gone?

W-Am Actually, [45]**you missed a big announcement—Greg will be retiring at the end of March.** He plans on slowly turning over responsibilities to Sarah, who will be the new artistic director. He'll start training her next Monday.

M-Au Oh, really? Well, I'm sorry to see Greg go, but I think Sarah will do a great job. [46]**I'm going to go find her and tell her how pleased I am.**

여: **히데키, 마드리드 여행은 어땠어요?**
남: **근사한 휴가를 보냈어요.** 제가 묵던 호텔에 워크숍이 열려서 사람들로 붐볐지만, 여행은 전반적으로 아주 좋았어요. 제가 없는 사이 사무실에 흥미로운 일이 있었나요?
여: 실은, **당신은 중요한 공지를 못 들었네요. 그렉이 3월 말에 퇴직할 거래요.** 그는 책임 업무를 서서히 신임 미술 감독인 세라에게 넘길 계획이에요. 다음 주 월요일부터 세라를 교육하게 될 거예요.
남: 아, 정말이요? 음, 그렉이 떠날 거라니 아쉽네요, 하지만 세라가 아주 잘할 거예요. **그녀를 찾아가서 내가 얼마나 기쁜지 얘기해야겠어요.**

어휘 host 주최하다 crowded 붐비는 overall 전반적으로 while ~하는 동안 retire 퇴직[은퇴]하다 turn over responsibilities to ~ 책임[맡은 일]을 ~에게 넘겨주다 artistic director 미술 감독 train 교육하다

44

What did the man do in Madrid?

(A) He took a vacation.
(B) He met a client.
(C) He attended a workshop.
(D) He inspected a project site.

남자는 마드리드에서 무엇을 했는가?

(A) 휴가를 갔다.
(B) 고객을 만났다.
(C) 워크숍에 참석했다.
(D) 프로젝트 현장을 점검했다.

어휘 inspect 점검하다, 검사하다 site 현장, 장소

해설 세부 사항 관련 - 남자가 마드리드에서 한 일

대화 맨 처음에 여자가 남자에게 마드리드 여행은 어땠는지(how was your trip to Madrid?)를 물었고, 이에 대해 남자가 멋진 휴가를 보냈다(I had a wonderful holiday.)고 했으므로 정답은 (A)이다.

▸▸ **Paraphrasing** 대화의 **had a wonderful holiday**
→ 정답의 **took a vacation**

45

What happened at the office while the man was gone?

(A) A renovation project was started.
(B) A negotiation was rescheduled.
(C) A retirement was announced.
(D) Some supplies were damaged.

남자가 없는 동안 회사에 무슨 일이 있었는가?

(A) 보수 공사가 시작되었다.
(B) 협상 일정이 재조정되었다.
(C) 퇴직 발표가 있었다.
(D) 일부 공급품이 파손되었다.

해설 세부 사항 관련 - 남자가 없는 동안 사무실에서 있었던 일

여자의 두 번째 대사에서 남자가 중요한 공지를 못 들었는데 그건 바로 그렉이 3월 말에 퇴직을 한다는 것(you missed ~ at the end of March.)이라고 했으므로 정답은 (C)이다.

46

What will the man offer to Sarah?

(A) His assistance
(B) His congratulations
(C) Some instructions
(D) Some incentives

남자는 세라에게 무엇을 해주겠는가?

(A) 지원
(B) 축하
(C) 설명
(D) 인센티브

어휘 instructions 설명(서), 지시 incentive 인센티브, 장려(책)

해설 세부 사항 관련 - 남자가 할 일

대화 맨 마지막에 남자는 세라를 찾아가서 자신이 얼마나 기쁜지 얘기하겠다(I'm going to go find her and tell her how pleased I am.)고 했으므로 정답은 (B)이다.

▸▸ **Paraphrasing** 대화의 **tell her how pleased I am**
→ 정답의 **His congratulations**

47-49 3인 대화

M-Cn Hi, Fred and Carol. Brief update—[47]**management wants us to explore the idea of adding some organic lotions to our current line of skin care products.** Any thoughts?

M-Au It sounds like a good strategy.

W-Am Well, we should review the sales data for our existing products first... [48]**Fred, when do you expect to finish the revenue report?**

M-Au Oh, I just have to check a few more figures.

W-Am Great. We'll have more to discuss soon, then.

M-Cn Yes. And that reminds me—[49]**tomorrow is Wednesday. Don't forget that we're scheduled to sit down with our wholesale distributor.** Let's make sure we're well prepared.

남1: 안녕하세요, 프레드와 캐럴. 짧게 소식을 전할게요. **경영진에서 우리의 현재 기초 화장품군에 유기농 로션 몇 가지를 추가하는 아이디어를 연구해 보기를 원해요.** 어떤 의견이 있나요?
남2: 좋은 전략 같은데요.
여: 글쎄요, 먼저 기존 제품들의 매출 자료를 검토해야겠어요… **프레드, 수익 보고서 작성이 언제 끝날 것 같아요?**
남2: 아, 수치 몇 개만 더 확인하면 돼요.
여: 잘됐네요. 그럼 곧 논의할 내용이 더 많아지겠어요.
남1: 네, 그러고 보니… **내일이 수요일이네요. 우리가 도매 유통업체와 회의할 예정이라는 것 잊지 마세요.** 우리 반드시 잘 준비해요.

어휘 brief 간단한, 짧은 update 최신 정보 management 경영진 explore 탐구하다, 연구하다 organic 유기농의 skin care 피부 보호 thought 생각, 안 strategy 전략 review 검토하다 sales data 매출 자료 existing 기존의 revenue 수익 figure 수치 remind 상기시키다 wholesale distributor 도매 유통업체

47

What are the speakers mainly discussing?

(A) Discontinuing facility tours
(B) Updating a software program
(C) Expanding a product line
(D) Holding a career fair

화자들이 주로 논의하는 것은 무엇인가?

(A) 시설 견학 중단
(B) 소프트웨어 프로그램 업데이트
(C) 제품군 확대
(D) 채용 박람회 개최

어휘 discontinue (계속하던 것을) 중단하다 expand 확대[확장]하다

해설 전체 내용 관련 - 대화의 주요 내용

대화 맨 처음에 경영진이 현재 기초 화장품군에 유기농 로션 몇 가지를 추가하는 아이디어를 연구해 보길 원한다(management wants us to explore the idea of ~ skin care products.)고 했고 화자들이 이것에 대해 의견을 나누고 있으므로 정답은 (C)이다.

▸▸ **Paraphrasing** 대화의 **adding** → 정답의 **expanding**

48

What does the woman ask Fred about?

(A) A potential venue
(B) A financial report
(C) A contract renewal
(D) An advertising approach

Test 9

여자는 프레드에게 무엇에 관해 물어보는가?
(A) 가능한 장소
(B) 재무 보고서
(C) 계약 갱신
(D) 광고 접근법

어휘 potential 잠재적인, ~의 가능성이 있는 venue 장소, 개최지 contract 계약(서) renewal 갱신, 재계약 approach 접근(법)

해설 세부 사항 관련 - 여자의 문의 사항
여자의 첫 번째 대사에서 프레드에게 수익 보고서 작성이 언제 끝나는지(Fred, when do you expect to finish the revenue report?)를 물었으므로 정답은 (B)이다.

▸▸ Paraphrasing 대화의 the revenue report
→ 정답의 A financial report

49

What will the speakers most likely do on Wednesday?
(A) Mail some documents
(B) Create a digital video
(C) Meet with a distributor
(D) Prepare a travel itinerary

화자들은 수요일에 무엇을 할 것 같은가?
(A) 문서 우편 발송
(B) 디지털 동영상 제작
(C) 유통업자와 회의
(D) 여행 일정 준비

해설 세부 사항 관련 - 화자들이 수요일에 할 일
대화 맨 마지막에 남자가 내일이 수요일이고 도매 유통업체와 회의가 있다는 걸 잊지 말라(tomorrow is Wednesday ~ with our wholesale distributor.)고 했으므로 정답은 (C)이다.

▸▸ Paraphrasing 대화의 sit down with our wholesale distributor
→ 정답의 Meet with a distributor

50-52

M-Cn Are you going to the marketing conference this spring? [50]**The program just went up on the Web site**, and some of the sessions look like they could be really helpful for us.

W-Br I haven't talked about it with my manager yet, but I'm interested, as long as it's within our budget. Where is it going to be held?

M-Cn At the Diamond Lake Conference Center in Centerville. [51]**I've heard that it's a really nice place.** Have you been there before?

W-Br No, but I'd like to go. I'll check out the conference's schedule of events. [52]**I hope Lindsey North is leading a session again this year.** She's always really interesting.

남: 올봄에 마케팅 컨퍼런스에 갈 예정인가요? **방금 웹 사이트에 일정표가 올라왔는데** 몇 개의 과정이 우리에게 정말 도움이 될 것 같군요.
여: 제가 상사분과 아직 얘기를 나누진 못했지만 관심이 있어요. 우리 예산을 초과하지 않는다면요. 어디에서 열리나요?
남: 센터빌에 있는 다이아몬드 레이크 컨퍼런스 센터에서요. **정말 근사한 곳이라고 들었어요.** 전에 가본 적 있나요?
여: 아니요, 하지만 가보고 싶어요. 컨퍼런스 일정을 확인해봐야겠네요. **올해에도 린지 노스가 과정을 진행하면 좋겠어요.** 그녀는 늘 아주 흥미롭거든요.

어휘 program 일정표, 차례표 session 과정, 회기 as long as ~하는 한, ~이기만 하면 within one's budget ~의 예산 범위 내에서 schedule of events 행사 일정

50

Where did the man see a conference schedule?
(A) In a trade journal
(B) On a posted notice
(C) In an e-mail
(D) On a Web page

남자는 컨퍼런스 일정을 어디에서 보았는가?
(A) 업계 잡지에서
(B) 게재된 공지에서
(C) 이메일에서
(D) 웹 페이지에서

해설 세부 사항 관련 - 남자가 컨퍼런스 일정을 본 곳
남자의 첫 번째 대사에서 일정표가 방금 웹 사이트에 올라왔다(The program just went up on the Web site)고 했으므로 정답은 (D)이다.

▸▸ Paraphrasing 대화의 on the Web site
→ 정답의 On a Web page

51

What does the man say about the conference center?
(A) It is nearby.
(B) It was built recently.
(C) It is owned by a city government.
(D) It has a good reputation.

남자는 컨퍼런스 센터에 관해 뭐라고 말하는가?
(A) 가깝다.
(B) 최근에 지어졌다.
(C) 시 정부 소유이다.
(D) 평판이 좋다.

어휘 reputation 평판

해설 세부 사항 관련 - 컨퍼런스 센터에 관한 남자의 언급
남자의 두 번째 대사에서 컨퍼런스 센터가 정말 멋진 곳이라고 들었다(I've heard that it's a really nice place.)고 했으므로 정답은 (D)이다.

52

What does the woman hope the conference includes?

(A) A networking opportunity
(B) A returning speaker
(C) A device demonstration
(D) A brainstorming session

여자는 컨퍼런스에 무엇이 포함되기를 바라는가?

(A) 인맥을 쌓을 기회
(B) 다시 오는 연사
(C) 기기 시연회
(D) 브레인스토밍 과정

어휘 networking (정보나 조언을 얻기 위한) 개인적 정보망의 형성 brainstorming 브레인스토밍, 난상 토론(회의에서 현안에 대해 각자가 생각나는 대로 의견을 말하고 최선책을 마련하는 일)

해설 세부 사항 관련 - 여자가 컨퍼런스에 포함되길 바라는 것

여자의 두 번째 대사에서 올해에도 린지 노스가 과정을 진행하면 좋겠다(I hope Lindsey North is leading a session again this year.)고 했으므로 정답은 (B)이다.

53-55 3인 대화

M-Au I'm joined today on Channel Eight News by executives from Euphoria Factory, the ice cream company. [53]**Your company launched an online campaign last month which asked consumers what new ice cream flavor they would like to see.** What prompted this?

W-Am Well, we value our customers and their feedback. We wanted them to help shape our brand.

M-Au Did a lot of people respond?

W-Br More than expected. [54]**We were surprised to receive over one million responses.**

M-Au So what were the results?

W-Br Well... [55]**Euphoria is proud to announce a pistachio ice cream flavor will go on the market in February.**

W-Am Yes, it'll join all our other flavors on shelves at retailers across America.

남: 오늘 채널 8 뉴스에는 아이스크림 회사인 유포리아 팩토리의 임원들을 모셨습니다. **귀사에서 지난달에 소비자들에게 어떤 아이스크림 맛이 새로 나오기를 원하는지를 묻는 온라인 캠페인을 시작하셨는데요.** 이것을 하게 된 계기가 무엇인가요?

여1: 글쎄요, 저희는 고객들과 그들의 의견을 소중히 여깁니다. 고객들이 저희 브랜드를 형성하는 데 도움을 주시기를 원했습니다.

남: 응답한 사람이 많은가요?

여2: 예상보다 많았습니다. **저희는 100만 개가 넘는 응답을 받아서 놀랐어요.**

남: 그래서 결과가 어땠나요?

여2: 음… **저희 유포리아는 피스타치오 맛 아이스크림이 2월에 시장에 출시될 것임을 발표하게 되어 뿌듯합니다.**

여1: 네, 그것이 미국 전역의 소매점들에 있는 저희 회사의 다른 맛 아이스크림들에 합류하게 될 것입니다.

어휘 be joined by ~와 함께하다 executive 이사, 임원 launch 시작하다 consumer 소비자 flavor 맛 prompt 촉발하다 value 귀하게 여기다 shape 형성하다 more than expected 예상보다 많은 be proud to + 동사원형 ~하게 되어 자랑스럽다 retailer 소매점

53

What did Euphoria Factory do last month?

(A) It lowered its prices.
(B) It published a newsletter.
(C) It surveyed the public.
(D) It hired a new executive.

유포리아 팩토리는 지난달에 무엇을 했는가?

(A) 가격을 내렸다.
(B) 회사 소식지를 발행했다.
(C) 여론 조사를 했다.
(D) 신임 임원을 채용했다.

해설 세부 사항 관련 - 유포리아 팩토리가 지난달에 한 일

남자의 첫 번째 대사에서 유포리아 팩토리가 다음에 나올 아이스크림 맛을 소비자들에 묻는 온라인 캠페인을 지난달에 시작했다(Your company launched ~ ice cream flavor they would like to see.)고 했으므로 정답은 (C)이다.

▸▸ Paraphrasing 대화의 consumers → 정답의 the public

54

What were the women surprised by?

(A) A number of participants
(B) An increase in expenses
(C) The simplicity of a procedure
(D) The results of an analysis

여자들은 무엇 때문에 놀랐는가?

(A) 참여자 수
(B) 비용 증가
(C) 절차의 단순성
(D) 분석 결과

해설 세부 사항 관련 - 여자들을 놀라게 한 것

두 번째 여자의 첫 번째 대사에서 자신들이 100만 개가 넘는 응답을 받아서 놀랐다(We were surprised to receive over one million responses.)고 했으므로 정답은 (A)이다.

▸▸ Paraphrasing 대화의 over one million responses
→ 정답의 A number of participants

55

According to the women, what will happen in February?

(A) Some consumers will win prizes.
(B) Some restaurants will open.
(C) A new item will become available.
(D) A retail store will have a sale.

여자들에 따르면, 2월에 무슨 일이 있겠는가?

(A) 일부 소비자들이 상을 받을 것이다.
(B) 일부 식당들이 문을 열 것이다.
(C) 새로운 상품을 구입할 수 있게 될 것이다.
(D) 한 소매점이 할인 판매를 할 것이다.

어휘 have a sale 할인 (판매)하다

해설 세부 사항 관련 - 2월에 발생할 일

두 번째 여자의 두 번째 대사에 유포리아는 피스타치오 맛 아이스크림을 2월에 시장에 출시할 것임을 발표하게 되어 뿌듯하다(Euphoria is proud to announce ~ in February.)고 했으므로 정답은 (C)이다.

▸▸ **Paraphrasing** 대화의 **a pistachio ice cream flavor**
→ 정답의 **a new item**

56-58

W-Br Accounting department, Tammy speaking.

M-Cn Hi. It's Ray in Sales. I'm having a problem with the new expense management system. [56]**Last week I requested repayment for a client dinner that I put on my credit card, but I haven't received a response yet.**

W-Br Hmm, your request should have been handled by now. [57]**Wait—you're checking the system's "My Activity" page, right? That's where you need to look.**

M-Cn Oh, I haven't done that, actually. Just a moment... Ah, yes, I see. Sorry—I expected an e-mail response, like before.

W-Br No problem. In fact, [58]**I think I'll send everyone a notice re-explaining this part of the new system.** You're not the first person who's been confused.

여: 회계부의 태미입니다.

남: 안녕하세요. 영업부의 레이입니다. 새로운 경비 관리 시스템에 문제가 생겼어요. **지난주에 제 신용카드로 결제한 고객 접대 저녁 식사 비용 지급을 요청했는데요. 아직 답변을 받지 못했어요.**

여: 음… 지금쯤이면 요청이 처리됐어야 하는데요. **잠깐만요. 시스템에서 "나의 활동" 페이지를 확인하고 계신 거죠, 그렇죠? 거기를 보셔야 해요.**

남: 아, 사실 그렇게 하진 않았어요. 잠깐만요… 아, 네, 보이네요. 죄송해요. 예전처럼 이메일로 답변이 올 줄 알았어요.

여: 괜찮습니다. **실은 새로운 시스템의 이 부분을 다시 설명하는 공지를 전 직원에게 보내야겠더라고요.** 혼선을 겪은 게 당신이 처음은 아니거든요.

어휘 accounting 회계 expense 비용 management 관리 repayment 상환 response 응답 handle 다루다 notice 공지, 알림 be confused 혼선을 겪다, 헷갈리다

56

What is the conversation mainly about?

(A) A business dinner
(B) Some sales data
(C) Some training sessions
(D) A reimbursement process

대화는 주로 무엇에 관한 것인가?

(A) 업무상의 저녁 식사
(B) 매출 자료
(C) 교육 세션
(D) 경비 환급 절차

어휘 reimbursement 상환, 배상

해설 전체 내용 관련 - 대화 주제

남자의 첫 번째 대사에서 지난주에 남자의 신용카드로 결제한 고객 접대 식사 비용 지급을 요청했는데 아직 답변을 못 받았다(Last week I requested repayment ~ I haven't received a response yet.)고 했고 이에 여자가 지금쯤 처리됐어야 한다며 대응하고 있으므로 정답은 (D)이다.

▸▸ **Paraphrasing** 대화의 **repayment** → 정답의 **reimbursement**

57

What does the man imply when he says, "I haven't done that, actually"?

(A) The woman has supplied helpful information.
(B) Another person deserves praise for a success.
(C) He was unable to meet a deadline.
(D) He is not qualified to give the woman advice.

남자가 "사실 그렇게 하진 않았어요"라고 말한 의도는 무엇인가?

(A) 여자가 유용한 정보를 제공했다.
(B) 다른 사람이 성공에 대해 칭찬받을 만하다.
(C) 그가 마감기한을 지킬 수 없었다.
(D) 그가 여자에게 충고를 할 만한 자격이 없다.

어휘 supply 제공하다 deserve ~할 만하다 praise 칭찬 meet a deadline 마감기한을 지키다 qualified 자격이 있는

해설 화자의 의도 파악 - 그렇게 하지 않았다는 말의 의도

인용문 바로 전 대사에서 여자가 시스템에서 "나의 활동" 페이지를 확인하고 있는지(you're checking the system's "My Activity" page, right?) 물어본 후, 바로 거기를 봐야 한다(That's where you need to look.)고 했다. 이에 남자가 사실 그렇게 하진 않았다고 했고 이후에 문제가 해결됐으므로, 남자가 놓친 유용한 정보를 여자가 제공했다는 의도가 내포되어 있음을 알 수 있어 정답은 (A)이다.

58

What does the woman decide to do?

(A) Recalculate some estimates
(B) Approve some requests
(C) Upgrade a computer system
(D) Issue a written clarification

여자는 무엇을 하기로 마음먹는가?

(A) 견적 재계산
(B) 요청 승인
(C) 컴퓨터 시스템 업그레이드
(D) 서면 설명 제공

어휘 estimate 견적 approve 승인하다 clarification 설명, 해명

해설 세부 사항 관련 – 여자가 한 결정

여자의 마지막 대사에서 새로운 시스템의 이 부분을 다시 설명하는 공지를 전 직원에게 보내야겠다(I think I'll send everyone a notice re-explaining this part of the new system.)고 했으므로 정답은 (D)이다.

▸▸ **Paraphrasing** 대화의 **send everyone a notice**
→ 정답의 **Issue a written clarification**

59-61

W-Am Gabriel, [59]**I've noticed some customers have a hard time recognizing who our store employees are because our uniforms are black and we don't stand out.** Maybe we should change them to a brighter, eye-catching color like yellow or orange.

M-Au Yes, that's a good idea. A lot of our products are black, so we'll be easy to spot in bright clothing. Let's mention this to Ms. Reynolds tomorrow during our staff meeting.

W-Am Oh, [60]**I'll be using one of my vacation days tomorrow.** How about we schedule some time with her on Monday?

M-Au [61]**After the new shipment of televisions and refrigerators comes in?** Sure. That works for me.

여: 게이브리얼, **우리 매장 직원 유니폼이 검은색이라 눈에 잘 띄지 않아서 일부 고객들이 누가 우리 직원들인지 알아보는 데 어려움이 있다는 걸 알았어요.** 아마 유니폼을 노랑이나 주황처럼 더 밝고 눈에 잘 띄는 색으로 바꿔야 할 것 같아요.

남: 네, 좋은 생각이네요. 대다수의 우리 제품들이 검은색이니까 우리가 밝은 옷을 입고 있으면 쉽게 눈에 띌 거예요. 내일 직원 회의 때 레이놀즈 씨한테 이 얘기를 하죠.

여: 오, **내일은 제가 하루 휴가를 쓸 거예요.** 월요일에 그녀와 시간을 잡아보면 어떨까요?

남: **텔레비전과 냉장고가 새로 입고된 후에요?** 괜찮아요. 전 좋아요.

어휘 notice 알아채다 have a hard time -ing ~하는 데 어려움을 겪다 recognize 알아보다, 인식하다 stand out 눈에 잘 띄다, 도드라지다 eye-catching 시선을 끄는, 눈에 잘 띄는 spot 발견하다 shipment 선적(물), 배송(품) come in 들어오다, 입고되다

59

What are some customers having a difficult time doing?

(A) Finding some merchandise
(B) Understanding a policy
(C) Filling out some forms
(D) Identifying staff members

일부 고객들이 무엇을 하는 데 어려움을 겪고 있는가?

(A) 제품 찾기
(B) 방침 이해하기
(C) 양식 작성하기
(D) 직원들을 알아보기

어휘 fill out 작성하다 identify 신원을 확인하다

해설 세부 사항 관련 – 일부 고객들이 어려움을 겪는 일

대화 맨 처음에 여자가 직원 유니폼이 검은색이라 눈에 잘 띄지 않아 일부 고객들이 누가 매장 직원들인지 알아보는 데 어려움이 있음을 알게 되었다(I've noticed some customers ~ and we don't stand out.)고 했으므로 정답은 (D)이다.

▸▸ **Paraphrasing** 대화의 **recognizing who our store employees are**
→ 정답의 **Identifying staff members**

60

What will the woman most likely do tomorrow?

(A) Distribute a schedule
(B) Reserve a conference room
(C) Take a day off
(D) Set up some equipment

여자는 내일 무엇을 할 것 같은가?

(A) 일정표 배포
(B) 회의실 예약
(C) 하루 휴가 내기
(D) 장비 설치

해설 세부 사항 관련 – 여자가 내일 할 것

여자의 두 번째 대사에서 내일 휴가를 하루 쓰겠다(I'll be using one of my vacation days tomorrow.)고 했으므로 정답은 (C)이다.

▸▸ **Paraphrasing** 대화의 **use one of my vacation days**
→ 정답의 **Take a day off**

Test 9

61

Where most likely do the speakers work?

(A) At an electronics store
(B) At a clothing retailer
(C) At a supermarket
(D) At a plant shop

화자들은 어디에서 일할 것 같은가?

(A) 전자제품 매장
(B) 의류 소매점
(C) 슈퍼마켓
(D) 꽃가게

해설 전체 내용 관련 – 화자들의 근무지

남자의 두 번째 대사에서 텔레비전과 냉장고가 새로 입고된다(the new shipment of televisions and refrigerators comes in)고 했으므로 정답은 (A)이다.

62-64 대화 + 좌석 배치도

W-Br Hi, I'm calling because I have a question about your ferry from Obreon to Tassel. [62]**Does it have wireless Internet service for mobile devices?**

M-Au Yes, but you'll have to pay a fee for it.

W-Br That's fine. I'd like to buy a ticket for the first ferry on Saturday.

M-Au Sure. That will be departing at eight A.M. Do you have any seating preferences?

W-Br Uh, won't I choose my seat on board the ferry?

M-Au No, [63]**the Obreon-Tassel ferry only has reserved seating.**

W-Br Oh, [63]**I'm surprised to hear that.** Um... I guess I'd like a window seat.

M-Au All right, [64]**I'll reserve the last available window seat for you.** How will you be paying?

여: 안녕하세요. 오브레온에서 태슬로 가는 페리에 대해 질문이 있어 전화했습니다. **모바일 기기용 무선 인터넷 서비스가 제공되나요?**
남: 네. 하지만 요금을 내셔야 할 거예요.
여: 괜찮아요. 토요일 첫 번째 페리 티켓을 사고 싶습니다.
남: 네. 오전 8시에 출발합니다. 원하시는 좌석이 있나요?
여: 음, 페리에 타서 좌석을 선택하는 것 아닌가요?
남: 아니요. **오브레온에서 태슬로 가는 페리에는 예약 좌석만 있습니다.**
여: 아, **뜻밖이네요.** 음… 저는 창가 쪽 좌석이 좋겠네요.
남: 알겠습니다. **마지막 남은 창가 쪽 좌석을 예약해 드릴게요.** 지불은 어떻게 하시겠습니까?

어휘 wireless 무선의 fee 요금 depart 출발하다, 떠나다 seating 좌석 preference 선호, 선호하는 것 on board 탑승하여, 승선하여 reserve 예약하다 available 이용 가능한

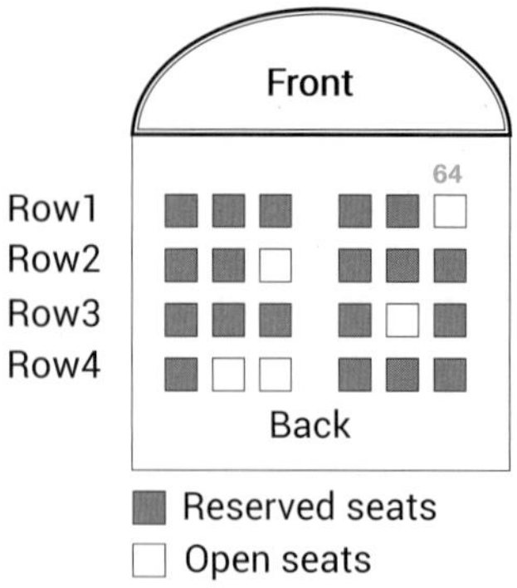

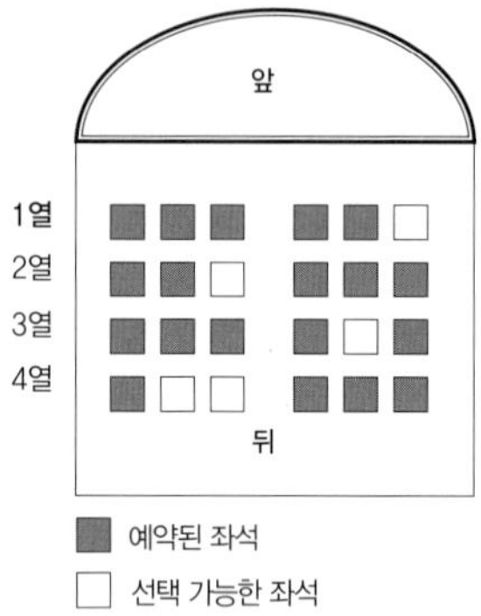

62

What does the woman inquire about?

(A) Using a dining service
(B) Bringing additional luggage
(C) Parking at the ferry terminal
(D) Accessing the Internet

여자는 무엇에 대해 문의하는가?

(A) 식사 서비스 이용
(B) 추가 수하물 지참
(C) 페리 터미널 주차
(D) 인터넷 접속

어휘 additional 추가의 access 접속하다

해설 세부 사항 관련 – 여자의 문의 사항

여자의 첫 번째 대사에서 모바일 기기를 위한 무선 인터넷 서비스가 제공되는지(Does it have wireless Internet service for mobile devices?) 물었으므로 정답은 (D)이다.

63

What is the woman surprised to learn about the ferry?

(A) Its passengers must book a particular seat.
(B) There is a fee for using its electrical outlets.
(C) It departs at later times on weekends.
(D) It makes several stops along its route.

여자가 페리에 대해 뜻밖이라고 생각한 사실은 무엇인가?
(A) 승객은 특정 좌석을 예약해야 한다.
(B) 콘센트 사용 요금이 부과된다.
(C) 주말에는 늦게 출발한다.
(D) 노선상에서 여러 번 정차한다.

어휘 passenger 승객 particular 특정한 electrical outlet 콘센트

해설 세부 사항 관련 – 뜻밖이라고 여겨지는 사실
남자의 세 번째 대사에서 오브레온에서 태슬로 가는 페리에는 예약 좌석만 있다(the Obreon-Tassel ferry only has reserved seating.)고 했다. 이에 여자가 뜻밖이라고(I'm surprised to hear that.) 했으므로 정답은 (A)이다.

64
Look at the graphic. Which row will the woman sit in?
(A) Row 1
(B) Row 2
(C) Row 3
(D) Row 4

시각 정보에 따르면, 여자는 어느 줄에 앉을 것인가?
(A) 1열
(B) 2열
(C) 3열
(D) 4열

해설 시각 정보 연계 – 여자가 앉을 줄
남자의 마지막 대사에서 하나 남은 창가 쪽 좌석을 예약해 주겠다(I'll reserve the last available window seat for you.)고 했다. 좌석표를 보면 창가 쪽 좌석이 남은 곳은 1열뿐이므로 정답은 (A)이다.

65-67 대화 + 건물 안내판

M-Cn Hi, I'm a new driver with DXT Courier, and [65]**I'm delivering some supplies to a company in this building.** I'm just checking... [66]**Their office is in Suite 2.** That's on the second floor, right?

W-Am Yes, that suite takes up the entire floor. Once you get off the elevator, you'll see the entrance door.

M-Cn Great, thank you. Oh, one more thing. I'm parked out front in a green-colored zone—do I need a permit?

W-Am No, you're fine. [67]**The green area is specifically for visitors. For future reference, note that the orange zone is reserved for employees.**

남: 안녕하세요. 저는 DXT 택배의 신입 기사인데, **이 건물에 있는 한 회사에 물품을 배달하러 왔습니다.** 그냥 확인하는 건데… **그 회사 사무실이 2호실에 있네요.** 2층에 있는 것 맞나요?
여: 네, 층 전체가 사무 공간이에요. 일단 승강기에서 내리시면 출입문이 보일 거예요.
남: 잘됐네요. 고맙습니다. 아, 한 가지만 더요. 차를 초록색 구역 앞에 주차했는데, 허가증이 필요한가요?
여: 아뇨, 괜찮습니다. **초록색 구역은 방문객 전용입니다. 앞으로 참고하시도록 알려드리자면, 주황색 구역은 직원들을 위해 따로 정해 놓은 것이니 유의해 주세요.**

어휘 courier 택배 회사, 배달원 take up 차지하다 entire 전체의 get off 내리다 entrance door 출입문 zone 구역 permit 허가증 for future reference 앞으로 참고하도록 be reserved for ~를 위해 따로 정해 놓다

Building Directory

Suite	Company
1	Garnet Associates
[66]2	Osage Consulting
3	Madison Research
4	Spencer Solutions

건물 안내

호실	회사
1	가넷 어소시에이츠
2	**오세이지 컨설팅**
3	매디슨 리서치
4	스펜서 솔루션즈

65
What is the purpose of the man's visit?
(A) He is checking a security system.
(B) He is going to a job interview.
(C) He is making a delivery.
(D) He is repairing an elevator.

남자의 방문 목적은 무엇인가?
(A) 보안 시스템을 확인하려고
(B) 구직 면접을 보려고
(C) 배달을 하려고
(D) 승강기를 수리하려고

해설 세부 사항 관련 – 남자의 방문 목적
남자의 첫 번째 대사에서 이 건물 내 한 회사에 물품을 배송하러 왔다(I'm delivering some supplies to a company in this building.)고 했으므로 정답은 (C)이다.

▸▸ Paraphrasing 대화의 **deliver** → 정답의 **make a delivery**

Test 9

66

Look at the graphic. Which company will the man visit?

(A) Garnet Associates
(B) Osage Consulting
(C) Madison Research
(D) Spencer Solutions

시각 정보에 의하면, 남자는 어느 회사를 방문할 것인가?

(A) 가넷 어소시에이츠
(B) 오세이지 컨설팅
(C) 매디슨 리서치
(D) 스펜서 솔루션즈

해설 시각 정보 연계 – 남자가 방문할 회사

남자의 첫 번째 대사에서 자신이 배달하는 회사 사무실이 2호실에 있다(Their office is in Suite 2.)고 했는데 건물 안내판을 보면 2호실 회사의 이름이 오세이지 컨설팅(Osage Consulting)으로 나와 있으므로 정답은 (B)이다.

67

What does the woman say about the parking areas?

(A) They are located behind the building.
(B) Some of them have a user fee.
(C) They are designated by color.
(D) They require printed permits.

여자는 주차 구역에 대해 뭐라고 말하는가?

(A) 건물 뒤편에 있다.
(B) 일부 구역에는 사용료가 있다.
(C) 색깔로 지정해 놓았다.
(D) 인쇄된 허가증이 필요하다.

어휘 designate 명시하다, 나타내다 require ~을 필요로 하다

해설 세부 사항 관련 – 주차 구역에 대한 여자의 말

대화 맨 마지막 여자의 말(The green area is specifically for visitors ~ reserved for employees.)을 통해 주차 구역이 색깔 별로 지정되어 있음을 알 수 있으므로 정답은 (C)이다.

68-70 대화 + 차트

W-Br Hi, Tim. This is last-minute, but... [68]**there's a live concert in the park this Saturday.** It has a great lineup of musicians. Here's the flyer.

M-Au Oh, that looks fun! Are others from our office going? Maybe we can get a group discount.

W-Br Only four of us can go. But, anyway, [69]**we qualify for the corporate sponsor price**— our firm actually helped fund the event.

M-Au I didn't know that. Well... how can I order a ticket?

W-Br Jenna, our budget assistant, is handling the paperwork. I still need to get my ticket, so [70]**I'll call her right now and ask her to order one for you, too.**

여: 안녕하세요, 팀. 이게 촉박하긴 한데… **이번 토요일에 공원에서 라이브 콘서트가 있어요.** 출연하는 음악가들이 대단해요. 여기 전단이 있어요.
남: 아, 재미있어 보이네요! 우리 사무실의 다른 직원들도 가나요? 어쩌면 단체 할인을 받을 수도 있을 것 같은데요.
여: 우리 중 네 명만 가요. 하지만 어쨌든 **우리는 후원사 가격 우대를 받을 수 있어요.** 우리 회사가 실제로 이 행사에 자금을 후원했어요.
남: 저는 몰랐네요. 음… 제가 입장권을 어떻게 주문할 수 있죠?
여: 예산 담당 보조인 제나가 서류 업무를 담당해요. 저도 아직 티켓을 구해야 하니까… **지금 제나에게 전화해서 당신 것도 한 장 주문해 달라고 부탁할게요.**

어휘 last-minute 막판의, 최종 순간의 lineup 출연진 group discount 단체 할인 qualify for ~할 자격이 있다 corporate sponsor price 후원사 우대가 fund 자금을 조달하다 paperwork 서류 업무[작성]

Admission price per person

University student	$5
[69]Corporate sponsor	$8
Groups of 20 or more	$10
General admission	$15

일인당 입장료

대학생	5달러
후원사	**8달러**
20명 이상 단체	10달러
일반 입장	15달러

68

What kind of event are the speakers discussing?

(A) A music concert
(B) A film festival
(C) A museum exhibit
(D) A theater performance

화자들은 어떤 행사에 관해 논의하고 있는가?

(A) 음악 콘서트
(B) 영화 축제
(C) 박물관 전시회
(D) 극장 공연

해설 전체 내용 관련 – 논의 중인 행사의 종류

여자의 첫 번째 대사에서 이번 주 토요일에 공원에서 라이브 콘서트가 있다(there's a live concert in the park this Saturday)고 했으므로 정답은 정답은 (A)이다.

69

Look at the graphic. Which ticket price will the speakers most likely pay?

(A) $5
(B) $8
(C) $10
(D) $15

시각 정보에 의하면, 화자들은 어떤 입장권 요금을 지불할 것 같은가?

(A) 5달러
(B) 8달러
(C) 10달러
(D) 15달러

해설 시각 정보 연계 – 지불할 입장권 요금

여자의 두 번째 대사에서 후원사 가격 우대를 받을 수 있다(we qualify for the company sponsor price)고 했다. 입장료 표를 보면 후원사(Corporate sponsor)는 8달러라고 되어 있으므로 정답은 (B)이다.

70

What will the woman probably do next?

(A) Rent a vehicle
(B) Print some paperwork
(C) Post a flyer on a wall
(D) Contact a coworker

여자는 다음에 무엇을 하겠는가?

(A) 차량 렌트
(B) 문서 출력
(C) 벽에 전단지 게시
(D) 동료에게 연락

해설 세부 사항 관련 – 여자의 다음 행동

대화 맨 마지막에 여자가 지금 제나에게 전화해서 남자의 표도 한 장 주문해 달라고 부탁하겠다(I'll call her ~ for you too.)고 했으므로 정답은 (D)이다.

▸▸ **Paraphrasing** 대화의 **call her** → 정답의 **contact a coworker**

PART 4

71-73 안내

W-Am OK, let's talk about the last item on today's agenda. Just like last year, management has provided a generous budget for a fun activity to reward everyone's hard work, and [71]**the events organizing committee has come up with three potential plans for us to choose among. Now, voting will again take place through e-mail.** [72]**In response to feedback from last year, though, you'll now have a full week to make your choice.** That should be plenty of time to consider each option. Uh, the e-mail describing the proposals is going out today, so look over it and then discuss it with each other. [73]**It could be helpful to hear other people's thoughts.**

자, 오늘의 마지막 안건에 대해 얘기해 보죠. 작년과 마찬가지로, 경영진에서 모두의 노고를 치하하기 위해 오락 활동에 쓸 넉넉한 예산을 지급했고요 **행사 조직 위원회는 우리가 선택할 수 있는 세 가지 가능한 계획안을 제시했습니다. 자, 투표는 이번에도 이메일을 통해 이뤄지겠습니다. 하지만 작년의 피드백을 반영하여, 이제 여러분에게는 한 주 동안 선택할 시간이 있습니다.** 각 선택사항들을 고려하기에 충분한 시간일 것입니다. 음, 제안사항들을 기술한 이메일이 오늘 발송될 예정이니까 살펴보시고 서로 얘기 나눠 주십시오. **다른 사람의 의견을 듣는 것도 도움이 될 수 있습니다.**

어휘 agenda 의제, 안건 management 경영진 provide 제공하다 generous 후한, 넉넉한 budget 예산 reward 보상하다 committee 위원회 come up with ~를 제시하다, 제안하다 potential 가능성 있는, 잠재적인 voting 투표 take place 개최되다, 일어나다 in response to ~에 응하여 plenty of 많은 describe 기술하다, 묘사하다 proposal 제안 look over 살펴보다

71

What will the listeners do soon?

(A) Travel abroad
(B) Reorganize a work space
(C) Answer inquiries from clients
(D) Vote on proposals

청자들은 곧 무엇을 할 것인가?

(A) 해외 여행하기
(B) 업무 공간 재구성하기
(C) 고객 문의에 답변하기
(D) 제안사항들에 대해 투표하기

어휘 abroad 해외로 reorganize 재조직하다, 재편성하다

해설 세부 사항 관련 – 청자들이 할 일

지문 초반부에 화자가 청자들에게 행사 조직 위원회가 선택할 수 있는 세 가지 가능한 계획안을 제시했다고 한 후 투표는 이메일을 통해 이뤄진다(the events organizing committee ~ take place through e-mail.)고 했으므로 정답은 (D)이다.

Test 9

72

According to the speaker, what has changed about a process?

(A) The time frame
(B) The budget
(C) The supervising committee
(D) The method of communication

화자에 따르면, 절차상 변경된 것은 무엇인가?

(A) 기간
(B) 예산
(C) 감독위원회
(D) 의사소통 방법

어휘 process 과정, 절차 time frame (어떤 일에 쓰이는) 기간, 시간 supervise 감독하다 method 방법

해설 세부 사항 관련 – 절차상 변경된 사항

지문 중반부에 화자가 작년의 피드백을 반영하여 이제 청자들에게는 한 주 동안 선택할 시간이 있다(In response to feedback ~ a full week to make your choice.)고 했으므로 정답은 (A)이다.

73

Why should the listeners speak to each other?

(A) To share their opinions
(B) To point out some mistakes
(C) To confirm some preparations
(D) To describe their roles

청자들은 왜 서로 이야기를 나눠야 하는가?

(A) 의견을 나누기 위해
(B) 실수를 지적하기 위해
(C) 준비사항을 확인하기 위해
(D) 역할을 설명하기 위해

어휘 point out 지적하다 confirm 확인해 주다, 확정하다 preparation 준비 describe 기술하다 role 역할

해설 세부 사항 관련 – 청자들이 이야기를 나눠야 하는 이유

지문 마지막에 화자가 청자들에게 다른 사람의 의견을 듣는 것도 도움이 될 수 있다(It could be helpful to hear other people's thoughts.)고 했으므로 정답은 (A)이다.

▸▸ Paraphrasing 지문의 hear other people's thoughts
→ 정답의 share their opinions

74-76 전화 메시지

M-Cn Hi, Ms. Daniels. [74]**This is Arnold Chen calling from World-Plus Lighting Fixtures.** You had ordered the new Model 10 ceiling lights for in-store pickup this Friday. Unfortunately, they won't be available until next Tuesday. [75]**Our supplier encountered a production issue because a shipment of glass arrived at their factory several days late.** I apologize for the inconvenience. Your business is important to us, so [76]**I'd like to offer you—at no charge—a deluxe maintenance kit that includes chemicals and tools for cleaning fixtures in high places.** It will be here waiting for you when you pick up your order.

안녕하세요, 대니얼스 씨. **저는 월드플러스 조명 설비의 아놀드 첸입니다.** 신형 모델 10 천장등을 주문하시고 이번 주 금요일에 매장에 들러 찾아가시기로 하셨는데요. 유감스럽게도, 다음 주 화요일에야 전등이 들어옵니다. **납품 업체의 공장에 유리가 며칠 늦게 도착하는 바람에 생산에 차질이 생겼거든요.** 불편을 끼쳐 드려 사과 드립니다. 고객님의 거래는 저희에게 중요하니 **제가 높은 곳에 설치된 부착물들을 청소할 수 있는 화학 약품과 도구가 들어 있는 최고급 유지보수 공구 상자를 무료로 드리려고 합니다.** 주문하신 물품을 찾으러 오실 때 여기에 도구 상자가 준비돼 있을 겁니다.

어휘 lighting 조명 fixture 부착물 ceiling 천장 in-store pickup 매장 방문 수령 unfortunately 안타깝게도 supplier 공급업체 encounter 맞닥뜨리다 production issue 생산 차질 inconvenience 불편 at no charge 공짜로, 무료로 deluxe 최고급의 kit 공구 상자 pick up 찾아 가다

74

What kind of company does the speaker work for?

(A) A print shop
(B) A camera manufacturer
(C) A lighting equipment store
(D) A photography studio

화자는 어떤 회사에서 일하는가?

(A) 인쇄소
(B) 카메라 제조업체
(C) 조명 장비 판매점
(D) 사진 스튜디오

해설 전체 내용 관련 – 화자의 회사 업종

지문 초반부에 화자가 자신을 월드플러스 조명 설비의 아놀드 첸(This is Arnold Chen calling from World-Plus Lighting Fixtures.)이라고 소개했으므로 정답은 (C)이다.

75

What does the speaker say caused a problem?

(A) A broken piece of machinery
(B) A product redesign
(C) A delayed shipment
(D) A shortage of workers

화자는 무엇 때문에 문제가 생겼다고 말하는가?

(A) 기계 부품 고장
(B) 제품 재디자인
(C) 배송 지연
(D) 근로자 부족

해설 세부 사항 관련 – 생산 문제의 원인

지문 중반부에 납품 업체의 공장에 유리가 며칠 늦게 도착하는 바람에 생산에 차질이 생겼다(Our supplier encountered ~ several days late.)고 했으므로 정답은 (C)이다.

▸▸ **Paraphrasing** 지문의 **a shipment of glass arrived at their factory several days late** → 정답의 **a delayed shipment**

76

What does the speaker offer the listener?

(A) A formal letter of apology
(B) An extended warranty
(C) Some discount rates
(D) Some free cleaning goods

화자는 청자에게 무엇을 제공하는가?

(A) 공식 사과 편지
(B) 보증 기간 연장
(C) 할인 요금
(D) 무료 청소용품

해설 세부 사항 관련 – 화자가 제공하는 것

지문 후반부에 화자가 청자에게 높은 곳에 설치된 부착물들을 청소할 수 있는 화학 약품과 도구들이 들어 있는 고급 유지보수 공구 상자를 무료로 제공하겠다(I'd like to offer you ~ cleaning fixtures in high places.)고 했으므로 정답은 (D)이다.

▸▸ **Paraphrasing** 지문의 **at no charge** → 정답의 **free**

77-79 안내

W-Br [77]**Thank you for attending Tech-Den Plus's seminar for freelance graphic designers.** Today I'll show you how to present your portfolio and make the best possible impression on potential clients. Before we start, [78]**I just want to remind everyone that your seminar registration grants you free access to all of our Web lectures and slideshows.** I'll explain this "members only" resource more at the end of today's session. OK. Now, to start off, [79]**I'd like to hand out some actual paper flyers and brochures that have successfully attracted customers.** Then we'll talk about why they work. Here we go.

프리랜서 그래픽 디자이너들을 위한 테크덴 플러스의 세미나에 참석해 주셔서 감사합니다. 오늘 저는 잠재 고객들에게 여러분의 작품집을 제시하고 가능한 한 최선의 인상을 남기는 방법을 여러분께 보여드리겠습니다. 시작하기 전에 **모두에게 알려드리고 싶은 것은 세미나 등록으로 저희의 인터넷 강의와 슬라이드 쇼를 전부 무료로 이용하실 수 있다는 점입니다.** 이 '회원 전용' 자료에 관해서는 오늘 모임이 끝날 때 더 자세히 설명해 드리겠습니다. 자, 우선 **성공적으로 고객들의 이목을 끈 실제 종이 전단과 안내 책자들을 나눠 드리려고 합니다.** 그런 다음 왜 이것들이 효과가 있는지 얘기해 보겠습니다. 시작하지요.

어휘 portfolio 작품집[포트폴리오] impression 인상 potential 잠재적인 grant free access to ~에 무료로 접근하게 하다 lecture 강의 resource 자료, 자원 hand out 나누어 주다 brochure 안내 책자, 브로셔 attract 이목[흥미, 관심]을 끌다 work 효과가 있다

77

Who most likely are the listeners?

(A) Graphic designers
(B) Freelance writers
(C) Career counselors
(D) Real estate developers

청자들은 누구일 것 같은가?

(A) 그래픽 디자이너들
(B) 프리랜서 작가들
(C) 진로 상담가들
(D) 부동산 개발업자들

해설 전체 내용 관련 – 청자들의 신분

지문 맨 처음에 화자가 청자들에게 프리랜서 그래픽 디자이너들을 위한 테크덴 플러스 세미나에 참석해 줘서 감사하다(Thank you for attending Tech-Den Plus's seminar for freelance graphic designers.)고 했다. 이를 통해 청자들이 그래픽 디자이너라는 것을 알 수 있으므로 정답은 (A)이다.

78

What is included with the seminar?

(A) Refreshments
(B) Transportation vouchers
(C) Online content
(D) In-person consulting

세미나에는 무엇이 포함되어 있는가?

(A) 다과
(B) 교통 이용권
(C) 온라인 콘텐츠
(D) 1:1 컨설팅

어휘 refreshments 다과 transportation 수송, 교통 in-person 직접의

해설 세부 사항 관련 – 세미나에 포함된 것

지문 중반부에 화자가 청자들 모두에게 상기시키고 싶은 것은 세미나 등록으로 인터넷 강의와 슬라이드 쇼를 전부 무료로 이용할 수 있다는 점(I just want to remind ~ and slideshows.)이라고 했으므로 정답은 (C)이다.

▸▸ **Paraphrasing** 지문의 **all of our Web lectures and slideshows** → 정답의 **online content**

Test 9

79

What does the speaker say she will distribute to the listeners?

(A) Promotional materials
(B) A list of topics
(C) A sign-up sheet
(D) Computer passwords

화자는 청자들에게 무엇을 나눠 주겠다고 말하는가?

(A) 홍보 자료
(B) 주제 목록
(C) 참가 신청서
(D) 컴퓨터 비밀번호

해설 세부 사항 관련 - 청자들에게 배부할 것

지문 후반부에 화자가 청자들에게 고객들의 이목을 끄는 데 성공한 실제 종이 전단과 안내 책자들을 나눠주겠다(I'd like to hand out ~ attracted customers.)고 했으므로 정답은 (A)이다.

▸▸ **Paraphrasing** 지문의 **paper flyers and brochures**
→ 정답의 **promotional materials**

80-82 전화 메시지

M-Cn Hi, [80]**this is Jared from Jackson Auto Center.** I'm calling to remind you that it's been six months since your vehicle got regular maintenance service here, so we suggest you schedule an engine tune-up for this month. [81]**You can book your visit by going to our Web site at www.jackson-auto.com and clicking the "Schedule" link.** Also, [82]**I wanted to mention that we have our deluxe car seat covers back in stock, but there are two or three of them left,** and... they're very popular with our customers. So ask one of our representatives about them when you come in, if that interests you. Thanks.

안녕하세요. **저는 잭슨 오토 센터의 재러드입니다.** 고객님의 자동차가 이곳에서 정기 점검 서비스를 받은 지 6개월이 되었으니 이번 달에 엔진 정비 일정을 잡으시라고 전화 드립니다. **저희 웹 사이트 www.jackson-auto.com에 방문하셔서 '일정' 링크를 클릭하시고 방문 예약을 하시면 됩니다.** 또한, **고급 좌석 커버의 재고가 있다는 말씀도 드리고 싶습니다. 2~3개가 남아 있는데··· 고객들에게 인기가 아주 많습니다.** 그러니 관심이 있으시면 방문하셔서 저희 직원에게 문의하세요. 감사합니다.

어휘 regular 정기적인 maintenance 점검, 정비 tune-up 정비 book 예약하다 in stock 재고가 있는, 물건이 있는

80

Where does the speaker most likely work?

(A) At a building cleaning service
(B) At a landscaping company
(C) At an automobile repair shop
(D) At a home improvement store

화자는 어디에서 일할 것 같은가?

(A) 건물 청소 용역업체
(B) 조경회사
(C) 자동차 수리점
(D) 주택 개량용품 판매점

해설 전체 내용 관련 - 화자의 근무지

지문 맨 처음에 화자가 자신을 잭슨 오토 센터의 재러드(this is Jared from Jackson Auto Center.)라고 소개했으므로 정답은 (C)이다.

▸▸ **Paraphrasing** 지문의 **Jackson Auto Center**
→ 정답의 **an automobile repair shop**

81

Why does the speaker urge the listener to visit a Web site?

(A) To obtain driving directions
(B) To watch an instructional video
(C) To complete a feedback survey
(D) To make an appointment

화자가 청자에게 웹 사이트를 방문하라고 촉구하는 이유는 무엇인가?

(A) 운전 길 안내를 얻도록
(B) 교육용 영상을 보도록
(C) 피드백 설문지를 작성하도록
(D) 약속을 잡도록

해설 세부 사항 관련 - 웹 사이트 방문을 권장하는 이유

지문 중반부에 화자가 청자에게 웹 사이트에 들어가서 '일정' 링크를 클릭하여 방문 예약을 할 수 있다(You can book your visit by ~ the "Schedule" link.)고 했으므로 정답은 (D)이다.

▸▸ **Paraphrasing** 지문의 **book your visit**
→ 정답의 **make an appointment**

82

Why does the speaker say, "they're very popular with our customers"?

(A) To apologize for long waiting lines
(B) To encourage a quick purchase
(C) To suggest posting a user review
(D) To recommend a substitute item

화자가 "고객들에게 인기가 아주 많습니다"라고 말한 이유는 무엇인가?

(A) 대기 행렬이 길어 사과하려고
(B) 빨리 구매하도록 독려하려고
(C) 이용 후기를 올리는 걸 제안하려고
(D) 대체 품목을 추천하려고

어휘 post 게재하다 substitute 대체의, 대용의

해설 화자의 의도 파악 – 고객들에게 인기가 아주 많다는 말의 의도

지문 후반부에 화자가 고급 자동차 좌석 커버 재고가 있다는 걸 언급하고 싶었고 2~3개 정도 남아 있다(I wanted to mention ~ two or three of them left)고 했다. 그리고 그 상품이 고객들에게 인기가 아주 많다고 했다. 이 인용문은 해당 상품이 인기가 아주 많으니 빨리 구매하라는 뜻을 전달한 것이므로 정답은 (B)이다.

83-85 담화

M-Au Thank you for inviting me to your bookstore to talk about a new product we're marketing at Melovic Supply. It's called Book-Pak Plus, and [83]**it's a full line of cardboard mailing boxes designed to protect books during shipment.** [84]**What makes this product different from our competitors' offerings is that it is available in a wide variety of different dimensions**—there's a box for every size of book. And [85]**if you purchase Book-Pak Plus in large quantities, you'll get our ten-percent bulk-order discount.** No coupon is ever needed. Now, I'll pass around some sample boxes so you can see which ones might work for you.

귀하의 서점에 초청해 주셔서 저희 멜로빅 서플라이에서 홍보 중인 신제품에 관해 이야기하도록 해 주셔서 감사합니다. 그것은 북팩 플러스라고 불리며, **배송 도중에 도서를 보호하도록 설계된 판지 우편물 상자 제품군입니다. 이 제품이 저희 경쟁사들의 제품과 다른 점은 여러 종류의 아주 다양한 크기들이 있다는 것입니다.** 모든 도서의 규격에 맞는 상자가 있습니다. 그리고 **대량으로 북팩 플러스를 구매하시면 10퍼센트의 대량 주문 할인을 받으실 수 있습니다.** 쿠폰은 필요 없습니다. 자, 상자 견본들을 돌릴 테니 어떤 상자들이 여러분께 맞을지 살펴보시기 바랍니다.

어휘 market (상품을) 내놓다, 광고하다 be called ~로 불리다 line 제품군 cardboard mailing box 판지로 만든 우편물 상자 protect 보호하다 competitor 경쟁사, 경쟁자 dimension 크기 in large quantities 대량으로 bulk-order discount 대량 주문 할인 pass around (여러 사람이 보도록) 돌리다

83

What is the speaker trying to sell?

(A) Customized stationery
(B) Display furniture
(C) Packaging material
(D) Printing paper

화자는 무엇을 팔고자 하는가?

(A) 맞춤형 문구
(B) 진열 가구
(C) 포장 재료
(D) 인쇄 용지

해설 세부 사항 관련 – 화자가 판매하려는 것

지문 초반부에 화자가 판매하려는 것은 배송 도중에 도서를 보호하도록 설계된 판지 우편물 상자 제품군(it's a full line of ~ during shipment.)이라고 했으므로 정답은 (C)이다.

▸▸ **Paraphrasing** 지문의 **cardboard mailing boxes**
→ 정답의 **packaging material**

84

According to the speaker, what is special about the product?

(A) It is imported.
(B) It is lightweight.
(C) It comes in many sizes.
(D) It is made from recycled goods.

화자에 따르면, 이 제품은 어떤 점이 특별한가?

(A) 수입품이다.
(B) 무게가 가볍다.
(C) 다양한 크기로 나온다.
(D) 재활용품으로 만든 것이다.

해설 세부 사항 관련 – 제품의 특별한 점

지문 중반부에 화자의 제품이 경쟁사들의 제품과 다른 점은 여러 종류의 아주 다양한 크기들이 있다는 점(What makes this product ~ different dimensions)이라고 했으므로 정답은 (C)이다.

▸▸ **Paraphrasing** 지문의 **it is available in a wide variety of different dimensions**
→ 정답의 **It comes in many sizes.**

85

How can listeners receive a discount?

(A) By placing a large order
(B) By using a special coupon
(C) By referring other customers
(D) By downloading a mobile app

청자들은 어떻게 할인을 받을 수 있는가?

(A) 대량으로 주문해서
(B) 특별 쿠폰을 사용해서
(C) 다른 고객들을 소개함으로써
(D) 모바일 앱을 다운로드해서

어휘 refer 소개하다

해설 세부 사항 관련 – 할인을 받을 수 있는 방법

지문 후반부에 대량으로 구매하면 10퍼센트의 대량 주문 할인을 받을 수 있다(if you purchase Book-Pak Plus ~ bulk-order discount.)고 했으므로 정답은 (A)이다.

▸▸ **Paraphrasing** 지문의 **purchase Book-Pak Plus in large quantities** → 정답의 **place a large order**

Test 9

86-88 방송

W-Am Welcome to *Morning Talk*. Today's guest is Nancy Tilden. [86]**In her twenty-year career as a professional event planner, Ms. Tilden has coordinated everything from small luncheons to major trade shows.** And, [87]**next month at Central University, she will start teaching our region's first-ever certification course for her profession.** During today's show, she'll share some basic tips on how to make any event run more smoothly. [88]**We invite all our listeners to send in questions for our guest by e-mail at contact@morning-talk.com or by text message at 45602.** Ms. Tilden, thank you for joining us in the studio.

〈모닝 토크〉 청취자 여러분을 환영합니다. 오늘의 초대 손님은 낸시 틸든 씨입니다. **20년 동안 전문 행사 기획자로 일해 온 틸든 씨는 소규모 오찬부터 주요 무역 박람회까지 온갖 행사를 조직해왔습니다.** 그리고 **다음 달에 센트럴 대학교에서 우리 지역 최초로 그녀의 전문 분야에 대한 인증 과정을 가르칠 예정입니다.** 오늘 방송에서 그녀는 어떤 행사든 더 순조롭게 진행되도록 하는 방법에 관한 몇몇 기본적인 조언들을 들려줄 것입니다. **청취자 여러분 모두 초대 손님에게 질문이 있으시면 contact@morning-talk으로 이메일을 보내거나 45602번으로 문자를 주시기 바랍니다.** 틸든 씨, 스튜디오에 나와 주셔서 감사합니다.

어휘 career 경력 professional 전문적인 coordinate 조직하다, 조정하다 luncheon 오찬 first-ever 최초의 certification course 인증 과정 profession 전문 직업[직종] smoothly 순조롭게, 매끄럽게 send in ~을 제출하다, 응모하다

86

What most likely is Ms. Tilden's area of expertise?

(A) Event coordination
(B) Data security
(C) Financial planning
(D) Fitness training

틸든 씨의 전문 분야는 무엇일 것 같은가?

(A) 행사 조직
(B) 데이터 보안
(C) 재정 기획
(D) 체력 훈련

해설 세부 사항 관련 – 틸든 씨의 전문 분야

지문 초반부에 20년 동안 전문 행사 기획자로서 일해 온 틸든 씨는 소규모 오찬부터 주요 무역 박람회까지 온갖 행사를 조직해왔다(In her twenty-year career ~ trade shows.)고 했으므로 정답은 (A)이다.

87

What does the speaker say will happen next month?

(A) A broadcast will have a guest host.
(B) A documentary will be released.
(C) A book will be published.
(D) A new class will be offered.

화자는 다음 달에 무슨 일이 있을 거라고 말하는가?

(A) 방송에 객원 진행자가 나올 것이다.
(B) 다큐멘터리가 공개될 것이다.
(C) 책이 출판될 것이다.
(D) 새로운 수업이 제공될 것이다.

해설 세부 사항 관련 – 다음 달에 발생할 일

지문 중반부에 다음 달부터 지역 최초로 그녀의 전문 분야(전문 행사 기획자)에 대한 인증 과정을 강의할 예정(next month at Central University, she will ~ her profession.)이라고 했으므로 정답은 (D)이다.

▸▸ **Paraphrasing** 지문의 **our region's first-ever certification course** → 정답의 **a new class**

88

What are listeners encouraged to do?

(A) Donate to a charity organization
(B) Take a tour of a radio station
(C) Attend a regional conference
(D) Submit questions electronically

청자들은 무엇을 하도록 권장 받는가?

(A) 자선 기관에 기부
(B) 라디오 방송국 견학
(C) 지역 총회에 참석
(D) 전자기기를 이용해 질문 제출

어휘 donate 기부하다 regional 지역의 electronically 전자기기를 이용해

해설 세부 사항 관련 – 청자들에 대한 권장 사항

지문 후반부에 화자가 청취자 모두 초대 손님에게 할 질문이 있으면 이메일을 보내거나 문자 메시지를 달라(We invite all our listeners ~ by text message at 45602.)고 했으므로 정답은 (D)이다.

▸▸ **Paraphrasing** 지문의 **send in questions for our guest by e-mail** → 정답의 **Submit questions electronically**

89-91 전화 메시지

M-Cn Ed, it's Ji-Soo. [89 90]**I just got your message asking if my department could get you a Chaworth chair instead of the Fleckstrom one. I understand that a Chaworth would be a better fit for you, but...** I've already completed your paperwork. Now that your original request for the Fleckstrom chair is in the system, an informal request to change it isn't enough. [91]**I'm e-mailing you the "Modify/Cancel a Request" form right now, so please fill it out and return it to me.** If you do that soon, it shouldn't be a problem to get you that Chaworth chair.

에드, 저는 지수입니다. **방금 플렉스트롬 의자 대신 채워스 의자를 저희 부서에서 구해드릴 수 있는지 문의하신 메시지를 받았습니다. 채워스가 더 잘 맞는다는 점은 이해합니다만**··· 이미 결재 문서 작업을 완료했습니다. 플렉스트롬 의자에 대한 원래 요청서가 시스템에 입력되어 있기 때문에 비공식적인 변경 요청으로는 충분하지 않습니다. **이메일로 "요청서 수정/취소" 양식을 지금 보내 드릴 테니 작성하셔서 저에게 다시 보내주십시오.** 바로 해 주시면 채워스 의자를 드리는 데 문제 없을 겁니다.

어휘 department 부서 instead of ~ 대신에 complete 완료하다 paperwork 문서 작업 now that ~이므로 request 요청 informal 비공식적인 modify 수정하다, 변경하다 cancel 취소하다 fill out 작성하다, 기입하다

89

What department does the speaker most likely work in?

(A) Legal
(B) Purchasing
(C) Production
(D) Technical Support

화자는 어느 부서에서 일하겠는가?

(A) 법무 부서
(B) 구매 부서
(C) 생산 부서
(D) 기술지원 부서

어휘 legal 법률과 관련된 purchase 구매하다 production 생산 technical 기술의

해설 전체 내용 관련 – 화자가 근무하는 부서

지문 초반부에 화자가 방금 플렉스트롬 의자 대신 채워스 의자를 구해 줄 수 있는지 문의한 청자의 메시지를 받았다(I just got your message ~ instead of the Fleckstrom one.)고 했으므로 정답은 (B)이다.

90

What does the speaker imply when he says, "I've already completed your paperwork"?

(A) A problem has been resolved.
(B) A task was reassigned.
(C) A process is ahead of schedule.
(D) A change will be difficult to make.

화자가 "이미 결재 문서 작업을 완료했습니다"라고 말한 의도는 무엇인가?

(A) 문제가 해결됐다.
(B) 업무가 재배정되었다.
(C) 절차가 일정보다 빠르게 진행된다.
(D) 변경하기가 어려울 것이다.

어휘 resolve 해결하다 reassign 다시 맡기다 ahead of schedule 일정보다 빠른

해설 화자의 의도 파악 – 이미 결재 문서 작업을 완료했다는 말의 의도

인용문 앞 문장에서 화자는 플렉스트롬 의자 대신 채워스 의자를 구해 줄 수 있는지 문의한 청자의 메시지를 받았다면서 채워스가 더 잘 맞는다는 점은 이해한다(I just got your message ~ a better fit for you)고 했다. 그런 다음 이미 결재 문서 작업을 완료했다고 했는데, 문맥상 이 인용문은 구매 물품을 변경하기가 어려울 것이라는 의도를 나타낸 것이므로 정답은 (D)이다.

91

What does the speaker instruct the listener to do?

(A) Send him another form
(B) Return his telephone call
(C) Cancel an upcoming trip
(D) Check his e-mail frequently

화자는 청자에게 무엇을 하라고 알려주는가?

(A) 다른 양식 전송하기
(B) 답신 전화하기
(C) 다가오는 여행 취소하기
(D) 이메일을 자주 확인하기

어휘 upcoming 앞으로 있을, 다가오는 frequently 자주, 빈번히

해설 세부 사항 관련 – 청자들이 할 일

지문 후반부에 화자가 이메일로 "요청서 수정/취소" 양식을 보낼 테니 작성해서 다시 보내달라(I'm e-mailing you ~ fill it out and return it to me.)고 했으므로 정답은 (A)이다.

92-94 회의 발췌

W-Br Thanks, all, for attending this early meeting. [92]**As phone operators here in the customer service department**, you normally get a lot of calls from people checking on the status of their shipments. Well, you'll probably get even more of these inquiries today. Uh... there's a big parade in the city. So [93]**we may need to tell some customers to be patient while our delivery drivers deal with the traffic challenges.** Now, [94]**I'd like you to work in pairs and practice handling this kind of incoming call.** One of you should play the part of the operator and the other should play a customer.

이렇게 이른 회의에 참석해 주셔서 모두에게 감사합니다. **이곳 고객지원부의 전화 상담원들로서** 여러분은 평소에 배송 상황을 확인하는 고객들로부터 많은 전화를 받습니다. 자, 오늘은 아마도 이런 문의를 훨씬 더 많이 받게 될 것입니다. 어··· 도심에서 대규모 행진이 있습니다. 그러니 **우리는 택배 기사들이 교통 문제를 처리하는 동안 일부 고객들에게 참고 기다려 달라고 말해야 할 수 있습니다.** 이제, **둘씩 짝지어서 이런 종류의 착신 전화를 처리하는 연습을 해보시기 바랍니다.** 여러분 중 한 분은 상담원 역할을 하고, 다른 한 분은 고객 역할을 하십시오.

어휘 operator 전화 상담원 normally 통상적으로 status 상황 inquiry 문의 parade 행진, 행렬 patient 인내하는, 참는 deal with ~을 다루다, 처리하다 traffic challenge 교통 문제 in pairs 둘씩 짝지어 practice 연습하다 incoming call 착신 전화 play the part of ~의 역할을 하다

92
Who are the listeners?
(A) Truck drivers
(B) Computer technicians
(C) Customer service representatives
(D) Warehouse workers

청자들은 누구인가?
(A) 트럭 운전사
(B) 컴퓨터 기사
(C) 고객 서비스 직원
(D) 창고 직원

해설 전체 내용 관련 - 청자들의 신분
지문 초반부에 화자가 청자들이 고객지원부의 전화 상담원(As phone operators here in the customer service department)이라고 했으므로 정답은 (C)이다.

93
What does the speaker imply when she says, "there's a big parade in the city"?
(A) A banner will be seen by many people.
(B) Some deliveries may take a long time.
(C) Some staff members may be absent.
(D) A neighborhood will be noisy.

여자가 "도심에서 대규모 행진이 있습니다"라고 말한 의도는 무엇인가?
(A) 많은 사람들이 현수막을 볼 것이다.
(B) 일부 배송에 시간이 오래 걸릴지도 모른다.
(C) 일부 직원들이 결근할지도 모른다.
(D) 인근 동네가 시끄러울 것이다.

해설 화자의 의도 파악 - 도심에서 대규모 행진이 있다는 말의 의도
지문 중반부의 인용문 뒤에 화자가 택배 기사들이 교통 문제들을 처리하는 동안 일부 고객들에게 참고 기다려 달라고 말해야 할지도 모른다(we may need to tell some ~ traffic challenges.)고 했는데, 인용문은 행진으로 인해 배송이 지연될 수도 있다는 의도를 담은 것이므로 정답은 (B)이다.

94
What does the speaker ask the listeners to do?
(A) Put on a uniform
(B) Move some equipment
(C) Work with a partner
(D) Use a Web site

화자는 청자들에게 무엇을 하라고 요청하는가?
(A) 유니폼 착용
(B) 장비 운반
(C) 짝과 함께 연습
(D) 웹 사이트 이용

해설 세부 사항 관련 - 화자의 요청 사항
지문 후반부에 화자가 청자들에게 둘씩 짝지어서 착신 전화를 처리하는 연습을 하길 바란다(I'd like you to work in pairs and practice handling this kind of incoming call.)고 했으므로 정답은 (C)이다.

▸▸ Paraphrasing 지문의 work in pairs
→ 정답의 work with a partner

95-97 안내 + 시간표

W-Am Attention, passengers. [95]**The Norselton Metro Transit Authority has an important announcement regarding Train 379.** [96]**As of September first, Train 379 will no longer stop at Frantine Station.** Based on our analysis of commuting patterns in the greater Norselton region, we believe this adjustment will improve our service's overall efficiency. All posted timetables in the station will be updated on August thirty-first to reflect this change. [97]**Remember, opinions and suggestions about transit services can be shared on our Web site by clicking the red button labeled "Talk to Us".** Thank you, and have a nice day.

승객 여러분께 알려드립니다. **노셀턴 지하철 교통당국에서 379호 열차에 관한 중요 공지사항을 알립니다. 9월 1일부로 379호 열차는 프랜틴역에 더 이상 정차하지 않겠습니다.** 노셀턴 광역권에서 이뤄진 출퇴근 패턴 분석 내용을 바탕으로 볼 때, 이번 조정 내용은 서비스의 전체적인 효율성을 향상시킬 거라고 여겨집니다. 역에 게시된 모든 시간표는 변경사항을 반영하여 8월 31일에 업데이트 될 것입니다. **저희 웹 사이트에서 빨간색 "의견 말하기" 버튼을 클릭하시면 교통 서비스에 관한 의견 및 제안을 공유하실 수 있음을 기억하세요.** 감사합니다. 좋은 하루 되십시오.

어휘 attention 주목하세요, 알립니다 passenger 승객 transit 교통 체계, 수송 authority 당국 regarding ~에 관해 as of ~일자로 no longer 더 이상 ~ 하지 않는 based on ~에 근거하여 analysis 분석 commute 통근하다 region 지역 adjustment 조정 improve 향상시키다, 개선하다 overall 전체의 efficiency 효율성 reflect 반영하다 suggestion 제안 southbound 남쪽으로 향하는 departure 출발

WEEKDAY SCHEDULE FOR FRANTINE STATION

Southbound Trains

Train	Departure Time
Train 315	5:00 A.M.
Train 383	5:18 A.M.
Train 324	5:30 A.M.
[95]Train 379	5:45 A.M.

프랜틴역 평일 시간표	
남행열차	
열차	출발 시간
315호 열차	오전 5:00
383호 열차	오전 5:18
324호 열차	오전 5:30
379호 열차	오전 5:45

95

Look at the graphic. Which departure time does the announcement concern?

(A) 5:00 A.M.
(B) 5:18 A.M.
(C) 5:30 A.M.
(D) 5:45 A.M.

시각 정보에 의하면, 안내방송은 어느 출발 시간에 관한 것인가?

(A) 오전 5:00
(B) 오전 5:18
(C) 오전 5:30
(D) 오전 5:45

어휘 concern 관련되다, ~에 관한 것이다

해설 시각 정보 연계 - 안내 방송에 언급된 열차의 출발 시간

지문 초반부에 화자는 노셀턴 지하철 교통당국에서 379호 열차에 관한 중요 공지사항을 알린다(The Norselton Metro Transit Authority has an important announcement regarding Train 379.)고 했다. 열차표를 보면 379호 열차 출발 시간은 오전 5시 45분이므로 정답은 (D)이다.

96

What is the speaker announcing?

(A) A permanent change to a route
(B) A delay caused by bad weather
(C) A plan for maintenance work
(D) A new feature available on a train

화자는 무엇을 알리고 있는가?

(A) 노선 영구 변경
(B) 악천후로 인한 지연
(C) 유지보수 작업 계획
(D) 열차 내에서 새로 이용 가능한 기능

어휘 permanent 영구적인 delay 지연 maintenance 유지, 관리 feature 특색, 특징 available 이용 가능한

해설 세부 사항 관련 - 화자가 알리는 것

지문 중반부에 화자가 9월 1일부로 379호 열차는 프랜틴역에 더 이상 정차하지 않는다(As of September first, Train 379 will no longer stop at Frantine Station.)고 했으므로 정답은 (A)이다.

97

What does the speaker remind the listeners about?

(A) The locations of some timetables
(B) A way to give feedback
(C) The color of a special bus line
(D) Some rules for train passengers

화자는 청자들에게 무엇에 대해 상기시키는가?

(A) 시간표 위치
(B) 피드백 제공 방법
(C) 특별 버스 노선의 색상
(D) 열차 승객을 위한 규칙

어휘 location 위치

해설 세부 사항 관련 - 화자가 상기시키는 사항

지문 후반부에 화자가 교통 당국 웹 사이트에서 빨간색 "의견 말하기" 버튼을 클릭하면 교통 서비스에 관한 의견 및 제안을 공유할 수 있음을 기억하라(Remember, opinions and suggestions about transit services can be shared on our Web site by clicking the red button labeled "Talk to Us".)고 하여 화자는 피드백 제공 방법을 상기시키고 있음을 알 수 있으므로 정답은 (B)이다.

98-100 회의 발췌 + 그래프

M-Au Great news, everyone. [98]**Ever since that trade magazine named our company's portable hand tools the "Best Choice" for professional contractors, sales have been increasing.** We have a chance of surpassing our expected revenues this year. Now, [99]**we're in the middle of the quarter in which we normally sell the most products**, and I want to avoid the drop that usually follows it. [100]**I recommend that we promote our products at the upcoming trade fair in Lonsing**. I'll research the details of reserving exhibit space for us. OK, let's keep up the good work.

아주 좋은 소식이 있습니다, 여러분. **그 업계 잡지가 우리 회사의 휴대용 손 공구들을 전문 도급업자들을 위한 '최선의 선택' 상품으로 선정한 이래로 매출이 꾸준히 증가하고 있습니다.** 우리는 올해에 우리의 예상 수익을 초과할 가능성이 있습니다. 자, **우리는 통상적으로 제품을 가장 많이 판매하는 분기에 들어섰으며,** 대개 그 후에 이어지는 매출 하락을 막기를 원합니다. **저는 우리가 다가오는 론싱 무역 박람회에서 우리 제품들을 홍보할 것을 권해 드립니다.** 제가 전시 공간 예약에 관한 세부 사항을 알아보겠습니다. 자, 계속해서 잘해 봅시다.

어휘 name 지정하다 portable 휴대용의 contractor 도급업자 surpass 초과하다, 뛰어넘다 expected revenue 예상[기대] 수익 promote 홍보하다 upcoming 다가오는 trade fair 무역 박람회 details 세부 사항 reserve 예약하다 exhibit space 전시 공간 keep up the good work 계속 잘하다

Test 9

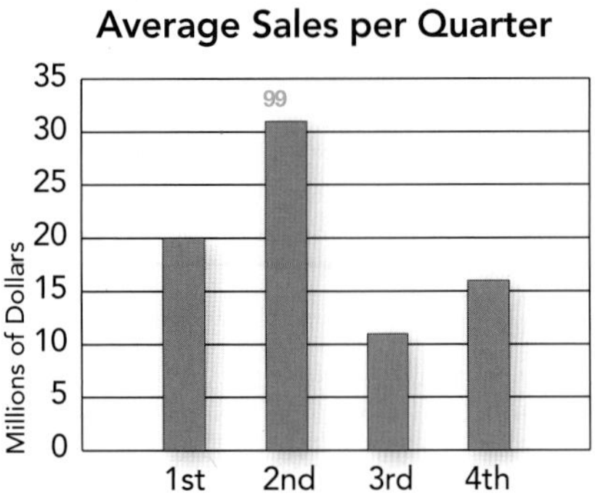

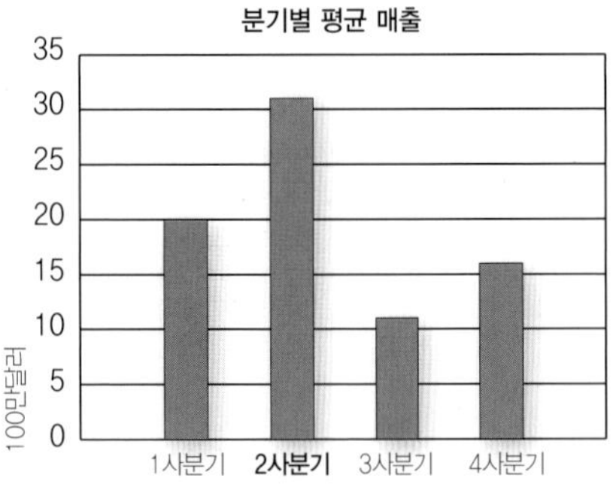

98

What type of products does the speaker's company most likely sell?

(A) Mobile phones
(B) Construction tools
(C) Inventory management software
(D) Casual footwear

화자의 회사는 어떤 종류의 제품을 판매할 것 같은가?

(A) 휴대폰
(B) 건축 공구
(C) 재고 관리 소프트웨어
(D) 캐주얼 신발류

해설 세부 사항 관련 - 화자의 회사가 판매하는 제품

지문 초반부에 그 업계 잡지가 화자 회사의 휴대용 손 공구들을 전문 도급업자들을 위한 '최선의 선택'으로 지정한 이래로 매출이 꾸준히 증가하고 있다(Ever since that trade magazine named ~ have been increasing.)고 했다. 이를 통해 화자의 회사가 휴대용 손 공구를 판매하는 업체임을 알 수 있으므로 정답은 (B)이다.

▸▸ **Paraphrasing** 지문의 **portable hand tools**
→ 정답의 **construction tools**

99

Look at the graphic. When is the meeting taking place?

(A) In the first quarter
(B) In the second quarter
(C) In the third quarter
(D) In the fourth quarter

시각 정보에 의하면, 회의는 언제 열리고 있는가?

(A) 1사분기
(B) 2사분기
(C) 3사분기
(D) 4사분기

해설 시각 정보 연계 - 회의를 하고 있는 시기

지문 중반부에서 통상적으로 제품을 가장 많이 판매하는 분기에 들어섰다(we're in the middle of the quarter in which we normally sell the most products)고 했다. 그래프를 보면 2사분기의 판매 기록이 가장 높은 것으로 나와 있으므로 정답은 (B)이다.

100

What does the speaker suggest?

(A) Offering additional price discounts
(B) Sponsoring a sporting event
(C) Participating in a trade show
(D) Advertising more on social media

화자는 무엇을 제안하는가?

(A) 가격 추가 할인
(B) 스포츠 행사 후원
(C) 무역 박람회 참가
(D) 소셜 미디어 광고 확대

어휘 additional 추가적인 participate in ~에 참가하다

해설 세부 사항 관련 - 화자의 제안 사항

지문 후반부에 화자가 청자들에게 다가오는 론싱 무역 박람회에서 제품들을 홍보할 것을 권장한다(I recommend that we promote our products at the upcoming trade fair in Lonsing.)고 했다. 즉, 무역 박람회에 참가할 것을 제안하는 것이므로 정답은 (C)이다.

▸▸ **Paraphrasing** 지문의 **the upcoming trade fair**
→ 정답의 **a trade show**

TEST 10

1 (A)	2 (D)	3 (C)	4 (B)	5 (A)
6 (C)	7 (B)	8 (C)	9 (A)	10 (A)
11 (C)	12 (B)	13 (B)	14 (A)	15 (C)
16 (B)	17 (B)	18 (C)	19 (A)	20 (A)
21 (C)	22 (B)	23 (A)	24 (C)	25 (A)
26 (C)	27 (B)	28 (A)	29 (A)	30 (C)
31 (B)	32 (C)	33 (D)	34 (D)	35 (C)
36 (A)	37 (D)	38 (D)	39 (C)	40 (C)
41 (A)	42 (C)	43 (B)	44 (D)	45 (A)
46 (B)	47 (C)	48 (D)	49 (B)	50 (A)
51 (B)	52 (A)	53 (D)	54 (A)	55 (D)
56 (D)	57 (C)	58 (A)	59 (B)	60 (A)
61 (A)	62 (B)	63 (B)	64 (C)	65 (C)
66 (C)	67 (A)	68 (B)	69 (B)	70 (A)
71 (B)	72 (D)	73 (B)	74 (A)	75 (A)
76 (C)	77 (C)	78 (C)	79 (D)	80 (D)
81 (D)	82 (A)	83 (B)	84 (B)	85 (A)
86 (A)	87 (B)	88 (D)	89 (B)	90 (D)
91 (A)	92 (D)	93 (C)	94 (C)	95 (D)
96 (D)	97 (B)	98 (A)	99 (C)	100 (B)

PART 1

1 M-Cn

(A) He's carrying some bags.
(B) He's sweeping leaves from a path.
(C) He's holding onto a railing.
(D) He's taking off his jacket.

(A) 남자가 봉투들을 들고 가고 있다.
(B) 남자가 길에서 나뭇잎을 쓸고 있다.
(C) 남자가 난간을 붙잡고 있다.
(D) 남자가 재킷을 벗고 있다.

어휘 carry 들고 가다, 나르다 sweep (빗자루로) 쓸다 path 길 hold onto ~을 꼭 잡다 railing 난간 take off (옷을) 벗다

해설 1인 등장 사진 – 사람의 동작 묘사
(A) 남자가 봉투들을 들고 가는(carrying some bags) 모습이므로 정답.
(B) 남자가 나뭇잎을 쓸어내는(sweeping leaves) 모습이 아니므로 오답.
(C) 남자가 난간을 붙잡은(holding onto a railing) 모습이 아니므로 오답.
(D) 남자가 재킷을 벗고 있는(taking off his jacket) 모습이 아니므로 오답.

2 W-Br

(A) Some travelers are getting off of an airplane.
(B) People are walking down an aisle.
(C) Luggage is being put in an overhead compartment.
(D) The seats are facing the same direction.

(A) 일부 여행객들이 비행기에서 내리고 있다.
(B) 사람들이 통로를 걸어가고 있다.
(C) 짐이 머리 위 짐칸에 놓이고 있다.
(D) 좌석들이 같은 쪽을 향해 있다.

어휘 get off ~에서 내리다 aisle 통로 luggage 짐, 수하물 overhead compartment 머리 위 짐칸 face ~쪽을 향하다 same 같은 direction 방향

해설 2인 이상 등장 사진 – 사람 또는 사물 중심 묘사
(A) 승객들이 비행기에 탑승한 상태이지 지금 내리고 있는(are getting off of an airplane) 모습은 아니므로 오답.
(B) 사진에 통로가 보이지만 사람들이 통로를 걷고 있는(are walking down an aisle) 모습은 아니므로 오답.
(C) 짐이 머리 위 짐칸에 놓이고 있는(is being put in an overhead compartment) 모습이 아니므로 오답.
(D) 기내 좌석들이 모두 같은 쪽을 향해 있는(are facing the same direction) 모습이므로 정답.

3 W-Am

(A) A man is entering a doctor's office.
(B) A woman is adjusting her glasses.
(C) They're sitting next to each other.
(D) They're organizing some documents.

(A) 남자가 병원에 들어가고 있다.
(B) 여자가 안경을 고쳐 쓰고 있다.
(C) 사람들이 나란히 앉아 있다.
(D) 사람들이 서류를 정리하고 있다.

어휘 doctor's office (개인) 병원, 의원 adjust (매무새 등을) 바로잡다 next to each other 나란히 organize 정리하다 document 문서, 서류

Test 10

해설 2인 이상 등장 사진 - 사람의 상태 묘사

(A) 의사로 보이는 남자의 모습에서 연상할 수 있는 병원(a doctor's office)을 이용한 오답.

(B) 여자가 안경을 쓰고 있는 상태이지 안경을 고쳐 쓰고 있는(is adjusting her glasses) 모습은 아니므로 오답.

(C) 두 사람이 나란히 앉아 있는(sitting next to each other) 모습이므로 정답.

(D) 두 사람이 차트를 보고 얘기하는 모습이지 서류를 정리하고 있는(organizing some documents) 모습은 아니므로 오답.

4 M-Cn

(A) A man is repositioning a projector.
(B) Mugs have been set on a table.
(C) Some window blinds are being raised.
(D) A group of people are eating a meal.

(A) 한 남자가 영사기를 옮기고 있다.
(B) 머그잔들이 테이블 위에 놓여 있다.
(C) 창문 블라인드들이 올려지고 있다.
(D) 한 무리의 사람들이 식사를 하고 있다.

어휘 reposition 위치를 바꾸다, 다른 장소로 옮기다 mug 머그잔 set ~을 (특정 장소에) 두다, 놓다 meal 식사

해설 2인 이상 등장 사진 - 사람 또는 사물 중심 묘사

(A) 사진에 영사기(a projector)가 보이지 않으므로 오답.

(B) 머그잔들이 테이블 위에 놓여 있는(have been set on a table) 모습이므로 정답.

(C) 사진에 창문 블라인드(Some window blinds)가 보이지만 창문 블라인드를 올리고 있는 모습이 아니므로 오답.

(D) 사람들이 회의를 하는 중이지 식사를 하고 있는(are eating a meal) 모습은 아니므로 오답.

5 M-Au

(A) A lamp is reflected in a computer monitor.
(B) An office window overlooks a field.
(C) Printed materials have been left on a desk.
(D) Pencils have been laid out near a keyboard.

(A) 램프가 컴퓨터 화면에 비친다.
(B) 사무실 창문에서 들판이 바라보인다.
(C) 인쇄된 자료가 책상 위에 놓여 있다.
(D) 키보드 근처에 연필들이 놓여 있다.

어휘 reflect (거울, 유리 등에 물체를) 비추다 overlook 내려다보다 field 들판 material 자료 leave 남기다, 두다 lay out 배치하다, 펼치다

해설 실내 사물/배경 묘사 사진 - 다양한 사물의 위치 묘사

(A) 램프가 컴퓨터 화면에 비치는(is reflected) 모습이므로 정답.

(B) 사무실 창문에서 건물들이 보이지 들판이 보이지는(overlooks a field) 않으므로 오답.

(C) 책상 위에 인쇄된 자료(printed materials)가 없으므로 오답.

(D) 연필들이 연필꽂이에 꽂혀 있지 키보드 근처에(near a keyboard) 놓여 있지 않으므로 오답.

6 W-Br

(A) A server is talking to some diners.
(B) Menus are being stacked on a tablecloth.
(C) Some items are on a serving tray.
(D) A kitchen worker is washing a glass.

(A) 웨이터가 식사 손님들에게 말을 하고 있다.
(B) 메뉴들이 식탁보 위에 쌓이고 있다.
(C) 물건들이 서빙 쟁반 위에 있다.
(D) 주방 직원이 유리잔을 씻고 있다.

어휘 diner 식사 손님 stack 쌓다 tablecloth 식탁보 tray 쟁반

해설 1인 등장 사진 - 사람 또는 사물 중심 묘사

(A) 식사 손님들에게 말을 거는(is talking) 웨이터는 없으므로 오답.

(B) 사진에 메뉴들(menus)은 보이지 않으므로 오답.

(C) 서빙 쟁반 위에 물건들이 있는(are on a serving tray) 상태이므로 정답.

(D) 유리잔을 씻는(is washing) 직원은 없으므로 오답.

PART 2

7

M-Au How many days will Greg be away?

W-Am (A) For a vacation.

(B) Three in total.

(C) I'll tell her.

그렉은 며칠간 자리를 비울 예정입니까?

(A) 휴가차요.

(B) 총 3일이요.

(C) 그녀에게 얘기할게요.

어휘 be away 부재 중이다, 떨어져 있다 vacation 휴가 in total 통틀어

해설 결근 일수를 묻는 How many 의문문

(A) 연상 단어 오답. 질문의 be away에 대해 자리를 비울 이유 측면에서 연상 가능한 vacation을 이용한 오답.

(B) 정답. 결근 일수를 묻는 질문에 총 3일(Three in total.)이라는 구체적인 기간으로 응답하고 있으므로 정답.

(C) 질문과 상관없는 오답. 결근 일수를 묻는 질문에 그녀에게 얘기하겠다(I'll tell her.)는 대답은 맥락에서 벗어난 응답이므로 오답.

8

M-Cn Where did you buy this pen?

W-Am (A) That'll be two dollars.

(B) I liked the color.

(C) At the bookstore.

이 펜은 어디서 샀나요?

(A) 2달러예요.

(B) 저는 그 색이 좋았어요.

(C) 서점에서요.

어휘 bookstore 서점

해설 구입 장소를 묻는 Where 의문문

(A) 연상 단어 오답. 질문의 buy에서 연상 가능한 two dollars를 이용한 오답.

(B) 연상 단어 오답. 질문의 pen에서 연상 가능한 color를 이용한 오답.

(C) 정답. 달력을 어디에서 구입했는지에 대해 서점(bookstore)이라는 구체적인 장소로 응답하고 있으므로 정답.

9

W-Br Could you help me put labels on these boxes?

M-Cn (A) I'd be happy to help.

(B) Many different sizes.

(C) Some old computer parts.

이 상자들에 표 붙이는 것을 도와주시겠어요?

(A) 기꺼이 돕지요.

(B) 아주 다양한 사이즈요.

(C) 일부 오래된 컴퓨터 부품이요.

어휘 label 라벨, 꼬리표 part 부품, 부분

해설 부탁/요청의 의문문

(A) 정답. 상자에 라벨 붙이는 것을 도와 달라는 요청에 대해 기꺼이 도와주겠다(I'd be happy to help.)는 수락의 표현으로 응답하고 있으므로 정답.

(B) 연상 단어 오답. 질문의 boxes에 대해 크기 측면에서 연상 가능한 different sizes를 이용한 오답.

(C) 질문과 상관없는 오답. 상자에 라벨 붙이는 것을 도와달라는 부탁에 일부 오래된 컴퓨터 부품(Some old computer parts.)이라는 대답은 맥락에서 벗어난 응답이므로 오답.

10

W-Br Are you going to call the caterer about the change?

M-Au (A) I don't have her number.

(B) Kate's change of clothes.

(C) We ate at a restaurant.

변경 사항에 대해 음식 공급업자에게 전화할 건가요?

(A) 저는 그녀의 전화번호를 몰라요.

(B) 케이트가 갈아입을 옷이요.

(C) 우리는 식당에서 먹었어요.

어휘 caterer 음식 공급업자

해설 통화 여부를 확인하는 be동사 Yes/No 의문문

(A) 정답. 변경 사항에 대해 음식 공급업자에게 전화를 할 것인지에 대해 No를 생략한 채 전화번호를 가지고 있지 않다(I don't have her number.)는 말로 전화하지 않을 것임을 우회적으로 표현한 것이므로 정답.

(B) 단어 반복 오답. 질문의 change를 반복 이용한 오답.

(C) 연상 단어 오답. 질문의 caterer에서 연상 가능한 restaurant을 이용한 오답.

11

M-Au You've used this software before, haven't you?

M-Cn (A) Please fill in this spreadsheet.

(B) In the user manual.

(C) Yes, but that was years ago.

전에 이 소프트웨어를 사용해 본 적이 있죠, 그렇지 않나요?

(A) 이 스프레드시트를 작성해 주세요.

(B) 사용설명서 안에요.

(C) 네, 하지만 몇 년 전 일이에요.

어휘 fill in (서식을) 작성하다, (빈 자리를) 채우다 spreadsheet 스프레드시트 user manual 사용설명서

해설 소프트웨어를 사용한 경험을 묻는 부가의문문

(A) 연상 단어 오답. 질문의 software에서 연상 가능한 spreadsheet를 이용한 오답.

(B) 연상 단어 오답. 질문의 this software에 대해 사용법 측면에서 연상 가능한 user manual을 이용한 오답.

(C) 정답. 이 기계를 전에 사용해 본 적이 있는지에 대해 먼저 Yes로 긍정적 응답을 한 후, 하지만 몇 년 전 일이었다(but that was years ago)고 부연 설명을 하고 있으므로 정답.

12

M-Cn Why did you arrive late to work today?

W-Am (A) Sure, if that's what you need.

(B) Because I missed the bus.

(C) Before the afternoon shift.

왜 오늘 늦게 출근했나요?

(A) 물론이죠, 그게 필요하시다면요.

(B) 버스를 놓쳐서요.

(C) 오후 교대 시간 전에요.

어휘 late 늦게 miss 놓치다 shift 교대 근무 (시간)

해설 늦게 출근한 이유를 묻는 Why 의문문

(A) Yes/No 불가 오답. 늦게 출근한 이유를 묻는 Why 의문문에 Yes나 Sure 또는 No와 같은 긍정/부정 응답이 불가능하기 때문에 오답.

(B) 정답. 오늘 왜 늦게 출근했는지에 대해 버스를 놓쳤기 때문(Because I missed the bus.)이라는 구체적인 이유를 제시하고 있으므로 정답.

(C) 연상 단어 오답. 질문의 work에서 연상 가능한 afternoon shift를 이용한 오답.

13

M-Au Didn't Ga-Yoon make an agenda for the meeting?

W-Br (A) The whole department.

(B) Not that I know of.

(C) Where is Conference Room Four?

가윤이 회의 안건을 작성하지 않았나요?

(A) 부서 전체요.

(B) 제가 알기로는 아니에요.

(C) 4호 회의실이 어디죠?

어휘 agenda 회의 안건, 의제 whole 전체의 department 부서 conference room 회의실

해설 목록 작성 여부를 묻는 부정의문문

(A) 연상 단어 오답. 질문의 meeting에서 연상 가능한 department를 이용한 오답.

(B) 정답. 가윤 씨가 회의 안건을 작성했는지에 대해 아닌 걸로 알고 있다(Not that I know of.)는 말로 부정적 응답을 하고 있으므로 정답.

(C) 연상 단어 오답. 질문의 meeting에서 연상 가능한 Conference Room을 이용한 오답.

14

W-Am The park's operating hours have been reduced because of budget cuts.

M-Cn (A) I'm sorry to hear that.

(B) The staff parking area.

(C) He's on the operations team.

예산 삭감 때문에 공원 운영 시간이 줄었어요.

(A) 그렇다니 유감이네요.

(B) 직원 주차장이요.

(C) 그는 운영 팀에 있어요.

어휘 operating hours 운영 시간 reduce 줄이다 budget cut 예산 삭감

해설 사실/정보 전달의 평서문

(A) 정답. 예산 삭감(budget cuts)으로 공원 운영 시간(operating hours)이 줄었다는 말에 유감(I'm sorry to hear that.)이라고 응답하고 있으므로 정답.

(B) 유사 발음 오답. 질문의 park와 부분적으로 발음이 동일한 parking을 이용한 오답.

(C) 유사 발음 오답. 질문의 operating과 부분적으로 발음이 동일한 operations를 이용한 오답.

15

W-Br When will you take your lunch break?

M-Au (A) The café next door.

(B) Take as many as you want.

(C) As soon as I finish reading this report.

언제 점심 드실 거예요?

(A) 옆 집 카페요.

(B) 원하시는 만큼 가지고 가세요.

(C) 이 보고서를 다 읽는 대로요.

어휘 lunch break 점심 시간 as many as ~만큼 많이 as soon as ~하자마자

해설 점심 식사 시점을 묻는 When 의문문

(A) 연상 단어 오답. 질문의 lunch에서 연상 가능한 café를 이용한 오답.

(B) 단어 반복 오답. 질문에 나온 take를 반복한 오답.

(C) 정답. 점심을 언제 먹을지 묻는 질문에 보고서를 다 읽는 대로(As soon as I finish reading this report.)라는 상대적 시점을 제시하고 있으므로 정답.

16

W-Br What award was your book nominated for?

M-Cn (A) By an authors' organization.

(B) Best Historical Fiction.

(C) You really deserve it.

당신의 책은 어떤 상 후보에 올랐지요?

(A) 저자들 단체에 의해서요.

(B) 최고의 역사 소설상이요.

(C) 당신은 정말 받을 자격이 있어요.

어휘 award 상 nominate (후보로) 지명하다, 추천하다 organization 조직, 단체 historical fiction 역사 소설 deserve ~를 받을 자격이 있다

해설 상의 종류를 묻는 What 의문문

(A) 연상 단어 오답. 질문의 book에서 연상 가능한 authors를 이용한 오답.

(B) 정답. 책이 어떤 상의 후보에 올랐는지 묻는 질문에 대해 최고의 역사 소설(Best Historical Fiction)이라는 구체적 시상 분야를 언급하므로 정답.

(C) 연상 단어 오답. 질문의 award에 대해 수상 자격 측면에서 연상 가능한 deserve it을 이용했으나, 후보에 오른 사람이 질문자에게 이 말을 하는 것은 논리에 맞지 않으므로 오답.

17

W-Am How can I tell if the batteries need to be replaced?

M-Au (A) Two should be enough for it.

(B) This light will start flashing.

(C) Oh, that's my favorite place.

배터리 교체가 필요한지 제가 어떻게 알 수 있나요?

(A) 두 개면 충분할 겁니다.

(B) 이 등이 깜박이기 시작할 겁니다.

(C) 오, 그곳은 제가 가장 좋아하는 곳입니다.

어휘 tell ~을 분간[구별]하다 if ~인지 어떤지 replace 교체하다 flash 불이 깜빡이다

해설 식별 방법을 묻는 How 의문문

(A) 질문과 상관없는 오답. 수량을 묻는 How many 의문문에 어울리는 응답이므로 오답.

(B) 정답. 어떻게 배터리 교체 시점을 알 수 있는지에 대해 이 불이 깜빡이기 시작할 것(This light will start flashing.)이라는 구체적인 확인 방법을 알려주고 있으므로 정답.

(C) 유사 발음 오답. 질문의 replaced에 대해 부분적으로 발음이 동일한 place를 이용한 오답.

18

M-Cn Should I reschedule the building permit inspection, or not?

W-Br (A) It used to be an office building.

(B) The city planning department.

(C) Yes—we need more time to prepare.

건축 허가 조사 일정을 변경해야 할까요, 아닐까요?

(A) 한때는 사무용 건물이었어요.

(B) 도시 계획 부서요.

(C) 네, 저희는 준비할 시간이 더 필요해요.

어휘 reschedule 일정을 변경하다 building permit 건축 허가 inspection 조사, 검토 used to + 동사원형 (한때) ~했다

해설 일정 변경 여부를 묻는 조동사(should) Yes/No 의문문

(A) 단어 반복 오답. 질문에 나온 building을 반복한 오답.

(B) 연상 단어 오답. 질문의 building에서 연상 가능한 city를 이용한 오답.

(C) 정답. 일정을 변경해야 하는지에 대해 먼저 Yes로 긍정적 응답을 한 후, 준비할 시간이 더 필요하다(we need more time to prepare.)는 부연 설명을 하고 있으므로 정답.

19

W-Am This medicine is sold at most pharmacies, right?

M-Au (A) I've definitely seen it on display at Cardell's.

(B) The patient in Room 405.

(C) No, it's a medical seminar.

이 약은 대부분의 약국에서 판매되죠?

(A) 카델즈에 진열된 건 분명히 봤어요.

(B) 405호실 환자요.

(C) 아니요, 의학 세미나예요.

어휘 medicine 약 pharmacy 약국 definitely 분명히 on display 전시된, 진열된 patient 환자 medical 의학의, 의료의

해설 약국에서의 판매 여부를 확인하는 부가의문문

(A) 정답. 이 약을 대부분의 약국에서 파는지에 대해 카델즈에 진열된 건 봤다(I've definitely seen it on display at Cardell's.)는 우회적인 답변을 하고 있으므로 정답.

(B) 연상 단어 오답. 질문의 medicine에서 연상 가능한 patient를 이용한 오답.

(C) 파생어 오답. 질문의 medicine과 파생어 관계인 medical을 이용한 오답.

20

M-Au How about sending an electronic invoice for the work?

W-Br (A) This client prefers a paper one.

(B) Sorry, I already spent it.

(C) Once a month.

그 작업에 대해 전자 청구서를 보내는 게 어때요?

(A) 이 고객은 종이로 된 걸 선호해요.

(B) 미안해요, 전 이미 써 버렸어요.

(C) 한 달에 한 번이요.

어휘 electronic 전자의 invoice 송장, 청구서 prefer 선호하다 spend (돈 등을) 쓰다

해설 제안/권유의 의문문

(A) 정답. 작업에 대해 전자 청구서를 보내자는 제안에 대해 No를 생략한 채 고객이 종이 송장을 선호한다(This client prefers a paper one.)며 거절 이유를 제시하고 있으므로 정답.

(B) 연상 단어 오답. 질문의 invoice에서 연상 가능한 spent를 이용한 오답.

(C) 연상 단어 오답. 질문의 sending에 대해 보낸 횟수 측면에서 연상 가능한 Once a month.를 이용한 오답.

21

M-Cn How do I access my bank account online?

W-Br (A) You can pay bills more easily.

(B) Yes, both savings and checking.

(C) Have you registered a password yet?

제 온라인 은행 계좌에 어떻게 접속하나요?

(A) 청구서 요금을 더 쉽게 지불할 수 있어요.

(B) 네, 보통 예금과 당좌 예금 둘 다요.

(C) 비밀번호는 이미 등록하신 건가요?

어휘 access 접속하다 bank account 은행 계좌 savings (account) 보통 예금 (계좌) checking (account) 당좌 예금 (계좌) register 등록하다

해설 온라인 계좌 접속 방법을 묻는 How 의문문

(A) 연상 단어 오답. 질문의 account에 대해 지불 측면에서 연상 가능한 pay bills를 이용한 오답.

(B) Yes/No 불가 오답. 접속 방법을 묻는 How 의문문에 Yes/No 응답이 불가능하기 때문에 오답.

(C) 정답. 어떻게 온라인 계좌에 접속할 수 있는지에 대해 비밀번호를 이미 등록했는지(Have you registered a password yet?)를 되물으며, 비밀번호를 입력해야 접속할 수 있음을 우회적으로 알려주고 있으므로 정답.

22

W-Am Who's designing the invitations for the club banquet?

M-Au (A) That's what the organizer said.

(B) One of our members is a graphic designer.

(C) I appreciate your inviting me.

클럽 만찬 초대장은 누가 디자인하고 있나요?
(A) 주최자가 그렇게 말했어요.
(B) 우리 회원 중 한 사람이 그래픽 디자이너예요.
(C) 저를 초대해 주셔서 감사합니다.

어휘 invitation 초대장 banquet 연회, 만찬 organizer 조직자, 주최자 appreciate 감사하다

해설 초대장 디자인을 누가 하고 있는지 묻는 Who 의문문

(A) 연상 단어 오답. 질문의 club banquet에서 연상 가능한 organizer를 이용한 오답.

(B) 정답. 누가 초대장을 디자인하는지에 대해 회원 중 한 사람이 그래픽 디자이너(One of our members is a graphic designer.)라는 말로 회원 중 한 사람이 디자인할 것이라는 의미를 우회적으로 표현한 것이므로 정답.

(C) 파생어 오답. 질문의 invitations와 파생어 관계인 inviting을 이용한 오답.

23

M-Cn Is this the updated list of exhibitors at the trade show?

W-Am (A) It looks like the old one.

(B) Kojima Tools' demonstration.

(C) No, the first show is on April eighth.

이게 무역 박람회 전시업체의 최신 목록인가요?
(A) 그건 예전 것 같네요.
(B) 코지마 툴즈의 시연이요.
(C) 아니요, 첫 번째 쇼는 4월 8일이에요.

어휘 update ~을 갱신[개정]하다 exhibitor 전시업체 trade show 무역 박람회 demonstration 시연, (상품의) 실물 선전

해설 업데이트된 일정표인지 확인하는 be동사 Yes/No 의문문

(A) 정답. 여행 일정표가 최신본인지를 묻는 질문에 No를 생략한 채 예전 것인 것 같다(It looks like the old one.)며 부정적 응답을 하고 있으므로 정답.

(B) 연상 단어 오답. 질문의 exhibitors에서 연상 가능한 Kojima Tools를 이용한 오답.

(C) 단어 반복 오답. 질문에 나온 show를 반복 이용한 오답.

24

M-Au Which photograph are you going to use with this article?

W-Br (A) Thanks, it took me a while to write.

(B) Look straight into the camera, please.

(C) There aren't a lot of options.

이 기사에 어느 사진을 쓸 생각이세요?
(A) 고마워요. 작성하는 데 시간이 좀 걸렸어요.
(B) 카메라를 똑바로 봐 주세요.
(C) 선택의 여지가 많지 않아요.

어휘 article 기사 take a while 시간이 좀 걸리다 look straight into ~을 똑바로 보다 option 선택(권)

해설 선택사항을 묻는 Which 의문문

(A) 연상 단어 오답. 질문의 article에서 연상 가능한 write를 이용한 오답.

(B) 연상 단어 오답. 질문의 photograph에서 연상 가능한 camera를 이용한 오답.

(C) 정답. 기사에 어느 사진을 쓸 생각이냐는 질문에 선택의 여지가 많지 않다(There aren't a lot of options.)며 아직 결정하지 않았음을 우회적으로 표현하고 있으므로 정답.

25

W-Am Where should I order the banner for the anniversary party?

M-Cn (A) Talk to Sarah about that.

(B) How about the back wall?

(C) A simple message of congratulations.

기념 파티에 쓸 현수막을 어디서 주문해야 하죠?
(A) 그건 세라에게 문의해 보세요.
(B) 뒷벽은 어때요?
(C) 간단한 축하 메시지요.

어휘 banner 배너, 현수막 anniversary 기념일 congratulation 축하

해설 주문할 상점을 묻는 Where 의문문

(A) 정답. 기념 파티에 쓸 현수막을 주문할 곳을 묻는 질문에 구체적 상점 이름을 알려주는 것 대신 세라에게 얘기해 보라(Talk to Sarah about that.)는 말로 알고 있을 만한 사람을 알려주고 있으므로 정답.

(B) 연상 단어 오답. 질문의 banner에 대해 설치 장소 측면에서 연상 가능한 back wall을 이용한 오답.

(C) 연상 단어 오답. 질문의 anniversary에서 연상 가능한 congratulations를 이용한 오답.

26

M-Au I figured out why the packaging machine broke down.

W-Br (A) It's just down the street.

(B) No, the package wasn't delivered.

(C) Will it take long to fix it?

포장 기계가 고장 난 이유를 알아냈어요.
(A) 길 저쪽에 있어요.
(B) 아니요, 그 소포는 배송되지 않았어요.
(C) 고치는 데 오래 걸릴까요?

어휘 figure out ~을 알아내다 packaging 포장 break down 고장나다 package 소포; 포장하다

해설 사실/정보 전달의 평서문

(A) 단어 반복 오답. 평서문의 down을 반복 이용한 오답.

(B) 파생어 오답. 평서문의 packaging에서 -ing를 빼고 반복 이용한 오답.

(C) 정답. 수리하는 데 오래 걸릴지(Will it take long to fix it?)를 물으며 고장 상태의 정도를 확인하므로 정답.

27

W-Br Why don't we make a corporate donation to a local charity?

W-Am (A) We're a major corporation.

(B) I like that idea.

(C) It was extremely helpful.

지역 자선단체에 기업 기부를 하면 어떨까요?

(A) 우리 회사는 주요 기업이에요.

(B) 그거 좋은 생각이네요.

(C) 그것은 아주 도움이 되었어요.

어휘 make a donation 기부하다 corporate 기업의 charity 자선단체 major corporation 주요 기업 extremely 극도로

해설 기업 기부를 권하는 제안 의문문

(A) 파생어 오답. 질문의 corporate과 파생어 관계인 corporation을 이용한 오답.

(B) 정답. 지역 자선단체에 기업 기부를 하자는 제안에 대해 좋은 아이디어(I like that idea.)라는 말로 동의를 나타내고 있으므로 정답.

(C) 질문과 상관없는 오답. How 의문문에 어울리는 응답이므로 오답.

28

M-Au Didn't you get the survey I e-mailed to you?

W-Am (A) It wasn't in my inbox.

(B) There's no mail on Sundays.

(C) I decided not to.

제가 이메일로 보냈던 설문 조사를 받지 않았나요?

(A) 제 받은 편지함에는 없었어요.

(B) 매주 일요일에는 우편물이 없습니다.

(C) 하지 않기로 결정했어요.

어휘 survey (설문) 조사 inbox 받은 편지함

해설 이메일 수신 여부를 묻는 부정의문문

(A) 정답. No를 생략한 채 받은 편지함에는 없었다(It wasn't in my inbox.) 고 못 받았음을 알리는 우회적 표현이므로 정답.

(B) 유사 발음 오답. 질문의 e-mailed와 부분적으로 발음이 동일한 mail을 이용한 오답.

(C) 연상 단어 오답. 질문의 survey에서 연상 가능한 decided를 이용한 오답.

29

W-Br Do you want to change the flight's departure date or return date?

M-Cn (A) Actually, I'm canceling the trip.

(B) He departed from Rome.

(C) First-class section.

항공편의 출발 날짜를 변경하기를 원하세요, 아니면 돌아오는 날짜를 변경하기를 원하세요?

(A) 실은, 그 여행을 취소하겠습니다.

(B) 그는 로마에서 출발했어요.

(C) 일등석이요

어휘 departure 출발 cancel 취소하다 depart 출발하다

해설 구를 연결한 선택의문문

(A) 정답. 항공편의 출발 날짜나 돌아오는 날짜를 변경할 것인지 묻는 질문에 변경이 아니라 여행 자체를 취소하겠다(I'm canceling the trip)는 제3의 답변을 한 것이므로 정답.

(B) 파생어 오답. 질문의 departure와 파생어 관계인 departed를 이용한 오답.

(C) 연상 단어 오답. 질문의 flight에서 연상 가능한 First-class를 이용한 오답.

30

M-Cn Have you reviewed the latest version of the grant proposal?

W-Br (A) It wasn't late—the deadline's today.

(B) A research project on alternative energy.

(C) I think it's ready to be submitted.

보조금 제안서 최신 버전을 검토하셨나요?

(A) 마감일이 오늘이니까 늦은 게 아니었어요.

(B) 대체 에너지에 대한 연구 프로젝트요.

(C) 제출할 준비가 된 거 같습니다.

어휘 latest 최근의 grant 보조금 proposal 제안(서) deadline 마감일 alternative energy 대체 에너지 be ready to + 동사원형 ~할 준비가 되다 submit 제출하다

해설 검토 여부를 묻는 조동사(have) Yes/No 의문문

(A) 유사 발음 오답. 질문의 latest와 부분적으로 발음이 동일한 late를 이용한 오답.

(B) 연상 단어 오답. 질문의 grant에서 연상 가능한 research를 이용한 오답.

(C) 정답. 보조금 제안서 최신 버전을 검토했는지에 대한 질문에 제출할 준비가 된 거 같다(I think it's ready to be submitted.)는 우회적인 답변을 하고 있으므로 정답.

31

W-Am Why are we postponing the ceremony to next week?

M-Au (A) Until the end of the month.

(B) You've seen the weather forecast.

(C) A post with the meeting agenda details.

왜 기념식을 다음 주로 연기하는 거죠?

(A) 이달 말까지요.

(B) 일기 예보 보셨잖아요.

(C) 회의 안건 세부 사항이 적힌 게시글이요.

어휘 postpone 연기하다 ceremony 기념식 weather forecast 일기 예보 post 게시(글) meeting agenda 회의 안건 details 세부 사항

해설 연기 이유를 묻는 Why 의문문

(A) 연상 단어 오답. 질문의 week에서 연상 가능한 month를 이용한 오답.

(B) 정답. 기념식을 다음 주로 연기한 이유를 묻는 질문에 일기 예보를 보지 않았나(You've seen the weather forecast.)며 날씨가 이유임을 우회적으로 표현했으므로 정답.

(C) 유사 발음 오답. 질문의 postponing과 부분적으로 발음이 동일한 post를 이용한 오답.

PART 3

32-34

M-Cn Good afternoon, ma'am. [32]**Would you like to try our department store's new hand lotion?** It leaves your skin feeling smooth and refreshed, and it comes in a variety of scents.

W-Br Thanks, but actually... I think that might cause problems for me. [33]**My skin is very sensitive, so I have to be very careful about the types of creams I put on it.**

M-Cn I understand. [34]**Here's a coupon for two dollars off the item anyway.** It doesn't expire until December, so maybe you'd like to keep this in mind for a gift.

남: 안녕하세요, 고객님. **저희 백화점의 새 핸드 로션을 한번 발라 보시겠어요?** 피부가 부드럽고 상쾌해집니다. 다양한 향이 있어요.

여: 고맙지만, 실은 … 저한테 문제를 일으킬 수도 있을 것 같아요. **전 피부가 아주 민감해서 바르는 크림의 종류에 굉장히 주의해야 하거든요.**

남: 그러시군요. **아무튼 여기 이 제품의 2달러 할인 쿠폰을 드립니다.** 12월까지 쓰실 수 있으니 선물용으로 기억해 두시면 좋겠네요.

어휘 smooth 매끄러운 refreshed 상쾌한 a variety of 다양한 scent 향 sensitive 민감한, 예민한 anyway 어쨌든 expire 만료되다 keep ~ in mind ~을 잊지 않고 있다

32

What does the man encourage the woman to do?

(A) Explore a new department
(B) Complete a customer survey
(C) Sample a product
(D) Join a rewards program

남자는 여자에게 무엇을 하라고 권하는가?

(A) 새 부서 조사하기
(B) 고객 설문조사 작성하기
(C) 제품 견본 써 보기
(D) 보상 프로그램 등록하기

어휘 explore 조사하다, 탐험하다 sample (경험 삼아 잠깐) 시도해 보다 reward 보상, 이익

해설 세부 사항 관련 – 남자의 권유 사항

남자의 첫 번째 대사에서 여자에게 백화점의 새 핸드 로션을 한번 써 보겠냐(Would you like to try our department store's new hand lotion?)고 권유했으므로 정답은 (C)이다.

▸▸ **Paraphrasing** 대화의 **try our department store's new hand lotion**
→ 정답의 **Sample a product**

33

What problem does the woman have?

(A) She does not live nearby.
(B) She does not have much money.
(C) She is in a hurry.
(D) She has a health issue.

여자는 어떤 문제를 갖고 있는가?

(A) 근처에 살지 않는다.
(B) 돈이 많지 않다.
(C) 급하다.
(D) 건강 관련 문제가 있다.

해설 세부 사항 관련 – 여자의 문제점

여자의 대사에 자신의 피부는 아주 민감해서 바르는 크림의 종류에 굉장히 주의해야 한다(My skin is very sensitive ~ I put on it.)고 했으므로 정답은 (D)이다.

▸▸ **Paraphrasing** 대화의 **My skin is very sensitive.**
→ 정답의 **She has a health issue.**

34

What does the man give to the woman?

(A) A free cosmetics item
(B) A sales receipt
(C) An application form
(D) A discount voucher

남자는 여자에게 무엇을 주는가?

(A) 무료 화장품
(B) 판매 영수증
(C) 지원서 양식
(D) 할인 쿠폰

해설 세부 사항 관련 – 남자가 여자에게 주는 것

남자의 두 번째 대사에 여기 그 제품에 대한 2달러 할인 쿠폰을 드린다(Here's a coupon for two dollars off the item anyway.)고 했으므로 정답은 (D)이다.

▸▸ **Paraphrasing** 대화의 **a coupon for two dollars off the item** → 정답의 **a discount voucher**

35-37

W-Am Excuse me. [35]**I just wanted to let you know that I really like the music you've been playing here in the café.** It creates the perfect relaxing atmosphere. [36]**Who's the pianist?**

M-Au [36]**Her name's Maria Martinez, and she's actually from right here in Daynesville.**

W-Am Wow, she definitely has a lot of talent.

M-Au If you like what you hear that much, you've got to see her live. She sings here regularly on the weekends. [37]**I'll get you a list of her upcoming shows.** Just a moment.

여: 실례합니다. **이 카페에서 틀어 주신 음악이 정말 좋다고 알려드리고 싶어요.** 정말로 편안한 분위기를 만들어 주네요. **피아노 연주자가 누구죠?**

남: **그녀의 이름은 마리아 마르티네즈이고 사실은 바로 여기 데인즈빌 출신입니다.**

여: 와, 분명 재능이 많은 분이네요.

남: 들으신 음악이 그렇게 좋으시다면, 그녀의 라이브 공연을 보셔야 해요. 주말마다 정기적으로 이곳에서 공연을 하거든요. **제가 앞으로 있을 그녀의 공연 목록을 가져다 드릴게요.** 잠시만요.

어휘 relaxing 마음을 편안하게 해 주는 atmosphere 분위기 definitely 분명히 talent 재능 have got to + 동사원형 ~해야 한다 regularly 정기적으로 upcoming 곧 다가오는

35

What does the woman say she likes about the café?

(A) The artwork on display
(B) The food
(C) The background music
(D) The furniture

여자는 카페에 관해 무엇이 좋다고 말하는가?

(A) 전시된 미술품
(B) 음식
(C) 배경 음악
(D) 가구

해설 세부 사항 관련 - 여자가 카페에 관해 좋아하는 것

대화 맨 처음에 여자가 카페에서 틀어 주는 음악이 정말 좋다는 점을 남자에게 알려주고 싶었다(I just wanted to ~ at this café.)고 했다. 즉, 배경 음악이 마음에 들었던 것이므로 정답은 (C)이다.

36

Who is Ms. Martinez?

(A) A local performer
(B) A business owner
(C) A talent agent
(D) A café manager

마르티네즈 씨는 누구인가?

(A) 지역 출신 음악가
(B) 업체 주인
(C) 탤런트 에이전트
(D) 카페 매니저

해설 세부 사항 관련 - 마르티네즈 씨의 신분

여자가 첫 번째 대사에서 피아노 연주자가 누구인지(Who's the pianist?) 묻자 남자가 그녀의 이름은 마리아 마르티네즈이고 여기 데인즈빌 출신(Her name's Martinez ~ here in Daynesville.)이라고 했으므로 정답은 (A)이다.

37

What does the man say he will do for the woman?

(A) Bring her a menu
(B) Add her name to a list
(C) Clear her table
(D) Give her a schedule

남자는 여자를 위해 무엇을 해 주겠다고 말하는가?

(A) 여자에게 메뉴를 가져다 주기
(B) 목록에 여자의 이름 추가하기
(C) 여자의 테이블 치워주기
(D) 여자에게 일정표 주기

해설 세부 사항 관련 - 남자가 여자를 위해 할 일

대화 맨 마지막에 남자가 여자에게 앞으로 있을 공연의 목록을 주겠다(I'll get you a list of her upcoming shows.)고 했으므로 정답은 (D)이다.

▸▸ **Paraphrasing** 대화의 **a list of her upcoming shows**
→ 정답의 **a schedule**

38-40

M-Cn Hey, Jenny. [38]**Have you seen Michael this morning? I can't seem to find him anywhere.** He was supposed to help me with the preparations for my presentation.

W-Br He's not here. I heard that he called in sick.

M-Cn Oh no, really? That could be a problem. [39]**I need the projector and video conferencing system set up, and I have no idea how to do that myself.**

W-Br Don't worry. Samantha is covering for him. [40]**I'll text you her extension number.** She should be able to help you.

남: 안녕하세요, 제니. **오늘 아침에 마이클 봤어요? 그가 어디 있는지 찾을 수가 없네요.** 제가 진행할 프레젠테이션 준비를 도와주기로 했거든요.

여: 그는 여기 없어요. 오늘 전화로 병가를 냈다고 들었어요.

남: 아 이런, 정말요? 그럼 문제가 되겠는데요. **영사기와 화상 회의 시스템을 설치해야 하는데 제가 어떻게 하는지 몰라서요.**

여: 걱정 마세요. 서맨사가 마이클을 대신해서 업무를 보고 있어요. **서맨사의 내선 번호를 문자로 보내 줄게요.** 서맨사가 당신을 도와줄 수 있을 거예요.

어휘 be supposed to + 동사원형 ~하기로 되어 있다 preparation 준비 call in sick 전화로 병가를 내다 projector 영사기, 프로젝터 video conferencing 화상 회의 set up 설치하다 cover ~를 대신해서 일하다 extension number 내선 번호

38

What does the man want to know?

(A) Who will give a presentation
(B) When an event starts
(C) How to find some data
(D) Where a coworker is

남자는 무엇을 알고 싶어하는가?

(A) 누가 프레젠테이션을 할지
(B) 행사가 언제 시작되는지
(C) 데이터를 어떻게 찾는지
(D) 동료가 어디에 있는지

해설 세부 사항 관련 – 남자가 알고 싶은 것
대화 맨 처음에 남자가 여자에게 오늘 아침에 마이클을 봤는지 물으며 그가 어디 있는지 찾을 수가 없다(Have you seen ~ him anywhere.)고 했다. 즉, 남자는 직장 동료를 찾고 있는 것이므로 정답은 (D)이다.

39

What problem does the man mention?

(A) He is not feeling well.
(B) He is late for a meeting.
(C) He cannot set up some equipment.
(D) He has misplaced some files.

남자는 어떤 문제를 언급하는가?

(A) 그가 몸이 좋지 않다.
(B) 그가 회의에 늦었다.
(C) 그는 장비 설치를 못한다.
(D) 그는 파일을 어디에 두었는지 잊었다.

해설 세부 사항 관련 – 남자가 언급하는 문제점
남자의 두 번째 대사에서 자신이 프로젝트와 화상 회의 시스템을 설치해야 하는데 어떻게 하는지 모른다(I need the projector ~ how to do that myself.)고 했으므로 정답은 (C)이다.

▸▸ **Paraphrasing** 대화의 **the projector and video conferencing system**
→ 정답의 **some equipment**

40

What does the woman say she will do?

(A) Review a slide show
(B) Prepare a conference room
(C) Send some contact information
(D) Confirm a number of attendees

여자는 무엇을 할 것이라고 말하는가?

(A) 슬라이드 쇼 검토하기
(B) 회의실 준비하기
(C) 연락처 보내기
(D) 참석 인원 확인하기

어휘 review 검토하다 attendee 참석자

해설 세부 사항 관련 – 여자가 할 일
대화 맨 마지막에 여자가 서맨사의 내선 번호를 문자로 보내주겠다(I'll text you her extension number.)고 했으므로 정답은 (C)이다.

▸▸ **Paraphrasing** 대화의 **text you her extension number**
→ 정답의 **Send some contact information**

41-43 3인 대화

W-Br Hello. Could we get two adult tickets for the contemporary art exhibit?

M-Cn I'm sorry, but [41]**we stopped selling tickets for that exhibit at seven-thirty because it closes at eight o'clock**. It'll open again tomorrow at ten.

W-Am Actually, we're leaving town tomorrow morning. [42]**We were just here in Kemperling for a few days to compete in a regional softball tournament.**

W-Br Could you recommend something else for us to do at this time of day?

M-Cn Well, [43]**there's nothing better than walking in the sand near Kemperling Pier.** It's beautiful to see the sun set over the ocean, and you'll find a lot of great places to eat around there.

여1: 안녕하세요. 현대 미술 전시회 성인 표 두 장 주시겠어요?
남: 죄송합니다만, **7시 30분에 전시회 입장권 판매를 마감했어요. 전시회가 8시에 끝나거든요.** 내일 10시에 다시 문을 열 겁니다.
여2: 사실 저희가 내일 오전에 이 마을을 떠나요. **저희는 지역 소프트볼 토너먼트 경기에 참가하느라 여기 켐퍼링에 며칠 머물렀던 거라서요.**
여1: 저희가 하루 중 이맘때에 할 다른 뭔가를 추천해 주실 수 있을까요?
남: 글쎄요, **켐퍼링 부두 근처의 모래사장을 걷는 것이 가장 좋습니다.** 바다 위로 해가 지는 것을 보는 게 아름답고, 그 주변에 먹을 수 있는 훌륭한 식당도 많이 있습니다.

어휘 contemporary art 현대 미술 exhibit 전시회 compete in ~에 참가[출전]하다 recommend 추천하다 at this time of day 이맘때에 pier 부두

41

What does the man mention about the exhibit?

(A) It will be closing for the day soon.
(B) Its ticket price has increased.
(C) Its venue has changed.
(D) It has sold out.

남자는 전시회에 대해 뭐라고 말하는가?

(A) 당일은 곧 끝날 예정이다.
(B) 입장권 가격이 인상됐다.
(C) 장소가 변경됐다.
(D) 매진되었다.

어휘 venue 장소, 개최지

해설 세부 사항 관련 - 전시회에 대한 남자의 말

남자의 첫 번째 대사에서 전시회가 8시에 끝나기 때문에 7시 30분에 전시회 입장권 판매를 마감했다(we stopped selling tickets ~ at eight o'clock.)고 했다. 이를 통해 전시회가 곧 끝날 것임을 알 수 있으므로 정답은 (A)이다.

▸▸ Paraphrasing 대화의 it closes at eight o'clock.
→ 정답의 It will be closing for the day soon.

42

Why have the women come to Kemperling?

(A) To go to a conference
(B) To help with a festival
(C) To participate in a competition
(D) To spend time with friends

여자들이 켐퍼링에 온 이유는?

(A) 총회에 가기 위해
(B) 축제를 돕기 위해
(C) 시합에 참가하기 위해
(D) 친구와 함께 시간을 보내기 위해

해설 세부 사항 관련 - 여자들의 캠퍼링 방문 이유

두 번째 여자의 첫 번째 대사에서 지역 소프트볼 토너먼트 경기에 참가하기 위해 이곳 켐퍼링에 며칠 머물렀다(We were just here ~ in a regional softball tournament.)고 했으므로 정답은 (C)이다.

▸▸ Paraphrasing 대화의 a regional softball tournament
→ 정답의 a competition

43

What does the man recommend?

(A) Walking through a garden
(B) Visiting a beach
(C) Attending a concert
(D) Opening a restaurant

남자가 권하는 것은 무엇인가?

(A) 정원 산책
(B) 해변가 방문
(C) 음악회 참석
(D) 레스토랑 개업

해설 세부 사항 관련 - 남자의 권장 사항

남자의 두 번째 대사에서 켐퍼링 부두 근처의 모래사장을 걷는 것이 가장 좋다(there's nothing better ~ in the sand near Kemperling Pier.)고 했으므로 정답은 (B)이다.

▸▸ Paraphrasing 대화의 walking in the sand near Kemperling Pier
→ 정답의 visiting a beach

44-46

M-Au Hi, Ms. Baxter. It's Shinji. [44]**I know I'm supposed to start my shift at the store at ten, but I won't be there until about ten-thirty.** I'm really sorry, but my car broke down, and I'm waiting for the bus now.

W-Am Please get here as soon as you can. [45]**Our shoe sale started today, so we're overloaded with customers.**

M-Au I'll do my best. In the meantime, I've trained Robert to work the cash register at checkout. [46]**Maybe you could have him cover that responsibility until I get there.**

W-Am Yes, I'll do that. We don't want our customers waiting too long to make their purchases.

남: 안녕하세요, 벡스터 씨. 신지입니다. **매장 근무를 10시에 시작해야 하는 것은 알지만 거의 10시 30분이 되어서야 도착할 것 같아요.** 정말 죄송합니다만 제 차가 고장 나서 지금 버스를 기다리고 있어요.

여: 가능한 한 빨리 오세요. **오늘 신발 할인을 시작해서 손님이 너무 많거든요.**

남: 최선을 다할게요. 그동안 제가 로버트에게 계산대의 금전 등록기에서 일하도록 가르쳐 줬는데요. **아마도 제가 도착할 때까지는 그에게 그 일을 맡도록 시키실 수 있을 겁니다.**

여: 네, 그렇게 할게요. 고객들이 물건을 사는 데 너무 오래 기다리게 하고 싶지는 않으니까요.

어휘 shift 교대 근무 (시간) break down 고장 나다 be overloaded with ~가 너무 많이 주어지다 in the meantime 그 동안에 cash register 금전 등록기 checkout 계산대 make a purchase 물건을 사다

44

Why is the man calling the woman?

(A) To switch shifts with her
(B) To check a work schedule
(C) To request time off
(D) To inform her of a late arrival

남자가 여자에게 전화를 건 이유는 무엇인가?

(A) 여자와 교대 근무 시간을 바꾸기 위해
(B) 근무 일정을 확인하기 위해
(C) 휴가를 신청하기 위해
(D) 늦게 도착할 것을 알리기 위해

해설 전체 내용 관련 - 남자가 전화를 건 이유

남자의 첫 번째 대사에서 매장 근무를 10시에 시작해야 하는 걸 알지만 거의 10시 30분이 되어야 도착할 것 같다(I know I'm supposed to ~ about ten-thirty.)고 했다. 즉, 남자는 여자에게 지각하게 될 것을 알리기 위해 전화를 한 것이므로 정답은 (D)이다.

45

According to the woman, why is the store busier than usual?

(A) A promotional sale has begun.
(B) Another employee is absent.
(C) New merchandise has been launched.
(D) A holiday is coming soon.

Test 10

여자에 따르면, 매장이 평소보다 바쁜 이유는 무엇인가?
(A) **판촉 할인이 시작됐다.**
(B) 또 다른 직원이 결근했다.
(C) 신제품이 출시됐다.
(D) 휴일이 곧 다가온다.

해설 세부 사항 관련 – 매장이 평소보다 바쁜 이유
여자의 첫 번째 대사에서 오늘 신발 할인을 시작했기 때문에 손님이 너무 많다(Our shoe sale started today, so we're overloaded with customers.)고 했으므로 정답은 (A)이다.

▸▸ Paraphrasing 대화의 **Our shoe sale started today.**
→ 정답의 **A promotional sale has begun.**

46
What does the man suggest?
(A) Hiring some temporary workers
(B) Assigning a task to a coworker
(C) Providing training to a colleague
(D) Asking another branch for assistance

남자가 제안하는 것은 무엇인가?
(A) 임시직 근로자를 고용하는 것
(B) **동료에게 업무를 배정하는 것**
(C) 동료에게 교육을 제공하는 것
(D) 다른 지점에 도움을 요청하는 것

어휘 temporary 임시의 assign ~을 배정하다 coworker 직장 동료 colleague 동료

해설 세부 사항 관련 – 남자의 제안 사항
남자의 두 번째 대사에서 로버트에게 계산대의 금전 등록기에서 일하도록 가르쳐 줬으니 그에게 자신의 책무를 맡길 수도 있다(Maybe you could have him cover that responsibility until I get there.)고 했다. 즉, 남자는 직장 동료인 로버트에게 업무를 맡길 것을 제안한 것이므로 정답은 (B)이다.

▸▸ Paraphrasing 대화의 **have him cover that responsibility**
→ 정답의 **assigning a task to a coworker**

47-49

W-Br Mr. Perkins, a local tour operator came in today and asked about leaving some brochures here. [47]**Have you thought about getting one of those brochure holder racks that some other hotels have?**

M-Cn No, I haven't. But it seems like a good idea. It would certainly be useful for our guests. Let's see, [48]**where could we put a rack?**

W-Br Most guests come in through the main entrance. The brochures could catch their attention as they pass by.

M-Cn So next to the plant over there? That could work. All right. [49]**I'll get on the Internet and try to buy a rack for a reasonable price.** Thanks for the idea, Eva.

여: 퍼킨스 씨, 지역 관광업자가 오늘 와서는 여기에 브로슈어를 놓는 것에 대해 물어봤어요. **다른 호텔들에 있는 그런 브로슈어 받침대 하나를 두는 거에 대해 생각해 보셨어요?**
남: 아니요, 없는데요. 하지만 좋은 생각인 거 같습니다. 우리 고객들한테 확실히 도움이 될 거 같아요. 봅시다, **받침대를 어디에 놓을까요?**
여: 고객 대부분이 중앙 출입구를 통해 들어오잖아요. 고객들이 지나갈 때 브로슈어가 그들의 시선을 끌 수 있어요.
남: 그럼 저기 식물 옆에요? 그거 괜찮겠네요. 좋아요. **제가 인터넷에 접속해서 적당한 가격의 받침대를 구입해 볼게요.** 아이디어 고마워요, 에바.

어휘 local 지역의 tour operator 관광업자 brochure 브로슈어, 안내책자 rack 걸이, 받침대 certainly 분명히 through ~을 통해서 catch one's attention ~의 시선[관심]을 끌다 pass by 지나가다 plant 식물 get on the Internet 인터넷에 접속하다 reasonable price 적당한 가격

47
What is the main topic of the conversation?
(A) A hotel policy
(B) An informational brochure
(C) A display stand
(D) A tour course

대화의 주제는 무엇인가?
(A) 호텔 정책
(B) 안내용 책자
(C) **진열대**
(D) 관광 코스

어휘 policy 정책 informational 정보를 주는 display stand 진열대

해설 전체 내용 관련 – 대화의 주제
여자의 첫 번째 대사에서 남자에게 다른 호텔들에 있는 그런 브로슈어 받침대 하나를 두는 거에 대해 생각해 보았는지(Have you thought about getting ~ some other hotels have?) 물었고 이와 관련된 내용이 이어지고 있으므로 정답은 (C)이다.

▸▸ Paraphrasing 지문의 **one of those brochure holder racks**
→ 정답의 **A display stand**

48
Why does the woman say, "most guests come in through the main entrance"?
(A) To emphasize the importance of cleaning an area often
(B) To recommend an angle for a photograph
(C) To express concern about an inconvenience
(D) To suggest a useful location for an item

여자가 "고객 대부분이 중앙 출입문을 통해 들어오잖아요"라고 말한 이유는 무엇인가?
(A) 특정 구역을 자주 청소하는 것의 중요성을 강조하려고
(B) 한 사진 촬영 각도를 추천하려고
(C) 불편 사항에 대해 우려를 표현하려고
(D) **어떤 물건을 놓는 데 유용한 위치를 제안하려고**

어휘 emphasize 강조하다 angle (시선의) 각도 concern 우려 inconvenience 불편, 불편한 것 location 위치

해설 화자의 의도 파악 – 고객 대부분이 중앙 출입문을 통해 들어온다고 말한 이유

인용문 바로 전 대사에서 남자가 받침대를 어디에 놓을지(where could we put a rack?) 물어봤다. 이에 여자가 고객 대부분이 중앙 출입문을 통해 들어온다고 했으므로, 받침대를 놓는 데 유용한 위치를 제안하려고 한 말임을 알 수 있어 정답은 (D)이다.

49

What does the man say he will do?

(A) Move some decorations
(B) Try shopping online
(C) Make a price list
(D) Work overtime tonight

남자는 무엇을 하겠다고 말하는가?

(A) 장식품 이동
(B) 온라인 쇼핑 시도
(C) 가격표 작성
(D) 오늘 밤 초과 근무

어휘 decoration 장식, 장식품 price list 가격표 work overtime 초과 근무를 하다

해설 세부 사항 관련 – 남자가 할 일

남자의 마지막 대사에서 인터넷에 접속하여 적당한 가격의 받침대를 구입해 보겠다(I'll get on the Internet and try to buy a rack for a reasonable price.)고 했으므로 정답은 (B)이다.

50-52

W-Br Joshua, [50]**are you done with the preparations for the workshop on Thursday? It's important that all the staff members learn how to use the new billing software.**

M-Au I'm almost finished. [51]**Yesterday I went through the user manual in detail and made an outline of the most important points.** Now I just have to create a few practice activities for people to do.

W-Br Great. It sounds like you have everything under control. And [52]**this is perfect timing because we've just hired several new employees.** So, we would've had to hold the workshop anyway.

여: 조슈아, **목요일에 있을 워크숍 준비는 마쳤나요? 모든 직원이 새로운 청구용 소프트웨어 사용법을 익히는 것이 중요해요.**

남: 거의 끝났습니다. **어제 사용 설명서를 자세히 훑어보고 가장 중요한 부분들을 요약했어요.** 이제 직원들이 해볼 실습 활동만 만들면 돼요.

여: 잘했네요. 모든 것을 잘 하고 있는 걸로 보이네요. 그리고 **신입 직원도 여러 명 고용했으니 타이밍이 완벽해요.** 어쨌든 워크숍을 열어야 했으니까요.

어휘 be done with ~를 끝내다 billing 청구서 발송 almost 거의 go through ~을 살펴보다 in detail 자세히, 세부적으로 outline 개요, 요약 practice 실습 under control 통제[관리, 감독]하에 있는

50

What is the conversation mainly about?

(A) A training session
(B) A contract renewal
(C) An interview process
(D) A software problem

대화의 주요 내용은 무엇인가?

(A) 교육 과정
(B) 계약 갱신
(C) 면접 절차
(D) 소프트웨어 문제

해설 전체 내용 관련 – 대화의 주제

대화 맨 처음에 여자가 남자에게 목요일에 있을 워크숍 준비는 마쳤는지를 물었고 모든 직원들이 새로운 청구용 소프트웨어의 사용법을 익히는 것이 중요하다(are you done with ~ billing software.)고 했다. 이를 통해 대화의 주제가 워크숍임을 있음을 알 수 있으므로 정답은 (A)이다.

▸▸ **Paraphrasing** 대화의 **the workshop**
→ 정답의 **a training session**

51

What did the man do yesterday?

(A) He contacted a manufacturer.
(B) He summarized a manual.
(C) He issued a bill.
(D) He practiced a talk.

남자는 어제 무엇을 했는가?

(A) 제조업체에게 연락했다.
(B) 설명서를 요약했다.
(C) 청구서를 발급했다.
(D) 강연 연습을 했다.

어휘 summarize ~을 요약하다 issue ~을 발행[발급]하다

해설 세부 사항 관련 – 남자가 어제 한 일

남자의 대사에서 어제 사용 설명서를 자세히 훑어보고 가장 중요한 부분들을 요약했다(Yesterday I went through ~ important points.)고 했으므로 정답은 (B)이다.

▸▸ **Paraphrasing** 대화의 **made an outline**
→ 정답의 **summarized a manual**

52

What does the woman mention about the business?

(A) Its workforce has recently expanded.
(B) It invests heavily in new technology.
(C) It will relocate to another city.
(D) It currently has several job openings.

여자는 회사에 대해 뭐라고 말하는가?
(A) 최근에 직원 수가 늘었다.
(B) 신기술에 대거 투자하고 있다.
(C) 다른 도시로 이전할 예정이다.
(D) 현재 공석이 몇 개 있다.

어휘 workforce 작업 인원, 전 종업원 expand (크기·수량 등에서) 확장하다, 확대되다 relocate 이전하다 opening 공석

해설 세부 사항 관련 – 회사에 대한 여자의 말
여자의 두 번째 대사에서 신입 직원도 여러 명 고용했으니 타이밍이 완벽하다(this is perfect timing ~ employees.)고 했으므로 정답은 (A)이다.

▸▸ Paraphrasing 대화의 **we've just hired several new employees**
→ 정답의 **Its workforce has recently expanded.**

53-55 3인 대화

W-Am [53]**Leon, Albert, what's your progress on tomorrow's article on the plan to build a new city hall?** I'd like a quick update.
M-Cn Sure. I just spoke to the mayor's office on the phone and got some good quotes. And Albert is almost finished confirming all of the background information.
M-Au [54]**All I have left to check is the amount of money that's being put aside for construction.**
W-Am So you two won't have any problems meeting the deadline?
M-Cn Right. In fact, we should be finished before dinner.
W-Am Great. [55]**I'll go see what pictures the photo editor has to go along with the story.** Keep up the good work.

여: **리안, 앨버트, 새 시청 건설 계획에 관한 내일 기사 진척 상황이 어때요?** 최근 상황을 간단히 알고 싶네요.
남1: 네. 방금 전화로 시장 사무실 쪽과 얘기를 했고요, 쓸만한 인용문구가 생겼어요. 그리고 앨버트가 모든 배경 정보 확인을 거의 끝냈습니다.
남2: **저는 건설을 위해 따로 떼어둘 돈 액수만 확인하면 됩니다.**
여: 그럼 두 분 다 마감일 맞추는 데 전혀 문제 없을까요?
남1: 네. 사실, 저녁 식사 전에 끝날 거 같습니다.
여: 좋아요. **저는 가서 기사에 어울릴 만한 사진으로 사진 에디터한테 어떤 게 있는지 확인해 볼게요.** 계속 수고해 주세요.

어휘 progress 진전, 진척 상황 article 기사 city hall 시청 mayor 시장 on the phone 전화로 quote 인용문 confirm 확인하다 background 배경 amount 양, 액수 put aside 따로 떼어두다 construction 건설 have a problem ~ing ~하느라 애를 먹다 meet the deadline 마감일을 맞추다

53
What activity are the speakers discussing?
(A) Participating in a city event
(B) Registering for a government permit
(C) Revising some construction plans
(D) Reporting on a local news story

화자들은 어떤 활동에 대해 얘기하고 있는가?
(A) 시 행사 참여
(B) 정부 허가 신청
(C) 건설 계획안 변경
(D) 지역 뉴스 보도

어휘 activity 활동 participate in ~에 참여하다 register for ~에 등록하다[신청하다] permit 허가 revise 변경하다 report on ~에 대해 보고[보도]하다

해설 전체 내용 관련 – 얘기되고 있는 활동
여자의 첫 번째 대사에서 새 시청 건설 계획에 관한 기사 진척 상황이 어떤지(what's your progress on tomorrow's article on the plan to build a new city hall?) 물어봤고 남자들이 이에 답하고 있는 것으로 보아, 화자들은 지역 뉴스 보도에 대해 얘기하고 있다는 사실을 알 수 있으므로 정답은 (D)이다.

54
What information does Albert say he needs to verify?
(A) The budget for a project
(B) The next step of a procedure
(C) The start time of a meeting
(D) The name of an official

앨버트는 자신이 어떤 정보를 확인해야 한다고 말하는가?
(A) 프로젝트 예산
(B) 절차상의 다음 단계
(C) 회의 시작 시간
(D) 담당 관리의 이름

어휘 verify 확인하다 budget 예산 procedure 절차 official 공무원

해설 세부 사항 관련 – 앨버트가 확인해야 하는 정보
첫 번째 남자의 첫 번째 대사에서 앨버트가 두 번째 남자임을 알 수 있다. 두 번째 남자의 첫 번째 대사에서 건설을 위해 따로 떼어둘 돈 액수만 확인하면 된다(All I have left to check is the amount of money that's being put aside for construction.)고 했으므로 정답은 (A)이다.

55
What will the woman most likely do next?
(A) Reschedule a dinner
(B) Drive to a building site
(C) Edit a draft of an article
(D) Look at some photographs

여자는 다음에 무엇을 하겠는가?
(A) 저녁 식사 일정 조정하기
(B) 건설 현장으로 운전하기
(C) 기사 초고 편집하기
(D) 사진 검토하기

어휘 reschedule 일정을 조정하다 building site 건설 현장 edit 편집하다 draft 초고, 초안

해설 세부 사항 관련 – 여자가 할 일

여자의 마지막 대사에서 기사에 어울릴 만한 사진으로 사진 에디터한테 어떤 게 있는지 확인하겠다(I'll go see what pictures the photo editor has to go along with the story.)고 했으므로 정답은 (D)이다.

56-58

M-Cn Well, now that the first week of classes is almost over, [56]**what do you think of the new series of course books?**

W-Am I like them—especially the beginner-level book. It has a lot of interesting ideas for in-class activities. How about you?

M-Cn The intermediate-level book seems to have too much material. [57]**I'm worried that I won't be able to teach all eight lessons by the end of the semester.**

W-Am You'll probably need to skip some parts, then.

M-Cn Yes, but which ones? Actually, I have the book here—[58]**could you look over it and make some recommendations?**

W-Am Oh, my class is about to start. [58]**Umm... are you free tomorrow morning?**

남: 음, 수업 첫 주가 이제 거의 끝나가는데, **새 교재 시리즈 어떻게 생각해요?**

여: 마음에 들어요. 특히 초급 수준 교재가요. 교실 내 활동에 관한 흥미로운 아이디어가 많더라고요. 당신은 어때요?

남: 중급 수준 교재는 자료가 너무 많은 것 같아요. **학기가 끝날 때까지 8개 과를 다 못 가르칠까 봐 걱정이에요.**

여: 그럼 아마도 몇 부분은 빼야 되겠는데요.

남: 네, 그런데 어느 부분을요? 실은, 제가 지금 책을 가지고 있는데요, **이거 훑어보시고 제안을 해주실 수 있으세요?**

여: 아, 제 수업이 시작하려고 해요. **음… 내일 아침에 시간 되세요?**

어휘 now that 이제 ~이니까[~인데] be over 끝나다 course book 교재, 교과서 in-class 수업 중의, 수업 시간의 intermediate 중급의 seem to + 동사원형 ~인 것 같다 material 자료 skip 건너뛰다, 생략하다 look over 훑어보다 make a recommendation 추천하다, 제안하다 be about to + 동사원형 막 ~하려는 참이다

56

What has recently changed for the speakers?

(A) The length of their class sessions
(B) The skill level of their students
(C) The classrooms they teach in
(D) The textbooks they use

화자들에게 최근 무엇이 바뀌었는가?

(A) 수업 시간의 길이
(B) 학생들의 실력 수준
(C) 가르치는 교실
(D) 사용하는 교재

어휘 length 시간, 길이 session (수업, 활동 등의) 시간, 세션 textbook 교과서, 교재

해설 세부 사항 관련 – 최근에 바뀐 것

남자의 첫 번째 대사에서 여자에게 새 교재 시리즈를 어떻게 생각하는지(what do you think of the new series of course books?) 물어보았으므로 정답은 (D)이다.

57

What is the man concerned about?

(A) Explaining a concept clearly
(B) Keeping listeners interested in a topic
(C) Finishing a certain number of lessons
(D) Impressing a supervisor

남자는 무엇에 대해 걱정하는가?

(A) 개념을 분명하게 설명하는 것
(B) 청자들이 주제에 계속 관심을 갖게 하는 것
(C) 일정 수의 과를 끝마치는 것
(D) 관리자에게 좋은 인상을 주는 것

어휘 be concerned about ~을 걱정하다 concept 개념 clearly 분명하게 keep A interested in ~ A가 ~에 계속 관심을 갖게 하다 impress 감동시키다, 좋은 인상을 주다 supervisor 관리자

해설 세부 사항 관련 – 남자의 우려 사항

남자의 두 번째 대사에서 학기가 끝날 때까지 8개 과를 다 못 가르칠까 봐 걱정이 된다(I'm worried that I won't be able to teach all eight lessons by the end of the semester.)고 했으므로 정답은 (C)이다.

58

What does the woman imply when she says, "my class is about to start"?

(A) She cannot fulfill a request immediately.
(B) She needs to access some materials as soon as possible.
(C) The man is invited to observe her class.
(D) The man will have to leave the room.

여자가 "제 수업이 시작하려고 해요"라고 말한 의도는 무엇인가?

(A) 요청을 즉시 이행할 수 없다.
(B) 가능한 한 빨리 자료를 봐야 한다.
(C) 남자는 여자의 수업을 참관할 수 있다.
(D) 남자가 교실에서 나가야 할 것이다.

어휘 fulfill 이행하다 request 요청 immediately 즉시 be invited to + 동사원형 ~하도록 초대[요청]받다 observe 관찰하다

해설 화자의 의도 파악 – 수업이 시작하려고 한다는 말의 의도

인용문 바로 전 대사에서 남자가 책을 훑어보고 제안을 해 줄 수 있는지(could you look over it and make some recommendations?) 요청했다. 이에 여자가 수업이 시작하려 한다며 내일 아침 시간이 되는지(are you free tomorrow morning?) 물어보았으므로 정답은 (A)이다.

59-61

M-Au Hi, Isabelle. [59]**I thought I might run into you at this conference.**

W-Br Hey, James. Yeah, [59]**I think the company sent one person from each branch.**

M-Au So, how are things going in Charleston?

W-Br Great so far. Of course, I miss you and my other coworkers at the Roseville branch. But [60]**I love being just a ten-minute drive from the office.** I used to have to drive over an hour each way.

M-Au I'm sure that gives you a lot more free time. So, are you staying for the afternoon sessions?

W-Br Yes—but you know those don't start until one-thirty. [61]**How about getting some lunch?** It'll give us a chance to catch up.

남: 이사벨, 안녕하세요. **이 컨퍼런스에서 당신과 마주칠지도 모른다고 생각했어요.**

여: 제임스, 안녕하세요. 네, **회사가 각 지점에서 한 명씩 보낸 것 같아요.**

남: 그런데, 찰스턴 지점은 어떻게 돌아가나요?

여: 지금까지는 아주 좋아요! 물론, 당신과 다른 로즈빌 지점 동료들이 그리워요. 하지만 **사무실에서 차로 10분 거리에 사는 게 너무 좋아요.** 전에는 편도로 한 시간 넘게 운전해야 했으니까요.

남: 분명 자유 시간이 훨씬 많아졌겠군요. 참, 오후 시간들을 위해 남아 있을 건가요?

여: 네, 하지만 알다시피 1시 30분이 되어야 시작해요. **점심을 먹는 건 어때요?** 그동안 서로 어떻게 지냈는지 얘기할 기회가 되겠네요.

어휘 run into ~와 마주치다 branch 지점 miss 그리워하다 catch up 그동안 있었던 일을 이야기하다

59

Where most likely is the conversation taking place?

(A) At a bus stop
(B) At an industry event
(C) At the man's office
(D) At a personal celebration

대화는 어디서 이루어지고 있는 것 같은가?

(A) 버스 정류장
(B) 업계 행사
(C) 남자의 사무실
(D) 개인적인 축하 행사

해설 전체 내용 관련 - 대화의 장소

대화 맨 처음에 남자가 여자에게 인사를 하며 이번 컨퍼런스에서 마주칠지도 모른다는 생각을 했다(I thought I might run into you at this conference.)고 했다. 이에 대해 여자도 남자에게 인사를 한 후, 회사가 각 지점에서 한 명씩 보낸 것 같다(I think the company sent one person from each branch.)고 했다. 즉, 화자들은 컨퍼런스에서 우연히 만나 대화를 하고 있는 것이므로 정답은 (B)이다.

▸▸ **Paraphrasing** 대화의 **at this conference** → 정답의 **at an industry event**

60

What advantage of her new job is the woman especially pleased about?

(A) The short commute
(B) The flexible hours
(C) The high salary
(D) The friendly staff

여자는 새 일의 어떤 점을 특히 좋아하는가?

(A) 짧은 통근 거리
(B) 탄력적 근무시간
(C) 높은 급여
(D) 친절한 직원

어휘 commute 통근 (거리) flexible 융통성 있는, 유연한

해설 세부 사항 관련 - 여자의 새 일에 대한 이점

여자의 두 번째 대사에서 사무실에서 차로 10분 거리에 사는 게 아주 좋다(I love being just a ten-minute drive from the office.)고 했다. 즉, 여자는 짧은 통근 거리를 마음에 들어 하는 것이므로 정답은 (A)이다.

▸▸ **Paraphrasing** 대화의 **just a ten-minute drive from the office** → 정답의 **the short commute**

61

What does the woman suggest?

(A) Having a meal together
(B) Collaborating on a proposal
(C) Sharing transportation
(D) Arranging a branch visit

여자는 무엇을 제안하는가?

(A) 함께 식사하기
(B) 공동으로 제안서 작성하기
(C) 교통편 함께 타기
(D) 지점 방문 주선하기

어휘 collaborate 협력하다, 공동으로 작업하다

해설 세부 사항 관련 - 여자의 제안 사항

대화 마지막에 여자가 남자에게 점심을 먹는 건 어떻겠냐(How about getting some lunch?)는 제안을 했으므로 정답은 (A)이다.

▸▸ **Paraphrasing** 대화의 **getting some lunch** → 정답의 **having a meal**

62-64 대화+쿠폰

W-Br You're in luck, sir. [62]**We did have more of the Y77 model in the stockroom. Here it is.**

M-Au Thanks! I really appreciate your help. When I didn't see any on the shelf, I was worried that you were sold out. So, I guess that's everything I need. I'd like to use this coupon, please.

W-Br All right. [63]**You'll get twenty percent off your item.**

M-Au Great. And I'm buying it for a friend. [64]**If he doesn't like it, can I bring it back to the store and get my money back?**

W-Br Sure, as long as you do so within thirty days.

여: 운이 좋으시네요, 손님. **창고에 Y77 모델이 더 있었어요. 여기 있습니다.**

남: 고마워요! 도와주셔서 정말 감사합니다. 선반에 없었을 때 다 팔렸을까 봐 걱정했어요. 이거면 될 것 같아요. 이 쿠폰을 사용할게요.

여: 알겠습니다. **20퍼센트 할인을 받으실 겁니다.**

남: 잘됐네요. 그리고 이건 친구를 위해 사는 거예요. **친구가 맘에 들어 하지 않으면 매장으로 다시 가져와서 환불받을 수 있나요?**

여: 물론이죠. 30일 이내에 그렇게 하신다면요.

어휘 be in luck 운이 좋다 stockroom 창고 be sold out 다 팔리다, 매진되다 within ~ 이내에 sleeping bag 침낭

Springer's Goods

Tents	10% off
[63]Backpacks	20% off
Sleeping Bags	25% off
Flashlights	30% off

스프링어스 굳즈

텐트	10% 할인
배낭	20% 할인
침낭	25% 할인
손전등	30% 할인

62

Why does the man thank the woman?

(A) She expedited an order for him.
(B) She checked a storage area for an item.
(C) She explained some product features.
(D) She gave him a coupon.

남자는 왜 여자에게 고마워하는가?

(A) 남자를 위해 급히 주문을 했다.
(B) 물건을 찾기 위해 보관 장소를 확인했다.
(C) 제품의 특성을 설명했다.
(D) 남자에게 쿠폰을 주었다.

어휘 expedite 신속히 처리하다 feature 특징

해설 전체 내용 관련 – 남자가 고마워하는 이유

여자의 첫 번째 대사에서 남자에게 창고에 Y77 모델이 더 있었다고 하면서 물건이 여기 있다(We did have ~ Here it is.)고 했다. 이에 대해 남자가 고맙다고 한 것이므로 정답은 (B)이다.

▸▸ Paraphrasing 대화의 the stockroom
→ 정답의 a storage area

63

Look at the graphic. What is the man buying?

(A) A tent
(B) A backpack
(C) A sleeping bag
(D) A flashlight

시각 정보에 의하면, 남자가 구매하고 있는 것은?

(A) 텐트
(B) 배낭
(C) 침낭
(D) 손전등

해설 시각 정보 연계 – 남자가 구매하는 것

여자의 두 번째 대사에서 남자가 20퍼센트 할인을 받을 것(You'll get twenty percent off your item.)이라고 했다. 그리고 쿠폰을 보면 배낭(Backpacks)이 20퍼센트 할인으로 명시되어 있으므로 정답은 (B)이다.

64

What does the man ask about?

(A) An instruction manual
(B) A delivery option
(C) A return policy
(D) A closing time

남자는 무엇에 대해 물어보는가?

(A) 사용 설명서
(B) 배송 선택 사항
(C) 반품 규정
(D) 폐점 시간

해설 세부 사항 관련 – 남자의 문의 사항

남자의 두 번째 대사에서 친구를 위해 사는 건데, 만약 친구가 맘에 들어 하지 않으면 매장으로 다시 가져와서 환불을 받을 수 있는지(If he doesn't like it, ~ money back?)를 물어봤다. 즉, 남자는 반품 규정에 대해 문의한 것이므로 정답은 (C)이다.

65-67 대화 + 지도

M-Cn OK, what's our next job?

W-Am [65]**The schedule says we're taking the Darby-brand washing machine to Mr. Wade's apartment and setting it up.**

M-Cn Great. The van will be lighter after that. Where should I go? [66]**We're on Powell now.**

W-Am Let me see... [66]**We just passed Bryant Lane, right? Then take a left on the first street after Sanders Road. Mr. Wade's place is on that block.**

M-Cn Will do. Uh, [67]**when we get there, I'll stay in the van. I'll just need you to go through the main entrance of the building** and check that there's a clear path for our cart. We shouldn't unload anything before we're sure.

남: 자, 다음 일은 뭐죠?

여: **스케줄에 따르면 다비 브랜드의 세탁기를 웨이드 씨 아파트에 가지고 가서 설치하는 거예요.**

남: 좋아요. 그거 끝나면 밴이 가벼워지겠네요. 어디로 가야 하죠? **지금 우리는 파월 가에 있어요.**

여: 한번 보고요… **우리가 방금 브라이언트 가를 지나쳤죠? 그럼 샌더즈 가를 지나 첫 번째 길에서 좌회전이요. 웨이드 씨 집이 그 블록에 있어요.**

남: 알겠습니다. 어, **도착하면 저는 밴 안에 있을게요. 당신이 건물 중앙 출입문으로 들어가** 우리 카트가 걸리지 않고 들어갈 수 있는지만 확인해 주세요. 확인하기 전까지는 아무것도 내리면 안 되거든요.

어휘 washing machine 세탁기 set up 설치하다 go through ~을 지나가다[통과하다] main entrance 중앙 출입문 clear (막히는 데 없이) 훤히 뚫린 path 길 unload 짐을 내리다 boulevard 대로

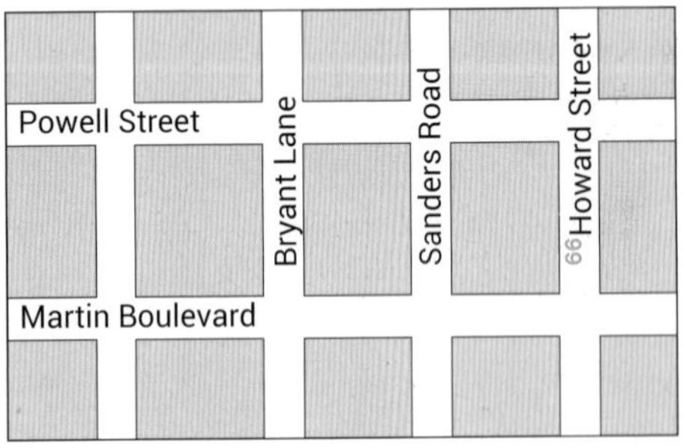

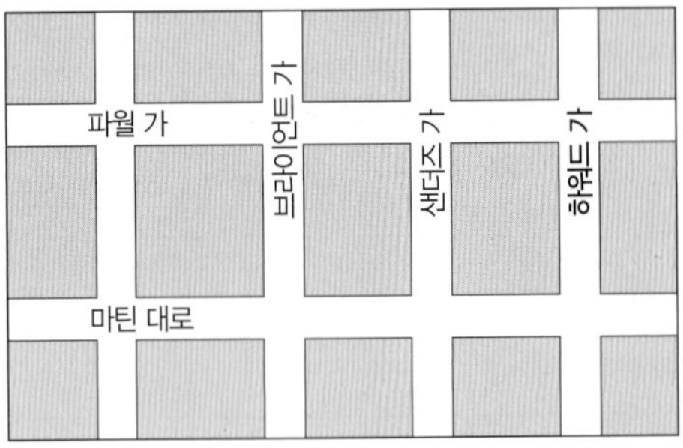

65

What will the speakers do at Mr. Wade's residence?

(A) Wash the windows
(B) Repair some plumbing
(C) Install an appliance
(D) Trim some trees

화자들은 웨이드 씨 집에서 무엇을 할 것인가?

(A) 창문 청소
(B) 배관 수리
(C) 가전 제품 설치
(D) 나무 가지치기

어휘 residence 거주지 plumbing 배관 appliance 가전 제품 trim 다듬다, 잘라내다

해설 전체 내용 관련 – 웨이드 씨 집에서 할 일

여자의 첫 번째 대사에서 스케줄에 따르면 다비 브랜드 세탁기를 웨이드 씨 아파트에 설치하기로 되어 있다(The schedule says we're taking ~ apartment and setting it up.)고 했으므로 정답은 (C)이다.

▸▸ **Paraphrasing** 지문의 **washing machine** → 정답의 **appliance**

66

Look at the graphic. Which street is Mr. Wade's apartment on?

(A) Bryant Lane
(B) Sanders Road
(C) Howard Street
(D) Martin Boulevard

시각 정보에 의하면, 웨이드 씨의 아파트는 어느 거리에 있는가?

(A) 브라이언트 가
(B) 샌더즈 가
(C) 하워드 가
(D) 마틴 대로

어휘 boulevard 대로

해설 시각 정보 연계 – 아파트가 위치한 거리

남자의 두 번째 대사에서 자신들이 파월 가에 있다(We're on Powell now.)고 했다. 이어 여자가 브라이언트 가를 지나왔음을 확인하며, 샌더즈 가를 지나 첫 번째 길에서 좌회전하라(take a left on the first street after Sanders Road.)고 방향을 알려주었고, 웨이드 씨 집이 그 블록에 있다(Wade's place is on that block.)고 했다. 지도를 보면 파월 가에서 브라이언트 가를 지나온 상태에서 샌더즈 가를 지나 첫 번째 길에서 좌회전한 곳은 하워드 가이므로 정답은 (C)이다.

67

What does the man ask the woman to do when they arrive?

(A) Enter a building
(B) Unload some tools
(C) Wait in a vehicle
(D) Make a phone call

남자는 여자에게 그들이 도착할 때 무엇을 해 달라고 요청하는가?

(A) 건물에 들어가기
(B) 연장 내려 주기
(C) 차량 안에서 기다리기
(D) 전화하기

해설 세부 사항 관련 – 도착 시 남자가 여자에게 해달라고 한 요청

남자의 마지막 대사에서 도착하면 자신은 밴에 있겠다(when we get there, I'll stay in the van.)고 한 후, 여자에게 건물 중앙 출입문으로 들어가 달라(I'll just need you to go through the main entrance of the building)고 했으므로 정답은 (A)이다.

▸▸ Paraphrasing 지문의 go through the main entrance of the building → 정답의 Enter a building

68-70 대화 + 전화번호부

M-Au Ms. Crafton, [68]**the staff performance reviews have all been submitted.**

W-Am Great, Jong-Kyu. How are they?

M-Au Well, [68]**I was hoping to sit down with you to talk about them.**

W-Am [69]**I'm sorry, but my schedule's pretty full this week.**

M-Au Oh. In that case, I can just send you the results by e-mail. But I do want to mention something now—one employee received ratings below our minimal standard.

W-Am I see. [70]**I'll have to talk to their manager. Who's the employee?**

M-Au [70]**David Brogan in Accounting.**

W-Am OK. Thank you for bringing that to my attention.

남: 크래프턴 씨, **직원 인사고과가 모두 제출되었어요.**
여: 좋아요, 종규. 어때요?
남: 글쎄요, **같이 앉아서 그것에 대해 얘기 나누고 싶은데요.**
여: **미안하지만, 이번 주 내 일정이 아주 꽉 찼어요.**
남: 오. 그렇다면 그냥 이메일로 평가 결과를 보내드릴 수 있어요. 하지만 지금 뭔가 좀 얘기하고 싶어요. 한 직원이 최저 기준 아래 등급을 받았어요.
여: 알겠어요. **내가 관리자에게 얘기해 볼게요. 직원이 누구죠?**
남: **경리부의 데이비드 브로건입니다.**
여: 알았어요. 그 문제를 내게 상기시켜줘서 고마워요.

어휘 performance 실적, 성과 review 검토, 평가 submit 제출하다 rating 등급, 순위 below ~보다 아래의 minimal 최소의 standard 기준 bring A to one's attention A에 ~의 관심을 가져오다

Department	Manager	Extension
[70]Accounting	Angela Watkins	29
Human Resources	Jong-Kyu Kang	43
Marketing	Elias Cohen	18
Product Development	Prisha Acharya	37

부서	관리자	내선번호
경리부	안젤라 와킨스	29
인사부	종규 강	43
마케팅부	엘리아스 코헨	18
제품개발부	프리샤 아차리아	37

68

What are the speakers mainly discussing?

(A) A company retreat
(B) Employee evaluations
(C) Design specifications
(D) A machine's performance

화자들은 주로 무엇에 관해 논의하고 있는가?

(A) 회사 야유회
(B) 직원 인사고과
(C) 디자인 명세서
(D) 기계의 성능

해설 전체 내용 관련 – 대화의 주요 내용

대화 초반부에 남자가 직원 인사고과가 모두 제출되었다(the staff performance reviews have all been submitted)면서 같이 앉아서 그것에 대해 얘기를 나누고 싶다(I was hoping to sit down with you to talk about them)고 했으므로 정답은 (B)이다.

▸▸ Paraphrasing 대화의 staff performance reviews → 정답의 employee evaluations

69

What problem does the woman mention?

(A) She is not authorized to give an approval.
(B) She does not have time to meet the man.
(C) She has not received the results of a test.
(D) She does not understand a document.

여자는 어떤 문제에 대해 언급하는가?

(A) 여자는 승인할 수 있는 권한이 없다.
(B) 여자는 남자와 만날 시간이 없다.
(C) 여자는 테스트 결과를 받지 않았다.
(D) 여자는 문서를 이해하지 못한다.

어휘 authorize 권한을 부여하다 approval 승인

해설 세부 사항 관련 – 여자가 언급한 문제점

남자의 두 번째 대사에서 같이 앉아서 인사고과에 대해 얘기를 나누고 싶다고 하자 여자는 미안하지만 이번 주 일정이 꽉 찼다(I'm sorry, but my schedule's pretty full this week.)고 대답했다. 즉, 여자는 일정이 빠듯해서 남자와 만날 시간이 없다는 것이므로 정답은 (B)이다.

Test 10

70
Look at the graphic. Who will the woman call?

(A) Ms. Watkins
(B) Mr. Kang
(C) Mr. Cohen
(D) Ms. Acharya

시각 정보에 의하면, 여자는 누구에게 전화를 걸 것인가?

(A) 와킨스 씨
(B) 강 씨
(C) 코헨 씨
(D) 아차리아 씨

해설 시각 정보 연계 – 여자가 전화를 걸 대상

대화 후반부에서 여자가 관리자와 얘기해 보겠다면서 직원이 누구인지(I'll have to talk to their manager. Who's the employee?)를 묻자 남자가 경리부의 데이비드 브로건(David Brogan in Accounting.)이라고 했다. 전화번호부를 보면 경리부의 부서장은 안젤라 와킨스이므로 정답은 (A)이다.

▸▸ **Paraphrasing** 대화의 **talk to** → 질문의 **call**

PART 4

71-73 담화

M-Au All right, everyone. In a minute we'll open the gates to Cedar National Park. [71]**I hope you enjoy connecting with nature today as you explore our many mountain paths.** Maps of the trails are posted throughout the park. If you have a problem, [72]**please refer to the card I've given all of you, which has the contact information for the ranger's office printed on it.** Luckily, our park has pretty good mobile phone reception. And finally, it's going to be a beautiful sunny day today, but the temperature will be quite hot. So, [73]**don't forget to stop for a rest frequently so that you don't get overheated.** Have a great time!

좋습니다, 여러분. 잠시 후에 세다 국립공원의 문을 열도록 하겠습니다. **오늘 많은 산길을 탐사하시는 동안 자연과의 유대를 즐기시길 바랍니다.** 공원 도처에 산길 지도가 게시되어 있습니다. 문제가 있으면 **제가 여러분 모두에게 드린 카드를 참조하세요. 거기에 공원 관리소의 연락처가 인쇄되어 있습니다.** 다행히도, 저희 공원은 휴대전화 수신율이 아주 좋습니다. 그리고 마지막으로, 오늘은 날씨가 화창하지만 기온이 꽤 높을 것입니다. 그러니 **잊지 마시고 자주 멈춰서 휴식을 취해, 체온이 지나치게 올라가지 않도록 하십시오.** 그럼 즐거운 시간 보내십시오!

어휘 national park 국립공원 connect with ~와 연결되다, 친해지다 explore 탐사하다, 답사하다 path 길 trail 산길, 오솔길 post 게시하다 throughout ~의 도처에 refer to ~을 참조하다 contact information 연락처 ranger (공원) 관리인 quite 상당히, 꽤 rest 휴식 frequently 자주 overheated 과열된

71
Why most likely are the listeners visiting the park?

(A) To take a class
(B) To go on a hike
(C) To clean it up
(D) To conduct research

청자들이 공원을 방문한 이유는 무엇이겠는가?

(A) 수업을 받기 위해
(B) 하이킹을 하기 위해
(C) 공원을 청소하기 위해
(D) 연구를 실시하기 위해

해설 세부 사항 관련 – 청자들의 방문 이유

지문 초반부에 화자가 청자들에게 오늘 많은 산길을 탐사하면서 자연과의 유대를 즐기길 바란다(I hope you enjoy connecting with nature today as you explore our many mountain paths.)고 했다. 이를 통해 청자들이 하이킹을 하려는 것임을 알 수 있으므로 정답은 (B)이다.

▸▸ **Paraphrasing** 지문의 **explore our many mountain paths**
→ 정답의 **go on a hike**

72
What has the speaker given to the listeners?

(A) A bag of supplies
(B) An admission ticket
(C) A map of a site
(D) An informational card

화자는 청자들에게 무엇을 주었는가?

(A) 물품 가방
(B) 입장권
(C) 현장 지도
(D) 정보가 적힌 카드

해설 세부 사항 관련 – 청자들에게 준 것

지문 중반부에 화자가 청자들 모두에게 준 카드에 공원 관리소의 연락처가 인쇄되어 있다(please refer to the card I've given all of you, which has the contact information for the ranger's office printed on it)고 했으므로 정답은 (D)이다.

▸▸ **Paraphrasing** 지문의 **the card**
→ 정답의 **an informational card**

73
What does the speaker remind the listeners to do?

(A) Drink plenty of water
(B) Take regular breaks
(C) Stay in a group
(D) Wear sun protection

화자는 청자들에게 무엇을 하라고 상기시키는가?
(A) 물 많이 마시기
(B) 규칙적으로 휴식 취하기
(C) 단체로 머물기
(D) 자외선 차단제 바르기

어휘 plenty of 많은 break 휴식 시간

해설 세부 사항 관련 – 청자들에게 상기시키는 것
지문 후반부에 화자가 청자들에게 자주 멈춰서 휴식을 취해 체온이 지나치게 올라가지 않도록 하라(don't forget to stop for a rest frequently so that you don't get overheated.)고 당부했으므로 정답은 (B)이다.

▸▸ Paraphrasing 지문의 **stop for a rest frequently**
→ 정답의 **take regular breaks**

74-76 소개

M-Cn [74]**Thank you for coming to our ceremony. We're here to celebrate the start of the construction project for Griffsen Services' new headquarters.** I'm Al Herrera, Griffsen's vice president of logistics. Uh, first, did each of you get a pamphlet as you came in? [75]**They feature a beautiful software-generated drawing of the new building's finished form**, so you'll want to pick one up. Now, it's my pleasure to introduce Jonas Marsh, our CEO and first speaker. [76]**I'm sure you all know Mr. Marsh, as he has received a lot of media attention for his strong leadership in guiding Griffsen through some tough times.** It is certainly thanks to him that we're able to take this exciting step. Ladies and gentlemen, Jonas Marsh!

기념식에 와 주셔서 감사합니다. 그리프슨 서비시즈 새 본사 건설 프로젝트의 시작을 축하하기 위해 자리를 마련했습니다. 저는 알 헤레라고요, 그리프슨의 물류 책임 부사장입니다. 음, 우선, 여러분 들어오시면서 팸플릿 받으셨습니까? **그 안에 새 건물의 완성된 형태를 컴퓨터 프로그램으로 구현한 멋진 그림이 들어 있습니다.** 그러니까 한 부씩 가지시는 게 좋을 거 같습니다. 자, 저희 CEO이면서 첫 번째 발표자이신 조나스 마시 씨를 소개하게 되어 기쁩니다. **여러분 모두 마시 씨를 아실 거라고 생각하는데요. 어려운 시기에 그리프슨을 이끄는 데 강한 지도력을 발휘하셔서 언론의 많은 관심을 받으셨기 때문이죠.** 이처럼 흥분되는 발걸음을 내딛을 수 있게 된 것도 분명 그분 덕택입니다. 신사 숙녀 여러분, 조나스 마시 씨입니다!

어휘 headquarters 본사 vice president 부사장 logistics 물류 (업무) pamphlet (광고 등을 위한) 소책자, 팸플릿 feature (특징으로) 포함하다 generate 만들어내다 pleasure 기쁨 CEO 최고경영자(= chief executive officer) be sure (that) ~을 확신하다 media attention 언론의 관심 thanks to ~덕분인, ~때문인

74

What type of event is taking place?
(A) A groundbreaking ceremony
(B) A shareholder meeting
(C) A product launch
(D) A guest lecture

어떤 종류의 행사가 벌어지고 있는가?
(A) 기공식
(B) 주주 총회
(C) 제품 출시
(D) 초청 강연

어휘 take place 발생하다, 일어나다 groundbreaking ceremony 기공식 shareholder 주주 launch 출시

해설 전체 내용 관련 – 행사의 종류
맨 처음에 화자가 청자들에게 기념식에 와 줘서 감사하다면서 그리프슨 서비시즈 새 본사 건설 프로젝트의 시작을 축하하기 위해 자리를 마련했다(Thank you for coming ~ for Griffsen Services' new headquarters.)고 했으므로 정답은 (A)이다.

75

What does the speaker say is included in a handout?
(A) A computerized image
(B) A detailed timeline
(C) A list of features
(D) A financial summary

화자는 유인물에 무엇이 포함되어 있다고 말하는가?
(A) 컴퓨터를 이용해 만든 이미지
(B) 상세한 시간표
(C) 제품 특성에 대한 목록
(D) 재무 요약

어휘 computerized 컴퓨터로 작성한 detailed 상세한 feature 특성, 기능 financial 재정의, 재무의 summary 요약

해설 세부 사항 관련 – 유인물에 포함된 사항
지문 중반부에 화자가 청자들에게 팸플릿을 받았는지 물어 본 후 그 안에 새 건물의 완성된 형태를 컴퓨터 프로그램으로 구현한 멋진 그림이 들어 있다(They feature a beautiful software-generated drawing of the new building's finished form)고 했으므로 정답은 (A)이다.

▸▸ Paraphrasing 지문의 **software-generated drawing**
→ 정답의 **A computerized image**

Test 10

76

What is Mr. Marsh famous for?
(A) Receiving an award
(B) Designing a building
(C) Managing a company
(D) Leading a media campaign

마시 씨는 무엇으로 유명한가?

(A) 수상 이력
(B) 건물 설계
(C) 회사 경영
(D) 미디어 캠페인 주도

어휘 be famous for ~으로 유명하다 design 설계하다 manage 경영하다 lead 이끌다

해설 세부 사항 관련 - 마시 씨가 유명한 이유

지문 후반부에 화자가 청자들에게 마시 씨를 언급하며 어려운 시기에 그리프슨을 이끄는 데 강한 지도력을 발휘해서 언론의 많은 관심을 받았다(I'm sure you all know Mr. Marsh ~ through some tough times.)고 했으므로 정답은 (C)이다.

▸▸ **Paraphrasing** 지문의 **guiding Griffsen**
→ 정답의 **Managing a company**

77-79 담화

W-Br Welcome to today's training session for Lang Electronics. In your new position, [77]**your main responsibility will be to handle comments and questions from customers over the phone.** In order to make our service as efficient as possible, [78]**the first thing you'll need to do is find out exactly what the issue is.** That way, you'll know whether you can help the person yourself or if you'll have to get a technician involved. During today's training, I'll assign you to small groups so you can role-play various situations. But before that, [79]**I've got a brief film for you to watch that outlines the main skills you'll need to develop.**

오늘 랭 전자 교육 과정에 오신 것을 환영합니다. 여러분의 새 직책에서 **주요 업무는 전화로 고객들의 의견과 문의를 처리하는 일입니다.** 우리 서비스를 최대한 효율적으로 하기 위해서 **여러분이 가장 먼저 해야 할 일은 문제가 무엇인지 정확히 파악하는 것입니다.** 그럼으로써 여러분은 해당 고객을 혼자서 도울 수 있을지, 아니면 기술자를 참여시켜야 할지 알 수 있을 겁니다. 오늘 교육 중에 여러분을 소그룹으로 배정하여 다양한 상황의 역할극을 해 볼 수 있게 할 것입니다. 하지만 그에 앞서 **여러분이 개발해야 할 주요 직무 기술을 요약한 짧은 영상을 보시겠습니다.**

어휘 efficient 효율적인 technician 기술자 involve (다른 사람을) 끌어들이다, 연루시키다 assign 배정하다 role-play 역할극을 하다 various 다양한 brief 짧은 outline 개요를 서술하다

77

Who most likely are the listeners?

(A) Electronics technicians
(B) Corporate trainers
(C) Call center workers
(D) Retail salespeople

청자들은 누구일 것 같은가?

(A) 전자제품 기사
(B) 회사 교육 담당자
(C) 콜센터 직원
(D) 소매점 판매원

해설 전체 내용 관련 - 청자들의 신분

지문 초반부에 청자들의 주요 업무는 전화상으로 고객들의 의견과 질문을 처리하는 일(Your main responsibility will ~ over the phone.)이라고 했다. 청자들이 고객과 전화 상담을 담당하는 콜센터 직원임을 알 수 있으므로 정답은 (C)이다.

78

According to the speaker, what should the listeners focus on first?

(A) Promoting new merchandise
(B) Earning a customer's trust
(C) Identifying the problem
(D) Preparing a work space

화자에 따르면, 청자들의 첫 번째 주안점은 무엇이어야 하는가?

(A) 신제품 홍보
(B) 고객의 신뢰 확보
(C) 문제점 파악
(D) 작업 공간 준비

어휘 merchandise 제품, 상품 identify ~을 확인하다, 식별하다

해설 전체 내용 관련 - 청자들의 첫 번째 주안점

지문 중반부에 서비스를 최대한 효율적으로 하기 위해서 가장 먼저 해야 할 일은 문제가 무엇인지 정확히 파악하는 것(the first thing you'll need to do is find out exactly what the issue is.)이라고 했으므로 정답은 (C)이다.

▸▸ **Paraphrasing** 지문의 **find out exactly what the issue is**
→ 정답의 **identify the problem**

79

What does the speaker plan to do next?

(A) Introduce a colleague
(B) Distribute handouts
(C) Assign groups
(D) Show a video

화자는 다음에 무엇을 할 계획인가?
(A) 동료 소개하기
(B) 인쇄물 나누어 주기
(C) 그룹 배정하기
(D) 동영상 보여 주기

해설 세부 사항 관련 - 화자의 다음 행동
지문 맨 마지막에 화자가 청자들에게 필요한 주요 직무 기술을 요약해 놓은 짧은 영상을 준비했다(I've got a brief film for you to watch that outlines the main skills you'll need to develop.)고 했으므로 정답은 (D)이다.

▸▸ **Paraphrasing** 지문의 **a brief film** → 정답의 **a video**

80-82 방송

W-Am A month after the Hillsville City Council approved a measure to open a local history museum in the Clement Building, the project is progressing smoothly. [80]**Keith Finley has been hired to manage the new institution's operations**, and [81]**he reports that plans are being made to move items from the Hillsville Public Library's history exhibit to the site.** However, Mr. Finley also points out that [81]**the Clement Building is much larger than the library's one-room exhibit.** It's five stories high. As a result, [82]**local residents are encouraged to contribute their own vintage items, related to daily life, that have historical significance.** These will be labeled with a plaque indicating the owner. For more information, call 555-0188.

힐스빌 시 의회에서 클레멘트 빌딩에 지역 역사 박물관을 개관하려는 조치를 승인한 한 달 후, 그 프로젝트는 순조롭게 진행되고 있습니다. **새 기관의 운영을 관리하기 위해 키스 핀리가 채용되었는데, 그는 힐스빌 공립도서관의 역사 전시물을 이곳으로 옮길 계획이라고 발표했습니다.** 그러나 핀리 씨는 **클레멘트 빌딩은 도서관의 단일실 전시관보다 훨씬 크다는 점도 언급했습니다. 그것은 5층 건물입니다.** 이에 따라 **지역 주민들에게 일상 생활과 관련된, 역사적으로 의의가 있는 빈티지 물품들을 기증하도록 권장하고 있습니다.** 기증품들에는 소유주를 명시한 명판을 붙여둘 것입니다. 더 자세한 내용을 알고 싶으신 분은 555-0188로 전화하십시오.

어휘 approve 승인하다 measure 조치, 수단, 대책 progress 진척되다, 진행시키다 institution 기관, 제도 operation 운영, 경영 exhibit 전시회, 전시물 story (건물의) 층 resident 주민 contribute 기증하다, 기부하다 related to ~에 관련된 historical 역사적인 significance 의의, 중요성 label ~에 표를[딱지를, 라벨을] 붙이다 plaque 명판 indicate 나타내다

80

Who most likely is Mr. Finley?
(A) A city council member
(B) A journalist
(C) A professor
(D) A museum director

핀리 씨는 누구일 것 같은가?
(A) 시 의회 의원
(B) 언론인
(C) 교수
(D) 박물관장

해설 세부 사항 관련 - 핀리 씨의 신분
지문 초반부에 새 역사 박물관의 운영 관리를 위해 키스 핀리가 채용됐다(Keith Finley has been hired to manage the new institution's operations)고 했으므로 정답은 (D)이다.

81

What does the speaker imply when she says, "It's five stories high"?
(A) A structure is easy to find.
(B) A building has a great view.
(C) Maintenance costs will be high.
(D) There is a lot of space to fill.

화자가 "그것은 5층 건물입니다"라고 말한 의도는 무엇인가?
(A) 그 건물은 찾기 쉽다.
(B) 건물의 전망이 좋다.
(C) 관리비가 비쌀 것이다.
(D) 채워야 할 공간이 많다.

어휘 maintenance cost 관리비

해설 화자의 의도 파악 - 5층 건물이라는 말의 의도
지문 중반부에 핀리 씨가 힐스빌 공립도서관의 전시물이 박물관으로 옮겨질 것이지만 클레멘트 빌딩은 도서관의 단일실 전시관보다 훨씬 크다(he reports that ~ one-room exhibit)고 했다. 이어서 건물이 5층 높이라고 했는데 이는 힐스빌 도서관에서 전시물을 받더라도 여전히 채워야 할 박물관 내 공간이 많다는 의미를 내포한 것이므로 정답은 (D)이다.

82

What are local residents asked to do?
(A) Donate everyday objects to a museum
(B) Share opinions about an exhibit
(C) Come to a fund-raising event
(D) Volunteer to work at an institution

지역 주민들은 무엇을 하도록 요청받는가?
(A) 박물관에 일상 용품 기증
(B) 전시회에 대한 의견 개진
(C) 기금 마련 행사 참석
(D) 기관에서 자원봉사

어휘 donate 기증[기부]하다 share 이야기하다, 공유하다

해설 세부 사항 관련 – 지역 주민들에 대한 요청 사항

지문 후반부에 지역 주민들에게 역사적으로 의의가 있는 일상 생활과 관련된 빈티지 물품들을 기증하도록 권장하고 있다(local residents ~ historical significance.)고 했으므로 정답은 (A)이다.

▸▸ **Paraphrasing** 지문의 contribute their own vintage items, related to daily life
→ 정답의 donate everyday objects

83-85 공지

M-Au [83]**I just want to give you all an update on what's happening this weekend. We've hired professional movers to pack up the office and transport everything to our new building on Crestview Avenue.** Now, we've already labeled all of the desks. If you want to keep your same chair, label it with your name and department. [84]**If you don't do that**, there won't be much we can do **if you can't find your chair after it's unpacked**. Similarly, [84]**we can't guarantee that items won't get damaged.** So [85]**I recommend taking your personal property with you when you leave on Friday.** You can bring it to the new site on Monday.

여러분 모두에게 이번 주말에 있을 일을 알려드리고자 합니다. 사무실 짐을 꾸려서 크레스트뷰 애비뉴에 있는 새 건물로 모두 옮길 전문 이사 업체를 고용했습니다. 이제, 이미 모든 책상에 꼬리표를 붙여 두었습니다. 같은 의자를 계속 갖고 계시려면 이름과 부서를 적어 꼬리표를 붙이십시오. **만약 그렇게 하지 않으면, 짐을 푼 후에 여러분의 의자를 찾지 못하더라도 저희가 할 수 있는 일은 많지 않습니다.** 마찬가지로, **물건이 손상되지 않을 거라 보장할 수도 없습니다.** 그러니 **금요일에 퇴근할 때 개인 소유물을 가져가시기 바랍니다.** 월요일에 새 장소로 다시 가져오시면 됩니다.

어휘 professional 전문적인 mover 짐을 나르는 사람, 이사 업체 pack up 짐을 꾸리다 transport 운반하다, 나르다 guarantee 보장하다 get lost 분실되다 property 소유물

83

According to the speaker, what will happen over the weekend?

(A) A construction project will begin.
(B) The business will move to another location.
(C) New office furniture will be delivered.
(D) Some rooms will be professionally painted.

화자에 따르면, 주말에 무슨 일이 있을 것인가?

(A) 건설 프로젝트가 시작될 것이다.
(B) 회사가 다른 곳으로 이사할 것이다.
(C) 새 사무용 가구가 배송될 것이다.
(D) 방 몇 개를 전문가가 페인트칠할 것이다.

해설 세부 사항 관련 – 주말에 있을 일

지문 맨 처음에 화자가 이번 주말에 있을 일을 공지하겠다(I just want to give you all an update on what's happening this weekend.)고 하면서 사무실 짐을 꾸려서 크레스트뷰 애비뉴에 있는 새 건물로 모든 걸 옮길 전문 이사 업체를 고용했다(We've hired ~ Crestview Avenue.)고 했다. 회사가 주말에 다른 곳으로 옮긴다는 것을 알 수 있으므로 정답은 (B)이다.

▸▸ **Paraphrasing** 지문의 our new building
→ 정답의 another location

84

Why does the speaker say, "there won't be much we can do"?

(A) To apologize for an error
(B) To give a warning
(C) To show disappointment
(D) To disagree with a suggestion

화자가 "저희가 할 수 있는 일이 많지 않습니다"라고 말한 이유는 무엇인가?

(A) 잘못을 사과하기 위해
(B) 주의를 주기 위해
(C) 실망감을 표시하기 위해
(D) 제안에 반대하기 위해

해설 화자의 의도 파악 – 할 수 있는 일이 많지 않다는 말의 의도

지문 중반부에서 만약 꼬리표를 붙여두지 않으면 짐을 푼 후에 의자를 찾지 못하더라도 할 수 있는 일이 많지 않다(if you don't do ~ after it's unpacked.)고 했다. 그리고 이어서 물건이 손상되지 않도록 보장해 줄 수도 없다(we can't guarantee that items won't get damaged)고 했다. 즉, 할 수 있는 일이 많지 않다는 인용문은 이사할 때 발생할 수 있는 분실이나 손상에 대해 미리 주의를 주기 위한 것이므로 정답은 (B)이다.

85

What does the speaker advise the listeners to do?

(A) Remove personal items from an office
(B) Report property damage to him
(C) Arrive early on Monday
(D) Indicate a brand preference

화자는 청자들에게 무엇을 하라고 조언하는가?

(A) 사무실에서 개인 용품을 치울 것
(B) 재산 피해를 자신에게 보고할 것
(C) 월요일에 일찍 도착할 것
(D) 브랜드 선호도를 표시할 것

어휘 remove 치우다

해설 세부 사항 관련 – 청자들에게 상기시키는 일

지문 후반부에 화자가 청자들에게 개인 소유물은 금요일에 퇴근할 때 가져가라(I recommend taking your personal property with you when you leave on Friday.)고 했으므로 정답은 (A)이다.

▸▸ **Paraphrasing** 지문의 **taking your personal property**
→ 정답의 **Remove personal items**

86-88 광고

W-Am Do you suffer from stress, back pain, or headaches? If traditional medicine isn't working for you, why not give yoga a try? [86]**At the Core Studio, we offer classes at various levels to help you practice yoga in a relaxing environment.** Our instructors are highly experienced and capable. In addition, [87]**we're open early in the morning through late in the evening to make sure you can easily find a workout time that's just right for you.** And, [88]**for the entire month of April, we're giving you a chance to try our services for free. Simply visit www.mycorestudio.com and download a voucher for a complimentary admission.**

스트레스나 허리 통증, 두통에 시달리십니까? 전통적인 약이 효과가 없다면 요가를 한번 해 보시면 어떨까요? **코어 스튜디오에서는 다양한 수준의 수업을 제공하여 여러분이 편안한 환경에서 요가 연습을 하도록 도와드립니다.** 저희 강사들은 경험이 풍부하며 역량을 갖추고 있습니다. 아울러 **저희는 여러분에게 꼭 맞는 운동 시간을 쉽게 찾으실 수 있도록 아침 일찍부터 밤 늦게까지 문을 엽니다.** 그리고 **4월 한 달 내내 저희 서비스를 무료로 받으실 수 있는 기회를 제공합니다. www.mycorestudio.com에 방문하셔서 무료 입장 쿠폰을 다운받으시기만 하면 됩니다.**

어휘 suffer from ~로 고통 받다 back pain 허리 통증 headache 두통 traditional 전통적인 medicine 약품 give ~ a try ~를 한 번 해 보다 practice 연습하다 instructor 강사 highly experienced 경험이 풍부한, 매우 노련한 workout 운동 entire 전체의 complimentary 무료의 admission 입장(권)

86

What kind of business is being advertised?

(A) A fitness facility
(B) An art school
(C) A hair salon
(D) A medical clinic

어떤 종류의 사업체를 광고하고 있는가?

(A) 피트니스 시설
(B) 미술 학교
(C) 미장원
(D) 병원

해설 전체 내용 관련 – 광고하고 있는 업종

지문 초반부에 코어 스튜디오에서는 다양한 수준의 수업을 제공하여 편안한 환경에서 요가 연습을 하도록 도와준다(At the Core Studio, we offer classes at ~ relaxing environment.)고 했다. 즉, 요가 수업을 진행하는 피트니스 시설을 광고하는 것이므로 정답은 (A)이다.

87

What does the speaker mention about the business?

(A) It has recently been renovated.
(B) Its hours of operation are convenient.
(C) Its practices are environmentally-friendly.
(D) It now offers a new service.

화자는 사업체에 관해 뭐라고 언급하는가?

(A) 최근 개조됐다.
(B) 영업 시간이 편리하다.
(C) 업무 관행이 환경친화적이다.
(D) 현재 새로운 서비스를 제공한다.

어휘 operation 영업, 운영 practice 관행; 업무

해설 세부 사항 관련 – 화자가 언급한 것

지문 중반부에 고객들에게 맞는 운동 시간을 쉽게 찾을 수 있도록 아침 일찍부터 밤 늦게까지 문을 연다(we're open early in the morning through late in the evening ~ right for you.)고 했으므로 정답은 (B)이다.

▸▸ **Paraphrasing** **we're open early in the morning through late in the evening** → 정답의 **Its hours of operation are convenient.**

88

According to the speaker, what can Web site visitors do in April?

(A) See a floor plan
(B) Download an e-book
(C) Chat with a consultant
(D) Obtain a free pass

화자에 따르면, 웹 사이트 방문자들이 4월에 할 수 있는 것은?

(A) 평면도 보기
(B) 전자책 다운로드하기
(C) 상담자와 이야기하기
(D) 무료 입장권 얻기

해설 세부 사항 관련 – 4월에 할 수 있는 것

지문 후반부에 4월 한 달 내내 서비스를 무료로 받아볼 수 있는 기회를 제공한다(for the entire month of April, we're giving you a chance to try our services for free.)며 사이트에 방문해서 무료 입장 쿠폰을 다운받으라(Simply visit ~ complimentary admission.)고 했으므로 정답은 (D)이다.

▸▸ **Paraphrasing** 지문의 **a voucher for a complimentary admission** → 정답의 **a free pass**

89-91 전화 메시지

M-Cn Hi, Ms. Takahashi. This is Kenny McCormick from Coplin, Incorporated. We're excited that you'll be visiting us next week to tour our manufacturing facility. [89]**I'm calling to find out whether or not you'd like to take in a show on your first night here.** There's a popular musical running at the Ramsey Theater that you might want to see. [90]**The theater is within walking distance of the Emerald Hotel, where you'll be staying.** But I know you might be tired from your flight, so it's completely up to you. [91]**I'll e-mail you the brochure for the show, and then you can just let me know if you'd like to see it.** Thanks.

다카하시 씨, 안녕하세요. 저는 코플린 주식회사의 케니 맥코믹입니다. 다음 주에 저희 제조 시설을 둘러보러 오신다니 기대가 큽니다. **이곳에서 묵으실 첫날 밤에 공연을 보실 것인지 여부를 확인하기 위해 전화 드립니다.** 아마 보고 싶어하실 것 같은 인기 있는 뮤지컬이 램지 극장에서 상연되고 있습니다. **극장은 투숙하실 에메랄드 호텔에서 걸어서 갈 수 있는 거리 안에 있습니다.** 하지만 비행기를 타고 오셔서 피곤하실 테니, 전적으로 귀하가 원하시는 바에 달려 있습니다. **공연 안내 책자를 이메일로 보내드릴 테니, 관람하고 싶으신지 여부를 저에게 알려 주십시오.** 감사합니다.

어휘 manufacturing facility 제조 시설 run (연극을) 공연하다, (영화 등을) 상영하다 within walking distance 도보 거리 이내에 tired 피곤한, 지친 completely 완전히, 전적으로 up to ~에 달려 있는

89

Why is the speaker calling?

(A) To notify the listener of a difficulty
(B) To inquire about a preference
(C) To invite the listener on a tour
(D) To confirm some flight details

화자는 왜 전화하는가?

(A) 청자에게 어려움을 알려 주기 위해
(B) 선호하는 것을 물어보기 위해
(C) 청자를 견학에 초청하기 위해
(D) 항공편 세부 사항을 확정하기 위해

어휘 notify 알리다, 통지하다 preference 선호하는 것

해설 전체 내용 관련 – 화자가 전화하는 이유

지문 초반부에 화자가 다카하시 씨의 방문 첫날 저녁에 공연을 보고 싶은지 확인하기 위해 전화를 했다(I'm calling to find out ~ first night here.)고 했다. 즉, 화자는 다카하시 씨가 공연 관람을 선호하는지 문의하기 위해 전화한 것이므로 정답은 (B)이다.

90

What does the speaker say about the Ramsey Theater?

(A) It hosts live shows every evening.
(B) It is a popular destination for tourists.
(C) It offers discounts to its members.
(D) It is near the listener's accommodations.

화자가 램지 극장에 대해 이야기한 것은?

(A) 매일 저녁 라이브 공연을 연다.
(B) 관광객들에게 인기 있는 장소다.
(C) 회원들에게 할인을 해 준다.
(D) 청자의 숙소 근처에 있다.

어휘 host 주최하다 destination 목적지 accommodation 숙소

해설 세부 사항 관련 – 램지 극장에 대한 화자의 언급

지문 후반부에 극장은 숙소인 에메랄드 호텔까지 걸어서 갈 수 있는 거리 안에 있다(The theater is within ~ be staying.)고 했으므로 정답은 (D)이다.

▸▸ **Paraphrasing** 지문의 **within walking distance of the Emerald Hotel**
→ 정답의 **near the listener's accommodations**

91

What does the speaker say he will do?

(A) E-mail the listener
(B) Call the listener again
(C) Reserve some tickets
(D) Print a brochure

화자는 무엇을 할 것이라고 얘기하는가?

(A) 청자에게 이메일을 보내기
(B) 청자에게 다시 전화하기
(C) 표를 예약하기
(D) 안내 책자를 인쇄하기

해설 세부 사항 관련 – 화자가 미래에 할 일

지문 맨 마지막에 화자가 청자에게 공연 안내 책자를 이메일로 보내 줄 테니 공연을 보고 싶으면 알려 달라(I'll e-mail you ~ to see it.)고 했다. 즉, 화자는 청자에게 공연 정보를 보내 줄 것이므로 정답은 (A)이다.

92-94 뉴스 보도

W-Br And finally, [92]**a major development in the city's mayoral election.** At a news conference held yesterday, Joanna Garza announced that she would challenge Mayor Griffin's campaign for reelection. This is significant because [93]**Mayor Griffin has been criticized for not supporting Norbinton businesses. In contrast,** Ms. Garza owns an expanding chain of laundry shops.

Unsurprisingly, [93]**the Norbinton Business Owners Association issued a statement this morning supporting her candidacy**. Still, at the press conference, Ms. Garza did not reveal her views on several important city issues. Instead, [94]**she said her plans would be described on her campaign Web site, which is being tested now and will go live soon**. For WQEO Radio, I'm Sophia Beattie.

그리고 마지막으로, **시장 선거의 새로운 주요 국면 소식입니다.** 어제 열린 기자 회견에서 조애나 가르자가 그리핀 시장 재선 운동에 맞서 도전하겠다고 발표했습니다. 이건 중요한 소식인데요, **그리핀 시장이 노르빈턴의 사업체들을 후원하지 않는다고 비난을 받아왔기 때문입니다. 그에 반해서, 가르자 씨는 확장 중인 세탁소 체인점들을 소유하고 있습니다.** 당연히 **노르빈턴 사업주 협회에서는 오늘 아침 가르자 씨의 출마를 지지하는 성명을 발표했습니다.** 그런데도 기자 회견에서 가르자 씨는 몇몇 중요한 시 쟁점에 관해 자신의 의견을 밝히지 않았는데요. 대신, **가르자 씨는 자신의 계획을 선거 운동 웹 사이트에서 설명할 거라고 말했는데, 웹 사이트는 지금 테스트 중이고 곧 개시될 예정입니다.** WQEO 라디오의 소피아 비티였습니다.

어휘 major 주요한 development 새로운 국면 mayoral 시장의 election 선거 news conference 기자 회견(= press conference) challenge 도전하다 campaign 선거 운동 significant 중요한, 의미 있는 criticize 비난하다, 비판하다 in contrast 대조적으로 own 소유하다 expand 확장하다 laundry shop 세탁소 unsurprisingly 놀랄 것 없이, 당연히 association 협회, 연합 issue 발표하다 statement 진술, 성명 candidacy 입후보, 출마 reveal 밝히다 instead 그 대신 describe 말하다, 설명하다 go live 작동을 시작하다

92

What is the broadcast mainly about?

(A) An economic development plan
(B) A business association
(C) A news provider
(D) A political contest

방송은 주로 무엇에 관한 내용인가?

(A) 경제 개발 계획
(B) 업체 연합
(C) 뉴스 제공자
(D) 정치적 경쟁

어휘 broadcast 방송; 방송하다 political 정치의

해설 **전체 내용 관련 – 방송의 주제**

지문 초반부에 화자가 시장 선거의 새로운 주요 국면 소식(a major development in the city's mayoral election.)이라고 했으므로 정답은 (D)이다.

93

What does the speaker imply when she says, "Ms. Garza owns an expanding chain of laundry shops"?

(A) Ms. Garza is usually very busy.
(B) Ms. Garza could benefit from a proposal.
(C) Ms. Garza is a good candidate for a position.
(D) Ms. Garza does not require financial support.

화자가 "가르자 씨는 확장 중인 세탁소 체인점들을 소유하고 있습니다"라고 말한 의도는 무엇인가?

(A) 가르자 씨는 대개 매우 바쁘다.
(B) 가르자 씨는 제안으로부터 이익을 얻을 수도 있다.
(C) 가르자 씨는 어떤 직책에 적합한 후보자이다.
(D) 가르자 씨는 재정 지원이 필요하지 않다.

어휘 benefit from ~에서 이익을 얻다 candidate 후보자

해설 **화자의 의도 파악 – 가르자 씨는 확장 중인 세탁소 체인점들을 소유하고 있다는 말의 의도**

화자가 인용문 바로 앞 문장에서 그리핀 시장이 노르빈턴의 사업체들을 후원하지 않아서 비난을 받아왔다(Mayor Griffin has been criticized for not supporting Norbinton businesses.)고 했다. 그에 반해 가르자 씨는 세탁소 체인점들을 소유하고 있다면서 노르빈턴 사업주 협회에서 오늘 아침 가르자 씨의 출마를 지지하는 성명을 발표했다(the Norbinton Business Owners Association ~ supporting her candidacy.)고 했으므로 정답은 (C)이다.

94

According to the speaker, what did Ms. Garza say will happen soon?

(A) A new shop will open.
(B) An advertisement will be broadcast.
(C) A Web site will be launched.
(D) A public discussion will be held.

화자에 따르면, 가르자 씨는 곧 어떤 일이 있을 것이라고 말했는가?

(A) 새로운 가게가 문을 열 것이다.
(B) 광고가 방송될 것이다.
(C) 웹 사이트가 개시될 것이다.
(D) 공개 토론회가 열릴 것이다.

어휘 launch 시작하다, 출시하다 discussion 토론(회)

해설 **세부 사항 관련 – 곧 일어날 일**

지문 후반부에 화자가 가르자 씨는 자신의 계획을 선거 운동 웹 사이트에서 설명할 거라고 말했는데, 웹 사이트는 지금 테스트 중이고 곧 개시될 예정(she said her plans would be described ~ and will go live soon.)이라고 했으므로 정답은 (C)이다.

▸▸ **Paraphrasing** 지문의 **will go live** → 정답의 **will be launched**

Test 10

95-97 회의 발췌 + 기능 리스트

M-Cn OK, let's begin. Today we're discussing issues we've been having with our new file-sharing program, PlozWare. Don't get me wrong—[95]**ever since we've started using it, both our garden planning and maintenance activities have been going more smoothly overall.** But there have been a few difficulties. For one, [96]**I've noticed that sometimes new details aren't being added to shared files like the project master plan spreadsheets.** Uh, outdated details aren't being deleted, either. But I think I've figured out why. You can see that I've pulled up the "Features" screen on the projector. [97]**We're going to talk about the one in the top right-hand corner.** Is anyone unfamiliar with it?

자, 시작합시다. 오늘은 새 파일 공유 프로그램 플러즈웨어와 관련해 우리가 겪고 있는 문제점을 얘기해 보겠습니다. 오해하지 마세요. **우리가 그걸 사용한 후부터 정원 설계와 관리 작업 둘 다 전반적으로 좀 더 순조로워졌습니다.** 하지만 몇 가지 어려움이 있는데요. 첫째로, **때때로 새로운 사항이 종합사업계획 스프레드시트 같은 공유 파일에 추가가 되지 않는 걸 발견했어요.** 음, 쓸모 없어진 사항도 삭제가 안 되고요. 하지만 왜 그런지 알 수 있을 거 같습니다. 제가 영사기에 "기능" 화면을 띄워 놓은 거 보고 계시는데요. **상단 오른쪽 끝에 있는 것에 대해 얘기하겠습니다.** 이거 생소한 사람 있나요?

어휘 ever since ~한 이래로 죽 maintenance 유지, 보수 go smoothly 순조롭게 진행되다 overall 전반적으로 notice 알아채다, 주목하다 details 세부 사항 outdated 시대에 뒤진, 시기가 지난 delete 삭제하다 figure out 파악하다, 이해하다 pull up 띄우다, 당겨 올리다 feature 특징, 기능 unfamiliar with ~에 익숙하지 않은 data sync 데이터 동기화(= data synchronization) remote deletion 원격 삭제 sharing control 공유 제어 file recovery 파일 복구

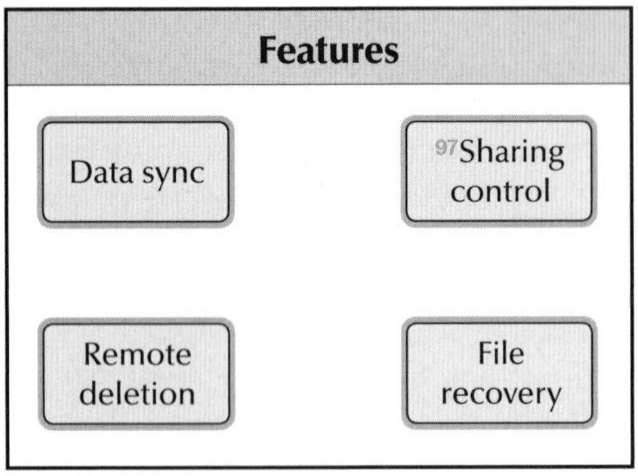

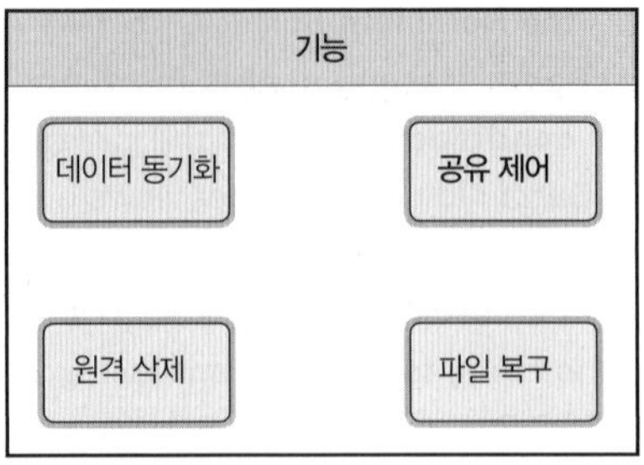

95

Where most likely does the speaker work?

(A) At a magazine publisher
(B) At a telecommunications firm
(C) At an architectural agency
(D) At a landscaping company

화자는 어디에서 일하겠는가?

(A) 잡지 출판사
(B) 통신사
(C) 건축 사무소
(D) 조경 회사

어휘 publisher 출판사 telecommunications firm 통신 회사 architectural agency 건축 사무소 landscaping 조경

해설 전체 내용 관련 - 화자의 근무지

지문 초반부에 화자의 회사가 새 프로그램을 사용한 후부터 정원 설계와 관리 작업 둘 다 전반적으로 좀 더 순조로워졌다(ever since we've started ~ going more smoothly overall.)고 했으므로 정답은 (D)이다.

96

According to the speaker, what is the problem with some files?

(A) They cannot be located.
(B) They were deleted.
(C) They were released publicly.
(D) They are not being updated.

화자에 따르면 일부 파일의 문제점은 무엇인가?

(A) 위치를 찾을 수가 없다.
(B) 삭제되었다.
(C) 일반에게 공개되었다.
(D) 업데이트되지 않는다.

어휘 locate 위치를 찾다 release 공개하다, 발표하다 publicly 공개적으로

해설 세부 사항 관련 - 일부 파일의 문제점

지문 중반부에 화자가 때때로 새로운 사항이 종합사업계획 스프레드시트 같은 공유 파일에 추가가 되지 않는다는 것을 발견했다(I've noticed that sometimes ~ like the project master plan spreadsheets.)고 했으므로 정답은 (D)이다.

▸▸ **Paraphrasing** 지문의 new details aren't being added
→ 정답의 not being updated

97

Look at the graphic. Which feature will the speaker talk about next?

(A) Data sync
(B) Sharing control
(C) Remote deletion
(D) File recovery

시각 정보에 의하면, 화자는 다음에 어떤 기능에 대해 이야기하겠는가?

(A) 데이터 동기화
(B) 공유 제어
(C) 원격 삭제
(D) 파일 복구

해설 세부 사항 관련 - 화자가 다음에 말할 기능
지문 후반부에 화자가 상단 오른쪽 끝에 있는 것에 대해 얘기하겠다(We're going to talk ~ top right-hand corner.)고 했는데 리스트를 보면 오른쪽 상단에 있는 기능은 공유 제어(Sharing control)이므로 정답은 (B)이다.

98-100 전화 메시지 + 주문서

W-Am Hi, this is Michelle Gray from Lynn International. I placed an order with you on March second, but I'd like to make a change to it. [98]**When I was counting up the tables we'll have for our March fifteenth banquet at the Ogden Center, I overlooked the main table at the front.** So, [99]**I'd like to order five more centerpieces** so I can put them in a row on the main table. That won't be a problem, right? Oh, and [100]**when the flowers are delivered to the Ogden Center, please use the side entrance off Samson Street, as the main entrance will be closed for repairs.** Thank you.

안녕하세요, 저는 린 인터내셔널의 미셸 그레이입니다. 3월 2일에 그쪽에 물건을 주문했는데 한 가지 변경을 하고 싶습니다. **3월 15일에 오그던 센터에서 열릴 저희 연회에 쓸 테이블을 세어보았는데 앞에 놓을 중앙 테이블을 간과했어요.** 그래서 중앙 테이블에 일렬로 놓을 수 있도록 **다섯 개의 중앙부 꽃 장식물을 추가 주문하려 합니다.** 그게 문제가 되지는 않겠죠, 그렇죠? 오, 그런데 **오그던 센터로 꽃이 배달될 때 샘슨 가로 나 있는 옆문을 이용해 주세요. 정문은 보수 작업 때문에 폐쇄될 겁니다.** 감사합니다.

어휘 count up ~을 세다 banquet 연회 overlook 간과하다 centerpiece (테이블 등의) 중앙부 장식 in a row 일렬로 quantity 수량 petal 꽃잎 arch 아치(모양의 것)

Jill's Flower Shop Order for Lynn International, March 2	
Item Description	**Quantity Requested**
Rose petals (pink, 20-ounce bag)	3
Entrance arch (white, 35 inches)	5
[99]Summer Mix centerpiece	25
Individual rose (pink)	30

질스 플라워숍 린 인터내셔널, 3월 2일 주문	
물품 내역	요청 수량
장미 꽃잎 (분홍색, 20온스 봉지)	3
아치형 입구 장식 (흰색, 35인치)	5
서머 믹스 중앙 장식물	25
개별 장미 (분홍색)	30

98

Why does the speaker want to change an order?

(A) She forgot to count one of the tables.
(B) A budget for supplies has been reduced.
(C) She has decided on a new theme for the party.
(D) More guests will attend than originally expected.

화자는 왜 주문을 변경하고 싶어하는가?

(A) 테이블 중 하나를 세지 않았다.
(B) 물품 예산이 축소되었다.
(C) 새로운 파티 주제를 결정했다.
(D) 당초 예상보다 많은 손님들이 참석할 것이다.

어휘 theme 주제, 테마

해설 세부 사항 관련 - 주문을 변경하고 싶은 이유
지문 초반부에 화자가 3월 15일 오그던 센터에서 열릴 연회에 쓸 테이블을 계산할 때 앞에 놓을 중앙 테이블을 간과했다(When I was counting up ~ at the front.)고 했으므로 정답은 (A)이다.

▸▸ **Paraphrasing** 지문의 overlook the main table
→ 정답의 forget to count one of the tables

Test 10

99

Look at the graphic. Which quantity does the speaker ask to change?

(A) 3
(B) 5
(C) 25
(D) 30

시각 정보에 의하면, 화자는 어떤 수량을 변경해 달라고 요청하는가?

(A) 3
(B) 5
(C) 25
(D) 30

해설 시각 정보 연계 - 변경을 요청한 수량

지문 중반부에 화자가 중앙부 꽃 장식물을 다섯 개 더 주문하고 싶다(I'd like to order five more centerpieces)고 했다. 그리고 주문서를 보면 서머 믹스 중앙 장식물(Summer Mix centerpiece)의 수량이 25개로 명시되어 있으므로 정답은 (C)이다.

100

What does the speaker explain to the listener?

(A) What to bring for identification
(B) How to access a venue
(C) Where to mail an invoice
(D) When to make a delivery

화자는 청자에게 무엇에 대해 설명하는가?

(A) 신원 확인을 위해 가져올 것
(B) 장소에 들어오는 법
(C) 송장을 우편으로 보낼 곳
(D) 배달할 시기

어휘 identification 신원 확인 access ~에 접근[진입]하다

해설 세부 사항 관련 - 청자에게 설명하는 것

지문 맨 마지막에 화자가 청자에게 정문은 보수 작업 때문에 폐쇄될 것이니 배달할 때 샘슨 가로 나 있는 옆문을 이용해 달라(when the flowers are delivered ~ for repairs.)고 했으므로 정답은 (B)이다.